Cocktails & Dreams
Perspectives on Drug and Alcohol Use

WILSON R. PALACIOS
University of South Florida

PEARSON
Prentice
Hall

Upper Saddle River, New Jersey 07458

Library of Congress Cataloging-in-Publication Data

Cocktails and dreams : perspectives on drug and alcohol use / [edited by] Wilson R. Palacios.
    p. cm.
  Includes bibliographical references and index.
  ISBN 0-13-098751-4
  1. Substance abuse—Research. 2. Addicts—Identification—Methodology.
3. Group identity—Research. 4. Ethnology—Research—Methodology.
5. Qualitative research. I. Palacios, Wilson R. HV4998 .C63 2005
362.29—dc22

                                            2003023951

Publisher: Stephen Helba
Executive Editor: Frank Mortimer, Jr.
Assistant Editor: Korrine Dorsey
Production Editor: John Probst, GTS Companies/York Campus
Production Liaison: Barbara Marttine Cappuccio
Director of Manufacturing and Production: Bruce Johnson
Managing Editor: Mary Carnis
Manufacturing Buyer: Cathleen Petersen
Creative Director: Cheryl Asherman
Cover Design Coordinator: Miguel Ortiz
Cover Designer: Carey Davies
Cover Image: Mark Richards, PhotoEdit
Editorial Assistant: Barbara Rosenberg
Marketing Manager: Tim Peyton
Formatting and Interior Design: GTS Companies/York Campus
Printing and Binding: Phoenix Book Tech Park

Pearson Education LTD.
Pearson Education Singapore, Pte. Ltd
Pearson Education, Canada, Ltd
Pearson Education—Japan
Pearson Education Australia PTY, Limited
Pearson Education North Asia Ltd
Pearson Educaçion de Mexico, S.A. de C.V.
Pearson Education Malaysia, Pte. Ltd

10 9 8 7 6 5 4 3 2 1
ISBN 0-13-098751-4

Dedication

❖

For my partner, Polly Palacios

Contents

❖

Preface

> No understanding of a world is valid without representation of those members' voices.
>
> *Michael Agar, The Professional Stranger, Second Edition*

The purpose of *Cocktails & Dreams: Perspectives on Drug and Alcohol Use* is to provide students with an enhanced understanding of drug subcultures through a qualitative (interpretive) research perspective. On a general level, qualitative research operates from an interpretive perspective because its primary objective is to identify and describe the personal experiences of participants and their respective social settings. The twenty-two chapters contained in this edited book represent a diverse group of qualitative researchers from the United States and abroad. Although their research design is qualitative, their methods range from traditional "street" ethnography, focus group based research, and/or field interviews with participants who use drugs such as marijuana, "crack" or powder cocaine, heroin, methamphetamine, and methylenedioxymethamphetamine (MDMA or "Ecstasy"). In addition, chapters are included that focus on the misuse of alcohol.

Several chapters also present the obstacles confronted by individuals when entering drug treatment programs. Such articles focus on how race/ethnicity, gender, and social class may at times operate against the individual's commitment to a drug-free lifestyle. The issues raised by many of the featured authors in this edited book are complex and multidimensional, as human behavior truly is; yet I hope students and instructors will find many of the issues raised to be thought-provoking and poignant for classroom discussions.

This edited book is divided into four sections: (1) Qualitative Research Methods and Illicit Substance Use Research; (2) Pursuing Other Forms of Communication; (3) After the Party Is Over; and (4) Emerging Issues: Managing Drug Use and Misuse. Each section is preceded by brief comments by the editor and is followed by questions to stimulate classroom discussion.

This volume may readily be used as a supplemental text in a course focusing on drug use and abuse or as a stand-alone text for a course on controversial issues in criminal justice, criminology, and sociology. The text may also be used in a research methods course. The readings contained in this edited book do not glamorize the use of drugs or its participants, nor does it endorse any particular political perspective concerning the use of drugs. As an ethnographer who has worked with several drug subcultures, I understand the professional obligation of being true to one's participants and the mechanics of good social research. I hope both students and instructors alike perceive this working philosophy throughout this volume.

Acknowledgments

❖

Many persons assisted in making this edited volume a reality. Primary were my senior undergraduate students, Mistie Smalls and Denise Bellini, who helped in scouring the library stacks for journal holdings of the articles presented herein. Second I owe a great debt to those faculty members across the country who anonymously reviewed the proposal for this text. I also owe a debt of gratitude to those authors whose work is presented here. The selections represent a broad range of qualitative research in the area of drug use and abuse.

The Department of Criminology staff at the University of South Florida also assisted my efforts. These individuals, Brian Brady and Victoria Gojmerac, provided invaluable support. Our librarian, Matt Torrence, assisted me in negotiating with many of the publishers who hold the copyrights for the articles reprinted in this edition. I also want to thank Dr. Paul F. Cromwell (Wichita State University) for his support during this whole process. In addition, I want to thank the following reviewers: Scott Decker, University of Missouri, St. Louis, Missouri; and Alex Del Carmen, University of Texas, Arlington, Texas. Finally, I wish to thank the editors and the entire production team at Prentice-Hall—Kim Davies, Frank Mortimer, Korrine Dorsey, Evelyn Perricone, John Probst, Barbara Cappuccio and Susan Beauchamp. Their words of encouragement and patience were extremely comforting.

Wilson R. Palacios
University of South Florida
Tampa, FL

Qualitative Research Methods and Illicit Drug Use Research

❖

> Until the criminologist learns to suspend his personal distaste for the values and
> lifestyles of the untamed savages, until he goes out into the field to the cannibals and
> head-hunters and observes them without trying to civilize them or turn them over to
> colonial officials . . . he will only be a jail house or court house sociologist.
>
> *Ned Polsky, Hustlers, Beats, and Others*

INTRODUCTION

The above cautionary statement by Polsky is as prophetic as it is timeless. Qualitative researchers who work with various drug subcultures are bound not only by a professional commitment to sound social scientific research—they also have a personal commitment to their research participants of reporting a balanced and minimally biased representation of their lives. The selections in section I present the historical significance of qualitative research among such a diverse community of participants, the challenges and risks encountered by such researchers, and the heightened degree of sensitivity these men and women in the field have for such concurrent issues as race, ethnicity, gender, and the sociopolitical context of their work.

The first chapter, Professor Kevin W. Whiteacre's "Criminal Constructions of Drug Users," represents a treatise against the theoretical and methodological dogma that has dominated much of criminology and the attempts made to study the illicit substance user. Professor Whiteacre calls for a new criminological discourse concerning this particular type of research, and moreover, argues for a new approach in drug intervention and prevention programs. Although he does not specifically address qualitative research methods as the key in this "new" dialogue, he does advocate an interpretive perspective as a guiding theoretical framework.

The second chapter, "The Role of Ethnography in Substance Abuse Research and Public Policy: Historical Precedent and Future Prospects," by Harvey W. Feldman and Michael R. Aldrich, presents a historical timeline concerning the development of ethnography as a research method or tool for understanding the social context of drug-using behavior. Furthermore, Professors Feldman and Aldrich demonstrate how ethnography has been used in addressing emergent drug and concurrent health problems in the United States.

In the third chapter, "The Multiple Roles of Qualitative Research in Understanding and Responding to Illicit Drug Use," Professor Tim Rhodes provides a historical overview of the role qualitative research has played in understanding substance-using behavior. This selection introduces the reader to the utility of adopting a qualitative perspective and how such a particular research design both informs and enhances traditional quantitative drug studies.

In the fourth selection, "Determining Drug Use Patterns Among Women: The Value of Qualitative Research Methods," Professor Claire Sterk-Elifson presents a qualitative mixed-method approach (i.e., in-depth interviewing, focus groups, and social and ethnographic mapping with participant observation) in the study of female drug users in the Atlanta, Georgia, area. Professor Sterk-Elifson's chapter demonstrates the strength that qualitative research methods bring to the study of women and their complex lives.

1

Criminal Constructions of Drug Users

Kevin W. Whiteacre
Indiana University

INTRODUCTION

Criminology, in its reliance on legalistic definitions of drug users and abusers, its study of the poor and powerless "users," and its exoticization and differentiation of the objects of study, has helped construct particular images and definitions of drug users. The concepts of drug users and subcultures have been reified, appearing as if they are real entities. Arguably, such images and connotations are produced largely through the media (Brownstein 1996; Reinarman and Levine 1997). But less recognized is the role that researchers and scholars play in the production of these images. This chapter seeks to identify how some academic research, criminology in particular, may contribute to the creation of drug-user identities.

Scholars are increasingly recognizing criminology's role, or at least complicity, in the actual production of criminal categories and images. Criminology's foundation in individualization and differentiation (Garland 1985, 115) and its corresponding methodologies has encouraged a particular constructed view of the world and the criminals inhabiting it. Critics have argued that criminology's reliance on government funding subjects its "agenda" to the influences of legislators', policy-makers', and practitioners' current concerns (Maguire 1997, 141). Milakovich and Weis (1975) even argue that to predict the findings of any study, one need only know the agency conducting it, the method of funding, and the implicit values to be upheld. Or more insidiously, the social scientist cannot help but simply defend the reality of his or her world—thus reproducing that reality under the guise of

Kevin W. Whiteacre. Prepared expressly for this edition.

social science (Taylor, et al. 1973, 33). Regardless, the conclusion of many critics is that much knowledge is an artifact of the way it was produced.

Because any account of a phenomenon can disqualify other accounts (Miller 1993), presenting only certain patterns of drug use within particular contexts could well ignore the infinite other possible presentations. Thus, criminological practice creates certain truths about drugs and drug users (Goode 1972). The focus on causation and identifying differences, coupled with a historical tradition of fear and misunderstanding of certain drugs, has led to pathological images of drug use in much criminological writing.

By no means is criminology, or more generally academia, singularly responsible for the construction of images of drugs or drug users. First, criminology is obviously no monolithic entity engaged in a narrow and closed study. Within the field, there are many different approaches to the study of drug use. Nor has the discipline remained static over time. There have been, however, some discernible approaches in enough of the mainstream publications to justify an analysis of how criminology may be influencing the construction of drug-use images.

Second, criminology is not constructing these images in a vacuum constrained only by methodology and personal choice. Researchers are working and living within a cultural milieu characterized by prevailing assumptions about illicit drugs and users. In other words, when researchers think of "drug users," they are already prejudiced by certain cultural connotations—addiction, disease, violence, hedonism, and so on—associated with the term. The nature of this context and the resulting constructs serve as the subject of this chapter.

Nor do the constructed objects passively accept their identities. Certainly, the law, media, public, and drug users themselves have all played important roles in the development of drug subcultures. The interaction between media and criminal justice officials in creating images of drug users and drug panics has been well-documented by researchers (Brownstein 1996; Reinarman and Levine 1997). Moreover, Becker (1963) and others have noted the importance of *moral entrepreneurs* in constructing the identities of deviants.

The intervening effects of criminological research and theory in the study of drugs, however, have been underinvestigated. Phillipe Bourgois (1995, 18) points out that "under [a] . . . microscope everyone has warts and anyone can be made to look like a monster." By submitting drug users to the scrutiny of field observation and/or surveys, researchers call attention to and emphasize a distortion of the users' personal foibles and idiosyncrasies, thus perpetuating the myth that drug users are somehow pathologically different from other individuals. This chapter explores how and why criminology, as practiced in the United States, produces these images of drug use and users.

RESEARCH METHODS

The criminal justice system's current shift toward "know-nothing managerialism" (Cohen 1992, 19) has fostered a return to emphasis on simple measurement of phenomena (i.e., the predominance of numbers as a descriptive medium; Maguire 1997). Various instruments developed to measure drug use such as the Arrestee Drug Abuse Monitoring Program (ADAM), the National Household Survey on Drug Abuse (NHSDA), Monitoring the Future, and the Drug Abuse Warning Network (DAWN) present little more than trends in the magnitude of use. Thus, reliance on the criminal justice system, which assumes any increase in use is *bad* and any decrease is *good,* will lead mainstream criminology farther away from any understanding and closer to mere descriptives of broad trends.

Additionally, the task of the "expert" criminologist has included not only explaining deviance but also reforming it. Viewing any illicit drug use as behavior in need of correction, criminological research is usually only interested in finding what makes drug users different from nonusers in order to stop all illicit drug use. When viewing the object of study through the legalistic definition of drug abuse, criminology often fails to appreciate the subjective distinctions between use patterns as understood by the users.

Eve Sedgwick's (1990) work on homosexuality suggests a means for considering drug research. She notes that the study of homosexuality is problematic because there are few people or institutions studying it that see homosexuality as a positive, much less prized, trait. Studies rarely provide advice on how to make sure one's kids turn out gay. On the other hand, there is an "unimaginably" large number of institutions endeavoring to prevent it (Sedgwick 1990). Similarly, with a few notable exceptions in the growing approach of harm reduction, very few researchers are concerned with how to encourage responsible drug use. Instead, drug use is studied with the goal of prevention and the eradication of certain drug users.

This is why Sedgwick is wary of studies of homosexuality. As long as cultural norms view homosexuality as pathological, any causal model—for instance, the nature/nurture debate—will be engaged under the assumption of pathology. This influence of culture prevents any science from being truly "objective" or value free. Thus, researchers can transform learning theory into epidemiology: "'Heroin use—like marijuana, alcohol, cigarettes, slang, clothing fads and popular music—spreads within groups of closely associated youths by a process of peer emulation and influence' [Hunt and Chambers 1976, 3]. Or to put the matter a bit differently, drug use spreads like an infectious disease" (Wilson and Herrnstein 1985, 371).

One might be hard pressed, however, to find this "disease model" applied to the spread of popular music or clothing fads. Infectious disease is reserved for explaining illicit drug use.

In their discussion of control theory, Gottfredson and Hirschi (1990) likewise allow prejudicial assumptions to taint their analysis. These assumptions lead them to take the drugs and crime relationship out of its political and legal context by simply connecting the two through an underlying shared trait. According to the authors, "Crime and drug use are connected because they share features that satisfy the tendencies of criminality. *Both provide immediate, easy, and certain short-term pleasure*" (41, emphasis added). Yet, all recreation can be described this way. *Recreation* is defined as nothing more than any play or activity "that amuses oneself." Monday Night Football or "Must See TV," renting movies, and going to the opera all satisfy the basic human urge for amusement, yet these activities are conspicuously absent from the discussion. An implicitly problematic explanation is reserved for recreation (or any desire) conventionally defined as deviant.

Is drug use somehow *more* recreational because it is more effective or more fun? Certainly, the process of acquiring, preparing, and consuming drugs is more difficult and requires more planning than going to the movies. Hirschi and Gottfredson allow cultural definitions of drug use as hedonism to taint their discussion and then further perpetuate this definition under the mantle of social science.

This desire to *explain* drug use—to search for its causes—results in a continuous stream of publications showing whatever statistically significant (though rarely robust) differences between users and nonusers that can be found. In fact, journal editors are unlikely to publish studies that do not find significant differences (Spender 1981). One feminist editor of a journal points out the problem in the study of females:

> It becomes very difficult to have findings of 'no difference' reported in the literature, because if the purpose of research is to find where [the objects of study] are deficient, and the deficiency cannot be located, then the experiment can be classified as a failure (rather than as a 'breakthrough' to a reconceptualization of the problem). (Spender 1981, 192)

Studies failing to find differences between users and nonusers fail to find causation, which is the primary mission of criminological theory. The publication of only those studies that find "significant" differences continues to construct the separate categories of users and nonusers according to a growing array of tested variables. Assuming their own cultural expressions and identities as the norm, dominant groups, including criminologists, then construct these discovered differences as dysfunction (Young 1990, 59). Illicit drug users then become identified as the problematic "Other."

Thus, the literature is filled with studies demonstrating differences between drug users and nonusers without ever really telling us very much about the users or their subjective experiences. For instance, social learning theory has been tested countless times by the study of adolescent marijuana use (Akers and Cochran 1985; Akers et al. 1979; Winfree et al. 1989; Bahr and Hawks 1993). The studies repeatly find that one of the best predictors of marijuana use is the extent of association with other marijuana users. Although these studies may help in testing theory, for example, by comparing the effects of social control variables versus social learning variables, they are of little use for a better understanding of the subjective experiences of drug users and they serve to enhance the mirage of the users' Otherness.

Studies investigating the differences (or the causes of use) between drug users and nonusers also develop a system of *auxiliary* traits (Becker 1963) that seem to distinguish between the two. Users are identified, not because they use certain drugs of interest, but also because the discovered differences purportedly leading them to use the drugs provide further secondary characteristics of users. The predictors of use are then seen as secondary social and psychological characteristics of users.

So now, users under study are different from nonusers on as many variables for which the researcher can fit into the statistical model and find significant results. These auxiliary traits then come to further distinguish users from nonusers. Marijuana users are not distinct just because they use marijuana but also because they share other characteristics such as low self-control (Gottfredson and Hirschi 1990), impulsivity (Wilson and Herrnstein 1985), or retreatism (Merton 1938).

In this way, research and the public policy it supports has defined certain users of certain substances as the Other. This serves the dual purpose of defining everyone else's legitimized substance use as normal and safe while also providing a dangerous Other. Fighting to eliminate (or cure) this Other makes us feel safer. "It is only by exaggerating the difference between within and without, above and below, male and female, with and against, that a semblance of order is created" (Douglas 1966, 4). Meaning is the result of difference and relationship (Storey 1998, 74). Good and moral cannot exist without bad and immoral, or clean without dirty, and so on.

According to Manderson (1995), illicit drug use may represent the violation of boundaries (e.g., the hypodermic needle's cross between the outer and inner worlds) or exclusion.

Manderson suggests that the drug subculture represents an "unwanted construction," which makes the uninitiated uncomfortable. "There is always a certain unpleasantness occasioned by being present at an alien ritual" (Manderson 1995, 803).

These seemingly unwanted constructions are, rather, *necessary* to counteract our fear of actual similarity with "drug users." The Other is not opposed to and facing the subject. It is next to it, too close for comfort (Young 1990, 144). ". . . [T]he most dangerous Other is always the one least distinguishable from oneself, the one that might really *be* oneself" (Lenson 1995, 8, emphasis in original). It is precisely because anyone can suddenly become a drug user, by the simple act of having his or her recreation labeled as such, that constructing the drug-using Other is so necessary. It establishes one's own identity in contrast, and in the process legitimates one's own means of fulfilling desire. We have reified a drug subculture and exoticized it. In the process of exoticizing, we have distanced ourselves so far as to make ourselves uncomfortable—both because we no longer understand it and because we sense its actual impending closeness.

Moreover, there is a considerable imbalance of studies involving impoverished or powerless groups of drug abusers. Criminological research, in general, focuses on the less powerful segments of society, the young more than the old, and the poor more than the wealthy (Pepinsky and Jesilow 1984). High school drug use surveys and the Arrestee Drug Abuse Monitoring Program in jails focus on the less powerful, more marginalized drug users. It seems quite unlikely that wealthy "respectable" community members, having more to lose, would come forward about their drug use when surveyed by the National Household Drug Abuse survey.

Additionally, the crack scare of the 1980s and the AIDS epidemic led to a further concentration of studies on residents of the inner cities. Primarily urban minorities use crack, and indigent heroin addicts have been the concern for studies about needle sharing and AIDS epidemiology. In reality, however, this is a small minority of the illicit drug-using population. Studies such as Beck and Rosenbaum's (1994) ethnography of mostly middle class ecstasy users are exceptional for their rarity.

The linkage between particular drugs and feared or rejected groups or political causes has historically served as a powerful theme in the American perception of drugs. David Musto (1973) chronicled how (White) American culture, in previous moral panics over some drugs, developed a fear of illicit drugs through their association with undesirable subgroups of society. Cocaine was linked to Blacks, marijuana was linked to Mexican immigrants, and opium was linked to Chinese immigrants. Research focusing on such groups of drug users is both a product of and a contributing force to an historically based cultural milieu associating illicit drug use with poor minorities.

This focus on isolated inner city drug markets allows researchers to make broad generalizations, such as "illicit drug markets are criminal by definition. They are essentially organized around the distribution and use of illicit substances. *In this environment, there is no meaningful definition of community*" (Wilson 1996, emphasis added). When "this environment" refers to socially and economically isolated, culturally disorganized communities, it may very well be true. Such a description, however, would be unrecognizable to members of Adler's (1993) cohesive networks of drug-dealing business partners and friends. For that matter, most drug users in better environmental circumstances would disagree entirely with this characterization of the "drug market."

There are a number of reasons why research focuses inordinately on addicted and powerless drug users. In the case of harder drugs like cocaine and heroin, many researchers just do not believe controlled use is common or even possible:

> The National Commission on Marijuana and Drug Abuse reported in 1973 that 90 percent of Americans disagreed with the statement, 'You can use heroin occasionally without ever becoming addicted to it.' The existence of hundreds of articles about heroin addiction, as opposed to only a few on any other pattern of use, attests to the research community's agreement with that view. (Zinberg 1995, 147)

With titles of books on heroin such as *It's So Good Don't Even Try It Once* (Smith and Gray 1972), researchers do not seem to agree with this view so much as they have perpetuated it. Researchers and professionals are the sources of the information used by the media and public. Although researchers are increasingly recognizing that the number of controlled heroin users may equal or even exceed the number of addicts (Kaplan 1983), historically, researchers simply assumed almost all heroin use was or became abusive (Zinberg 1995).

Most important, the research methods used influence the study population. Many studies use data from Drug Use Forecasting (DUF) or Arrestee Drug Abuse Monitoring (ADAM), which track drug-use trends of arrestees. Using a population already overrepresented by the poor and minorities inevitably leads to studies reflecting such distortions. Other studies identify their population through services such as needle exchange programs, publicly provided drug treatment, or other services used primarily by the addicted and poor.

To find and study middle- and upper-class illicit drug users is difficult because they are understandably hesitant to come forward about their use. Usually, such individuals are found once they have entered treatment for drug-abuse problems. (Exceptions, of course, do exist. See, for example, Siegel 1977, and Beck and Rosenbaum 1994, to name just two.)

Finally, some criminologists may be hesitant to acknowledge and study successful individuals who are controlled users of illicit drugs because they present, according to the U.S. Office of National Drug Control Policy, "a *highly* contagious" example to potential drug users (White House 1989, 11, emphasis in original). Zimring and Hawkins (1992, 16) point out that it is the nonaddicted drug users "who are most conspicuously thumbing their noses at the state authority."

Grace (1986) suggests that social scientists rarely verbalize any explicit discursive assumptions (about illicit drugs and users). That is, there seems to be little reflexive acknowledgment of the discourse's own kind of coincident biases toward the objects of study. Instead, sometime in the past "someone began talking *as if* such and such things were true. In good time others followed the lead, accepting some of the same terms and metaphors and adding more of their own, until eventually a full-fledged jargon of the familiar sort came into being" (Grace 1986, 20). The turn-of-the-century moral crusades against opiates, cocaine, and marijuana set the foundation for popular perceptions of and professional inquiry into illicit drugs and drug use. Criminologists have simply built upon it.

In his seminal work on *Orientalism,* Said (1978) suggests that a scholar is just a specialist in a particular field of knowledge already constructed historically and culturally by an entire society. Before criminology or sociology began studying illicit drug use, American culture had already developed a fear of drugs—particularly when associated with disadvantaged and feared groups. The anecdotes of the early 1900s, telling of violent crimes committed by kids while high on marijuana and of violent black males who could not be stopped by bullets while high on cocaine, helped to build a tradition suspicious of unconventional drugs. Therefore, studies of disadvantaged minority drug users and studies aiming to "correct" the drug-use problem speak to a common sense notion of drugs held by the general public and its professionals. New continuing studies of the same style further reinforce and restate cultural norms that were almost a century in the making.

LANGUAGE AND THE DRUG USER

Drugs, and even more so drug users, have been constructed through legal and cultural processes. In popular media as well as academic research, people who use legal drugs are not called drug users whereas those who use illegal drugs are. Someone who smokes tobacco is a *smoker,* but someone who smokes marijuana is a *drug user*. Though both substances are recognized as drugs, one *smokes* cigarettes, whereas someone else *uses* marijuana.

The academic literature often uses drug use and abuse interchangeably when discussing illegal drugs. Legal definitions of drug abuse—any use of illegal drugs—have come to provide the analytical definitions for many researchers, regardless of the actual behavior patterns under study. Scholars talk of certain populations being at a "higher-than-average *risk* of drug use" (Zimring and Hawkins 1992, 198, emphasis added). "Risk" emphasizes only the potential dangers of drug use and is generally reserved for proscribed drugs.

Language plays a most important role in society and culture. It constructs reality (Grace 1986). Criminologists, while in the process of studying a reality, actually play a role in creating it through the discourse of the field and use of language. The contexts of discussions involving drugs or drug users influence their conceptual elements and thus their very meaning. The issue here is not so much "faulty" research on drug use as it is the importance of how drug use is talked about even if it is not the object of study per se.

For instance, a criminological essay about domestic abuse off-handedly mentions the importance of arresting "drug dealers, thieves, and rapists" (Hirschel et al. 1992). The idea of drug users now includes, at least peripherally, murderers and rapists. Likewise, a textbook on criminal justice lists the "basic rules of society: do not murder, rob, sell drugs, commit treason" (Cole and Smith 1998, 404). Again, selling drugs is associated with the most serious predatory crimes and even treason against one's country.

In a discussion of peacemaking methodology, Caulfield and Evans (1997) list the "core issues" related to "drug-oriented behavior" including "alienation, a drug-oriented culture, an addiction-based culture, instant gratification, cure-alls via over-the-counter medication, and economic structures that place more value on drugs than on employment with a realistic minimum wage" (106–107). Doubtlessly, such variables are associated with drug *abuse* and some drug use, but the absence of any benign or even neutral "causes" of drug use represents cultural assumptions rather than any attempt at a thorough listing of variables associated with drug use.

Another example is provided in Wonders's (1999, 118) discussion of an aspect of "positionality," through which we attribute meaning to things that then take on those given meanings:

> If the state claims that young people who use drugs are criminal (rather than 'ill,' as is done in many other industrialized countries), then the state has played an active role in shaping the identity of teenagers and others who used drugs—it has changed who they are.

While describing how the state imposes a criminal meaning on drug use, Wonders charitably offers up an alternative identity—sick person. In her own discussion of positionality, she has criticized one definition and suggested another (a dubious improvement for the user) to take its place. Rather than merely being a criminal, a drug user may now be sick instead. This is exactly how scholars can unreflexively construct identities of their objects of study—even while being critical of how others are doing it. These are studies in which drug use is not even the focus of study, yet it is talked about in ways that conform to popular images of illicit drug use, thereby further reifying those images.

Supporting the continued prohibition of illicit drugs, Wilson (1990, 28) argues that if illicit drugs are legalized, "to the lives and families destroyed by alcohol we will have added countless more destroyed by cocaine, heroin, phencyclidine (PCP), and whatever else *a basement scientist can invent*" (emphasis added). In a sentence, Wilson manages to perpetuate particular images of the illicit drug scene (even if made licit). It is probably not accidental that marijuana or LSD was not mentioned in the list of illicit drugs that will destroy lives. Again, the "hard" drugs, like heroin, cocaine, and PCP stand in as representatives for the whole gamut of illicit drugs.

More important, the imagery of a "basement scientist" connotes something unsavory or dirty about the class of drugs to which he refers. Although pharmaceutical companies are responsible for the development and current production of the majority of abused drugs, Wilson clearly identifies drugs of abuse as illicit/underground drugs.

The use of this imagery draws on cultural preconceptions about illicit drugs and concurrently adds new dimensions to the connotations of "drugs." Drug users are not just people who ingest chemical entities that alter their physiology, they are symbolically associated with disease, the subterranean, and low self-control. "The images which we associate with drug use have taken on profound emotional significance partly because of the kinds of things they have come to symbolize and partly because this symbolism is fraught with ambiguity" (Manderson 1995, 800).

DIRECTIONS IN RESEARCH

Of course, not all research perpetuates the hegemonic notions of drug-user pathology. Much critical work has challenged these images of drug users, and the growing literature on harm reduction suggests new directions for research on drug use. Works such as Reinarman and Levine's (1997) edited book *Crack in America* and Beck and Rosenbaum's (1994) study of Ecstasy users help expose the myths and panics surrounding certain types of drug-use behaviors, as well as class, race, and other biases underlying these reactions. Grossman and associates (1974) have identified some positive character traits associated with marijuana use among college students. They found that openness to experience and creativity were associated with moderate marijuana use, where as nonusers were more authoritarian and "narrow in interests."

Deconstructing pathological motivations behind certain legal and public reactions to specific drug-use behaviors also allows a more informative critique of public policy. Moreover, recognizing the positive motivations behind drug use and the pathological motivations behind the unequally enforced prohibition against some drug use helps balance the conversation. Identifying healthy drug-use patterns can inform our approaches to dealing with destructive drug use. Perhaps there are no good or bad drugs, only good or bad relationships with drugs (Weil and Rosen 1998). Doubtless, there is a relationship between components of unhealthy drug use and unhealthy policy responses to drugs.

With its focus on pathology and correction, research runs the risk of essentially having nothing to say to the large number of people who do choose to use drugs regardless of the messages. Research itself, then, may actually contribute to drug-related harm through its sheer irrelevance (see Cohen 1993, 68). The growing movement toward harm reduction is based on the recognition that many policy and research approaches to some drugs may indeed be responsible for some of the problems with which those drugs have been associated.

In harm reduction, drug use is viewed as neither right nor wrong. It is simply one of a multitude of behaviors in which people engage. Though some proponents of harm reduction may view abstinence as an ideal, they focus on the more immediately realistic goal of reducing the harms related to the use of substances. Recognizing that we cannot eliminate drug use altogether, harm reductionists aim to minimize its potential dangers (Rosenbaum 1996, 10). That is, harm reduction focuses on decreasing risk and severity of adverse consequences of use without necessarily decreasing the actual level of consumption (Single 1997).

Risk reduction programs in Europe and Australia are based on a morally neutral view of drug use. Rather than condemning the use of certain drugs, the programs seek to discover how unhealthy relationships can be avoided while perhaps encouraging healthier drug use. Drug users themselves have built much of the harm reduction movement. In fact, it is the users who have historically shared the norms, traditions, and mores that have helped others minimize the negative consequences of drug use (Becker 1963; Zinberg and Harding 1982).

Research must seek appreciation for the subjective realities of drug users themselves. The challenge lies in finding ways to conduct research with and learn from illicit drug users without objectifying or pathologizing them (Whiteacre and Pepinsky 2002). Peacemaking criminology and its emphasis on balanced conversation, or drawing out the voices least heard (Pepinsky 1998), can provide a foundation for new approaches. Drawing out the voices of drug users suggests looking for ways to allow them to tell their own stories. It becomes a discourse *of* drug users rather than *about* them (Whiteacre and Pepinsky 2002).

Until the cultural constructions of drug use and drug users are recognized and dealt with, there is little hope for meaningful policy reform. Without new methodologies and approaches in research to build links with drug users of all types rather than just those in prison or treatment, policy will continue to reflect the assumptions of prejudice and ignorance.

REFERENCES

Adler, P. A. 1993. *Wheeling and dealing*. New York: Columbia University Press.

Akers, R. L., and J. K. Cochran. 1985. Adolescent marijuana use: a test of three theories of deviant behavior. *Deviant Behavior* 6:323–46.

Akers, R. L., M. D. Krohn, L. Lanza-Kaduce, and M. Radosevich, 1979. Social learning and deviant behavior: a specific test of a general theory. *American Sociological Review* 44:636–55.

Bahr, S. J., and R. D. Hawks, 1993. Family and religious influences on adolescent substance abuse. *Youth and Society* 24:4.

Beck, J., and M. Rosenbaum, 1994. *Pursuit of Ecstasy*. New York: State University of New York Press.

Becker, H. S. 1963. *Outsiders*. New York: The Free Press.

BOURGOIS, P. 1995. *In search of respect: Selling crack in El Barrio*. New York: Cambridge University Press.

BROWNSTEIN, H. H. 1996. The media and the construction of random drug violence. In *Examining the justice process,* ed. J. A. Inciardi. Fort Worth, TX: Harcourt Brace College Publishers.

CAULFIELD, S. L. S. and A. R. EVANS. 1997. Peacemaking criminology: A path to understanding and a model for methodology. In *Thinking critically about crime,* ed. B. MacLean and D. Milovanovic. Vancouver: Collective Press.

COHEN, JULIAN. 1993. Achieving harm reduction in drug-related harm through education. In *Psychoactive drugs and harm reduction: From faith to science,* eds. Nick Heather, Alex Wodak, Ethan A. Nadelmann, and Pat O'Hare. London: Whurr Publishers.

COHEN, S. 1992. *Against criminology.* New Brunswick, NJ: Transaction Publishers.

COLE, G. F., and SMITH. C. E. 1998. *The American system of criminal justice.* Belmont, CA: West/Wadsworth.

DOUGLAS, M. 1966. *Purity and danger.* London: Ark Paperbacks.

GARLAND, D. 1985. The criminal and his science. *The British Journal of Criminology* 25(2):109–37.

GARLAND, D. 1992. Criminological knowledge and its relation to power: Foucault's geneaology and criminology today. *British Journal of Criminology* 32(4):413–25.

GOODE, E. 1972. *Drugs in American society.* New York: Knopf.

GOTTFREDSON, M. R., and T. HIRSCHI. 1990. *A general theory of crime.* Palo Alto, CA: Stanford University Press.

GROSSMAN, JAN, RONALD GODSTEIN, and RUSSELL EISENMAN. 1974. Undergraduate marijuana and drug use as related to openness to experience. *Psychiatric Quarterly* 48(1):86–92.

HIRSCHEL, J. D., I. W. HUTCHINSON, C. W. DEAN, and A. MILLS. 1992. The law enforcement response to spouse abuse: Past, present and future. *Justice Quarterly* 9(2):247–83.

HUNT, L. G., and C. D. CHAMBERS. 1976. *The heroin epidemics: A study of heroin use in the United States, 1965–1975.* New York: Spectrum Publishers.

KAPLAN, J. 1983. *The hardest drug: Heroin and public policy.* Chicago: University of Chicago Press.

LENSON, D. 1995. *On drugs.* Minneapolis: University of Minnesota Press.

MAGUIRE, M. 1997. Crime statistics, patterns, and trends: Changing perceptions and their implications. In *The Oxford handbook of criminology,* eds. M. Maguire, R. Morgan, and R. Reiner. Oxford: Clarendon Press.

MANDERSON, D. 1995. Metamorposes: Clashing symbols in the social construction of drugs. *The Journal of Drug Issues* 25(4):799–816.

MERTON, R. K. 1938. Social structure and anomie. *American Sociological Review* 3:672–82.

MILAKOVICH, M. E., and K. WEIS. 1975. Politics and measures of success in the war on crime. *Crime and Delinquency* 21(1):1–10.

MILLER, L. J. 1993. Claims-making from the underside. In *Reconsidering social constructionism,* eds. J. A. Holstein and G. Miller. New York: Aldine De Gruyter.

PEPINSKY, H. E. 1998. Empathy works, obedience doesn't. *Criminal Justice Policy Review* 9(2):141–167.

PEPINSKY, H. E., and P. JESILOW. 1984. *Myths that cause crime.* Cabin John, MD: Seven Locks Press.

REINARMAN, C., and H. G. LEVINE. eds. 1997. *Crack in America.* Berkeley: University of California Press.

ROSENBAUM, MARSHA. 1996. *Kids, drugs, and education.* Oakland, CA: The National Council on Crime and Delinquency.

SAID, E. W. 1978. *Orientalism.* New York: Vintage Books.

SEDGWICK, E. K. 1990. *Epistemology of the closet.* Berkeley: University of California Press.

SIEGEL, R. K. 1977. Cocaine: recreational use and intoxication. In *Cocaine: 1977,* eds. R. C. Petersen and R. C. Stillman. Bethesda, MD: National Institute on Drug Abuse.

SINGLE, ERIC. 1997. Towards a harm reduction approach to alcohol-problem prevention. In *Harm reduction: A new direction for drug policies and programs,* Patricia G. Erickson, Diane M. Riley, Yuet W. Chueng, and Patrick O'Hare, eds., Toronto: Toronto University Press.

SMITH, D. E., and G. R. GAY, eds. 1972. *It's so good don't even try it once: Heroin in perspective,* Upper Saddle River, NJ: Prentice Hall.

SPENDER, D. 1981. The gatekeepers: A feminist critique of academic publishing. *Doing feminist Research,* ed. H. Roberts. London: Routledge & Kegan Paul.

STOREY, J. 1998. *An introduction to cultural theory and popular culture.* Athens: The University of Georgia Press.

TAYLOR, I., P. WALTON, and J. YOUNG. 1973. *The new criminology: For a social theory of deviance.* London: Routledge & Kegan Paul.

WEIL, ANDREW, and WINIFRED ROSEN. 1998. *From chocolate to morphine.* Boston, MA: Houghton Mifflin Company.

WHITE HOUSE. 1989. *National drug control strategy.* Washington, DC: U.S. Government Printing Office.

WHITEACRE, KEVIN W., and HAL PEPINSKY. 2002. Controlling drug use. *Criminal Justice Policy Review* 13(1):21–31.

WILSON, J. Q. 1990. Against the legalization of drugs. *Commentary,* February.

WILSON, W. J. 1996. *When work disappears: The world of the new urban poor.* New York: Knopf.

WILSON, J. Q., and R. J. HERRNSTEIN. 1985. *Crime and human nature.* New York: Simon & Schuster.

WINFREE, I. T., C. T. GRIFFITHS, and C. S. SELLERS. 1989. Social learning theory, drug use, and American Indian youths: A cross-culture test. *Justice Quarterly* 6(3):395–415.

WONDERS, N. A. 1999. Postmodern feminist criminology and social justice. *Social justice/criminal justice,* ed. B. A. Arrigo. CA: West/Wadsworth.

YOUNG, I. M. 1990. *Justice and the politics of difference.* Princeton, New Jersey: Princeton University Press.

ZIMRING, F. E., and G. HAWKINS. 1992. *The search for rational drug control.* New York: Cambridge University Press.

ZINBERG, N. E. 1995. Nonaddictive opiate use. In *The American drug scene,* eds. J. A. Inciardi and K. McElrath. Los Angeles, CA: Roxbury Publishing Company.

ZINBERG, NORMAN E., and WAYNE M. HARDING. 1982. *Control over intoxicant use.* New York: Human Sciences Press.

2

The Role of Ethnography in Substance Abuse Research and Public Policy

Historical Precedent and Future Prospects

Harvey W. Feldman and Michael R. Aldrich

❖

INTRODUCTION

Perhaps the best way to begin is to answer the question: What is ethnography? One of the earliest definitions of ethnography was provided by A.H. Beatty in 1896, who wrote, "Ethnography is purely descriptive, dealing with characteristic social and political conditions of people, irrespective of their possible physical relations or affinities" (Wiseman and Aron 1970, 238). The definition sounds old fashioned, formal, and somewhat unclear, but it serves as a starting point.

James Spradley, who died in 1982, was an ethnographer affiliated with the University of Washington in Seattle and the author of *You Owe Yourself a Drunk: An Ethnography of Urban Nomads* (Spradley 1970), a landmark study of the way alcoholics move through the criminal justice system. He called ethnography "the science of cultural description" and claimed that "through a painstaking process of participant observation one slowly comes to apprehend the insider's view of life" (Spradley 1977, 13).

Reprinted with permission from E. V. Lambert (ed.), *The Collection and Interpretation of Data from Hidden Populations*. National Institute on Drug Abuse (NIDA) Research Monograph. 98. Rockville, MD.

Jennifer James defined ethnography as "the study of cultures from within" (James 1977, 180). James Walters, who worked the streets of Philadelphia, called ethnography "an analytic description of behaviors that characterize and distinguish cultures or sociocultural groups" (Walters 1980, p. 17). Jacqueline Wiseman and Marcia Aron, in their book *Field Projects for Sociological Students* (1970), said, "Ethnographic research is an investigator's application of his sociological methods and skills to a specific scene in order to learn enough about its people, situations and human relations to be able to present the reader with a slice of life" (Wiseman and Aron 1970, p. 237). Finally, George Beschner, an adapted ethnographer affiliated with the National Institute on Drug Abuse (NIDA), once described ethnography as "the study of a culture or social group from the perspective of its members" (Feldman et al. 1979, 4).

To sum up these definitions, there are perhaps three essential features they touch on. First, even though ethnography is a scientific method, it requires an artist's touch or even better, an artist's soul, rather than being the simple application of a technical approach to analyze human behavior.

Second, clearly the aim is to get an insider's view of a culture or social group, with emphasis on being authentic and on being accurate. To achieve that, the ethnographer has to go where members of the culture or social group carry out their activities and observe members by watching them carefully, asking the right questions, and by listening.

Finally, like many others in scientific fields, it is the ethnographer's task to assemble data in a way that makes sense and that reflects actual phenomena. How detailed the final product will be is subject to debate. The old view of ethnography as cultural description required that the product be absolutely thorough. To achieve this completeness may have required several years of living among the populations under study, so that each piece of the culture was understood in its relationship to all the others. As ethnography moved more and more into the arena of applied sciences, where its influence may have been determined by its ability to respond with data in a timely fashion, completeness may have been sacrificed to significance.

The more recent view, because of some developments in ethnography and its use in government's management of social and health problems, is that the ethnographer must gain a quick but accurate understanding of a phenomenon in order to act on it. The use of ethnography for understanding the spread of the human immunodeficiency virus (HIV) within intravenous (IV) drug-using populations is a recent example of the application of ethnographic research methods to a health problem with complex social implications; it will be discussed later in this chapter. Ethnography is a useful device for understanding a phenomenon quickly, so that findings can be converted into public health policies and control measures. As ethnography grows in importance as a tool for obtaining information quickly for policymakers, it risks losing its reputation for completeness. Ronald Cohen, an anthropologist, said in "The Logic of Generalization" that "scientific findings and explanations are always partial, and they always leave something out" (Cohen 1970, 31).

Generally, ethnography is the term used to describe almost all qualitative research, from strictly interviewing, which is its most limited form, to extensive observation from some selected social role that allows an insider's view. Many ethnographers prefer fieldwork, which means spending time where members of a group spend their time, seeing what goes on, and then asking questions about the observations.

HERODOTUS: THE BEGINNINGS OF DRUG ETHNOGRAPHY

Where and when did ethnography's connection to substance abuse begin? Drug ethnography as a research method is a fairly recent development. The first recorded example in Western literature is found in Herodotus in his description of the Scythians, who were nomadic horsemen of Central Asia somewhere around the fifth century BC. Briefly, Herodotus claimed that, after the burial of a king, the Scythians purified themselves by fixing three sticks in the ground, tied together at the top and tightly covered with felt. Inside this little tent they put a dish with red-hot stones in it. Then they took hemp seed, crept under the tent, and threw it on the red-hot stones. And, to quote Herodotus:

> It smolders at once and sends up such billows of smoke that no Greek vapor-bath could surpass it. The Scythians howl with joy in these vapor-baths, which serve them instead of bathing, for they never wash their bodies with water. (Aldrich translation)

Herodotus is often accused of making up wild tales, and, in his *Histories,* (De Selincourt 1954) he often says he does not believe them himself. But this account of bathing in marijuana vapors was verified in 1948 when a Russian archaeologist (Rudenko 1970) dug up a Scythian tomb barrow in Siberia and found, next to well-preserved corpses, six poles about 18 inches high, a felt blanket, a copper cauldron with stones in it, and a leather medicine bag containing hemp seeds, quickfrozen in ice since about the fifth century BC. So Herodotus was verified in every particular, except that there were six sticks instead of three. This demonstrates another point: ethnographers have difficulty counting.

COLUMBUS AND PANE: THE DISCOVERY OF DIMETHYLTRYPTAMINE (DMT)

The first ethnography in America came from Christopher Columbus and a friar he hired on his second voyage (1493–1496). The friar's name was Ramon Pane, and his special task was to record native customs. Columbus noticed the Tainos of Haiti sniffing a dust that made them "become like drunken men" (Wassen 1967, 235). Pane investigated and found that this powder, called *cohoba* by the natives, was snuffed by chiefs and shamans to communicate with the spirits. Pane noted a bizarre outcome, which today would be considered psychedelic: "Consider what a state their brains are in, because they say the cabins seem to them to be turned upside down and the men are walking with their feet in the air" (Wassen 1967, 238).

At first the Europeans thought *cohoba* was tobacco and dismissed the visions Pane reported as heathen nonsense. Pane commented, "They speak many things incoherently" (Wassen 1967, 238). The Tainos were exterminated about 50 years later, and not until 1916 was a botanist able to identify cohoba as a hallucinogenic drug made from the beans of a tree, *Anadenanthera peregrina* (Safford 1916). The active ingredient was identified in the 1950s as dimethyltryptamine or DMT. Not until 1972, when Altschul reviewed ethnographic reports of surviving tribes who used this snuff, did the meaning of the visions reported by Columbus and Pane become clear:

> the person, who is seated with his head turning to one side and his arms around his knees, becomes at first unconscious, then wakens and, with his face turned toward the ceiling, speaks unintelligibly; the Indians say that the house in which the powder is taken then appears to be upside down and they themselves seem to be walking on air. (Altschul 1972, p. 13)

So it took from 1496 to 1972 for the discovery of DMT to make sense. The lesson from this for ethnography and ethnographers, as well as for all scientists, is to keep pursuing analysis of the data; sooner or later, it will begin to make sense.

VESPUCCI, CIEZA, AND ACOSTA: BUT WHY DO THEY DO IT?

In 1504, Amerigo Vespucci gave the first ethnographic report of coca chewing, as he found it in 1499 on a little island off South America. Watching the natives put coca and powdered lime in their mouths so "their cheeks bulged with the leaves . . . which they chewed like cattle," he wondered why: "They did this frequently, a little at a time; and the thing seemed wonderful, for we could not understand the secret, or with what object they did it." After asking for drinking water and being offered coca instead, Vespucci guessed that "they kept this herb in their mouths to stave off thirst" (Aldrich and Barker 1976, 3).

Fifty years later, Cieza de Leon, an ethnographer in South America during the Spanish Conquest, asked directly: "When I asked some of these Indians why they carried these leaves in their mouth . . . they replied that it prevents them from feeling hungry, and gives them great vigor and strength" (Aldrich and Barker 1976, 3). At first this notion was dismissed as pure imagination, but when the Spaniards discovered that the natives would not work the silver mines of Potosi without coca, they allowed them to chew it. By 1570, Jose de Acosta said that the traffic in coca at Potosi had exceeded a half million pesos a year (von Hagen 1959).

From these very early ethnographic reports of drug use, a lesson can be learned that has modern application. Ethnography takes place in a cultural context, affecting both the observer and the observed. Drug ethnography, in particular, is a matter of one group with a certain viewpoint studying another group with quite a different viewpoint. A value and a limitation of ethnography is that it occurs in a specific place and time. This should always be remembered while collecting and interpreting data from "hidden populations" or populations whose behavior we might not like or find socially undesirable.

DE QUINCEY: THE INDUSTRIAL CONTEXT

Depending on how strictly we want to hold to a definition of ethnography, the modern era for drug ethnography probably began with Thomas De Quincey in his 1822 *Confessions of An English Opium-Eater*. De Quincey was an ethnographer in many ways and was the first to consider opiate use in the modern industrial context. At an early age, he ran away from home and lived in the streets of London, mingling with thieves, prostitutes, and other social outcasts. He wrote:

> At no time in my life have I ever been a person to hold myself polluted by the touch or approach of any creature that wore a human shape. On the contrary, it has been my pride to converse familiarly . . . with all human beings . . . that chance might fling my way, a practice which is friendly to the knowledge of human nature. (Ward 1966, 42)

This is a great quote for all ethnographers to remember. Having disdain for social classes, particularly if those classes are the very subjects of study, is the basis for bias that will distort and probably destroy objectivity. De Quincey's message is timely: ethnographers cannot present an accurate portrait of a population whom they dislike, distrust, or look down on.

De Quincey began his study of opium users by observing men he noted were distinguished for talent or eminent station. He preserved the anonymity of his contacts by leaving blanks for the names of famous addicts. Later, in an 1856 revision of his *Confessions,* he revealed that they included Samuel Taylor Coleridge, the famed poet and critic and author of "The Rime of the Ancient Mariner"; Sir William Wilberforce, the man most responsible for abolishing slavery throughout the English Empire; and many other prominent British figures. Following this, he began exploring opium use among the lower classes, and, as a participant observer, he moved into the real world of the opium system of the time—users, suppliers, their bosses, and working conditions. Here he noted, among other things, that one immediate reason for working-class opium abuse was "the lowness of wages, which, at that time, would not allow them to indulge in ale or spirits" (Ward 1966, p. 24–25). The result was an enlightening description of opiate abuse in the context of the onrushing Industrial Revolution. De Quincey's conclusion was that, in this context, opiate use cut across all classes of society, which was also noted in America by Fitz Hugh Ludlow (1867).

THE ETHNOBOTANISTS: PERILS OF PARTICIPANT OBSERVATION

In the 19th century, many botanists were drug ethnographers. Richard Spruce, who spent much of his life collecting plants in the Amazon, was the "great granddaddy" of them all. In 1851 through 1852, he found himself in Brazil among a head-hunting tribe of the Rio Vaupes, who had never seen a white man before. He asked about a drink called *caapi* that their sorcerers used, and they urged him to try some. He managed to down a cupful, and the tribal leaders, anxious to show him all their drugs, plied him with manioc beer, a two-foot-long cigar (Spruce had never smoked before) and a large bowl of palm wine. Overcome with a strong inclination to vomit, he retired to a hammock, drank coffee, and passed out (Wallace 1908). Despite this negative experience, he was sufficiently impressed to gather specimens of the vine from which the drink was made. He correctly identified it as *Banisteriopsis caapi,* also called yage, which is now known to contain the hallucinogen harmine. More than a century later, Schultes subjected Spruce's specimens to chemical analysis and found them "comparable with freshly collected plant material" (Schultes and Hofmann 1980, 168). Another lesson for qualitative research: if possible, with the permission of the respondents, collect evidence to verify observations. More importantly, Spruce reminds us that "participant observation" can be a contradiction in terms. The question is, how much does one participate in order to be allowed to observe? In extreme cases, one's life may depend on the answer.

Other ethnobotanists who have conducted drug research in this century include La Barre, Whose book *The Peyote Cult* (La Barre 1938) is a key reference on the Native American Church; Schultes (1937), whose early work on peyotism among the Kiowa (Vestal and Schultes 1939) led to 40 years of studying Amazon drug plants; Wasson (1980), who discovered the modern use of psilocyben mushrooms in Mexico, which led to a complete revision of our understanding of native uses of such plants; and, more recently, Davis (1985), whose fieldwork in Haiti revealed that the drug used in voodoo to make men into zombies is from a West Indian puffer fish. Understanding the use of each of these drugs within their respective cultures was the contribution of ethnographers, in these cases, ethnobotanists.

In our urban milieu, ethnographers themselves must answer the question of how deeply to participate in the activities of a social group or a culture. Field researchers have always been warned about the dangers of "going native." Arthur Vidich (1955) stated that, in doing so, researchers lose their objectivity. Vidich's advice is sound: the development of mutually beneficial research relationships should not depend on demonstrating to respondents the researcher's trustworthiness by becoming involved in activities that are either personally repugnant, ethically questionable, physically dangerous, or outright illegal. It is not necessary to share needles with IV drug users to study needle sharing and the way that activity may affect the acquired immunodeficiency syndrome (AIDS) epidemic; researchers' credibility is at risk both within the scientific community and with respondents if researchers do not clearly identify themselves as nonparticipants in illegal activities. As often as not, an invitation to share drugs or commit a crime is a test of whether researchers are who they say they are—researchers rather than agents of social control. These are, of course, individual decisions that should always be made on the basis of pursuing information, not from insecurity or for thrill seeking.

THE DEVELOPMENT OF MODERN DRUG ETHNOGRAPHY

Probably the first important drug ethnography for modern times in America was carried out, appropriately enough, in Chicago, the home base for field research in America. Being within the famed "Chicago school" of social research, it was an extensive one-man study by Bingham Dai titled simply *Opium Addiction in Chicago* (Dai 1937). Dai's study was a combination of field research and the psychoanalytic approach. It is important because it captured the evolving opiate scene between the latter nineteenth century, when drugs were freely available in the United States, and the changes brought about by the Harrison Act of 1914.

Dai divided his respondents, who were predominantly white, into two categories: those addicted to morphine through medical treatment, and those addicted primarily due to the influences of other drug addicts and "peddlers," through what Dai called "pleasure parties," or association with pimps, prostitutes, pool rooms, gambling houses, and homosexuals. Dai's method was the indepth life history interview. Given his psychoanalytical background, it was not surprising to find his observations cast in terms like "infantile" personalities, excessive dependence on others, and a tendency to withdraw or escape from social responsibility (Dai 1937). The fact that he drew many of his cases from the Psychopathic Hospital in Chicago may account for his tendency to identify psychopathology as the underpinning of all drug abuse.

Alfred Lindesmith, who had helped Dai gather respondents, used qualitative interviewing techniques to develop definitions of addiction—probably the first in the world derived from ethnographic research—and published them in 1947 in the landmark book called *Opiate Addiction* (Lindesmith 1947). His work in the 1940s and 1950s changed the theoretical perspective toward addicts. Based on his findings and conclusions, he argued against what he believed were the severe limitations of the public policy of prohibition that grew out of the Harrison Act. Lindesmith criticized and contradicted the enforcement policy of the Federal Bureau of Narcotics at the time, which he described in *The Addict and the Law* (Lindesmith 1965).

Lindesmith's ethnographic work contributed to a scientific understanding of the meaning of addiction and was used to juxtapose two views of the phenomenon: drug addiction as crime and drug addiction as disease. That juxtaposition was, in fact, the title of a report, *Drug Addiction: Crime or Disease?*, issued by a Joint Committee of the American

Bar Association and the American Medical Association (1961). The Federal Bureau of Narcotics argued against the report before it was published, which resulted in the publication of what had originally been only an internal report, and Lindesmith's research became the basis of public discussion about the management of drug addiction in America for the next 30 years.

From the 1940s to the 1960s, most of the ethnographic studies in the drug field shifted the emphasis from asking why people used drugs to asking how they went about getting involved in drug use and how they remained involved. Rather than looking for underlying causes, ethnographers began to find their search for etiological influences in the social world rather than the internal world of experimenters. This period constituted the first major shift away from psychoanalytic theory and a medical model of addiction to a more sociological perspective. The concept of drug use as a "career" became very useful. Building on the work of Everett Hughes (1984) who introduced the study of occupations into sociology, Howard Becker (1963) took the career model and applied it to deviant careers in general and drug users specifically. This conceptual shift had broad implications and was the basis for what came to be viewed as a new sociological movement called "labeling theory." When applied to the field of addiction, it provided a different perspective that included an analysis of individual drug users and of public policy, as well as a legal framework within which such activities took place. In this way, Becker's concepts helped structure the way drug ethnographers began to collect and analyze data. This shift in concept was evident in his own study, "Becoming a Marijuana User" (Becker 1953).

At approximately the same time, other small ethnographic studies of drug users were in progress. One of these became most influential, namely Harold Finestone's (1957) study of black heroin addicts in Chicago entitled "Cats, Kicks, and Color." Many in the field of drug ethnography, while impressed with the influence of this single study, were critical of it, because it seemed less a description of heroin addicts than a description of low-income street blacks in Chicago in general, whether or not they were involved in heroin use. In carrying out interviews in an office rather than spending time among heroin users in their natural settings, Finestone apparently mistook a general black perspective as something peculiar to heroin users. In noting that they employed a special argot of slang terms, for example, the word "bread" for money, or because they had a preference for "cool jazz," he attributed these characteristics to addicts when, in fact, they were common among street blacks almost everywhere during the 1950s. Finestone's fame will rest not so much on having carried out top-level ethnography as it will on the use of his work by later sociologists who, in scouring the literature for descriptions of drug users, found the drug ethnography library of the period relatively barren except for Finestone's study.

In an attempt to develop a broad theory of delinquency, Richard Cloward and Lloyd Ohlin (1960) aimed to unite the previously disparate theories of structural functionalism and anomie as developed by Robert Merton (1957) and Emile Durkheim (1951) with the tradition of differential association as developed by Shaw and McKay (1942) and Sutherland (1947). In their book *Delinquency and Opportunity: A Theory of Delinquent Gangs,* Cloward and Ohlin attempted to portray several delinquent subcultures, one of which was a "retreatist" subculture of addicts, which was based on a theoretic category developed by Merton, Cloward's mentor. The only empirical study that provided actual descriptions of addict behavior and supported this perspective was Finestone's short description in "Cats, Kicks, and Color." It became the sole basis of support for a theory that was soon to achieve national prominence. Had the work of Cloward and Ohlin occurred a few years later, they would have had available to them numerous studies to draw from, but, at the time, Finestone's was one of few descriptive studies of heroin addicts available. Because of the importance of the Cloward and Ohlin opportunity theory and its use as the underpinning of the Mobilization for Youth delinquency project in New York City, the "trial balloon" for the 1960s antipoverty program, their minitheory of addicts as double failures within a retreatist subculture became a persistent theme.

Along with the explosion of drug use in the 1960s, primarily among youth (Mandel and Feldman 1988) and various populations throughout the United States, there was also a rise in the funding for ethnographic research that came principally from NIDA and its predecessor, the Center for Drug Studies, under the National Institute of Mental Health, through a woman most contemporary drug ethnographers look upon with great respect, Eleanor Carroll. She was a strong advocate on behalf of ethnography and field research and did much to advance the field.

The 1960s produced what has been referred to as the "era of iconoclasts" in the drug field. This involved a shift away from the classic question that Lindesmith posed about addiction as crime or disease. Several ethnographers, operating independently in different parts of the country, asked instead, "How about neither?" Building on the career model and going directly into the hangouts of drug users, these ethnographers moved away from trying to understand drug use as a consequence of the physical and/or psychological effects of drugs to exploring how the activity of drug use itself was viewed within the community contexts where it took place. A consistent conclusion was that drug use should be viewed not as a pathology so much as a status-enhancing activity within certain communities where street action and high-risk behavior were highly valued.

The *Add Center Project Final Report: The World of Youthful Drug Use* by Herbert Blumer (1967), one of the old-timers of the Chicago School, was a key document in the move toward a different view of drug use. Much of the report was written by Alan Sutter, who mixed easily with street drug users and was probably the first to note that drug use seemed less an issue of pathology and more a means to acquire social status and reputation within an environment that valued risk-taking behavior. This view was supported by concurrent studies by Edward Preble (Preble and Casey 1969) and Feldman (1968).

Almost all these developments in the 1960s were snapshots of special population: Sutter (1966; Sutter 1969; Sutter 1972) with blacks in Oakland; Polsky (1967) with pool hustlers; Feldman with Italians in Boston (Feldman 1973; Feldman 1974, 1977); Carey and Mandel (1968) with amphetamine use in the San Francisco Bay Area; and Preble and Casey (1969; Preble 1980a) in New York City with Puerto Ricans and mixed white ethnic heroin addicts. The rise in the number of ethnographic studies continued into the 1970s: Sherri Cavan (1972) with hippies in the Haight; Irving Soloway's 1974 study of methadone clients (Soloway 1974); major studies of marijuana use in Jamaica (Rubin and Comitas 1975) and Costa Rica (Carter 1980); Patricia Cleckner's work on cocaine users in Miami (Cleckner 1976a, 1976b; Cleckner 1977); Jennifer James's ethnography of prostitutes in Seattle (James 1976; James 1977); Joan Moore's now classic study of Mexican-American "homeboys" in Los Angeles (Moore 1974); and the Feldman et al. (1979) study of phencyclidine (PCP) users. The ethnographers in the PCP study worked in four cities: Wayne Wiebel in Chicago, Jennifer James in Seattle, Patricia Cleckner in Miami, and James Walters in Philadelphia. As ethnographers became interested in special populations, Marsha Rosenbaum and Sheigla

Murphy conducted research to improve the understanding of females who injected heroin (Rosenbaum 1981), of women in methadone maintenance programs (Rosenbaum and Murphy 1987; Murphy and Rosenbaum 1988), and, more recently, of professionals who use methylenedioxymethamphetamine (Rosenbaum and Morgan 1988).

Coming into the 1980s, there has been a dual research emphasis on street dealing and drug trafficking and on the out-of-treatment drug user. Three studies of drug dealing have added greatly to our understanding of that illegitimate business: Allen Fields's (1984, 1986) study of young street "weedslingers," Bruce Johnson's (1985) study of heroin dealers, and Patricia Adler's (1985) study of cocaine traffickers.

Two ethnographic works focused on addicts who have never been in treatment: *Life with Heroin* (Hanson et al. 1985), and—important for understanding how some addicts can move away from heroin use without entering formal treatment programs—Patrick Biernacki's *Pathways from Heroin Addiction* (Biernacki 1986), which won the Charles Cooley award offered by the Society for the Study of Symbolic Interactionism last year.

The tendency of 1970s ethnographic work was to shift away from a focus on ethnicity and culture to studies that were largely drug specific. During this period, there was a growing concern over the emergence of new drugs. It was widely believed that each drug had its won special subculture; and it was the contribution of ethnographers that revealed the clear existence of polydrug users and the way they sifted and sorted through a variety of drug options. What came out of the 1970s ethnographic research, however, was a clearer picture of social subgroups, not by drug of preference necessarily, but in demographic configurations based on age, sex, race, ethnicity, and neighborhood affiliation. Collectively, many of these studies challenged the notion of the existence of "drug subcultures" and showed that a better understanding of drug-using behavior might be achieved by studying drug users within particular community contexts where such behaviors occur.

FUTURE ETHNOGRAPHY IN DRUG/AIDS INTERVENTION AND PREVENTION

What emerged from these studies was an accumulation of information that supplemented and improved national data collections on drug abuse. For example, in the PCP study (Feldman et al. 1979), surveys that the Federal government sponsored were examined and compared to data collected from young people in natural social groups in four cities. It was possible to identify in those four cities certain patterns of PCP use. For example, there was an interest in identifying as precisely as possible when the fad of PCP began and when momentum developed such that youth in a wide variety of social settings in different parts of the United States began to experiment with PCP. It was possible to establish the year 1973 as the date of entry in all four cities, with a clear rise in use in 1974 and a leveling off in 1975. When the national survey data were examined, especially the surveys of high school seniors, it was found that, for those peak years of experimentation in 1973 and 1975, there was no mention of PCP use among young drug users. In other words, the PCP phenomenon entered the world of youth and diminished without the national data system ever identifying it. What became obvious to many researchers in the 1970s was that ethnography was a useful supplement and, in many ways, a far sharper instrument for collecting information about emerging drug patterns and the ways drug users adapted to them than had previously been thought.

The discovery that ethnography might well be useful as a method for identifying new drug use trends gave rise to serious discussions about employing ethnographic field stations (Feldman 1980; Preble 1980b). There were two important conferences held to develop this idea, which resulted in two publications: the book, *Street Ethnography: Selected Studies of Crime and Drug Use in Natural Settings* (Weppner 1977), which has Ed Preble's prophetic article, "Methadone, Wine and Welfare," and the NIDA monograph, *Ethnography: A Research Tool for Policymakers in the Drug & Alcohol Fields* (Akins and Beschner 1980).

These publications evolved from two meetings sponsored by NIDA, which were held to discuss the utility of funding ethnographic field stations: the first, in 1976, in Key Biscayne, and the second, in Chicago, on ethnography as the basis for State and local planning in the drug and alcohol fields. The first meeting was cosponsored by the Drug Enforcement Administration (DEA). There was general agreement that ethnographic methods would be extremely useful in identifying new drug trends. There was similar agreement that the connection of ethnography with the DEA might be problematic, and many of the ethnographers in attendance were reluctant to have a close association with that agency while collecting data from populations involved in illegal activities. As a result, several ethnographers in attendance opposed common research undertakings; and the idea of ethnographic field stations was shelved for the time.

At the Chicago meeting of 1979, which was sponsored solely by NIDA, the concept of ethnographic field stations was reexamined and endorsed as a unique method for collecting data to be utilized for planning and policy-making purposes. It was not supported by government funding sources through the 1980s, however, until the emergence of the AIDS epidemic.

From the exchange of ideas between ethnographers and policymakers during these national meetings and from ethnographic studies themselves, some new prevention and education strategies began to emerge. For example, most of the publicity on the dangers of PCP use came through the national media, with such television news shows as "60 Minutes" and others, which emphasized the connection between PCP use and violence and/or psychotic behavior. However, research on the violence associated with PCP use indicated that there were few such incidents of violence, other than panic reactions to hospital personnel or police attempting to employ physical constraints. Instead, it appeared that any drug-associated violence was not precipitated by ingesting the drug necessarily but by medical personnel and police who were ill-informed on how to manage adverse reactions. What emerged quite clearly from this study was that PCP was a powerful drug and that youth knew it to be a powerful drug. In fact, its very reputation, reinforced by the national media, was the motivation that prompted users to take it in the first place. The drug did have adverse effects; but these effects, according to the users themselves, were not the ones the media publicized. Rather than the dramatic incidents of violence, the condition young people identified as most problematic was called "burning out," a state of cloudiness and forgetfulness resulting from prolonged consumption of the drug, which was basically an anesthetic. It was this condition of "burning out" that eventually led to a lessening of interest in PCP use among most youth throughout the country.

Probably the most important use of ethnography in the drug field is now in progress. With the development of the AIDS epidemic among IV drug users, there is an urgency to mobilize our finest scientific resources to address what has the potential of becoming a national crisis and has become one already in New York City and northern New Jersey. If the

Surgeon General is correct in saying that he does not anticipate a cure for AIDS and that a vaccine is in the distant future, then the urgency must be to keep new infections to a bare minimum. In San Francisco and Chicago, where ethnography has been something of a tradition, it has been found that the most effective approach to carrying the prevention-education message to IV drug users and their sexual partners has been through an aggressive strategy of outreach based on ethnography.

Right now, IV drug users are truly members of a hidden population whose behaviors must be understood by those responsible for managing the HIV epidemic in order to mount an effective intervention. One response has been to support ethnographers to develop studies that can quickly grasp relationships between needle sharing and the epidemic in ways that traditional research methods cannot (Feldman et al. 1984; Feldman and Biernacki 1988; Wiebel 1988).

In addition to providing street-based intervention with a conceptual basis for managing the AIDS epidemic among IV drug users and their sexual partners, ethnography can make continuing contributions to drug research in general. One area of interest is that of the heroin addict and his or her resistance to change. Ethnography and the experience of street-based interventions have accumulated evidence that the notion that IV drug users are hard to reach and resistant to change may be in serious error. The experience of street-based efforts in San Francisco, Chicago, and now several other cities has demonstrated that addicts are receptive and responsive to educational campaigns and will change certain behaviors as long as the necessary changes do not require alterations of customs, values, and lifestyles that are essential to their identities and cultural associations. While this may run counter to the conventional wisdom regarding addict behavior, it suggests a wider universality that can be applied to other social groups and cultures. Through ethnography, it is possible to apply this finding to IV drug users and the HIV epidemic. In San Francisco, Chicago, and the other cities where an ethnographic approach has been employed, there has been success in changing needle-sharing and needle-cleaning behaviors in a relatively short period of time (Watters 1987; Watters et al. 1988). The strategy of employing ethnography as the forerunner to aggressive outreach to IV drug users at risk for HIV infection has now been expanded to 27 major American cities.

As these ethnographically based projects develop, one result may be the creation of a structure for the delivery of health care, early intervention, and social services to inner-city communities that is new and more closely tailored to the needs of urban populations. Ethnographically oriented outreach AIDS prevention projects may be a model for a variety of health and social services in the future.

CONCLUSION

In summary, ethnography has made significant contributions to the substance abuse field. History has shown that ethnography has successfully penetrated a wide variety of drug-using populations from the time of Herodotus to our present day. Invariably, ethnographers have presented "different" views of drug users, some which have contradicted popular conceptions. These analytic descriptions may be closer to the way drug users are seen and responded to within their own sociocultural context than to the portrait painted by some health professionals. In this sense, ethnography has challenged theories of etiology and provided new concepts that are practical and utilitarian. Similarly, ethnography has identified problems in maintaining accurate updates on patterns of drug use and the emergence of drug fads by noting limitations of current national data systems; it has suggested ways to modify and augment the present arrangements. Finally, ethnography has demonstrated and continues to demonstrate its usefulness in applied research. With the emergence of the HIV epidemic as a problem of potentially catastrophic proportions, ethnography has the flexibility for use in short-term exploratory research efforts and in day-to-day outreach intervention by trained health educators, among populations that have been viewed as difficult, if not impossible, to access and change.

The challenge for drug ethnographers will be to fulfill the promise of their potential by addressing the major social and health problems of the day. For now, management of the AIDS epidemic should hold the highest priority. If success in that effort is achieved, thousands of drug users, their families, and their neighbors may never experience the epidemic, helped by a delivery of health services that will benefit nondrug users as well as the "hidden populations" who are the subjects of present concern.

REFERENCES

ADLER, P.A. *Wheeling and Dealing: An Ethnography of an Upper-Level Drug Dealing and Smuggling Community.* New York: Columbia University Press, 1985.

AKINS, C., and BESCHNER, G., eds. *Ethnography: A Research Tool for Policymakers in the Drug & Alcohol Fields.* National Institute on Drug Abuse Services Research Branch, DHHS Pub. No. (ADM)80-946. Washington, DC: Supt. of Docs., U.S. Govt. Print. Off., 1980.

ALDRICH, M.R., and BARKER, R.W. Historical aspects of cocaine use and abuse. In: Mule', S.J., ed. *Cocaine: Chemical, Biological, Clinical, Social and Treatment Aspects.* Cleveland: CRC Press, 1976. pp. 3–11.

ALTSCHUL, S.v.R. *The Genus Anadenanthera in Amerindian Cultures.* Cambridge: Botanical Museum, Harvard University, 1972.

BECKER, H.S. Becoming a marijuana user. *Am J Sociol* 59:235–242, 1953.

BECKER, H.S. *Outsiders: Studies in the Sociology of Deviance.* Glencoe, IL: Free Press, 1963.

BIERNACKI, P. *Pathways from Heroin Addiction: Recovery Without Treatment.* Philadelphia: Temple University, 1986.

BLUMER, H.; SUTTER, A.; AHMED, S.; and SMITH, R. *Add Center Project Final Report: The World of Youthful Drug Use.* Berkeley, CA: University of California, 1967.

CARTER, W.E., ed. *Cannabis in Costa Rica: A Study of Chronic Marihuana Use.* Philadelphia: Institute for the Study of Human Issues, 1980.

CAREY, J.T., and MANDEL, J. A San Francisco Bay Area speed scene. *J Health Soc Behav* 9:164–174, 1968.

CAVAN, S. *Hippies of the Haight.* St. Louis: New Critics Press, 1972.

CLECKNER, P.J. Blowing some lines: Intracultural variations among Miami cocaine users. *J Psychedelic Drugs* 8:37–42, 1976a.

CLECKNER, P.J. Dope is to get high: A preliminary analysis of intracultural variation in drug categories among heavy users and dealers. *Addict Dis* 2:537–552, 1976b.

CLECKNER, P.J. Cognitive and ritual aspects of drug use among young black urban males. In: DuToit, B.M., ed. *Drugs, Rituals and Altered States of Consciousness.* Rotterdam: A.A. Balkema, 1977. pp.149–168.

CLOWARD, R.A., and OHLIN, L.E. *Delinquency and Opportunity: A Theory of Delinquent Gangs.* Glencoe, IL: Free Press, 1960.

COHEN, R. The logic of generalization: Generalizations in ethnology. In: Naroll, R., and Cohen, R., eds. *A Handbook of Method in Cultural Anthropology*. New York: Columbia University Press, 1970. pp. 31–50.

DAI, B. *Opium Addiction in Chicago*. Shanghai: Commercial Press, 1937. (Reprint, Montclair, NJ: Patterson Smith, 1970.)

DAVIS, W. *The Serpent and the Rainbow*. New York: Simon and Schuster, 1985.

DE SELINCOURT, A. *Herodotus: The Histories*. Harmondsworth, England: Penguin, 1954.

DURKHEIM, E. *Suicide: A Study of Sociology*. Glencoe, IL: Free Press, 1951.

FELDMAN, H.W. Ideological supports to becoming and remaining a heroin addict. *J Health Soc Behav* 9(2):131–139, 1968.

FELDMAN, H.W. Street status and drug users. *Trans/Soc* 10(4):32–38, 1973.

FELDMAN, H.W. Street status and the drug researcher: Issues in participant observation. Washington, DC: Drug Abuse Council, 1974.

FELDMAN, H.W. A neighborhood history of drug switching. In: Weppner, R.S., ed. *Street Ethnography: Selected Studies of Crime and Drug Use in Natural Settings*. Beverly Hills: Sage, 1977. pp. 249–278.

FELDMAN, H.W. Introduction: Background and purpose of the ethnographers' policymakers' symposium. In: Akins, C., and BESCHNER, G., eds. *Ethnography: A Research Tool for Policymakers in the Drug & Alcohol Fields*. National Institute on Drug Abuse Services Research Branch. DHHS Pub. No. (ADM)80-946. Washington, DC: Supt. of Docs., U.S. Govt. Print. Off., 1980. pp.1–7.

FELDMAN, H.W.; AGAR, M.H.; and BESCHNER, G. *Angel Dust: An Ethnographic Study of PCP Users*. Lexington, MA: Lexington Books, 1979.

FELDMAN, H.W., and BIERNACKI, P. The ethnography of needle sharing among intravenous drug users and implications for public policies and intervention strategies. In: Battjes, R.J., and Pickens, R.W., eds. *Needle-Sharing Among Intravenous Drug Abusers: National and International Perspectives*. National Institute on Drug Abuse Research Monograph 80. DHHS Pub. No. (ADM)88-1567. Washington, DC: Supt. of Docs., U.S. Govt. Print. Off., 1988. pp. 28–39.

FELDMAN, H.W.; MANDEL, J.; and FIELDS, A. In the neighborhood: A strategy for delivering early intervention services to young drug users in their natural environments. In: Friedman, A.S., and Beschner, G.M., eds. *Treatment Services for Adolescent Substance Abusers*. National Institute on Drug Abuse Research Monograph Series. DHHS Pub. No. (ADM)84-1342. Washington, DC: Supt. of Docs., U.S. Govt. Print. Off., 1984. pp. 112–128.

FIELDS, A.B. "Slinging weed": The social organization of street-corner marijuana sales. *Urban Life* 13(2–3):274–280, 1984.

FIELDS, A.B. Weedslingers: Young black marijuana dealers. In: Beschner, G., and Friedman, A.S., eds. *Teen Drug Use*. Lexington, MA: Lexington Books, 1986. pp. 85–104.

FINESTONE, H. Cats, kicks, and color. *Soc Prob* 5(7):3–13, 1957.

HANSON, B.; BESCHNER, G.M.; WALTERS, J.M.; and BOVELLE, E. *Life with Heroin: Voices From the Inner City*. Lexington, MA: Lexington Books, 1985.

HUGHES, E.C. The study of occupations (1959). *The Sociological Eye: Selected Papers*. New Brunswick, NJ: Transaction Books, 1984. pp. 283–297.

JAMES, J. Prostitution and addiction: An interdisciplinary approach. *Addict Dis* 2:601–618, 1976.

JAMES, J. Ethnography and social problems. In: Weppner, R.S., ed. *Street Ethnography: Selected Studies of Crime and Drug Use in Natural Settings*. Beverly Hills: Sage, 1977. pp. 179–200.

JOHNSON, B.D.; GOLDSTEIN, P.J.; PREBLE, E.; SCHMEIDLER, J.; LIPTON, D.S.; SPUNT, B.; and MILLER, T. *Taking Care of Business: The Economics of Crime by Heroin Abusers*. Lexington, MA: Lexington Books, 1985.

Joint Committee of the American Bar Association and the American Medical Association on Narcotic Drugs. *Drug Addiction: Crime or Disease?* Bloomington, IN: Indiana University, 1961.

LA BARRE, W. *The Peyote Cult*. New Haven: Yale, 1938. (2nd ed. New York: Schocken, 1969.)

LINDESMITH, A.R. *Opiate Addiction*. Bloomington, IN: Principia Press, 1947. (2nd ed. *Addiction and Opiates*. Chicago, IL: Aldine, 1968.)

LINDESMITH, A.R. *The Addict and the Law*. Bloomington, IN: Indiana University, 1965.

LUDLOW, F.H. What shall they do to be saved? *Harper's Magazine* 35:377–387, 1867.

MANDEL, J., and FELDMAN, H.W. The social history of teenage drug use. In: Beschner, G., and Friedmann, A.S., eds. *Teen Drug Use*. Lexington, MA: Lexington Books, 1986. pp. 19–42.

MERTON, R.K. *Social Theory and Social Structure*. Glencoe, IL: Free Press, 1957.

MOORE, J.; CEREA, L.; GARCIA, C.; GARCIA, R.; and VALENCIA, F. *Homeboys*. Philadelphia: Temple University Press, 1974.

MURPHY, S., and ROSENBAUM, M. Money for methadone. II: Unintended consequences of limited-duration methadone maintenance. *J Psychoactive Drugs* 20(4):397–402, 1988.

POLSKY, N. *Hustlers, Beats, and Others*. Chicago: Aldine, 1967.

PREBLE, E. Problems utilizing ethnography in a single state agency. In: Akins, C., and Beschner, G., eds. *Ethnography: A Research Tool for Policymakers in the Drug & Alcohol Fields*. National Institute on Drug Abuse Services Research Report. DHHS Pub. No. (ADM)80-946. Washington, DC: Supt. of Docs., U.S. Govt. Print. Off., 1980a. pp. 90–100.

PREBLE, E. What an ethnographic field station looks like. In: Akins, C., and Beschner, G., eds. *Ethnography: A Research Tool for Policymakers in the Drug & Alcohol Fields*. National Institute on Drug Abuse Services Research Report. DHHS Pub. No. (ADM)80-946. Washington, DC: Supt. of Docs., U.S. Govt. Print. Off., 1980b. pp. 64–71.

PREBLE, E., and CASEY, J.J. Taking care of business: The heroin user's life on the streets. *Int J Addict* 4(1):1–24,1969.

ROSENBAUM, M. *Women on Heroin*. New Brunswick, NJ: Rutgers University Press, 1981.

ROSENBAUM, M. *Surrender to Control: Women on Methadone*. Final report to the National Institute on Drug Abuse, unpublished manuscript.

ROSENBAUM, M., and MORGAN, P. Ecstasy use among professionals: An ethnography. Presented at the meeting of the American Society of Criminology, November 1988.

ROSENBAUM, M., and MURPHY, S. Not the picture of health: Women on methadone. *J Psychoactive Drugs* 19(2):217–226, 1987.

RUBIN, V., and COMITAS, L. *Ganja in Jamaica: A Medical Anthropological Study of Chronic Marihuana Use*. Scotch Plains, NJ: Mouton/MacFarland, 1975.

RUDENKO, S.I. *Frozen Tombs of Siberia: The Pazyryk Burials of Iron-Age Horsemen*. Berkeley: University of California, 1970.

SAFFORD, W.E. Identity of cohoba, the narcotic snuff of ancient Haiti. *J Wash Acad Sci* 6:548–562, 1916.

SCHULTES, R.E. Peyote and the American Indian. *Nature* 30(3):155–157, 1937.

SCHULTES, R.E., and HOFMANN, A. *The Botany and Chemistry of Hallucinogens*. 2nd ed. Springfield, IL: Charles C Thomas, 1980.

SHAW, C.R., and MCKAY, H.D. *Juvenile Delinquency and Urban Areas*. Chicago: University of Chicago, 1942.

SOLOWAY, I.H. Methadone and the culture of addiction. *J Psychedelic Drugs* 6:1–99, 1974.

SPRADLEY, J.P. *You Owe Yourself A Drunk: An Ethnography of Urban Nomads*. Boston: Little, Brown and Co., 1970.

SPRADLEY, J.P. FOREWORD. In: Weppner, R.S., ed. *Street Ethnography: Selected Studies of Crime and Drug Use in Natural Settings*. Beverly Hills: Sage, 1977. pp. 13–16.

SUTHERLAND, E.H. *Principles of Criminology*. 4th ed. Philadelphia: J.P. Lippincott, 1947.

SUTTER, A.G. The world of the righteous dope fiend. *Issues in Criminology* 2(2):177–222, 1966.

SUTTER, A.G. Worlds of drug use on the street scene. In: Cressey, D., and Ward, D.A., eds. *Delinquency, Crime and Social Process*. New York: Harper and Row, 1969.

SUTTER, A.G. Playing a cold game: Phases of a ghetto career. *Urban Life and Culture* 1(1): 77–91, 1972.

VESTAL, P.A., and SCHULTES, R.E. *The Economic Botany of the Kiowa Indians as It Relates to the History of the Tribe.* Cambridge, MA: Botanical Museum, 1939.

VIDICH, A.J. Participant observation and the collection and interpretation of data. *Am J Sociol* 60(4):354–360, 1955.

VON HAGEN, V.W. *The Incas of Pedro de Cieza de Leon.* Norman, OK: University of Oklahoma, 1959.

WALLACE, A.R. *Richard Spruce: Notes of an Ethnobotanist on the Amazon and Andes.* London: Macmillan, 1908. (Reprint, New York: Johnson Reprint, 1970.)

WALTERS, J. What is ethnography? In: Akins, C., and Beschner, G., eds. *Ethnography: A Research Tool for Policymakers in the Drug & Alcohol Fields.* National Institute on Drug Abuse Services Research Branch. DHHS Pub. No. (ADM)80-946. Washington, DC: Supt. of Docs., U.S. Govt. Print. Off., 1980. pp. 15–20.

WARD, A. *Confessions of An English Opium-Eater, by Thomas De Quincey.* New York: Signet, 1966.

WASSEN, S.H. Anthropological survey of the use of South American snuffs. In: Efron, D.H.; Holmstedt, B.; and Kline, N.S., eds. *Ethnopharmacologic Search for Psychoactive Drugs.* National Institute of Mental Health. PHS Pub. No. 1645. Washington, DC: Supt. of Docs., U.S. Govt. Print. Off., 1967. pp. 233–289.

WASSON, R.G. *The Wondrous Mushroom: Mycolatry in Mesoamerica.* New York: McGraw-Hill, 1980.

WATTERS, J.K. Preventing human immunodeficiency virus contagion among intravenous drug users: The impact of street-based education on risk behavior. Presented at the Third International Conference on AIDS, Washington, DC, 1987.

WATTERS, J.K.; CHENG, Y.-T.; LEWIS, D.; JANG, M.; and CARLSON, J. Drug-use profile, risk participation, and HIV exposure among intravenous drug users in San Francisco. Presented at the Fourth International Conference on AIDS, Stockholm, June 1988.

WEPPNER, R.S., ed. *Street Ethnography: Selected Studies of Crime and Drug Use in Natural Settings.* Beverly Hills: Sage, 1977.

WIEBEL, W.W. Combining ethnographic and epidemiologic methods in targeted AIDS interventions: The Chicago model. In: Battjes, R.J., and Pickens, R.W., eds. *Needle-Sharing Among Intravenous Drug Abusers: National and International Perspectives.* National Institute on Drug Abuse Research Monograph 80. DHHS Pub. No. (ADM)88-1567. Washington, DC: Supt. of Docs., U.S. Govt. Print. Off., 1988. pp. 137–150.

WISEMAN, J., and ARON, M. Field Projects for Sociological Students. Cambridge, MA: Schenkman, 1970.

ACKNOWLEDGMENTS

This work was supported in part by U.S. Public Health Service grants 1 R18 DA 05879-01 and 1 R01 DA 05015-01 from the National Institute on Drug Abuse. Patrick Biernacki and Jerry Mandel reviewed various portions of this paper.

3

The Multiple Roles of Qualitative Research in Understanding and Responding to Illicit Drug Use

Tim Rhodes

It is said that the beginnings of modern qualitative research on drug use can be traced to De Quincey's *Confessions of an English Opium Eater* (1822), where the method employed was akin to participant observation (Feldman and Aldrich, 1990). As applied research, the methodological origins of qualitative research may be traced to social interactionism in sociology, which emerged in the 1920s and 1930s, led by the Chicago school (Znaniecki, 1934; Carey, 1975). These developments emphasised the socially situated nature of individual action, and demonstrated the value of integrating multiple qualitative methods to understand the subjective meanings and social contexts of behaviour, giving rise to a number of ethnographies in criminality and deviance (Anderson, 1923; Shaw, 1930; Whyte, 1955). The experience of addiction and dependency itself, for example, was found to have a social, rather than merely physiological, basis in socially situated understandings of what constituted withdrawal (Lindesmith, 1947). This was the genesis of qualitative research as a means of understanding drug use and its interpretation as socially constructed, and of encouraging intervention developments coherent with local practices in different cultural settings.

Building on the principles of social and symbolic interactionism, qualitative studies in the field of illicit drug use have been of note, not only for the social explanations of drug use and addiction they provided, but also for their insights into applied qualitative methodology and theorising on deviance (Becker, 1953; 1963; Agar, 1973; 1980; Weppner, 1977).

Reprinted with permission from Gloria Greenwood and Kathy Robertsun, *Understanding and Responding to Drug Use: The Role of Qualitative Research.* European Monitoring Centre for Drugs and Drug Addiction Scientific Monograph Series, Volume 4.

The clandestine nature of many drug use behaviours and subcultures has provided ideal terrain for the development of what are now considered classic ethnographies of drug use, deviance and normality (Becker, 1953; Sutter, 1966; Preble and Casey, 1969; Agar, 1973; Jackson, 1978). In the tradition of ethnography, the focus of such research was to 'make sense' of the social world of drug use from the perspectives of drug users. Drawing on a variety of techniques, including direct observations and face-to-face interviews, these studies sought to describe the everyday context of behaviours and lifestyles otherwise misunderstood or hidden from view.

Popular perceptions of drug users as passive or deviant were countered by drug ethnographies of the 1960s and 1970s which discovered purposeful and active meanings in drug use in the context of the drug user's lifestyle (Hughes, 1961; Becker, 1963; Preble and Casey, 1969; Feldman et al., 1979). As demonstrated by ethnographies of the use of LSD (Becker, 1970), PCP (phencyclidine) (Feldman et al., 1979), heroin in urban areas (Hughes, 1961; Preble and Casey, 1969; Agar, 1973), methadone (Preble and Miller, 1977) and alcohol (Spradley, 1970), popularly misunderstood behaviours were found to be rational and normal when understood from the perspectives of drug users, and when 'situated' within the social contexts in which they occurred.

While the dominant methodological approach in contemporary drugs research remains quantitative, there has been increasing receptivity to the use of qualitative methods as a means of understanding and responding to drug use (Agar, 1980; 1995; Rosenbaum, 1981; Adler, 1985; Pearson, 1987; Power, 1989; Moore, 1993; Ratner, 1993; Taylor, 1993; Gamella, 1994; 1997; Kaplan and Verbraek, 1999; Rhodes, 1999; Roldan and Gamella, 1999). This is particularly the case with regard to informing the development of policy and community interventions (Hughes, 1977; Atkins and Beschner, 1980; Feldman and Aldrich, 1990; Brooks, 1994; Agar, 1999).

The public health urgency surrounding HIV transmission associated with drug use provides a key example. Here, qualitative research has been demonstrated to be ideally suited to conducting studies among hidden populations 'at risk', as well as a means of identifying and interpreting 'risk behaviours' associated with drug use, and of developing social interventions in response (Murphy, 1987; Ouellet et al., 1991; McKeganey and Barnard, 1992; Sterk, 1993; Rhodes, 1995; 1997; Grund et al., 1996; Koester, 1996; Power et al., 1996; Wiebel, 1996; Bourgois, 1997). Research into AIDS has highlighted the role of qualitative research in both understanding the social context of drug use and risk behaviours, as well as in responding with pragmatic recommendations for intervention and policy developments.

At its most fundamental, the role of qualitative research into illicit drug use can therefore be envisaged as a means of understanding the lived experiences and meanings of drug use from the perspectives of drug users themselves. Additionally, as a means of understanding action as socially organised, qualitative research aims to understand how the lived experiences and meanings associated with drug use are influenced by different social, cultural and economic contexts. At the outset, qualitative research aims to describe the context-based nature of drug use and the social meanings that such behaviours are perceived to have. Qualitative research thus proceeds on the assumption that it is possible to gain insight into the factors producing social behaviour primarily through engaging with the lives of participants themselves. The role of ethnography, for example, has been described as an attempt to 'record how individuals perceive, construct, and interact within their social and economic environment' (James, 1977, p. 180).

While ethnography may have a higher status in the field of addictions than elsewhere, there still very much remains a 'divide' between quantitative and qualitative approaches to drugs research (Health, 1995; McKeganey, 1995; Pearson, 1995). This is neither helpful nor appropriate in developing understanding of the interplay of individual, social and contextual factors influencing drug use (Agar, 1995). All methods are tools, and each necessarily reveals and conceals different aspects of the phenomena under study (Denzin, 1970). The challenge for future drugs research is to recognise the pragmatic utility and methodological desirability of using multiple methods, in order to encourage research which understands the epidemiology and the social context of drug use. With this in mind, the multiple roles of qualitative research in understanding and responding to drug use are summarised below.

THE MULTIPLE ROLES OF QUALITATIVE DRUGS RESEARCH

Reaching and Researching Hidden Populations

The first consideration is both methodological and practical. Illicit drug use is a hidden activity and, in most countries, the majority of drug users remain hidden from treatment and agency-based services. Those in contact with services are often unrepresentative of the broader population of drug users, and this may be the case with regard to patterns of drug use, risk behaviour and health status. This has led researchers to consider sampling designs capable of reaching hidden populations, whose 'membership is not readily distinguished or enumerated based on existing knowledge and/or sampling capabilities' (Wiebel, 1990, p. 6). Overcoming such sampling problems, including those of access, bias and trust, has encouraged considerable methodological innovation in sampling design (Lambert, 1990; Carlson et al., 1994; Council of Europe, 1997; Sifaneck and Neaigus, 1999). A key characteristic of such innovation is the use of ethnographic theoretical sampling techniques, emphasising inductive approaches to targeted social networks and snowball, purposive and quota sampling (Biernacki and Waldorf, 1981; Carlson et al., 1999).

In the absence of pre-existing or representative sampling frames, sampling methods in surveys of drug use largely utilise data from multiple sources, in order to target theoretically driven quotas of drug users and/or social networks using a variety of chain-referral techniques (Biernacki and Waldorf, 1981; Cohen, 1989; Diaz et al., 1992; Hendriks et al., 1992). Emphasising theoretical and methodological realism over scientific idealism, such approaches commonly use ethnography to inform the development of numeric sampling quotas—in particular geographical or social environments—as well as in participant recruitment and follow-up (Carlson et al., 1999).

The use of ethnographic fieldworkers and key informants, including those with indigenous or privileged access, has become a common feature of such designs, aiming to maximise access and rapport as well as ethnographic descriptions of networks and settings (Hughes, 1977; Hendriks et al., 1992; Griffiths et al., 1993; Power, 1995). While the use of snowball sampling methods borrows from ethnographic methodology, particularly as far as gaining access, rapport and informing sampling design are concerned, such studies need not be 'ethnographic' in the data they collect, nor in the analyses they undertake. However, qualitative sampling methods have become key features of quantitative studies of drug use (Biernacki and Waldorf, 1981; Carlson et al., 1994; 1999).

Understanding the Experience and Meaning of Drug Use

Behaviours communicate social meanings. Both the nature of knowledge itself and the process by which it is acquired shape the lived experience and perceived meanings of drug use. Two key tenets of qualitative research are to describe the social meanings participants attach to drug use experiences and the social processes by which such meanings are created, reinforced and reproduced (Moore, 1993; Rhodes, 1995; Agar, 1997). Illicit drug use is a social activity and the process of drug taking derives symbolic importance, and has social meaning, depending on the contexts of use (Becker, 1953; Grund, 1993). Qualitative research is therefore concerned with descriptions of how drug use is 'lived' and interpreted through social interactions. Whereas epidemiological research concentrates on delineating the distribution of patterns of drug use and its consequences, qualitative research aims to appreciate why such behaviours occur and how they are understood in different contexts among different social groups (Rhodes, 1995).

Because of their inductive and iterative approach to data collection and hypothesis generation, qualitative methods are ideally suited to identifying and describing the lived experience of drug use from participant perspectives. Whereas deductive designs, as well as most quantitative research, tend to be construct-driven—defining categories or variables of interest a priori on the basis of pre-existing hypotheses and theoretical frameworks—inductive designs aim to construct interpretations on the basis of data as they emerge from participant descriptions and observations (Agar, 1980; Layder, 1993). To oversimplify, the ethnography of drug use is data-driven, and thus hypothesis-generating, and leads to the discovery of subjective meaning, whereas the epidemiology of drug use is construct-driven, and thus hypothesis-testing, and leads to the charting of (presumed-to-be) objective measures of drug use.

Examples abound of the contribution of qualitative research to discovering how the meanings of drug use are socially organised. The ethnographies conducted by Howard Becker on marijuana and LSD use, for example, describe how drug use behaviours are a function of the social meanings they are perceived to communicate to participants (Becker, 1953; 1963; 1970). As his studies illustrate, the lived experience of the effects of drugs only comes to have meaning in the context of individuals' expectations of drug effects, which are themselves a function of the social organisation of knowledge in particular social networks or settings (Becker, 1953; 1970). The subjective meanings participants attach to their drug use, as with any behaviour, 'arise in the course of social interaction which itself is situated within wider cultures—"or subcultures"—of meaning and understanding' (Becker, 1970, p. 311). Qualitative research is therefore necessary if researchers and interventionists are to grasp how drug use experiences are differently interpreted by social groups in different settings.

A more recent example concerns ethnographic descriptions of HIV-related risk behaviour associated with injecting drug use. These studies have shown that needle and syringe sharing is not simply the product of risk perception or risk calculus, but that such practices also depend on the symbolic meanings they are perceived to have among participants (Murphy, 1987; Zule, 1992; Barnard, 1993; Grund, 1993). While commonly categorised a priori as 'risk behaviour' by construct-driven research paradigms, syringe sharing may alternatively be interpreted by participants as a symbol of trust and reciprocity, particularly within close friendships and sexual relationships (Zule, 1992; Grund, 1993). Qualitative understandings of the social meanings of epidemiologically defined risk behaviours help provide an appreciation of why such practices occur in certain situations or contexts, even given individuals' knowledge of the health risks involved (Rhodes, 1997).

Understanding the Social Contexts of Drug Use

The social meanings of behaviours are context-dependent. As noted, qualitative research aims to understand the nexus of meaning and context (Agar, 1995; 1997). Here, the role of qualitative research is to distinguish how drug use patterns, and their meaning and interpretation, differ by social, cultural and economic context. The social context of drug use is made up of an interplay of factors, including individual and group subjective interpretations of drug use, the physical, interpersonal and social settings in which drug use occurs, and wider structural and environmental factors. Building on notions of symbolic interactionism—the study of how the social meanings of behaviour are created and reinforced through social interaction itself (Denzin, 1970)—social context is viewed as a key process, influencing how the meanings and practices of drug use are socially organised (Becker, 1963; 1970).

A variety of studies have illustrated how individuals' beliefs and interactions associated with drug use are influenced by context. Following the example above, the meanings and practices of needle and syringe sharing have been found to depend on the influence of perceived social or network norms and expectations (Barnard, 1993; Wiebel, 1996; Rhodes and Quirk, 1996; Power et al., 1996); particular interpersonal and social relationships (Zule, 1992; Barnard, 1993; Rhodes and Quirk, 1998); the physical and social settings in which drug use occurs (Ouellet et al., 1991; Ruggiero, 1993; Turnbull et al., 1996; Wiebel, 1996); and wider structural, economic and policy factors (Pearson, 1987; Fraser and George, 1988; Grund et al., 1992; Gamella, 1994; Bourgois, 1997). The ethnographic work of Ouellet et al. (1991) and Wiebel (1996), for example, shows how different Chicago 'shooting galleries' have different rules for the sale or rent of injecting equipment, which, in turn, sustain different social norms influencing individuals' drug use and HIV risk behaviour. Here, the 'micro-setting' is envisaged as a key contextual factor influencing proximity to risk and opportunities for risk reduction. In contrast, studies by Grund et al. (1992) and Watters (1996) illustrate how the 'macro-setting'—in this case, the policy and economic context—influences the formation of drug users' social and support networks, which, in turn, impact on individual and group opportunities for risk reduction.

Other examples concern the contribution of qualitative findings to understanding the influence of social context on drug trends. Studies by Pearson (1987), Fraser and George (1988) and Gamella (1994), for example, show how exogenous factors—such as policing, housing and heroin availability—influence the social relationships maintained or lost within particular geographical or social networks, which, in turn, influence patterns of purchasing and dealing, and the diffusion of new drug trends. Of key interest here is the dual importance of social relationships in mediating initiation and use, and the influence of macro contextual factors in creating or sustaining social relationships conducive to drug use (Pearson, 1987; Gamella, 1994). In a quite different study, Henderson (1996) describes how patterns of ecstasy use are, to a large extent, socially organised within the social mores of rave and dance club cultures. Like Becker's work on LSD and marijuana (Becker, 1953; 1970), she finds the behavioural manifestations of the effects of ecstasy are contained within this particular context. The social contexts of drug use environments mediate the social meanings and practices of drug use, and qualitative research has a pragmatic contribution to make to the development of interventions and policies that are coherent with ideas of social and environmental change.

Informing Quantitative Research

A well-established role of qualitative research is to inform the design of quantitative measures of drug use. Here, qualitative research aims to inform the construction of meaningful constructs or measures in quantitative studies, as well as to shape appropriate analyses and their interpretation (Wiebel, 1990; 1996). A key example in HIV prevention research concerns the identification and interpretation of risk behaviours associated with drug use. The practices of 'front-loading' and 'back-loading', for example, were identified on the basis of direct observations of drug injecting in Rotterdam (Grund et al., 1991). Similarly, ethnographic observations in Denver and El Paso identified a variety of other 'indirect' sharing practices, at the time previously unexplored (Koester et al., 1990; Koester, 1996; Wiebel, 1996). These included the shared use of 'cookers', 'cottons' and rinse water among participants, even after they had made attempts to reduce HIV transmission risks by flushing out their syringes with bleach. In each case, drug injectors were found to be unwittingly engaging in risk behaviour (Wiebel, 1996). These practices have since entered the battery of epidemiological measures designed to assess the prevalence and distribution of risk associated with equipment sharing (Jose et al., 1993; Hunter et al., 1995; Ingold and Toussirt, 1997).

In addition to identifying drug use behaviours or theoretical constructs for subsequent epidemiological measurement, qualitative data play a key role in interpreting the findings generated from quantitative research. It has been demonstrated, for example, that data from qualitative interviews may be used to help interpret and substantiate the findings of quantitative surveys and statistical models (Barnard and Frischer, 1995). While statistical modelling may identify correlational relationships between variables, it does not adequately assess why or how these relationships exist, nor explain what these associations mean. The triangulation of multiple methods and data sources, and the combined use of quantitative and qualitative methods in particular, enables the researcher to cross-check findings in order to increase the validity of the interpretations made (Denzin, 1970).

Complementing and Questioning Quantitative Research

As a complement to epidemiological research, which traditionally centres on the interplay between 'agent', 'host' and 'environment', the role of qualitative research has been described as an attempt to provide closer understandings of how 'host' interacts with 'environment' (Agar, 1997). As noted above, qualitative understandings of the meaning and context of drug use are crucial for informing epidemiological studies. This has led towards the development of 'ethno-epidemiologies' of drug use (Agar, 1995; 1997). These involve attempts to better situate epidemiological measures and analyses within participant, rather than outsider, frameworks of interpretation, as well as attempts to encourage paradigm shifts in contemporary epidemiology from an overemphasis on risk factor approaches towards emphasising the social–environmental determinants of drug use (Agar, 1995; Pearce, 1996; Susser and Susser, 1996). As Michael Agar indicates, 'ethnography isn't just a methodological add-on; it is a conceptual and theoretical means to a necessary epidemiological end' (Agar, 1997, p. 1166). In this respect, ethnography and epidemiology converge, where the 'failures' of modern risk factor epidemiology (Susser and Susser, 1996) encourage a realisation of the need for epidemiological constructs to be ethnographically explored, as well as for ethnography to inform the development of epidemiological measures.

> The first need is to restore 'host' and 'environment' to central importance in epidemiological analysis, to defocus on 'agent' and celebrate the two other corners of the epidemiological triad. From 'host' it isn't difficult to derive a focus on *'meaning'*, for it is a truism that human hosts live in a symbolic and material world. And it isn't difficult to arrive at 'context' from 'environment', since a concern with context reveals the layers of circumstance, ranging from immediate situation to political economy, in which the 'hosts' shape their lives. The need to restore the importance of host and environment, then, requires the study of meaning and context. And the investigation of meaning and context is exactly the research task that ethnography is designed to accomplish. (Agar, 1997, p. 1166)

There is general consensus that quantitative methods can learn from qualitative methods, as well as vice versa, and that methods provide a set of complementary tools to investigation, rather than necessarily indicating a particular logic of inquiry or explanation (Hartnoll, 1995). There is agreement that 'methodological identity' should not be preserved at 'the cost of greater understanding' (McKeganey, 1995). However, the long-standing divide between 'qualitative-inductive' and 'quantitative-deductive' approaches exists for a reason. Every method, to some extent, shapes the findings it produces, yet qualitative methods are better suited to questioning deductive modes of explanation than the other way round (Pearson, 1995; Rhodes, 1995). Quantitative–qualitative differences are helpful if all methods are appropriately applied to the research question in hand and if both can be scientifically critical of the other (Hartnoll, 1995; Pearson, 1995).

An ethnographically informed epidemiology of drug use is a challenge which continues to escape most drugs research, and few contemporary epidemiological studies of drug use either attempt or adequately achieve an understanding of drug use in its environment (ACMD, 1998). An additional role played by qualitative research, therefore, is that it has the potential to question the application and interpretation of a priori epidemiological constructs, as well as the logic of deductive research (Moore, 1993; Rhodes, 1995; 1997; Bloor, 1997; Romani, 1997). This is particularly important given the considerable resistance to paradigm shifts within epidemiology, and the paradigm predominance of positivism more generally (Susser and Susser, 1996).

The tenets of induction and hypothesis generation encourage analyses grounded in the perspectives of participants, of which the researcher is one, and thus aim to make visible the subjective and inter-subjective meanings of action (Agar, 1997). Qualitative drugs research is both iterative and reflexive (Moore, 1993). In adopting a different epistemological logic in the formation of interpretation and judgment from deductive approaches, it both complements and challenges the assumed objectivity of common-sense understandings of drug use. Induction enables the discovery of plural—and competing—interpretations of drug use and addiction which often fall outside the interpretative frameworks championed by positivist and conventional epidemiological research. As David Moore has noted of his ethnography of recreational drug use, whereas dominant research and policy discourses talk of 'drug-related "problems" and "harm" and how to reduce their incidence', participants were found to emphasise the benefits of drug use in their 'talk of "big nights" and "speeding"' (Moore, 1993, p. 17). Studies oriented to explorations in ethnoepidemiology have illustrated how 'drug use', 'addiction' and 'problems' associated with drug use are, in part, socially constructed by the paradigms, methods and findings of research (Bloor, 1997). Qualitative methods are, of course, not immune to this process (since all acts of re-search are forms of interaction and interpretation), but they aim to be reflexive about the process of interpretation, and do not blindly purport to capture objectivity.

It is important to reiterate that drug users are the experts on their lived experiences of drug use. No research method or design has the capacity to capture objective empirical 'facts', and it is pretence or rhetoric which says otherwise (Moore, 1993). This is obvi-ously of concern when particular methods or forms of research purport to capture objec-tivity by virtue of their own claims, institutional self-legitimation, and symbolic or scientific capital. There remains very much a divide in paradigms of inductive and de-ductive science, as well as in applied qualitative and quantitative methods (McKeganey, 1995; Heath, 1995; Pearson, 1995). The role of qualitative methods is undervalued, and they rarely reach their potential, because they are commonly envisaged as a mere com-plement or supplement to positivist research (viewed as producing hard or objective facts and as 'real science'). The challenge for the future clearly involves the use of multiple methods in drugs research and this also requires recognition of the paradigmatic differ-ences underpinning induction and deduction. Not only is there a need to ground epidemi-ology within participant interpretative frameworks of what is meaningful, but there is an equal need to realise the contribution of qualitative research in questioning 'expert' understandings, the discourses of drug use within which they operate, and their perpetua-tion by an over-reliance on positivist paradigms.

Developing Effective Intervention and Policy Responses

The pivotal role of qualitative research in informing the design of drug interventions and policies is twofold. Firstly, it is important to target interventions in accord with local drug use norms and practices. This also demands an appreciation of how different social and economic contexts influence drug use, as well as drug users' capacity for initiating and sustaining behaviour change. Secondly, an understanding of the social processes shaping everyday drug use is a necessary prerequisite for developing interventions which are mean-ingful and useful to drug users themselves. A wealth of research highlights the pragmatic contribution of qualitative research o intervention and policy development, particularly with regard to the design and evaluation of community-based initiatives (Hughes, 1977; Feldman and Aldrich, 1990; Brooks, 1994; Larson, 1999).

In keeping with the multiple roles of qualitative research summarised above, ethnographic contributions to drug intervention developments—including policy—have emphasised the importance of:

- understanding drug users' perceived needs for, and experiences of, interventions;
- understanding service providers' perceptions of service need, organisation and effectiveness; and
- exploring the social and contextual processes influencing the effectiveness of intervention delivery and impact (as with qualitative process evaluation).

Examples have included: treatment ethnographies exploring drug users' experiences of methadone and other forms of drug treatment (Preble and Miller, 1977; Korf and Hoogenhout,

1990; Keene and Raynor, 1993; Schroers, 1995); help-seeking and service utilisation (Hartnoll and Power, 1989); general practice (McKeganey, 1988); health promotion and community interventions (Jamieson et al., 1984; Brooks, 1994; Blanken and Tenholter, 1995; De Ruyver et al., 1995; Sheridan and Barber, 1996; Shiner and Newburn, 1996); responses to policy (Grund et al., 1992; Bieleman et al., 1993); developing links between ethnography and community outreach (Hughes, 1977; Sterk, 1993; Wiebel, 1996); and understanding the impact of prison setting on drug use (Turnbull et al., 1996).

Here, qualitative research is viewed not as a means of knowledge generation for its own ends but as a means of 'action-oriented' research and intervention development (Power, 1995; Rhodes et al., 1999). The increasing receptivity to the use of qualitative methods is less indicative of wider paradigm shifts in method than it is an outcome of the realisation that qualitative methods in particular have immense practical utility for developing local responses to drug use (Feldman and Aldrich, 1990; Wiebel, 1996). This has led to the development of models of qualitative action research (Power, 1995) and of rapid assessment and response using multiple qualitative methods (Rhodes et al., 1999). The development and evaluation of effective responses require an understanding of the interplay between the meanings and contexts of drug use, as well as of intervention need, feasibility and appropriateness. Qualitative research is ideally positioned to provide the data necessary for evidence-based practice.

CONCLUSIONS

In conclusion, I envisage multiple roles for qualitative research in understanding and responding to drug use. Qualitative methods are viewed as a complement to quantitative methods, and it should be emphasised that all methods are tools for capturing different aspects of drug use and its consequences. The challenge for future drugs research is to enlist qualitative methods as fundamental components of multi-method studies of drug use. Qualitative methods and, more generally, inductive designs, complement their quantitative and deductive counterparts in capturing the interplay between the meanings and contexts of drug use.

If one challenge for future drugs research is to realise the opportunities afforded by multiple methods, a second challenge is to recognise the importance of developing ethnomethodological studies of drug use. To deny the differences between inductive and deductive designs, as well as their respective links with qualitative and quantitative methods in contemporary drugs research, is also to underplay the additional role of qualitative research in challenging common-sense interpretations of drug use, often unwittingly reinforced and reproduced by positivist paradigms. In the absence of qualitative research, there is a danger of perpetuating understandings of drug use which are devoid of relevance or meaning for participants. This, in turn, can encourage the formation of policy or the development of interventions which are inappropriate or ineffective, and, at worst, counterproductive. Qualitative research is a prerequisite for understanding and responding to drug use.

ACKNOWLEDGEMENTS

Sections of this introduction draw on Rhodes, T. and Moore, D. (1999, forthcoming) 'On the qualitative in drugs research', *Addiction Research,* special issue on qualitative research in the addictions.

REFERENCES

ADLER, P. (1985) *Wheeling and Dealing: an Ethnography of an Upper-Level Drug Dealing and Smuggling Community,* New York: Columbia University Press.

Advisory Council on the Misuse of Drugs (ACMD) (1998) *Drug Use and the Environment,* London: Home Office.

AGAR, M. (1973) *Ripping and Running: a Formal Ethnography of Urban Heroin Users,* New York: Academic Press.

AGAR, M. (1980) *The Professional Stranger: an Informal Introduction to Ethnography,* New York: Academic Press.

AGAR, M. (1995) 'Recasting the "ethno" in "epidemiology"', *Medical Anthropology,* 16, 1–13.

AGAR, M. (1997) 'Ethnography: an overview', *Substance Use and Misuse,* 32, 1155–1173.

AGAR, M. (1999, forthcoming) 'Qualitative research and public policy', in T. Rhodes (Ed.) *Qualitative Methods in Drugs Research,* London: Sage.

ANDERSON, N. (1923) *The Hob,* Chicago: University of Chicago Press.

ATKINS, C. and BESCHNER, G. (Eds.) (1980) *Ethnography: a Research Tool for Policy-Makers in the Drug and Alcohol Fields,* US Department of Health and Human Services (Publication No ADM 80–946).

BARNARD, M. A. (1993) 'Needle sharing in context', *Addiction,* 88, 805–812.

BARNARD, M. and FRISCHER, M. (1995) 'Combining quantitative and qualitative: researching HIV-related risk behaviours among drug injectors', *Addiction Research,* 2, 351–362.

BECKER, H. (1953) 'Becoming a marijuana user', *American Journal of Sociology,* 59, 235–242.

BECKER, H. (1963) *Outsiders: Studies in the Sociology of Deviance,* London: Free Press.

BECKER, H. (1970) 'History, culture and subjective experience: an exploration of the social bases of drug-induced experiences', in H. Becker (Ed.) *Sociological Work,* Chicago: Aldine.

BIELEMAN, B., TEN DEN, C. and KROES, L. (1993) 'De wijze waarop heroïnegebruikers reageren op drugsmaatregelen (The way in which heroin users react to drug policy measures)', *Tijdschrift voor Alcohol, Drugs en andere Psychotrope Stoffen,* 19(2), 107–115.

BIERNACKI, P. and WALDORF, D. (1981) 'Snowball sampling: problems and techniques of chain referral sampling', *Sociological Methods and Research,* 10, 141–163.

BLANKEN, P. and TENHOLTER, J. (1995) 'Convenience advertising als medium voor AIDS-preventie onder risico jongeren (Convenience advertising as a medium for AIDS prevention among youth at risk)', Rotterdam: Addiction Research Institute (IVO)/Erasmus University.

BLOOR, M. (1997) 'Addressing social problems through qualitative research', in D. Silverman (Ed.) *Qualitative Research: Theory, Method and Practice,* London: Sage.

BOURGOIS, P. (1997) 'Social misery and the sanctions of substance abuse: confronting HIV risk among homeless heroin addicts in San Francisco', *Social Problems,* 44, 155–173.

BROOKS, C. (1994) 'Using ethnography in the evaluation of drug prevention and intervention programs', *International Journal of the Addictions,* 29, 791–801.

CAREY, J. (1975) *Sociology and Public Affairs: the Chicago School,* London: Sage.

CARLSON, R., WANG, J., SIEGAL, H., FLACK, R. and GUO, J. (1994) 'An ethnographic approach to targeted sampling: problems and solutions in AIDS prevention research among injection drug and crack-cocaine users', *Human Organisation,* 53, 279–286.

CARLSON, R., WANG, J., SIEGAL, H., et al. (1999, forthcoming) 'Ethnography and targeted sampling', in T. Rhodes (Ed.) *Qualitative Methods in Drugs Research,* London: Sage.

COHEN, P. (1989) *Cocaine Use in Amsterdam in Non-Deviant Subcultures,* Amsterdam: Instituut voor Sociale Geografie, Universiteit van Amsterdam.

Council of Europe, Pompidou Group (1997) *The Handbook on Snowball Sampling,* Strasbourg: Council of Europe.

DE RUYVER, B., SOENENS, A., VAN DAELE, L. and VANDERBEKEN, T. (1995) *Straathoek werk in Vlaanderen: Opstellen van een theoretische concept voor straathoek werk. Inhoudelijke en methodische ondersteuning van de veldwerkers en hun coodinatoren (Outreach projects in Flanders: Formulating a theoretical concept of outreach work in view of intrinsic and methodological support to workers and their employers)*, King Baudouin Foundation, Research Group Drug Policies.

DENZIN, N. (1970) *The Research Act*, Chicago: Aldine.

DIAZ, A., BARRUTI, M. and DONCEL, C. (1992) *The Lines of Success? A Study on the Nature and Extent of Cocaine Use in Barcelona*, Barcelona: Laboratori de Sociologia.

FELDMAN, H. W., AGAR, M. and BESCHNER, G. M. (Eds.) (1979) *Angel Dust: an Ethnographic Study of PCP Users*, Lexington, MA: Heath/Lexington Books.

FELDMAN, H. and ALDRICH, M. (1990) 'The role of ethnography in substance abuse research and public policy', in E. Lambert (Ed.) *The Collection and Interpretation of Data from Hidden Populations*, Rockville: National Institute on Drug Abuse (Monograph 98).

FRASER, A. and GEORGE, M. (1988) 'Changing trends in drug use: an initial follow-up of a local heroin community', *British Journal of Addiction*, 83, 655–663.

GAMELLA, J. (1994) 'The spread of intravenous drug use and AIDS in a neighbourhood in Spain', *Medical Anthropology Quarterly*, 8, 131–160.

GAMELLA, J. (1997) *Las rutinas del yonqui activo: un modelo cognitivo, Jornadas sobre Programas de Intercambio de Jeringuillas*, Ministerio de Sanidad y Consumo.

GRIFFITHS, P., GOSSOP, M., POWIS, B. and STRANG, J. (1993) 'Reaching hidden populations of drug users by privileged access interviewers', *Addiction*, 88, 1617–1626.

GRUND, J.-P. C. (1993) *Drug Use as a Social Ritual: Functionality, Symbolism and Determinants of Self-Regulation*, Rotterdam: Instituut voor Verslavingsonderzoek.

GRUND, J.-P. C., FRIEDMAN, S. R., STERN, L. S., JOSE, B., NEAIGUS, A., et al. (1996) 'Syringe-mediated drug sharing among injecting drug users: patterns, social context and implications for transmission of blood-borne pathogens', *Social Science and Medicine*, 42, 691–703.

GRUND, J.-P. C., KAPLAN, C., ADRIAANS, N. F. P. and BLANKEN, P. (1991) 'Drug sharing and HIV transmission risks: the practice of "frontloading" in the Dutch injecting drug user population', *Journal of Psychoactive Drugs*, 23, 1–10.

GRUND, J.-P. C., STERN, L. S., KAPLAN, C. D., ADRIAANS, N. F. P. and DRUCKER, E. (1992) 'Drug use contexts and HIV-consequences: the effect of drug policy on patterns of everyday drug use in Rotterdam and the Bronx', *British Journal of Addiction*, 87, 381–392.

HARTNOLL, R. (1995) 'A difficult business', *Addiction*, 90, 762–763.

HARTNOLL, R. and POWER, R. (1989) *A Study of Help-Seeking and Service Utilisation*, London: Institute for the Study of Drug Dependence.

HEATH, D. (1995) 'Quantitative and qualitative research on alcohol and drugs: a helpful reminder', *Addiction*, 90, 753–755.

HENDERSON, S. (1996) '"E types and dance divas": gender research and community prevention', in T. Rhodes and R. Hartnoll (Eds.) *AIDS, Drugs and Prevention: Perspectives on Individual and Community Action*, London: Routledge.

HENDRIKS, V. M., BLANKEN, P. and ADRIAANS, N. F. P. (1992) *Snowball Sampling: a Pilot Study on Cocaine Use*, Rotterdam: Addiction Research Institute, Erasmus University.

HUGHES, H. (1961) *The Fantastic Lodge: the Autobiography of a Drug Addict*, New York: Fawcett World Library.

HUGHES, P. (1977) *Behind the Wall of Respect: Community Experiments in Heroin Addiction Control*, Chicago: University of Chicago Press.

HUNTER, G. M., DONOGHOE, M. C. and STIMSON, G. V., et al. (1995) 'Changes in the injecting risk behaviour of injecting drug users in London, 1990–1993', *AIDS*, 9, 493–501.

INGOLD, F. R. and TOUSSIRT, M. (1997) *Étude Multi-Centrique sur les Attitudes et les Comportements des Toxicomanes Face au Risque de Contamination par la VIH et les Virus d'Hépatites*, Paris: IREP.

JACKSON, B. (1978) 'Deviance as success: the double inversion of stigmatised roles', in B. A. Babcock (Ed.) *The Reversible World*, Ithaca: Cornell University Press.

JAMES, J.(1977) 'Ethnography and social problems', in R. Weppner (Ed.) *Street Ethnography,* Beverly Hills, CA: Sage.

JAMIESON, A., GLANZ, A. and MACGREGOR, S. (1984) *Dealing with Drug Misuse: Crisis Intervention in the City,* London: Tavistock.

JOSE, B., FRIEDMAN, S. R. and NEAIGUS, A., et al. (1993) 'Syringe-mediated drug-sharing (backloading): a new risk factor for HIV among injecting drug users', *AIDS,* 7, 1653–1660.

KAPLAN, C. and VERBRAEK, H. (1999) 'The changing nature of Dutch drugs ethnography', *Addiction Research* (submitted).

KEENE, J. and RAYNOR, P. (1993) 'Addiction as a "soul sickness": the influence of client and therapist beliefs', *Addiction Research,* 1, 77–87.

KNIPE, E. (1995) *Culture, Society and Drugs: the Social Science Approach to Drug Use,* Prospect Heights, IL: Waveland Press.

KOESTER, S. (1996) 'The process of drug injection: applying ethnography to the study of HIV risk among IDUs', in T. Rhodes and R. Hartnoll (Eds.) *AIDS, Drugs and Prevention: Perspectives on Individual and Community Action,* London: Routledge.

KOESTER, S., BOOTH, R. and WIEBEL, W. (1990) 'The risk of HIV transmission from sharing water, drug mixing containers and cotton filters among intravenous drug users', *International Journal on Drug Policy,* 1, 28–30.

KORF, D. J. and HOOGENHOUT, H. P. H. (1990) *Zoden aan de dijk: Heroïnegebruikers en hun ervaringen met en waardering van de Amsterdamse drughulpverlening (What good is that? Heroin users and their experiences with and appraisal of the drug treatment services in Amsterdam),* Amsterdam: Instituut voor Sociale Geografie, Universiteit van Amsterdam.

LAMBERT, E. (Ed.)(1990) *The Collection and Interpretation of Data from Hidden Populations,* Washington, DC: National Institute on Drug Abuse.

LARSON, A. (1999, forthcoming) 'Fostering ownership of illicit drug research by marginalised communities', in T. Rhodes (Ed.) *Qualitative Methods in Drugs Research,* London: Sage.

LAYDER, D. (1993) *New Strategies in Social Research,* Cambridge: Polity Press.

LINDESMITH, A. (1947) *Opiate Addiction,* Bloomington, IN: Principia Press.

McKEGANEY, N. (1988) 'Drug abuse in the community', in S. J. Cunningham-Burley and N. McKeganey (Eds.) *Readings in Medical Sociology,* London: Routledge.

McKEGANEY, N. (1995) 'Quantitative and qualitative research in the addictions: an unhelpful divide', *Addiction,* 90, 749–751.

McKEGANEY, N. and BARNARD, M. (1992) AIDS, *Drugs and Sexual Risk: Lives in the Balance,* Milton Keynes: Open University Press.

MOORE, D. (1993) 'Ethnography and illicit drug use: dispatches from an anthropologist in the field', *Addiction Research,* 1, 11–15.

MURPHY, S. (1987) 'Intravenous drug use and AIDS: notes on the social economy of needle sharing', *Contemporary Drug Problems,* 14, 373–395.

OUELLET, L., JIMENEZ, A., WENDELL, J. and WIEBEL, W. (1991) 'Shooting galleries and HIV disease: variations in places for injecting illicit drugs', *Crime and Delinquency,* 37, 64–85.

PEARCE, N. (1996) 'Traditional epidemiology, modern epidemiology and public health', *American Journal of Public Health,* 86, 678–683.

PEARSON, G. (1987) *The New Heroin Users,* London: Blackwell.

PEARSON, G. (1995) 'The quantitative–qualitative dispute: an unhelpful divide, but one to be lived with', *Addiction,* 90, 759–761.

PLANT, M. (1975) *Drug Takers in an English Town,* London: Tavistock.

POWER, R. (1989) 'Participant observation and its place in the study of illicit drug use', *British Journal of Addiction,* 84, 43–52.

POWER, R. (1995) 'A model of qualitative action research amongst illicit drug users', *Addiction Research,* 3, 165–181.

POWER, R., JONES, S., KEARNS, G. and WARD, J. (1996) 'An ethnography of risk management amongst illicit drug injectors and its implications for the development of community-based interventions', *Sociology of Health and illness,* 18, 86–106.

PREBLE, E. and CASEY, J. (1969) 'Taking care of business: the heroin user's life on the street', *International Journal of the Addictions,* 4, 1–24.

PREBLE, E. and MILLER, T. (1977) 'Methadone, wine and welfare', in R. Weppner (Ed.) *Street Ethnography,* Beverly Hills: Sage.

QUIRK, A., HOLLAND, J. and HARTNOLL, R. (1991) *Hard to Reach or Out of Reach?* London: Tufnell Press.

QUIRK, A., LILY, R., RHODES, T. and STIMSON, G. V. (1998) *Opening the Black Box: a Qualitative Study of Methadone Treatment Process,* London: Centre for Research on Drugs and Health Behaviour.

RATNER, M. (1993) *Crack Pipe as Pimp,* New York: Lexington.

RHODES, T. (1995) 'Researching and theorising "risk": notes on the social relations of risk in heroin users' lifestyles', in P. Aggleton, G. Hart and P. Davies (Eds.) *AIDS: Sexuality, Safety and Risk,* London: Taylor and Francis.

RHODES, T. (1997) 'Risk theory in epidemic times: sex, drugs and the social organisation of risk behaviour', *Sociology of Health and Illness,* 19, 208–227.

RHODES, T. (Ed.) (1999, forthcoming) *Qualitative Methods in Drugs Research,* London: Sage.

RHODES, T., HARTNOLL, R. and HOLLAND, J. (1991) *Hard to Reach or Out of Reach? An Evaluation of an Innovative Model of Outreach Health Education,* London: Tufnell Press.

RHODES, T. and MOORE, D. (1999) 'On the qualitative in drugs research', *Addiction Research* (submitted).

RHODES, T. and QUIRK, A. (1996) 'Heroin, risk and sexual safety: some problems for interventions encouraging community change', in T. Rhodes and R. Hartnoll (Eds.) *AIDS, Drugs and Prevention,* London: Routledge.

RHODES, T. and QUIRK, A. (1998) 'Drug users' sexual relationships and the social organisation of risk', *Social Science and Medicine,* 46, 161–183.

RHODES, T., STIMSON, G. V., FITCH, C., et al. (1999) 'Rapid assessment, injecting drug use and public health', *The Lancet.*

ROLDAN, A. A. and GAMELLA, J. (1999) 'The limits and scope of ethnography', *Addiction Research* (unpublished paper).

ROMANÍ, O. (1997) 'Etnografía y drogas: discursos y prácticas', *Nueva Antropología,* 16(52), 39–66.

ROSENBAUM, M. (1981) *Women on Heroin,* Brunswíck, NJ: Rutgers University Press.

RUGGIERO, V. (1993) 'Brixton, London: a drug culture without a drug economy', *The International Journal of Drug Policy,* 4, 83–90.

SCHROERS, A. (1995) *Szenealltag im Kontaktcafe (Everyday life of the scene in a street corner agency),* Berlin: Verlag für Wissenschaft und Bildung.

SHAW, C. (1930) *The Jack-Roller,* Chicago: University of Chicago Press.

SHERIDAN, J. and BARBER, N. (1996) 'Drug misusers' experiences and opinions of community pharmacists and community pharmacy services', *The Pharmaceutical Journal,* 2370, 325–327.

SHINER, M. and NEWBURN, T. (1996) *Young People, Drugs and Peer Education: an Evaluation of the Youth Awareness Programme,* London: Home Office.

SIFANECK, S. J. and NEAIGUS, A. (1999) 'Assessing, sampling and screening hidden populations: heroin sniffers in New York City', *Addiction Research* (submitted).

SILVERMAN, D. (1985) *Qualitative Methodology and Sociology,* Aldershot: Gower.

SPRADLEY, J. P. (1970) *You Owe Yourself a Drunk: an Ethnography of Urban Nomads,* Boston: Little Brown.

STERK, C. (1993) 'Outreach among drug users: combining the role of ethnographic field assistant and health educator', *Human Organisation,* 52, 162–168.

SUSSER, M. and SUSSER, E. (1996) 'Choosing a future for epidemiology: from Black Box to Chinese Boxes to Eco Epidemiology', *American Journal of Public Health,* 86, 674–677.

SUTTER, A. (1966) 'The world of the righteous dope fiend', *Issues in Criminology,* 2, 177–222.

TAYLOR, A. (1993) *Women Drug Users: an Ethnography of Female Injecting,* Oxford: Clarendon.

THRASHER, F. (1927) *The Gang,* Chicago: University of Chicago Press.

TURNBULL, P., DOLAN, K. A. and STIMSON, G. V. (1991) *Prisons, HIV and AIDS: Risks and Experiences in Custodial Care,* Horsham: AVERT.

TURNBULL, P., POWER, R. and STIMSON, G. V. (1996) '"Just using old works": injecting risk behaviour in prison', *Drug and Alcohol Review,* 15, 251–260.

WATTERS, J. (1996) 'Americans and syringe exchange: roots of resistance', in T. Rhodes and R. Hartnoll (Eds.) *AIDS, Drugs and Prevention: Perspectives on Individual and Community Action,* London: Routledge.

WEPPNER, R. S. (Ed.) (1977) *Street Ethnography,* Beverly Hills, CA: Sage.

WHYTE, W. F. (1955) *Street Corner Society,* Chicago: University of Chicago Press.

WIEBEL, W. (1990) 'Identifying and gaining access to hidden populations', in E. Lambert (Ed.) *The Collection and Interpretation of Data from Hidden Populations,* Washington, DC: National Institute on Drug Abuse.

WIEBEL, W. (1996) 'Ethnographic contributions to AIDS intervention strategies', in T. Rhodes and R. Hartnoll (Eds.) *AIDS, Drugs and Prevention: Perspectives on Individual and Community Action,* London: Routledge.

ZNANIECKI, F. (1934) *The Method of Sociology,* New York: Farrer and Rhinehart.

ZULE, W. A. (1992) 'Risk and reciprocity: HIV and the injection drug user', *Journal of Psychoactive Drugs,* 24, 243–249.

4

Determining Drug Use Patterns Among Women

The Value of Qualitative Research Methods

Claire Sterk-Elifson

INTRODUCTION

The use of illicit drugs such as cocaine and heroin continues to be a social problem in society. Despite numerous studies addressing potential reasons for initiation and continuation of drug use and possible links between drug use, crime, and violence; the health consequences of drug use; and the impact of drug use on the individual user as well as on the community and society at large, many questions have remained unanswered. Drug use is a complex behavior that can be understood only when studied in the larger sociocultural context in which it occurs.

Much of the current knowledge regarding drug use is derived from large-scale quantitative studies. The two most well-known population-based surveys are the National Household Survey on Drug Abuse (NHSDA), a cross-sectional survey including multistage probability samples, and the Monitoring the Future Project, which includes sequential cohorts of high-school students and young adults (Johnston et al. 1991; NIDA 1994). Additional survey data are derived from institutionally based studies. Two examples of such studies are the Drug Abuse Warning Network (DAWN), which shows weighted estimates of the number of drug mentions among emergency room admissions in a nationwide sample of hospitals, and the Drug Use Forecasting (DUF) Survey, which yields drug use estimates

Reprinted with permission from Elizabeth Y. Lambert, Rebecca S. Ashery, and Richard H. Needle, *Qualitative Methods in Drug Abuse and HIV Research,* National Institute on Drug Abuse Research Monograph 157.

derived from urine screening for drugs among arrestees. These and other epidemiological data sets provide information on drug use prevalence and incidence, however, explanations for trends are not available. To provide such answers requires insight into drug-using behaviors and related norms and practices guiding these behaviors (Des Jarlais et al. 1986; Sterk-Elifson 1993).

Furthermore, the various survey data are not necessarily congruent. Recently, the population-based surveys showed declining rates of drug use, whereas the institutionally based survey revealed an increase in morbidity and mortality rates (National Institute of Justice 1993; NIDA 1994). Studies involving a qualitative research paradigm may explain these contradicting findings through an indepth exploration of drug use.

Due to its illegal nature, reliable and valid information on drug use is difficult to collect. The underlying nature of qualitative research may make this method the most appropriate for studying hidden populations (Abramson 1992; Herdt et al. 1991; Spradley 1979). Qualitative methods require the investigator to spend considerable time with the group under study; to develop contacts with key respondents and build trust relations; and to learn the language, norms, values, attitudes, and behaviors of the group. Qualitative research does not seek to test existing theoretical frameworks; rather, it is deductive and aims to gain an indepth understanding of the group under study and to derive a theoretical framework from the qualitative data.

Studies utilizing a qualitative approach are not new to the substance abuse field. Studies have focused on issues such as the structure of drug users' daily lives (Preble and Casey 1969), drug-using careers among heroin users (Waldorf 1973), the use of language among heroin users (Agar 1973), the social roles among drug users (Stephens 1991), and drug dealing among cocaine and crack users (Adler 1985; Williams 1989).

The majority of the available studies involve male drug users, and sometimes include a subsample of female users as a comparison group (Chein et al. 1964; Hser et al. 1987). The use of illicit substances such as heroin and cocaine has traditionally been associated with males; however, since the 1970s drug use by females has become more prevalent and received more attention in drug use studies.

Initially, female drug users primarily were studied in the context of involvement in prostitution activities. Findings from several studies indicated that drug use functioned as a strategy to cope with the stresses related to prostitution (Goldstein 1979; James 1976). It has also been suggested that prostitution mainly serves as a means to support a drug habit (Cushman 1972). More recently, the link between prostitution and drug use has been shown to be highly complex (Sterk 1990; Sterk and Elifson 1990).

Other qualitative studies involving women focused on the impact of heroin use on their lives and described how the women's heroin use narrowed their options in life (Rosenbaum 1981; Taylor 1993). Since the emergence of crack cocaine on the drug market in the 1980s, females' drug use increasingly received attention as the male–female ratio was more equal than among users of other drugs. In addition, the exchange of sex for crack by female users received substantial attention (Inciardi et al. 1993; Ratner 1993).

Female drug users increasingly are acknowledged as a group worth studying in itself as opposed to serving simply as comparison groups in studies of male drug users. Drug use among women differs from that among men due to factors such as the reproductive role of women and the societal expectation of women to conform to a traditional role as opposed to engaging in deviant behaviors. From a methodological viewpoint, female drug users are more "hidden" than their male counterparts. This is partly due to their limited numbers and their largely subordinate position in the drug subculture.

The main data collection strategies utilized in the existing qualitative studies involve participant observation (Adler 1985; Williams 1989) and indepth interviewing (Goldstein 1979; Rosenbaum 1981; Waldorf 1973). Participant observation requires firsthand involvement by the researcher in order to observe behaviors in the natural setting, to identify patterns, and to discover "rich points" or "cues" (Adler 1993; Agar 1993; Becker 1963). Indepth interviewing involves guided but open-ended interviews in which the respondent identifies the salient issues within the context of the topic under study. As the researcher learns more about the topic, the interviews with subsequent respondents will include this knowledge. In other words, the content of each interview becomes a sounding board for information collected in previous interviews. The ultimate product is an indepth cultural model of the social reality from the respondents' point of view, the so-called emic perspective (Pike 1990).

Quantitative and qualitative research paradigms supplement each other. Quantitative methods are an excellent research tool to collect trend data, to identify risk behaviors and markers, and to develop predictor models for drug use or certain drug use patterns. On the other hand, qualitative methods are relevant when seeking to understand the sociocultural context of drug use.

This chapter focuses on the use of qualitative methods in the Female Atlanta Study (Project FAST), a qualitative study of female drug users. First, a brief overview of Project FAST is presented. This is followed by a discussion of the main data collection strategies: ethnographic mapping and participant observation, indepth interviewing, and focus groups and consensus building. A separate section focuses on safety issues in qualitative research.

A BRIEF OVERVIEW OF PROJECT FAST

The main purpose of Project FAST was to identify the impact of drug use patterns on the lives of female drug users. The two main drugs and routes of administration included are injected heroin and/or cocaine and crack cocaine use. The study sought to explain changes in drug use patterns among women and the impact of the drug use pattern on the women's lives and on related issues such as the support of the drug habit and the set and setting of use. The set and setting of use refer to the sociocultural context of use (e.g., the people present and the type of drugs used).

When the principal investigator started approaching key respondents who had assisted in previous research projects, one of their first questions was the name of the study. The first step in the working relationship with the community consultants was thus to select a name for the project. They pointed out that the name needed to be short, catchy, and not directly refer to drug use. "Project FAST" was the chosen name.

Data collection for Project FAST occurred between June 1992 and June 1994. The overall research design was collaborative, meaning that female drug users were involved in all stages of the research process ranging from identifying initial research questions and procedures for data collection and data analysis. The main data collection strategy was indepth interviewing, supplemented by ethnographic or social mapping including participant observation. Where appropriate, quantitative measures were included (e.g., demographic characteristics, self-esteem, and knowledge of HIV and AIDS).

A total of 14 community consultants was involved in the data collection process. One-half of the community consultants were female, 10 were African American, 2 caucasian, and 2 Hispanic (1 Mexican-American woman and 1 Puerto Rican woman). All but two community consultants had been drug users (N = 8) or currently used drugs (N = 4). The community consultants assisted in the recruitment of women for indepth interviews and collected data for the ethnographic mapping.

Potential respondents identified through ethnographic mapping were asked to participate in a brief street interview to further determine eligibility and, if eligible, were invited for a longer indepth interview. The brief street interview included topics such as first name, date of birth, main community consultant, drug use during the last 4 weeks, and treatment history during the last year. The main purpose of the brief street interview was a final screen for eligibility to participate in the study. Participation was voluntary, respondents were paid, and no personal identifiers were recorded.

To be eligible for an indepth interview, a woman had to live in the Atlanta metropolitan area, be 18 years of age or older, and be an active drug user. For injecting drug users (IDUs), being an active drug user was defined as injecting at least 4 days per week during the last year; crack cocaine users had to use at least 3 grams of cocaine per week or use daily during the last year.

A total of 164 female drug users participated in the study and were interviewed about topics such as family background, reproductive history, drug use and drug treatment experiences, violence and abuse, health history including HIV and AIDS, and social support. Interviews were conducted at a variety of locations ranging from a downtown university office to various community settings. Prior to the interview, women were asked to sign an informed consent form and were briefed extensively about the reporting requirements for child abuse. The interviews were tape recorded and transcribed. The length of the interviews ranged between 1½ hours to 4 hours, depending on the respondent.

The majority of the women (73 percent) were between 21 and 40 years old, were African American (58.5 percent), graduated from high school or had a graduate equivalency diploma (GED) (60.9 percent), had never been married (51.2 percent), and had at least one child (76.8 percent). Approximately two-thirds of the women were primarily crack cocaine smokers, while the remaining one-third were primarily heroin and/or cocaine injectors. Slightly over four-fifths of the women were polydrug users and combined their primary drug of use with other drugs such as marijuana and alcohol.

DATA COLLECTION STRATEGIES

Ethnographic Mapping and Participant Observation

The main goals of the ethnographic mapping were to identify geographical areas where drug use occurred, to explore the dominant drug use patterns, and to identify female drug users in each selected geographic area. Ethnographic mapping involves recording the physical as well as the social infrastructure by geographic area; mapping data were collected through participant observation and informal conversations.

The first decision in the ethnographic mapping process involved selecting geographical areas appropriate for the study. An initial list of 25 geographical areas (ZIP Code areas) was compiled based on epidemiological indicators such as data from local law enforcement agencies, emergency rooms, and drug treatment centers. This list was presented to the community consultants who assisted in the selection of neighborhoods within the ZIP Code areas, added neighborhoods known for drug use but not included based on the epidemiological indicators, and shared their knowledge about the drug scene in each neighborhood. Based on these discussions and some initial mapping and observations, 15 neighborhoods were selected for ethnographic mapping.

Members of the research team, including the community consultants, started the mapping process by conducting a walkthrough observational survey of the neighborhood and noting drug copping areas and buildings. In addition, information was collected through informal conversations with local drug experts, local nonusing residents, and local drug users. A total of 15 individuals participated in the ethnographic mapping. This effort allowed development of basic knowledge of drug use in the neighborhoods and establishment of initial contact with drug users. Based on the ethnographic mapping, neighborhoods were divided according to key characteristics. For example, neighborhoods were characterized as primarily crack areas or shooting (heroin and/or cocaine) areas, residential versus transient drug use areas, and public versus hidden drug use areas. Specific attention was paid to the presence and the varying roles of female drug users. Distinctions were made between and within neighborhoods (e.g., female drug-using street prostitutes versus crackhouse prostitutes, women in the drug business, and women who use drugs but depend on a partner for drugs and/or money and never profile themselves as users in public settings).

Sampling in qualitative studies strives to represent a wide range of experiences. Generally, the sampling frame emerges as the investigation progresses. In other words, the researchers work with a sampling process as opposed to the predetermined sampling frame and procedures typically used in quantitative studies. The ethnographic mapping provided baseline data for the identification of a range of neighborhoods from which a wide variety of female drug users could be recruited, while at the same time permitting flexibility and openness to inclusion of new neighborhoods.

Participant observation—the observation of human behaviors and actions—is a major component of ethnographic mapping and becomes more important as the research progresses. As knowledge and understanding increase, the observations become more focused. In addition, the observation information is verified by having multiple observers in the neighborhood across time periods. For example, several observers in a neighborhood reported that women were actively involved in drug dealing, while other observers in the same neighborhood reported the female drug users were primarily involved in prostitution. These conflicting reports were further explored to determine if they were due to observation bias or differences within the neighborhood. In this example, the contradictory reports stemmed from differences within the neighborhood. While one observer had gained access to the drug-using street prostitutes, another established contact with women involved in the drug business. However, there was no direct overlap between the networks of women who were prostitutes and those who participated in the drug business.

Further exploration of this issue revealed that one of the observers felt uncomfortable observing drug transactions but not street prostitution. Similarly, community consultants familiar with injection drug use had difficulty conducting participant observation among crack users. Each participant observer brings personal biases into the study, which may lead to biased observations and reporting as well as role conflict for the observers (e.g., when the observer feels uncomfortable reporting certain findings) (see Sterk-Elifson 1993 for further discussion). The potential for biased data collection and reporting in Project FAST was reduced through strategies such as having several people conduct participant observation in the same neighborhood, discussing findings in staff meetings, and exploring differences in findings through detailed and focused participant observation.

Bias also occurred due to responses from the field. For example, Hispanic female drug users, primarily Mexican-American and Puerto Rican women, were more open about their drug-using and sexual behaviors to the Hispanic female community consultant than to the caucasian, African-American, and male community consultants. The Hispanic women shared the same cultural background, including language. In this case, the shared background enhanced the relationship between researcher and subjects. One has to be careful, however, when assuming that a shared background is required. One of the caucasian community consultants was rejected by caucasian female drug users who were much more open to African-American consultants. The key factor in the success of the community consultants is a combination of feeling comfortable with the women and being accepted by them.

Conducting ethnographic mapping targeted at female drug users differs from this process with males in a number of ways due to the number of female drug users relative to that of men, the ways in which women support their habit, the women's relationships with male users, and the stigmatization of female drug users as failures. For example, the researchers experienced difficulty in approaching female IDUs who had a relationship with a male user. On several occasions researchers were only able to establish contact after having sought approval from the male partner. Similar difficulties occurred when approaching female drug-using prostitutes who worked for a pimp.

In summary, the information from the ethnographic mapping was used to gain access to and increase knowledge of female drug users, to make sampling decisions, and to create initial contacts with female drug users for the indepth interview component of the study. As the study progressed, the ethnographic mapping information was compared with the interview information. While it took time to gain entrance into the drug-using communities and to develop trust, this period was also used to collect basic information. The time needed to "get in" varied by and within neighborhoods and depended on numerous factors in addition to those mentioned previously; these include the weather, police actions in the neighborhood, and drug availability. For example, everyone on Project FAST remembers the feeling of frustration when the police opened a storefront "miniprecinct" in a community where project members had just gained access.

INDEPTH INTERVIEWS

Indepth interviews were conducted with 164 women, all of whom resided in the areas targeted in the ethnographic mapping effort. These women were not a convenience sample; rather, they represented a cross-section of female drug users in the neighborhoods included in the study. Theoretical sampling was employed to ensure the inclusion of such a sample. As the investigators learned more about female drug users in the selected neighborhoods, relevant distinctions between the various types of female drug users emerged (e.g., through differences between women from different racial/ethnic backgrounds, length of drug use, means of support of the drug habit, way of introduction into drug use, and reproductive status). Based on this theoretical knowledge regarding important differences, sampling decisions were made to ensure the inclusion of a broad representation of female drug users.

Indepth interviews were conducted with each woman selected through theoretical sampling. These interviews differ from survey-based interviews in that the researcher does not use an instrument with standardized questions and response categories, but instead employs an interview guide with open-ended responses. By focusing on the salient issues as identified from the female drug users' point of view, the interviewer is able to develop an insider's perspective of females' drug use. This approach required that the interviewer be a careful listener, constantly integrate the information, probe for elaborations when necessary, and verify throughout the interview if the interviewer's interpretations are correct. The following is an example of such an interaction.

Respondent: When I get high I just lose it . . . I mean, I can't stop 'til all my rock is gone and then I'll start bugging other folks for a hit.

Interviewer: Tell me about that, how do you bug people and how do you know who to bug?

Respondent: There's too many tricks. You can stare at them and the person may give you some just to get rid of you. Sometimes, I start messing with my pipe, like making a lot of noise and cussing, or I'll pace around a person who is just about to take a hit . . . I mean, you tell me. There's a million ways.

Interviewer: But what if you try to bug the wrong person?

Respondent: You see, that what the trick is. You have to know; you just have to know. It's having the smarts. I can't tell you, a person knows. I myself won't go to a sucker who I know wants sex. I'll look for someone who owes me.

Interviewer: Let me see if I get this right. You bug people who owe you first, you stay away from guys who want sex, and what else?

Respondent: To tell you the truth, I'll do anything to get high. I mean, I don't want to and I'll try to forget it as soon as I can.

Interviewer: So, you may do something but you will not tell me about it because it is something you want to forget and you may not acknowledge it to yourself because it makes you feel bad about yourself?

This example indicates the importance of asking the respondent to elaborate on issues such as bugging, sharing drugs, and selecting individuals for a hit of crack. It also shows how indepth interviewing allows the interviewer to capture the complexities of the women's stories and to explain contradictions in a woman's story. Women, like the respondent in the interview, will not address certain issues out of fear for negative labeling by themselves and by others (Klein 1983; Waterston 1993).

Almost all women contended that female drug users are seen as "bad women," while male users "can get away with much more." The women frequently introduced topics that appeared to be linked to the image of bad women. The two most salient areas identified were the junction of the drug use and the mother role and the ways in women support their drug habit. Many women revealed everyday tensions between their drug use and their mother role. In terms of the support of the drug habit, the women discussed how prostitution or sex-for-drug exchanges were an easy route for women to take, and how this made them vulnerable to abuse. The interviews with the women revealed relevant issues that are not discussed in the literature on male drug users. Female drug users need to be asked different questions than those traditionally raised in studies among male users.

Some components of the interview were more structured and included cognitive techniques such as free listing and pile sort. These techniques provided insight into individual practices and perceptions of the relationship between beliefs, norms, and events. It was not uncommon for women to respond to exercises using these techniques by referring to and elaborating on statements made earlier in the interview. Several women mentioned physical and sexual abuse when free listing about female drug use, which in turn facilitated discussions about abuse. While the interviewers initially focused on the women's experiences as victims, the free listing and pile sorting indicated that women were also perpetrators in abusive situations.

The nature of indepth interviewing assumes that the interviewer and the respondent engage in a dialog in which both partners are coequals (Oakley 1986). Female drug users are not accustomed to being asked about their opinions, their behaviors, and the meaning of their actions. While this also may be true for male drug users, the situation for women is more extreme as they generally are seen as "secondary citizens" by male users and often are not taken seriously by male drug users.

Indepth interviewing, as opposed to questionnaire-based interviewing, implies that the interviewer is an important research tool as well. The content of the indepth interview depends on the relationship between the researcher and the respondent. For example, while some interviewers felt comfortable asking about sex for crack, others would probe less often and, as a consequence, get less detailed information. Similar differences may have occurred depending on how comfortable the respondent felt with the interviewer. In several interviews involving an African-American interviewer and respondent, respondents made reference to both women having the same racial background and a shared understanding of the world, while they ignored any differences in socioeconomic status (see Collins 1990 and Hooks 1989 for further discussion). Overall, however, no major differences were identified within Project FAST based on the racial composition of the interviewer–respondent dyad.

Data analysis of indepth interviews occurs both sequentially and concurrently. After the completion of five interviews, the interviewers began to analyze the data by identifying salient issues across interviews and contradictions between interviews. Based on this preliminary data analysis, topics were added to or deleted from the interview guide. Thus, the breadth and depth of the questions grew as the study progressed. If a woman did not voluntarily address issues identified as salient in previous interviews, the interviewer made a special effort to collect data on these topics.

Focus Groups

Several focus groups were conducted with women who were interviewed as well as women who were not. The main reason for conducting focus groups was to verify data interpretations. During a focus group individuals participate in a guided discussion with each other about the meanings of the findings in the presence of staff members. Focus groups provide the researchers with another level of analysis and consensus building, this time between participants in the focus group.

An example was a focus group in which drug use among pregnant women was discussed. Some members of the group emphasized harm reduction among pregnant users, while others stated that pregnancy did not affect drug use. The discussion led the focus group members to distinguish between heavy crack users who exchange sex for crack and those users who do not engage in sex-for-crack exchanges. When the focus group leader introduced findings from the participant observation and the interviews regarding drug use during pregnancy, it appeared that it was almost impossible to distinguish between the two types of crack users. However, apparently all the pregnant crack users engaged in harm reduction, but the extent of behavioral change varied between women and for each woman (Sterk-Elifson et al. 1994). The women who were heavy users and exchanged sex for crack were not a homogenous group, nor did the same woman respond uniformly all the time. While a woman may not use crack but instead drink alcohol in the company of a friend, she may smoke in a crack house. Several women also reported that they would quit using once they felt the baby move, which was a clear reminder of their pregnancy.

Focus groups were used as a consensus-building strategy regarding the data interpretations of the one-to-one indepth interviews and of the participant observation information from the ethnographic mapping. Qualitative data often are analyzed from the researcher's perspective, creating a situation in which the emphasis is on the insider's perspective of females' drug use during data collection but not during data analysis. Focus groups provide qualitative researchers with an additional tool in the data analysis and theory development process, which is common in grounded theory (Glaser 1978; Glaser and Strauss 1967; Strauss and Corbin 1990). Constantly comparing information from different data collection sources is referred to as "triangulation of the data" (Fielding and Fielding 1986). Triangulation increased the validity of the data and allowed identification and exploration of various cultural models of drug use among female drug users.

SAFETY

Due to the nature of ethnographic mapping, specifically the direct and intense involvement of the researchers with the drug-using communities, the safety of the researchers becomes an important aspect of the research process. During the initial stages of the ethnographic mapping in Project FAST, researchers always entered the field in teams of two. The exceptions involved four community consultants who had extensive drug contacts in the neighborhoods where they were working. As the research proceeded, the project field workers, including the community consultants, were viewed less as "professional strangers" (Agar 1980). As the researchers established rapport in the field and developed personal contacts, it became more common for an individual to work alone. Each time researchers were in the field, they were instructed to call in their location, the expected time of arrival and departure, and, if available, the name of a street contact.

It is almost impossible to anticipate difficulties in the field, but clear safety guidelines reduce the potential for trouble. Furthermore, anybody who felt uncomfortable during the ethnographic mapping process was encouraged to leave the field immediately.

Ethnographic mapping and participant observation may also present frustrations for the research staff as is illustrated in the following excerpt from a researcher's field notes.

> For weeks now we have been hearing about a get-off house down the street. No one seems to know exactly what is going on. Melissa has promised me for the fifth time that she will get us in, but today she backed out again . . . (the first two times she did not show up, the third time she said that her connection was not there; the fourth time she had something else to do) and

> this time she said that her connection has changed his mind and was not about to let a white girl come in . . . She said that he had been watching me in the neighborhood and someone even told him I was cool . . . He told Melissa that he didn't see what he was going to get out of this . . . Just as I was about to leave, a guy walked up and Melissa kicked me while whispering, "that's him." I am pissed and not about to have him play more games with me; however, as soon as he walks up I force a smile on my face and become very friendly . . . I never would take these kind of sexist comments (such as "oh, there is another pussy on the block") if it wasn't for my crazy desire to get into Mr. Big T's house.

These field notes indicate that the researcher was faced with the same sexism and disrespect experienced by female drug users and that the researcher needed to react in a way that would not escalate the situation.

Similar safety guidelines were applied to the indepth interviews, specifically those conducted in the community setting. The challenge during the interviews was to ensure privacy and confidentiality while at the same time ensuring the interviewers' safety. As is common in qualitative research among drug users, all project members have their war stories. However, no one associated with Project FAST has been seriously injured, partly due to the established relationships with female drug users and their associates.

Another dimension is the safety of the respondents. Women were stopped by the police because they were observed talking with a researcher, which was viewed as confirmation of their drug use. Others were challenged by boyfriends or relatives for sharing their stories with the researchers. Developing safety guidelines is an important component of conducting qualitative research. For Project FAST the guidelines were continuously modified as new insights were developed and new relationships in the field were established.

CONCLUDING REMARKS

Qualitative and quantitative research paradigms answer different questions but operate in a complementary fashion. The findings from qualitative research can be used in quantitative research to identify salient content areas, to develop response categories for close-ended questions, and to phrase the questions and answers in culturally appropriate language. At the same time, findings from quantitative studies can identify areas for further qualitative explorations.

Both methodologies have their strengths and weaknesses. Quantitative surveys and epidemiological research currently dominate the drug abuse research field, but recently health concerns (particularly the onset of the AIDS epidemic) have underscored the need for studies based on qualitative approaches (Herdt and Lindenbaum 1992). For example, drug users who may have admitted to needle sharing may be less likely to do so now that needle sharing has been identified as risk behavior for HIV transmission. However, the qualitative nature of Project FAST made it more difficult deceive the investigators. If needle sharing was observed in certain neighborhoods or shooting galleries and users from these sites reported not engaging in needle sharing, the researchers were in a position to challenge this report. Furthermore, due to the dialog between interviewer and respondent during indepth interviews, it also was more difficult for the respondent to distort the information. Frequently findings from the participant observation were used to challenge respondents during indepth interviews and appeared to encourage respondents to divulge more accurate information.

Research on substance abuse is critical to identifying ways to prevent drug use initiation and to develop intervention strategies to reduce any potential harm from drug use to the user, the user's community, and society at large. Successful prevention and intervention programs require a clear understanding of risk behaviors. In other words, effective programs and policies must be based on a valid theoretical understanding of drug use and abuse. Drug use and abuse can be addressed effectively with knowledge of underlying norms, values, and attitudes of drug users. This approach has been validated in drug abuse treatment, where programs specifically targeting women and their children appear more successful in attracting women than male-oriented programs.

At the same time qualitative research has its weaknesses, including limited samples, difficulties in replication, and the use of nonstandardized instruments. Replication of such studies is problematic for a number of reasons such as changes in the research setting and researcher bias.

In many ways qualitative research among female drug users is not different from that among male drug users. However, studying female users differs from studying male users. Female drug use is less common than use among men, which increases the difficulty of reaching women. Female drug users tend to occupy a subordinate position in the drug world, which frequently causes their lives to be controlled by males; researchers may need to establish a relationship with the male partner prior to being able to reach the women. Women fear legal repercussions such as the loss of custody of their children. Participant observation revealed that it was not uncommon for community members, relatives, and other drug users to view female users as worthless. This negative perception caused a number of women to deny their drug use, which made it more difficult to interview them.

A quantitative study of female drug users could have included a larger sample of women; however, it would have lacked the depth of information derived from the qualitative study. A good example of the way that qualitative and quantitative data complemented each other involved drug use during pregnancy. Pregnancy and drug use are viewed as incompatible, even among female users. However, many respondents reported continued drug use during pregnancy, largely related to the sociocultural context in which they live. While a survey would have shown that a substantial number of female drug users continued to use drugs, the indepth interviews revealed various harm reduction strategies among pregnant female drug users. These included using drugs less frequently or in smaller amounts and shifting to alcohol use, which because of its legality was viewed as less harmful. These findings were further confirmed in the participant observation and the focus group information.

For many of the female drug users who participated in Project FAST, drug use was one of many problems in their lives. Several women indicated that they used drugs to temporarily forget the stress of everyday life. Uncovering the complexities of subjects' lives is one of the main strengths of qualitative research, especially when studying oppressed individuals who engage in illegal behaviors.

REFERENCES

ABRAMSON, P. Sex, lies, and ethnography. In: Herdt, G., and Lindenbaum, S., eds. *The Time of AIDS: Social Analysis, Theory and Method*. Newbury Park, CA: Sage Publications, 1992. pp. 101–123.

ADLER, P.A. *Wheeling and Dealing: An Ethnography of an Upper-Level Drug Dealing and Smuggling Community*. New York: Columbia University Press, 1985.

ADLER, P. Ethnography and epidemiology: Building bridges. *Proceedings of the 1992 Community Epidemiology Working Group*. Rockville, MD: National Institute on Drug Abuse, 1993. pp. 531–543.

AGAR, M. *Ripping and Running: A Formal Ethnography of Urban Heroin Users*. New York: Academic Press, 1973.

AGAR, M. *The Professional Stranger*. Lexington: Lexington Books, 1980.

AGAR, M. Ethnography: An aerial view. *Proceedings of the 1992 Community Epidemiology Working Group*. Rockville, MD: National Institute on Drug Abuse, 1993. pp. 520–530.

BECKER, H. *Outsiders: Studies in the Sociology of Deviance*. Glencoe, IL: Free Press, 1963.

CHEIN, I.; GERARD, D.; LEE, R.; and ROSENFELD, E. *Narcotics, Delinquency and Social Policy: The Road to H*. London: Tavistock, 1964.

COLLINS, P. *Black Feminist Thought: Knowledge, Consciousness, and the Politics of Empowerment*. New York: Routledge, 1990.

CUSHMAN, P. Methadone maintenance treatment of narcotic addiction. *NY State J Med* 72:1752–1769, 1972.

DES JARLAIS, D.; FRIEDMAN, S.; and STRUG, D. AIDS and needle sharing within the intravenous drug use subculture. In: Feldman, D., and Johnson, T., eds. *The Social Dimensions of AIDS: Method and Theory*. New York: Praeger, 1986. pp. 111–125.

FIELDING, N., and FIELDING, J. *Linking Data*. Newbury Park, CA: Sage, 1986.

GLASER, B. *Theoretical Sensitivity*. Mill Valley, CA: Sociological Press, 1978.

GLASER, B., and STRAUSS, A. *The Discovery of Grounded Theory: Strategies for Qualitative Research*. New York: Aldine de Gruyter, 1967.

GOLDSTEIN, P. *Prostitution and Drug Use*. Lexington, MA: Lexington Books, 1979.

HERDT, G.; LEAP, W.; and SOVINE, M., eds. Sex, AIDS, and anthropology. Special issue. *J Sex Res* 28, 1991.

HERDT, G., and LINDENBAUM, S. *The Time of AIDS: Social Analysis, Theory, and Method*. Newbury Park, CA: Sage, 1992.

HOOKS, B. *Talking Black: Thinking Feminist, Thinking Black*. Boston: South End Press, 1989.

HSER, Y.; ANGLIN, D.; and BOOTH, W. Sex differences in addict career. *Am J Drug Alcohol Abuse* 13:231–251, 1987.

INCIARDI, J.; LOCKWOOD, D.; and POTTIEGER, A. *Women and Crack Cocaine*. New York: MacMillan, 1993.

JAMES, J. Prostitution and addiction: An interdisciplinary approach. *Int J Addict* 2:601–618, 1976.

JOHNSTON, L.; O'MALLEY, P.; and BACHMAN, J. *Drug Use among American High School Seniors, College Students, and Young Adults, 1975–1990*. Vol. 1. High School Seniors. Rockville, MD: National Institute on Drug Abuse, 1991.

KLEIN, R. How to do what we want to do: Thoughts on feminist methodology. In: Bowles, G., and Klein, R., eds. *Theories of Women's Studies*. London: Routlege and Kegan, 1983. pp. 88–104.

National Institute of Justice. Arrestee drug use. *Drug Use Forecasting*. Washington, DC: Supt. of Docs., U.S. Govt. Print. Off., 1993.

National Institute on Drug Abuse. *National Household Survey on Drug Abuse: Population Estimates, 1993*. Rockville, MD: National Institute on Drug Abuse, 1994.

OAKLEY, A. Interviewing women: A contradiction in terms. In: Oakley, A., ed. *Telling the Truth about Jerusalem*. Oxford: Basil Blackwell, 1986.

PIKE, K. On The emics and etics of Pike and Harris. In: Headland, T.; Pike, K.; and Harris, M., eds. *Emic and Etics: The Insider/Outsider Debate*. Newbury Park, CA: Sage, 1990. pp. 28–47.

PREBLE, E., and CASEY, J. Taking care of business: The heroin user's life on the street. *Int J Addict* 4:1–24, 1969.

RATNER, M., ed. *Crack Pipe as Pimp: An Ethnographic Investigation of Sex-for-Crack Exchanges.* Lexington, MA: Lexington Books, 1993.

ROSENBAUM, M. *Women on Heroin.* New Brunswick, NJ: Rutgers University Press, 1981.

SPRADLEY, J. *Participant Observation.* New York: Holt, Rinehart, and Winston, 1979.

STEPHENS, R. *The Street Addict Role: A Theory of Heroin Addiction.* Albany: State University of New York Press, 1991.

STERK, C. *Living The Life: Female Prostitutes and Their Health.* Rotterdam: Erasmus University Press, 1990.

STERK, C., and ELIFSON, K. Drug-related violence and street prostitution. In: DeLaRosa, M.; Lambert, E.; and Gropper, B., eds. *Drugs and Violence: Causes, Correlates, and Consequences.* National Institute on Drug Abuse Research Monograph 103. NIH Pub. No. 94-3715. Washington, DC: Supt. of Docs., U.S. Govt. Print. Off., 1990.

STERK-ELIFSON, C. Outreach among drug users: Ethnography and health education. *Hum Organ* 52:162–168, 1993.

STERK-ELIFSON, C.; DOLAN, K.; and HURST, D. "Drug Use Patterns During Pregnancy." Paper presented at Technical Review on Women and Drug Use, Rockville, MD, June 13–14, 1994.

STRAUSS, A., and CORBIN, J. *Basics of Qualitative Research: Grounded Theory Procedures and Techniques.* Newbury Park, CA: Sage, 1990.

TAYLOR, A. *Women Drug Users: An Ethnography of a Female Injecting Community.* Oxford: Claridon Press, 1993.

WALDORF, D. *Careers in Dope.* Englewood Cliffs, NJ: Prentice Hall, 1973.

WATERSTON, A. *Street Addicts in the Political Economy.* Philadelphia: Temple University Press, 1993.

WILLIAMS, T. *Cocaine Kids.* Reading, MA: Addison Wesley, 1989.

QUESTIONS FOR THOUGHT AND DISCUSSION

Chapter 1: "Criminal Constructions of Drug Users," by Kevin W. Whiteacre

1. What are some traditional methodological approaches used in studying drug-using behavior?
2. How has criminology approached the study of drug-using behavior?
3. What has been the traditional relationship between public policy and criminology as it relates to drug-using behavior?
4. What particular perspective does the author advocate in studying drug users?

Chapter 2: "The Role of Ethnography in Substance Abuse Research and Public Policy: Historical Precedent and Future Prospects," by Harvey W. Feldman and Michael R. Aldrich

1. Please define the ethnographic tradition.
2. Who were some of the earlier ethnographers?
3. How do modern drug ethnographies differ from the earlier work of ethnobotanists?
4. What role did ethnographers play in the early days of the HIV/AIDS epidemic?

Chapter 3: "The Multiple Roles of Qualitative Research in Understanding and Responding to Illicit Drug Use," by Tim Rhodes

1. What are some methodological challenges in working with hidden populations?
2. Why is it important to understand the social contexts of drug use?
3. How does qualitative research complement and enhance quantitative research?
4. How can drug intervention methods be improved using a qualitative perspective?

Chapter 4: "Determining Drug Use Patterns Among Women: The Value of Qualitative Research Methods," by Claire Sterk-Elifson

1. How does a qualitative perspective enhance our understanding of gender and drug-using behavior?
2. What was the particular research strategy employed by members of the Project FAST team?
3. How was the project enhanced by the use of both ethnographic mapping and participant observation?
4. What were some of the benefits of employing interviews and focus groups as part of data collection?

WORLD WIDE WEB SITES

Qualitative European Drug Research
    http://qed.emcdda.org/

Qualitative Research Bibliography
    http://www.twu.edu/as/ws/biblio.htm

The Qualitative Report
  http://www.nova.edu/ssss/QR/qualres.html

QualPage: Resources for Qualitative Research
  http://www.qualitativeresearch.uga.edu/QualPage/

Street Drugs
  http://www.streetdrugs.org/

Drug Abuse Warning Network
  http://dawninfo.samhsa.gov/

National Institute on Drug Abuse
  http://www.nida.nih.gov/NIDAHome1.html

Centers for Disease Control
  http://www.cdc.gov/nchs/index.htm

Pursuing Other Forms
of Communication

❖

Alcoholism is a search for a common language, or at least, it is a compensation for a language that has been lost. The use of drugs does not imply the overestimation of the value of langue but of silence. Drunkenness exaggerates communication; drugs destroy it. Young people's preference for drugs reveals a change in contemporary attitude toward language and communication.

Octavio Paz, Alternative Currents

INTRODUCTION

The pursuit of expanding one's own consciousness through the use of drugs is a timeless practice. Whether part of shaman tradition, an adjunct to introspection, reliving and reconciling events in one's life, or as perceived by "outsiders," for purely hedonistic reasons, the following selections in section II showcase these varying accounts. Also in this section, chapters are featured that highlight a very common drug problem throughout college campuses; binge drinking. The reader will also find a chapter that focuses on the marijuana underground economy of northern England. While drugs such as alcohol, marijuana, and heroin have unrelated chemical properties, users of such substances do so in order to "take the edge off" from life. While it may seem to function as a temporary mediator from such stress, it may simultaneously open the door to a host of unanticipated behavioral, medical, and social problems.

In the first selection, "Becoming a Marihuana User," Howard S. Becker offers a classic symbolic interactionist (SI) perspective whereby the user's motives and disposition for using marijuana are best understood as a social-experiential process that either mitigates or enhances the use of such a drug. Setting aside the known pharmacological properties of marijuana, Becker demonstrates how individuals ascribe meaning, motive, and interpretation to such behavior.

In the second selection, "The High, the Money, and the Fame: The Emergent Social Context of 'New Marijuana' Use among Urban Youth," Jean J. Schensul, Cristina Huebner, Merrill Singer, Marvin Snow, Pablo Feliciano, and Lorie Broomhall offer a contemporary application of Becker's original thesis. By focusing on cultural factors, social rituals, and meanings associated with the use and distribution of high-potency marijuana ("New Marijuana"), the authors reopen a long-standing question on whether marijuana is truly a gateway to "harder" drugs.

The third selection, "Urban Crop Circles: Urban Cannabis Growers in the North of England," is an ethnographic portrait of commercial cannabis growers, its structure, social networks and relationships, their motivation for the "business," and its connection to the larger cannabis market in England. As such, Garfield Potter and Simeon Dann detail a less than monolithic cannabis market as is so commonly perceived by "outsiders."

In the fourth selection, "'You Become Really Close . . . You Talk about the Silly Things You Did and We Laugh': The Role of Binge Drinking in Female Secondary Students' Lives," Australian researchers Margaret Sheehan and Damien Ridge present narratives from women who struggle to construct meaning from their drinking episodes. Sheehan and Ridge offer a culturally specific harm-reduction policy that is holistic and embedded in local realities.

The fifth selection, "Race and the Culture of College Drinking: An Analysis of White Privilege on Campus," Robert L. Peralta examines the importance of considering social-structural and institutional circumstances in accounting for differences in alcohol consumption among White and Black undergraduates. By implementing an open-ended qualitative interview protocol, Peralta offers a new perspective worth considering when attempting to account for such behavioral differences regarding alcohol consumption between racial groups.

In the sixth selection, "Fantasy Island: An Ethnography of Alcohol and Gender Roles in a Latino Gay Bar," researchers Carlos F. Cáceres and Jorge I. Cortiñas employ participant observation, qualitative in-depth interviews, and analysis of historical data to demonstrate how alcohol serves as both as a facilitator and mediator towards social and sexual (behavioral) diversity among a collective of Latino males. Cárceres and Cortiñas discuss the significance of their findings from a public health perspective.

The seventh selection, "Gen-X Junkie: Ethnographic Research with Young White Heroin Users in Washington, DC," Mr. Todd G. Pierce of the Nova Research Company, presents a social network portrait of middle-class heroin users from the Washington, DC, area. By employing a variety of qualitative methods (i.e., qualitative in-depth interviews, participant observation, and life histories) Pierce constructs a social network scheme of a group of heroin users not previously studied. Public health implications and future research directives and initiatives are discussed.

The eighth selection, "Drug Use in Nepal: The View from the Street" by Joel M. Jutkowitz, Hans Spielmann, Ulrich Koehler, Jagdish Lohani, and Anil Pande, presents the life histories of a group of street children in Kathmandu. The researchers offer a multidimensional portrait of young heroin users who have publicly and privately encountered cultural, economic, and familial strains as a result of their drug use.

5

Becoming a Marihuana User[1]

Howard S. Becker

The use of marihuana is and has been the focus of a good deal of attention on the part of both scientists and laymen. One of the major problems students of the practice have addressed themselves to has been the identification of those individual psychological traits which differentiate marihuana users from nonusers and which are assumed to account for the use of the drug. That approach, common in the study of behavior categorized as deviant, is based on the premise that the presence of a given kind of behavior in an individual can best be explained as the result of some trait which predisposes or motivates him to engage in the behavior.[2]

This study is likewise concerned with accounting for the presence or absence of marihuana use in an individual's behavior. It starts, however, from a different premise: that the presence of a given kind of behavior is the result of a sequence of social experiences during which the person acquires a conception of the meaning of the behavior, and perceptions and judgments of objects and situations, all of which make the activity possible and desirable. Thus, the motivation or disposition to engage in the activity is built up in the course of learning to engage in it and does not antedate this learning process. For such a view it is not necessary to identify those "traits" which "cause" the behavior. Instead, the problem becomes one of describing the set of changes in the person's conception of the activity and of the experience it provides for him.[3]

This paper seeks to describe the sequence of changes in attitude and experience which lead to *the use of marihuana for pleasure*. Marihuana does not produce addiction, as do alcohol and the opiate drugs; there is no withdrawal sickness and no ineradicable craving for the drug.[4] The most frequent pattern of use might be termed "recreational." The drug is used

Reprinted with permission from Howard S. Becker, "Becoming a Marihuana User," *American Journal of Sociology,* 1953, vol. 59, pp. 235–42.

occasionally for the pleasure the user finds in it, a relatively casual kind of behavior in comparison with that connected with the use of addicting drugs. The term "use for pleasure" is meant to emphasize the noncompulsive and casual character of the behavior. It is also meant to eliminate from consideration here those few cases in which marihuana is used for its prestige value only, as a symbol that one is a certain kind of person, with no pleasure at all being derived from its use.

The analysis presented here is conceived of as demonstrating the greater explanatory usefulness of the kind of theory outlined above as opposed to the predispositional theories now current. This may be seen in two ways: (1) predispositional theories cannot account for that group of users (whose existence is admitted)[5] who do not exhibit the trait or traits considered to cause the behavior and (2) such theories cannot account for the great variability over time of a given individual's behavior with reference to the drug. The same person will at one stage be unable to use the drug for pleasure, at a later stage be able and willing to do so, and, still later, again be unable to use it in this way. These changes, difficult to explain from a predispositional or motivational theory, are readily understandable in terms of changes in the individual's conception of the drug as is the existence of "normal" users.

The study attempted to arrive at a general statement of the sequence of changes in individual attitude and experience which have always occurred when the individual has become willing and able to use marihuana for pleasure and which have not occurred or not been permanently maintained when this is not the case. This generalization is stated in universal terms in order that negative cases may be discovered and used to revise the explanatory hypothesis.[6]

Fifty interviews with marihuana users from a variety of social backgrounds and present positions in society constitute the data from which the generalization was constructed and against which it was tested.[7] The interviews focused on the history of the person's experience with the drug, seeking major changes in his attitude toward it and in his actual use of it and the reasons for these changes. The final generalization is a statement of that sequence of changes in attitude which occurred in every case known to me in which the person came to use marihuana for pleasure. Until a negative case is found, it may be considered as an explanation of all cases of marihuana use for pleasure. In addition, changes from use to nonuse are shown to be related to similar changes in conception, and in each case it is possible to explain variations in the individual's behavior in these terms.

This paper covers only a portion of the natural history of an individual's use of marihuana,[8] starting with the person having arrived at the point of willingness to try marihuana. He knows that others use it to "get high," but he does not know what this means in concrete terms. He is curious about the experience, ignorant of what it may turn out to be, and afraid that it may be more than he has bargained for. The steps outlined below, if he undergoes them all and maintains the attitudes developed in them, leave him willing and able to use the drug for pleasure when the opportunity presents itself.

I

The novice does not ordinarily get high the first time he smokes marihuana, and several attempts are usually necessary to induce this state. One explanation of this may be that the drug is not smoked "properly," that is, in a way that insures sufficient dosage to produce real symptoms of intoxication. Most users agree that it cannot be smoked like tobacco if one is to get high:

> Take in a lot of air, you know, and . . . I don't know how to describe it, you don't smoke it like a cigarette, you draw in a lot of air and get it deep down in your system and then keep it there. Keep it there as long as you can.

Without the use of some such technique[9] the drug will produce no effects, and the user will be unable to get high:

> The trouble with people like that [who are not able to get high] is that they're just not smoking it right, that's all there is to it. Either they're not holding it down long enough, or they're getting too much air and not enough smoke, or the other way around or something like that. A lot of people just don't smoke it right, so naturally nothing's gonna happen.

If nothing happens, it is manifestly impossible for the user to develop a conception of the drug as an object which can be used for pleasure, and use will therefore not continue. The first step in the sequence of events that must occur if the person is to become a user is that he must learn to use the proper smoking technique in order that his use of the drug will produce some effects in terms of which his conception of it can change.

Such a change is, as might be expected, a result of the individual's participation in groups in which marihuana is used. In them the individual learns the proper way to smoke the drug. This may occur through direct teaching:

> I was smoking like I did an ordinary cigarette. He said, "No, don't do it like that." He said, "Suck it, you know, draw in and hold it in your lungs till you . . . for a period of time."
>
> I said, "Is there any limit of time to hold it?"
>
> He said, "No, just till you feel that you want to let it out, let it out." So I did that three or four times.

Many new users are ashamed to admit ignorance and, pretending to know already, must learn through the more indirect means of observation and imitation:

> I came on like I had turned on [smoked marihuana] many times before, you know. I didn't want to seem like a punk to this cat. See, like I didn't know the first thing about it—how to smoke it, or what was going to happen, or what. I just watched him like a hawk—I didn't take my eyes off him for a second, because I wanted to do everything just as he did it. I watched how he held it, how he smoked it, and everything. Then when he gave it to me I just came on cool, as though I knew exactly what the score was. I held it like he did and took a poke just the way he did.

No person continued marihuana use for pleasure without learning a technique that supplied sufficient dosage for the effects of the drug to appear. Only when this was learned was it possible for a conception of the drug as an object which could be used for pleasure to emerge. Without such a conception marihuana use was considered meaningless and did not continue.

II

Even after he learns the proper smoking technique, the new user may not get high and thus not form a conception of the drug as something which can be used for pleasure. A remark made by a user suggested the reason for this difficulty in getting high and pointed to the next necessary step on the road to being a user:

> I was told during an interview, "As a matter of fact, I've seen a guy who was high out of his mind and didn't know it."
>
> I expressed disbelief: "How can that be, man?"
>
> The interviewee said, "Well, it's pretty strange, I'll grant you that, but I've seen it. This guy got on with me, claiming that he'd never got high, one of those guys, and he got completely stoned. And he kept insisting that he wasn't high. So I had to prove to him that he was."

What does this mean? It suggests that being high consists of two elements: the presence of symptoms caused by marihuana use and the recognition of these symptoms and their connection by the user with his use of the drug. It is not enough, that is, that the effects be present; they alone do not automatically provide the experience of being high. The user must be able to point them out to himself and consciously connect them with his having smoked marihuana before he can have this experience. Otherwise, regardless of the actual effects produced, he considers that the drug has had no effect on him: "I figured it either had no effect on me or other people were exaggerating its effect on them, you know. I thought it was probably psychological, see." Such persons believe that the whole thing is an illusion and that the wish to be high leads the user to deceive himself into believing that something is happening when, in fact, nothing is. They do not continue marihuana use, feeling that "it does nothing" for them.

Typically, however, the novice has faith (developed from his observation of users who do get high) that the drug actually will produce some new experience and continues to experiment with it until it does. His failure to get high worries him, and he is likely to ask more experienced users or provoke comments from them about it. In such conversations be is made aware of specific details of his experience which he may not have noticed or may have noticed but failed to identify as symptoms of being high:

> I didn't get high the first time . . . . I don't think I held it in long enough. I probably let it out, you know, you're a little afraid. The second time I wasn't sure, and he [smoking companion] told me, like I asked him for some of the symptoms or something, how would I know, you know . . . . So he told me to sit on a stool. I sat on—I think I sat on a bar stool—and he said, "Let your feet hang," and then when I got down my feet were real cold, you know.
>
> And I started feeling it, you know. That was the first time. And then about a week after that, sometime pretty close to it, I really got on. That was the first time I got on a big laughing kick, you know. Then I really knew I was on.

One symptom of being high is an intense hunger. In the next case the novice becomes aware of this and gets high for the first time:

> They were just laughing the hell out of me because like I was eating so much. I just scoffed [ate] so much food, and they were just laughing at me, you know. Sometimes I'd be looking at them, you know, wondering why they're laughing, you know, not knowing what I was doing. [Well, did they tell you why they were laughing eventually?] Yeah, yeah, I come back, "Hey, man, what's happening?" Like, you know, like I'd ask, "What's happening?" and all of a sudden I feel weird, you know. "Man, you're on, you know. You're on pot [high on marihuana]." I said, "No, am I?" Like I don't know what's happening.

The learning may occur in more indirect ways:

> I heard little remarks that were made by other people. Somebody said, "My legs are rubbery," and I can't remember all the remarks that were made because I was very attentively listening for all these cues for what I was supposed to feel like.

The novice, then, eager to have this feeling, picks up from other users some concrete referents of the term "high" and applies these notions to his own experience. The new concepts make it possible for him to locate these symptoms among his own sensations and to point out to himself a "something different" in his experience that he connects with drug use. It is only when he can do this that he is high. In the next case, the contrast between two successive experiences of a user makes clear the crucial importance of the awareness of the symptoms in being high and re-emphasizes the important role of interaction with other users in acquiring the concepts that make this awareness possible:

> [Did you get high the first time you turned on?] Yeah, sure. Although, come to think of it, I guess I really didn't. I mean, like that first time it was more or less of a mild drunk. I was happy, I guess, you know what I mean. But I didn't really know I was high, you know what I mean. It was only after the second time I got high that I realized I was high the first time. Then I knew that something different was happening.
> [How did you know that?] How did I know? If what happened to me that night would of happened to you, you would've known, believe me. We played the first tune for almost two hours—one tune! Imagine, man! We got on the stand and played this one tune, we started at nine o'clock. When we got finished I looked at my watch, it's a quarter to eleven. Almost two hours on one tune. And it didn't seem like anything.
> I mean, you know, it does that to you. It's like you have much more time or something. Anyway, when I saw that, man, it was too much. I knew I must really be high or something if anything like that could happen. See, and then they explained to me that that's what it did to you, you had a different sense of time and everything. So I realized that that's what it was. I knew then. Like the first time, I probably felt that way, you know, but I didn't know what's happening.

It is only when the novice becomes able to get high in this sense that he will continue to use marihuana for pleasure. In every case in which use continued, the user had acquired the necessary concepts with which to express to himself the fact that he was experiencing new sensations caused by the drug. That is, for use to continue, it is necessary not only to use the drug so as to produce effects but also to learn to perceive these effects when they occur. In this way marihuana acquires meaning for the user as an object which can be used for pleasure.

With increasing experience the user develops a greater appreciation of the drug's effects; he continues to learn to get high. He examines succeeding experiences closely, looking for new effects, making sure the old ones are still there. Out of this there grows a stable set of categories for experiencing the drug's effects whose presence enables the user to get high with ease.

The ability to perceive the drug's effects must be maintained if use is to continue; if it is lost, marihuana use ceases. Two kinds of evidence support this statement. First, people who become heavy users of alcohol, barbiturates, or opiates do not continue to smoke marihuana, largely because they lose the ability to distinguish between its effects and those of the other drugs.[10] They no longer know whether the marihuana gets them high. Second, in those few cases in which an individual uses marihuana in such quantities that he is always high, he is apt to get this same feeling that the drug has no effect on him, since the essential element of a noticeable difference between feeling high and feeling normal is missing. In such a situation, use is likely to be given up completely, but temporarily, in order that the user may once again be able to perceive the difference.

III

One more step is necessary if the user who has now learned to get high is to continue use. He must learn to enjoy the effects he has just learned to experience. Marihuana-produced sensations are not automatically or necessarily pleasurable. The taste for such experience is a socially acquired one, not different in kind from acquired tastes for oysters or dry martinis. The user feels dizzy, thirsty; his scalp tingles; he misjudges time and distances; and so on. Are these things pleasurable? He isn't sure. If he is to continue marihuana use, he must decide that they are. Otherwise, getting high, while a real enough experience, will be an unpleasant one he would rather avoid.

The effects of the drug, when first perceived, may be physically unpleasant or at least ambiguous:

> It started taking effect, and I didn't know what was happening, you know, what it was, and I was very sick. I walked around the room, walking around the room trying to get off, you know; it just scared me at first, you know. I wasn't used to that kind of feeling.

In addition, the novice's naive interpretation of what is happening to him may further confuse and frighten him, particularly if he decides, as many do, that he is going insane:

> I felt I was insane, you know. Everything people done to me just wigged me. I couldn't hold a conversation, and my mind would be wandering, and I was always thinking, oh, I don't know, weird things, like hearing music different . . . . I get the feeling that I can't talk to anyone. I'll goof completely.

Given these typically frightening and unpleasant first experiences, the beginner will not continue use unless he learns to redefine the sensations as pleasurable:

> It was offered to me, and I tried it. I'll tell you one thing. I never did enjoy it at all. I mean it was just nothing that I could enjoy. [Well, did you get high when you turned on?] Oh, yeah, I got definite feelings from it. But I didn't enjoy them. I mean I got plenty of reactions, but they were mostly reactions of fear. [You were frightened?] Yes. I didn't enjoy it. I couldn't seem to relax with it, you know. If you can't relax with a thing, you can't enjoy it, I don't think.

In other cases the first experiences were also definitely unpleasant, but the person did become a marihuana user. This occurred, however, only after a later experience enabled him to redefine the sensations as pleasurable:

> [This man's first experience was extremely unpleasant, involving distortion of spatial relationships and sounds, violent thirst, and panic produced by these symptoms.] After the first time I didn't turn on for about, I'd say, ten months to a year . . . . It wasn't a moral thing; it was because I'd gotten so frightened, bein' so high. An' I didn't want to go through that again,

> I mean, my reaction was, "Well, if this is what they call bein' high, I don't dig [like] it." . . . So
> I didn't turn on for a year almost, accounta that . . . .
>
> Well, my friends started, an' consequently I started again. But I didn't have any more, I
> didn't have that same initial reaction, after I started turning on again.
>
> [In interaction with his friends he became able to find pleasure in the effects of the drug
> and eventually became a regular user.]

In no case will use continue without such a redefinition of the effects as enjoyable.

This redefinition occurs, typically, in interaction with more experienced users who, in a number of ways, teach the novice to find pleasure in this experience which is at first so frightening.[11] They may reassure him as to the temporary character of the unpleasant sensations and minimize their seriousness, at the same time calling attention to the more enjoyable aspects. An experienced user describes how he handles newcomers to marihuana use:

> Well, they get pretty high sometimes. The average person isn't ready for that, and it is a little
> frightening to them sometimes. I mean, they've been high on lush [alcohol], and they get higher
> that way than they've ever been before, and they don't know what's happening to them. Because
> they think they're going to keep going up, up, up till they lose their minds or begin doing weird
> things or something. You have to like reassure them, explain to them that they're not really flip-
> ping or anything, that they're gonna be all right. You have to just talk them out of being afraid.
> Keep talking to them, reassuring, telling them it's all right. And come on with your own story,
> you know: "The same thing happened to me. You'll get to like that after awhile." Keep coming
> on like that; pretty soon you talk them out of being scared. And besides they see you doing it
> and nothing horrible is happening to you, so that gives them more confidence.

The more experienced user may also teach the novice to regulate the amount he smokes more carefully, so as to avoid any severely uncomfortable symptoms while retaining the pleasant ones. Finally, he teaches the new user that he can "get to like it after awhile." He teaches him to regard those ambiguous experiences formerly defined as unpleasant as enjoyable. The older user in the following incident is a person whose tastes have shifted in this way, and his remarks have the effect of helping others to make a similar redefinition:

> A new user had her first experience of the effects of marihuana and became frightened and hys-
> terical. She "felt like she was half in and half out of the room" and experienced a number of
> alarming physical symptoms. One of the more experienced users present said, "She's dragged
> because she's high like that. I'd give anything to get that high myself. I haven't been that high
> in years."

In short, what was once frightening and distasteful becomes, after a taste for it is built up, pleasant, desired, and sought after. Enjoyment is introduced by the favorable definition of the experience that one acquires from others. Without this, use will not continue, for marihuana will not be for the user an object he can use for pleasure.

In addition to being a necessary step in becoming a user, this represents an important condition for continued use. It is quite common for experienced users suddenly to have an unpleasant or frightening experience, which they cannot define as pleasurable, either be-cause they have used a larger amount of marihuana than usual or because it turns out to be a higher-quality marihuana than they expected. The user has sensations which go beyond any conception he has of what being high is and is in much the same situation as the novice, uncomfortable and frightened. He may blame it on an overdose and simply be more careful in the future. But he may make this the occasion for a rethinking of his attitude toward the drug and decide that it no longer can give him pleasure. When this occurs and is not followed by a redefinition of the drug as capable of producing pleasure, use will cease.

The likelihood of such a redefinition occurring depends on the degree of the individual's participation with other users. Where this participation is intensive, the individual is quickly talked out of his feeling against marihuana use. In the next case, on the other hand, the experience was very disturbing, and the aftermath of the incident cut the person's participation with other users to almost zero. Use stopped for three years and began again only when a combination of circumstances, important among which was a resumption of ties with users, made possible a redefinition of the nature of the drug:

> It was too much, like I only made about four pokes, and I couldn't even get it out of my mouth, I was so high, and I got real flipped. In the basement, you know, I just couldn't stay in there anymore. My heart was pounding real hard, you know, and I was going out of my mind; I thought I was losing my mind completely. So I cut out of this basement, and this other guy, he's out of his mind, told me, "Don't, don't leave me, man. Stay here." And I couldn't.
>
> I walked outside, and it was five below zero, and I thought I was dying, and I had my coat open; I was sweating, I was perspiring. My whole insides were all . . . , and I walked about two blocks away, and I fainted behind a bush. I don't know how long I laid there. I woke up, and I was feeling the worst, I can't describe it at all, so I made it to a bowling alley, man, and I was trying to act normal, I was trying to shoot pool, you know, trying to act real normal, and I couldn't lay and I couldn't stand up and I couldn't sit down, and I went up and laid down where some guys that spot pins lay down, and that didn't help me, and I went down to a doctor's office. I was going to go in there and tell the doctor to put me out of my misery . . . because my heart was pounding so hard, you know . . . . So then all week end I started flipping, seeing things there and going through hell, you know, all kinds of abnormal things . . . . I just quit for a long time then.
>
> [He went to a doctor who defined the symptoms for him as those of a nervous breakdown caused by "nerves" and "worries." Although he was no longer using marihuana, he had some recurrences of the symptoms which led him to suspect that "it was all his nerves."] So I just stopped worrying, you know; so it was about thirty-six months later I started making it again. I'd just take a few pokes, you know. [He first resumed use in the company of the same user-friend with whom he had been involved in the original incident.]

A person, then, cannot begin to use marihuana for pleasure, or continue its use for pleasure, unless he learns to define its effects as enjoyable, unless it becomes and remains an object which he conceives of as capable of producing pleasure.

IV

In summary, an individual will be able to use marihuana for pleasure only when he goes through a process of learning to conceive of it as an object which can be used in this way. No one becomes a user without (1) learning to smoke the drug in a way which will produce real effects; (2) learning to recognize the effects and connect them with drug use (learning, in other words, to get high); and (3) learning to enjoy the sensations he perceives. In the course of this process he develops a disposition or motivation to use marihuana which was not and could not have been present when he began use, for it involves and depends on conceptions of the drug which could only grow out of the kind of actual experience detailed above. On completion of this process he is willing and able to use marihuana for pleasure.

He has learned, in short, to answer "Yes" to the question: "Is it fun?" The direction his further use of the drug takes depends on his being able to continue to answer "Yes" to this question and, in addition, on his being able to answer "Yes" to other questions which arise as he becomes aware of the implications of the fact that the society as a whole disapproves of the practice: "Is it expedient?" "Is it moral?"[12] Once he has acquired the ability to get enjoyment out of the drug, use will continue to be possible for him. Considerations of morality and expediency, occasioned by the reactions of society, may interfere and inhibit use, but use continues to be a possibility in terms of his conception of the drug. The act becomes impossible only when the ability to enjoy the experience of being high is lost, through a change in the user's conception of the drug occasioned by certain kinds of experience with it.

In comparing this theory with those which ascribe marihuana use to motives or predispositions rooted deep in individual behavior, the evidence makes it clear that marihuana use for pleasure can occur only when the process described above is undergone and cannot occur without it. This is apparently so without reference to the nature of the individual's personal makeup or psychic problems. Such theories assume that people have stable modes of response which predetermine the way they will act in relation to any particular situation or object and that, when they come in contact with the given object or situation, they act in the way in which their makeup predisposes them.

This analysis of the genesis of marihuana use shows that the individuals who come in contact with a given object may respond to it at first in a great variety of ways. If a stable form of new behavior toward the object is to emerge, a transformation of meanings must occur, in which the person develops a new conception of the nature of the object.[13] This happens in a series of communicative acts in which others point out new aspects of his experience to him, present him with new interpretations of events, and help him achieve a new conceptual organization of his world, without which the new behavior is not possible. Persons who do not achieve the proper kind of conceptualization are unable to engage in the given behavior and turn off in the direction of some other relationship to the object or activity.

This suggests that behavior of any kind might fruitfully be studied developmentally, in terms of changes in meanings and concepts, their organization and reorganization, and the way they channel behavior, making some acts possible while excluding others.

NOTES

1. Paper read at the meetings of the Midwest Sociological Society in Omaha, Nebraska, April 25, 1953. The research on which this paper is based was done while I was a member of the staff of the Chicago Narcotics Survey, a study done by the Chicago Area Project, Inc., under a grant from the National Mental Health Institute. My thanks to Solomon Kobrin, Harold Finestone, Henry McKay, and Anselm Strauss, who read and discussed with me earlier versions of this paper.

2. See the following for examples of this approach, Eli Marcovitz and Henry J. Meyers, "The Marihuana Addict in the Army," *War Medicine* VI (December 1944), 382–391; Herbert S. Gaskill, "Marihuana, an Intoxicant," *American Journal of Psychiatry* CII (September 1945): 202–4; Sol

Charen and Luis Perelman, "Personality Studies of Marihuana Addicts," *American Journal of Psychiatry* CII (March 1946): 674–82.

3. This approach stems from George Herbert Mead's discussion of objects in *Mind, Self, and Society* (Chicago: University of Chicago Press, 1934), pp. 277–280.

4. Cf. Roger Adams, "Marihuana" *Bulletin of the New York Academy of Medicine* XVIII (November 1942): 705–730.

5. Cf. Lawrence Kolb, "Marihuana," *Federal Probation* II (July 1938): 22–25; and Walter Bromberg, "Marihuana: A Psychiatric Study," *Journal of the American Medical Association*, CXIII (July 1, 1939): 11.

6. The method used is that described by Alfred R. Lindesmith in his *Opiate Addiction* (Bloomington: Principia Press, 1947), chap. i. Also, I would like to acknowledge the important role Lindesmith's work played in shaping my thinking about the genesis of marihuana use.

7. Most of the interviews were done by the author. I am grateful to Solomon Kobrin and Harold Finestone for allowing me to make use of interviews done by them.

8. I hope to discuss elsewhere other stages in this natural history.

9. A pharmacologist notes that this ritual is in fact an extremely efficient way of getting the drug into the blood stream. R. P. Walton, *Marihuana: America's New Drug Problem* (Philadelphia: J. B. Lippincott, 1938), 48.

10. "Smokers have repeatedly stated that the consumption of whiskey while smoking negates the potency of the drug. They find it very difficult to get 'high' while drinking whiskey and because of that smokers will not drink while using the 'weed'" cf. New York City Mayor's Committee on Marihuana, *The Marihuana Problem in the City of New York* (Lancaster, PA: Jacques Cattell Press, 1944), 13.

11. Charen and Perelman, op. cit., p. 679.

12. Another paper will discuss the series of developments in attitude that occur as the individual begins to take account of these matters and adjusts his use to them.

13. Cf. Anselm Strauss, "The Development and Transformation of Monetary Meanings in the Child," *American Sociological Review* XVII (June 1952): 275–286.

6

The High, the Money, and the Fame

The Emergent Social Context of "New Marijuana" Use Among Urban Youth

Jean J. Schensul, Cristina Huebner, Merrill Singer, Marvin Snow,
Pablo Feliciano, and Lorie Broomhall

❖

INTRODUCTION

In 1995, when the National Institute on Drug Abuse (NIDA) published findings of its Monitoring the Future study,[1] researchers and policy makers alike were confronted with evidence of a growing rate of marijuana use among middle- and high-school-aged youth (Swan 1995). For the third year in a row, the study found statistically significant increases in the percentage of eighth graders who reported using marijuana during the last year, with rates more than doubling from 6.2% in 1991 to 13% in 1994 (UMNIS 1994). Among tenth and twelfth graders, marijuana consumption was up for the second year in a row (UMNIS 1996). While the rates of adolescent marijuana use were still considerably lower than the record levels of the 1970s, by the early 1990s, the downward trend had begun to reverse as marijuana began making a strong comeback as a desired drug among U.S. youth. Before long, the secretary of Health and Human Services director, Donna Shalala, announced a co-ordinated national initiative to counter this trend.

Shalala's pronouncement follows a long history of efforts to thwart marijuana use in the United States, especially during the twentieth century. Despite these campaigns, "[a]ccording to every reliable, systematic study that has ever been conducted on the subject, marijuana is by far the most commonly tried and used illegal drug in every population, social group, community, and milieu in American" (Goode 1984, 85). As a hardy and adaptable wild plant, marijuana (*Cannabis sativa*) grows naturally and abundantly around the world and in many parts of the United States and hence is easily accessible. Human consumption of marijuana is an ancient pratice with the earliest reports of its use for psychotropic effects dating to the fifth century B.C. (Feldman and Aldrich 1990). Intentional cultivation of marijuana in the New World, especially for fiber, dates to the colonial period. During the nineteenth century, the drug, like cocaine and heroin, was legally dispensed and widely sold as an ingredient in various patent medicines. Neighborhood pharmacies sold marijuana as a tincture produced by companies like Parke-Davis and Squibb to treat various illnesses and emotional conditions (Walton 1938).

Domestic concern about marijuana use was minimal until the Great Depression, which enhanced popular hostility toward ethnic minority populations, especially toward Hispanics in the Southwest and blacks in the South, groups that were seen as competing for jobs with white workers. As Musto (1987) has shown, Congressional passage of the Marihuana Tax Act in 1937, a law that in effect banned marijuana use, was closely tied to anti-Mexican and anti-black sentiments. Despite passage of the law, by the 1940s, marijuana smoking had become a fixture among avant garde musicians and other artists. Even Malcolm X, prior to his conversion to Islam and subsequent emergence as a charismatic African-American leader, spent several years during and after World War II selling marijuana cigarettes ("reefers") to musicians in Harlem and marketing marijuana sticks to performers in a number of East Coast cities (Malcolm X 1968).

This association linking the arts, nonconventional lifestyles, and marijuana helped to create a street image of the marijuana user as a glamorous figure worthy of emulation. By the 1950s, marijuana had become a routine feature of inner-city youth subculture, and by the mid- to late 1960s, its use as a psychedelic had spread to suburban youth as well along with a broad social, media, and economic infrastructure promoting the growth and use of marijuana and marijuana products and reinforcing the social use of marijuana and its importance in personal-psychological development (Becker 1953; Johnson 1973).

By the mid-1980s, rap music, was signaling the "unofficial" transition from alcohol to marijuana as the drug of preference among inner-city youth. Perkins (1996, 260–61) notes:

> The titleholder for eclectic rap is Cypress Hill, whose 1991 *Cypress Hill* and 1993 *Black Sunday* reveal one obsession—marijuana. Hip hop's priests of the blunt invoke the Book of Genesis in "Legalize It": "I have given you all the seeds and herbs of the land." Led by MC B-Real, whose nasal twang speaks of the blessing of cannabis, they have more than any other force, revived "reefer madness" and introduced it to a new generation as an alternative to alcohol, particularly malt liquor.

Until the 1980s, most of the marijuana available to urban youth in the United States was grown in Mexico or elsewhere in the Caribbean or Latin America and was imported illegally. "Commercial" or regular marijuana is characterized by relatively low levels of THC (tetrahydrocarbinol, the main psychoactive ingredient in marijuana), ranging from

1–5%. Over the past two decades, however, marijuana production and distribution has undergone significant changes, including a notable increase in domestic production, expansion of indoor growth of plants on a large scale along with utilization of hydroponic growing methods, and genetic manipulation of plant characteristics. The result has been the production of new varieties on the domestic market, associated with different features and "highs." The THC level of some types of marijuana has jumped five-fold to between 10% and 25%, and the street price for high-potency marijuana brands has climbed dramatically (cf. Fields 1984, 1986). In addition, while regular marijuana continues to be widely available and used, the "new marijuana," as we refer to it in this paper, has become deeply ingrained in key aspects of inner-city youth culture, including language, music, visual media, clothing, parties, and other social gatherings.

It is likely that inner-city youth have been using high-potency marijuana for some time. Contemporary younger users in Hartford say that new brands of marijuana, much stronger than "regular" marijuana, have been on the streets for over a decade. National studies, however, provide little information about drug varieties, how they are mixed, or the contexts in which they are used. Indeed, the emergence of new marijuana use occurred during a period of rapid decline in the number of studies being conducted on marijuana. As Kalant and colleagues (1999) note, the number of scientific and clinical publications on marijuana listed in *Index Medicus* increased from an average of less than ten a year in the decade prior to 1967 to 300–350 a year from the mid- to late 1970s (following popular concern about the movement of marijuana use from the inner city to the suburbs), only to fall to less than 100 a year thereafter (associated with drops in funding for cannabis research). Thus we have little detailed information about the emergent use of more potent forms of marijuana. In this light, this paper, which is based on a broader, ongoing NIDA funded ethnographic and epidemiological study of the pathways to heavy drug use among youth and young adults in Hartford, Connecticut,[2] examines the sociocultural context of new marijuana use as an emergent drug trend among inner-city youth.

METHODS

This paper is based on ten months of ethnographic research with adolescents and young adults in Hartford, Connecticut, who use marijuana regularly or who are associated with other youth who do so. The primary purpose of our ethnographic research has been to gain a deeper understanding of the context of marijuana, cocaine, and heroin use among youth in the city. We were also interested in finding out what drugs young people were using, in what order they were initiating use, and where and how they were obtaining and using marijuana and other drugs. To accomplish these goals, members of our research team conducted in-depth interviews with young male and female injection drug users to find out about drug-use sequencing, the role of marijuana in their lives, and the relationship between marijuana and other drugs. The staffs of youth-serving agencies in Hartford provided us with the contexts and contacts for conducting a total of ten focus group sessions with 71 young people ranging in age from 14 to 20 who were either using marijuana or exposed to its use in their schools, their neighborhoods, or their families. In these focus groups, participants discussed their perceptions of drug and marijuana use, drug availability, drug preferences, drug costs, and other factors associated with the drug trade. Several members of the research team engaged in participant observation and informal interviewing in a number of clubs and other relatively public social settings favored by youth in different parts of the city in an effort to gain a baseline understanding of the role of these locations in the distribution and use of marijuana and other related drugs. Project staff also conducted a preliminary content analysis of selected music, movies, and magazines popular among urban youth that reflect values, social usage, and general information about the new forms of marijuana.

A central component of fieldwork was involvement with networks of young new marijuana users. Network researchers on the team identified and became engaged with two large, widely dispersed social networks of young adult new marijuana users and distributors working in different parts of the city, one predominantly Hispanic, the other primarily African American and Caribbean-West Indian. After identifying index youth through their own personal or agency networks, they gained rapport with them, interviewed them, met their close friends, learned about their connections, and participated in various aspects of their lives. The index informants were both 20 years old, and their personal networks included over 150 associates, male and female, between 18 and 35 years of age. By participating in these networks, project researchers were able to obtain information on how money is raised to purchase marijuana, how marijuana is acquired and smoked, where smoking occurs and with whom, the difference between occasional and regular social use of new marijuana, and why young people are so devoted to smoking new marijuana.

In sum, to date, our approach to understanding new marijuana use among inner-city (primarily African-American and Latino) youth in Hartford has (1) been largely exploratory; (2) involved several different methods of data collection, including both qualitative and quantitative approaches (although this paper primarily reports out ethnographic findings); (3) focused on both younger users and sellers (who are also all users) of new marijuana; and (4) focused on understanding cannabis consumption within the context of socio-cultural factors that structure use patterns in our target population.

Understanding the use of new marijuana as an emergent trend among urban youth, we believe, requires a focus on the following core topics that will be used to structure this paper: (1) youth perceptions of new marijuana as contrasted with regular marijuana; (2) patterns of use and user experience of the new marijuana ("the high"); (3) the economy of the new marijuana market in relation to regular marijuana ("the money"); (4) the status and prestige that users and other youth attribute to the use of the new marijuana ("the fame"); and (5) the ways in which new marijuana is embedded in hip hop culture and the popular media. Through an exploration of these issues, we will show how the new marijuana has become a driving force, both economically and socially, for a growing number of inner-city adolescents and young adults. We begin this examination by positioning our ethnographic findings relative to the reports of the major American epidemiological monitoring studies intended to track drug-use patterns including marijuana use.

STUDIES OF EPIDEMIOLOGICAL TRENDS IN MARIJUANA USE AMONG YOUTH

Several longitudinal studies monitor trends and identify emergent patterns in drug consumption among adolescents and adults in the United States. One such study, the National Household Survey on Drug Abuse (NHSDA) identified a steady increase in the percentage of adolescents reporting marijuana use between 1992 and 1996 with the number of new marijuana users among youth between the ages of 12 and 17 increasing from 1.4 million in 1991 to 2.4 million in 1994 and 1995 (SAMHSA 1998:42). However, the NHSDA does not report on the emergent use of new marijuana or the underlying social and cultural patterns associated with its use. The Monitoring the Future study of the National Institute on Drug Abuse, which tracks drug use in secondary school students, found a similar pattern for eighth and tenth graders in 1996 (NIDA 1997).

The Community Epidemiology Work Group (CEWG) of the National Institute of on Drug Abuse is a network of drug researchers located in major metropolitan areas around the United States (as well as in some other countries) which meets semiannually to share findings on ongoing city-by-city surveillance of drug-use patterns based on epidemiological and ethnographic data collection. In 1996, the CEWG reported the presence of indoor hydroponics in several areas of the country (CEWG 1998). CEWG identified inter-city differences in available marijuana prices and THC purity as reflected in Table I.

TABLE I   Community Epidemiology Work Group Findings on Marijuana Prices by City*

City	Marijuana Type	Price Per Ounce
Atlanta	Commercial**	$100–$125
	Indoor Sinsemilla	$200–$250
Boston	Commercial	$75–$300
	Sinsemilla	$200–$300
Chicago	Commercial	$60–$70
	High quality	$110–$200
Honolulu	"Low quality"	$250–$500
	"High quality"	$400–$800
Miami	Commercial	$65–$180
	Sinsemilla	$250–$600
San Francisco	Commercial	$40–$100
	Sinsemilla	$200–$600
San Diego	Commercial	$50–$75
	Sinsemilla	$200–$400
Seattle	Commercial	
	Sinsemilla	$200–$350
Washington, DC	Commercial	$150–$250
	Sinsemilla	$150–$500

Modified from Exhibit 36 and Exhibit 28, Epidemiologic Trends in Drug Abuse (CEWG 1997:62, 1998:57).

* All categories in this table are based on CEWG terminology. "Commercial" refers to regular marijuana; other terms refer to what we term new marijuana in this article, containing high levels of tetrahydrocannabinol (THC).

**Commercial marijuana contains from 2–4% THC; sinsemilla contains from 8–20% THC with percentages varying by city (CEWG 1998).

In Table I, researchers in a number of cities report the concurrent availability of high-potency new marijuana and lower potency, foreign-grown regular (i.e., imported) marijuana with considerable inter-city differences in THC levels and prices of regular and new marijuana. In New York City, which appears to be a key source for the new marijuana available in Hartford, CEWG researchers Frank and Gales (1997:178–179) report the following:

> In casual conversation with users and dealers, field researchers find that widespread use of marijuana may be partially due to a change in attitude and perception. Many drug users tend to opt for marijuana in preference to crack, which is regarded as a low-status drug. . . . [Y]ounger users about age 15–30 continue to prefer smoking blunt cigars loaded with marijuana. . . . An ounce of [regular] marijuana sells for approximately $70–$80, while the pound price varies. "Skunk" [a type of new marijuana] sells for about $800 per pound; "Chocolate," currently the most popular brand, commands $1,000–$1,200 per pound.

A CEWG researcher (Falkowski 1998, 137) from Minnesota reports on the identification of a "sophisticated indoor grower [who] boasted flavored marijuana plants (chocolate, vanilla, etc.)." Brief mention of new marijuana availability, variety, and cost are included in the city reports for several other CEWG cities, for example, the existence of a "pot-cottage crime industry" in Miami (Hoffer and Mendelson 1998) and reports of "narcotic-like effects" from smoking small quantities of genetically manipulated new marijuana in Denver (Holland and Whitman 1998). However, like the other monitoring mechanisms noted above, there remains a paucity of information on the actual attitudes, use patterns, and marketing practices associated with the appearance of new marijuana in the CEWG reports. The Hartford study attempts to clarify some of these aspects of new marijuana use.

USER PERCEPTIONS: HIGH-POTENCY NEW MARIJUANA VERSUS LOWER-POTENCY REGULAR MARIJUANA

It is evident from field observation and interviews with youth that there are clear differences between the old (i.e., regular) marijuana and the varieties of new marijuana, both of which are readily available in Hartford as well as in other areas of the Northeast. While both the old and new forms of marijuana are derived from the *Cannabis sativa* plant, a major botanical difference between these two forms is the THC level. Informants say that the new marijuana is engineered to produce only female buds, which are believed to contain much higher levels of THC. Additionally, the new marijuana has no seeds, hence the name "sinsemilla," (meaning "without seeds" in Spanish, see Table I above). The new marijuana looks, smells, and tastes different; sells for a considerably higher price per unit weight than regular marijuana; and is said to produce a much more intense high. When asked about the difference, a regular user said, "Anybody that sells it, they could tell you the difference. It's a big difference. . . . You could just tell them that this [the higher cost] is the difference. Yeah, and the looks of it, the smell of it, the taste of it, it is just a whole different ball game." Terminologically, on the streets, regular marijuana often is called "regular weed" or "ses." In Hartford, the new marijuana most often is referred to as "bud" (a term previously in use in some locales for regular marijuana as seen in the quote below) or as "exotic."

Users can differentiate many different types of "bud," based on a number of factors, including how the plants were grown; where they were cultivated either within or beyond the continental United States (e.g., special value is placed on new marijuana from Hawaii);

the distinctive look and color of the plants when they reach full maturity and after they are processed into a smokeable product; the aroma given off by the plants before and while they are being smoked; the effects produced by smoking; and the unit cost in ounces or pounds.

Regular marijuana, as purchased on the street in Hartford, is brownish in color and appears to be dry. Bud has a much deeper green color than its regular counterpart, lacks seeds, and, if it is good quality, has a chunky appearance. Bud also exhibits some exotic features in contrast to regular marijuana. For example, one brand of bud sold on the street contains small, white, moist, fuzzy balls, a second is colored lime green, another contains orange "hair-like" tendrils; and yet another is characterized by its purple tint. When asked about different types of bud, one key informant said, "OK, there's bud, there is one that is bud, then you have hydro, you have purple haze, you have redline, you have Hawaian, you have Brinson. . . . That weed came from uh Redman [the rap musician]. . . . Like, he's the first person to ever start talking about Brinson weed." The nine most common types of bud currently sold in Hartford are Bud (in this case labelling a specific subtype), Hydro (or Dro), Brinson, Hawaiian (or Orange), Purple Haze, Brown Purple Haze, Redline, Arizona Red, and Bristol. The most popular varieties on the street are Bud, Hydro, and Brinson. Another informant summed up the differences among types of new marijuana by saying, "Bottom line is everybody grow they own weed a different way, and then they name it what they want."

While users clearly distinguish between varieties of regular marijuana and varieties of bud, most of the youth to whom we have spoken say that ultimately it doesn't really matter which type of bud is smoked because all types produce a better high than regular marijuana. As one informant put it, the "high" the users get from smoking bud is "off the hook" (i.e., wild or intense) and makes you "bent" (extremely intoxicated), as opposed to the "nice" or "mellow" high produced by regular marijuana. Respondents themselves attribute the difference to higher THC levels in new marijuana compared to regular marijuana. This sense that the new marijuana is significantly better than and different from regular marijuana extends to the long-term effects of protracted use. Reflecting contemporary ideas in popular health and nutrition, users describe bud as being purer and healthier because it smells and tastes better than regular marijuana. Unlike inhaling regular marijuana smoke, they say, inhaling new marijuana smoke does not hurt and less of it is required to obtain the desired psychotropic effects.

THE NEW MARIJUANA MARKET (THE "MONEY")

When one of our key informants was asked to explain the difference between regular marijuana and bud, he stated, "The difference is in the price and the price speaks for itself." The difference in the quality of the "high" elevates the street value of the new varieties of marijuana. One key informant told us that Hartford distributors can purchase regular marijuana locally for $60 to $80 per ounce, depending on the source and sell it for from 50% to 100% above the purchase price. A common terminology describes the quantities or units in which marijuana is sold on the street: a $5 bag of marijuana is called a "a nick"; $10 worth is called a "dime bag"; $20 worth is called a "dub sac" or a "deuce bag"; $25 worth is called either a "quarter" or is referred to as a "dub sac plus a nick." Bud, by comparison, is considerably more expensive than regular marijuana, selling locally for $450 to $700 per ounce. According to the street market, a bud dealer should at least double his/her money. One of our key informants said, "Sellin' bud you gonna double yo' money and sometimes get even $200 more. But, if you smokin' some of yo' own stash or givin'play [giving friends a reduced price] you gonna make $900 instead of a 'g.'" Unlike regular marijuana, bud is sold only in $15 and $30 bags respectively, which are referred to as "a 15 bag" or "a 30 bag," although some prized brands such as Brinson are more expensive. As one informant said, from bud "you make mad profit even dipping into your own supply" (i.e., even when smoking some of it yourself).

SPARKING OFF: ACHIEVING AND EXPERIENCING THE NEW MARIJUANA "HIGH"

Bud's street popularity rests on its perceived ability to produce a unique high. The most important dimensions of the "bud high" are the social context of consumption, "setting," and users' attribution of a "set" of meanings to their experience (Zinberg 1984). Users heighten their experience with bud by learning appropriate terminology and a set of associated beliefs about the drug and by participating in rituals that socialize new users into proper use while reinforcing close relationships among group members.

Informants generally concur that bud is usually consumed "with the boys," not alone. They agree that even though some people do it, smoking bud alone isn't "worth it" because the best part of the experience is sharing the high with someone who is "on the same level." Sincere,[3] one of our key informants, stressed that most of the time he and his "boys" pool their money together to see how much they can afford. Then they decide whether to buy a bag of bud that yields one "L" (an L is a "blunt," a cigar filled with bud, considered to be the basic smokeable unit of new marijuana) or a bag of regular marijuana that yields about two to three Ls or even four if you "got play" (a reduced price). The difference for them is that it is possible to get "really bent" (quite high) from a single "piece" or L, whereas regular marijuana produces a less intense immediate high, but the larger amount that can be purchased with the same amount of money makes it possible to smoke multiple times throughout the day. Usually bud wins.

Bud is ingested by smoking. Among the alternative forms of smoking are rolling a small amount of marijuana in cigarette paper as a "joint," smoking it with a "bat" or a "bong" (a water pipe), or inserting it into a "blunt." Only with considerable practice is it possible to gain the skill required to prepare a blunt effectively. If the blunt is loose, too much air passes through it causing the bud to burn too rapidly. Also, a blunt that is improperly rolled will burn on one side and not on the other. When this happens, Latino users refer to it in Spanish as *el canoe* because of its appearance. Within a network of drug users, certain members tend to become known for their rolling skills and are usually relied on to prepare blunts for the whole group. Two of our informants complained that when "amateurs" are involved, the blunt is not wrapped tightly enough. By contrast, a "professional" knows how to pack a blunt so that the cigar leaves stay very tight, and the tobacco and marijuana burn evenly.

Preparing a blunt begins with buying a cigar. Currently, the cigars most often chosen for the preparation of blunts are Garcia Vega (regular, green tube, blue tube, and brown tube), Phillies, White Owl, and Dutch Masters because they burn slowly and do not detract from the taste of the marijuana. "The boys" choose the cigar most appropriate for the type of session or "cipher" (name for a group session in which bud is used) they are planning. For example, Garcia Vegas packaged in tubes are larger than other cigars, and they burn more slowly. They thus are considered more appropriate for use with bigger quantities of bud or for longer sessions.

The cigar is cut lengthwise and the inner tobacco is removed along with the "cancer piece." The cancer piece is a short layer of cigar leaf found at one end in between the internal green layer of tobacco and the external brown wrapping. All participants, when questioned, recognized that the entire cigar is carcinogenic. However, they believe a street myth that identifies the "cancer piece" as that part of the tobacco that causes cancer, so they remove it. Removal of the "cancer piece" they explained, is part of the "rolling tradition."

Depending on the quantity of bud to be rolled, the cigar may be cut lengthwise a second time, leaving one piece that is about two-thirds of the leaf and discarding the rest. This is done in order to reduce the amount of tobacco leaf being smoked in relationship to the amount of bud. The edges of the cigar leaf are licked and rubbed flat. Then the bud is placed inside the leaf and rolled tightly. An experienced roller may re-roll the blunt more and more tightly until it is perfect. The outer edge of the cigar leaf is licked and smoothed firmly onto the body of the rolled blunt. Finally, a flame is passed over the blunt to dry and seal all of the edges. The blunt is now ready to "spark up" (light) and "pass around."

When "the boys" get together to smoke a blunt, the event is called a "cipher" or a "session." These terms denote a ritual in which members of a crew or clique pass a blunt around until it is gone. Our network members say that "with good bud, after one or two pulls [inhalations] you begin to feel the effects of the high." A cipher can take place at someone's house, in a car, or anywhere "on the block," defined by network members as their territory. The following description, taken from fieldnotes gathered through participant observation, is typical of a session:

> The Owl walks towards the glass table and uncovers the fruit bowl which is filled with marijuana. "I've been waiting all day to smoke this s__t" "What kind of marijuana is this?" I[researcher] ask. "Tropical bud" says G-Money. "Some of the best s__t you could ever smoke." "Roll a piece," states La. G-Money sits down and unwraps a Garcia Vega. He wets the Garcia by putting half in his mouth, turns it around and wets the other half. La hands him a razor blade and he splits the Vega down the middle. He empties the tobacco into a small wastebasket. "You smoke?" asks G-Money. "No" I reply. "Neither did La until he tried some bud from New York. He's been smoking ever since." The bud is green with orange and red fibers, similar to photographs we have seen in *High Times*. G-Money tears the tip of the Vega and splits the top portion which is done very slowly. He peels off a piece of paper—"the cancer part." G-money re-licks the Vega to seal the split end. He grabs a few buds from the bowl. "Roll a fat one" states Swatch. G-money crunches up the bud and lines it in the Vega. "Spark it up" states the Owl. G-Money passes the blunt to the Owl. The Owl lights the blunt and takes two hits and passes. Each member repeats the process until it is passed to the Owl. He takes another hit and attempts to pass it to Swatch who motions no with his hand. Each member now refuses to take another hit. "This is some good s__t" states the Owl.

Bud is never wasted or thrown away. If a blunt is not smoked completely, i.e., there is some bud remaining in the blunt, it is saved for later use. At the end of the week, network members collect any leftover bud "roaches" and roll them into a special blunt which they call "the resonator." As one key player emphasized, "You can never get bored of bud. Bud is bud. You can never waste it. Me and my boys have a saying 'it's bud, you gotta hit it'. If it were a blunt of regular weed, we might toss the end, but if it's bud you gotta hit it til it's all gone."

CELEBRITY, REPUTATIONS (THE "FAME"), AND THE ROLE OF GENDER RELATIONS

On the street, males who distribute and/or smoke bud are looked up to and respected by their peers. They become known as having connections with successful "players." If they gain expertise and influence in the drug business, they can make and can be seen spending a great deal of money. Not all distributors gain large amounts of wealth, however, either because they cannot generate the connections or because they choose to maintain a safe balance between salaried employment and involvement in illegal activities.

A man who is skillful at making "mad money" and has established intricate distribution and use networks is known as "Big Willie." This term seems to have crossed ethnic boundaries and is used equally often in African-American and Hispanic/Latino communities. Anyone referred to as "Big Willie" has achieved a high level of fame and respect among bud-user networks and is looked to as a social icon. A network member explained, "You don't f__k with Big Willies cause they got the connex." Big Willies often spend weekend nights driving around in their souped-up or rented cars, visiting clubs, and observing their "soldiers" at work at local gates.

The clubs offer Big Willies the opportunity to display their wealth on weekends by demonstrating their expensive cars, clothes, jewelry, and watches and by spending large amounts of money on expensive alcohol for their "boys" and their women. In this way they reinforce their prestige and enhance their social standing with their peers. At the same time, clubs offer safe locations where distributors can meet, confirm social connections, discuss new deals, and set the stage for the ritual display of wealth, power, and social connections.

While smoking or dealing in bud enhances the street reputation of young men, young women are subject to the reverse set of standards. Reflecting popular rap lyrics and cross-cultural traditional patterns of gender relations (see Weeks et al. 1996; Sobo 1995; Zambrana 1982), male informants talk about two different kinds of women: "thug girls" and "wifeys" or "boos." Women who smoke bud and are involved in the business side of the bud scene, are referred to as "thug girls," a term referring to young women who are "down" with the ways of the street. Like men, they also acquire reputations for doing their own drug dealing or for holding drugs, drug money, and weapons for male associates. Thug girls can make a considerable amount of money either as independent dealers or as important accessories to a man's business; it is likely that they can establish broad connections in the bud world but only through other men. Despite their money and connections, thug girls do not necessarily gain the same public fame and respect as Big Willies. One key informant, Sincere, says, "They [women] makin' money, but they not so paid. There are girls who hustle a lot and better than a lotta guys, but I ain't never seen one driving a Lexus. Naw I ain't seen that yet."

Thug girls are not viewed as likely candidates for long-term relationships. Instead, as business associates, they are susceptible to having temporary relationships with a number of distributors. The reputation for being sexually available that they may acquire as they search for financial and emotional stability harms their potential for long-term relationships with male partners.

Young women who choose to avoid smoking bud publicly, remove themselves from the social and economic settings where bud is used and exchanged, and focus on their studies and/or church activities are never referred to as thug girls. They are seen as desirable longer-term love partners, and after having gained the status of girlfriend, are referred to as "wifey," "boo," or "shorty." Young men involved in drug use or distribution say they do not turn to wifeys to hold bud money or drug stashes. According to some key informants who work with drug-using youth, this does not mean that young women are avoiding drugs. They may be using bud or other forms of marijuana or alcohol at home, at private parties, and among female friends, but their drug use is private. The male pattern of keeping a serious girlfriend "safe from" the life of the streets while maintaining multiple sexual and drug partnerships is reflected in other literature regarding the struggles of urban low-income women in their relationships with their male partners (Carovana 1991; Fullilove et al. 1990; Gupta and Weiss 1993).

CULTURAL CONTEXT: THE NEW MARIJUANA SCENE

Local ideas about and attitudes towards bud, bud-use norms, and the language used to refer to new forms of marijuana are directly influenced by and, in turn, influence the media and popular youth culture reflected in magazines, movies, music, and music videos (cf. Stephens et al. 1998). Our informants have introduced us to a variety of magazines that focus on the production, distribution, and use of bud or on the hip hop youth subculture that at times overtly and at times covertly sanctions and celebrates its consumption. *High Times, Cannabis, Hemptimes, The Source, Blaze, Rap Pages,* and *Vibe* are all magazines devoted to the growth, development, marketing, and use of marijuana and marijuana products, which are sold by companies located in Canada, the United States, and the Netherlands. Their catalogs provide detailed descriptions of the highs associated with various brands of new marijuana such as the following excerpts:

> Afghani #1—Very strong physical, practically narcotic high.
> Amstel Gold—Smokes soft with a citruslike aroma and has a good high. Easy to grow, grows with long compact resinous buds.
> Chitral—Good harvest, nice herbal taste and strong "physical high."
> Euforia—[T]he famous Skunk high, taste not too sweet as our other Skunk selections.
> Haze Skunk—Truly superior sweet taste. The high is incredibly clear and up energy.
> Thai—Very strong and energetic "up" high.
> Western Winds (Kali Mist)—An almost pure Sativa with a soaring cerebral high. (Marc Emery Direct Seed Sales 1999:2–4)

These magazines are supported by companies that advertise the sale of equipment and supplies needed for indoor cultivation of enhanced marijuana and other expensive products that can be smoked or ingested such as "Kind Budz from Jamaica," "Northern Heights herbal hash oil," and "Chronix totally organic" (Dream World 1999:62). They also feature a number of products, such as "Urine Luck," (Spectrum Labs 1999:95) "Urine Pure," "Test Pure," and "Naturally pure Yourealitea Quick Flush" capsules and tea (Naturally Pure Enterprises 1999:69), that claim to mask the presence of THC in the urine, enabling users to pass urine tests even after smoking.

Additionally, as noted in the reference to Cypress Hill above, marijuana is an important element in rap music and hip hop culture. As a recent cover story of *Times Magazine,* "It's a Hip-Hop Nation" (Farley 1999), illustrates, rap music reflects the inner-city street experience of rap artists, many of whom endured poverty and racism as they were growing up.

Most rap songs hold great symbolic value for members of bud networks, validating and reinforcing their behaviors and lifestyles.

Some types of bud first become popular because a successful rap artist makes reference to them in his/her song lyrics, resulting in a surge in the demand for and price of a particular type of bud. For example, Redman's (a popular rap artist) rap song "Whateva Man" refers to a type of bud that, according to the song lyrics, came from "his boy Branson" (Redman 1996b):

> Yo, I'm rollin with a forty pack of niggaz
> Get my weed from Branson cause his sack's bigger. (Redman 1999)

The new bud on the streets was named Branson (or Brinson) and became so popular that it was sold in Hartford only in $40 bags. As a result, Branson's popularity and the profits that distributors realized soared.

Hip hop music helps to launch and sustain new street trends in the use of bud and the behaviors surrounding its acquisition and consumption. At the same time, because of the strong subcultural emphasis on "staying real" (close to the social roots of the music), street language and behaviors influence trends in the music. The lyrics of many popular rap songs include references to "getting blunted" (high on marijuana blunts), smoking "hydro," having a session or "cipher," or "getting paid" (making a lot of money on drugs). For example, Gang Starr (1996) raps in their song, "Take two and pass":

> Take two [pulls] and pass so we can get blunted. . . . I think, write, and rhyme when I'm done getting blunted . . . and let the lala [marijuana] enhance our mind. . . . [E]ven in the mornin' a blunt adds spice and a blunt can spruce up your day. (Gang Starr 1996)

On her track "The Rain (Supa Dupa Fly)," Missy "Misdemeanor" Elliot (1998) raps, "I take a puff, puff me some indo [weed]. . . . I smoke my hydro on the D-Low [Down Low, meaning concealed or hidden]." In "Hits from the Bong," the rap group Cypress Hill (1993) describes how to prepare a blunt for smoking, the comparative value of blunts and bongs (water pipe) as alternative routes of new marijuana consumption, and the challenges of smoking bud in a bong:

> I like a blunt or a big fat cone, but my double-barrel bong is getting me stoned. There's water inside don't spill it. It smells like s__t on the carpet. . . . Still it goes down smooth when I get a clean hit of the skunky, phunky, smelly green s__t.

Redman (1996b), in "Smoke Buddah [Marijuana]" raps:

> I got that sh–to get your whole clique high, We can get high, but act funny N' I'm a whip out! N' they gonna whit out N' blow notes like Michele, Cuz you tried to jump tha cypher N' it goes (This a-way!) Smoke on N' on, you don't stop.

These snips of popular songs by well known rap groups illustrate the reciprocal relationship among street slang, promotional advertising of marijuana and associated products, and the culture associated with bud use and the songs of rap artists.

Youth with entrepreneurial skills who become large-scale new marijuana distributors čan earn between $35,000 and $80,000 per month or even more. A common attitude shared by young distributors is that the wisest path is to "make big money, smoke some, and chill with your crew." In other words, the emphasis is on avoiding activities that invite public notice and police intervention. As a central member in one of the youth networks we are studying commented, "We ain't tryin' to go to jail."

Instead, successful distributors of new marijuana and other drugs in Hartford and elsewhere in the Northeast are exploring ways to reap the financial benefits of the illicit drug business, save or invest their earnings and move out of the drug trade as quickly as possible. For example, one 20-year-old key informant told us that in a matter of months, he would have enough to retire for the rest of his life and planned to invest his earnings in legitimate business developments. It is widely known that a group of young adults in the north end of Hartford was investing in businesses supporting hip hop culture. They have launched their own DJ businesses, record labels, hip hop clothing designs, and music groups. Supa Buddah (pseudonym), a recorded rap group started by four Latino youth from Hartford is one such group. At least six other businesses started by people who obtained their venture capital by distributing bud have been established in Hartford. These are mainly clothing/gear stores that sell the latest hip hop fashions. In addition to employing youth directly, many of these businesses utilize the skills of others in their networks. For example, one of Sincere's boys is the logo designer for all of the gear sold in Word-Up Clothing (pseudonym). The networks that begin on the streets are "steadfast" (loyal) and play an important role in the establishment of legitimate businesses, which help to stabilize their neighborhoods. These businesses provide a means for youth to display their artistic and musical talents, which otherwise would have no other productive outlet.

Many of the young artists and entrepreneurs who derive their inspiration from street culture have already produced significant amounts of wealth, much of which is spent locally in neighborhood shops and strip malls, bolstering city and suburban economies. Their labels and businesses for the most part will serve local and regional markets. A very few among them, such as Tupac Shakur and Redman, may, like basketball stars, become nationally recognized, holding out to aspiring young adults in local neighborhoods the hope for upper-middle-class success and continuing wealth.

CONCLUSION

Our broad study of pathways in drug use among inner-city youth was launched with the intention of identifying routes and factors in the transition from initial experimental drug use to heavy drug use, "hard" drug use, and drug injection among inner-city youth. This study follows almost a decade of interviewing adult heroin and cocaine addicts and garnering from them stories and interview data concerning the development of their addictive and often risky drug-use patterns. While most of our adult participants reported early and continued marijuana use, our primary focus in these earlier studies was on drugs and drug-use practices involved in the transmission and spread of HIV disease. Consequently, we failed to notice fully significant changes, such as the emergence of high-potency marijuana use among adolescent and young adult drug-user networks, in the very neighborhoods we were studying. This type of inattention to new marijuana use has characterized the illicit drug research field generally.

Inner-city adolescents, by contrast, have focused considerable attention on the new marijuana. Our current research points to the presence of several factors, all with important political, economic, and social dimensions, that contribute to the appeal of new marijuana and the sense of excitement that energizes the contemporary new marijuana market (Baer et al. 1997). First, there is money to be made. Young people know from experience that they can make more money more quickly selling new marijuana than they can pursuing legal employment. In the inner city, where jobs for youth are scarce, of low status, and poorly paid, this is a significant motivator.

Second, selling and using new marijuana has become an important way of gaining status, prestige, and popularity among peers as well as money that can be spent on consumer and display goods and possessions that demonstrate personal success. New forms of marijuana expand the marijuana market, and a distributor's reputation can rise dramatically with access to newer brands and the ability to sell multiple varieties of bud to multiple audiences. Use of the new brands operates similarly. Having access to the "hottest" brands of new marijuana indicates that one has good social connections and has the resources to use only the best. Again, social discrimination is a significant factor here. Avenues of personal success and social achievement are limited among the inner-city poor. Access to bud, by contrast, is relatively unlimited.

Third, among users, scarcity polarization (Ditto and Jemmott 1989), sensation-seeking (Zuckerman 1987), self-fulfilling prophecy (Snyder et al. 1977), and cognitive dissonance (Festinger 1957) all appear to be important factors contributing to the attractiveness of newer forms of marijuana and the expansion of the new marijuana market. Young users know that some types of bud, such as Brinson, are available only in limited quantities that sell at comparatively high prices. When they finally acquire it, their sense of expectancy and exhilaration may augment their drug experience. It has long been known among drug users and researchers that "set" and "setting" (user expectations and the social context of use) are at least as important, if not more so, than drug pharmacology (Beardsley and Kelly 1999). Thus the street reputation of new marijuana as being especially euphoric, the street emphasis on the unusually powerful highs that are experienced with particular hard-to-get brands of bud, and the higher costs associated with these brands contribute to the subjective drug experiences of users.

Fourth, individuals in our study population have easy access to several glossy magazines that glorify marijuana use. While the drug that they praise is illegal, magazines promoting its use are not and can be purchased from several mainstream bookstore chains. Once acquired, these magazines are disseminated person to person through youth social networks. Commonly, these magazines, which detail carefully subtle differences (in taste, smell, appearance, cost, and subjective effects), describe new marijuana using terminology and photographs that are suggestive of sexual relationships. It has long been a Madison Avenue insight that "sex sells," and this lesson has not been lost on the new marijuana market.

Finally, new marijuana is closely intertwined with other arenas of the contemporary youth subculture, such as rap music. Products of the commercial music industry, including CDs, radio, music television, and live concerts, are all redundant, heavily accessed forms of entertainment among urban youth. All of these entertainment formats feature music that touts marijuana use generally and especially new marijuana use. Individuals who are looked up to by youth regularly sing the praises of "firing up" a blunt and getting high. While such songs have helped to make a number of performers quite wealthy, their success, in turn, serves to legitimize the use of illicit substances for younger audiences who are just coming of "drug-use age."

In short, there are multiple yet connected factors, all of which are shaped in one way or another by the politics and economics of contemporary society (including ethnic/race relations, social inequality, and profit-making) that have contributed to the emergence and growth of new marijuana consumption among inner-city youth. The qualitative data presented in this paper illustrate how urban young people access regular and new forms of marijuana and how embedded these new forms of marijuana are in their lives. According to our pilot survey data, among marijuana-using youth, 66% use new marijuana.

To date, however, our data show that most marijuana-using youth, even those using high-potency marijuana, report that they have little interest in moving beyond marijuana to use other drugs or other forms of drug consumption. In fact, their descriptions of cocaine and heroin users reveal a clear and deep social division between younger drug users who only use marijuana and those who use cocaine, crack, or heroin. Nevertheless, other data collected ethnographically by our ethnographic team, as well as through our surveys with older drug users in Hartford, suggest that in addition to bud, regular marijuana laced with other drugs designed to "intensify the high" is readily available and in use in Hartford. Marijuana intensifiers in regular use include marijuana resin (chocolate), "embalming fluid," PCP, cocaine, or heroin. Surveys of older injection drug users and some youth indicate that the age of initiation of these combination drugs is one or two years later than either regular or new marijuana. It is significant that the youth we have interviewed do not show the same reservations about experimenting with these marijuana intensifiers as they do with respect to drugs like cocaine and heroin alone. In fact, when pressed, a number of them have said they have at least experimented with these additives.

What are the implications from a public health standpoint of the growing adoption of high-potency new marijuana among inner-city youth? While research on the health effects of marijuana use remain equivocal (Kalant et al. 1999; Solowij 1998), as Solowij (1999, 212) concludes, based on a review of the animal literature, there is convincing evidence that chronic administration of large doses of THC are associated with "long-lasting impairments in learning and memory functions, EEG and biochemical alterations, impaired motivation and impaired ability to exhibit appropriate adaptive behavior." Studies of prolonged high-dosage cannabis use in humans have not identified gross indications of "brain damage" (Rubin and Comitas 1975; Comitas 1976), but more subtle alterations in brain function and performance have been detected (Biegon and Kerman 1995; Fletcher et al. 1996; Naus 1984; Page et al. 1988; Wert and Raulin 1986). Biomedical and clinical epidemiological researchers, consequently, have expressed concern that high-potency marijuana exposure may be particularly problematic during adolescence "when neuroendocrine, cognitive and affective functions and structures of the brain are in the process of integration. . . . [R]esearch needs to investigate the possibility that more severe consequences may occur in adolescents exposed to cannabinoids, than in those who commence cannabis use at a later age" (Solowij 1999, 213).

Finally, there is the drug-use pathway issue that has been central to the marijuana discourse for decades: namely is marijuana a gateway to "harder" drugs? As indicated, most of our informants reported that neither they nor their friends have plans to use "harder" drugs. They view bud as an endpoint in their drug-use careers. As we have noted, however, other evidence from our study of drug-use transitions suggests that ending drug use with bud may be a pattern for some but not for all youth. Rather, we believe that new marijuana and marijuana with additives may be, at least for some youth, transitional to more regular, "hard" drug use and may be strategically marketed by illicit drug distributors to young users specifically for this reason. These are issues we are continuing to explore in our ongoing research. In this instance, ethnography stands as a critical tool for monitoring the prescience of our informants' assertions as well as our own.

NOTES

1. Monitoring the Future is an annual epidemiological investigation of national trends in substance use among adolescents and young adults funded by the National Institute of Drug Abuse and conducted by the University of Michigan.
2. NIDA grant #DA 11421; Principal Investigator: Jean J. Schensul, Ph.D.; Co-Principal Investigators: Margaret Weeks, Ph.D., Merrill Singer, Ph.D.; Research team members include Raul Pino, M.D., Lorie Broomhall, Ph.D., Essie Hayes, Mark Convey, and Mariajose Romero of the Institute for Community Research and Cristina Huebner, B.A., Marvin Snow, B.A., and Scott Clair, Ph.D., of the Hispanic Health Council.
3. Youth often choose not to reveal their family names and are known on the street by street names. All of the names cited in the text are pseudonyms based on these street names.

REFERENCES

BAER, H., M. SINGER, and I. SUSSER (1997). Medical Anthropology and the World System: A Critical Perspective. Westport, CT: Bergin and Garvey.

BEARDSLEY, P. and T. KELLY (1999). Acute Effects of Cannabis on Human Behavior and Central Nervous System Functions. *In* The Health Effects of Cannabis. H. Kalant, W. Corrigall, W. Hall, and R. Smart, eds. Pp. 127–170. Toronto: The Addiction Research Foundation, Centre for Addiction and Mental Health.

BECKER, H. S. (1953). Becoming a Marijuana User. American Journal of Sociology 59:235–242.

BIEGON, A. and I. KERMAN (1995). Quantitative Autoradiography of Cannabinoid Receptors in the Human Brain Post-Mortem. *In* Sites of Drug Action in the Human Brain. A. Biegon and N.D. Volkow, eds. Pp. 65–74. Boca Raton, FL: CRC Press.

CAROVANO, K. (1991). More than Mothers and Whores: Redefining the AIDS Prevention Needs of Women. International Journal of Health Services 21:131–142.

COMITAS, L. (1976). Cannabis and Work in Jamaica: A Refutation of the Amotivational Syndrome. Annals of the New York Academy of Sciences 282:24–32.

Community Epidemiological Work Group (CEWG) (1997). Epidemiological Trends in Drug Abuse, vol. 1. Highlights and Executive Summary. Rockville, MD: National Institute on Drug Abuse. (1998). Epidemiological Trends in Drug Abuse, vol. 1. Highlights and Executive Summary. Pp. 57–58. Rockville, MD: National Institute on Drug Abuse.

CYPRESS Hill (1993). Hits from the Bong. *On* Black Sunday. Ruffhouse/Columbia.

DITTO, P. H. and J. B. JEMMOTT, III (1989). From Rarity to Evaluative Extremity: Effects of Prevalence Information on Evaluations of Positive and Negative Characteristics. Journal of Personality and Social Psychology 57:16–26.

Dream World (1999). Advertisement. High Times, January:62.

FALKOWSKI, C. L. (1998). Drug Abuse Trends in the Minneapolis/St. Paul Metropolitan Area. *In* Epidemiological Trends in Drug Abuse, vol. 2. Proceedings. Community Epidemiology Work Group. Pp. 133–146. Bethesda, MD: DHHS/PHS National Institute of Drug Abuse.

FARLEY, C. J. (1999). It's a Hip-Hop Nation. Time Magazine, February 8: 54–66.

FELDMAN, H. and M. ALDRICH (1990). The Role of Ethnography in Substance Abuse Research and Public Policy: Historical Precedent and Future Prospects. *In* The Collection and Interpretation of

Data from Hidden Populations. E. Lambert, ed. Pp. 12–30. NIDA Research Monograph #98. Rockville, MD: National Institute on Drug Abuse.

FESTINGER, L. (1957). A Theory of Cognitive Dissonance. Evanston, IL: Row, Peterson.

FIELDS, A. B. (1984). "Slinging Weed": the Social Organization of Street Corner Marijuana Sales. Urban Life 13(2–3):274–280. (1986). Weed Slingers: Young Black Marijuana Dealers. *In* Teen Drug Use. G. Beschner and A. A. Friedman, eds. Pp. 85–104. Lexington, MA: Lexington Books.

FLETCHER, J., J. B. PAGE, D. FRANCIS, K. COPELAND, M. NAUS, C. DAVIS, R. MORRIS, D. KRAUSKOPF, and P. SALZ (1996). Cognitive Correlates of Long-Term Cannabis Use in Costa Rican Men. Archives of General Psychiatry 53:1051–1057.

FRANK, B. and J. GALES (1997). Current Drug Trends in New York City. *In* Epidemiological Trends in Drug Abuse, vol. 2. Proceedings. Pp. 172–188. Rockville, MD: National Institute on Drug Abuse.

FULLILOVE, M., R. FULLILOVE, III, K. HAYNES, and S. GROSS (1990). Black Women and AIDS Prevention: A View towards Understanding the Gender Rules. Journal of Sex Research 27:47–64.

GANG STAR (1996). Take Two and Pass. *On* The Best of Gang Star. Gold Rush.

GOODE, E. (1984). Drugs in American Society. New York: Knopf.

GUPTA, G. and E. WEISS (1993). Women's Lives and Sex: Implications for AIDS Prevention. Culture, Medicine and Psychiatry 17:301–316.

HALL, J. N. and M. WHITMAN (1998). Drug Use in Miami-Dade Country, Florida. *In* Epidemiological Trends in Drug Abuse, vol. 2. Proceedings. Community Epidemiology Work Group. Pp. 114–132. Bethesda, MD: DHHS/PHS National Institute of Drug Abuse.

HOFFER, L. and B. MENDELSON (1998). Drug Use Trends in Denver and Colorado. *In* Epidemiological Trends in Drug Abuse, vol. 2. Proceedings. Community Epidemiology Work Group. Pp. 70–82. Bethesda, MD: DHHS/PHS National Institute of Drug Abuse.

JOHNSON, B. (1973). Marijuana Users and Drug Sub-Cultures. New York: Wiley.

KALANT, H., W. CORRIGALL, W. HALL, and R. SMART, eds. (1999). The Health Effects of Cannabis. Toronto: The Addiction Research Foundation, Centre for Addiction and Mental Health.

MALCOLM X. (1968). The Autobiography of Malcolm X. London; Penguin.

MARC EMERY Direct Seed Sales (1999). Marc Emery Direct Seed Sales Mail-Order Catalog. Cannabis Culture. January–February: 2–8.

MISSY "Misdemeanor" Elliot (1998). The Rain. *On* The Rain (Supa Dupa Fly). Elekt.

MUSTO, D. (1987). The American Disease: Origins of Narcotic Control. New York: Oxford University Press.

National Institute on Drug Abuse (NIDA) (1997). The Monitoring the Future Study: Trends in Prevalence of Use of Various Drugs for Eighth, Tenth, Twelfth Graders, College Students, and Young Adults, with Five Year Trends Noted. Rockville, MD: National Institute on Drug Abuse.

Naturally Pure Enterprises (1999). Advertisement. High Times, January: 69.

NAUS, G., ed. (1984). Marijuana in Science and Medicine. New York: Raven Books.

PAGE, J. B., J. FLETCHER, and W. TRUE (1985). Psychosociocultural Perspectives on Chronic Cannabis Use: The Costa Rican Follow-Up. Journai of Psychoactive Drugs 20:57–65.

PERKINS, W. E. (1996). Droppin' Science. Philadelphia: Temple University Press.

REDMAN (1996a). Smoke Buddah. *On* Muddy Waters. Def Jam. (1996b). Whateva Man. *On* Muddy Waters. Def Jam. (1999). Lyrics. Electronic document. Ishan's Rap/R&B Page. Ishan Issadeen, web-master.http://www.geocities.com/SouthBeach/Boardwalk/3028/lyrics.html.

RUBIN, V. and L. COMITAS (1975). Ganja in Jamaica: A Medical Anthropological Study of Chronic Marijuana Use. The Hague: Mouton.

SNYDER, M., E. D. TANKE, and E. BERSCHEID (1977). Social Perception and Interpersonal Behavior: On the Self-Fulfilling Nature of Social Stereotypes. Journal of Personal and Social Psychology 35:656–666.

SOBO, E. J. (1995). Choosing Unsafe Sex: AIDS-Risk and Denial among Disadvantaged Women. Philadelphia: University of Philadelphia Press.

SOLOWIJ, N. (1995). Cannabis and Cognitive Functioning. Cambridge: Cambridge University Press. (1999). Long-Term Effects of Cannabis on the Central Nervous System. *In* The Health Effects of Cannabis. H. Kalant, W. Corrigall, W. Hall, and R. Smart, eds. Pp. 195–265. Toronto: The Addiction Research Foundation, Centre for Addiction and Mental Health.

Spectrum Labs (1999). Advertisement. High Times, January:95.

STEPHENS, T., R. BRATHWAITE, and S. TAYLOR (1998). A Model for Using Hip-Hop Music for Small Group HIV-AIDS Prevention Counseling with African American Adolescents and Young Adults. Patient Education and Counseling 38:127–137.

Substance Abuse and Mental Health Services Administration (SAMHSA) (1998). National Household Survey on Drug Abuse, Main Findings. Rockville, MD: Department of Health and Human Services/Substance Abuse and Mental Health Services Administration.

SWAN, N. (1995). Marijuana, Other Drug Use Among Teens Continues to Rise. NIDA Notes 10(2):8–9.

University of Michigan National Information System (UMNIS) (1994). Trends in Prevalence of Various Drugs for 8th Graders, 10th Graders, and High School Seniors. Monitoring the Future Study Press Release. Rockville, MD: National Institute on Drug Abuse. (1996). Marijuana and Tobacco Use Still Rising among 8th and 10th Graders. Monitoring the Future Study press release. Rockville, MD: National Institute on Drug Abuse.

WALTON, R. (1938). Marijuana—America's New Drug Problem. Philadelphia: Lippincott.

WEEKS, M. R., M. SINGER, M. GRIER, and J. J. SCHENSUL (1996). Gender Relations, Sexuality and AIDS Risk among African American and Latina Women. *In* Gender and Health: An International Perspective. C. Sargent and C. Brettell, eds. Pp. 238–270. New York: Prentice Hall.

WERT, R. and M. RAULIN (1986). The Chronic Cerebral Effects of Cannabis Use: Psychological Findings and Conclusions. The International Journal of the Addictions 21:629–642.

ZAMBRANA, R., ed. (1982). Work, Family and Health: Latina Women in Transition. Monograph 7, Hispanic Research Center. New York: Fordham University.

ZINBERG, N. (1984). Drug Set and Setting. New Haven: Yale University Press.

ZUCKERMAN, M. (1987). Biological Connection between Sensation Seeking and Drug Abuse. *In* Brain Reward Systems and Abuse. J. Engel and L. Oreland, eds. Pp. 165–176. New York: Raven Press.

7

Urban Crop Circles

Urban Cannabis Growers in the North of England

Garfield R. Potter and Simeon L. Dann
University of Sheffield

> Homegrown cannabis found in Sheffield is so powerful it is virtually hallucinogenic. . . . Almost 80 per cent of cannabis consumed in Sheffield is grown locally in highly controlled conditions—making the drug 'rocket fuel' in the words of the city's most senior drug officer.
>
> *Sheffield Star, October 2001*

INTRODUCTION

Cannabis growing as a criminal enterprise, supplying drug markets with domestically produced rather than imported cannabis, is a relatively new feature of United Kingdom marijuana markets. In a period of six or seven years, locally grown marijuana has gone from being the preserve of a few cannabis connoisseurs to making up 80% of all marijuana smoked in South Yorkshire, England. Evidence suggests that in the United Kingdom "soapbar"[1] costs less than ever.[2] At the same time quality and availability of prime skunk[3] cannabis has increased in the South Yorkshire area, while the price has dropped significantly.[4] Advanced growing techniques have become widespread and the equipment has become cheaper.[5] This has led to a change in the dynamics of marijuana markets. An alternative localized supply chain rooted in homegrown[6] cannabis is challenging the

---

Garfield Potter and Simeon L. Dann. Prepared expressly for this edition.

traditional model of large-scale, import-led cannabis markets. This alternative supply chain seems to exist in two forms: "cooperative"-style marijuana production has radically different features from the common image of the import-led market. Often, the cooperative-style market is not as deeply involved in the "criminal underworld" as the importers market; it is less organized, is less hierarchical, and operates on a smaller scale. There is less overlap with harder drugs and other forms of organized crime. The ethos of the individuals involved is, for want of a better phrase, more left wing than that of the more traditional drug-dealing gangs and organized crime syndicates.

Corporate-style[7] marijuana production more closely resembles the stereotypical model of drug dealers with all the connotations of hierarchical "organized crime." Although the latter type of cannabis-growing organization may be responsible for a larger share of the market, cooperative growers are far from insignificant and appear to be growing in size and related market influence. More individuals appear to be involved in this model, although total cannabis production may be less than for corporate-style growers. This chapter serves as an introduction to the homegrown commercial cannabis market in the United Kingdom, describing the range of participants, exploring their relationships to each other, and drawing up a model of the domestically produced marijuana market. Using ethnographic research methods, we draw a working model of cannabis-growing networks by exploring the roles of individuals and groups within this network. We look at how the participants relate to one another to form a distinct but informal network for cannabis production and distribution consisting of individuals, partnerships, cooperatives, and more structured corporate growing operations. Each of these approaches to commercial cannabis growing will be examined in terms of the motives and methods of those involved and of relationships between individuals within the wider growing community.

THE STRUCTURE OF DRUG MARKETS
IN THE UNITED KINGDOM

Drug markets are often portrayed as being controlled by organized crime groups and drug cartels. The market is seen as a pyramidal structure following simple rules: Fewer individuals are involved in the top levels of the market dealing in large quantities of drugs and money distributed in wholesale. As one moves down through the layers of the distribution network, a greater number of drug dealers control a smaller quantity of drugs. Deals consist of smaller units of drugs selling for higher prices per unit weight. At the bottom end of the market, drug dealers sell retail quantities to consumers. The distribution network is seen as hierarchical—the higher up the pyramid, the more influence, power, and money involved.

Dorn et al. (1992) outline the most recent and broadest picture of UK drug dealing and its evolution over time. Looking at drug dealing across five decades, the authors suggest that in the 1950s and 1960s drug dealing followed a very different model to the one we see now. "'Dealing was different in those days: no violence, no rip-offs, people actually trusted each other. When you bought or sold, dealer and client invariably sat down and got stoned together—partly sampling the wares but partly social. Nowadays it all seems to be sell and run.' (Harry, the cannabis dealer)".[2] It is only as time goes on, perhaps as the quantity of illegal drugs consumed and, correspondingly, the value of the market have expanded, that the market has increasingly been dominated by organized criminals and drug-dealing syndicates. Substantially increased profits in the sector have been paralleled by dominance of those involved in large-scale drug distribution, often overlapping with other forms of organized crime and increasingly backed up with violence when competing for a share in the market.

Like Dorn et al. and many others, we believe that the popular image of drug dealing as a hierarchical, violent, organized "business" is misplaced, but that is not to say that it is wrong. Although it may be true that many areas of the drug trade are dominated by these stereotypical drug and/or crime barons, particularly at the production and/or importation end, we contend that there is an alternative, parallel distribution network. We explore this idea within the context of homegrown cannabis, where this pattern is most noticeable.

METHODOLOGY

This chapter reports on preliminary findings of an ongoing research project on cannabis growing in England. Employing ethnographic research methods, our aim is to portray a core section of our research subjects in the wider cannabis-growing network. Although it is too early to be able to generalize with any certainty, we believe that the patterns of relationships between those involved in domestic marijuana cultivation portrayed here are repeated elsewhere in the United Kingdom.

The research is largely qualitative—principally participant observation and semi-structured interviews. The sample was assembled through snowballing—key figures were identified through personal contacts, participation in the local underground music, clubbing, student and recreational drug-using scenes, as well as through conversation with suppliers of cannabis seeds and horticultural and hydroponics shops. As individuals got to know us and know more about our work, they began not only to open up more but also introduced us to their friends and other contacts. Initially, we just socialized with our subjects, getting to know them and their lifestyles. Over a number of years, friendships and trust developed and opportunities for participant observation increased. We got to examine grow rooms, participate in the mechanics of growing, harvesting, and distributing the crop, and witnessed the sometimes incredibly complex interactions between different players within the scene. A series of tape-recorded interviews began, although not all our contacts were willing to participate in this strand of the research, fearing possible legal repercussions or just wishing "to be safe." Further information was taken from local and national media, the Internet,[8] and local and national police statistics.

In this chapter, we have concentrated on the case studies of a selection of individual participants in a cannabis-growing network centered on South Yorkshire in northern England. We have chosen these particular examples because they reflect both a cross section of the individuals involved in cannabis growing and the roles they play, along with a working example of the nature and importance of relationships within the wider cannabis dealing and growing network. By talking about individual members and groups, we hope to show the range of people who currently grow cannabis in this area, and to provide insight on their reasons for growing. Case studies were constructed largely from field notes and were backed up with interview quotations when this data was available. Although we have deliberately chose many individuals from the same circle of cannabis growers to highlight the nature of relationships and individual roles, the patterns described here were repeated elsewhere.

CANNABIS CULTIVATORS IN THE UNITED KINGDOM

Cannabis Growing as a Criminal Enterprise

Cannabis is the most widely used illegal drug in Europe and the United States. Although much research has been directed at drug trafficking from smuggling down to street-level dealing, little research has been directed to those in *production* of cannabis, or indeed any other drug. Whereas most cannabis consumed in the Western world would traditionally be imported from Africa and Asia (for the European market) and South America and the Caribbean (for North American consumers), increasingly domestic production is occurring in these countries. Whereas research into cannabis production for the import market has been somewhat limited by problems associated with international research, (primarily problems of access to cannabis producers in what are largely Third-World countries), research into domestic cannabis growers has recently begun to take off, especially in the United States.

Ours is not the first attempt at a typology of commercial cannabis producers. Ralph Weisheit (1990, 1991) has done a large amount of research into domestic marijuana cultivation in Illinois. He identified three main types of cannabis grower based on their attitudes toward and reasons for growing: namely *Hustlers* (entrepreneurs attracted to cannabis growing not purely for the financial reward, although this is important, but also for the challenge of operating such an enterprise), *Pragmatists* (who turn to cannabis growing to meet financial needs rather than for greed), and *Communal Growers* (whose prime motivation lies in pride at being able to produce a good-quality product) (*ibid.*). Although there is some overlap between his categorization and ours, we have approached the question from a different angle, concentrating not just on motivation but also on relationships to other growers and to the wider cannabis market.

The Range of Cannabis Growers in the United Kingdom

There are many different types of cannabis growers in the United Kingdom. A wide variety of growing methods are employed; some grow cannabis outdoors with little or no human intervention beyond planting and harvesting, others grow indoors in flowerpots or greenhouses. An increasing number of cannabis growers are employing more advanced technology: hydroponics-growing setups, high-intensity lighting on timer switches, carbon filters (for removing the smell), and fans. While some cannabis growers are happy, even proud, to cultivate in a purely organic environment, others are equally happy to use chemical feeds, fertilizers, insecticides, and fungicides. Some grow many small plants while others grow fewer plants but to a larger size. Some growers grow from seed[9]; other growers take cuttings from existing plants or even breed their own varieties.

Although most growers grow purely for their own consumption, or that of their friends, others grow primarily or exclusively for profit—some of them on a very large scale. For those studying drug markets and drug distribution networks, these growers are critical. Increasingly well-organized individuals or groups of growers are producing enough cannabis to have a significant effect on the traditional import-led cannabis market in the United Kingdom. Here we have attempted a typology of those involved in cannabis production in the United Kingdom, looking at the differing approaches to commercial cannabis production and distribution.

Growing for Personal Use

The majority of cannabis growers grow for their own use rather than for financial gain. These growers are fairly common and are not a new phenomenon. What seems to be new is the increased use of technology by even the smallest scale cannabis growers. Although many people still employ the traditional methods of a patch of ground, a selection of seeds, and the natural growing cycle, more and more people are utilizing scientific advances in hydroponics and plant breeding. Our first two case studies show two distinct but effective approaches to growing cannabis for personal use.

> "Jill," now a middle-aged professional and keen amateur gardener, has been smoking cannabis since her university days. Her consumption dropped while she was bringing up her two children, but she now smokes one or two joints most evenings to unwind. She sees the criminal side of the general drug trade as an "ugly and predictable by-product of current drug laws." About seven to eight years ago, in an effort to minimize her contact with what she sees as the "seedier" side of the cannabis culture, she decided to utilize her gardening know-how and greenhouse to try to grow a handful of plants for her own use. Now, using nothing more than seeds from previous crops and simple horticultural knowledge she grows almost enough every year to meet her smoking requirements. When she has finished harvesting she dries the crop and stores it in the freezer until such time as it is required. While she still occasionally has need to visit dealers, these visits are kept to an absolute minimum. While she will occasionally give away a couple of buds[10] to friends, this is infrequent in order to preserve her stocks and money never changes hands.
>
> "Alan" is now in his early 20s. He has recently graduated from university and currently lives in a large shared house with a mixture of students and graduates. He has been smoking on and off for about 7 years, but with periods of abstinence that have lasted up to a year. Although he currently smokes a lot—his household of 9 goes through over an ounce of skunk a week—he would prefer to ingest his cannabis in food or drink form. Ideally he would like to "infuse [cannabis] in alcohol, and develop a method of ingestion that doesn't involve smoking" but never seems to have enough spare skunk to invest to this end. He recently started growing two plants in a cupboard using hydroponics, chemical fertilizers, a carbon filter and a six hundred watt grow lamp. He expects to harvest about six to eight ounces of top bud per crop and is keeping any leaves and 'shake'[11] to put in vodka. His plants started as cuttings, which, along with the growing equipment and lights, came from a friend, "Weedhopper" (subject of a separate case study, below). In exchange for this loan and horticultural expertise Weedhopper will receive half of the crop. Alan has no definite plans for his share of the crop; we asked him if he'd considered selling it:
>
> "I haven't decided yet! I mean, if it gets sold, then there still really won't be that much need for it to be sold outside of these walls. In which case probably what will happen is I'll give it away and accept gifts for the rest of the year. I certainly don't agree with the old axiom that you shouldn't give to receive. Glad to give to receive!"

Cannabis is an easy plant to grow. It grows in almost any climate with a minimum of intervention; however, a bit of extra care and attention can significantly improve the quality and quantity of a crop. Jill transferred techniques used for growing tomatoes and general gardening knowledge into a successful cannabis-growing venture, resulting in a product of better quality than that available from her local dealers. Alan used a modern hydroponics system along with sodium lights, timer switches, electric fans, and a carbon filter to much the same effect. The unifying feature of those that grow their own cannabis is that they smoke regularly and intend on smoking (or otherwise consuming) their crop or share it with friends rather than selling it. Despite the differing approaches seen here, both Jill and Alan share common motives and ideologies. The developments in hydroponics technology have led to the situation that while a grower like Jill needs a quiet, secluded greenhouse to grow her cannabis, Alan can produce as much, if not more, cannabis of a better quality than Jill in the privacy of his own bedroom wardrobe.

The vast majority of cannabis growers are growing for their own consumption or for the use of their cannabis-smoking friends. They come from a wide variety of backgrounds—we have seen the professional middle-age woman and the unemployed recent graduate. Our research included many other examples from across the socioeconomic spectrum. These growers do not even consider any potential profits from their crops—whatever they grow saves them from having to buy as much (or any) cannabis from other sources. There are financial benefits whereby home-grown cannabis means less has to be bought with cash—the motivation of "thrift" identified by Warner (1986, 2000). Beyond this limited financial incentive, motivation to grow is often rooted in pride, practicality, and/or personal ethics. Growers are proud to be able to produce their own smoke, as noted by Warner (*ibid.*) and as particularly relevant to Weisheit's "Communal growers" (Weisheit 1991). Practical considerations include the desire for a regular, reliable, and good-quality supply of cannabis. From an ethical viewpoint, a desire to avoid the black market (for reasons of quality and purity of supplies, or as a stand against organized crime, criminal profit, or harder-drug connections associated with dealers) was frequently cited by our respondents.

Other Not-for-Profit Growers

Not all personal-use growers operate individually. We have seen how Alan had a working relationship with "Weedhopper," who is actually in it for some financial reward and is the subject of a separate case study that follows. Other not-for-profit growers pool knowledge and resources: Individuals grow their own cannabis, but may help each other out and may stagger their growing cycles and share their harvests so that individuals have a constant supply of fresh skunk without having to buy any.

There is another group of cannabis growers who operate on a not-for-profit basis. In the United Kingdom many individual or groups of cannabis growers exist who supply medicinal users with cheap or free cannabis for self-medication. Interesting as these growers are, they are not discussed in this chapter as they fall outside our current subject group, and are probably worthy of an entire chapter of their own. All we need to consider here is that again a wide range of methods are employed, often using high-tech growing setups, and again a wide range of people are often involved including (perhaps unsurprisingly considering the context) many doctors. Further information on medical growing cooperatives is easily obtainable from the Internet.[12]

Commercial Cannabis Growers

Of the urban commercial cannabis growers that are the subject of our study,[13] distinctions can be made in relation to the organization of growing operations and the motivation behind growing. Although financial gain is, by definition, a key motivating factor, it is not the only one. Considering the risks and effort involved in cannabis production, there are easier ways of making more money in both the licit and illicit economies. In particular, smaller-scale growers do not see huge financial rewards and, therefore, tend to be motivated by other goals and ideologies as much as, if not more than, money. Initially, we split our typology by the size and structure of the growing operation(s) as this also reflects the motivation and ideology of those involved as well as the approach to growth and distribution of cannabis.

Small-Scale for-Financial-Profit

The amount of cannabis produced by one plant varies considerably with plant variety and growing conditions, and is a reflection on the abilities of the individual grower. The highest yield from one observed plant was 14 ounces, but this was well above average. Growers generally obtained between 3 and 8 ounces of dried cannabis per plant with the more experienced growers getting better results. For the purposes of calculations, . . . we allowed 5 ounces of cannabis per plant—an estimate that seems to be backed up by our observations. With this in mind, we can begin to understand the potential income available to cannabis growers.

A standard bedroom wardrobe can easily accommodate two or three skunk plants under a single growing light. With the average grow cycle among our group lasting from 10–14 weeks, one 2-plant wardrobe could easily produce 10 ounces of skunk every three months. In the local market, this would currently fetch between £100 and £135 per ounce,[14] or up to £1350 per grow, £5400 over a year. Given this minimal effort and risk (see notes on the "10-plant rule" later in this chapter), the temptation to supplement a student loan or low income is clearly visible. Because local dealers tell us of clients who smoke an ounce a week or more, profits are not necessarily as high as first appears for cannabis growers, but even if a grower smokes more than he grows, a cash lump sum can always be useful.

> "G," currently a postgraduate student, was paying his own way through a master's degree. Despite a reasonably termed bank loan, part-time work, and occasional forays into drug dealing, he found the economical pressures too great and fell behind on his rent. After some encouragement from a friend ("Weedhopper"), he set up a hydroponics grow-room of two plants. Weedhopper, who arranged in return to take 60% of the sales profit, provided cuttings, equipment and expertise. Six and a half ounces of top bud were eventually sold to a local dealer; "G" paid his rent arrears and was left with enough skunk to see him through many weeks of smoking. Although the operation was profitable, having cleared his pressing debts he did not feel the need to grow again 'unless it's legalized, of course!'

G and his girlfriend smoked about an eighth of an ounce of cannabis a week at this time. Over a year, this would have equaled $8\frac{1}{2}$ ounces, which is far more than his share of the total crop produced. Therefore, it cannot really be said that he grew his plants to make a profit. In his own words: "I needed cash quick. I paid off my debts, had free weed for a month. Then I went back to buying from my regular dealer." The financial motivation here was perhaps not so much greed as a combination of need and convenience, and the income was hardly a profit when offset by cannabis spending over the rest of the year.

> "JJ" was a university undergraduate. Having been a heavy cannabis smoker since his early school days he went on to deal cannabis and other drugs throughout his university career. After becoming heavily in debt, he began to investigate other avenues for making cash. A brief

and expensive foray into cocaine dealing merely landed him in more debt, so when he was offered a job as a caretaker for a crop of skunk—to be grown in his cellar—he jumped at the chance. All he had to do was the basic day-to-day management of the crop while his employer, a man referred to as "mysterious Bob," visited the house every few days, checked the crop, and issued instructions for the next few days' care. Unfortunately, he was involved in a drug bust at a fellow dealer's house which led to the police searching his house and finding ten plants. He eventually got arrested and was sent to prison for three months. He told us: "The thing is I had to own up to the weed because it was 'mysterious Bob' who was actually doing the funding and growing of it and everything. I actually did nothing for it, but I got like 60% of the crop for taking the risk."

Although JJ and G were using very similar growing methods and both sought financial reward for their efforts, there were clear differences in their approaches. JJ was heavily involved in the local drug-dealing scene and was introduced to growing through his drug-dealing associates. "Mysterious Bob" was very much JJ's "boss" in that he had the ultimate say over every aspect of the growing operation. The relationship between G and Weedhopper was one primarily based in friendship. G had ultimate control over every stage of the growth and harvest, although he respected Weedhopper's expertise. This is a very important distinction in the way that commercial cannabis cultivation is structured in relation to the wider cannabis (and other drugs) market, and a point we shall return to later.

"Bob," now 25, is currently unemployed. He graduated from university about three years ago and managed to get a well-paying job but had to leave due to mental health problems. When he first stopped working he was keen not to claim benefits and looked around for an alternative means of supporting himself. After many conversations with Weedhopper, he decided to start growing to provide for himself without the need to claim benefits. He grows nine plants at any one time (plus a mother plant for cloning from), but these are divided equally in three stages of growth so that he harvests three plants every month. He usually harvests around eight ounces a month of prime top bud. He sells most of this for 120 pounds per ounce, thus enabling him to pay rent, buy food, socialize, and repay the substantial debts that he accrued at university.[15]

Whereas both JJ and G saw cannabis growing as a one time only or occasional way to make some quick cash, Bob needed something to give him a more regular income. A larger-scale grow room, while still fitting comfortably into his one-bedroom flat and divided to accommodate three staggered growing stages, gave Bob a regular income and a way to survive without relying on jobs or benefits. He was his own boss, growing as much cannabis as he needed to meet his monthly expenditures. He could have easily doubled or tripled his income with little extra effort, but chose not to because of a combination of a lack of greed and a fear of unnecessary risk. His system was a little more complicated than ones we have discussed so far, necessitating more time and effort from him. As such, his growing was something of a job—it needed regular hours with carefully planned holidays. The rewards included an earned reputation for growing some of the best skunk around[16] and the ability to live a relatively hassle-free life away from "the real world."

"This whole thing's kinda like a transitional period. Having been a student and not used to working in the real world, I can't go straight into an environment like that, I mean from one extreme to the other. I've done it before and had a really bad time and thought f__k that s__t, I'm not doing that." (Bob)

Motivation in this case is financial, but is a practical consideration rather than greed or desire, which is somewhat reminiscent of Weisheit's pragmatists. Bob had tried "real work"—he had been a well-paid software engineer—but found that the rigid hours and social contact did not go well with his mental health condition.

A small-scale growing setup can easily provide individuals with a reasonable standard of living without working, or allow the low-income individuals to live above their usual means. With six plants growing at a time, Bob was earning around £800–£1000 a month (tax free). As we have said, he could have grown far more and expanded his profits considerably, but he chose not to; he was growing so that he could lead a quiet life. Although it was still a job of sorts to him, the actual amount of time and effort needed to support his lifestyle was minimal and he could avoid the stress he associated with formal employment. Others, however, are not so laid back in their approach to life and treat growing cannabis as a serious business.

Large-Scale for-Profit

Many of those we talked to during our research referred to a "10-plant rule".[17] The common belief among growers and others in legal service is that although judges and magistrates consider many things before delivering their verdict (and/or deciding on sentence), one key factor is involved: the number of plants of being grown. The consensus of those we spoke to[18] was that below ten plants would probably result in the avoidance of a custodial sentence, possibly landing the miscreant with only a police caution. In reality, work by the Independent Drug Monitoring Unit (IDMU) (taken from the Web site on March 20, 2001) says that "growing more than 2–3 plants can result in an 'intent' charge, if not conviction." The most important aspect is not so much quantity grown as evidence showing intent to supply,[19] but it is the grower's perception of the existence of this 10-plant rule that is important rather than the reality of the situation. Of course, a larger number of plants is harder to explain away as being for personal use only. As such, growing larger quantities of cannabis is more than just scaling up the operation—other factors, namely risk, need to be taken into consideration. As the risks increase, the money becomes more important, and the ideological motivations of the self-sufficient grower or medicinal supplier are drowned out in the larger scale-growing operations.

> "Iain" used to grow his own plants for his own consumption and that of his friends. A "greenfingered hippie," he was very good at producing top quality skunk on a regular basis. Being justly proud of his produce he was generous with giving out samples and this eventually "got [him] noticed." Some of the more serious players in the local drug scene approached him with an offer he couldn't refuse. They were to provide equipment, finances, houses, and security and he was to provide his knowledge. He was to receive a percentage of the skunk produced as a wage.[20] The operation grew from 3 or 4 houses scattered around the city to 8 and then 11. Getting more skunk than he could possibly smoke himself, Iain found he could make himself a handsome profit as a dealer, but after a while decided he wanted to get out. On trying to end the relationship, which he perceived to be getting "far too dodgy," he found himself facing death threats if he didn't carry on. Faced with an ultimatum like that, he moved to a different city.

Cannabis growing can produce vast profits if conducted on a large enough scale. Eleven houses with three or four growing rooms in each house, with an average of twelve plants per room, can each be cropped every three months. At 5 ounces a plant, that amounts to over

7920 ounces (220 kilograms) of cannabis grown every year, selling wholesale at £3500 per kilo (local prices). This amounts to over £750,000 each year, minus overheads.[21] However, as the scale of growing increases, so do the efforts, overheads, and risks involved. Not only must an entrepreneur monitor many more plants spread over a larger area—possibly with the help of employed growers such as Iain—he must manage larger systems, rent larger premises, sell a larger crop, and sometimes employ a workforce. In terms of risk, the entrepreneur faces not only a higher risk of being caught (more employees, more and bigger growing premises, more drug arrests involving their produce) and greater sentences, but also a higher risk of being ripped off by others in the criminal underworld. As Iain's case shows, cannabis production on this scale can incorporate some of the more unpleasant elements of organized crime in the drug world.

> "Charlie" is a young professional. He worked for a major company and therefore earned a good salary. He supplemented this income by supplying cannabis in wholesale to dealers. He used this money to pay not only for mundane things like the mortgage on his house but also for a flamboyant lifestyle, which included expenses such as his sports car. He very rarely smokes marijuana. A few years ago he had the idea of growing his own skunk in order to make more profit. He was unwilling to use his own house for this because of the risks involved, so he experimented with the system of growing in other peoples houses and employing them to look after the crop, either for a wage or for a cut of the final crop. This proved unsatisfactory; the first few grows were so problematic that the final crops were substandard if they grew to harvest at all. In one case a whole crop was almost ruined when the janitor got into the habit of checking on the plants during their "dark" periods. In order to circumnavigate the problems he'd been having Charlie decided to rent houses under false names and then use them for the sole purpose of growing a crop. By using this arrangement, he successfully separated cannabis growing from the more conformist aspects of his life, and only those he chose to tell knew anything about his decision to grow on a large scale. He only had to visit the grow house every few days, so contact with the crop was kept to a minimum and thus the perceived risks of such a large grow were minimized. The operation was a success and repeated several times, though the quality of the cannabis was not as good as others available in the area. Charlie has ideas for an even larger enterprise that he plans to grow "somewhere out in the country, in a farm or something."

Here we can see a fine example of what some have called "the opportunistic irregular."[22] Charlie had no real belief in the sanctity of marijuana, unlike many of our other respondents—indeed he does not really smoke marijuana at all. Rather, he had seen an opportunity to make money and had taken it, and when he had seen an opportunity to cut down on his expenditure and make more money, he had grasped the chance. Even when he was overseeing a large growing operation, he would be selling more cannabis than he produced, but spending considerably less on his wholesale purchases.

The small-scale growers we talked to were not greedy. They saw growing as a way to make money for necessary expenses—urgent debts or a comfortable but minimal lifestyle. Iain's employers and Charlie, on the other hand, are examples of those who see the fuller potential of cannabis cultivation in funding an active social life and expensive tastes. Problems of increased risk and effort were weighed against increased profits and these entrepreneurs operated to the level they were happy with. Charlie compromised by growing less than he would have liked to maintain a low profile. Iain's boss opted for greater profits, but employed strong-arm tactics to further protect himself. In both situations, there is no doubt that profit is a primary motive, but other factors come into play. Charlie in particular could be seen to be an entrepreneur with parallels to Weisheit's (1990, 1991) hustlers. Money was important, but equally the challenge of operating and maintaining an illegal industry seemed to be a key motivating factor. Successfully running a business and avoiding the law seemed to give him as much satisfaction as actually making profits. Charlie was a well-paid middle-class professional with intelligence and business sense who could have made a fortune in legitimate enterprises if he so wished, whereas Iain spoke of employers involved in many illegitimate enterprises who came from less advantaged backgrounds. They operated more along the traditional lines of organized criminal gangs—again, we see how people from a wide variety of backgrounds can be involved in cannabis growing, even on the larger scale. In cannabis-growing operations of this scale, the financial motivation becomes more important while the ideological and "ethical" motivations become less relevant.

Cooperatives

An alternative method of avoiding the restrictions of the 10-plant rule was evident among many—perhaps the majority—of our study group.

"Jason" started smoking cannabis at school. While studying at the university, he realized that many of his circle of friends grew or dealt, and with their help started growing cannabis.

Interviewer:	And why did you decide to start growing?
Jason:	'Cause I was sick of having to go find for and score decent stuff, and plus for it was a way of making a bit of cash' cause I was skint.
I:	And how did you get started? There's quite a lot of expertise involved in setting up these systems.
J:	Aye! Through friends. Friends that were in the trade.
I:	They just provided you with information? Or equipment?
J:	Both.

Jason described a circle of friends who were all heavy smokers, all "cannabis connoisseurs." Many of them began growing their own cannabis through a combination of the desire for a reliable source, quality of skunk, and potential financial gain. A few of the members of this growing circle had horticultural backgrounds and were studying related subjects at university. In Jason's own words:

"It's more like a group of growers. They all help each other snip and like whoever's just cropped all the others will help shift it, and it all goes for the same price. I mean if I give it to someone and they want to sell it for a bit more than fair enough. Commercially it all goes for the same."

Individual members of the group all had equal status—each grew their own plants in their own house and could ultimately decide what they wanted to do with their crop. However, they operated on a cooperative basis for mutual benefit. They staggered harvesting to ensure a constant supply of quality cannabis and sold surplus supplies through a single "designated dealer," splitting profits equally among themselves. Although the group was strictly egalitarian in principle, in reality two of the members had considerably more influence. Both Weedhopper and "Jonah" (see below) had considerable cannabis-growing experience. Both were studying degree subjects related to plant sciences. Although operating as a separate entity to the group, their dealer, "M," was an important individual to them. The roles of these key individuals are discussed in the following text.

During a period of two to three years, this group thrived, providing a constant supply of top-quality skunkweed to a market hungry for this commodity. Although there were sometimes as many as twenty people (or more) in the cooperative, individual members dipped in and out depending on other pressures such as work, finances, or general laziness. Most growers in this cooperative chose to keep below ten plants; however, some grew more, especially if cash was tight. Unlike Iain's story, no threats or other intimidation was used to keep members in check, and members saw themselves as equal partners rather than employed growers. They had an understanding that if any individual was busted or suffered crop failure, the other members would help cushion the loss from their own crops. Within this circle, all members saw equal shares of profits (in proportion to their crop size), benefits, risk, and chores, such as harvesting and packaging. Although successful, this group, which we feel typifies our concept of a "growing cooperative," dissolved when the majority of the founding members finished their university careers and eventually moved away.

Although equal within the previous group, certain members, along with their dealing contact, all had other involvement in the wider cannabis-growing scene.

"Jonah," "M" and "Weedhopper" met about 5 years ago through their mutual interest in cannabis and overlapping social lives. We have looked at their roles within the cooperative we described previously, but all three had a wider involvement in the local cannabis market. Jonah and M had plenty of experience in growing their own cannabis although neither of them grew in their own houses at the time of this research. Weedhopper grew intermittently, although he gave up briefly when working for one of the largest wholesale growing-light specialists in the country (he didn't want to compromise his job or his own involvement in cannabis growing). All three often socialize together as well as being involved with numerous small- and large-scale cannabis growers across the region. The three of them were founding members of the cooperative described previously—M didn't grow within this cooperative but he sold the cannabis for everyone. Despite their friendship, Jonah and M operate independently, sometimes cooperating with each other, sometimes competing with each other. Both have a history of dealing cannabis and other substances going back years before they met each other. Weedhopper is younger and relatively less experienced. He also prefers not to deal, hating the "donkey work" and the high risk/low profit ratio. He is vocal in his condemnation of the current laws and cannabis society, often getting evangelical on the subject. In the utopia of Weedhopper, as many people as possible would grow a few plants, thus getting rid of "Babylon" and the financial and criminogenic realities of dealing. (Weedhopper, for example, hates the idea of friends making money off friends while recognizing the practical need for an income.)

Key Individuals and Wider Networks

Within the cooperative we have outlined Jonah, M, and Weedhopper were cornerstones of many separate growing projects. The three of them had a lot of cannabis-growing experience and some related scientific and technical knowledge. In addition to this role, both Jonah and M, but especially Jonah, supplied other cooperative members with growing equipment. Jonah explained to us how, when he was introducing new people to cannabis growing, he would lend them his equipment and expertise in exchange for half of the crop. If they wished to grow again, he would usually offer to sell them the equipment, with the growers not having to pay until after the harvest of their second crop. Having taught them the basics, Jonah was happy for these new growers to set up independently of him, and would continue to offer advice and growing tips if asked. Jonah was also a supplier of cuttings of a top-grade, high-yield skunk to people he was helping to set up and anyone else who wanted one (sometimes for free, but sometimes at £10 per cutting).

At one point in our research he boasted, "Everyone's growing what I'm growing!" Although this of course was not strictly true, it was evident that many growers we observed were growing the strain of cannabis he had bred himself and supplied to others. That strain had something of a revered status among the local smoking cognoscenti; during our research, another grower smoked a few buds and was so won over he asked for some cuttings immediately. Others in our study, notably "Hoover" (a local dealer), observed that many customers would time their visits so that they could obtain this skunk in preference to the strain he obtained from other sources. Jonah and M were operating in the wider cannabis-growing and dealing network in much the same way they operated in the cooperative we have described. Jonah would set up people with grow rooms and M would usually operate as Jonah's dealer, distributing his share (or the entirety) of the harvests. Although much of Jonah's cannabis would pass through M's hands, it was not an exclusive arrangement. Jonah would sometimes sell through other people, cutting M out of the chain, and M would often deal cannabis that had had nothing to do with Jonah. Between the two of them, they seemed responsible for a large percentage of the skunk available through local dealers and were personally connected to the growth and distribution of hundreds of kilograms of top-quality skunk in the period during which we studied them. Neither, however, made a fortune out of dealing; both also relied on legitimate work as a source of income.

> Weedhopper has been inspired both by Jonah's methods and his experience as a member of the cooperative and has taken it upon himself to set up other people with grow rooms. A pleasant, intelligent, sociable character he is well known to many, both in and out of the cannabis community, and in the course of the numerous friendships he strikes up the fact he knows a great deal about growing cannabis usually crops up at some point. Like Jonah he usually takes 50% of the first crop in return for equipment and tuition/advice, and will sell people equipment should they need it. Through his many contacts in the cannabis-growing community—as well as his friends from the cooperative and because he used to work for a hydroponics and lighting equipment shop where many of the staff and customers had experience in growing cannabis—he could readily get hold of cheap equipment. Weedhopper had been involved in the setting up of upwards of twenty new grow rooms at the time of the research and as such had helped introduce a large quantity of marijuana—and marijuana growers—to the local market. However he never seemed to make much money or be that bothered about making money; his interests in seeing people grow cannabis stemmed more from a sense of apostolic duty than commercial rewards. He believed in promoting good quality cannabis and cutting out the "gangster element" from the equation, and he had a general interest in ecology.

These key individuals have important roles to play in shaping the wider cannabis market. With knowledge and experience, one individual can be instrumental in setting up many growing operations. With a liberal attitude toward other growers, those they introduce to cannabis growing will often set up their own grow rooms—on a more independent footing— at a later date. Thus, cannabis growing spreads through a population.

Key individuals link many separate cannabis-growing operations—in our example, Weedhopper was heavily involved in the cooperative and was also instrumental in setting up many partnerships and assisting many small-scale independent growers (such as G, Alan, and Bob). He also worked for a lighting specialist and socialized with many other growers in local pubs and nightclubs. Through individuals such as he, different sections of the wider cannabis-growing/dealing network become more tightly linked. Information—on growing techniques, police activity, market prices and the like—becomes disseminated through the entire group.

To summarize, we have seen different units operating within a wider cannabis-growing network. The unit of commercial cannabis growing is the growing operation or grow room. Individuals may have small grow rooms of their own or they may be involved in a larger growing operation. Groups of individuals come together to form partnerships, or cooperatives, where more than one person shares the work in one or more grow rooms. Some individuals may work on a larger scale in which all the grow rooms in an operation are theirs, but they need the help of others to run the operation. Key individuals are involved in many grow operations—they may be active members of a particular cooperative while also setting up other partnerships or starting off other individuals who are separate from this main cooperative.

These individuals, and the nongrowing dealers to whom they sell, often overlap with the corporate grow and import led markets—in our example, Jonah and M were both involved in smuggling cannabis themselves, and many other growers would often be involved in dealing imported cannabis as well. Further overlap between the corporate and cooperative growers occurs through social events and mutual friends and acquaintances. Although the organized criminals in charge of corporate growing operations may have little to do with their cooperative-style counterparts, those who are actually overseeing the day-to-day cannabis growing often have similar ideologies and use the same supply shops. Many "employed growers" from the corporate model move into cooperative growing and the reverse can also be true.

Individual growing operations are often interlinked through key individuals and other areas of overlap so that the wider cannabis growing scene, and the even wider cannabis dealing scene, can actually be seen as a large interlinked network or web. All of the growers/dealers involved are always in it for some form of gain. However, there is a difference between the cooperatively structured operations (less concerned for profit, noticeably influenced by "ethical" considerations) and the hierarchically structured corporate-style growing business (concerned almost exclusively with profit and power).

Motivation to Grow Cannabis

There are three categories of motives that seem to influence cannabis growers: financial, practical, and ideological/ethical. Financial motives range from "thrift" (Warner 1986, 2000) (having to spend less or no money on buying cannabis) through to "greed" (a desire for money for personal pleasure). In between these extremes, we have those with more practical or specific financial aims such as clearing debts, supplementing a limited income, or providing an alternative to legitimate employment. Within the category of greed we also have a range, from acquiring specific but limited luxuries, to wishing for a lifestyle beyond the individual's legitimate means up to wanting as much money as possible.

Practical motivation covers the desire to ensure a regular supply or certain standard of quality of cannabis for personal use (although excesses will often be sellable). Ideological and/or ethical motivation includes the following: the individual's desire to distance him- or herself (and others) from the established drug market [avoiding the related adulteration of drugs, connection to (and pushing of) other, harder drugs, and connections to violence and other, often "organized," crime]; pride in producing one's own (often of superior quality) cannabis; promotion of legalization of marijuana; and supplying to medical users. Cannabis growing may occur as a result of any of these motives, or as a combination of them. It is the difference in the relative importance of different motives that seems to interplay with the different approaches to cannabis growing that we have seen. A general rule is that as the size of the growing operation increases, financial incentives become more relevant. However, the relationship is not that straightforward and nonfinancial motivations can play an important part in even the largest cannabis-growing enterprises.

Urban Commercial Cannabis Cultivators: Networks, Relationships, and Motivations

It becomes important at this point to define exactly what we mean by a cannabis grower. Clearly, anybody who has knowledge of cannabis plants on their property is a cannabis grower. Equally, those who do not grow cannabis on their own premises, but are actively involved in assisting[23] someone else in growing cannabis are, cannabis growers. For our purposes, anyone with an active interest—that is, some personal gain or return (be it in cannabis, money, or otherwise)—is a grower even if they do not have an active involvement in the actual growing operation. Looking at our group of subjects, it becomes clear that different growers operate along different lines. The most telling differences lie in the motivation behind growing and the relationships between different members of the wider network. Differences in these attitudes are largely reflected in differences in the size of the growing operations.

At one end of the growing spectrum we have *not-for-profit growers*—those growing for themselves and their friends' personal consumption, or those growing to supply medical users. Although methods of growing can range from minimal to advanced technology, motivation to grow is rooted in reasons other than financial gain. Financial advantage may provide an element of motivation in that growing one's own cannabis is much cheaper than buying it, but generally these growers smoke more than they produce themselves. More important reasons for growing one's own cannabis range from the purely altruistic (such as supplying medicinal users), to the pride and satisfaction of producing one's own cannabis or supplying friends with a high-quality smoke, to a more practical motivation such as maintaining a readily available supply and reducing contact with established dealers, harder drugs, and other crime. These individuals do not really act as dealers and there is no need to try to fit them into a wider typology of drug traffickers.

Beyond this, we have growers who make money by selling their product. An obvious distinction within this group is the amount an individual grows, although this is not straightforward because individuals may be involved in many different relationships over many different growing projects in varying stages at any one time. What is more telling is the individual attitude toward growing for profit and the nature of growers' relationships with others in the growing community. Within the *for-profit growers* category we have *independents,* who operate largely independent of other growers. They may receive help or advice from friends with growing experience, but this is nothing more than friendly advice—there is not necessarily any reciprocal assistance and there is no financial[24] transaction. Although there is no real reason for a ceiling on the size of an individual grower's operation, all the ones we have encountered usually keep to 10 or less plants. Bigger grow rooms are perceived to involve more risk (both in the chances of getting caught and the potential sentence if caught) and more work: When cannabis growing operated on a larger scale, it ceased to be an independent enterprise.

Independents do not make much money: a 10-plant system harvesting every 3 months would be worth between £16,000 and £24,000 per year. Although this may be on a par with a graduate salary, constrictions of space or fear of the increased risks of more plants means most independent growers produce much less than this. They tend to use the extra money to supplement low- or medium-paid jobs, often providing extra for having a good time or acquiring a few luxuries, or for paying off debts. Some independents do use their illicit income as an alternative to work, even if they could earn more money in formal employment. Independent growers are cannabis smokers who use some of their own crop and take pride in growing well (or, for the less experienced growers, in being able to grow at all). Although financial incentives may be a primary reason for growing, they are not the exclusive reason and independents can in no way be considered greedy. This quote from Bob highlights a more pragmatic incentive.

> "Well, I was basically not happy in the job I was in[25] and in that situation its difficult to step back and look at yourself and think well I'm in a situation I really shouldn't be in. Your head's full of stress, especially if you do have stress problems and a family history of stress problems so I just thought 'f__k it', get away. So I looked for alternative sources of income. The only one being profitable enough to sustain graduate and student loan repayments and everything that has to go out i.e. £800 a month is Skunk. I mean I could do other stuff like getting to dealing all sorts of pills and speed for example but I mean, especially after what happened to [an ecstasy-dealer friend] going down and that I don't want to even go there whereas this, I might get off with a caution."

In reference to Weisheit's categories of marijuana growers, independents can be seen to be closest to pragmatists. Cannabis growing is a way to make some extra money to cover debts, to avoid unwanted employment, or to provide some luxuries that would otherwise be beyond the grower's means.

Cooperative growers are best described as groups of friends. Like-minded small-scale cannabis growers may join together to maximize their growing efficiency and conduct what is essentially both a business and a hobby in a more sociable environment. By pooling knowledge and resources (such as growing equipment, different strains of cannabis), coordinating their growing cycles (ensuring a regular supply of good-quality cannabis), offering mutual practical assistance (grow room maintenance, harvesting), and providing each other with support and backup (covering the losses from a failed crop, taking care of a grow room when its owner is away), cooperative members can maximize their impact on the local cannabis market.

By agreeing on prices and distributing income on an egalitarian model, the individual members guarantee a regular income protected from uncertainties such as crop failure or police action. Profits are on a par with independent growers, but effort and risk are reduced and quality can benefit from the width of the cooperative members' experience. At the smallest level, cooperatives can consist of only two individuals, and it is not necessary for both of them to be actively growing. Relationships in which one person provides equipment and expertise whereas the other provides space and day-to-day maintenance and retains ultimate control of the crop with an agreed split on either the crop or the sale profit operate on the same principles that define our cooperatives.

Cooperative growers closely resemble Weisheit's communal growers—a degree of "love of cannabis" and a certain amount of pride in growing it are as important as financial motives. Individuals within the community share information, advice, and equipment while maintaining friendly competition and relations. Some individuals are also pragmatists in the same way that independent growers are, but find being in a cooperative enhances their growing ability. Cooperatives work on an egalitarian or nonhierarchical basis: no one is in charge of anyone else and each grower has ultimate control over his crop. This distinguishes them from *corporate growers,* who seek to maximize profits primarily by increasing their output.

Corporate growers have many active grow rooms at any one time in a variety of different properties. Sometimes a property is bought or rented exclusively for growing; at other times space in other people's houses will be utilized. In either scenario, the corporate grower or growers pay *employed growers,* either in money or in cannabis, to do the day-to-day management of the crop. The corporate grower or a representative checks the crop every few days, issuing instructions concerning growing procedure or security issues. Corporate growers often have a wider involvement in dealing in cannabis and/or other drugs and may also enjoy a well-paid job; they are motivated by the large financial rewards.

Corporate growers are hustlers in Weisheit's typology. They show an entrepreneurial approach to the whole business—their primary concern is to make money, but there is also a certain attraction in operating a successful illicit enterprise. Whereas all other categories of cannabis grower have some passion for cannabis as a drug and/or as a plant, corporate growers do not necessarily share this interest—some of them never smoke it.

Employed growers tend to have a degree of involvement in the wider cannabis scene: they will often be growers themselves whose experience and ability has been recognized or they will have been dealers at some point, thus showing their willingness to operate within the illegal cannabis economy. In either case, they have more than a passing familiarity with cannabis and have a history of breaking the law over cannabis- or drug-related issues. For any employed grower, the primary incentive is money.

Key people link individual cooperatives and corporations, and even link independent and not-for-profit growers into the wider homegrown cannabis network. Such individuals may be involved in a wide range of separate growing projects acting independently, in numerous partnerships, in cooperatives, and even in corporate growing operations. They tend to have extensive knowledge and experience in cannabis growing, and have access to plenty of growing equipment for their use or for that of others. These key individuals share the best elements of both the entrepreneur and the communal grower—they see the opportunity to make some money out of a hobby and they have a passion for cannabis as a drug, as a plant, and as a *cause celebre.*

Taking the integrated growing operation—the total output of growers in a definable unit—as a base rather than an individual, we have a model based on relationships between individuals associated with growing. Independent growers operate independently in a commercial sense but exist in the wider network with support from other growing friends or associates, or those with a legitimate role in the wider network. Individual growers may exist in a *cooperative* or may be part of a *corporation* (as employers or employees). Independents, cooperative members, and corporation members are all linked into the wider *network* through relationships with other network members. Many members of different cooperatives or corporations will know each other socially and certain *key individuals* will participate in or be known to many groups of growers. A further linking role in the wider network is provided by those with a "legitimate" role in cannabis growing such as management and workers at shops that supply growing equipment or hemp seeds. Note that many of those we spoke to who were in such jobs had at least some experience in growing cannabis.

Unsurprisingly, when we look at the market as a whole, we find it resembles not so much a pyramid as a web. There are many corporate growing setups, many more cooperatives, and many independent growers. Many of the individuals involved in these setups have contacts elsewhere in the wider cannabis-dealing community. There are also substantial overlaps with the import-led cannabis market—many dealers are supplied from both local and overseas sources, many growers are involved in smuggling, lots of participants in the network have overlapping social lives and frequent the same pubs, clubs, and social events. Individuals drift between roles or fill many at the same time. Both the market as a whole and the individuals within it are dynamic, and although some cells within the network may be more structured, more hierarchical, and more organized than others, the prevailing model is of a tangled web of individuals who relate to each other in a variety of different ways.

CONCLUSIONS AND DISCUSSION

Lots of people grow cannabis, with an increasing number of them using high-technology growing techniques resulting in larger, more potent yields. Not all grow commercially, but the potential profits are tempting. For many, growing cannabis serves as a solution to practical and ethical problems associated with buying cannabis on the black market. Growing creates a reliable and regular supply for themselves and those they know that is separate from the black market. It can be an enjoyable and social pastime, which is often more important than any financial reward (although money is a welcome extra incentive). As growing operations become bigger, money becomes more of an issue and the social, practical, and ideological aspects are less apparent.

In relation to this, we have identified two separate models of large-scale commercial cannabis production. Cooperative growing circles consist of individuals who are motivated as much by the social and ideological aspects of growing cannabis as the financial ones. Having a supply of good-quality cannabis is important to the individuals and they take pride in what they grow. They like to spread good cannabis around relatively cheaply (they are often opposed to the more established profit-oriented and criminogenic drug-dealer networks) and encourage others to grow their own crops. They often have left-wing and liberal ideologies, and are generally, and often vociferously, in favor of cannabis legalization. Corporate growers are primarily concerned about profit. Pride in the crop plays virtually no role and some do not even smoke. They often have involvement with other forms of crime and with hard drugs. They are protective of their interests and are often willing to resort to violence.

The emergence of the cooperative-style cannabis growers as a rival market supplier to the established corporate model seems to be a result of many factors. On the one hand, improved technology has made cannabis growing more and more accesible. On the other hand, an increasing number of cannabis smokers are becoming disillusioned with the established drug markets and the associated crime, violence, and hard drugs. As the number of smokers goes up in the United Kingdom so the views of the minority of consumers who have concerns about the quality of their cannabis and the activities of those who supply it become more relevant. The alternative cooperative model we have seen in relation to cannabis growing (but which seems to exist to some extent in the distribution of imported cannabis as well) can exist and operate as a viable rival to the established corporate model because there are enough consumers of cannabis who want this alternative supply. Within the United Kingdom, the political and public rhetoric of recent years is also perceptively more liberal—small-scale growers no longer feel as threatened by the risks of breaking the law. On top of these three aspects (growing technology, market forces, liberalization of attitudes towards cannabis), the location of our study got an international airport only recently and is a long way from the sea—imported cannabis needs to travel farther, through more layers of the drug supply network, to reach the area. Imported cannabis is often of a lower quality and a higher price as well as being less readily available than in other parts of the United Kingdom—this may explain why the phenomena we have explored in this chapter seem more advanced in South Yorkshire than elsewhere in Britain.

Although our studies have centered on the homegrown cannabis distribution network, it is possible that the alternative cooperative model of distributors exists elsewhere in the drug-dealing world. Cannabis is an exceptional drug in many ways. It is a drug that can be easily produced (grown) by anyone, anywhere. Cannabis use is generally not associated with addiction, violence, or other criminal activity[26] in the same way that harder drugs (particularly heroin and crack cocaine) are. It is the most widely used drug but it is also the one with the least potential profit (in weight-for-weight terms, and therefore in distribution terms) for black marketeers. There is little doubt that the unique status of this illegal drug has helped foster the alternative dealing model we have outlined. Having said this, it seems likely that similar cooperative supply networks will begin to emerge for other drugs. Ecstasy and other dance drugs are becoming increasingly popular while also becoming easier to manufacture—already in South Yorkshire there are homemade Ecstasy suppliers offering an alternative source of the drug often at cheaper prices. In short, cooperative models may emerge in other drug markets to challenge corporate-style dealers. This alternative model of drug distribution needs to be recognized if we are to understand the workings of illegal drug markets.

NOTES

1. Soapbar is common UK slang for low-quality resin (usually from North Africa) such as that which dominates the British cannabis market—Moroccan resin accounted for 42% of the total UK cannabis market (resin and herbal) in the late 1990s (Atha 2001).
2. House of Commons Select Committee on Home Affairs Memoranda (2001). Anecdotal evidence and communications with local dealers suggest that in South Yorkshire, this trend is greater than for the national average.

3. Although originally the name for a specific strain of cannabis, the word *skunk* has become something of a generic name for all high-potency weed cannabis varieties.

4. Although national evidence suggests that skunk prices have changed little in recent years (*ibid.*) local smokers and dealers suggest skunk prices in South Yorkshire have dropped significantly in the last five years or so from a norm of £25 per eighth of an ounce to a current average of £20.

5. Personal communications with local suppliers of hydroponics equipment and growing lights.

6. *Homegrown* is a term that needs clarification. To some smokers and dealers, homegrown cannabis is of inferior quality grown by amateurs in their back garden. To others (particularly local dealers we spoke to), homegrown cannabis is highly sought after—locally produced by experienced growers without suffering degradation caused by packaging and shipping. We use the term *homegrown* to cover all cannabis produced in the UK rather than imported from abroad.

7. Curtis and Wendel (2000) speak of corporate-style distributors in their attempt at developing a typology of drug dealers. We feel that the type of grower we refer to as "corporate" reflects their use of the word for dealers.

8. Particularly the UKCIA (United Kingdom Cannabis Internet Activists), a Web site and discussion group with many useful links.

9. Easily available by mail order, over the Internet, or over the counter from head shops.

10. The "bud" is the flowering part of the cannabis plant, the most potent part.

11. Grower and dealer slang for the lesser quality bottom-bud and leaves as opposed to the prime quality top-bud of a plant.

12. See, e.g., THC4MS.co.uk, or the directory section of UKCIA at www.Thc4ms.org.uk.

13. During the course of our research, we heard many stories of rural cannabis growers including farmers who grow large crops to subsidize their otherwise unproductive holdings. These diversifying farmers fall beyond the scope of this report.

14. More if sold in retail amounts of £20 per eighth of an ounce.

15. At the time, the average UK student left university with debts of over £10,000.

16. The dealer he sold to noted that customers "often timed their purchasing to coincide with [Bob's] crop."

17. Our phrase, not theirs.

18. This point was heavily discussed on the UKCIA e-mail discussion group where one participant, a barrister, had done some real research into sentencing in cultivation cases. Number of plants and grow room technology were found by him to be the two most decisive factors in sentencing. Other respondents in our face-to-face discussions frequently suggested that growing up to "about 10 plants" was safer than growing more, although other respondents felt that going over 5 plants would prove risky.

19. The more knowledgeable and cautious growers try to avoid possession of "dealing paraphernalia" such as bags or packaging, scales, or large sums of money on the same premises as their plants.

20. Iain would not disclose the value of the deal, but other growers we spoke to who had been made similar offers received between 10 and 60% of the crop or sale value. Twenty to thirty percent seemed to be normal.

21. The largest growing operation we came across consisted of about 1800 plants per crop—potentially £3.5 million in a year, less overhead.

22. See Dorn et al. (1992).

23. Through physical assistance, advice, supply of equipment, and so on.

24. A financial transaction does not have to involve money, but may involve a sellable quantity of marijuana. Friendly advice or help may be rewarded by a small gift of cannabis for personal use.

25. Software engineering on training pay of £18,000 p.a.

26. See Zimmer and Morgan (1997) for a thorough review of the scientific evidence of a wide range of cannabis-related issues.

REFERENCES

ATHA, M. J. 2001 Types of cannabis available in the UK. Retrieved 30th October 2001.

ATHER, M., and S. BLANCHARD. 2001. IDMU Web site www.idmu.co.uk. (Retrieved October 30, 2001).

CURTIS, R., and T. WENDEL. 2000. *Toward the development of a typology of illegal drug markets.* In *Illegal Drug Markets: From Research to Prevention Policy,* eds. M. Natarajan and M. Hough. Sydney: Willow Tree Press.

DORN, N., K. MURJI, and N. SOUTH 1992. *Traffickers: Drug markets and law enforcement.* London: Routledge.

House of Commons Select Committee on Home Affairs Memoranda. 2001. *Drug Trends Appendix C,* citing IDMU surveys (www.IDMU.co.uk). Retrieved 30th October 2001.

UKCIA 2002. United Kingdom Cannabis Internet Alliance Web site and e-mail discussion group monitored. January 2001–December 2002, www.ukcia.co.uk.

WARNER, R. 1986. *Invisible hand: The marijuana business.* New York: Beech Tree Books.

WEISHEIT, R. A. 1990. Domestic marijuana growers: Mainstreaming deviance. *Deviant Behavior* 11:107–129.

——— 1991. The intangible rewards from crime: The case of domestic marijuana cultivation. *Crime and Delinquency* 37(4): 506–527.

ZIMMER, L., and J. P. MORGAN, 1997. *Marijuana myths marijuana facts: A review of the scientific evidence.* New York: The Lindesmith Center.

8

"You Become Really Close ... You Talk about the Silly Things You Did, and We Laugh"

The Role of Binge Drinking in Female Secondary Students' Lives

Margaret Sheehan and Damien Ridge
Deakin University, Melbourne, Australia

❖

INTRODUCTION

Young Australian women grow up in a society where historically alcohol has been widely used and enjoyed (Hamilton, 1987; Bell, 1996; Banwell, 1991; Woolcock, 1991; Sheehan, 1994). Although social norms and expectations can work to limit or conceal women's drinking, a cultural shift is underway whereby negative attitudes regarding women's alcohol use have eased to some extent in recent years (Woolcock, 1991; Park, 1991), and drinking among young women has increased (Shanahan and Hewitt, 1999). Fifty percent of 12-year-old young women have used alcohol, and the figure rises to 95% for 17-year-olds (Letcher and White, 1998). Although they are aware of potentially negative outcomes, young men and women also realize that drinking alcohol has advantages including fun and greater social ease and confidence (Davey, 1994; Shanahan and Hewitt, 1999). In the current climate, the

Reprinted from "You Become Really Close ... You Talk About the Silly Things You Did, and We Laugh: The Role of Binge Drinking in Female Secondary Students' Lives" by Margaret Sheehan and Damien Ridge, *Substance Use and Misuse,* vol. 36(3), pp. 347–72, 2001. Copyright by Marvel Dekker.

concern of health policymakers has converged on young Australians who engage in 'heavy' or 'binge drinking.' However, definitions of binge drinking vary enormously within the community. The lay understanding of binge drinking seems more aligned with drinking continuously, quickly, and heavily. An important aspect of this common interpretation is the notion that the outcome from a binge will be significant or complete drunkenness. School surveys used in Victoria and Australia have generally defined binge drinking as five or more standards drinks in 'one session' with no time frame suggested for the session (Crundall, 1991). In the 1996 *Victorian Secondary Students and Drug Use Survey,* the definition for young women's binge drinking was revised from five or more drinks, down to three or more drinks in a session (Letcher and White, 1998). Davey (1994) in his work defined 'extreme binging' as 8–10 drinks in a session in an attempt to better draw a distinction between degrees of binging.

Binge drinking (when defined as three or more drinks in a session) is a common practice for female students and increases in prevalence with age. Twenty-four percent of year 7 and 58% of year 12 women reported binging on at least one occasion over a 2-week period (Letcher and White, 1998). Young women who binge drink were identified by the National Drug Strategy as an important group for public health interventions because of the higher risks they are exposed to compared with their nonbinging counterparts (National Drug Strategy Committee, 1992). These harms include death, falls and injury, violence, sexual assault, trouble with the law, and the breakdown of relationships. Significantly though, campaigns and school programs targeting young women's alcohol use have been primarily unsuccessful in reducing 'heavy' drinking behaviors (Makkai, 1993).

Little qualitative research relating to women's alcohol use has been undertaken, and studies have tended to neglect gender differences (Banwell, 1991; Broom, 1994; Astbury et al., 1992). Although the literature on the alcohol experiences of young women aged 14 to 17 is also lacking, there is some information on drinking patterns and reasons for use. It is known that the majority of drinking occurs on the weekend, young women have a preference for drinking spirits, and the drinking contexts include family homes, friends places, parks, the streets, pubs, and nightclubs (Crundall, 1991; Hibbert et al., 1992; New South Wales Drug and Alcohol Directorate, 1992). This research strongly supports the findings for other population groups that the major reasons young women report for drinking are to socialize, relax and have fun. Although important, this quantitative research provides only limited insight into the contexts and meanings underlying young women's drinking. Additionally, this literature tends to give an impression of homogeneity among young women, rather than a diversity of socioeconomic backgrounds, cultures, and geographic locations.

The study reported on in this article originally grew out of work with teachers and young women on a national alcohol education project entitled *'Rethinking Drinking'* (McLeod, 1997). This project aimed to provide accurate and relevant alcohol education for students in years 9 and 10. The current research aimed to explore young women's alcohol use and to understand the role it played in their lives. The quantitative data collected in the first research phase revealed that more than half of the young women had felt drunk as a result of their drinking. The focus groups, which were conducted with young women classified as 'heavy drinkers' elaborated on themes from the initial survey. The analysis from these group discussions forms the core of this article, which explores the ways in which young women use alcohol, the role of alcohol in their lives, and the harms and other outcomes that were experienced as a result of binging. Where appropriate, limited data from the survey is included in the paper to provide a comprehensive picture about some key aspects of the research.

There is a discourse within youth alcohol research that underage drinking is necessarily undesirable (Harris and Sheehan, 1995). This article takes as its starting point the premise that at some level alcohol plays a meaningful role in young peoples' lives (Pavis et al., 1997). The discussion explores the meanings behind the experiences of 'binge drinking,' especially in terms of mediating social relationships. The meanings of alcohol are explored with young women from a range of socioeconomic backgrounds. By viewing study participants as 'experts' in binging, this article moves beyond examining causes, and advances the voice of young women about the meaning of alcohol and binging within their own lives (Nimmagadda, 1999). These meanings are multiple and revolved around pleasure, gender expectations, socializing, relationships, fun, secrecy and transgression, danger, exploration, and independence. Additionally, the analysis situates 'binge drinking' within a broader framework of young womens' drinking and the narratives of young womens' lives. In doing so, the discussion problematizes harm minimization approaches that sidestep pleasure, while providing some insights into how harms might be addressed.

METHODS

The research was designed in two phases and carried out between May and September 1996. In the first phase, 850 young women in years 9 and 10 (aged 14–16) from nine different secondary schools across Victoria participated in completing an anonymous, 126-item self-report questionnaire (Sheehan, 1997). The instrument was used to collect data about consumption rates, drinking patterns, attitudes toward drinking, drinking situations, harmful experiences, positive experiences, reasons for drinking, and alcohol education lessons at school. The questionnaire was adapted from a well-established survey, *Victorian School Students Drug Use Survey,* and was also piloted with one group of year 9 and year 10 girls. The survey took between 25 to 40 minutes to complete and required a reading age of approximately 12 years. In the second phase, four focus groups were used to facilitate the exploration of issues that emerged from the survey in greater depth, allowing young women to describe experiences of alcohol in their own terms. The focus group method was chosen to allow participants to interact socially with each other and create dialogue around alcohol experiences in a manner consistent with their experiences of drinking. The focus groups included young women who completed the survey and had binge drank. The results of the initial survey were used in the construction of a themes list for a pilot focus group discussion around common alcohol harms and experiences. The themes covered in the focus groups included the following: level of consumption, harms experienced, positive stories, role of peers, attitudes regarding young women's drinking, storytelling around typical episodes of binging, influence of situations on harms, school alcohol education programs, and links between alcohol, and relationships/sex. With Monash University ethics clearance and Department of Education approval, four school survey sites were identified for follow-up focus groups, and young women were invited to volunteer by completing an attached form at the completion of the class survey. On the day of the survey, the researcher explained the aims of the focus groups and explained that focus group volunteer names would not be linked to their completed surveys. Immediately after the survey all volunteers were considered against the criteria of binging experiences and harms experienced. Forms were then detached from surveys to ensure subsequent anonymity. The volunteers were given a plain English statement about the focus group and a consent form for both the parent/carer and their own signatures. Volunteers who returned forms were contacted by telephone and arrangements were made directly with the study participant independently of the school. A focus group was then carried out in each of the four areas with a total of 23 girls involved, with $n = 7, 6, 5,$ and 4, respectively.

Sampling

Year 9 and year 10 female students were selected for the survey and focus groups with the goal of sampling students old enough to be engaged in relatively high levels of drinking, but not legally of age to purchase alcohol or drink on licensed premises. This aim was achieved, with almost 73% of survey participants having consumed alcohol in the previous month and around 58% stating they had 'felt drunk.' In selecting schools for the quantitative survey, strata categories of socioeconomic level, ethnic background, and geographic location (urban, peri-urban, and rural) directed the identification of seven postcode areas. The seven school sites (where a 'school site' means all those schools participating from a specific post code area) were ranked according to indices provided by the Australian Bureau of Statistics (ABS, 1991), on a scale of one to seven, where seven indicated the most disadvantaged site. Focus groups were conducted at four sites only because of the constraints on resources available to the project (ABS rankings in parentheses): Country (6), Metropolitan Eastern (3), Metropolitan Fringe (2), and Low Income (7). Focus group participants were selected using criterion sampling from those volunteers who reported drinking regularly and who binge drank or consumed alcohol at harmful levels on a regular basis according to National Health and Medical Research Council (1992) guidelines. Students also needed to have experienced at least three alcohol related harms (from a list of 20 categorized as emotional, social, physical or sexual on the 'harms chart' in the survey) to be included. Where feasible, attempts were made to include close friends in each group discussion to facilitate dialogue. This was possible when young women volunteered information during the telephone contact about friends who had also volunteered.

Focus Group Sketches

County ($n = 4$)   Girls in this group were relatively reserved, although they willingly shared stories about alcohol in their lives. They decided to change out of their school uniforms before the focus group, and wore jeans and tee shirts, all plain colors. They didn't wear makeup. Although they were not phased by the research they were perhaps a little wary of me being from the city, maybe because *'things like drinking are different in the country,'* but also I suspected they were feeling self-conscious about what they said and how they behaved. Initially, this group was uncomfortable and would not accept any food but with a little persuasion gratefully accepted. These girls enjoyed school but were bored with options outside school. They didn't giggle together like other groups, yet shared knowing smiles and told their stories in an honest, matter-of-fact way. They didn't waste words.

Metro Eastern ($n = 5$)   This group of girls all had boyfriends and interestingly defined themselves as such. *"We are the girlfriends, you know the girls with boyfriends."* Being a girlfriend was a status thing. This group of girls pursued current fashion trends with beads and clips in hair, heavy platform runners, tight short tops, and loose baggy jeans frayed at the bottom; none were in uniform. Of all groups these young women seemed the least connected to each other, and, while acquainted, were not all peers. Interestingly three of them lived in single-parent families and experienced significant freedom in their outside school time. There was greater diversity in this group than others, with young women variously friendly, wary, open, and confident. They all seemed flattered that they were to be the subject of research, as they said *'life was often so boring.'* Academic aspects of school were not regarded as all that important.

Lower Income (*n* = 6)   The lower income girls were more alternative in appearance and dress including body piercing, dreadlocks, and petticoats as outer garments. The fact that one girl was homeless and another living out of home seemed more a fact of life than a problem. School was mentioned as only a part of life with another whole world away from school. For their age, their group seemed independent and worldly, however, there was a sense of close connection, looking after and out for each other, perhaps a sisterhood that was not so evident in other groups. They were interested in my research but not excited by their inclusion in it—they understood that I needed them. Most were assertive, occasionally bold, and two of them overtly angry. They were what you might call *"in your face,"* but nothing about them was intimidating. One of the young women was very articulate. This group used explicit language freely, not seeking my approval, and quickly established a dialogue that excluded school. They wanted me to like them, but didn't care if I didn't—and I did—they were very likeable.

Fringe (*n* = 7)   Girls in this group were very outgoing, friendly, excited, and chatty; a few of them had very loud voices. They laughed, giggled, and let out an occasional scream as they engaged in the group. They spoke across and over each other, but they accommodated their peers' views when necessary. Their slight lack of confidence showed in their surprise at my interest in them and their gratitude for my treating them as adults. The fact that this was the largest group may have contributed to the feeling that they were part of a larger gang, or maybe the stories about everyone hanging out together made me think of them as more of a gang than any of the other groups. School was the hub of their lives, and they spoke positively about the social aspects. They all wore the school uniform, but half wore heavy eye makeup, jewelry, and nail polish seemingly more as a fashion statement than rebellion. Some girls seemed to have extensive knowledge of life, but fewer had such experiences. They spoke a lot about gender differences often referring to boys as their mates, brothers, friends, sometimes with a resigned acceptance that life is different for girls than boys.

Data Collection and Analysis

The focus groups were all led by the first author, a researcher and former teacher who has extensive experience working with young women. The surveys and discussions were conducted between May and September 1996, with the focus groups being scheduled within 6 weeks of the survey. The discussions were conducted in informal, relaxed settings away from the school premises, including a café, McDonalds, a community center, and a private home. In an attempt to find the most comfortable local venue young women were invited to suggest one. The range of choices available to the fringe and country focus groups were somewhat restricted compared with those of the city focus groups. Initially the venue appeared to influence both mood and group expectations. For example the young women arriving for the focus group at the community health center, being somewhat unfamiliar with them, were expecting a more formal meeting, while those entering McDonalds seemed relaxed and in familiar surrounds that fostered informality. The deliberate sharing of food including chips, chocolate, coke, and cake in all groups while talking resulted in a relaxed, informal atmosphere where many began to 'tell stories' about school. The smallest group in the country took the longest to warm up but all groups of young women spoke and interacted comfortably within the spaces they used for the focus group.

Discussion was based on the themes list, but tended to be more directed by the participants. Group discussions lasted from between 40 and 90 minutes. Focus groups were tape-recorded and fully transcribed. The transcripts were coded manually using a themes approach after the researcher thoroughly familiarized herself with the transcripts. Themes were also generated by contrasting the transcripts with the survey results and the general literature. Aspects of the analysis were triangulated (e.g., against survey data, data revealed after focus groups), and this has allowed for comparison of information for congruence of meaning.

RESULTS

The Meaning of Drinking, Binging, Risk and Harm

The survey and focus group results confirmed that young women primarily drink for fun, enjoyment, and to feel good. The other top responses were 'to relax,' 'to be popular and mix with friends,' and 'to cheer up/forget worries.' The theme of drinking because of boredom was strong both in the country focus group and the group on the metropolitan fringe. To 'pick up guys' or 'get on with someone' was mentioned in all focus groups, and the link between alcohol, relationships, boys, and sex was raised repeatedly by young women in group discussions. The majority of young women surveyed had experienced positive outcomes from their drinking (56%), with only 19% in the survey reporting that they could recall negative or bad experiences from their own perspective. However, highlighting the gap between young peoples' and professional interpretations of alcohol use-related harms, 75% of young women reported experiencing at least one alcohol use-related harm (as defined by the researcher), with the mean number of harms being 4.6. Here, the researcher included physical, sexual, emotional, and social harms (e.g., lying to parents, conflict with friends, making a fool of yourself, trouble getting home, damage to property, and vomiting). These kinds of harms did not particularly feature in participant stories as being harms worthy of consideration. In fact, the notion of linking harm and alcohol did not sit easily with these womens' narratives.

> "I wouldn't really say that having an argument with your friend was a real harm. It's not like getting killed in a car, bashed up, raped, or something . . . I mean they're real problems." (Lower Income)

> "The worst harms for girls are to do with getting really drunk and getting taken advantage of by boys and ending up being with someone and you might not remember." (Fringe)

> "No it's not . . . the worst harm is like dying, getting killed in a car, wandering away and falling unconscious, or drowning. We've had that happen to one of our friends (not drown), but she got lost and she was unconscious." (Fringe)

As mentioned previously, the majority of drinkers emphasized positive alcohol experiences. The most common positive experiences reported in an open-ended questioning were 'increased fun at an event,' 'feeling happy and in control,' 'increased confidence around boys,' and 'feeling more relaxed.' The focus groups expanded on the theme of fun and enjoyment with women telling stories about adventures, pranks, conquests, and increased intimacy.

Figure 8–1 shows that the lower income school site recounted the highest incidence of harms (40%), yet they also reported the highest level of positive memories (73%). Focus groups revealed that the two categories of experience were interconnected with the good and not so good times occurring as part of that one experience. The risks and occasional negative outcomes from drinking were all considered as part of the total experience and bigger story. There appears to be no clear distinction between positive and negative times, as all alcohol experiences subsequently contribute to the whole, becoming the 'good' anecdote. The horrible hangover the next morning or the uncomfortable situation with a boy do not exist on their own. They are accepted elements of the socializing that afforded a good time, a pleasurable interaction, and a shared experience that can be savored and recounted with embellishment if necessary.

> "Our friend was drunk and walking around the party hugging and kissing everyone and crying saying if anything happened to you I'd be so sad—I really love you. It was hilarious—then she fell over and cut her leg—that wasn't so funny." (Metro East)

> "I was having the best time and dancing and pretending to sing into the microphone, you know, and Karen was doing her spitting beer through her teeth trick. Then I felt the room start to spin and I thought, 'Oh my god, I'm gunna chuck' and I did, about ten times." (Metro East)

The question "How will you feel tomorrow?", which was the key message of a youth alcohol mass media campaign (Commonwealth Department of Health and Family Services, 1996), in many cases from a young woman's perspective could be answered simply: "pretty good," "very pleased," "happy," "amused," "pissed off if you've been caught out," and

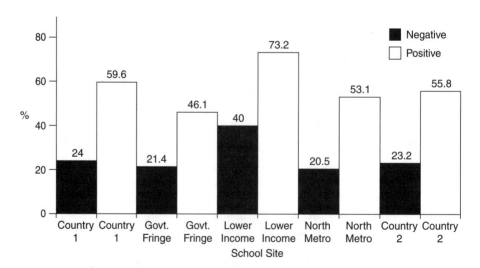

FIGURE 8–1   School site positive and negative drinking experiences

"looking forward to the next time." Even if a harm occurs as judged by the health professional or parent, the assumption that the prevailing memory will be a negative one does not necessarily follow from young women's stories.

As argued in the introduction, the culture of alcohol use has changed, and it is more acceptable than ever for young women to use alcohol (Broom, 1994). The norms that govern alcohol's social acceptability today allow much greater alcohol intake than in the past. In fact, Park (1991) notes that what is now considered socially acceptable is no longer synonymous with safe levels of alcohol use. Many of the stories in the current study included tales of consumption of large amounts of alcohol as an acceptable part of the drinking ritual regardless of the consequences.

> "Three glasses of wine and I'll be pretty tipsy, and then another two or three on top of that and I'll be obviously drunk. I'd be really confident socializing and having a party and then another two and I'd be on the floor . . . I've got the worst alcohol tolerance really." (Fringe)

> "On a Friday you'd go over to your friends place and just have a nice quiet drink or something, maybe share a bottle of vodka (large bottle) between three of us—you wouldn't get really pissed or anything." (Metro East)

In terms of 'binge drinking,' young women's interpretations are considerably removed from some professional definitions that would classify young women consuming three glasses of wine over a whole evening as binge drinking. This social drinking (for instance, sharing 22 standard drinks between three people as in the quote above) by young women juxtaposed against professional definitions of hazardous levels of drinking highlights the gap between public health policy directions, social norms, and young women's lived experiences of alcohol. Although the National Goals and Target document identified the reduction of binge drinking from 14% to 10% by the year 2000 (Nutbeam et al., 1993), one young woman explained:

> "It's not even seen by us as anything major—I mean everyone drinks, some people get really pissed others stay in control . . . there are plenty of worse things . . . we could be doing drugs and stuff." (Country)

Some professional constructions of 'risk' ascribed to binging assume that drinking risks are somewhat separated out from and somehow more significant than everyday risks in life. Such constructions of risk do not make sense within these young women's stories. Alcohol is rarely used for the sole purpose of feeling inebriated. On the contrary, alcohol is fully entangled in socializing, playing a meaningful role in pleasure and fun, the negotiation of relationships, belonging to the group, and the expression of interpersonal feelings such as belonging and anger. Many authors now argue that young people are not members of a special high-risk category (Wyn and White, 1997; Ridge, 1994). Nevertheless, experimentation and risk-taking with substances is a feature of growing up in Western industrialized societies. Learning to use alcohol in various social contexts, including by making mistakes, needs to be grasped as an important task for young people (Lowe et al., 1993; Pavis et al., 1997).

Although there may be an argument for protecting young women from identifiable harms, there tends to be a confused professional discourse about protecting them from their own ignorance or their peers. The notion that they know better, are led by their peers, are ill-informed, or drink for negative reasons, denies young women credit for their drinking choices.

Many drinking stories highlighted the choices young women made, and as such they had considerable agency. They plan their drinking, sometimes control their intake, or deliberately use alcohol to alter their mood and their experiences of interpersonal dynamics.

> "As soon as you're drunk you think, 'I'm going to stop now because I'm going to save my alcohol.' If you keep drinking what's the point." (Low Income)

> "I'd sort of had enough but I kept on drinking because I'm usually really shy and when I drink I mix more easily and have a better time." (Country)

Story-Telling and Secrets

It became clear to the researcher that the story-telling around alcohol involved narratives that had been told and retold within the group many times. These alcohol narratives were effective in drawing together and creating a coherent account of a range of social experiences that might otherwise be interpreted in individualized, fragmented, and less positive ways. The voices of these young women telling their stories are loud, occasionally bold, yet sometimes confused and embarrassed. Regardless of the harms involved, the narratives were generally threaded together by a chorus of laughter borne of happy memories shared among friends. Young women insisted in both the survey and the focus groups that they drink because it is fundamentally fun and pleasurable. Here, in the comfort and company of friends, narratives of drinking can be important in group identification and bonding.

> "When you drink with people you become really close to them . . . you talk about the silly things you did, and we laugh . . . the other day we were laughing so much we were crying with laughter." (Lower Income)

Young womens' stories revealed a tendency to hide the extent of their drinking from outsiders including adults and other young people who might judge them. These young women understand that their drinking has a contested status. The perceived stigma of drinking meant that the young women interviewed had difficulties voicing their binging experiences outside of their own drinking group. Adults were not to be trusted and drinking secrets were well-guarded.

> "They talk about a harm minimization approach but if they find out there's been a party where people got pissed, they want to know all your business and probably phone your parents and then send you to the counselor." (Metro East)

> "My mother would kill me if she knew I drank; she thinks I'm a goody-two-shoes and also because I've got asthma she thinks I shouldn't drink." (Fringe)

A number of stories highlighted the reality of drinking being illegitimate and the social sanctions involved. One informant was suspended from school for "getting pissed at the social," and numerous girls were grounded, lectured to, or otherwise punished for drinking. Social sanctions are accepted as part of the territory by the informants, being incorporated into the 'good story' of binging.

> "My parents made me go to a drug and alcohol counselor after they found out I spewed at a party. My mum said, 'I don't want you to turn into a teenage alcoholic' . . . as if . . ." (laughter). (Metro East)

Young women reported that outside their own group of peers their drinking was not considered entirely acceptable, although there was a begrudging acceptance that they drank. In this sense, their use of alcohol was not a secret they anguished over. Rather, aspects of their stories needed to be hidden in a pragmatic sense to protect their own interests.

> "My mum knows that we all drink but she'd rather not know about it she says—just be sensible—She's got no idea of what we actually do or how much we really drink." (Fringe)

> "She [the mother] said she doesn't really mind if I have a drink or two, but she doesn't want me drinking and getting really drunk. I said, 'Why don't you trust me?' She said, 'I do, it's just you never know how other people are going to behave.' She lets me go out without asking too many questions and, she says, 'Don't let me down.' Sometimes I have to lie to her or just tell half the truth, just so I don't let her down, of course (all laugh). You know I don't want her worrying about me, being such a caring daughter and all (more laughter)." (Fringe)

Young women have learned that they need to keep quiet, and this silence appears to serve a meaningful role in terms of the group identification. These young women share the secret of binging. They bond and identify around binging because they share meaningful and 'good' stories, as well as the expectation to hide the extent of their drinking, be it from parents, teachers, health educators, or boys.

> "Lots of us get drunk . . . I'm not sure about the geeks, we don't mix with them but I heard them talking about their party and they were going to be drinking, I thought, 'Oh my God, if the geeks drink, everyone must drink,' I can't imagine them pissed, not that they'd really tell anyone. They'd be more scared than us of getting caught . . ." (Metro East)

Additional possibilities for the editing and self-censorship of young women's drinking stories are discussed later in this article, including the power of stereotypes of femininity and a lack of comfort by health professionals about the ethics of exploring behaviors of young people that are deemed deviant or illegal.

The Social Terrain

The Role of Alcohol and Binging in Mediating Social Relations

The role that alcohol plays in young women's lives needs to be understood within the context of their social and sexual relations as they deal with the challenges involved in growing up. Young women's stories of alcohol and binging can generally be understood as stories about relationships and exploring the possibilities for greater independence. The majority of stories highlight the importance of social connection in relations as a key feature in young womens' lives where alcohol works as a facilitator. Shared with friends, alcohol enhanced social relations, helped young women to relax and feel good after a week at school, socialize, and engage in all kinds of young women's business.

> "Your closeness with your friends gives you this amazing quality of life feeling, and I think, 'Isn't life great, it makes me basically happy all the time.'" (Lower Income)

> "I decided not to have a drink because I was working the next morning, and I was just standing there. They (her friends) were all drinking and having a good time and laughing, and I felt really left out so I had a few drinks and I had a good time too—I was really glad that I ended up drinking, not for the sake of drinking, but to be part of the group." (Country)

The stories of binging have a commonality in that alcohol plays an important role in mediating social relationships. For instance, establishing relations with boys is not without its stresses. Alcohol was important in exploring, developing, and even finishing relationships with boys. Although there are dangers (e.g., to reputation) that study participants were well aware of, young women were able to harness the sexual assertiveness that accompanied intoxication and put it to good use.

> "Some girls, if they like a guy, they'll just go for it if they've been drinking when normally they wouldn't . . . because they've been drinking the boys will think 'Ok this is good' . . . " (Fringe)

> "I was having a great time and I was pissed and so was he, and boys always talk more to you when they've been drinking . . . we were dancing and he kept smiling at me and I was smiling and laughing . . . I thought he was bad." (*Bad* here is meant as very desirable). (Fringe)

> "At the time, if they're drunk, it's a lot easier to talk to boys and you don't care so much about what you say so you loosen up." (Country)

It was clear to the interviewer that belonging to a group and feeling connected to a group was extremely important for these young women. Alcohol in many cases was being used to assist in the communication, to reduce the shyness, and sometimes in heightening the sensuality of sex.

Heterogeneity

The category of binge drinkers as targeted by health interventions assumes a discrete group of young women without necessarily acknowledging that this group may be heterogeneous. The results of the current analysis are consistent with rejections of universal and homogeneous categorizations of youth (Wyn and White, 1997). Social and alcohol use differences were evident between as well as within the five focus groups (Wilcox-Rountree and Clayton, 1999). Although, some young women had strong supportive networks of girlfriends who helped them cope with life's drama and challenges, other relied on boyfriends for support. Stories highlighted different amounts of leisure time, differing degrees of freedom, and differing levels of responsibility within the family. Social differences translated into differences in alcohol use, including consumption, drinking session environments, the role the friendship group plays, and the perceived stigma associated with drinking, as well as the interpretation of harm minimization messages directed at them. For instance, parental drinking patterns differed significantly from those informants who stated that a parent was an alcoholic, to both mothers and fathers who never drank. There were a few young women who drank with their mothers, and another who always gave her mother two Panadols and a cup of tea after her mother had been out with the girls. A number of young women were well aware that drinking breached family rules and expectations. Binge drinking occurred at "vodka and video nights," at parties with friends, in nightclubs, outside "no alcohol" discos, and by a range of girls. Some young women from the lower income area reported drinking cask wine because it was effective and cheap. This group also told stories of taking public transport late at night and engaging in minor vandalism when they were intoxicated. The lower income group of women occasionally engaged in aggressive acts while intoxicated.

"Well this isn't really a very nice story but I smeared cat s__t on the neighbor's undies when they were hanging on the line, she's such a b___h I still think she's a b___h when I'm sober, but I wouldn't have done that." (Lower Income)

"Just finding yourself with some complete stranger sitting on a station and thinking, 'Oh My God where am I?' . . . I find that when I'm drunk I get too confident, I get smart and rude, and I've gotten myself into plenty of situations where someone could have beaten the s__t out of me . . . when we used to go out as a group we'd walk up to people on train and get right next to them and yell as loud as we could to frighten them . . . sometimes they'd try to get away and we'd follow them (all laugh) just for fun." (Lower Income)

Gender Relations and Binging

It is clear within the literature that there is a double standard in relation to young men's and young women's drinking. Broom (1994) argues that alcohol is still socially disapproved of on a sex-specific basis, resulting in restrictions on young women's drinking behaviors. Gender was indeed a theme in many of the young womens' stories. Two pervasive themes in the current study included the importance of codes of femininity and the transgression of those codes. Young women's stories in the current study incorporate incidents where drinking was not condoned for them in the same way it was for their male counterparts. In particular, a number of young women told stories about being treated differently than their brothers. They frequently interpreted this differential treatment as being linked to their perceived vulnerability to sexual harm. Young women were amused, annoyed, and frequently resigned to the double standards they experienced.

"My mum saw my friends and me down the main street with some guys who were drinking. She said, 'I saw you hanging around the street—I hope you weren't drinking—you looked liked a bunch of little sluts.'" (Fringe)

"My brother is 18. Whenever my dad has a drink or a beer, he offers some to my brother yet my sister is 23, and he won't offer her a drink. When she and her boyfriend come over, my dad will offer her boyfriend a beer, but he still won't offer Linda a beer . . . One day she said, 'Aren't you going to offer me a beer?' and dad says, 'Well you can go get your own if you want one.' He still won't get her one." (Fringe)

"My boyfriend doesn't mind me drinking, but he doesn't like me drinking too much because he doesn't trust the other guys, so usually when I drink with him I stay pretty sober." (Metro East)

There was an initial reluctance to tell transgressive stories, with a constant checking with the group during the interview to ensure a particular story could be told. These young women knew they were playing with and sometimes pushing the boundaries of socially sanctioned femininity. The hesitancy young women displayed in voicing the 'awful' things they had done when drunk appeared related to a fear of being judged as 'not nice girls.' Nevertheless, given permission, time, and support by the interviewer to talk about the 'unfeminine,' rebellious, loutish, and aggressive behavior, young women were keen to tell their stories. The transgressions reported included vomiting and getting it stuck in their hair; fighting with their friends over boys, aggressive language, physically brawling with other girls and behaving in a 'sluttish' manner, including behaving in such a manner with boys considered to be 'creeps.'

"You'd be disgusted if you knew what I did—oh no I can't tell you, I was so horrible . . . no don't tell her . . . OK, I'll go and get a drink and you can tell her. (Laughs and leaves the room). (Lower Income)

"There's this school nut, and I don't get along with her very well. It's got to do with my boyfriend she likes him or something like that. At the school social we had both been drinking and we're standing in the middle of the floor yelling and screaming at each other and the two of us nearly got into a punch up . . . in our evening dresses. How classy is that?" (Metro East)

Although it is tempting to romanticize these transgressions as challenging feminine stereotypes, this 'coming out' was more about testing the water, frequently in the safety of numbers. In telling the stories, it was a sheepish group outing, not individuals confidently rebelling and going out on a limb. These young womens' stories are consistent with Broom's (1994) claim that regimes of femininity shape women's drug use, including choice of drug, the social environment of use, and the social response to use. Finally, the suggestion that young women ignore safe drinking messages in the quest for equality with their male counterparts (Ling and Spurritt, 1998) was not a theme in the focus groups.

"Sometimes they (boys) go on about how they drank a slab, and got so pissed and how drunk they were . . . I wish I could down a slab in front of them to shut them up but why would you bother?" (Fringe)

Harm Minimization

Despite differences in lay and professional discourses around harm, young women were keen to minimize harm in ways that were practical in their circumstances. Young women were not victims of their lack of decision-making skills. On the contrary, they were aware of and practiced a range of harm minimization strategies.

"What we do is take it in turn. If there was a party and we go along, she'd say to me, 'Are you going to be drinking?' and if I say, 'No, I really don't feel like it, she'll say, 'Will you look after me?' and I do the same sort of thing . . . but if it ended up she was drinking and I was drinking, I'd make sure someone I trusted looked after me. (Metro East)

Most were acutely aware of environments and situations that put them at risk, and implemented their own harm minimization strategies. One young woman reported that when she had to catch the last train home she would never be 'really off her face because she'd be an easy target.' However, young women acknowledged limitations to protection against sexual harm, stating that although they could protect themselves against sexual harm, if men wanted to get them they would, whether you were drunk or sober. Another harm minimization strategy reported was that of selecting drinking environments that were safer than others. Women tended to keep together in groups when they drank in parks, outdoor sports grounds, or in the city. Often, if there was access to a house this would be used for a party. Generally, young women thought drinking inside was safer than being on the street. They were well aware of the dangers of getting into a car with a drunk driver or driving themselves when drunk. Some also reported keeping friends out of cars. Through previous experiences, one young woman felt she had a propensity to 'crack onto just anyone' after she had been drinking too much. She established a deal with her friends that if she began to harass a certain male who she really liked, they would stop her to ensure that she didn't make a fool of herself and scare him away for good.

CONCLUSION

For the majority of young women in the sample, drinking and binging experiences are interpreted in meaningful and positive ways. Direct experiences of alcohol are woven together through individual and group narratives. It is through telling stories that these young women are able to make sense of and locate their drinking within their various social realities. As a stigmatized activity, binging for young women only takes on coherency of meaning through the good story. The power of narrative here has to do with the way that practical experiences associated with a marginalized activity are linked together with moral content, allowing embellishment, ongoing interpretation, and philosophies to be developed (Cruickshank, 1997). For instance, an ethic emerging from stories brimming with drama and fun was that women should try to look out for themselves and each other when binging involved a lack of control.

Group participants identify around, and bond through, their alcohol experiences and narratives. Here, harms encountered along the way tend to be filtered through enjoyable tales. Alcohol and binging tales contribute to the fabric of these young women's lives with a heady mix of enjoyment, pleasure, confidence, fun, closeness, secrecy, friendships, exploration of relationships, and sex. In contrast to some professional discourses, the lived experience of these women is that harm is rarely the outcome, and never exclusively on its own. If young women are going to identify with the messages of health promoters, there is an important acknowledgement that needs to be made first. Drinking alcohol is meaningful, part of relationship-building, and women make active interpretations and choices in their drinking. In addition, any attempts at marginalizing the activity is resisted through the power of narrative. For instance, women in the study provided many examples of the restrictions that codes of femininity potentially placed on them, in terms of drinking and its interpretation. The transgression of such feminine codes, although not a full scale defiance of social norms, was a significant theme in the stories and fits with the notion of narrative as a form of challenge to hegemonic discourses. Such limited transgressions are commensurate with the marginality of the activity backed up by multiple reasons for the disapproval of young women's drinking including: perceptions of impaired nurturing ability, greater accessibility as a sexual partner, the status of victim of sexual assault, and the release of emotions that do not always sit comfortably with notions of femininity such as anger (Gomberg, 1988).

Although it remains a challenge to minimize dangers in the more harmful practices related to young women's drinking, further exploring young women's narratives may provide a valuable way forward in promoting women's own indigenous protection strategies. The focus groups' interviews bore out that students already had a significant amount of knowledge and experience around drinking, and they implemented sensible indigenous harm minimization strategies. In addition, the current analysis questions the wisdom of public health policy and health promotion/education practice that singles out and prioritizes alcohol risks above other risks in everyday life. There were context-specific dangers experienced by young women, especially for those from lower socioeconomic backgrounds. The contexts in which they live and drink are dangerous. Being in a train station alone late at night is potentially dangerous, as is living in a home with domestic violence or living on the street, as was the case for one young woman in a focus group. By recognizing that young women drink and there are risks commensurate with other aspects of living, professionals can assist young women to more realistically appraise potentially harmful settings and situations, and further develop their own strategies and skills to minimize harm (Wyn and Sheehan, 1995). The current analysis supports calls for youth and school-based education programs that use a holistic welfare approach where relationships, family support, academic success and so called 'risky' sexual and drug use behaviors are all considered as part of a bigger picture (Glover, 1998; Fuller, 1999).

The findings discussed have a number of implications for future public health research and health promotion practice. First, results suggest that it would be beneficial for additional public health campaigns and initiatives to acknowledge the voice of young women. Additional research in the area of young women's alcohol use and other sensitive social health issues should include qualitative research methods in an attempt to examine the complex nature of the issue and to provide information not available from standard survey material. Furthermore, the term "binge drinking" for young women in this research was associated with extreme behavior and negative connotations, having limited resonance with them. In light of this finding, it appears important that "binge drinking" be problematized as moralistic and one that is counter-productive in engaging young women. A clear message for public health campaigns, especially those targeting underage drinkers, is the necessity to acknowledge, without prejudice and moralizing, the positive experiences and benefits of drinking as well as its negative consequences to properly engage and educate young women. This supports the continuation of a harm minimization approach as favored in Australia in the 1990s, rather than the current more conservative, regressive 'zero tolerance approach' being advocated for school education policy.

One shortcoming of this study was the small number of focus groups and hence the limited selection of young women. The diversity of young women and alcohol experiences hinted at in the findings points to the need for additional research that explores such differences. The inclusion of peers in the focus groups as in this study introduces the possibility that relationships and preexisting dynamics between members of the group are more important in the communication process than the needs of the researcher. Although at times "proving oneself" appeared to encourage exaggeration of alcohol use-related stories, the seeming closeness and familiarity with each other appeared to temper (through claims of disbelief and amusement) "tall" stories. Although possible exaggerations might be considered a limitation of the methodology, it is also possible to look at such embellishments as actually providing useful insights into the way that binging narratives and good anecdotes operated to draw friends together and create coherent meaning frameworks that resisted hegemonic expectations. Similarly, the subjectivity of the field researcher was crucial. She was once a student who used alcohol and experienced a number of binge drinking outcomes in her own school years. As it turned out, the first researcher's ability to relate to the narratives was an important consideration in the collection of data and the analysis. The researcher was able to empathize with the experiences of the study participants and communicate this understanding. She gained the sense that her particular approach gave the participants license to come forward with stories that might not ordinarily have been revealed to 'outsiders,' particularly adults. However, one cannot always be certain that the meaning given to the situation by the researcher corresponds exactly to the meaning given by the respondents.

REFERENCES

ASTBURY, J.; FRANK, L.; BURROWS, C. Changing the Research Story: Women and Drugs Research Workshop. In Women and Drug Research Workshop; Astbury, J., Frank, L., Burrows, C., Eds.; Addiction Research Institute of Victoria: Melbourne, 1992; 1–10.

Australian Bureau of Statistics. *Australian Bureau of Statistics Information Paper SEIFA*. Australian Bureau of Statistics: Melbourne, 1991.

BANWELL, C. I'm Not Really a Drinker: Women and Alcohol. In *Ladies a Plate;* Park, J., Ed.; University Press: Auckland, 1991.

BELL, I. Why Do People Use Drugs? In Perspectives on Drug Addiction; Wilkinson, C., Saunders, B., Eds.; Montgomery Press: Perth, 1996; 40–46.

BROOM, D. *Double Bind: Women Affected by Alcohol and Other Drugs*. Allen and Unwin: Melbourne, 1994.

Commonwealth Department of Health and Family Services. *How Will You Feel Tomorrow*. Australian Government Publishing Service: Canberra, 1996.

CRUIKSHANK, J. Negotiating with Narrative: Establishing Cultural Identity at the Yukon International Storytelling Festival. Am. Anthropologist 1997, *99* (1), 56–69.

CRUNDALL, I. Teenage Drug Use: The Survey. Substance 1991, *2*(1), 18–19.

DAVEY, J.; CLARKE, J. Come to the Cabaret and Get Legless: Tertiary Student 'Event' Drinking. Youth Stud. Aust. 1991, *10*(4), 30–35.

DAVEY, J. Young Women and Drinking. Youth Stud. Aust. 1994, *13*(3), 28–31.

FULLER, A. Promoting Resilience. *Turning the Tide Newsletter,* Issue 9, December 1999. Department of Education, Employment and Training: Melbourne, 1999.

GLOVER, S.; BURNS, J.; BUTLER, H.; PATTON, G. Social Environments and the Emotional Well-Being of Young People. Family Matters 1998, *49,* 11–16.

GOMBERG, I. The Psychosocial Aspects of Women and Alcohol Use. Healthright 1988, *9*(1), 12–15.

HAMILTON, M. The Social Environmental Perspective: Young People Drinking. In *Proceedings of Autumn School of Studies on Alcohol and Drugs;* St Vincent's Hospital, Department of Community Medicine: Melbourne, 1987; 30–34.

HARRIS, A.; SHEEHAN, M. Taking the Hiccups Out of Alcohol Education. Youth Stud. Aust. 1995, *14*(1), 41–45.

Health Department Victoria. *1989 Survey of Alcohol and Tobacco and Other Drug Use Among Victorian Secondary School Students*. Health Department: Melbourne, 1990.

HIBBERT, M.; CAUST, J.; PATTON, G. *The Health of Young People in Victoria: Adolescent Health Survey*. Centre for Adolescent Health: Melbourne, 1992.

LETCHER, T.; WHITE, V. *Australian Secondary Students' Use of Over-The-Counter and Illicit Substances in 1996*. Publications Production Unit, Department of Health and Aged Care: Canberra, 1998.

LING, M.; SPURRITT, T. Drug Education Evaluation: Focus Groups. *First International Conference on Drugs and Young People,* Melbourne, Australia, Melbourne Convention Centre, Nov 22–24, 1998.

LOWE, G.; FOXCROFT, D.; SIBLEY, D. *Adolescent Drinking and Family Life*. Harwood Academic Publishers: Switzerland, 1993.

MAKKAI, T. DRUGS. Anti-Social Behaviour and Policy Choices in Australia. In *The 1993 National Household Survey Report Series*. Australian Government Publishing Service: Canberra, 1993a.

MAKKAI, T. Awareness of the 'National Campaign Against Drug Abuse' and the 'Drug Offensive'. In *The 1993 National Household Survey Report Series,* Australian Government Publishing Service: Canberra, 1993b.

MCLEOD, J. *Rethinking Drinking: You're in Control. An Alcohol Education Program for Secondary Students. Reflections on the Development, Implementation and Strengths of the Program*. Youth Research Centre: Melbourne, 1997.

Munro, G. *Alcohol and Drug Education Programs in Schools.* Unpublished paper for Adolescent Health Seminar Series: Alcohol and Drug Issues in Australia. Centre for Adolescent Health: Melbourne, 1994.

Munro, G. Reducing Harm Through Education. Substance 1992, *3*(2), 8–11.

National Drug Strategy Committee. *National Drug Strategic Plan 1993–1997.* Australian Government Publishing Service: Canberra, 1992.

National Health and Medical Research Council. *Is There a Safe Level of Daily Consumption of Alcohol for Men and Women? Recommendations Regarding Responsible Drinking Behaviour*, 2nd Ed.; Australian Government Publishing Service: Canberra, 1992.

New South Wales Drug and Alcohol Directorate. *Survey of Drug Use by New South Wales Secondary School Students.* New South Wales Department of Health: Sydney, 1992.

Nimmagadda, J. A Pilot Study of the Social Construction of the Meanings Attached to Alcohol Use: Perceptions from India 1999, *34*(2), 251–267.

Nutbeam, D.; Wise, M.; Bauman, A.; Harris, E.; Leeder, S. *Goals and Targets For Australia's Health in the Year 2000 and Beyond.* Australian Government Publishing Service: Canberra, 1993.

Park, J. *Ladies a Plate.* Auckland University Press: Auckland, 1991.

Pavis, S.; Cunningham-Burley, S.; Amos, A. Alcohol Consumption and Young People: Exploring Meaning and Social Context. Health Educ. Res. 1997, *12*(3), 311–322.

Ridge, D.; Plummer, D.; Minichiello, V. Young Gay Men and HIV: Running the Risk? AIDS Care 1994, *6*, 371–378.

Shanahan, P.; Hewitt, N. *Developmental Research for a National Alcohol Campaign: Summary Report.* Commonwealth Department of Health and Aged Care: Canberra, 1999.

Sheehan, M. *In The Spirit of Fun: An Exploration of the Use and Meanings of Alcohol in Young Women's Lives.* Unpublished Master of Public Health thesis. Monash University: Melbourne, 1997.

Sheehan, M. *Alcohol Control and Drink Driving: The Social Context.* Australian Government Publishing Service: Brisbane, 1994.

Victorian Drug Strategy Section. *Secondary School Students and Drug Use Survey.* Victorian Department of Health and Community Services: Melbourne, 1993.

Wilcox-Rountree, P.; Clayton, R.R. A Contextual Model of Adolescent Alcohol Use across the Rural–Urban Continuum. Substance Use Misuse 1999, *34*(4–5), 495–519.

Woolcock, H. *Safe Driving Project Social History Report Drink Driving Prevention Project.* University of Queensland: Brisbane, 1991.

Wyn, J.; Sheehan, M. Re-Thinking Drinking: Rethinking Alcohol Education. In *24th International Medical Advisory Group Conference Proceedings.* Australian Associated Brewers: Sydney, 1995; 185–198.

Wyn, J.; White, R. *Rethinking Youth.* Allen and Unwin: St Leonards, New South Wales, 1997.

9

Race and the Culture of College Drinking

An Analysis of White Privilege on Campus

Robert L. Peralta
American University

> No, we regulate ourselves. It's not the university regulating us because we have to fight for the things we want so why jeopardize it by acting stupid? Why give them another reason to try to take something away from us that we fought so hard to get?
>
> *(Pam, African American respondent)*

Recent research documents the extent to which alcohol is used among college undergraduates. Presley and colleagues (1998) claim that 24.2% of their sample reported using alcohol 3 times a week or more. These patterns are consistent across epidemiological studies (O'Malley et al. 1998). Twenty-two percent of students in a study by Wechsler and colleagues reported binge drinking (defined as 5 or more drinks in a single sitting for men, 4 or more for women) in the last two weeks in 1998. Survey data suggests most college students feel drinking is a central part of social life (Wechsler et al. 1996). College students regard drinking as central for students in general and for groups such as athletes, social fraternities, and sororities. Indeed, 92% of students report that the social atmosphere on their campuses promotes alcohol use (Wechsler et al. 1996). While these survey results document behaviors and attitudes of the dominant college culture, less is known about the sociology of drinking for undergraduate minority students (for more insight into the sociology of alcohol use, see Peralta in press).

Robert L. Peralta. Prepared expressly for this edition.

We do know that White students appear to drink more than do non-White students. Compared with young Whites, young Blacks have consistently reported lower rates of alcohol use, drunkenness, and alcohol-related problems (Herd 1997; Jones-Webb 1998; Johnson and colleagues 1998; Wechsler et al. 1998). White college students, for example, self-reported drinking 6.6 drinks a week while non-White students consumed 3.4 drinks (Weschsler et al. 1998). Forty-seven percent of White students were classified as binge drinkers compared to 18% of Black, 25% of Asian, 38% of Hispanics, and 37% of "other" students. Disparities in drinking patterns speak to differences in drinking cultures and the social arrangements that produce them (see Pittman and White 1991).

This study explores drinking disparities by race through analyzing accounts of college drinking from African American and White students. I work toward developing an understanding of the social structural factors related to drinking in college as they pertain to Black and White students. The development of a sociostructural understanding of drinking for college students is informed by talking with undergraduates about these issues. Three intertwined themes emerged from the accounts of minority and White students. First, students talked about the importance and structure of university social space. Minority students asserted that campus was largely "White space" where students, staff, and professors were overwhelmingly White (see Feagin and colleagues, 1996, for a discussion of "White space"). It was within this White space that drinking took place. Student's accounts suggest that alcohol use provided a means for White students to participate in White culture and forge relationships with other White students. Those who were not White reported a disconnection from the college culture. In exploring this theme, I looked at how Black students viewed drinking from the perspective of being Black in predominantly White space.

The second theme emerging from these data concerned student's views on bias imposed by institution components of the university itself. African American students stated the university had official and unofficial policies in place that worked to limit their ability to pursue activities, such as drinking. Here I focus on the relationship between drinking behavior and institutional policy.

Finally, privilege emerged as a theme in discussions with African American students. African American students indicated, as numerical and racial minorities on campus, they felt pressure to be "model" citizens for fear of creating or perpetrating existing stereotypes indicative of their race. Here, I attempt to express their concerns involving drinking behavior and the potential for negative stereotypes to arise from engaging in such behavior.

Two overarching goals guide this chapter. The first is to begin understanding, from the perspective of undergraduates, some of the sociocultural mechanisms at work in undergraduate drinking. To achieve this goal, this chapter is organized to present the voices of the students to whom I spoke. The second goal was to connect what was learned from these experiences with the relevant existing literature on social structure. The final section of this chapter summarizes the findings and poses questions for future research.

METHOD

Procedure

This research was a part of a larger study on the drinking behaviors of college students (see Peralta, in press, for additional information). A qualitative research design was used to document participants' experiences with alcohol at a single university. Students responded to

TABLE 9–1   Student Interviews: Race by Gender N (%)

Race	Gender		Total
	Males	Females	
White	29 (71)	26 (70)	55 (71)
Black	10 (24)	10 (27)	20 (26)
Latino	1 (2)	1 (3)	2 (3)
Asian	1 (2)	— (—)	1 (1)
Total N (%)	41 (100)	37 (100)	78 (100)

class announcements in sociology and criminology courses and to ten posted notices placed in campus areas frequented by these youth. Minority students were purposely over sampled to give voice to those who have been traditionally excluded from research. Difficulty recruiting minority participants (African American and gay and lesbian students) prompted the use of $10 stipends to encourage their participation.

The University Office of Human Research granted ethical approval for the project. Seventy-eight interpersonal in-depth interviews lasting 45 minutes to 1 hour were conducted in the office of the primary investigator. Informed consent was given for participation and all respondents were assured confidentiality.

Respondents

A self-selected purposive sample of 78 undergraduate students was interviewed. Data were collected between 1997 and 2001. College class ranking ranged from freshmen to senior status. Students lived both on and off campus. Seventy-one percent ($N = 55$) of the sample was White and 26% ($N = 20$) was Black. Two respondents were of Hispanic origin and one respondent self described as Asian. Fifty-three percent ($N = 41$) were male; 47% were female ($N = 37$). Seventy-two percent ($N = 56$) self-identified as heterosexual, 22% ($N = 17$) self-identified as homosexual, and the remaining 6% ($N = 5$) self-identified as bisexual. The mean ($\pm$ SD) age was 20 years old $\pm$ 2.75. Thirty-two percent ($N = 24$) reported being freshmen at the time of the interview. Fifteen percent ($N = 11$) of the sample reported being a member of a fraternity or sorority (see Tables 9–1 through 9–3).

TABLE 9–2   Student Interviews: Sexuality by Gender N (%)

Sexuality	Gender		Total
	Male	Female	
Heterosexual	30 (73)	26 (70)	56 (72)
Homosexual	10 (24)	7 (19)	17 (22)
Bisexual	1 (2)	4 (11)	5 (6)
Total N (%)	41 (100)	37 (100)	78 (100)

TABLE 9–3   Student Interviews: Race by Sexuality N (%)

Race	Sexuality Hetero	Gay	Bisexual	Total
White	38 (68)	12 (71)	5 (100)	55 (71)
Black	18 (32)	2 (12)	— (—)	20 (26)
Latino	— (—)	2 (12)	— (—)	2 (3)
Asian	— (—)	1 (6)	— (—)	1 (1)
Total N (%)	56 (100)	17 (100)	5 (100)	78 (100)

Instrument

A semistructured open-ended interview guide consisting of 12 questions was developed and pilot tested by the primary author to study alcohol use among college students. Many questions were presented in projective form to reduce the response effect on threatening questions (see Sudman and Bradburn 1982). Demographic questions were asked in addition to questions about drinking quantity and frequency, attitudes toward drinking, reasons for drinking, expectations of alcohol use, and consequences of drinking. Some of the questions specific to the study were as follows: (1) What do you think of the idea of getting drunk? (2) What are your experiences with drinking on this campus? (3) What are your expectations for people who get drunk? (4) What goes through your mind when you see someone drinking or getting drunk? Probing questions were used when appropriate to facilitate further discussion. The interview was designed to be open enough to allow students to discuss in depth issues they thought pertained to alcohol use yet structured to keep the discussion focused on alcohol use on college.

Analysis

Grounded theory was the analytical technique used in this study, as the purpose was to explore issues related to drinking behaviors on a college campus. This technique allows respondents to inform the development of both theory and relevant hypotheses for testing in future research (see Lincoln and Guba 1985). All of the interviews were transcribed and coded. An initial content analysis was conducted for patterns of responses emerging from the data. After this initial analysis, a more thorough examination of the transcripts was conducted for emergent themes. Interrater reliability was utilized for verifying consistency in coding and interpretation. Specific concepts articulated by various respondents were grouped. These concepts included social space, control and power, identity, social control, and racism.

RESULTS

Drinking differences, in terms of attitudes, drinking behaviors, and experiences with alcohol differed qualitatively by race. These differences support existing epidemiological data. Whereas one White female in my sample of 26 White females reported never achieving intoxication, 4 out of 10 Black females reported never having felt intoxicated. Two Black males out of 10 similarly reported never having felt intoxicated. All White males reported having become intoxicated during college. Two Black females and one Black male reported complete abstinence whereas one White female reported near abstinence (she had had only two drinks in the past year).

What follows are three interrelated themes that emerged from the data. These themes are explained and supported using accounts from the respondents interviewed. These accounts explain in certain detail the social structural factors associated with the various drinking patterns found on the college campus where the study took place.

Social Space

Accounts reveal how the social locations of Blacks and Whites and the social spaces they occupy work to encourage or discourage specific drinking practices. The social location of an individual, that is, where in life a person is socioeconomically, racially, as a male or female, for example, and how this status fits into the community or social space at large—plays an important role in shaping the meaning and use of alcohol (see Feagin and colleagues 1996).

Talking to Black students at length about their experiences with college drinking flowed into discussions about segregation, discrimination, discomfort, and isolation. The following accounts taken from African American students first illustrate the concept of social space as it relates to isolation and segregation felt on a campus dominated by White students. Each quote thereafter illuminates the relationship between social space and alcohol use.

Frieda and Brenda, both African American females, talk about the isolation they felt in class and in campus as Black individuals.

Frieda: And I was the only Black in most of my courses and that is the way it is going to be everywhere I go, especially in my field.

Brenda: It's really segregated on this campus. Like if you walk through the student union you know, there's like the Black's table, they have like two tables and everything else is like White and it's so weird to look at. I always tell my friends "it's like we're in high school, look at this!"

Sandy describes the segregated nature of dormitory living at the university:

Sandy: Because of my program, I lived over at the freshman dorm. And there are about, seriously, ten Black people period on that side of campus. A lot of students in our program even dropped out back then or they moved because they didn't feel comfortable there.

Being in predominantly White space creates loneliness, boredom, and isolation. Being Black means not participating fully in the college culture. I asked Janice about her boredom:

Janice: [The university setting is] like a suburb as opposed to an urban area and it's just not a big place. And although there might be a large number of students here at the university it just seems that there's a lot more for Caucasian students to do, at least in my view because of the area. And what I'm used to and what my culture is and what I enjoy with my people and my culture so it's not always that easy to go and find things to do.

Eric, an African American male, contemplates decisions about which racial space to occupy and the differences in drinking between these two different social spaces:

> *Eric:*   Should I be with people that are my race? Those with the same type of background that I have and who are my true friends? I think that is the main reason I got back on the right track . . . made me slow down with the drinking. Which is what I really like about the Black community, 'cause most of the programs they put on are not about drinking. I mean some drinking does go on but it is not the main activity. Like at White parties the main activity is drinking. They hardly dance if they do dance. It is more of go there, drink, get drunk, and socialize. You really don't know anybody. I learned how to interact with White people that have never been around people of color before. I think a lot people here haven't experienced Black people before. You know? I think a lot of people are scared. And they have too many stereotypes.

When drinking takes place in White space, African Americans fear the potential for racism and discrimination to emerge. Brad states,

> Well, the whole thing about getting drunk is that it is supposed to make you a social magnet in the sense of you are looser with your tongue. People are, um, putting down the inhibitions, you know. Like that initial nervousness you had to talk to someone you see over on the side. You know if you have that barrier down, that nervousness, that fear of rejection, you know that you are going to talk to them. So I think that is one thing, but at the same time people are susceptible to verbal abuse, sexual abuse, just anything like I mentioned before. I don't want somebody to come out of their mouth with the "N" word cause I will be like "okay, this is what you really think; this is what is really in your head." And I don't want to hear that. I don't want to have to deal with that.

While White space characterizes the social landscape of the university, enclaves of Black space exist on the college campus where this study took place. These spaces, however, are generally tucked away within the private parameters of dorm room space, university space allotted to Black students for a fixed amount of time, or other Black spaces. Darren exemplifies this in his explanations of parties and states,

> If White students come to a flow [term used to describe an African American party], I wonder. I'm not racist, but I wonder how they knew about it and why they came. I think it is good that they came. But how did they hear about it or whatever? I think they are brave, you know? That's a good thing. It's a very good thing. Trying to break the color barrier.

Adrian compares Black parties and White parties:

> I've been to a couple of White parties. I hate to say "White parties" but let's be real. That's what it is. Normally White parties you go and everybody is just drinking. No music, maybe a little music here and there. But for the most part it is just socializing and drinking.

These statements exemplify the discomfort minority students feel while attending campus parties at a primarily White university. Part of their discomfort is expressed in their self-reported avoidance of the drinking culture. Related to issues of social space and how this social structural construct influences drinking behavior are institutional mechanisms. Administrative policies and action engaged in by university officials also help to shape drinking cultures.

Institutional Bias

The following accounts reveal how Black students believe that the university controls and allots certain social spaces to be used for drinking, thus unintentionally creating drinking spaces for certain groups. For example, social fraternities are in effect given drinking privileges while African American groups at the university are not granted similar privileges to drink. That is, the social space to engage in drinking behavior is not allocated equally. The following African American students vocalize this bias:

Eric: Alcohol is not central at Black gatherings 'cause that is how the university has set it up. Whites have more freedom that way.

Sandy: [Our functions are] a lot different than White fraternities and sororities 'cause we don't have the house and we do our activities on campus.

Eric: [It is how the] university is set up, I mean most Black parties are on campus. You go out and Black people, on this campus, in order to do something, you have to do it on campus. They might have after parties and sometimes there is alcohol there, but a lot time there isn't.

Robert: Do you have a [fraternity] house?

Michael: Naw, no, we don't.

Robert: Where do you meet?

Michael: We have a room over in the student center.

Frieda: Yeah, it is a totally different atmosphere in terms of alcohol and the way White students and Black students party. Like, they can go to fraternity houses and drink, things like that. The only way that [Black] students can drink is to do it in their rooms or off campus. I mean that is the way Black organizations work . . . If the party is on campus, it's like we have to pay for security. Whereas you can go to a fraternity house or a house on such and such avenue and drink openly and I've seen minority students who feel kind of like "what is that about?"

Not only is space formally controlled, so too is drinking behavior. African American students report being scrutinized by campus police more so than their White counterparts. Take the following accounts by African American students. Below, Brad talks about participating in an African American organization initiation ceremony and his experience with campus police.

We were out at the [dorm] on north campus and we were all kind of outside on the tennis courts cheering these people on and congratulating them and the police like just rolled up and just said "you know you guys are making a lot of noise; we have heard some complaints." I live right by a condemned frat house. It was a condemned frat house recently and they were sometimes really loud and there have been times when I called the police and told then they are making too much of a disturbance, and the police might just drive by and like they will come by and it will get quiet and then they will like drive back out. And it doesn't seem like the police really got out of the car. It was more like they see a cop coming down the street and they, like the cop turns around and goes away. There have been times [when] they [White students] were lighting fireworks and things. That to me is, I don't want to accuse public safety of being racist or anything but at the same time we have not always received the same treatment as others and we weren't even drinking outside. Obviously none of us *were* drunk, we were all just cheering on these people that were becoming a part of this organization.

Janice also states:

Minority students have a problem with campus safety. People might not be outright racist, but I think they have stereotypes in their head that Black students are this or that. And so they were [the university] actually last year talking about cutting out our party period and not letting any organization have a party. That's how bad it was going to get for us, whereas you know White students can party until they die, which they do, and it's not a problem.

Frieda states,

It seems like non-Blacks can get away with drinking, and then we have like get-togethers and it's like all the cops come. We're scrutinized a lot more. I mean I've been in places like in the dorms where you have, we call it a "flow," which is like a little get together and we would be in there and, you know, would be dancing and we would have drinks in there. Public safety would knock on our door and come and be like "we wanted to come around and check it out." And there was a White person down the hall with a cup in her hand and was standing out in the hallway and the cop didn't do anything and she was drinking outside her room with a cup in her hand! And it was just like that is real biased. How are you going to come to us and say "okay, well, you all need to do this and what are you doing?" and ask stupid questions when right down the hall somebody else is in violation too. We feel that if we have a party, if anything goes wrong, we'll be the first to get shut down, whereas if it's a frat party or a party on such and such street it won't get shut down.

Jimmy states his experiences at the university:

They have been mostly positive. Maybe some of the experiences have helped me and that is positive. Most of the bad stuff has happened with the police department. One incident happened when I was a freshman. My friends, all Black, and me were walking down the street and we were walking back from a party and it was around maybe 2 o'clock in the morning. And we were looking for a place to eat. And we were the only group, pretty much the only group of Black people downtown at that time and there was a whole bunch of White people around, I mean just a whole bunch of White people. And it so happened that a fight had just broken out and it had just ended while we were walking down and so the police were trying to clear everybody out. And the two or three, I don't know how many there were, but they started following us and the groups of White kids they were just standing there just on the corner doing nothing, just watching. And the cops did nothing to them. But they started following us and were like "alright, everybody move along." And we were like "alright." So we start walking. And we notice that they were following us down the street. And they were passing all the groups of White kids just standing on the corner watching. And they started putting on their gloves and stuff and then like touching on their billy clubs and holding it and stuff and they followed us for like a block. They were intimidating. I guess growing up in a city I should have experienced stuff like that, and I have, but it has never been that direct.

These accounts highlight the sentiments Black students felt about university policy and procedure as well as activity engaged in by campus police. African American students felt that bias embedded within the social structure of the university system itself shapes who can drink without penalty. Related to both social space and institutional bias are issues of race-based privilege. In the next section, privilege is defined and discussed in terms of drinking behavior.

Privilege

In this section, the definition of privilege entails the freedom from being singled out and tokenized as a representative of a specific "race." African Americans report not having the privilege to be free from constant race-based evaluation. Black students face the constant risk of adding to existing stereotypes, should they "slip up." White students do not carry the burden of having to represent their race because they do not stand out in White social space. Black students report feeling that they do not have the privilege of blending in. The following accounts illustrate the pressures some Black students report experiencing as they relate to alcohol use in the White social space of college existence. Michael states, for instance,

> Um, Black people at University X, we are out of our element. A group of Black kids is going to catch your eye a little bit more, you know? They are going to grab more attention than a group of White guys. You know that happens everywhere. I try not to be out there in public view where people can see. All that does is create more stereotypes like, all Black people, all they do is drink and get drunk. Yeah, I drink and I might get drunk, but they really don't know you (they only know your color). They are going off the fact that I am Black and I am drunk and that becomes the whole opinion of you. When I do go out to a club or something like that I definitely try not to get drunk. You know what I mean and if I do drink, I really don't come out or anything like that 'cause people, I don't even want to give them a chance to make a stereotype about me. If I am out there all drunk, then they will say "all those Black people, they are always drunk. All they do is this and that."

Robert:	Being watched, does that keep you from getting in trouble with drinking?
Michael:	I guess it does, but to have to be on your toes like that all the time? I shouldn't have to be on my toes like that all the time. It's crazy that I have to; it's not a good thing but it is a good thing. It's crazy, but that is the way it is. The fact that we have to stay on our toes keeps us out of trouble, but you know I would rather just do what I want to do and not have to worry about all that. Yeah, I would like to be able to do that. Is it possible? No, it is not.
Seth:	A bunch of Black guys walking, stumbling, they would be picked up right away. They are automatically assumed to be guilty of something. They are guilty before being proven innocent.
Robert:	Have you ever had any run-ins?
Seth:	No, not me. Cause when I go out in public I am usually with my White friends. When I am with my Black friends, we are in the safety and privacy of our own room. Away from like, you know. As far away as possible. So we are nowhere to be found.

Robert: So is this on purpose because . . .?

Seth: It's racism. Open blatantly racism. Who looks like the criminal? Who looks like the criminal to public safety and to the officers?

Robert: Story of officers following a group of Black guys—the cops were intimidating the . . .

Seth: Yeah, well, the police are intimidated. It is not just because, uh, the police are trying to be intimidating. They are intimidated themselves. "Which one of these, which one of these *brothas* gotta gun on 'em? Which one of these gang members have a gun or are carrying a nine and are gonna blow up something?" That's what the police are thinking. I'm just, I'm just like one of the White kids they saw but I have color so.

African American students suggest the social arrangements and drinking discussed here are a form of White privilege. Their conclusions about how these social relationships stem from privilege lead me to believe that this privilege is part of the foundation upon which domination rests. The privilege to drink openly and to be praised for this behavior works to inform the social audience who is privileged and who is not. Take the following accounts that reveal the frustration felt by African American students:

Michael: I think the White fraternities might drink a whole lot more than, like, Black just, like, from a stereotype. And from what I see, just passing by their houses, when they are having a party you see them doing it. Hanging out of the balconies or whatever. My whole theory is every body drinks. White, Black, purple. If you are going to drink it doesn't matter. Just some are allowed to and others are not.

Adrian: The football house is a house where all the football players live. It's a one-story house and nothing but football players live there. If one football player moves out, another moves in. It's known as the football house. And they have parties there; they are wild crazy fun. The ideal football party, there it is. All the stereotypes you think of it, that's it.

Robert: What is the race mix?

Adrian: [The majority are White.] Even most of the Black football players don't normally go but you might see a few scattered here and there. You know. But, um, like a lot of Black students that I know just Black students don't drink as much alcohol as White students do.

Christy, a White female college student, in the following statement reveals how a formal agent of social control undermined her sense of privilege. Her privilege to drink was interrupted and this angered her even though her behavior was clearly illegal. Christy angrily remembers:

That got me so mad, you have no idea. The cop, ugh, I have so many letters to write. Like pissed off letters to write, and this is one of them. He pulled me out of a group. I was in a group of four girls and a guy; he came up to me and asked me for ID and at first I gave him, I feel like an idiot now but I gave him, I told him the wrong name. I told the wrong name. A friend of mine did that once and the cop let her go. He wrote it down and let her go.

Robert: Was this at a party or . . .

Christy: This was at homecoming! This is *homecoming* with ice shots and kegs and cans and people throwing beer at each other on the field and he comes up to me and I was standing there like, and so I gave him the wrong name and I think that pissed him off! And he was like, "Christy, Christy, Christy, why are you lying to me?" I got defensive and he got the CB and he was like "we have a scared one here." I asked the dean, and she said that if a woman cop is not around, they would do a pat down. And he did that to me. I guess it is procedure and all, but he did that to me. He kept me there for like twenty minutes. I felt like violated. It was creepy.

Interestingly, most White students were oblivious to the presence of Black students, their functions, and their impact on university life. One White student, when asking about Black activity, responded in jest by saying "You mean there are Black students on campus?" White students did not discuss Black activity. White students did not readily understand the concept of "racialized space," whereas Black students openly discussed White and Black space issues. In other words, Black students were well aware of the social dynamics of racial segregation on campus. In and of themselves, White obliviousness and ignorance are indicative of White privilege (see McIntosh for discussion, 1993). White privilege is to not have to face or understand issues surrounding race, race relations, or racial inequality. Their world is one that is self-contained and protected and rarely penetrated by difference. This life experience is radically different from the life experience of Black students who must learn to work at adapting to White communities while maintaining ties to their Black communities.

TOWARD A SOCIAL STRUCTURAL UNDERSTANDING OF COLLEGE DRINKING

Epidemiological research on alcohol use patterns has revealed interesting and puzzling differences by race (Johnson and colleagues 1998; Caetano 1997; Caetano and Clark 1998) while other literature identifies interesting correlates pertaining to these varying rates of use (Wallace and Bachman 1991). The social location of the college campus proves to be no exception (Wechsler and colleagues 1998). Examining social structural issues pertaining to college life reveals interesting social explanations for some of these differences. Research documents feelings of disconnection with "college life" for Black students at traditionally White universities. This research suggests that Black students do not have as strong a connection to or fondness for the lived "college experience" as White students do (Feagin and colleagues 1996). These data support such conclusions. In interviewing Black students about college alcohol use, feelings of alienation appear to stem from a disinterest in and, for some, an altogether avoidance of the college drinking culture.

Literature suggests that Black students do not have as strong a bond with "college life" compared to White students (Feagin et al. 1996; Smith et al. 2000). Thus, Black students do not necessarily identify with college drinking cultures as they might identify with their culture of origin. This is because African American students do not necessarily feel welcomed, nor are they necessarily interested in assimilating into White college culture. Because African American students do not always identify with the White campus and therefore are not as apt to consider the university "home," Blacks may look to their Black friends and families as sites of connection, social reference, and leisure time.

Talking to Black students at length about their experiences with college drinking flowed into discussions about segregation, discrimination, discomfort, and isolation. These factors were not taken into consideration at the beginning of the study. This technique allowed for important and often overlooked themes about race relations and their impact on drinking behavior to emerge. The empirical evidence presented here documents how drinking cultures operate within social space and how social space in turn shapes behavior. Some students may or may not find the social space they occupy comfortable or compatible with their own social locations as Black men or women. The degree of comfort appears to have an effect on decisions to participate in drinking cultures.

In the data that are presented in this chapter, African American students describe discrimination, stereotyping, and prejudice in a social landscape that is supposed to be enlightened. The present research supports Feagin's et al. (1996) findings suggesting the traditional university campus is primarily White space where African Americans continue to face subtle and overtly racist ideology. In the accounts presented here, I illuminate how cultural, social, and political aspects of the campus environment revolve around Whiteness leaving little "space" for Blacks to openly socialize.

The formal institution of the university and the various social organizations associated with it control much of student social space and hence leisure activity. Nevertheless, informal aspects of social control prove to be quite influential in establishing and maintaining drinking norms regardless of formal laws and sanctions. The questions of who can drink openly; whose drinking is closely monitored; whose alcohol-related behavior is overlooked, pardoned, or praised; and whose drinking is stigmatized and by whom, have a profound influence on the extent and manner in which college students use alcohol. Thus, both formal and informal social control mechanisms intrinsic to the college institution shape the social processes of alcohol use and hence the drinking patterns reported in the literature.

Drinking cultures are exemplary of more than leisure-seeking behavior because drinking behavior is highly meaningful (West 2001). Indeed, based on these data, it appears drinking cultures help to form, shape, and maintain social hierarchies. On campus, it is those in privileged spaces and of privileged races that can drink openly, who can use alcohol to construct legitimate identities, and who can use alcohol to perform behavior that would otherwise be considered destructive.[1] Black students readily recognize the informal and formal social structural barriers that are imposed upon them. Black students talk about the barriers that curtail their drinking behavior and recognize at the same time the freedom with which White students drink and how they are enabled to drink by the university itself.

A deeper analysis of drinking behavior by race reveals how the reproduction of perceived social hierarchy is inextricably connected to drinking cultures arising from established social arrangements. Behaviors associated with drinking, such as vandalism and aggression, work to establish systems of domination on campus through fear. Thus, not only can we see how Whites and Blacks drink differently, we can also see how alcohol-related consequences contribute to establishing and maintaining social hierarchies. Social hierarchies are formally institutionalized by social structures, but it is in everyday interactions that hierarchies manifest themselves; it is in everyday action where hierarchies materialize. Open drinking behavior becomes a privilege.

Kantor (1977) states that "tokens" can never really be seen as they are and thus find themselves in a constant fight against stereotypes. "Role encapsulation" occurs when "token minorities" become encapsulated in limited roles. These roles may allow for security of place; however, they constrain minorities to specific areas of "permissible or rewarded" action. Because tokens are apt to receive attention due to their difference, their visibility creates what Kantor calls "performance pressures." This means minorities feel pressure to behave in a model fashion. Black students here assert that heavy or sloppy drinking would undermine attempts to rise above negative stereotypes, thus supporting Kantor's concept of role encapsulation.

Perhaps White students, as a result of their privilege, can move easily between the social worlds of family life and college drinking life. They can perhaps more easily adapt to both social locations because of fundamental familiarity and connection to the dominant structure. Students easily identify with students who are like themselves in terms of race, education, interests, and aspirations (Feagin et al. 1996). When drinking cultures are already in place before White students arrive on campus, White students may thus easily identify with White space and hence the drinking culture that is associated with this space.

Research in the future should examine these questions and more. It may prove worthwhile to examine if and how alcohol is used to perform or "do" gender within different social institutions (see West 2001). Future studies should also explore how quantity and frequency measures of alcohol use, for example, might be important markers of masculinity for youth in certain social contexts. It would be useful to document the different ways alcohol is used to express, construct, and perhaps deconstruct established gender roles. The effects of race, sexuality, and class on the meaning of alcohol-related violence is also in need of research (see Bachman and Peralta 2002; Cruz and Peralta 2001). Studies should address the issue of gender construction by using in-depth research techniques of qualitative methodology to better uncover the gender-laden meanings of alcohol use for students and nonstudents alike.

In conclusion, I interpret the social factors discussed earlier as collectively having an effect on Black student drinking. Blacks in this study were concerned with how they were perceived as individuals in a society they believe to be steeped in stereotypical images and beliefs about persons of their race. Black students report actively avoiding dishonoring their "race" by not participating in potentially stigmatizing behavior. Black students in this study did not necessarily feel welcomed, nor were they necessarily interested in attempting to assimilate into White space. Black students spoke of how college space is primarily White space and how drinking is a part of this White landscape. These are spaces in which Black students do not necessarily feel accepted, welcomed, or comfortable. The open and public use of alcohol by White students may maintain social space as White space, and hence contribute to the reproduction of racial differences in drinking cultures. Finally, these conditions possibly work to separate Black students from the dominant college culture. In sum, these social conditions may be playing a role in maintaining racial segregation on campus, thus producing disparate drinking cultures.

ACKNOWLEDGMENTS

I would like to thank Drs. Cynthia Robbins, Margaret L. Andersen, Ronet Bachman, Michelle Meloy, and J. M. Cruz for their comments and suggestions. I would like to thank Tricia Wachtendorf for data collection assistance, comments, and suggestions. Finally, I wish to thank the

American Sociological Association's Minority Fellowship Program and the Department of Sociology and Criminal Justice at the University of Delaware for assistance in funding this research.

NOTE

1. Of course, this works in multidirectional ways. Gays and lesbians are privileged within the "gay space" provided by the gay bar and heterosexuals are not. White individuals are the "guests" when they are in predominantly "Black space." Certain behaviors and expressions are forbidden depending upon one's identity status and the social space they find themselves in.

REFERENCES

BACHMAN, R., and R. L. PERALTA. 2002. The relationship between alcohol and violence in an adolescent population: Does gender matter? *Deviant Behavior* 23(1):1–19.

CAETANO, R. 1997. Prevalence, incidence and stability of drinking problems among Whites, Blacks and Hispanics: 1984–1992. *Journal of Studies on Alcohol* 58(6):565–73.

CAETANO, R., and C. L. CLARK. 1998. Trends in alcohol consumption patterns among Whites, Blacks, and Hispanics: 1984–1995. *Journal of Studies on Alcohol* 59:659–68.

CRUZ, J. M., and R. L. PERALTA. 2001. Family violence and substance use: The perceived effects of substance use within gay male relationships. *Violence and Victims* 16(2):161–72.

FEAGIN, J. R., V. HERNAN, and N. O. IMANI. 1996. *The agony of education: Black students at a White university.* London: Routledge.

HERD, A. D. 1997. Sex ratios of drinking patterns and problems among Blacks and Whites: Results from a national survey. *Journal of Studies on Alcohol* 58(1):75–82.

JOHNSON, F. W., P. J. GRUENEWALD, A. J. TRENO, and G. ARMSTRONG-TAFF. 1998. Drinking over the life course within gender and ethnic groups: A hyperparametric analysis. *Journal of Studies on Alcohol* 59(5):568–81.

JONES-WEBB, R. 1998. Drinking patterns and problems among African Americans: Recent findings. *Alcohol Health and Research World* 22(4):260–65.

JONES-WEBB, R., C. Y. HSIAO, P. HANNAN, and R. CAETANO. 1997. Predictors of increases in alcohol-related problems among Black and White adults: Results from the 1984 and 1992 National Alcohol Surveys. *American Journal of Drug and Alcohol Abuse* 23(2):281–299.

KANTOR, R. M. 1977. *Men and women of the corporation.* Boston: HarperCollins Publishers.

LINCOLN, Y. S., and E. G. GUBA. 1985. *Naturalistic inquiry.* Newbury Park, London: Sage Publications.

MCINTOSH, P. (1993)[1989]. White privilege: Unpacking the invisible knapsack. In *Experiencing race, class, and gender in the United States,* ed. V. Cyrus. Mountain View, CA: Mayfield Publishers.

O'MALLEY, P. M., L. D. JOHNSTON, and J. G. BACHMAN. 1998. Alcohol use among adolescents. *Alcohol Health & Research World* 22(2):85–94.

PERALTA, R. L. In press. Alcohol use and the fear of weight gain in college: Reconciling two social norms. *Gender Issues,* forthcoming.

PITTMAN, D. J., and H. R. WHITE, Eds. 1991. *Society, culture, and drinking patterns reexamined.* New Brunswick, NJ: Rutgers Center of Alcohol Studies.

PORTER, J. R., and R. E. Washington. 1993. Minority identity and self-esteem. *Annual Review of Sociology* 19:139–62.

PRESLEY, C. A., J. S. LEICHLITER, and P. W. MEILMAN. 1998. *Alcohol and drugs on American campuses: A report to college presidents, third in a series 1995, 1996, and 1997.* Published by the Core Institute, Southern Illinois University, Carbondale.

Smith, S. S., and Mignon R. Moore. 2000. Intraracial diversity and relations among African Americans: Closeness among Black students at a predominantly White university. *The American Journal of Sociology* 106:1–29.

Sudman, S., and N. M. Bradburn. 1982. *Asking questions: A practical guide to questionnaire design.* San Franscico: Jossey-Bass.

Wallace, J. M., and J. G. Bachman. 1991. Explaining racial/ethnic differences in adolescent drug use: The impact of background and lifestyle. *Social Problems* 38(3):333–37.

Wechsler, H., T. Nelson, and E. Weiztman. 1996. From knowledge to action: How Harvard's College Alcohol Study can help your campus design a campaign against student alcohol abuse. *Change* 32(1):38–43.

Wechsler, H., G. W. Dowdall, G. Maenner, J. Gledhill-Hoyt, and H. Lee. 1998. Changes in binge drinking and related problems among American college students between 1993 and 1997. *Journal of American College Health* 47(2):57–68.

Wechsler, H., B. E. Molnar, A. E. Davenport, and J. S. Baer. 1999. College alcohol use: A full or empty glass? *Journal of American College Health* 47(6):247–252.

West, L. A. 2001. Negotiating masculinities in American drinking subcultures. *The Journal of Men's Studies* 9(3):371–92.

10

Fantasy Island

An Ethnography of Alcohol and Gender Roles in a Latino Gay Bar

Carlos F. Cáceres and Jorge I. Cortiñas

INTRODUCTION

Although studies on sexuality in cultures of Latin-American/southern European origin are not numerous, it is widely accepted in current literature that the construction and discourse on sexuality in these cultures are different from those of Anglo-Saxon contexts in diverse regards (Parker 1991; Gilmore 1990; Brandes 1980). On one side, urban-popular discourses with a rigid gender-role segregation and a tension between good and bad women (that is, women suitable for marriage and women suitable for entertainment/pleasure, in both cases from a male's perspective), and, on the other side, official discourses showing a heavy influence from the teachings and dogmas of the Roman Catholic Church (which privilege premarital abstinence and marital monogamy) seem to be part of these sexual universes. The "moral conservativeness" of the latter, however, is said to be subsumed in the former's mandate of a role separation that demands chastity from women and imposes rites of passage to adult masculinity on men, in what has been called a double moral standard. A high degree of normative homophobia is also assumed, although the widespread practice of transvestism among some homosexually active men, as well as the high frequency of bisexual behavior, suggest that homosexuality is also constructed differently.

Adapted from "Fantasy Island: An Ethnography of Alcohol and Gender Roles in a Latino Gay Bar," by Carlos F. Cáceres and Jorge I. Cortiñas, *Journal of Drug Issues,* vol. 26(1), pp. 345, 1996. Copyright 1996 by *Journal of Drug Issues.* Adapted by permission.

The emergence of the AIDS epidemic during the last decade has shown a need to better understand the way in which different cultures police sexuality. The flexibility of cultural views about certain bisexual behaviors, for which men do not label themselves as "gay" or "bisexual," is being used to explain a shift in epidemiological patterns of HIV infection in Latin America (i.e., from a pattern predominantly affecting homosexual men to another with increasing involvement of women) (Pan American Health Organization 1993).

These features might be present as well among the different communities constituted as a result of immigration from Latin America during this century in several urban centers in the United States. Interestingly, Latino communities in the United States have experienced—and continue to experience—a disproportionate share of the AIDS burden, a phenomenon that is much more evident among women (The Panos Institute 1990). Although these communities are far from being homogeneous (on the basis of factors such as country and social class of origin of their members, time of arrival and generation-related issues, skin color and acculturation, social support, and resources), such diversity may be analyzed to develop a characterization of communities that offers operational utility. Nevertheless, the importance of a shared language and some major cultural features may determine commonalities that present social implications of several kinds.

This study was held in a geographical area where the numerous existing Latino communities, largely formed by immigrants from rural provinces of northern Mexico and, recently, from El Salvador (though with members from all other Latin-American countries) at first glance seem fairly religious and "traditional." At the same time, this area hosts one of the largest and best organized gay communities in the United States. Consequently, the emergence of a Latino immigrant culture in an area where the dominating gay culture holds significant power offers a special opportunity to explore an evolving social construction of sexuality among Latinos. The phenomenon of *transvestism,* and the social settings where it is expressed, may offer a key to a better understanding of parts of the cultural context of sexuality in this migrant community.

This report is focused on the roles of gender and alcohol use in the dynamics of a setting where several dimensions of relative marginality coalesce and construct a "hidden population," and where issues of HIV/STD prevention are consequently relevant. A qualitative study of social interaction took place at a Latino bar with transvestites (also called "vestidas," "*travesties,*" or, in the Anglo gay culture, "drag queens") in a centric area of the traditional Latino neighborhood (now increasingly gentrified) of a large urban area in the United States. Bars constitute a key reference point for important portions of the population in several communities, as they offer diverse options for the use of leisure time, and provide opportunities for socialization. Moreover, in Latino contexts, their social role holds a better profile than the one of their counterparts in Anglo contexts, where official discourses on alcohol consumption have become heavily medicalized. This particular bar, peculiar due to the centrality of transvestites, represents a unique setting where valuable insights can be obtained on the ways in which sexuality, homosexuality, bisexuality, and gender are understood among Latinos.

Finally it must be recalled that, due to the convergence of multiple marginalities (i.e., immigrant status, homosexuality, a bar with erotic meanings), the bar's clientele constitutes, in many ways, a truly hidden population in a North-American context. Better representations of this world will permit the development of sensitive social action programs that, particularly in the area of AIDS prevention, incorporate the subjects' perceptions of their world and their problems, as well as the potential solutions they foresee.

METHODS

A qualitative research approach based on ethnographic methods (see Glaser and Strauss [1967] on "Grounded Theory," for example) was used. Grounded Theory states that useful interpretations of the social reality may be developed from the detailed description of observations, its analysis to "discover" meaningful theoretical categories, and further elaboration over such categories in the direction of constructing a substantive theory which provides a valid interpretation of this social reality and forms the basis for its generalizability in other settings.

The convergence of multiple social stigmas construct the bar's clientele as a hidden population. The difficulties of access to it make a qualitative approach especially suitable, to the extent that probabilistic sampling is impossible and survey techniques imply a fair amount of knowledge of the target population's social universe which is not available in this case. Qualitative methodology will provide a strong basis for the understanding of a set of meanings, norms and values that are, indeed, constituting a subculture.

Three methods were employed:

(1) Participant Observation

The authors, fluent in both English and Spanish, accomplished participant observation during approximately weekly visits to the research setting between September and December 1992, usually on weekends for at least 1 hour between 9 p.m. and midnight. Approximately two-thirds of the authors' visits were done individually, while the others were done as a team. The authors repeatedly engaged in conversations with the patrons and the bartender, and introduced themselves as researchers who were doing a study on the bar life. Field notes were prepared for each visit, for further analysis.

(2) In-Depth Interviews

Four in-depth interviews with key informants were carried out in this study. Interviewees included a former dancer and current patron, a *travesti* performer, a postoperated transexual performer, and the bar owners. Interview guides with open-ended questions were used, and sessions were audiotaped with the interviewees consent. Subjects covered included the history of the bar, its current atmosphere, its clientele, the role of alcohol, the role of the show, and the interviewee's feelings and expectations regarding this social world.

(3) Historical Data

Historical data on the bar was obtained through some documents provided by the bar's owners.

Information gathered through the three methods was analyzed for the determination of theoretical categories, which further permitted the elaboration of a comprehensive representation of the bar's world. Due to time and budget constraints, this study was accomplished as a pilot exploration of a very complex social setting which might provide us and others with new information to be used in more specific approaches that employ qualitative and possibly quantitative techniques in the future.

THEORETICAL BACKGROUND

Gender and Sexuality

From a social constructionist perspective, gender and sexuality may be said to constitute two culturally elaborated structures that impose a value hierarchy on the array of possibilities of social diversity (Parker 1991). The two of them intersect in the domain of sexual gender roles. However, a culturally specific hegemonic gender structure provides a fundamental framework for the organization of social life regarding norms, meanings, and expectations connected to being a man or being a woman in all imaginable terrains, including economic activities, relationship to the family and other social institutions, power expectations, and social interaction in general. It manifests through what could be called hegemonic models of masculinity and femininity. This hegemonic gender structure, which itself evolves across time, is constantly challenged by alternative discourses on masculinity and femininity, which in fact determine its change over time. In many dimensions, the traditional gender structure is said to establish a more rigid role separation between males and females in societies of Iberic/southern European origin, such as those in Latin America (Gilmore 1990). In the traditional gender script in these societies, the main tensions around the fulfillment of normative masculinities refer to the dichotomy "hombre"/"maricón" ("man"/"faggot"). Men's masculinity must be proved through certain rites of initiation and constantly demonstrated through certain displays of seductive-erotic abilities, the capacity to fight, physical strength, and rudeness. Women's gender, on the contrary, is a natural attribute with no need of proof. The fundamental tension among women gravitates between "propriety" or "decency" (which constitutes a requisite for women's suitability for marriage and implies virginity and limited sexual interests) and the lack thereof, which corresponds to "bad girls" with whom men are supposed to display their manhood and cultivate precious sexual expertise, without ever thinking of marrying them. Although much of these traditional gender roles is rapidly changing, particularly in urban areas and among the upper and middle classes (due to the resocialization elicited by the media), the traditional discourses retain some of their influence and power, particularly among the current parental generations.

The structure of sexuality imposes a value hierarchy on the innumerable possibilities of sexual activities. The Judeo-Christian tradition is said to bestow the highest value upon penetrative, noncommercial, vaginal sex with reproductive intentions in the context of a monogamous, heterosexual, legally sanctioned union, and to impose a marginal flavor on, say, activities that combine several negatively valued attributes (such as commercial sex, anal penetration, "promiscuity," same-sex partners, lack of a legal union, lack of reproductive intentions). At the same time, however, at the level of desire, a parallel scale of attribution of erotic value may be said to exist, which tends to privilege activities and scenarios that from a moral perspective are clearly disdained (Parker 1991).

Male-to-female *travestism* is a rather frequent phenomenon among a fraction of homosexually active men in Latin-American urban cultures, particularly among the popular classes. In the traditional hegemonic view of homosexuality in these settings, the *travesti*, as the most public of homosexual characters, signified the generic homosexual. *Travestism* is mostly lived as a transgender lifestyle where men are resocialized into a mock femininity (manifested in cross-dressing, making-up, and patterns of socially sanctioned gender-specific behavior). *Travesties* are usually accepted in their communities as typical performers of certain economic activities (i.e., hairdressers, cooks, dancers, and also prostitutes) and in many cases as agents of sexual initiation of adolescents or as people who pay hegemonic "men" for sex, either occasionally or on a continuous basis (thus becoming a source of income for their male partners). In the gender structure, *travesties* are pseudofemales that essentially qualify as "loose girls." If there is such a thing as the traditional Latin-American sexuality structure, we could say it values sex between "men" and "*travesties*" as morally bad (although far less bad than officially "homosexual" sex, as *travesties* are pseudofemales); moreover, due to the ambiguity between moral and erotic dimensions of values mentioned above, it may be highly arousing for many men. Lay constructions of *travestism* are a mix of both essentialist views (i.e., often people explain *travestism* as the result of nature's mistakes: "The rebellion of a truly female soul oppressed within a male body"), and "constructionist" ideas (i.e., the "contagiousness" of transgender conditions and the risks they pose to "men" who socialize with *travesties* for too long without keeping a reasonable distance) (Epstein 1987).

Travesties have traditionally represented all homosexually active men in the public's mentality, although their acceptability in the middle and upper classes was always much lower than in the popular sectors. The reproduction of *travesti* socialization patterns in those sectors may be related to the lower degree of privacy surrounding people's sexual experiences (particularly those of adolescence), and it can be hypothesized that boys known to have had (usually coercive) sex with an older man in a passive role are easily pressed by others to share a social space with *travesties*. *Travestism* was constructed as the "necessary pathway" of men who had "failed to protect their manhood." Conversely, the higher degree of privacy of sexual activities among men in the middle and upper classes permits the construction of closeted patterns of homosexual experience, much closer to those of pre-Stonewall North America. An easy mistake, however, is to assume that this structural enforcement of the adoption of a transgender lifestyle among working class homosexual men radically denies cross-dressers both their subjectivity and, most crucially, their agency. It is inconsistent with the active political role *travesties* on stage and off play in many social settings in Latin America. Gloria Anzaldúa adopts a self-conscious posture of analysis that we think would be useful here. She insists that the preceding accounts, with their naturalized unquestioned and assigned dichotomy of male/female are the real problem. Stating a new, transgender identity, she writes:

> There is something compelling about both male and female, about having an entry into both worlds. Contrary to some psychiatric tenants, halves and halves are not suffering from a confusion of gender. What we are suffering from is an absolute despot duality that says we are able to be only one or the other. It claims that human nature is limited and can not evolve into something better. But I, like other queer people, am two in one body, both male and female. I am the embodiment of the *hetero gamos:* the coming together of opposite qualities within. (Anzaldúa 1987)

Leisure Time, Alcohol, and the Bar

A second cluster of issues to be considered as a prolegomenon to our discussion includes, in the first place, leisure time. In a civilization process that organized social life in the industrial settings of modernity, new norms and boundaries were essential in the transformation of lifestyles. The alienating labor regimes that characterized the emergence of capitalism and its social classes preserved leisure modalities and possibilities. Leisure was, after all, the time where life is enjoyed, the justification of people's efforts to survive on earth. Its modalities and possibilities varied not only with time, culture, and social class, but across other dimensions of diversity among people. Leisure strategies—valued upon the basis of socially constructed meanings—implied the social sanction of spaces, times, and contexts.

Now, many of these strategies were—and continue to be—built in the intersection of tensions such as those between the proper and the improper, the beautiful and the grotesque, the erotically arousing, and the disgusting. They define transgressive spaces (i.e., adult theaters, bars, brothels), times (i.e., Carnival, Halloween, Saturday nights) and characters (i.e., the prostitute, the erotic dancer, the drag queen) from whose marginality their leisure/pleasure potential is derived.

Bars are particularly important in this regard, despite significant differences in the ways such spaces are constructed cross-culturally (i.e., in relation to alcoholic content of drinks used, acceptable patterns of drinking in the bar and elsewhere, degrees of marginality of the bar, and its culture). In many Latin-American working class settings, as opposed to mainstream North American Anglo culture, drinking together continues to be not only acceptable but often encouraged among groups of people during leisure time, regardless of gender and age (although acceptable patterns vary upon their basis). As medicalization of alcohol consumption is also limited, the official prevalence of the social syndrome of alcoholism is probably lower than expectable from the patterns of consumption. On the contrary, liberal social drinking rests on the construction of alcohol use as an almost ritualistic necessity if people are to *have a good time*. As a disinhibitor it is supposed to bring joy and relaxation to social gatherings (McKirnan and Peterson 1989). This is not to say, however, that individual and social problems do not arise from alcohol use; the utility of Western biomedical categories to define and address them in this culture must, nevertheless, be analyzed.

Bars usually combine alcohol availability with that of other sorts of socially transgressive entertainment, namely gambling, erotic dancing, and both commercial and noncommercial casual sex. In consequence, they embody somewhat marginal leisure spaces where marginality is not necessarily due to alcohol consumption. This framework is to help us undertake the analysis of field data from a bar that combines the aforementioned features with tensions around gender and sexual transgression, and also around migration and culture. Regarding gender and sexuality, issues related to gay people's vulnerability to heavy drinking—explained due to expectations of intoxication as a tension reducer in a homophobic society, as well as due to the centrality of bars in the gay leisure culture—will have to be considered (Hall 1992; Tori 1989; Stall and Willey 1988). This implies a consideration of how "gay" the bar studied is, as well as a further problematization of drinking patterns among gays as evidence of a particular "vulnerability." Regarding migration and culture, issues to be considered include acculturation processes and the conflicts between fairly different constructions of homosexuality.

THE SETTING

The Bar's Story

In the early eighties, an unmarried heterosexual couple of business and life partners purchased an old coffee shop from its Anglo lesbian owners in the traditional Latino district of a large urban area in the United States. They served a steady but small lunchtime crew of heterosexual Latino men, but at night the place was nearly empty. After about a year and a half, a few Latino gay patrons began to frequent the bar. The owners treated them the way they treated all their customers, with attention and warmth, so they came back, with their friends. Little by little their numbers grew until "they had thrown out the straight people and were here to stay." Unwittingly, they had become heterosexual owners of a gay bar. The owners welcomed the sales that came with increased patronage and were pleased by what they saw as the better behaved and politer gay Latinos. To solidify their new consumer base, they began to host drag shows and beauty contests which were performed on a slab of wood laid out across the pool table. The heterosexual bartenders were replaced with gay ones. The crowd, younger than it is now, reacted enthusiastically. Soon the bar's tiny dimensions proved too small for the growing crowds, and in the mid-eighties the owners moved into a larger space in the surroundings. In this new locale, the bar continued to grow with expanded capacity and a proper stage for its performers, and began to attract Anglo patrons, who today constitute about 20% of the clientele. Though many of them may not understand the lyrics or how to dance a cumbia, they seem to enjoy themselves immensely. The announcements continue to be entirely in Spanish, and the music overwhelmingly so. The bar's reputation for safety has also been earned with constant vigilance from the owners and even the consuetudinary family occasionally attends its popular shows.

Despite their never having been married, the owners are often affectionately referred to as man and wife by many patrons. Over the years, the owners and the patrons grew quite fond of each other. Then the AIDS epidemic hit; patrons and performers began to get sick and die of what at first people thought was just a disease of white gay men. The owners visited people in the hospital, brought them meals, and held benefits to cover medical costs. The first local meetings and fundraisers held in response to the AIDS crisis among Latino gay men took place at the bar, long before government funding was available to meet their practical support and prevention needs.

The Current Social Setting: Activities, Patrons

Entertainment activities explicitly available at the bar include drinking, dancing (in a small space), listening to the music, talking, and watching TV (although the music volume is usually too loud for TV listening or relaxed conversation to be possible), playing pool or pinball, or watching the shows (i.e., a dancing/lip-syncing show by drag queens on Fridays and Saturdays at 11 p.m., or a male strip-tease show on Thursdays and Sundays). Besides these overt activities, other covert practices in the bar include: meeting potential sexual partners; some level of mild sexual contact (e.g., touching the buttocks or breast) during the tipping of performers or even while dancing or conversing.

Roughly, six kinds of people may be found among the bar's clients: (1) The drag queens (*travesties*) who, besides performing, attend as patrons. Not only are they very well accepted by all other patrons, but indeed their presence stands for the distinctive feature of the bar. Virtually adored, drag queens seem to be at the center of all social interactions on the busy nights. (2) Traditional, nongay-identified Latino men, many of whom are married or united to women, and behaviorally heterosexual or bisexual; they usually drink significant volumes of alcohol, meet friends, get invited drinks from other men, and flatter/dance with drag queens. They can be characterized as "machos latinos" (Caceres 1994). (3) Gay-identified Latino men, who drink (lesser amounts), dance, meet friends, and meet potential sexual partners. (4) Gay-identified Anglo men, who drink (lesser amounts), observe, look for sexual partners (i.e., people usually meeting the stereotype of Latino men, either gay or straight), and occasionally meet friends. (5) Latina lesbians, who watch the show, drink, and dance. (6) Finally, heterosexual Latino couple, who occasionally attend to drink, play pool, or talk. The latter two are clearly minoritarian groups, though they become easily integrated if present.

A Fantasy Island

"Fantasy Island" identifies a popular American TV show of the seventies, where the screenplay's version of magic realism portrayed the ritual materialization of the fantasies of people attending a fabulous resort. Though their wishes came true, visitors learned there was a price to pay. The metaphor of a *fantasy island* has already been used to describe the social meaning of bars. In many senses, the image works for our bar. For most of the patrons, the bar works as a social space where their "normal" sense of reality is suspended and a different set of rules comes into play. Albeit modest, the bar's decoration provides an unmistakable flavor of a perennial party. It is, indeed, the decoration we could find in the taverns of many small Mexican towns. Nationalist symbols and other pieces of mestizo pop art create an atmosphere that people find homey and friendly.

Traditional male migrants, usually married or united to women, find in the bar an environment where alcohol, "girls," and music are available, and where an occasional free drink can be obtained from gay patrons. As mentioned, "girls" in this case pertain to the sexual domain of the morally inappropriate yet erotically valued. *Travesti* femininity is constructed as the "wildest" of all, as one holding the most aggressive (that is, paradoxically, the most "masculine") attitude towards sex among feminine characters. As one patron put it, " . . . they want d__k" [" . . . quieren verga"] (field notes).

For gay-identified Latino men (not *travestied*), the bar may be experienced as a place at the same time gay and Latino, a wonderland where the essence of their two specificities (i.e., belongingness in a gay culture and in a Latino culture at the same time) are cared for. For gay Latinos still in the closet (usually younger and living with their families), as any other setting that might be considered part of a gay ghetto in the city, the bar may provide the opportunity to safely "liberate," one or two nights a week, what they probably see as a painfully "repressed" sexual identity.

The motivations of Caucasian gay patrons are probably different. They tend to have been somehow exposed to the Latino migrant culture before (through friends or lovers or at work), and to be fond of it, to seek interaction with a community they may find warmer, simpler, or just picturesque. Besides this, the myth of the Latin lover (hypersensual, exotic, "macho"), not exempt of a racist, colonialist appeal of sexual subjugation of (or subjugation by) individuals felt to be generally inferior, may be said to operate here.

If there is, however, a constituency for which the bar represents a *total* experience, it is that of *travesties*. The bar provides a public which not only does not punish, but celebrates their transgression of conventional gender roles. The setting, consequently, becomes a temple where an experience that is already perceived as highly self-actualizing and self-valuing by drag queens ("letting out the woman I have inside") is sanctified; an alternative world where they are at the center of everyone's attention. They are, indeed, what makes this bar special, in the best of the senses. The price for their fantasy (usually that of being "the best, the most beautiful, the most adored") is, however, high: spontaneity. Every single minute of their nights at the bar is a minute of performance. And it is not just performing "femininity": Depending on their moods, their publics', or the will to define a personal "style," they may perform a candid Dolores del Rio, a glamorous Maria Felix, or even a sensual, modern, outrageous Gloria Trevi. Of course, *travesties* are not the only ones who perform out of the stage—that is, act after the show—and other patrons negotiate their self-presentations and realities with similar ability depending on the public and their specific intentions.

A Home Away From Home: Safety

Another recurrent subject in the authors' formal and informal conversations with patrons was the image of the bar as a surrogate home. In this regard, there is a sense of a surrogate family among them. Indeed, for many of them, this "family" may be far more accepting and tolerant to difference than their biological family. To some extent, elements of care and respect that constitute the common sense norms of the place coalesce with referents of plain leisure and sexual flavor, resocializing people into a "new family," a family of choice that may fulfill some of their needs of emotional support in a nonjudgmental context. As this may be particularly important for Latinos who conserve much of their attachment to their biological families yet conceal their sexual orientation to them, the bar nurtures, relieves from guilt, and becomes an emotional shelter where the antihegemonic sexual mores not only refuse to automatically imply a flavor of darkness or perversion, but become an ideologic constituent of a new, positive, and valuable world. Patrons' practices that signify the feeling of a surrogate family include, for instance, complaints made to regulars about "having disappeared" while everybody "missed them," when in fact such absence might have been limited to a single weekend. Similarly, the disposition to protect each other from outsiders who transgress the norms of nonviolent, family-like interaction. Finally, this sense of family seems to be supported by the owners and has become evident in terms of solidarity with those affected by AIDS and concern for the prevention of this disease among these dear "relatives."

The relative safety the bar offers, as compared to other Latino bars, is a distinctive dimension of its identity that patrons highly appreciate. Social marginality and poverty that surround the lives of many rural Latin-American immigrants often become associated with violence and dependence on alcohol and/or other drugs. This bar, however, is seldom a violent place (field notes, November 28), and patrons of different groups do not feel at risk of being attacked. This feeling of safety and quietude is essential to the construction of the bar as both a fantasy island and a surrogate home. This is peculiar, given the volumes of alcohol consumed and the involvement of sensuality and seduction (and, inevitably, of competitions and jealousy). Patrons may, however, perceive and respect the norms and boundaries necessary to preserve the uniqueness of the bar.

GENDER TRANSGRESSION AND ALCOHOL USE IN A LEISURE SPACE

The Disruption and Dispersion of Gender

Recalling the quote of Anzaldúa (1987) cited above, crucial here is our abandonment of an analysis that treats cross-dressers as *faux* women, our rejection of the traditional tag of "female impersonator." After all, the point is never to look like an ordinary woman, the point is *never to pass. Travesties* at our bar are always dressed over the top, very showy, glamorous, and sexy. Certainly the audience never really believes, nor would they be interested if they were seeing a woman born woman lip syncing on stage (field notes, October 17).

In many ways, this identity constitutes the essence of the bar. The drag queens are, after all, the center of attention—the main attraction. As mediators of culture, their influence is enormous. If the containment strategies of dominant culture reveal an insistence that gender remain assigned and never elected, the disruption tactics of these *travesties* demonstrate their commitment to the opposite goal.

Increasingly, sociological treatments of gender as an investigative category have abandoned the traditional concern over freeing the subjugated universal woman form the universal man. Instead, the new focus is preoccupied with concerns over the assumptions of that very bifurcated, seemingly natural gender system. We have even moved beyond the simple critique of gender (that which is socially constructed) that left sex (the biological) as the sacrosanct purview of science. Even human bodies have become legitimate spheres of intervention, debate, and manipulation. This theoretical departure has mirrored, been influenced by, and contributed to parallel movements in contemporary feminist and lesbian/gay political praxis. Transgender political activity, prosex feminism, queer and antilesbian/gay theory, as well as women of color organizing, represent this trend. Anthropology has contributed by recounting the berdache of the Plain's Indians, the shaman of the Zuni, European hermaphrodites and others who refuse classification in two pronged gender systems.

In academia, Donna Haraway (1991) has emerged as the most articulate of this new breed of storytellers committed to radical, postmodern treatments of gender. Championing what she calls *cyborg feminism* she shows that biology is not just political science but becomes a legitimate target of intervention. The point is not to free our original selves from false consciousness, but to control pleasures, experiences, and powers in new ways. Strategic praxis is guided not by universals and metatheories but by an embracing of "permanently partial identities and contradictory stand points."

Examined in this light, the bar's suspension of gender becomes evident. Drag queens imitate women less than they exemplify drag queens, their performances sprinkled with interrogations of heterosexuality and identities dependent on genitalia, and their living bodies proving the agency of their election over the assignments of "nature." Over and over again their presence begs the question, *what is my gender?* Their performances insinuate that the audience's gender may be in doubt as well.

One of the *travesti* performers strides on stage in male drag, stripping to reveal female drag, while the audience knows underneath that she is really a "man," all the while singing "Sweet Dreams," the song Annie Lennox made famous in male drag. The levels of mediated reality become so layered that the truth of a foundation disappears (field notes, November 7). The lyrics say it all: ". . . *our lives are thinly disguised illusions that we willingly embrace.*" Beginning the set in male drag also makes the uniform of the corporate male just that: another type of drag. As much a costume as the performer's dress; their gender as much a construction.

Relations in the bar do not follow the segregation of sexes that Anglo gay communities experienced in the seventies. When another performer (the most sensuous of them, a postoperated Cuban transsexual) is on stage, she is openly courted by lesbians in the audience (field notes, November 28). The irony is not lost on anyone. The dance floor of the bar is further proof of the seemingly endless potential combinations of pairs across gender: "A very large and quiet drag queen dances with a small gay Latino man who seems lost in her bosom. An African American gay man dances with his white male partner. A Mexican *travesti* dances with a straight young Latino man. Two drag queens share a dance as well" (field notes, October 30). Even the identity of drag queens remains highly malleable and person-specific. The Mexican travesty self-identifies as a gay man who wears drag. The Cuban transsexual sees herself as a transgender person.

Our point is not that gender has ceased to exist at the bar. Indeed, at various times its presentation can seem all too familiar, as in the exaggerated *machismo* of the nongay identified (field notes, October 4) or the Chippendale bodies of the male strip-teasers (field notes, October 11). Our finding however is that a serious struggle is going on, and that, despite the power of the structures of gender and sexuality, gender is being pushed in new ways, shaped into new arrangements, dispersed over new surfaces. With drag (show drag, male drag, ranchera drag, etc.), hormones and silicone implants, makeup and jewelry, texts (song lyrics, pronouncements), and other tools, what nature gave people is revealed to be malleable to the human touch.

Alcohol: The (Re)creation of Private and Social Selves

The role of alcohol at the bar is complex and needs to be contextualized in several ways. The fact that the bar serves a large number of people not fitting into traditional constructions of heterosexuality means we should take into account recent work on the special relationship of the sexually marginalized to alcohol use and abuse (Stall and Willey 1988; McKirnan and Peterson 1989; Hall 1992; Tori 1989; Fifield 1977). That the bar is in many ways an inheritor of Mexican and Latino culture indicates that a familiarity with the role of alcohol in those cultures should also be considered. The stress of immigration is also relevant here. Perhaps easiest to miss is the obvious point that this is after all a bar and at least at some level is dependent on establishing an environment conducive to alcohol consumption.

The established higher prevalence of alcohol use among people with alternative sexualities as an aggregate has been explained, when constructing it as a problem, by stress caused by societal heterosexism and the expectations of intoxication as a tension reducer, or physical actualization of deeper internalized feelings of low self-worth. When it is not constructed as a problem, it is explained by the heavy use of bars as social resources and the corresponding role of alcohol as disinhibitor. To this the different incorporation of alcohol in social life among Latinos must be recalled. Although it is quite possible that all of these functions are served by alcohol at our bar, we observed its use as disinhibitor most often. Specifically, alcohol acquires an almost ritualistic necessity as the washing away of a certain part of the self, thus allowing the exploration of assumed identities taboo on the outside. Intoxication is not the only route by which alcohol achieves this, though often it is simply used as an indicator of license, its physical presence in the room sufficing to delineate our presence on Fantasy Island. Other times it becomes a tool by which to negotiate sexual intimacy.

We have already remarked that one of the main functions of the bar is the provision of an arena where access to certain modes of behavior and identity are not only allowed but celebrated. For some people, most notably the *travesties,* access to that liberated zone is achieved through crossing the threshold of the bar's entrance. The bar belongs to them.

Their attire and mannerisms are all the drug they need. Other patrons enter the bar and remain who they were on the outside, their inhibition and normative heterosexual behavior still intact. This is where alcohol comes in: Its consumption constitutes a second gate to fantasy island, the leaving behind of sobriety to achieve the level of license exemplified by other patrons.

With drink in hand men walk up to the performers, tip them, and maybe receive a kiss or are allowed (by themselves and the *travesti*) to pet or slap the legs or buttocks (field notes, September 12). Even drunk gay couples use the safety of the bar and alcohol to kiss each other in public. The most conservative-looking older Latino men can be seen, again with drink close by, sliding dollar bills down the briefs of a scantily clad beefcake dancer (field notes, October 2). Most obvious is the Latinos' use of alcohol as a license for homoerotic intimacy. But their prerequisites seem to include more than just being drunk; they seem to also need their suitors to be drunk. Not only must their ability to witness (and remember) be impaired, but so must the others'. The physiological state of intoxication is less crucial than the agreement that on some level (if only by one's presence in a bar and one's acting drunk) alcohol is a key player, even the causative player. The point is, then, to decrease the "normal" agency of the people involved. Alcohol use is the key element of a rite. Leisure time, social drinking (which is highly valued among men as a way of approaching others and sharing one's feelings and concerns; as a way of getting "more honest") and the relative loss of the ability to discern, to forget the rules (or its presumption), make up the context of frequent homoerotic approaches (after all, "flesh is weak").

The trafficking of alcohol is also an important prop to the negotiation of intimacy. The authors were often invited to have drinks and routinely declined them so as to avoid colliding with the meaning of a "yes" they did not share (field notes, September 26, October 4). When one of us erred by accepting a drink, he quickly found himself the object of unsolicited and aggressive advances. Offering to buy someone a drink is a useful query as to their interest in you; accepting a drink is an affirmation of mutual interest that entirely eclipses the seemingly "real" discussion regarding drinks. In similar fashion, alcohol serves as the currency by which Latino men who are not gay-identified sell their interest to gay suitors. Working-class men, maintaining exaggerated macho gestures that would allay theirs or others' misunderstandings about their identity can approach patrons and very frankly ask for free drinks. In exchange the patrons receive their company, proximity, and perhaps some mild physical contact. What is played with is the fantasy of actual sex happening later, to the extent that "macho" men count on their suitors' assumedly necessary attraction to them, to their "manliness," to their sex. In fact, the offering of free beers publicly legitimizes these men's approaches to gay men who are not *travesties,* though such approaches may well be motivated by more than just the drinks (i.e., by an interest in social or sexual contact with gay men). The presence of alcohol on the table, however, asserts the normative quality of a "macho" interest in drinking and the legitimacy of its obtention from gay men in exchange of some company. The extent to which sex takes place is assumed to depend on the ability of the gay suitors to arouse their essential masculine desire and their own ability (assumedly weakened by alcohol itself) to avoid it.

Drinking at our bar often assumed the almost bacchanalian air that is considered to have in working-class social settings in Latin America (Díaz-Guerrero 1975), in the sense that the obvious goal was not merely to drink, but to get collectively drunk. As long as one did not interfere with other patrons, people seemed free to be as drunk as they wanted to be.

Intoxication became both a goal and an important source of humor and conversation. Being drunk became itself yet another reason to celebrate by drinking some more. The antics of drunken persons were cause for collective amusement. When the D. J. failed to get the next record on, making five very obvious false starts, one patron yelled "Guarda la botella" ["put away the bottle,"] (field notes, September 12). Drunk men could also jump on stage with the performers, sometimes needing to be coaxed off (field notes, September 26), other times encouraged by the crowd to take off their shirt (field notes, October 30). All of this was not only permitted but seemed to entertain, providing another center of performance.

What is important here is not to romanticize such drinking as natural or culturally specific and therefore neutral. It is simply to point out the dangers of engaging in a Western, primarily recovery industry-driven functionalist analysis that relies heavily on drinking as an individualized and pathological response to the environment or life experiences of a person. Latin-American patterns of experiencing and using alcohol may be unrevealed by such paradigms. Nonetheless, it does seem clear that our initial exploration was valid in that here is certainly something "queer" about drinking at the bar. Again, we should remember Tori's findings that gay-identified Mexican immigrants drink more than comparable heterosexual Mexican immigrants (Tori 1989), though we should also recall that bars are central to both Anglo and Latino gay ghettos. What is perhaps most interesting is the way the two paradigms of drinking can coexist in the same moment, intersecting or even feeding on each other in a positive feedback loop.

Undiscussed so far is the fact that this bar has an economic as well as an aesthetic interest in encouraging drinking. Bartenders, like any others dependent on tips, will always have an incentive to serve people quickly and check frequently if they would like a refill. Additionally, whether intentionally or not, the hour-and-a-half drag shows on Friday and Saturday nights set up a time slot where there is little one can do but watch the show and drink. Conveniently, that time slot comes right before closing time which is when those seeking sexual intimacy most need to be uninhibited. On almost any night the music is turned up so loud that conversation is difficult, thus again privileging drinking as a primary activity. Aesthetically, the bar benefits from the festive and interactive air a drunk, and thus uninhibited, crowd gives the performances. Of passing notice is the primacy alcohol has at the bar as the drug of choice, thus resembling more its neighboring heterosexual Latino bars than those of the Anglo gay district, where "speed," "acid," or "ecstasy" are common.

CONCLUSIONS

In this paper we have reported on a study of social interaction at a Latino gay bar with drag queens in a large urban area of the United States carried out between September and December 1992. As mentioned, we have addressed the roles of alcohol and gender in the dynamics of a setting that is socially "marginal" in several ways and constructs a "hidden population" where issues of HIV/STD prevention are particularly significant. Besides presenting the bar as a leisure space perceived by its patrons to play under different conditions of reality (i.e., fitting the paradigm of the fantasy island) and to offer the warmth and intimacy of a surrogate family, of a "home away from home," we have explored the implications of different perspectives on the numerous roles of alcohol (and alcohol use), particularly as a facilitator of transgression, as a symbol of willingness to transgress the norms, and as a sign of permission to correspond to a transgressive approach. We have finally explored the role of the bar as a space where an active struggle for the reconstruction of gender is taking place through the disruption and dispersion of traditional gender categories.

As Anzaldúa (1987) remarks when talking about "the new mestiza" who " . . . copes by developing a tolerance for contradiction, a tolerance for ambiguity . . . [and] has a plural personality," the notion of plural personality is the key to understanding the partial, strategic, and contradictory identities that populate the bar. A necessary bastard race on the way to the creation of an entirely new culture. Crucially, the bar proposes not just "both a creature of darkness and light, but also a creature that questions the definitions of light and dark and gives them new meanings." A (re)invention of history that utilizes new symbols, new myths and "new perspectives toward the dark skinned, women and queers" (Anzaldúa 1987).

This is not to embrace a polemical enthusiasm that naively insists on seeing only the bar's liberatory facets, its value as a locus of resistance. This "fantasy island" has its shortcomings, and its new culture sometimes stumbles and other times seems very old. To some extent the role of alcohol and the low profile afforded women demonstrate the limits of its subversive potential. Nonetheless, the diversity of the clients, the fluidity of its genders, the mix of languages, and the plurality of its locations all point to the reality best explained by the theories of multiculturalism, strategic alliances, new societies, and emergent cultures.

As an interim society our bar's culture represents a social setting open to sexual diversity (in terms of meanings, desires, orientation, and behavior). Probably for this reason it hosts several groups that may differ importantly from each other, but whose diverse interests may intertwine, complement, or just converge peacefully. This remarkable coalescence sets up the appeal of the bar as a place where desires are accomplished, where a supportive, accepting, caring family can get together, and where patrons can feel protected from violence or from intolerance—and even actively protect that safety. Doubtless, drag queens provide the core of the bar's identity. They embody the accomplishment of the greatest fantasy; they suggest a wonderland with reconstructed genders. And inevitably alcohol represents a key element in the negotiation of access to wonderland and in its communal exploration.

In conclusion, the luminiscent side of our bar is overwhelmingly present when analyzing our observations and the insiders' interpretations therof. Clearly, the bar offers a positive alternative for congregation of patrons that is safe and supportive. From a social change perspective, this is relevant in at least two senses:

First, it provides a particularly important space of social support for people who experience diverse dimensions of marginality in their everyday life. This is also true with regard to the AIDS epidemic as a challenge to the bar's reference community: The nature of the place as a commercial leisure space has not been an obstacle for the organization of fundraising activities to support friends' treatment or to cooperate with prevention campaigns in the Latino community. AIDS and prevention needs are present in people's minds and talk. The first activist efforts in the city's Latino gay community scheduled their meetings at the bar. This understanding of "care for their people" resulting in overt talk about prevention may compensate the problems elicited by alcohol intoxication in the practice of safer sex.

Second, it also provides an interesting case study of community agency in regard to the creation of a leisure space that is both tolerant and fond of differences and overlooks the traditional gender construction, thus outlining some possible aspects of an utopic new society where such categories, reconstructed, offer new possibilities and new challenges.

ACKNOWLEDGMENTS

The research presented in this paper was prepared during the authors' stay at the School of Public Health, University of California at Berkeley. Special thanks are due to Dr. Patricia Morgan for her support. Financial assistance to Dr. Cáceres was provided by the Fogarty International Center, Grant TW-00003-05.

REFERENCES

ANZALDÚA, G. (1987). *Borderlands/La frontera: The New Mestiza*. San Francisco: Spinters/Aunt Lute.

BRANDES, S. (1980). *Metaphors of masculinity. Sex and status in Andalusian folklore*. Philadelphia: University of Pennsylvania Press.

CÁCERES, C. (1994). *New representations of male bisexuality in Latin America and the prevention of AIDS*. Abstracts Book, X International Conference on AIDS, Yokohama/Japan.

DÍAZ-GUERRERO, R. (1975). *Psychology of the Mexican: Culture and personality*. Austin: University of Texas Press.

EPSTEIN, S. (1987). Gay politics, ethnic identity: The limits of social constructionism. *Socialist Review* 93/94 (May-August 1987):9–54.

FIFIELD, L., J. LATHAN, and C. PHILIPS (1977). *Alcoholism in the gay community: The price of alienation, isolation and oppression*. Los Angeles: The Gay Community Services Center.

GILMORE D. (1990). *Manhood in the making. Cultural concepts of masculinity*. New Haven and London: Yale University Press.

GLASER, B., and A. STRAUSS (1967). *The discovery of grounded theory: Strategies for qualitative research*. New York: Aldine Publishing Company.

HALL, J. (1992). An exploration of lesbians' images of recovery from alcohol problems. *Health for Women International* 13:181–198.

HARAWAY, D. (1991). *Simians, cyborgs and women: The reinvention of nature*. New York: Routledge.

McKIRNAN, D., and P. PETERSON (1989). Psychosocial and cultural factors in alcohol and drug abuse: An analysis of a homosexual community. *Addictive Behaviors* 14:555–563.

Pan American Health Organization (1993). *Epidemiological surveillance of AIDS in the Americas. Quarterly Report: April-June 1993*. Washington D.C.: PAHO.

The Panos Institute (1990). *Triple jeopardy: Women and AIDS*. London: The PANOS Institute.

PARKER, R. (1991). *Bodies, pleasures and passions: Sexual culture in contemporary Brazil*. Boston: Beacon Press.

STALL R., and J. WILLEY (1988). A comparison of alcohol and drug use patterns of homosexual and heterosexual men: The San Francisco Men's Health Study. *Drug and Alcohol Dependence*, 22:63–73.

TORI, C. (1989). Homosexuality and illegal residency status in relation to substance abuse and personality traits among Mexican nationals. *Journal of Clinical Psychology*, 45(5):814–821.

11

Gen-X Junkie

Ethnographic Research with Young White Heroin Users in Washington, DC

Todd G. Pierce

INTRODUCTION: RESEARCH OBJECTIVES, DESIGN, AND POPULATION

Historically, both ethnographic and epidemiologic research conducted with injection drug users (IDUs) focuses on people from poor socioeconomic situations. They are easier to access on the streets, monetary incentives for interview participation is very attractive, the ethnographer can be fit within the IDUs world view (often as an HIV counselor, outreach worker, or case manager), and they are at the most risk for HIV because intravenous drug use or sex-for-crack exchanges are overrepresented in poorer populations.

Beyond the possible political implications, maintaining this exclusive and extended focus (fifteen some-odd years of HIV research with these populations) also limits our theoretical understanding of the nature of networks of IDUs and the gambit of risk behaviors. This project focuses on economically well-off White IDUs or those who grew up in that socioeconomic condition. "Studying up" or "sideways," meaning the study of people with either the same or greater levels of mainstream power (that of the researcher's), allows us to better understand the range of behaviors we are investigating while also allowing us to

Adapted from "Gen-X Junkie: Ethnographic Research with Young White Heroin Users in Washington, DC," by Todd G. Pierce, *Substance Use and Misuse,* vol. 34(14), pp. 2095–2114, 1999. Copyright Marcel Dekker, Inc., 1999.

create a better cultural comparative model. As Murphy (1987) points out, IDUs can be found in every part of our society, not just the inner city.

Ethnographic data for this study were based on a network analysis of the IDUs. These networks of IDUs were extracted from larger complex units of social analysis: metropolitan area, suburban communities, inner city or downtown club scenes, drug market and use areas, etc. (see Hannerz, 1980:170–201). The networks were made up of an "extremely complex interlinkage" (Hannerz, 1992:69) of networks with their own "perspectives" (*ibid.*) or world views on how they structure meaning within their perceived realities. For the purposes of this study, selected network variables (i.e., IDUs, young, White) were sampled for analysis. Network analysis can be a very powerful tool for social sciences (Aldrich, 1982:293) but to fully understand these networks we must also consider the interlinking networks that make up the sampled networks (i.e., the wider communities from which the network members come, their histories, economies, and so on) and must analyze both the group and individual levels within their social and cultural contexts (Curtis et al., 1995; see also Bott, 1957; Mitchell, 1969; Barnes, 1972).

The core sample for this study was drawn from a snowball sampling design and consisted of 12 White intravenous drug users (six male/six female) ranging in ages from 19 to 31. The snowball sample was achieved through the ethnographer's networking through the social networks of the IDUs first, and then introduced to the IDUs from their friends and other IDUs. The typical scenario would occur over a game of 8 ball (pool) where the ethnographer's opponent would ask what the ethnographer did for a living, and then when told that he studied heroin users, the opponent would say "Oh, I have a friend that you should meet. He's a junky." Then the ethnographer would give the opponent his business card and tell him to give it to the friend to arrange for a meeting.

In total, 12 egocentric networks were studied. The sample of networks contained two or three core or main members as well as periphery and outer periphery members. Primary analysis for each network was based on dyadic and triadic core relationships within each network (Neaigus et al., 1995). Each network had members that connected one network to the next (a "bridger"). Bridged networks contained White, Black, and Hispanic members. Most of the 12 IDUs in the main sample came from a White, suburban, middle- or upper-middle-class background. Several were from very "well-off" families. All had at least a high school education, while some had either a four-year college degree or some college. Other individuals in the study included eight who were either heroin or cocaine snorters, cocaine injectors, or rehabilitated heroin injectors. In addition to these eight, about 25 peripheral network members were included in the study. These members were part of the social environment of the 12 core IDUs and were either cocaine snorters or sexual conjugates (sex partners) of the core. The individuals and the networks studied were part of extremely complex micro- and macrocultural formations, which in turn influences their drug-use behaviors (see Grund et al., 1991; Singer et al., 1992; Watters, 1988, 1989).

Through intensive participant observation, the ethnographer accessed drug users within the music and club "scene" of Washington, DC, and created relationships with several heroin IDUs, which led to the meeting of other IDUs (the snowball). Ultimately, he was exposed to a multitude of aspects of the users' lives. These aspects included the activities and rituals of club life, after-hours bars, pool halls, family life and relations, sexual relationships, friendships, and involvement with the drug economy and other users.

All subjects for this project were informed of the ethnographer's research objectives and were guaranteed confidentiality. Almost all of the subjects for the study admitted to wanting to participate because of the money offered for the interviews, but later came to rather enjoy working with the ethnographer. After a time the ethnographer and the subjects became close friends and colleagues, working together in this ethnographer endeavor.

Research Methodology

A variety of ethnographic research methods were employed at different levels throughout the research. All methods were embedded within the context of intensive participant observation. The ethnographer participated in all life activities with most of the research subjects, save for drug use, though he did drink alcohol. An average of 50 hours of participant observation was conducted every week for approximately 104 weeks. The ethnographer often ate, slept, and socialized at informant's houses, as did the informants at the ethnographer's house. Toward the end of the research project, several subjects divulged their addictions to their families. Because the ethnographer knew the families, the subjects also told them what the ethnographer was up to. This compromised the ethnographer's research status, since the proverbial cat had been let out of the bag. But, in fact, this actually aided the family because they were able to talk to the ethnographer about addiction and were happy their family member was working with him. It aided in creating an open and respectful relationship for all parties concerned.

Life histories (Langness, 1965; see also Langness and Frank, 1981; Kroeber, 1961) were obtained from all of the core sample members. These interviews typically lasted 2 to 3 hours and were conducted either at the ethnographer's office, home, or a coffee shop. The respondents were paid $30 to $40 for the interview, depending on how long it took to do. The interviews investigated the respondent's life from birth to the present, covering all aspects of life, and focusing on drug use as it occurred.

Even recall interviews (Agar, 1980) were utilized to elicit data on past injection events to establish a self-report record of injection behaviors, their contexts, and network dynamics. The event recalls attempted to reconstruct specific events or instances within the respondent's recent life history. These interviews were conducted in coordination with the life histories and took place at the same time/place. Directed observations (developed for the Needle Hygiene Project but modified to include network-focused data collection for this project) (see Note 1) of injection events (see Note 2) were conducted with individual and multiperson injection events to record personal and network-based injection rituals. These observations were performed within the natural contexts of the individual's and network's injection locations. The observations aimed at data on network dynamics, needle hygiene practices, and other injection behaviors as they occurred within different times and spaces so as to capture variations on the injection theme in relation to contexts. All observational data were recorded in tables designed specifically for this task (previously utilized for the Needle Hygiene Project) and within field notes for future analysis.

Network plots, or diagrams that illustrate network connections and relations, were created with each informant. These plots depicted network membership, relationships, positions within other cultural and behavioral realms, and relations within socioeconomic structures (including relations within the drug economy and supply of drugs and needles). These plots were updated periodically and when changes occurred within the networks.

Informants regularly aided the ethnographer in keeping track of the plots and verified field note data for him during sporadic and periodic follow-up sessions as a means of insuring data reliability and to check the validity of data. Also, a comparative model was used within the analysis so as to help establish differences and ranges in behaviors and meanings within and between different types of networks. Different young White networks were compared for variations in structure, formation, changes over time, and possible dissolution. Also, the young White networks were compared to older Black IDU networks on which data had also been collected during the same years (see Note 3). These Black networks offered completely different structural dynamics than the White, which aided in creating a range of possibilities for comparisons. The exact same research methods were used with all networks. These comparisons will be utilized throughout the network descriptions to illustrate distinct differences between certain network characteristics and behaviors.

NETWORK ATTRIBUTES: FORMATION, CHANGE, AND DISSOLUTION

Network Formation

When studying the creation of an IDU network, you must first ask whether networks formed before or after drug use were put into the mix. In most cases the networks studied in DC turned to injecting drugs after network formation. This point is central for our understanding of risk networks because it helps us better understand the foundations of the network itself (thus a better understanding of the risk relations). In most cases the network members knew each other and had a relationship prior to drug use. Those who did not know their network before "using" acquired them after accessing key roles within their drug environment (i.e., drug running).

What was discovered in DC was that there were two general ways young White IDU networks formed. The first was a network relationship that stemmed from long-term friendships. The second was centered around IDUs that had an ability to cop dope successfully.

Cindy's network is a good example of a long-term friendship network. Her network had three main members who were IDUs, one of which was her boyfriend (her main sex partner). She also had a number of other sexual partners who were part of her network, but they were not IDUs. The main members of the network, Cindy (age 20), her boyfriend Jimmy (age 31), and her best friend Sandy (age 19), had had a relationship before shooting up together. Cindy and Sandy had known each other since the age of 13 or 14. They had literally grown up together and had been hanging out in the rock and roll "scene" since their early teenage years. Cindy had started injecting with one of her boyfriends when she was in her late teens. Sandy had acquired a snorting habit by using with several of her friends, but then asked Cindy to help her in administering her first injection. The ethnographer witnessed her first injection (Pierce, forthcoming:1), and interviewed Sandy the next day to discuss the event, and why she did it with Cindy:

> She's (Cindy) been an intravenous drug user for years, and she never wanted me to, she wouldn't, we hadn't done heroin together. We never have done heroin together until this [past] weekend, because she doesn't want me to get like her, she doesn't want me to shoot up heroin. She doesn't like this, but she saw that I was going to do it anyway. And she's lonely, really. She's very lonely. She's got her boyfriend, and he's not very nice to her, and she kind of didn't want me to do it, but she really like, I mean that's what she told me afterwards. She said "I really enjoy

doing this with you, even though it's very bad." Then she's like "Okay, fine. Let's get the heroin, let's get the needles. We'll do this." She taught me how to do it. I've seen it done before, I just never went that step until this weekend. (Pierce Interview: WX:14)

This scenario was common for most of the users in the study. In fact, all of the users "turned on" to injection through a friend who was using. In such cases the formation of both young White and Black injection networks came from much deeper sociocultural roots, i.e., neighborhood communities or schoolmates, than simply the need to inject. People are generally social beings, and form networks within their lives to satisfy different social needs they have (i.e., feeling accepted, belonging, loved). Different networks fulfill different needs. Some networks, like the family, may fulfill a need for stability or safety, others may be for advancement of knowledge, or adventure. Like many social activities, the first time one does something, it is usually done with somebody else who can experience it with you or show you how to do it.

In order to bring a network analysis to a deeper level here, we ask why and how people associate with each other in different cultural surroundings. Though anthropologists and sociologists alike have tackled this issue in some depth (indeed, historically this has been the mission of both disciplines), the topic cannot be given the proper attention in this discussion. But the bottom line is that most people do not experiment with heroin or start injecting it on their own. They are brought into a risk network of current users or they create a network of experimental users who eventually develop substantial habits (see Note 4). In order to fully understand the creation and the dynamics of a network, one must first understand the nature of its formation.

With experimentation comes new experiences and the feelings and knowledge that come with them. The evolution of a person's drug addiction is a learning process that is often learned with their network, but also on their own through trial and error. Sandy explains for us the feelings she had about injecting heroin as opposed to just snorting it:

> I'm used to needles because I have a bad history with asthma, and I'm just used to needles from getting blood drawn, and whatever, and I find it kind of . . . it's hard to explain, it's a lot more sexy, almost. It's a lot more, you're really getting into the whole feel of the high. It's part of . . . the preparation's almost like, it's an anticipation . . . you're not just spreading a few lines out and snorting it this time. You're now cooking it and you're putting a needle in your vein. It's, if you have time to kind of sit there and do it, like have the whole symbolism thing, it's, it makes it a lot more impressive in your mind. It's uh, I don't, it's hard to explain. It's almost a fun thing, but it's not fun. I mean the pain of the needle, or whatever, that's not fun, but it's, you've got these little toys to play with, and you've got all this stuff that you have, that's illegal. And if you get caught, you feel like s__t with it, but when you have it, it's almost like it's, it's more . . . almost like a toy . . . drugs. To play with, I don't know, it's not a happy thing, if you really think about it, but it gets you really excited about the whole thing and it's fun . . . It's almost like a permanent thing in your mind. You're really going to get high. It's really happening, you're really getting prepared for this whole thing, things like that, it's just the whole anticipation of getting high. You've got to do all [these things], it's part of the whole process. (Pierce Interview: WX:14)

How these new experiences are discussed and learned within a network and certain socioeconomic contexts are important for understanding the injection processes, the personal nature and the social nature of the drug-using rituals (see Note 5). Also, the behavior that is learned through trial and error as an individual IDU builds a habit is important because it illustrates how some behaviors are not taught or discussed. Many aspects of drug misuse were not discussed by network members, such as morning sickness from withdrawal symptoms. In one discussion with the ethnographer, early on in her addiction, Sandy had described having a headache all day long. The ethnographer asked her how much dope she was using. She replied "three or four bags a night." Essentially, she was binging on heroin, but only at night instead of a constant stream of use throughout the day. And she was unaware of the detox effects occurring in the morning. Nobody from her network had told her! Even though her network members were very experienced users. In fact, it was the ethnographer who had to educate her on her biophysical reactions to the drugs. "Man, you just don't know why you have these headaches all day do you? You're dope sick!" She was horrified upon learning this. It was as if the reality of her level of use had just set in. That's when her long uphill struggle to recovery started, after the fact. A few days after learning this she told the ethnographer her headaches were all better, now she "got off E" (see Note 6) in the morning with that coveted first shot of dope for the day.

This transference of cultural information (or lack of it) is important for understanding risk reduction in injection behaviors because it tells us how people learn (or do not learn) certain behavioral procedures for injecting drugs. And, to make matters more complicated, this transference of information happens differently for all subpopulations or microcultures.

The second type of network formation is centered around copping dope. Young, new, White IDUs generally have a lot of difficulty trying to cop dope off the street. They fall prey to more experienced IDUs who will "take" them for all they are worth. They are literally sitting ducks for a "hard-core" street junkie who knows the ropes. Also, dealers do not trust people whom they do not know well, and so will be reluctant to sell to them. Therefore, the young White user must earn his stripes on the streets by going through a series of rip-offs and takes, gaining access to a runner, and then establishing a steady relationship. Not all young White IDUs can or want to do this. It is a risky endeavor, and the stakes are high when playing the street game. Only a few users from this study were any good at copping their own dope; even fewer held the highly respected runner position.

What this meant was that users who were not very adept at copping for themselves sought out users who could do that for them (for a small fee, usually in the form of money or drugs). In the first type of network formation discussed earlier, the network members were forced to go through trial and error routines in order to cop. In most cases only one of the members would do the copping for the entire network. Some of these successful buyers would find routes to copping other than the streets, like a dealer at a night club or an acquaintance from another network who had access to the drug. If a trusting relationship could be established with that acquaintance, then maybe the buyer and his or her network would join up with the runner's network, thus expanding the network based on the need for drugs (on the seeker's side), the need for money (on the runner's side), and trust. The runner then becomes the bridger of the two networks (the runner's own network and that of the seeker).

A good example of such network formation was Ken's, a 25-year-old White male, with long brown hair and tattoos. He's a musician, works at different clubs as a doorman, and plays a good game of pool. He is the center of his network because he is a drug runner. He was taught how to deal drugs by an older Black man (Q) who had been running drugs for about 20 years, and who is also part of Ken's network. Ken has six network members, both male and female; all are White except for Q. His network members are not only customers for drugs, but they are also friends. He has known many of them for several years and socializes with them outside the context of injecting or scoring drugs. Although they pay him either in drugs or money for helping them score, the relationship doesn't stop there. They will often eat meals together, stay at each others apartments, go out on the town together, etc.

Ken is a bridger to Q's network which consists of about 30 people from different ethnic and socioeconomic backgrounds. Although Ken has injected with Q at Ken's apartment (which doubles as an exclusive shooting gallery), there is no risk of HIV infection between the two men or the two networks. This is because there is no direct or indirect sharing occurring during injection episodes. In networks that do directly or indirectly share drug-use equipment, bridgers can be a very high-risk agent for the network members because they can spread the virus from one network to the next. But because Ken's network is very safe in their drug-use behaviors, there is no (or extremely low) risk of infection.

There are other ways that networks form as well, most of which happen by the pure chance of being at the same place at the same time. A good example of this might be if one user sees another trying to cop some dope on the street and decides to approach the person to either aid in copping or to maybe ask if the person knows where they can get a good deal. They might even go as far as to pool their money in an attempt to cop a higher quantity of dope. This is rare, but it does happen.

IDUs from the study also reported making contacts at methadone clinics and NA meetings. In these environs it might be more risky to approach somebody because they are all supposed to be cleaning up. But they usually can tell if somebody is high, and so they approach them anyway. DC does not have a needle exchange program, and needles cannot be legally purchased without a prescription (a topic that will be covered later). But IDUs that I have worked with in Hartford, Connecticut have reported making network connections at needle exchange points (see Note 7). These connections are usually for the purpose of locating "good dope" rather than network expansion per se.

A nice example of how networks are created can be drawn from the ethnographer's own experiences when meeting the respondents for this project. The ethnographer was not familiar with DC nor its drug scene. He did not know anybody when he moved into town, but found in-roads to one or two IDUs located within the alternative punk scene (see Note 8) (from which the ethnographer himself hails). These in-roads occurred within the social networks of the IDUs and through participating in social activities (like pool, as described earlier). The ethnographer then had those IDUs introduce him to other IDUs in their network, or members of other networks. The chain of people made up the sample for the study: it is not much different for an IDU who moves into town and doesn't know anybody, let alone other IDUs. This sort of network begins with a superficial "weak link" or peripheral connection within a network (as opposed to long-term "core" connections like Cindy and Sandy's), but that changes over time as relationships are developed.

The differences found between the way younger White risk networks formed in comparison to older African American networks is revealing. Most of the Black IDUs studied had grown up in neighborhoods with a long history of drug economies. Many had relatives working within that economy as drug dealers, hustlers of some sort, and users. Their neighborhoods were inundated with drugs, and they quickly learned what it was all about at a young age. Many of the Black IDUs had histories of incarceration because of their dealings with the drug market. Many of the users (almost all of them) had grown up knowing each other, but had entered the drug scene at different points in their lives. Their networks were much larger than the Whites, yet they tended to have a small core network in which they created relationships based on either sexual relations or hustling schemes. The number of people they might inject with is much higher and changes more rapidly, but those people appear to be drawn from a limited number of people within their neighborhood.

The young White IDUs, in contrast, tend to come from suburban communities that do not have a visible active drug economy of nearly the scale that is found in poorer urban neighborhoods. They learn about drugs in their teenage years, and in many cases pass through a series of drugs before ending up on heroin (see Note 9). Their networks are small, with only a few people at the core (close sexual relations and best friends), and those networks are usually formed around trying to cop dope. They do not cop in their home neighborhoods (dealers are hard to find in Bethesda, MD), they do not use there frequently, and they have very few run-ins with the law.

In sum, one critical difference between the Black low-income (or informal economy incomes only) networks and White middle-class networks was that the Black networks were focused on getting money to buy the dope (they knew exactly how to go about getting it, but couldn't afford it), while the Whites were focused on purchasing it (they had sufficient economic means to afford it, but were not good at getting it). Exact opposites in that respect, but both working for the same goal: Dope.

Network Changes

Networks were tracked over time to examine changes in size, relationships, risk behavior, and drug-use activities such as copping and connections within the street economy. The core of the networks changed very little. When it did, it was often spurred on by one of the members cleaning up off drugs (rehabilitating) or through changes within relationships, e.g., two or more of the network members might get into a dispute over some topic, maybe over drugs or some other social issue. Over the one year of the study, the IDUs became better at copping for themselves as well as better at finding sources of new needles.

When rehabilitation of a person occurs it can cause the network to splinter into two or more separate groups, depending on that person's role within the network. Ken's group is a good example of this sort of spintering. Ken cleaned up about halfway through the study. This caused his network members to form three different networks with other IDUs or primary dyadic relations. As soon as Ken is taken out of the picture, a drastic change occurs as the remaining members scramble for resources. Because Ken was the main drug supply for many of the network members, they now had to find their own way to cop drugs. To lessen this burden, Ken gave several of the network members the information and phone numbers they would need to cop the drugs.

Each of the members still consider Ken a friend, but he "had to do what he had to do," which meant clean up. But they were then stuck for another way to get drugs. Also, the members reverted to their main partners as a core network for support. The network did not actually dissolve completely; it just changed on a drug-use level.

As discussed earlier, networks also change as the members meet other people who can cop for them or offer something the network can use, i.e., money. This brings us back full circle to network formation. Networks also change when members move to other cities. In most cases the original network is kept while members from the new location are added on, thus making the IDU who moved a bridger of two networks. This happened with Cindy's network. She moved with her boyfriend to a beach in Virginia where they created a large network for whom they ran drugs from DC. They would drive back and forth in her sports car every couple of days on drug runs. Cindy hid the 10 packs of dope in a condom that she inserted into her vagina, just in case the police pulled them over. This new "beach" network was abandoned as soon as the summer was over and Cindy moved back to DC.

Network Dissolution

The most drastic change that any network can go through is total dissolution. This can happen through extreme splintering or when all or most of the network members quit using drugs (kick, clean up, rehabilitate, etc.). This happened with Cindy's network. By the end of the study Cindy and Sandy had cleaned up, Cindy had broken up with her boyfriend, and all other members had been dropped, save for a few sex partners (who changed every couple of months). Her boyfriend continued to use, but with a new network. In Cindy's network case, two of the three main or core members had cleaned up, and this caused the network to dissolve completely. Although the network may have been created before any of the members were IDUs (meaning long-term friendship-based nets), upon dissolution those ties were in most cases severed as well. Many of the IDUs had to change their social environments in order to stay clean, which meant getting rid of old friends and the places they socialized at. Cindy's boyfriend was cut out of the picture completely, but Sandy was kept as a friend because they were trying to clean up together. Even though they remained friends, they did not socialize together as much as they used to. They both began to rebuild their lives separately by creating new networks of friends and relationships.

Another network that dissolved was centered around a 25-year-old woman named Carol and her 22-year-old boyfriend Jim. They had three main members to their network and several not so important members. In this network's case the main core people were very different in terms of social status. Carol had a B.A. in philosophy and was very driven toward an upwardly mobile lifestyle, while her boyfriend was an untrained artist who also played the drums and was using drugs at a higher rate than Carol. Jim lived at an apartment that was paid for by his mother's husband (stepfather), but was thrown out after he had attempted suicide. The stepfather thought it was bad for his image to have the stepson around, so he evicted him.

When Jim moved to a homeless shelter, he and Carol (who was living with her parents) decided they should kick their habits. In short, Carol was able to kick and he was not, even though they were both taking methadone. This caused a tremendous strain on their love relationship, and ultimately ended in dissolution of the relationship. During their attempt at kicking they had severed ties with the other network members, at least that is what Carol thought. Jim continued contact with several of them after they had supposedly broken up. She discovered this and eventually left town so that she could be away from the environment completely. In this case the core members of the network changed, the dynamics of the network changed, and a different network was maintained by one of the original core members. This is not a case of splintering, but rather a reorganization.

DRUG USE BEHAVIORS: NEEDLE PROCUREMENT, NEEDLE HYGIENE, AND HIV RISK

Unlike most IDU subpopulations, the young White IDUs in this study were extremely safe users. As noted by many researchers, seropositivity levels will vary from population to population based on several factors (Price et al., 1995; see also Allen et al., 1992; Berkelman et al., 1989; Des Jarlais et al., 1988; Quinn et al., 1989; Siegal et al., 1991). Actual seropositivity data for the sample networks were not gathered. Self-report data indicated that only one member of the study was HIV-positive, but he did not directly or indirectly share any of his drug-use paraphernalia. In fact, there was almost no direct or indirect sharing of syringes or drug-use equipment observed within any of the direct observations of injection events of the networks. Most of the IDUs studied have the resources to buy their own bags of dope, which decreases the chance of indirect sharing occurring. And because most come from a well-educated and well-off economic background, they have had access to a wealth of information about HIV, safe sex, safe drug use, and safe cleaning practices. Basic concepts of viral transmission were well known by all of the IDUs studied, which made them very conscious of their behaviors.

The young White subpopulation worked with might be considered sexually liberal due to the high rate of sexual partners they had. Several of the participants had an average of one new partner a month, in many cases they had co-occurring sexual relationships (affairs or multiple partners), and in some cases there was group sexual encounters (both two men and one woman, or two women and one man). These cases usually occurred when the participants were intoxicated (drunk), but were reportedly consensual events. New partners or new sexual adventures were always reported to the ethnographer as if they were telling stories of a great hunting expedition. One informant, Cindy, would even run up to the ethnographer with a smile and say, "I have a new one for my network plot!" And 9 times out of 10 she meant a new sexual partner. Although most are aware of and practice safe sex, there were many reports of unsafe sex, usually during sex when drunk.

Syringe procurement was usually done by buying the needles off the street or from a pharmacy. Although the latter is not legal in DC (you must have a prescription), it was easily done by a well-dressed young White person. The typical scenario was that the IDU cleaned themselves up, dressed up in their finest clothes, and came up with a line for why they needed the needles. One informant (Carol) said she needed them to inject vitamin B. In most cases the pharmacist took the line and made them sign a waver, releasing the pharmacy of any legal responsibilities they might have for selling the works to someone without a prescription.

When purchasing on the street, young White IDUs have to trek into some pretty rough areas to find sellers. A large network of Black sellers (the network discussed above in the discussion on network formation) sold works as their hustle. Most of the works they sell are new and in sealed packages. But in some cases they will use the needles and then try to sell them as new, without cleaning them first. This is looked down upon by most sellers, and they will often yell at those who do. It is considered a very bad thing to do, even among other needle sellers. But it does happen, which puts the young White user at risk when purchasing a needle from the street.

Awareness of needle hygiene and hygienic drug use is well known among this population. It is enforced by many of them in conversation and in practice. One of the networks worked with had an HIV-positive member who had contracted HIV from sharing needles in the 1980s. He was an older IDU, but was very aware of his HIV status and so made sure he did not share liquids or syringes with anybody else. He did not disclose his status to anybody besides the ethnographer, but promoted safe use within his network " . . . because it's the right thing to do."

As discussed earlier, direct sharing was extremely rare within the White networks that were observed. In fact, the only direct sharing observed was between two core members of a network that had two outer periphery members within it as well. This core is made up of a 31-year-old man named Tim and his 22-year-old girlfriend Lucy. They keep their own sets of works, but they get them mixed up on occasion.

Because they divide their bags of dope in liquid (they are a live-in couple and pool all resources), they do partake in indirect sharing. They also have unprotected sex. This does not create any real risks for them or their network because it is a contained sharing of fluids. They do not indirectly or directly share with anybody else, nor do they routinely have sex with other people (Lucy does have sex with other women on occasion). This would place her at some small risk of HIV transmission, in which case, if infected, she could then infect Tim. This is a possible risk, but slim in comparison to other risky behaviors (such as unprotected vaginal or anal sex and sharing needles). In sum, young White IDUs were found to be at little risk for HIV in comparison to older Black IDU networks. This had a lot to do with socioeconomic and educational levels as well as the level of drug use. While indirect sharing (though the sharing of cookers, cottons, or rinse water) is almost nonexistent in this population, it is the norm within the older Black population. While direct sharing of syringes/needles is close to nil within the younger White population, it does happen on occasions within the older Black networks.

Level of drug use and economic resources are key to understanding the differences between different types of IDU risk networks. The young White users who began to build up substantial heroin habits began to use up more than their economic resources could support. This eventually made them have to rely on street hustles to get by. By that time, when they had used their other resources, they had potentially gained access to dealers for whom they could run drugs. This helped them carry their habits for a while longer. That, too, would only last so long before they exceeded that resource. Then they were left to the streets with virtually no knowledge of the cultures of the street economy, and so they became prey to those who are accustomed to it, i.e., those who are from a poorer socioeconomic condition and who are very familiar with the streets. When this happens to young White middle-class heroin users, it is usually time for them to kick.

KICKING THE DOPE: ECONOMIC LOSS, CULTURAL STRESSES, AND TRANSITIONS

Heroin addiction has taken on many cultural symbols within the larger part of American society, both in the way it is imagined and in the ways we have treated it. These symbols are utilized by the user and the nonuser alike when discussing drug use and addiction. A young White heroin user's addiction is commonly couched within a context of personal trauma or depression. It is the saddened "rock star" or the depressed inner turmoil of the teenager. Their pain is imagined as being *inner* pain, with psychological issues that must be addressed. A poor Black user's addiction is often discussed in relation to larger *exterior* circumstances. He or she is often discussed in terms of systemic poverty and institution-alized racism. The "system" has gone wrong, not the addict. This is terribly interesting and important fact, and must be kept in mind when studying these sorts of microcultures. The users at both ends of the economic spectrum will often use this discourse. The White users often referred to personal problems in their lives that led them to drug use. The Black users often referred to a lack of jobs and opportunities and to poverty as being causes of their drug addictions.

Also, the way in which heroin addiction is discussed and illustrated by the popular media and academia reflects the same discourse used by the addicts themselves (see Note 8). It is common to see writings on heroin addiction (or drug addiction in general) among minorities being represented with statistics and graphical charts. This is a depersonalized way of representing real people. On the other hand, young White addicts are often repre-sented, especially in the media, through documentaries in a journalistic style—very per-sonal, very tragic. Interestingly enough, the users do read these types of reports or are at least familiar with the discourse, and mimic its rhetoric. This is the mimetic process that Taussig describes (1993) that often leads to mimetic excess: copies of copies of copies, for which there is no original. We are left only with creations of perceived realities con-trolled through specific discourses (e.g., journalism, social or medical sciences, anthro-pology, etc.).

Understanding how an addict perceives his or her addiction, how and why they be-came an addict, is important for trying to understand why they want to clean up, and how they do it.

Cleaning up off a heroin habit is an interesting topic because it relates to all the top-ics discussed above: The reasons why networks form, their changes, their dissolution, their risk behaviors, etc. What was discovered through watching several of the younger White IDUs enlarge their habit size was that they went through the phases of use and economic support discussed above, but they had also undergone stresses as they underwent transitions from the White suburban life they grew up with and knew so well to the urban ghetto and the street-based economies of the drug world. The users were quickly losing parts of their "selves" as the different cultural roles that created them, i.e., the student, the daughter or son, the champion horse rider, the hard worker, the brother or sister, etc., began to slip away as the drugs took over their lives (chemically, socially). They slowly but surely moved closer to the street environment, to the home of "the real junkies," the hardened street addict that researchers of today are so familiar with. They didn't realize that these street junkies were no different than themselves, just better at surviving within their own environment.

Beyond being traumatic to the young White user emotionally, heading to the street life can often be deadly as they do the wrong things in the street because they don't know the proper roles in that environment. Also, they must learn the street way of using, where you do NOT divide bags of dope in powder form because you might end up ripping someone else off of their 0.02 cc of dope or end up with less cut than them. Thus the users now find themselves in a world of higher risk for HIV and no way to get out, except to kick.

In most cases kicking came well before that point, not because they couldn't afford the drugs. Rather, it was also personal stresses that caused the kick. The fear of losing friends, family, and social status was enough stress to force the IDUs to clean up. These cul-tural and social forces can be a powerful influence in a person's life, more powerful than dope. When these things are slowly being torn away, and the user sees his or herself chang-ing both physically and culturally, it scares the living daylights out of them. And when the next stop is some street corner or a shooting gallery, it's often enough to help them try to kick. Although many of the White IDUs had visited such locations, it was only because they were trying to cop. But they were not part of that scene, and they didn't know how to act or play the role when there.

Kicking dope happened a lot with the young White IDUs in the study. Many of them had attempted it numerous times with some success. They might stay clean for a few months, a half a year, maybe a few years. But then they'd end up using again, building a habit, losing cultural identities, money ran short, and then kicking completely or ending up on the streets. In most cases kicking was done informally, without knowledge of their habit or clean up being divulged to anyone outside their drug use and close social networks. This was either done through "chipping" one's way down to detox (meaning they used less and less each day), the straight kick (no drugs to help the pain of withdrawal), or they used drugs purchased on the street to ease the pain of the kick (drugs that help you sleep it off were preferable). The ethnographer aided several IDUs who asked him to help them kick. One stayed at his apartment during the initial kick.

Compared to the older Black IDUs, the younger White IDUs attempted kicking much more. The process of using, stresses, and kicking discussed above occurred rapidly and multiple times for most, while the older Black IDUs were able to maintain a consistent habit for up to 20 years. This is because they have a limited economic resource that is determined, by and large, by their particular hustle. For instance, a needle seller knows he can sell only so many needles in a day, and so he pretty much knows how much dope he will be able to shoot in a day. This amount may vary on "good" days, but it is pretty constant. The White user, on the other hand, will build a large habit quickly, and thus he or she will "crash and burn" quickly, which leads to the repeated kicks. Many of the older Black IDUs talk about wanting to kick, but because they are from the streets they do not feel the cultural stresses that might influence a kick attempt at the same level by the younger Whites. Many of the older Black IDUs kicked only when forced to do so by the law (either when locked up or forced into a rehab clinic for a 21-day detoxification).

RECOMMENDATIONS: UNDERSTANDING VARIATION
IN NETWORKS AND HIV RISK

This research with young White IDUs offers the drug research and HIV intervention fields several insights. For one, through an ethnographic approach to network analysis, one that not only includes risk relations but also socioeconomic and cultural variables, we can bet-ter understand the possible range of HIV risk related behaviors among injection drug users. Also, through a understanding of the different processes IDUs from different socioeco-nomic backgrounds go through within their histories of drug use, we can better understand the root causes of drug addiction and rehabilitation.

Future ethnographic research with IDUs should attempt to create more culturally comparative research models that analyze networks across different ethnic, gender, and so-cioeconomic ranges. This will help assist harm reduction and HIV prevention more effec-tively because it will allow us to better understand the finer points and differences in drug addiction, drug-use behaviors, and HIV risk.

ACKNOWLEDGMENTS

Research for this study was conducted in Washington, DC, mainly in the Shaw, Adams Morgan, Dupont Circle, and Mount Pleasant neighborhoods, and the Virginian and Maryland suburbs of DC. This project was inspired through research for the National Opinion Research Center (NORC) in their research project entitled The Networks Project. NORC's project was a multisite epidemiological and ethnographic study of various intravenous drug users (IDU) networks performed in 1995–96. Access to the White IDU networks was gained during NORC's project, and continued with a more intensive research focus for the Community Epidemiology Work Group (CEWG) project under the direction of Dr. Michael Agar.

N O T E S

1. The Needle Hygiene Project (NHP) was a seven city ethnographic study that was conducted in 1993. The methodology for this project demanded that the ethnographers be able to collect comparative data across all sites. To do this, the ethnographers utilized a method they developed called "directed observation" of injection drug use behaviors. Todd Pierce, M.A., Michael Clatts, Ph.D., Steve Koester, Ph.D., and Lourie Price, Ph.D., developed this method and the NIDA Field Manual for this seven city project.

2. An injection event is defined as the observed time of injection behaviors. The parameters of the event are determined by the ethnographer's presence at the location of the behaviors (i.e., shooting galleries). The event can be brief or several hours long, and may include several actual injection "episodes." Data collected for "events" include the macro- and microlevel environmental situation of the event (i.e., location, time of day, police presence), how the money for drugs and syringe were obtained (the "hustle"), how drugs and injection equipment were actually obtained, how they were used, and by whom, throughout the event, and disposal of equipment, as well as all microcultural dynamics of the users in the event (power relations, etc.).

3. Twenty egocentric Black networks (10 male/10 female) were studied for this project, forming four separate clusters of networks. The exact same ethnographic methods used for data collection on the Whites were also used for the Blacks and Latinos that were part of the study. The Latinos from the study are not discussed in this article. In DC, Latino IDUs are uncommon, and were often bridgers or peripheral members of either Black or White networks.

4. I am making a generalization across all types of heroin users and injection networks here—White, Black, and Latino. Although there may be cases of individuals using on their own, it is very rare that they started using alone at the start of their injection use. It is also rare that they continue to use alone. Many "older" or seasoned IDUs will report being "loners," but with only a little ethnographic investigating it is found that they indeed have an extensive network of people they use with on occasion.

5. I am not supporting the "gateway" theoretical discussions here. On the contrary, there is an incredible difference between smoking marijuana and injecting heroin. Unfortunately, there is neither the time nor space to debate this topic within this text. One suggestion I can propose for this debate would be to consider gateway networks as a key factor to drug misuse. Social networks, including drug use networks, do not form due to a predetermined or acquired biophysical condition, i.e., drug misuse and the biochemical changes the brain goes through with this "disease." This can be illustrated by my argument that most first time experiences an individual has usually occur with someone else (smoking, drinking, sex, dancing, eating, and so on). The jury is still out on the genetically predetermined drug addict, which is also used in the gateway discourse. To that end of the debate I would have to pose the question: Is it because one or both parents were addicts,

or was it growing up in an environment of addicts where the youth is constantly surrounded with their behavioral routines?

6. "Get off E" is to satisfy the "craving" for heroin. The term is allegorical to a car that has an empty gasoline tank.

7. Research in Hartford, Connecticut, was conducted during 1990–1994 under the direction of Merrill Singer, Ph.D. at The Hispanic Health Council of Hartford, Connecticut, funded by HIN for the NIDA Cooperative Agreement and Needle Hygiene Project.

8. The "alternative" punk scene refers to the punk rock microcultures that had developed during the early 1970s and had developed and changed throughout the 80s and 90s. Although these microcultures (Hannerz 1992) differ in many ways, there are some common links in ideologies and cultural material (i.e., music, clothing style).

9. For popular representations of heroin addiction, see the texts *JUNKY* by W. S. Burroughs (1977) (which was first published as *JUNKIE* under the pen name William Lee). Also, see the writings of Jim Carroll [*The Basketball Diaries, Forced Entries* (1987)]. For recent articles in popular magazines, refer to *Details,* April 1996, pp. 68–70, Love in vein; or *Newsweek,* August 1996 lifestyle report, Rockers, models, and the *new* allure of heroin (emphasis added). From 1988 to 1997 a slew of major motion pictures were produced that either directly or indirectly illustrated the junky lifestyle. Also, on any given day in American you can see portrayals of junked out models *on the nod* in blue jeans and perfume commercials. Heroin chic!

REFERENCES

AGAR, M. (1980). *The Professional Stranger: An Informal Introduction to Ethnography*. New York, NY: Academic Press.

ALDRICH, H. (1982). The origins and persistence of social networks. In Peter Marsden and Nan Lin Man (Eds.), *Social Structure and Network Analysis*. Beverly, CA: Sage.

ALLEN, D. M., ONORATO, I. M., GREEN, T. A.; and the FIELD SERVICE BRANCH OF THE CDC (1992). HIV infection in intravenous drug users entering drug treatment, United States 1988 to 1989. *Am. J. Public Health* 82: 541–546.

BARNES, J. (1972). *Social Networks*. Reading, MA: Addison-Wesley.

BERKELMAN, R. L., HEYWARD, W. L., STEHR-GREEN, J. K., and CURRAN, J.W. (1989). Epidemiology of human immunodeficiency virus infection and acquired immunodeficiency syndrome. *Am. J. Med* 86: 761–770.

BOTT, E. (1957). *Family and Social Network: Roles, Norms, and External Relationships in Ordinary Urban Families*. London: Tavistock.

BURROUGHS, W. S. (1953). *JUNKY*. New York, NY: Penguin Books, Ace Books, 1977.

CARROLL, J. (1987). *Forced Entries: The Downtown Diaries: 1971–1973*. New York, NY: Penguin Books.

CURTIS, R., FREEDMAN, S., NEAIGUS, A., JOSE, B., GOLDSTEIN, M., and ILDEFONSO, G. (1995). Street-level drug markets: Network structure and HIV risk. *Soc. Networks* 17: 229–249.

DES JARLAIS, D. C., FRIEDMAN, S. R., and STRONEBURNER, R. L. (1988). HIV infection and intravenous drug use: Critical issues in transmission dynamics, infection outcomes, and prevention. *Rev. Infect. Dis.* 10: 151–158.

GRUND, J., KAPLAN, C., ADRIAANS, N. (1991). Needle sharing in the Netherlands: An ethnographic analysis. *Am. J. Public Health* 81: 1602–1607.

HANNERZ, U. (1980). *Exploring the City: Inquiries toward an Urban Anthropology*. New York, NY: Columbia University Press.

HANNERZ, U. (1992). *Cultural Complexity: Studies in the Social Organization of Meaning*. New York, NY: Columbia University Press.

KATEL, P., and HAGER, M. (1996). Rockers, Models and the New Allure of Heroin. *Newsweek* pp. 50–56, August 26.

KROEBER, A. E. (1961). *Ishi in Two Worlds: A Biography of the Last Wild Indian in North America.* Berkeley, CA: Sage Press.

LANGNESS, L. L. (1965). *The Life History Method in Anthropology.* New York, NY: Rinehart and Winston.

LANGNESS, L. L., and FRANK, G. (1981). *Lives: An Anthropological Approach to Biography.* Navato, CA: Chandler and Sharp.

MITCHELL, J. C. (1969). The concept and use of social networks. In J. C. Mitchell (ed.) *Social Networks in Urban Situations.* Manchester, UK: Manchester University Press.

MURPHY, S. (1987, Fall). Intravenous drug use and AIDS: Notes on the social economy of needle sharing. *Contemp. Drug Probl.* pp. 373–395.

NEAIGUS, A., FRIEDMAN, S., GOLDSTEIN, M., ILDEFONSO, G., CURTIS, R., and JOSE, B. (1995). Using dyadic data for a network analysis of HIV infection and risk behaviors among injection drug users. In R. Needle, S. C. Coyle, S. G. Genser, and R. T. Trotter (Eds.), *Social Networks, Drug Abuse, and HIV Transmission* (NIDA Research Monograph 151). Rockville, MD: NIDA.

PIERCE, T. G. (forthcoming). *Use Twice and Destroy: An Ethnography of Young White Heroin Users.*

PRICE, R., COTTLER, L., MAGER, D., and MURRAY, K. (1995). Injection drug use, characteristics of significant others, and HIV-risk behaviors. In R. Needle, S. C. Coyle, S. G. Genser, and R. T. Trotter (Eds.), *Social Networks, Drug Abuse, and HIV Transmission* (NIDA Research Monograph 151). Rockville, MD: NIDA.

QUINN, T. C., ZACARIAS, F. R. K., and ST. JOHN, R. K. (1989). HIV and HTLV-1 infections in Americans: A regional perspective. *Medicine* 68:189–209.

SCOTT, H., and DRAKE, S. (1996, April). Love in vein. *Details Magazine* (New York, NY), pp. 68–70.

SIEGAL, H. A., CARLSON, R. G., FALCK, R., LI, L., FORNEY, M. A., RAPP, R. C., BAUMGARTNER, K., MYERS, W., and NELSON, M. (1991). HIV infection and risk behaviors among intravenous drug users in low seroprevalence areas in the Midwest. *Am. J. Public Health* 81:1642–1644.

SINGER, M., ZHONGKE, J., SCHENSUL, J., WEEKS, M., and PAGE, J. (1992). AIDS and the IV drug user: The local context in prevention efforts. *Med. Anthropol.* 14:285–306.

TAUSSIG, M. (1993). *Mimesis and Alternity: A Particular History of the Senses.* New York, NY: Routledge, Chapman and Hall.

WATTERS, J. (1988). Meaning and context: The social facts of intravenous drug use and HIV transmission in the inner city. *J. Psychoactive Drugs* 20: 173–177.

WATTERS, J. (1989). Observations on the importance of social context in HIV transmission among intravenous drug users. *J. Drug Issues* 19: 9–26.

12

Drug Use in Nepal

The View from the Street

Joel M. Jutkowitz, Hans Spielmann, Ulrich Koehler, Jagdish Lohani, and Anil Pande

INTRODUCTION

The ethnography of drug use has a strong tradition to build on, a tradition that can be traced back to ancient history as Feldman and Aldrich have suggested (Feldman and Aldrich, 1990:12–22). An important part of that tradition is a focus on particular communities of drug users such as the recent study of the role of crack and its relationship to sex in the United States, *Crack Pipe as Pimp: An Ethnographic Investigation of Sex-for-Crack Exchanges* (Ratner, 1993). This study builds on that tradition but extends its application by looking into the cultural context of drug use, and above all heroin use, in Nepal, a country which has witnessed virtually no prior scientific studies of drug use (see Note 1). In keeping with the theme of this special issue, we focus further on a particular aspect of heroin use—among street children in the capital, Kathmandu.

Before examining this set of users, it is worthwhile to place drug use in Nepal in context. Nepal is not a major producer of drug crops as is, for example, the case with neighboring India, nor a major historical trafficking route, although in recent years there have been indications of increased movement of opiates through the country (see Note 2). Traditionally, there was widespread availability and use of marijuana (in leaf form and as hashish), some in connection with religious practices. Hinduism is the official religion of

Adapted from "Drug Use in Nepal: The View from the Street," by Joel M. Jutkowitz, Hans Spielmann, Ulrich Koehler, Jagdish Lohani, and Anil Pande, *Substance Use and Misuse,* vol. 32(7 + 8), pp. 987–1004,1997. Copyright by Marcel Dekker, Inc.

Nepal. Use of cannabis derivatives such as marijuana (locally referred to as ganja) and bhang (an infusion of cannabis) is often justified in connection with religious festivals because of the presumed predilection by one of principal figures of the Hindu pantheon, the God Shiva, for the drug (see Note 3).

The ease of availability of marijuana, a tolerant attitude toward drug use as well as an image of Nepal as Shangri-la, a mountain paradise, led to the growth of a drug-using "hippie" population in the country in the sixties and early seventies. In the seventies, stricter legislation and controls, as well as the social forces working within the hippie subculture, led to an end of this phenomenon, except for a few aging hangers-on. However, in the mid-seventies, cases of drug dependency on opiates, especially heroin, began to appear, growing in number according to observers over the past two decades.

Both official and unofficial estimates indicate that from virtually no cases in 1976, there were over 10,000 and even as high as 20,000 heroin addicts a decade later, concentrated in the Kathmandu valley (Kathmandu is the capital of Nepal, and the Kathmandu valley is a principal population center), but with cases also present in other urban areas. The existing legislation distinguishes between cannabis and other drugs in terms of the penalties provided. The idea of the legislation is to de-emphasize cannabis while continuing to express a legal concern for other drugs such as heroin. However, there is only limited enforcement of that legislation (see Note 4).

The "drug problem," as noted above, has evolved over the past two decades. From a problem that centered on foreigners utilizing marijuana and psychedelic drugs, the major concern is now one of Nepalis, particularly young men and women, using heroin. The Government of Nepal had been reluctant as drug use evolved to recognize the existence of the drug problem and its indigenous character. However, by the middle of the 1980s, the government and the royal family began to express a interest and awareness of the serious nature of drug consumption in their country. Even so, that awareness was tempered by the persistence of an image of the problem as one that came from abroad. When the King of Nepal's brother HRH Prince Dhirendra Bir Bikran Shah opened the Seventh International Conference of Non-Government Organizations on Drug Dependence, held in Kathmandu in September, 1985, he remarked,

> Drug dependence is a fairly recent phenomena in this country, but one which has assumed alarming proportions not in terms of absolute numbers but in terms of the rate of growth in a short period. The uniqueness of this problem in Nepal has been that, despite the free availability of soft drugs and (their) limited use in society . . . (and on) . . . religious occasions, till comparatively recent times, addiction and dependency syndrome developed late . . . probably as an outcome of exposure to certain distorted elements of outside culture. [Seventh International Conference of Non-Government Organizations on Drug Dependence (1985), p. 3.]

STUDY DESIGN

This study originated in a concern with the drug-use(r)-associated problems facing Nepali youth on the part of Youth Vision, a Nepali nongovernment organization. The field work for the study took place in the period 1990–1992. The study was funded by a grant through the US Embassy from the State Department's Bureau of International Narcotics Matters. Technical assistance in the design of the study was provided by the Asia Regional Narcotics Education (RNE) Project of USAID as part of a larger effort to promote research on the nature and extent of drug use in Asia. (The RNE Project supported drug prevalence surveys in Thailand, the Philippines, and Sri Lanka.)

Initially, there were a total of 30 subjects, but full data were completed on only 16 of the subjects. Some of those initially included voluntarily dropped out of the study. Others were not followed up after initial contact because of the limited time and resources available to the research team. (Funding for the study was fairly limited, and the research team worked on for a period on a voluntary basis.)

There was no assumption that the group would be statistically representative of the universe of heroin users in Kathmandu since the aim of the study was to portray the "heroin scene." The 16 subjects with full data represent a broad cross-section of the different elements that constitute that scene. The study employed a life history method that, through a series of interviews (a minimum of two, more if the subject was willing) with each subject, developed data on the personal history of each subject, his or her experiences with drug use, with drug-user treatment, current drug use, and current personal situation. The interviews were conducted in the native language of the speakers. Where interviews were conducted by nonnative speakers, one of the native speakers acted as interpreter.

Each subject was asked questions about his or her personal history, starting from early childhood, family background, relationships with other family members, education, employment, attitudes toward society, toward religion, toward other ethnic groups, interests and hobbies, and friends. With regard to drugs, each subject was asked about his or her personal history of use, the effects that had been felt, the relationship with other drug users, family patterns of drug use, drug use routine, modes of securing and financing drug use, consequences of drug use including relations with the law, and treatment of drug use.

In a study such as this, access is an important consideration. That access was secured by the research team because several of its members had a history of involvement in activities assisting the drug-using population of Kathmandu. This provided them both with the basic knowledge to understand the characteristics of the street environment and the drug scene in Kathmandu as well as initial credibility with the potential interviewees.

CHARACTERISTICS OF THE CASES

The 16 cases presented here reflect a cross-section of social characteristics and drug-use-associated problems found in the drug-user scene in Kathmandu. Those characteristics are discussed further below. To preserve the anonymity of the individuals studied, each individual is identified by consecutive letters of the alphabet (A–P) as well as by a term which characterizes his or her principal occupational activity. Table 12–1 summarizes selected characteristics of the cases in terms of their occupations, location in the social structure, and certain aspects of their drug use.

As Table 12–1 indicates, these drug users represent a wide variety of social situations and occupations. In a South Asian society such as Nepal which is multiethnic and multireligious, ethnicity, religion, and caste, related to the Hindu religion, represent important social markers. The group studied includes a member of the Hindu priestly caste (a Brahman) as well as other descendants of Indo-Aryan peoples who came up from the Indian subcontinent to form the modern Kingdom of Nepal. It includes Newars who are descendants of the indigenous inhabitants of the Kathmandu Valley. It also includes Tibetans from the north as well as Gurung, descended from hill people of west-central Nepal. The majority are Hindu,

TABLE 12–1 Selected Background Characteristics of the Individuals Studied

ID	Occupation	Ethnicity (sex)	Age	Education[a]	Marital status[b]	Drug use	Treatment	Involvement with law	Current use
A	Dealer	Tibetan/Buddhist (male)	40	H.S.	M	Heroin, marijuana, hashish	7–9 times	Yes	Heroin
B	Social worker	Newar high caste (male)	34	H.S.	M	Heroin, marijuana, hashish, morphine, opium, tranquilizers	4	No	Drug-free
C	Drifter	Newar high caste (male)	31	H.S.	Sep	Heroin, marijuana	7	No	Marijuana alcohol
D	Priest	Brahman high caste (male)	24	E.S.	S	Heroin	2	No	Tranquilizers
E	Laborer	Newar lower caste (male)	28	E.S.	M	Heroin	3+	No	Alcohol
F	Cassette packer	Newar lower caste (female)	27	None	M	Heroin, alcohol	None	No	Sedatives
G	Computer man	Minority religion (non-Hindu) (male)	27	College	S	Heroin, marijuana	None	No	Alcohol
H	Broker	Tibetan (male)	25	E.S.	S	Heroin, hashish	1	No	Heroin
I	Tailor	Low professional caste (male)	24	E.S.	S	Heroin, other opiates	5+	Yes	Alcohol

J	Guide	High caste (male)	24	College	S	Heroin, marijuana, alcohol	2	No	Alcohol
K	Dealer II	High caste Newar (male)	25	Apprenticeship	C	Heroin, other opiates, prescription drugs	7	No	none
L	Biker	High caste Newar (male)	23	H.S.	S	Heroin, hashish	6	No	Alcohol
M	Bag-seller[c]	Hindu Gurung caste (male)	20	E.S.	M	Heroin, prescription drugs, hashish	None	Yes	Heroin
N	Baker	High caste Buddhist Newar (male)	20	H.S.	S	Heroin, marijuana, codeine	5+	Yes	Heroin
O	Kid-beggar	Tamang Buddhist (male)	18	E.S.	Sep	Heroin, tranquilizers	2	No	Alcohol
P	Kid[c]	Gurung (male)	14	E.S.	S	Heroin, marijuana, hashish	None	Yes	Heroin, prescription drugs

[a]Highest level of education achieved. E.S. is elementary school, H.S. is high school. College signifies postsecondary schooling.
[b]S is single, M is married, Sep is separated, and C is cohabitating.
[c]These two lived on the streets at the time of the study. The others lived in some sort of regular dwelling.

but some are Buddhist and one from a minority religion. (Nepal, as noted above, is officially a Hindu kingdom.) (For a discussion of Nepali peoples, see Bahadur Bista, 1987.)

Although the use of heroin is penalized by the law, only six of the 16 had been in any way involved with the law. Two of those were the most vulnerable, M and P, who lived on the street. None, however, had had long jail sentences.

DRUG CAREERS

Some of the defining characteristics of a drug user that have been examined in the literature (see Note 5) are patterns of initiating use, the types of substances used, the form and frequency of that use, the social context of use, and the outcomes of use—outcomes in terms of the impact on lifestyle as well as on the health and well being of the individual drug user. Outcomes also refer to the consequences of use—these may include going to jail, seeking treatment and rehabilitation and even, as was the case with at least one of the subjects of this study, death. While the size of the population studied is small, the life histories of each of the subjects can offer a wide variety of data on all of these topics. Presenting each person's story would stretch beyond the limits of this article. It would also step beyond the intention of this special issue—to examine populations that have been displaced. Thus, we shall try to focus in large part on issues that relate to the displaced populations, although where appropriate we shall refer to cases outside the set of those who can be classified as displaced.

Foreign Devils Did It to Us

Starting with one of the broader issues of the relationship between displaced populations and drug use, we have referred to the common perception in Nepal that the drug-user problem remains a problem resulting from the influence of foreigners. The political elite often expresses this view, as was noted above. The view is a common one in the history of drug use, not only in Nepal but all over the world. In Thailand it was the Chinese who were traditionally blamed for opium use. David Musto, in his history of drug use in the United States, *The American Disease,* comments that a US congressman "Representative Porter in the 1920s denied any unusual appetite for narcotics in the United States, blaming our problem on the perfidy and greed of other nations" (Musto, 1987:248).

The cases in our study point to a far different picture of the origin of the drug-user(s) problem in Nepal. The set of 16 users included in this study display a variety of paths to heroin use. Some initiated use at a fairly early age (as young as 9), some at a far later age (as old as 28). The motivations they describe vary—curiosity, relationships with friends or relatives who were users, as a reaction to personal crises, as part of the context of a specific social setting. Many went through a gradual process of moving from one drug to another, while a few began directly with heroin. None of those interviewed had been drawn into drug use by foreigners, that is, as the consequence solely of direct contact with foreigners.

The individual we have called "the social worker" (Case B), demonstrates this variety of influences—starting with culturally acceptable patterns of use, having a peer group of drug users, moving from other drugs to an involvement with heroin. Because he was of the generation that grew up in Kathmandu when there were still "hippie" hangers-on, he had contact with them, but their role was most certainly not the deciding influence in his drug career. B began to use psychoactive substances as a child when his grandmother served him rice soaked in alcohol for breakfast. As a Newar, this constituted a traditional form of ingesting alcohol. B started smoking cigarettes when he was 14 years old. At the same age, he started smoking *ganja,* smoking it regularly with friends until he was around 18. He and his friends would sit around what is denoted as their "earth-room," a private smoking den—burning incense, listening to Western music and chatting, enjoying each other's company while passing around the "chilum," a cone-shaped pipe used for marijuana or hashish.

A similar pattern holds true for one of the displaced persons in the study, the individual we have called "the broker" (Case H). H demonstrates a common sequence—moving from other drugs to an involvement with heroin. H was born in Tibet but was taken to Nepal at the age of 3 when his family fled, apparently for political reasons. H left Kathmandu at the age of 10 to go to boarding school. His education was interrupted when his parents took him back to Tibet. He returned to Nepal after his father's death. For various reasons (the flight from Tibet, attendance at boarding school, the death of his father, and H's return to Kathmandu), H spent a good period of his adolescence separated from his family. As he explains the process, after living somewhat more than a year in Kathmandu, he was introduced to *charas* (hashish) by some Tibetan friends. (At the time he was unemployed.) For a few weeks he used both *charas* and *ganja* (marijuana) occasionally. He then observed this same group of friends using *brown sugar* [a form of heroin that is reputed in Kathmandu to have a higher degree of impurities (hence the brown color) and to originate in Bihar state in northern India]. After more or less a month of observing, he asked those same friends to let him try the drug. His curiosity was aroused, he said, because one friend told him "If you take this, you fly in the sky; it gives a beautiful trip." He was interested enough to pay the equivalent of a couple of dollars to secure that first try. He took *brown sugar* by "chasing the dragon." This practice is common throughout South and Southeast Asia and consists of placing the drug on a piece of metal foil, heating it from below, and inhaling the smoke through a rolled piece of paper, often a currency note. One explanation for the name is that as the heroin is heated, one has to chase the smoke (the heroin dragon) across the foil so that it does not escape.

This first trip made him feel terrible. He remembers that he vomited and that his face and the rest of his body itched all over. But, he did, as his friends had promised, "feel nice." After this initiation he started using heroin every day, getting his dose free from friends for the first several weeks. He observed that in these early weeks, despite throwing up, he had "a nice feeling" from the use. He continued to use the drug, developing a means of securing the necessary cost of maintaining his supply.

Here again there is no "western devil" promoting drug use. H's initiation appears to be a function of the peer group he chose (Tibetans like himself), the information he received regarding the effects of the drug, and his curiosity. Again the availability of the drugs also contributed as did the perceived positive effects of the drug as weighed against the immediate negative consequences.

Another displaced individual, a street child (a person whose home is in the street as opposed to one who spends a considerable portion of time on the street, but still has a home), demonstrates the contribution made by social setting, reinforced by peer group behavior. The kid, Case P, initiated use extremely early in life, when he was 9 years old. P started using *ganja* and *charas* when he began work collecting and "recycling" garbage. Some of the friends he worked with "chased" *brown sugar*. They urged him to try because they said it would help to keep him warm through the cold nights. (P always slept in the open, on the streets.) They gave him some puffs of *brown sugar* which made him extremely thirsty and caused him to vomit. But despite this experience, he enjoyed the drug and continued using it—ending up after several years injecting rather than smoking. Here again, there is also the presence of the positive and negative effects of the drug itself.

The literature, it can be noted, suggests the importance of a sorting out process among certain groups by the drug of choice, a process that contributes in Nepal to the reinforcement of use in the case of street children. Ingram in his study of the US military (Ingram, 1984) points to the manner in which the type of drug defined the social group. As he states,

> Alcohol bonded small face-to-face groups, while drugs bonded larger social categories that cut across small groups and cliques. However, the contents of the social interaction, exchange of goods and services, exercise of status claims, and bids for social power were clearly present in both drug and alcohol patterns. (Ingram, 1984:166.)

In a similar vein, Alcaraz et al. (1995) in their study of Bolivian street children also noted that those they studied often sorted themselves out into groups whose membership could be defined by whether or not they used drugs as well as by the type of drugs that were used (for example, glue and other inhalants as opposed to cocaine paste).

The cases point to the need to see the initiation of use in Nepal as a complex process, a set of variables that lead to use rather than a single factor (for instance, the assumption that foreigners caused the drug problem in Nepal). No one variable determines. Variables that play a role include: an early history of culturally acceptable use of substances such as alcohol, tobacco, and in certain circumstances, marijuana or hashish; the influence of peers or significant others; and of the specific social setting in which they operate. There are times when outside (i.e., foreign) influences are included in the mix, but never as a single overarching determinant of drug use. A user may begin at an early age or far later in life. Peer groups and significant others do play a role, but so does curiosity, the interest in a new experience. The initial experience itself does not have to be an entirely enjoyable one. According to subjects in the study, that experience often brings physical discomfort, nausea, vomiting, and dizziness at the same time that it provides a "high." While all of this is not new to the literature on drug use, it is reaffirmed in this non-Western cultural context.

At the same time, there are some factors specific to the Nepali scene. For example, there is the traditional association of forms of marijuana with certain religious contexts as earlier noted in the case of the Hindu deity Shiva. [One case, C, used *ganja* for the first time at the age of 11 in the company of *saddhus* (holy men) at a Hindu temple.] This may assist in facilitating the entrance of some users into the drug scene. There is also the relative availability of heroin in Kathmandu which facilitates maintenance of a user's dependency.

Drug, Set and Setting

This examination of entrance into drug use points to the utility of seeing the process of drug use in Kathmandu in the framework provided by Zinberg's drug, set (personality) and setting (1984:5). Following Zinberg's formulation, you need to understand the interaction of the pharmacological action of the specific drug or drugs being used, the attitudes and personality traits of the user, and the physical and social milieu of use in order to comprehend why a person uses a drug and how that drug affects a person.

In the case of heroin, the drug that is the focus of this study, the pharmacological effects include inducing a sense of euphoria, drowsiness, an insensitivity to pain, the possibilities of nausea, vomiting, and a dependency which is marked by withdrawal symptoms. In Nepal, heroin usually is available in two forms, *brown sugar,* which is usually smoked, and white heroin, which is injected.

In terms of personality traits, many of those in the study had low self-esteem, some were depressed. Many had little to show in the way of personal successes in school or in work and felt diminished as a consequence. Some came from dysfunctional families which again was reflected in their attitudes toward themselves. Some had broken with social taboos and felt rejection as a consequence—for example, by marrying a person not selected by their parents, a sharp break with cultural traditions.

Finally, in terms of social settings, many had peer groups which supported or promoted drug use (sometimes, in fact, where drug use was the focus of the group). Several were in precarious social situations, for example, maintaining themselves on the streets as scavengers of garbage, as beggars, brokers of illegal currency or of drugs.

Holding the type of drug constant (although there are certainly variations that resulted from whether or not heroin was inhaled or injected and differences as well in the quantities consumed), much of the variation among the cases was most certainly a function of the interaction between set and setting, that is, between personality traits of the individuals and the social and physical circumstances. Looking at several of the cases illustrates the terms of this interaction.

P, the kid, is certainly an individual who could call on very few resources. P at the age of 14 was effectively on his own, living on the streets of Kathmandu. P's father is one of the oldest heroin users in Kathmandu. P's stepmother does not want P to live with his father and her. P left his mother's house when he was 7. Sometimes he visits her, but never stays at her home. P's mother is remarried and her new husband does not like to have P "sticking around" according to P.

Thus, P is homeless, living on the streets of Kathmandu and generating income by begging and collecting garbage for recycling—plastic bags, metal scraps, and the like. About half of his daily income of around 80 to 100 rupees goes for drugs and remainder for meals and for watching videos.

P who, as noted earlier, injects heroin, prefers to do so with his friends in a deserted temple. P and his friends play the "in and out game" while injecting—drawing blood back into the syringe after the initial heroin dose is injected. The procedure is repeated as many as eight times and is a common practice among Nepali users who inject heroin. For the times when P does not have enough money to buy heroin, "somebody" will give him prescription drugs or he will buy the cotton wads used by his friends to prepare their heroin injections.

P has been robbed while he slept, arrested (four times) by the police, and been the victim of police extortions to avoid arrest and harassment. Despite these problems, P (the youngest of his group) indicated that he cherished his freedom. He was satisfied as well with the locality where he lived because of the cleanliness of the garbage. The area where he lives is one where there are a considerable amount of tourists who throw out their garbage in plastic bags, sometimes even throwing away items of considerable value. P and his friends defend that territory against other garbage collectors as their prized possession.

Thus, P combines a personal situation which has left him ostracized from his family with a desire for his personal freedom. He found a niche for himself which permits survival, provides a circle of friends, but is racked with risks, of arrest, of robbery, and of extortion. He clearly sits outside the normal social order. His displacement is absolute—after the study was completed he died, apparently of a heroin overdose.

H, the Tibetan discussed earlier, is also a street person. H is a broker, engaging in money changing and selling drugs on the street. In addition to the usual risks of street life and of drug use itself, H is at risk for HIV infection, a common feature of those studied given that 14 of the 16 at some time or another in their drug careers injected heroin. H started injecting heroin a year before the study, when he was 24. He devotes almost all of his income to buying heroin. While he and his friends receive clean needles and sterilized water from an American social worker, H says he and his friends "share syringes now and then." H knows that AIDS is a serious disease, connected with "having sex," but does not know any more about its transmission or prevention.

H's physical appearance is that of a street beggar. He does not appear to pay any attention to his physical well-being. His circle of friends are those linked to consuming heroin. His other significant set of relations are those he meets in the process of securing money for heroin. He does like to play with the children in his neighborhood and was observed teaching them games. He dreams of having his own business, an antique shop. He says that "if I leave this *brown sugar,* I think I have a chance. If I really leave, then my mother will give me money to open a shop."

His mother has made him the offer, but on the condition that he returns to his native Tibet. H does not believe that it will be possible for him to give up heroin while remaining in Nepal. "Here (in Kathmandu) I don't find any job; here, I don't have a good friend."

H's status on the street is a precarious one, but certainly not as great as that of P. He cannot find meaningful employment and friends he can count on. However, his prospects are greater because he can still draw on resources such as potential emotional and economic support from his family in Tibet. He has a broader range of choices, a function of his personal relationship with his family and the social opportunities that signifies. He also can generate greater financial resources in his role as "broker." In short, his life chances are greater than other denizens of the street.

Life with Heroin, Nepali Style

Beyond the lives of the socially marginal, it is worthwhile observing that, along lines suggested by Hanson et al. (1985), some heroin users in Nepal, much like some users in the inner cities of the United States as well as elsewhere in the society, can engage in conventional activities, managing their heroin use. Take as an example the case of J.

J has been able to maintain his daily use while functioning in a fairly active and responsible occupation—as a guide for mountain trekkers. J, who was 24 at the time of this study, had been dependent on heroin from the time he was 16.

He asserts that he had a heroin dependence he could control when needed. His approach while acting as a guide, he explained, was to use heroin once a day, in a dosage half his normal amount, taken covertly early in the morning. He would maintain this level of drug use while guiding hikers 6 to 8 hours a day for treks that lasted up to 6 weeks. In line with his concern not to display his dependency, he always dressed impeccably. He was determined not to show weakness to anybody. While J provided the study of evidence of his own self-doubt, he demonstrated a desire, carried out in his job, to maintain himself within the society's mainstream.

CONCLUSIONS

The study is an exploratory one. It opens up a need to further examine the complex, dynamic, multivariables associated with drug use and users—focusing on such issues as the relationship between the breakdown of traditional norms, of traditional family roles, and the reshaping of personal traits and social circumstances including the redefinition of the role of the family. It also points to a cost of the poverty and marginality that permeates Kathmandu—the youngest subject and a casualty (see Postscript) was essentially a societal castoff, outside his family, securing his livelihood in the most menial of forms—picking over society's garbage, whose closest circle of friends were involved as a group in drug use.

The study helps to dispel a myth—that the single causal factor that determines drug use is the presence of foreign influences. The cases point to a variety of interactions between social circumstances, personality, and the availability and impact of heroin and other drugs that result in the initiation of use and its continuation. There was a "hippie" subculture in Nepal, centered on Kathmandu, that no longer exists except in the case of a few aging hangers-on. That subculture was facilitated by easy and unsanctioned access to drugs. But the subjects in this study largely post-date the heyday of the subculture and have had little or no contact with its members. The "hippie" culture cannot be adjudged guilty as the single and sole cause of drug use among Nepalis.

This has important policy implications for the Nepali government as well as once more attacking what has been a persistent myth in the history of drug use in many parts of the world. The blame is placed on them, not on us. In the United States this has meant blaming the Chinese for opium, the Mexicans for marijuana, the African-Americans for cocaine (in the 1920s) (see Note 6). In Nepal, as we have noted, the foreign devil was the Western "hippie," but the data of this study document rather that there is a complex interaction in the case of heroin use between personality and social circumstance which takes advantage of availability. This means that to effectively deal with the problem(s) requires far more than condemning a factor that, in fact, is only a very small part (if it is any part at all) of the equation.

And as was pointed out, Nepal, like the inner cities of the United States, offers instances that demonstrate that heroin users are not "righteous dope fiends" but individuals who can seek to establish or reestablish meaningful relationships in their lives (H with his family), hold gainful employment and manage their drug use (the case of J).

As the literature repeatedly points out, the approach that needs to be taken in Nepal as elsewhere to deal with the drug-use(r)-associated issues involves a realization of its complexity, of the interaction above all between personality and social setting, understanding that social setting involves in and of itself an intricate relationship between political, social, and economic factors that set limits on the life chances of drug users. And as Wayne Weibel has suggested, the value added of this sort of qualitative research, which can reach displaced or hidden populations such as users in the street, is that it "is often the only means available for gathering sensitive and valid data from otherwise elusive populations of substance abusers" (Weibel, 1990:5). And the picture that can be painted through such qualitative tools can provide insights regarding the relationships that exist and which can be the groundwork for future research.

POSTSCRIPT

It is incumbent on researchers of drug use to remember the very human dimension of what they do. That dimension is even more evident when the work is ethnographic. Two tragic events underscored that dimension for the researchers involved in this study.

Three months after the last interview with C, he died of a heroin overdose. Four months after the last interview with P, the youngest subject in the study, he also died of a heroin overdose. We were told that both overdoses were accidental. C has a wife and children and other family members who mourn him. There will not be many people apart from his gang who will remember P, let alone grieve for him. But he will be missed by his gang and by the members of this research team. We are grateful to both C and P for their willingness to share their concerns and their happiness, however small. May their souls find eternal peace.

ACKNOWLEDGMENTS

This article was authored by Joel M. Jutkowitz, based on field research originally designed by Hans Spielmann and undertaken by a team that was led by Ulrich Koehler, Jagdish Lohani, and Anil Pande. The research was supported by grants from the US Department of State through the US Embassy/Nepal, from the United States Agency for International Development (USAID) Asia Regional Narcotics Education Project, and from the USAID Narcotics Awareness and Education Project. Development Associates Inc. administered the two USAID projects. Youth Vision, a Nepali NGO concerned with drug abuse prevention among other activities, provided the institutional framework for the study. The analysis and interpretations of the data contained in this article were made by Dr. Jutkowitz who takes full responsibility for any errors or omissions. All of the institutions mentioned, while providing support for the research, are in no way responsible for the contents of the article nor do the opinions expressed represent the opinions of the US government, the US Agency for International Development, Development Associates, or Youth Vision.

NOTES

1. There have been several quantitative studies of drug use that have focused on Nepali high school students as well as broad discussions of the sociological concomitants of drug use, but the study reported here is the first ethnographic study directly focusing on drug use. As a counterpart to the ethnographic study reported in this article, the US Embassy, with technical assistance from the United States Agency for International Development (USAID) Asia Regional Narcotics Education project, also supported a survey of drug use among students (Bhandari and Subba, 1992).
2. The Bureau of International Narcotics Matters, *International Narcotics Control Report* (Department of State, Washington, D.C., April 1994) notes that Nepal is "an attractive alternative trafficking route" (p. 237). The same report notes that there is no evidence of any significant Nepalese opiate production. This report is commonly referred to as the INCSR.
3. See Spencer and Navaratnam (1981:9) and Rubin and Comitas (1975) which refer to the cult of Shiva and its relationship to the use of cannabis. As Rubin notes "Cannabis is used in worship

and in offerings made on the fulfillment of vows and *bhang* (an infusion of cannabis) is customarily served at weddings and religious festivals" (1975:17).
4. The data is this paragraph are based on the author's interviews in 1987 with officials of the Nepali government as well as local observers of the Nepali drug scene. See J. M. Jutkowitz, *Asia Regional Narcotics Awareness Survey,* (Arlington, VA: Development Associates, 1987) Ch. IV. The 1994 INCSR (see note 2) reports a total of 25,000 users in the country, although this represents an estimate which does not result from national prevalence studies.
5. In discussing heroin, Robins writes about how a user initiates use, the frequency and amount of use, and the physical and social problems that seem to result from use in defining what he refers to as "addict careers" (1979, 325). A review of such ethnographic studies as Hanson et al. (1985) or Feldman et al. (1990) shows an attention to these sorts of questions as well as others related to the particular type of drug and its specific cultural setting.
6. For a discussion of the racial stereotyping of users of various drugs, see Musto (1987). Musto writes about the myths of the relationship between African-Americans and cocaine use (pp.7–8), Chinese and opium use (pp. 3–6), and Mexicans and marijuana use (p. 219).

REFERENCES

ALCARAZ, F., FLORES, N., ZAMBRANA, E., and BOURGOIS, P. (1995). *The Forgotten Children.* La Paz: National Secretariat of Health and Social Welfare.

BAHADUR BISTA, D. (1987). *People of Nepal,* 5th Ed. Kathmandu: Ratna Pustak Bhandar.

BHANDARI, B., and SUBBA, C. (1992). *Students and Drugs in Nepal.* Kathmandu: Drug Abuse Prevention Association Nepal.

FELDMAN, H. W., and ALDRICH, M. R. (1990). The role of ethnography in substance abuse research and public policy: Historical precedent and future prospects. In E. Y. Lambert (Ed.), *The Collection and Interpretation of Data from Hidden Populations* (NIDA Research Monograph 98). Rockville, MD: National Institute on Drug Abuse.

HANSON, B., BESCHNER, G., WALTERS, J. M., and BOVELLE, E. (1985). *Life with Heroin: Voices from the Inner City.* Lexington, KY: Lexington Books.

INGRAM, L. H. (1984). *The Boys in the Barracks: Observations on American Military Life.* Philadelphia, PA: Institute for the Study of Human Issues.

MUSTO, D. F. (1987). *The American Disease: Origins of Narcotic Control.* New Haven, CT: Yale University Press.

RATNER, M. (Ed.) (1993). *Crack Pipe as Pimp: An Ethnographic Investigation of Sex-for-Crack Exchanges.* New York, NY: Lexington Books.

ROBINS, L. N. (1979). Addict careers. In R. J. Dupont, A. Goldstein, and J. O'Donnell (Eds.), *Handbook of Drug Abuse.* Rockville, MD: National Institute on Drug Abuse.

RUBIN, V., and COMITAS, L. (1975). *Ganja in Jamaica: A Medical Anthropological Study of Chronic Marijuana Use.* The Hague: Mouton.

SEVENTH INTERNATIONAL CONFERENCE OF NON-GOVERNMENT ORGANIZATIONS ON DRUG DEPENDENCE (1985). *Publication No. 2.* Kathmandu: IFNGO.

SPENCER, C. P., and NAVARATNAM, V. (1981). *Drug Abuse in East Asia.* Oxford: Oxford University Press.

WEIBEL, W. (1990). Identifying and gaining access to hidden populations. In E. Y Lambert (Ed.), *The Collection and Interpretations of Data from Hidden Populations* (pp. 4–11) [National Institute on Drug Abuse Research Monograph 98, DHHS Publication (ADM) 90-1678] Washington, D.C.: US Government Printing Office.

ZINBERG, N. (1984). *Drug, Set and Setting: The Basis for Controlled Intoxicant Use.* New Haven, CT: Yale University Press.

QUESTIONS FOR THOUGHT AND DISCUSSION

Chapter 5: "Becoming a Marihuana User," by Howard S. Becker

1. Why is it important to understand the user's attitude and experience as it relates to continued marijuana use?
2. How does a person "learn" to use marijuana?
3. How does Professor Becker's theory contradict the traditional medical model used in understanding the behavior of the marijuana user?

Chapter 6: "The High, the Money, and the Fame: The Emergent Social Context of 'New Marijuana': Use among Urban Youth," by Jean J. Schensul, Cristina Huebner, Merrill Singer, Marvin Snow, Pablo Feliciano, and Lorie Broomhall

1. What are the cultural factors associated with the use of high-potency marijuana?
2. How do the ethnographic findings contradict epidemiological trends in marijuana use among youth?

Chapter 7: "Urban Crop Circles: Urban Cannabis Growers in the North of England," by Garfield R. Potter and Simeon L. Dann

1. What are the characteristics of commercial cannabis growers in England?
2. Please describe the typology of such growers.
3. How are the cannabis markets influenced by such diversity in its growers?

Chapter 8: " 'You Become Really Close . . . You Talk about the Silly Things You Did, and We Laugh': The Role of Binge Drinking in Female Secondary Students' Lives," by Margaret Sheehan and Damien Ridge

1. What role does alcohol play in the lives of these participants?
2. How does alcohol serve as a facilitator?
3. How is binge drinking related to gender relations?
4. What kind of public health model do the authors propose?

Chapter 9: "Race and the Culture of College Drinking: An Analysis of White Privilege on Campus," by Robert L. Peralta

1. What accounts for the difference in drinking patterns among White and Black students?
2. What three social structural mechanisms account for disparate drinking patterns?
3. How might institutional bias account for such behavioral differences among White and Black students?

Chapter 10: "Fantasy Island: An Ethnography of Alcohol and Gender Roles in a Latino Gay Bar," by Carlos F. Cáceres and Jorge I. Cortiñas

1. For the participants in the study, what function do bars serve?
2. How is social drinking defined by the participants?

3. Why do the authors make reference to the study site as a "Fantasy Island"?

4. What role does ethnicity play in understanding drinking, sexual behavior, and sexual identity?

Chapter 11: "Gen-X Junkie: Ethnographic Research with Young White Heroin Users in Washington, DC," by Todd G. Pierce

1. What are the social and behavioral dynamics of young White heroin users in the Washington, DC, area?

2. What are the differences between White and Black heroin users in this study?

3. What are the public health implications of the author's finding?

Chapter 12: "Drug Use in Nepal: The View from the Street," by Joel M. Jutkowitz, Hans Spielmann, Ulrich Koehler, Jagdish Lohani, and Anil Pande

1. Please describe the complex process surrounding the participants' drug-using history?

2. How is poverty related to the participants' drug-using experiences?

3. Are there gender and cultural differences among these participants?

WORLD WIDE WEB SITES

Web of Addictions Fact Sheet
http://www.well.com/user/woa/facts.htm

Marijuana Anonymous World Services
http://www.marijuana-anonymous.org

The Psychedelic Library
http://www.druglibrary.org/schaffer/lsd/lsdmenu.htm

The Multidisciplinary Association for Psychedelic Studies
http://www.maps.org/

Erowid: Alcohol
http://www.erowid.org/chemicals/alcohol/alcohol.shtml

Erowid: Heroin
http://www.erowid.org/chemicals/heroin/heroin.shtml

After the Party Is Over

> Like other really crucial experiences, drugs turn everyday reality topsy-turvy and force us to contemplate our inner selves. They do not open the doors of another world nor do they free our fantasy: rather, they open the doors of our world and bring us face to face with our phantoms.
>
> *Octavio Paz, Alternating Currents*

INTRODUCTION

The selections presented in this section stimulate more questions rather than provide definitive answers. For example, why do some people prefer powder versus "crack" cocaine? What is the allure of methamphetamine? Why do others indiscriminately replace one drug with another? How do women and men involved in the illegal distribution of crack cocaine confront erratic customers, violent competitors, and law enforcement? How could some people be willing to do *anything* for the opportunity to use a drug, while others could simply walk away from the experience? Is it possible for some drugs to have a legitimate role in mental health therapy? Do drugs remove the social boundaries between one's sexual identity and behavior? The purpose of the following chapters in section III is to guide the reader through such questions and possibly stimulate more inquisitive comments that had not been anticipated.

The first selection, "Rich Man's Speed: A Qualitative Study of Young Cocaine Users," by Professors Annabel Boys, Julie Dobson, John Marsden, and John Strang, presents qualitative data from thirty-four cocaine users recruited from the streets of London, U.K. Their objective is to examine patterns of cocaine use, associated health risks among such users, and the development of an anti-drug awareness campaign that mirrors the user profile as presented herein.

In the second selection, "Crack Dealing, Gender, and Arrest Avoidance," University of Missouri–St. Louis Professors Bruce A. Jacobs and Jody Miller present in-depth qualitative interviews with female crack dealers, and examine how these women initiate and sustain arrest avoidance techniques. The professors situate the women's arrest-risk management style within a gender-cultural ("street") specific scheme.

In the third selection, "Street Status and the Sex-for-Crack Scene in San Francisco," Professors Harvey W. Feldman, Frank Espada, Sharon Penn, and Sharon Byrd examine the contextual overlap between drug-using behavior (specifically crack cocaine), sexual histories, and the risk for HIV/AIDS exposure among a group of men and women in San Francisco, California.

   The fourth selection, "The Lives and Times of Asian-Pacific American Women Drug Users: An Ethnographic Study of Their Methamphetamine Use" by Professor Karen A. Joe, presents the first ethnographic account of Asian-Pacific American women drug users, and specifically, their coping strategies as they traverse both this specific drug subculture and their respective familial networks.

   In the fifth selection, "Negative Experiences on Ecstasy: The Role of Drug, Set, and Setting," Professors Karen McElrath and Kieran McEvoy present qualitative in-depth interviews of ninety-eight current or former users of MDMA/Ecstasy in Northern Ireland. The researchers present data focusing on the factors relating to negative experiences as self-reported by the participants. In addition, McElrath and McEvoy discuss how one's social–psycho–physiological state, or set, and environment shapes a person's overall drug experience.

13

"Rich Man's Speed"

A Qualitative Study of Young Cocaine Users

Annabel Boys, Julie Dobson, John Marsden, and John Strang
King's College London

INTRODUCTION

In recent years, results from social surveys have reinforced government concern about increasing cocaine use among young people in the UK. The most recent British Crime Survey found that 5% of 16–24-year-olds reported cocaine use in the past year. This represented a five-fold increase on reports to the 1994 survey (Ramsay *et al.*, 2001; Sharp *et al.*, 2001). Data gathered from a sample of 11–15-year-olds in England in 1998 suggest that around 1% of this age group had used cocaine in the past year (Goddard & Higgins, 1999).

Cocaine tends to be bracketed with heroin as the most harmful drugs currently used by young people (UKADCU, 1999). While young heroin users have received considerable attention from researchers, policy makers and education specialists (Parker *et al.*, 1998), cocaine use has only recently been recognized as a problem among young people and very little is known about who uses it and the types of harm experienced by users in this age group.

There are currently two forms of cocaine that are available in the UK: cocaine hydrochloride (a white crystalline salt, often referred to as 'powder cocaine') and a base form of the drug commonly known as 'crack cocaine' (Marsden *et al.*, 1998b). Cocaine hydrochloride is most commonly used intranasally, whereby a dose of the drug is sniffed

Adapted from ' "Rich Man's Speed": A Qualitative Study of Young Cocaine Users,' Annabel Boys, Julie Dobson, John Marsden, and John Strang, *Drugs: Education, Prevention, and Policy,* vol. 9(2), pp. 197–209, 2002. Taylor & Francis Ltd. http://www.tandf.co.uk/journals.

into the nose and absorbed mainly via the nasal mucosa. Cocaine in this form can also be swallowed or mixed with water for intravenous injection. Smoking cocaine hydrochloride is believed to be uncommon as the high temperatures required to make the drug vaporize result in the decomposition of most of the active ingredients, rendering this mode of use very inefficient (Jeffcoat *et al.*, 1989). In contrast, the much lower melting point of crack cocaine makes it more suitable for smoking. Users can either prepare crack cocaine from cocaine powder (by adding sodium bicarbonate and/or ammonia and heating the mixture to isolate solid crystals of 'crack'), or they may purchase the drug already in this form.

The speed with which cocaine reaches the brain, and thus the effects are felt, differs significantly according to the route of administration. If it is ingested orally, the effects are usually felt after 10–30 minutes; if intranasally administered, this time period drops to 2–3 minutes; if injected, it takes approximately 30–45 seconds; and finally, if the base form of the drug is smoked, it reaches the brain within 8–10 seconds (Vereby & Gold, 1988). The mode of administration is thought to be closely linked to the severity of consequences associated with use. Evidence shows a greater propensity for dependence on cocaine when it is smoked as crack or injected (Hatsukami & Fischman, 1996). A binge or episodic pattern is particularly common when crack cocaine is smoked, with large amounts being consumed over several hours and even days. This is likely to be due to the short duration of action, with the intense but brief euphoric rush encouraging compulsive further use (Gossop *et al.*, 1994). Tolerance to the effects experienced from cocaine use can develop rapidly, and consequently dependence liability appears to be greatest for smoking, followed by intravenous and lastly intranasal routes (Vereby and Gold 1988). However, it has been suggested that the use of cocaine powder intranasally may be a 'gateway behaviour' to using crack cocaine (Hatsukami & Fischman, 1996).

Recent focused studies of drug use in London have suggested that the latter part of the 1990s saw a marked increase in the number of young people using cocaine hydrochloride (Boys *et al.*, 1999b, 2000b). In a study of young nontreatment polydrug users (aged 16–22), over half reported that they had used cocaine powder and just over 40% of these had also used crack cocaine (Boys *et al.*, 2000b). This study also found that a substantial proportion of the powder cocaine users (43.5%) had *never* tried other stimulant drugs such as ecstasy and amphetamines. In contrast, national probability survey data suggest that levels of crack cocaine use have remained stable over the past 6 years at less than 1% (Ramsay *et al.*, 2001; Sharp *et al.*, 2001).

Although there has been little published on the characteristics of young cocaine users in England, a substantial body of research has examined cocaine powder consumption in Europe, Australia and North America (e.g., Cohen, 1994; Hammersley & Ditton, 1994; McCarthy & Hagan, 1996; Mugford, 1994). These studies have tended to describe the typical cocaine powder user as single, in their mid-20s and better educated than average. Users under the age of 20 years have been traditionally reported to be extremely rare (Cohen, 1994; Harrison, 1994) and in general, controlled use of cocaine powder has been described as the norm, with only a minority developing problems associated with their use (Drucker & Davies, 1994). However, little is known about the reasons why young people are attracted to using cocaine, their patterns of use or associated negative consequences.

This paper presents the results of a qualitative study designed to examine patterns of cocaine use and health risks among young users. The primary aims of the study were to profile patterns of cocaine use and to explore how cocaine hydrochloride (referred to as 'cocaine powder' throughout the rest of the paper) is perceived by users in relation to crack cocaine, amphetamines and ecstasy. Research in this area is fundamental to developing suitable educational and policy responses to target young stimulant users.

METHOD

Data were collected via in-depth face-to-face interviews, complemented by a short quantitative questionnaire. A team of five 'peer access interviewers' (PAIs) was employed to recruit and interview their cocaine-using peers. The use of PAIs has been promoted as a valuable means of collecting data from hidden populations of drug users (Brain *et al.,* 2001; Griffiths, 1998; Griffiths *et al.,* 1993; Power, 1994). Four of the interviewers had already been involved in interviewing respondents for other studies on young drug users conducted by the research centre, the fifth expressed an interest in interviewing work after being interviewed for the study herself. The PAIs underwent a one-day training course on interviewing skills and using the questionnaire. Each person received an interview manual developed specifically for the study. The manual provided a written reference source to consolidate material covered in the training sessions such as background to the study, confidentiality, interviewing techniques and notes clarifying potentially problematic questions. An informal approach to training was employed to try to ensure that participants were as relaxed as possible and felt able to ask questions throughout the sessions. Interviewers were also encouraged to contact the research staff if any further questions concerning the study arose after the initial training. Further training was provided during the course of the study when additional needs were identified through debriefing sessions or from checking completed questionnaires and interview tapes.

Respondents were recruited using 'snowballing' methods starting with individuals already known to the five interviewers. In this approach each individual that is accessed during the sampling stage is asked to nominate another suitable candidate for the study. This process is repeated until no new nominations are received or until sufficient recruits have been obtained. Snowball sampling has had a history of success in sampling hidden populations of drug users (e.g., Biernacki, 1986; Forsyth, 1996; Lenton *et al.,* 1997). All respondents had used cocaine powder within the year prior to interview. As resources were limited and consequently the sample size was also limited, interviewers were instructed to recruit a range of 'types' of user, including those who had stopped using the drug and some who were currently using several times each week. All participants were informed that the data collected were both anonymous and confidential and that participation was voluntary. The interviews took place in informal community settings such as cafés, parks and private houses.

In the first part of the interview, a brief, structured, interviewer-administered questionnaire was used to record sample demographic characteristics and consumption patterns of nine substances (tobacco, alcohol, cannabis, amphetamines, LSD, ecstasy, cocaine powder, crack cocaine and heroin). Items were based on frequency and quantity measures developed by Marsden *et al.* (1998a).

The second part of the interview used a semi-structured interview schedule to gather qualitative data on the following topics: patterns of cocaine use, context of use, negative effects from use, perceived risks associated with use and perceptions of cocaine relative to other stimulant drugs. Both parts of the interview were tape-recorded with the interviewee's consent. This facilitated quality control measures as it enabled the researchers to check that the interview protocol had been followed and that the questionnaire had been completed accurately. It also provided a means of checking (and correcting) any inconsistencies or anomalies in the quantitative questionnaires before the data were computer-coded. The semi-structured part of the interview (part 2) was transcribed and subjected to a content analysis based on methods described by Patton (1990). All interviewee names have been changed to protect anonymity.

RESULTS

The sample comprised 34 young people (10 males) between the ages of 18 and 28 (mean age of 22 years). A fifth of the sample ($n = 7$) were unemployed at the time of interview; just over half ($n = 18$) were in full-time work, two were working on a part-time basis and seven were in full-time education. Seven participants were living in council or housing association properties; just over a quarter were living with their parents; 15 in privately rented accommodation; two owned a property and one was sleeping on a friend's floor. Six of the interviewees had no formal educational qualifications.

Substance Use

In addition to cocaine powder, all respondents reported lifetime use of alcohol, cigarettes and cannabis. Most ($n = 32$, 94%) had also used amphetamines and 79% ($n = 27$) had used ecstasy. Ten reported that they had tried crack cocaine (29%). Table 13-1 presents data on lifetime prevalence of substance use together with the mean age of first use.

On average, respondents had tried seven out of the nine substances surveyed (range 4–9). Two people had tried them all.

The average age for first cocaine use was 18.4 years, although some were as young as 14 years when they first tried the drug. Several individuals had moved straight from cannabis to cocaine, without trying ecstasy or amphetamines first (similar patterns were

TABLE 13–1   Substance use history ($n = 34$)

Substance	n (%)	Mean age first use (years)	Range (years)
Alcohol	34 (100)	12.3	2–16
Cigarettes	34 (100)	12.2	6–18
Cannabis	34 (100)	14.5	11–21
Cocaine	34 (100)	18.4	14–23
Amphetamines	32 (94)	16.3	13–23
Ecstasy	27 (79)	17.3	13–23
LSD	19 (56)	15.9	11–21
Crack cocaine	10 (29)	19.4	15–23
Heroin	6 (18)	18.2	16–22

TABLE 13–2   Substance use during the year and 3 months prior to interview
($n = 34$)

Substance (number ever used)	Used in last 90 days (n)	Mean days used in past 90 (n)	Typical amount used (range)
Alcohol ($n = 34$)	34	44	9 (1–32)[a]
Cigarettes ($n = 34$)	31	69	12 (1–40)[b]
Cannabis ($n = 34$)	30	55	3.5 (0.1–25)[c]
Amphetamines ($n = 32$)	8	7	0.6 (0.1–1.5)[d]
Ecstasy ($n = 27$)	20	7	2.4 (0.25–8.0)[e]
LSD ($n = 19$)	1	2	1[e]
Cocaine powder ($n = 34$)	33	16	0.8 (0.1–4.0)[d]
Crack cocaine ($n = 10$)	2	3	0.6 (0.3–1.0)[d]
Heroin ($n = 6$)	1	5	0.13[d]

[a]Standard units of alcohol.
[b]Number of cigarettes.
[c]Number of cannabis cigarettes.
[d]Grams.
[e]Number of tablets.

found in our earlier study—Boys *et al.,* 1999b, 2000b). In particular, just over a fifth of the sample reported that they had never tried ecstasy.

When recent substance use was examined, a different picture emerged. On average, respondents had used five out of the nine different substances during the last 90 days (range 3–8). The most common substances (other than cocaine) were alcohol ($n = 34$, 100%), cigarettes ($n = 31$, 91%) and cannabis ($n = 30$, 88%). Use of the other stimulant drugs was much less common with just under 60% having used ecstasy and less than a quarter reporting amphetamine use during this time period. Table 13-2 presents data on prevalence, frequency and typical quantity of use for the nine substances during the 90 days prior to interview.

Cocaine Use

Two-thirds ($n = 23$, 68%) of the sample had used cocaine on at least 50 separate occasions and 12 (35%) reported over 100 occasions of use. Patterns of current cocaine use ranged from consumption on special occasions only, to using several grams each week. Fourteen (41%) of the respondents were using cocaine at least once each week at the time of interview. The average amount used on a typical occasion also varied considerably, ranging from one 'line' to 4 g, with an average of 0.84g (mode = 0.5 g).

The most popular route of administration for cocaine was intranasal ($n = 33$, 97%); one person reported that they mainly smoked it and a further five (15%) estimated that they smoked it on between 5% and 25% of using occasions. One female respondent explained that her history of amphetamine and cocaine use had resulted in nasal problems (mainly irritation of the mucous membranes and sinus problems) that made sniffing cocaine unpleasant. Consequently, she had started to rub the drug on to her gums instead. There were no reports of using cocaine by injection.

Differences in the perceived effects obtained from cocaine powder according to whether it was snorted or smoked appeared to motivate route of administration choices. For example, in the following extracts two female interviewees explain how they deliberately vary cocaine consumption methods:

> The effects from smoking it [cocaine] can make the effects of a line last longer—we smoke some every time we buy it—we do a line and I'll make a spliff [tobacco mixed with cocaine in a cigarette], then we do another line. (Lynsey, aged 24)

> I like to start with a couple of Charlie joints [tobacco mixed with cocaine in a cigarette], I put about a line's worth in one joint and then share that around so we have a couple of them and a few drinks . . . that eases you into it, it's not as strong as just doing a line straight away. (Sarah, aged 23)

There was widespread awareness among interviewees that cocaine could be smoked both with and without tobacco, but some confusion over the difference between smoking powder cocaine and cocaine in the form of crack. Several reported that they had first used cocaine accidentally by smoking a 'joint' (which they had thought contained only cannabis) that was passed to them in a social situation.

Context of Cocaine Use

Cocaine use generally took place with a group of friends and was described as a social activity. A few commonly used with just one other person (often a partner) and just one respondent habitually used the drug when alone. This particular young woman was using the most heavily out of all the interviewees (almost every day) and she no longer associated her use with socializing.

Using cocaine at home or at a friend's house was common. When in public places, pubs and bars were more popular locations for using the drug than night-clubs. This seemed to be due to the logistics of using cocaine in a night-club. Problems highlighted included the drug getting 'mashed-up' (getting sticky in the hot and sweaty atmosphere which made it impossible to take intranasally); long queues to use the toilets (where use commonly took place) and concerns that taking the drug in the toilets in pairs or in groups might attract attention. Most who used cocaine in association with going to night-clubs tended to limit consumption to when they were at home getting ready to go out and in a pub or bar before reaching the club.

Motivations for Using Cocaine

The most common positive effects reported from cocaine use were feeling more confident, feeling more sociable and having more energy. The increase in confidence seemed to be a major motivating factor for use, particularly as it helped to facilitate social interaction and reduce feelings of self-consciousness.

There was evidence that some users had motivations for choosing cocaine over other stimulant drugs. Explanations included preferring the less intense and easier to control effects of cocaine to those experienced from ecstasy or amphetamines. This point is illustrated by the following two quotes:

What do you like about the effects of cocaine?
The main thing is that you feel completely stable, rather than feeling like you've taken drugs. With other things you start to feel like you're losing control a bit, like you're going to spin out, make a fool of yourself, whereas cocaine makes you be able to think fairly quickly, can hear everything you're doing, your ability to communicate with other people is still intact, but you've got a sense of empowerment, confidence . . . you feel like you can handle it, like you can handle a lot and not feel spaced out . . . You could easily take cocaine and nobody would know that you're on it, it's quite easy to conceal it. (Toni, aged 27)

Pills [ecstasy tablets] are more of rushing feeling, you feel weird . . . whereas coke you're alert, don't feel as mangled. With pills you're trying to find a step, holding onto the wall, all your vision is going—I don't get that with coke and still get the dance-all-night feeling. (Jemma, aged 19)

The perception that the effects associated with cocaine are more predictable and shorter-lived than those associated with other stimulants is highlighted in the following excerpt from an interview with Sarah, a 23-year-old student:

Once you've done a whole pill [ecstasy tablet] there's nothing you can do to stop it. You can freak out on a pill and sometimes they can make you hallucinate. Whereas on coke the worst that can happen is just that you get a bit paranoid and it can be quite annoying but you know that you can do a line and then just wait and see how you feel and do another or whatever, you're in a lot more control I think, which people like. (Sarah, aged 23)

The shorter-lived effects associated with cocaine use were a clear attraction to Taz, a 24-year-old sales assistant, as this meant that using it did not impinge so much on other areas of his life:

It's a bigger choice to take an E than to have a line. I'd prefer to have a line as I know that I can have a couple of drinks and then go home. With E you need to think about the future—what you're doing the next day etc. (Taz, aged 24)

Additional reasons for preferring cocaine to other stimulant drugs included beliefs that the after-effects from the drug are less unpleasant and that use is less damaging to health in the long term.

Cocaine powder was widely associated with wealth, fashion and a glamorous lifestyle. It was described by several as 'rich man's speed' and regarded as a status symbol as the following two quotes illustrate:

It's because it's expensive and it's because it has connotations of rock stars. People hire a Rolls Royce because it makes them feel good and you would take cocaine to feel good in the same way. (Ben, aged 25)

It doesn't seem to get the bad press like other drugs, E, crack, heroin. Loads of famous people do coke—gives it a coolness. (Rob, aged 22)

It's all about the money . . . I think it's gonna keep spreading and I think it's ageless because it represents money to people—it's about status to people. (Jo, aged 28)

In contrast, amphetamines and ecstasy were regarded as less exclusive:

> Because it's expensive it's seen as more classy, compared with E's and speed. (Denise, aged 22)

In addition to the perception that cocaine was a more glamorous and 'classy' drug, some suggested that it was also more socially acceptable than other drugs. The following quote from a 21-year-old student illustrates this point:

> There's a massive coke scene in London, everyone's into it—even quite straight people who don't even smoke or do anything else will do cocaine and say it's OK. It's the one that's acceptable, maybe because of the glamour attached to it, the media world. (Jackie, aged 21)

A recurring theme was that cocaine is the ideal accessory for people who like to wear expensive fashionable clothes and who want to give the impression that they are wealthy. Once again, these observations about cocaine seemed to be in sharp contrast to other stimulant drugs such as ecstasy and amphetamines.

> Cocaine comes with a lot of material things like clothes, designers, the local pub with boys in Versace or whatever with their Charlie or their Charlie spliffs, trying to get the girls' cos the girls want coke off them . . . I see 17-year-olds using it in pubs. Showing off, fashion, drugs, money, mobile phones, that's why a lot of these youngsters get into dealing, it's more of a look to impress. (Ruth, aged 19)

For some, the fact that cocaine is relatively expensive seemed to have led to the conclusion that it is of better quality or 'purer' than other drugs and therefore less damaging or dangerous:

> I see speed as being the one that does the most damage, from what I've heard and learnt. That's why I don't take it as I've heard it's really bad for my body and I don't really like the hit, totally different, lot harder, more manic. The cheaper the drug the more damaging it is to you, that may be a really stupid thing to say, but if it's taken less time to prepare, cheaper chemicals going into it, I'd rather spend more and get a better hit. (Jude, aged 25)

Cocaine was often described as a safer alternative to amphetamines or ecstasy. For example, many expressed concern that the contents of an ecstasy tablet were unknown and potentially lethal:

> E's more dangerous, because of the effects. You don't know what you're doing with ecstasy and you don't know what's in the tablets. Whereas cocaine, it's pure so you know what you're taking, it's a lot different. (Chloe, aged 18)

Several respondents cited the high-profile media stories about the death of Leah Betts [1] as having had a significant impact on their views about ecstasy. This was particularly evident among those such as 20-year-old Karen, a full-time student, who had never tried ecstasy:

> *Have you ever used ecstasy?*
> No . . . it scares me. Leah Betts' campaign really affected me . . . Before Leah I was aware that people took them and died from them, but that campaign was just amazing . . . I wouldn't take one now. (Karen, aged 20)

The lack of similar high-profile stories about cocaine seemed to have led to the conclusion that it was a safer option as Yvonne, a 20-year-old student, explained:

> I think people don't really see the dangers of coke. Don't hear much about it, I know that it is addictive . . . unless something major comes out about the dangers of it I think its use will continue. A lot of people have been scared by what happened to Leah Betts. (Yvonne, aged 20)

Negative Experiences

The negative effects that participants had experienced from their cocaine use can be categorized in three groups: (1) short-term effects experienced while under the influence of cocaine; (2) after-effects experienced on the day following use (often referred to as the 'come-down' period); and (3) long-term effects.

1. *Short-term effects.* Short-term physical symptoms reported by the sample included nasal irritation or bleeding, tension in facial muscles and a dry mouth. Common short-term psychological effects were feelings of anxiety, paranoia and insomnia. The consumption of other drugs (particularly cannabis and/or alcohol) to help to cope with or to reduce these side-effects was widely described.

2. *After-effects.* After-effects experienced during the day following cocaine use or 'come-down' period included irritability, fatigue, feeling low or depressed, and being withdrawn. Again, using other drugs (such as alcohol or cannabis) to cope with these was commonly described.

3. *Long-term effects.* The recognition of long-term negative effects was relatively uncommon in this sample. The few respondents who recognized that they had experienced long-term effects in association with their cocaine use mentioned feeling paranoid, depressed and having relationship problems as a result of their use. Heavier cocaine use was also associated with users becoming less sociable and more withdrawn.

Using Cocaine with Other Substances

Using other psychoactive substances concurrently with cocaine was extremely common. By far the most popular substance to use in addition to cocaine was alcohol (though there were also reports of cannabis, ecstasy and amphetamine use). Virtually everyone interviewed reported that they regularly drank alcohol when using cocaine. Reports of drinking more heavily than usual while under the influence of cocaine were widely described, with several reporting that they often drank at least twice their usual alcohol intake. For a significant number of respondents, cocaine use was always accompanied by alcohol. Some used cocaine to moderate the undesirable effects of alcohol (such as feeling less in control and unsteady on their feet), so that they could continue to drink. In contrast, others used alcohol in a functional way to moderate the effects of cocaine: to help them to relax more, to take the edge off feelings of anxiety or paranoia and to help them to sleep at the end of the evening. As Kate, an unemployed 22-year-old, explained:

> I won't have cocaine without alcohol. Because when you have cocaine on its own it's a completely different buzz. You can get on a paranoid buzz if you have it on its own. The alcohol brings you on a level. (Kate, aged 22)

In the following excerpt, Sarah, a 23-year-old student who had been using cocaine intermittently over the past 2 years, describes how she typically uses alcohol when taking cocaine to ensure that she can sleep afterwards:

> Drink doesn't really have such an effect on you when you're on coke—you feel the need for
> the alcohol . . . you don't seem to get really drunk, but then if you drink enough, when you start
> coming down from the coke and it [the alcohol] starts having an effect on you then you become
> drunk and that helps you get to sleep—it sounds stupid, but it's like an equation, you have to
> get it just right.

Overall, respondents recognized very few risks associated with using cocaine and alcohol
together. A few mentioned that the after-effects or 'hangover' experienced the next day was
often worse after using cocaine and alcohol than after just using alcohol. However, there
was a tendency to attribute this to heavy alcohol use and a lack of sleep, rather than the cocaine consumption. Only one person (a 21-year-old female student) reported trying to avoid
alcohol when using cocaine. In contrast, many of the ecstasy users described drinking very
little or nothing when under the influence of ecstasy. This seemed to have been prompted
by harm-reduction information obtained from leaflets and other media targeting young
stimulant users.

Perceived Risks Associated with Cocaine Use

Most interviewees seemed to think that there were few long-term risks associated with cocaine unless use was particularly heavy. Almost all reported that they did not see themselves
ever having enough money to use cocaine with sufficient frequency to be at risk from physical harms or psychological addiction. Knowledge about reducing harms associated with
cocaine was notably scarce. While appropriate measures to take when using ecstasy were
widely described, only two people mentioned strategies relating to cocaine use. One of
these, Jemma, a 19-year-old secretary who was using approximately half a gram of powder
cocaine twice a week, describes the measures she takes when using cocaine in the following excerpt:

> I drink plenty of alcohol to bring myself down, drink lots of orange juice, don't take vitamin
> pills and I know I should . . . I don't know about the harmful effects and I don't know about
> safe ways to take Charlie. I don't think there is a safe way.

Another respondent indicated that they always tried to eat a meal before using cocaine. Participants stressed a need for more information about cocaine, related risks and how to avoid
them, similar to that provided for ecstasy users.

Crack Cocaine

Ten people (29%) reported that they had used cocaine in the form of crack. The age of first
use for this drug ranged from 15 to 23 years (mean = 19.3 years). One person had tried cocaine in this form on just one occasion, six estimated that they had used it between two and
ten times and one person had used it on over 100 separate occasions. Five respondents had
used this drug within the past year and two within the 3 months prior to interview. Just one
person indicated that they were currently using crack several times a week.

Despite the fact that almost a third of the sample had tried cocaine in this form, its image was in sharp contrast to that of powder cocaine. Virtually everyone (both those who had used it and those who had not) spoke about crack cocaine using negative language. Words such as 'dirty' and 'scummy' were chosen to describe this form of cocaine. Many spontaneously associated it with heroin when asked how they thought about crack, saying that it was used by 'junkies', 'low-life' and 'crack-heads'. Unlike cocaine in its powder form, crack was clearly not associated with socializing.

> I've never used crack and see it as a different image—coke I see as social, crack is more underclass and scummy. Doing crack, you wouldn't go out for the night. (Neil, aged 22)

Of particular concern was how poorly informed some respondents were about crack. Several were unaware that it is a smokeable form of cocaine. On hearing the interviewer's explanation of what crack is, two respondents realized that they had actually used crack unwittingly. Twenty-three-year-old Sarah, was one of these:

> 'I was confused about crack for a long time because I was smoking it without really realising it—I know that now, because you can smoke coke in a bong or in a joint . . . you can get like a little bottle with foil on the top same as you do with crack and smoke it like that—so I've done that before. When I've been offered a bong with white stuff on the top I've just assumed it's been coke, but looking back now it was actually crack. I didn't even ask, I just assumed it was coke because I knew he did coke as well and then I realized later . . . I should have realized at the time because I remember thinking it was quite a weird buzz and I really craved another shot at the bong . . . It was a very intense high, but that feeling at the end of the high really bothered me—that just really wanting some more. I know how addictive it [crack] is, it's really addictive and so I don't think I will do it again.

It was also common for interviewees to associate crack use with people who commit crime. Many (like Sarah) described crack cocaine as being very 'addictive', and explained that it was best avoided as it was very easy to become ensnared into heavy use. No one who was interviewed for this study spoke of this form of the drug in a positive light.

DISCUSSION

The profile of the cocaine users interviewed in this study challenges prior perceptions about the typical cocaine user noted in the introduction. Previous studies have suggested that the typical cocaine user is in their mid-20s and is better educated than average and that cocaine users under the age of 20 are extremely rare (Cohen, 1994; Harrison, 1994). In contrast, the average age for the first use of cocaine among the current sample was 18.4 years and ranged from 14 to 23 years. This raises the possibility that there may be a substantial population of people much younger than previously thought who are using cocaine. Evidence from the most recent British Crime Surveys (Ramsay & Partridge, 1999; Ramsay et al., 2001) supports these results, suggesting that approximately 3–4% of 16–19-year-olds have tried cocaine. These data highlight a need to educate young people about cocaine while they are still in compulsory education (i.e. under 16 years) to ensure that when and if the opportunity to initiate use presents itself, they are well equipped to make informed decisions about the drug. Similarly, characteristics of the sample clearly question the notion that cocaine users are 'better educated than average'.

Indeed, five participants had no qualifications at all. This again suggest that perceptions that cocaine users are generally from an older, more affluent section of society than users of other common illicit drugs may be inaccurate (although a larger study is required to confirm this).

Routes of Use

Given the pharmacological properties of cocaine powder, the finding that some respondents typically smoked cocaine powder as well as consuming it intranasally was not anticipated. It would be expected that this practice would result in such little effect being obtained by the user that it would be discarded in favour of an alternative means of administration. This practice raises particular concerns that the boundary between cocaine powder and crack may be becoming more blurred within this group. Indeed evidence from the interviews suggests that some users who regularly use cocaine powder in this way may be at increased risk of unintentionally initiating crack use. There is a need for more research in this area to examine the motivations behind smoking cocaine powder and to examine potential ways to decrease the likelihood of confusion between the two forms of cocaine.

Motivations for Using Cocaine

Cocaine use served a range of functions for the young people interviewed in this study, many of which could be described as enhancing social interactions. Similar functions for the use of other stimulants by non-treatment samples of young people have been described elsewhere (Boys *et al.,* 1999a, 1999c, 2000b, 2001). Many described using cocaine in social situations that were very similar to those in which they had chosen to use amphetamines or ecstasy in the past. For some, cocaine was used as a substitute for other stimulants. Motivations for this practice varied. Overall, the strongest influences seemed to be the perception that the effects from cocaine were more controllable and the after-effects less unpleasant. Those who could afford to pay more for a stimulant were in effect buying a less unpleasant 'come-down' as well as less unpredictable experiences while intoxicated. There was also evidence that high-profile stories in the media about ecstasy-related deaths had deterred people from choosing ecstasy and that some regarded cocaine as a safer alternative.

Negative Effects Associated with Cocaine Use

In general, respondents associated very few risks with cocaine use unless consumption was particularly heavy. As many were not in a financial position to use the drug more than intermittently, they did not class themselves as 'at risk'. However, when asked about negative effects that they had experienced from cocaine use, a substantial number were reported. Many of these were short-lived, experienced while under the influence of the drug and often moderated by the use of other substances such as alcohol or cannabis. More worrying were accounts of longer-lasting psychological symptoms such as feelings of depression, paranoia or lack of motivation. Overall, there was a notable lack of knowledge and awareness concerning potential negative effects or risks associated with cocaine use. This was in sharp contrast with users' knowledge about amphetamines and ecstasy. Similarly, few were able to describe measures to reduce harms associated with cocaine, whereas there was good awareness of appropriate harm-reduction strategies for ecstasy. These findings signal a need for efforts to raise awareness and disseminate more information about cocaine use and its associated risks and harms targeted at young people.

Cocaine and Alcohol

A particularly high level of alcohol consumption while using cocaine was described by the sample. Virtually everyone interviewed regularly drank alcohol when using cocaine and a significant proportion *always* drank alcohol while using the drug. Alcohol consumption under these circumstances tended to be heavier than normal, and some participants reported that they more than doubled their usual alcohol intake. Studies of adult cocaine users have noted similar patterns of substance use (e.g., Martin *et al.,* 1996). It has been observed elsewhere that concurrent substance use often serves a clear function for the user in terms of managing or enhancing the intoxicating effects experienced (Boys *et al.,* 2000a,b, 2001). Similar functions were evident in the current sample: alcohol either helped to moderate the less pleasant effects associated with cocaine use (such as anxiety, or insomnia) or cocaine was used to help manage undesirable effects from alcohol enabling the individual to drink more heavily. Many users avoided alcohol altogether when using ecstasy (behaviour seemingly prompted by harm-reduction information gleaned from a variety of media), unlike when using cocaine. Studies have shown that the compound produced in the body from the interaction between cocaine and alcohol (cocaethylene) takes longer to be eliminated (Andrews, 1997; Hart *et al.,* 2000; McCance-Katz *et al.,* 1998) and is more toxic than either drug alone (Andrews, 1997; NIDA, 1999). The combination of cocaine and alcohol has been found to produce greater euphoria and psychological well-being than either drug in isolation and it has been suggested that this may encourage heavier consumption, therefore increasing the toxic risk to the user (McCance-Katz *et al.,* 1998). Only one of the 34 cocaine users interviewed showed any awareness that combining alcohol and cocaine might carry additional risks for the user. This highlights a pressing need for efforts to raise awareness of these issues among young cocaine users and to stress the potential risks associated with such concurrent use.

Crack Cocaine

To date, estimates of crack cocaine use among young people in the UK have been considerably smaller than those for powder cocaine (Ramsay & Partridge, 1999). However, almost a third of the current sample reported that they had tried crack cocaine, and six of these had used it within the past year. Of particular concern was how poorly informed some of the respondents were about crack, several being unaware that it was a smokeable form of cocaine. The fact that two people realized during the course of the interview that they had actually used crack unwittingly suggests that the actual prevalence of crack use could be higher than reported. In common with Green *et al.*'s (1994) recreational cocaine users, the current sample universally regarded crack very negatively compared with cocaine in its powder form. However, the data indicate that in practice the boundary between the two forms of the drug may be becoming more blurred and initiation might occur unintentionally, particularly among users who are in the habit of smoking cocaine. While it is encouraging that respondents appeared to differentiate quite clearly between using cocaine as powder or crack, the possibility that some young people may confuse the two is cause for serious concern. These findings signal a pressing need for efforts to increase knowledge and awareness about crack cocaine together with further research to establish just how widespread use of this form of cocaine is among young powder cocaine users. Furthermore, this finding could have implications for UK drug prevalence surveys. In particular, questions about drug use could be clarified by including descriptions of the drugs named to help to enhance the accuracy of the resulting data.

Future Directions

The data presented here suggest that a greater focus on the needs of young cocaine users is required in the UK. While raising some important issues, limitations of this study include its relative size and local focus. The next step is to conduct a large-scale quantitative study of cocaine users to examine whether our findings are applicable to the larger population of cocaine users both in London and nationally. Such a study would play a vital role in informing appropriate education and policy responses at a national level.

The evidence presented suggests a need for a well-planned strategy to raise awareness on cocaine use and the related risks and harms. Initiatives following in the footsteps of the campaigns that have targeted ecstasy users over the past 10–15 years may help to redress the imbalance that appears to have resulted in some young people concluding that cocaine is the safer stimulant. We would strongly recommend that a variety of media should be exploited to deliver messages to as many young people as possible—both those who have already tried cocaine and those who have not. In particular, efforts should be made to educate young people about the relationship between cocaine powder and crack and the risks associated with use of the drug in either form. Furthermore, the results presented suggest that raising awareness of the potential risks associated with drinking heavily when using cocaine could be a useful and appropriate focus for harm-reduction efforts. Finally, given our observations that campaigns that have targeted ecstasy users may have contributed to a shift away from ecstasy use to cocaine use instead, we would urge that all stimulant drugs are targeted concurrently.

ACKNOWLEDGEMENTS

The research described in this paper was supported by funding from Action-on-Addiction. The views expressed are those of the researchers and are not necessarily those of the funders.

NOTE

1. Leah Betts died in November 1995 after taking an ecstasy tablet at her 18th birthday party. Her death was widely covered by the media and resulted in a national advertising campaign using billboards bearing an image of her in a coma to warn people of the potential dangers associated with ecstasy use.

REFERENCES

ANDREWS, P. (1997). Cocaethylene toxicity. *Journal of Addictive Diseases,* 16(3), pp. 75–84.

BIERNACKI, P. (1986). *Pathways from Heroin Addiction: recovery without treatment* (Philadelphia, PA: Temple University Press).

BOYS, A., FOUNTAIN, J., MARSDEN, J., GRIFFITHS, P., STILLWELL, G. & STRANG, J. (2000a). *Drug Decisions: a qualitative study of young people, drugs and alcohol.* London: Health Education Authority.

BOYS, A., MARSDEN, J., FOUNTAIN, J., GRIFFITHS, P., STILLWELL, G. & STRANG, J. (1999a). What influences young people's use of drugs? A qualitative study of decision-making. *Drugs: education, prevention and policy,* 6(3), pp. 373–89.

BOYS, A., MARSDEN, J. & GRIFFITHS, P. (1999b). Reading between the lines: is cocaine becoming the stimulant of choice for urban youth? *Druglink,* Jan/Feb, pp. 20–23.

BOYS, A., MARSDEN, J., GRIFFITHS, P., FOUNTAIN, J., STILLWELL, G. & STRANG, J. (1999c). Substance use among young people: the relationship between perceived functions and behavioural intentions. *Addiction,* 94(7), pp. 1043–50.

BOYS, A., MARSDEN, J., GRIFFITHS, P. & STRANG, J. (2000b). Drug use functions predict cocaine-related problems in young people. *Drug and Alcohol Review,* 19, pp. 181–90.

BOYS, A., MARSDEN, J. & STRANG, J. (2001). Understanding reasons for drug use among young people: a functional perspective. *Health Education Research,* 16(4), pp. 457–69.

BRAIN, K., PARKER, H. & BOTTOMLEY, T. (2001). Untreatable? Hidden crack cocaine and poly drug users. In H. Parker, J. Aldridge & R. Egginton (Eds), *UK Drugs Unlimited: new research and policy lessons on illicit drug use.* Hampshire: Palgrave.

COHEN, P. (1994). Cocaine use in Amsterdam in non-deviant subcultures. *Addiction Research,* 2(1), pp. 71–94.

DRUCKER, E. & DAVIES, J. (1994). Editorial—cocaine. *Addiction Research,* 2(1), pp. i–ii.

FORSYTH, A. J. M. (1996). Places and patterns of drug use in the Scottish dance scene. *Addiction,* 91(4), pp. 511–21.

GODDARD, E. & HIGGINS, V. (1999). *Smoking, Drinking and Drug Use Among Young Teenagers in 1998, Volume 1: England.* London: The Stationery Office.

GOSSOP, M., GRIFFITHS, P., POWIS, B. & STRANG, J. (1994). Cocaine, patterns of use, routes of administration and severity of dependence. *British Journal of Pyschiatry,* 164, pp. 660–64.

GREEN, A., PICKERING, H., FOSTER, R., POWER, R. & STIMSON, G.V. (1994). Who uses cocaine? Social profiles of cocaine users. *Addiction Research,* 2(1), pp. 141–54.

GRIFFITHS, P. (1998). *Qat Use in London: a study of qat use among a sample of Somalis living in London.* Home Office Drugs Prevention Initiative Paper 26. London: The Stationery Office.

GRIFFITHS, P., GOSSOP, M., POWIS, B. & STRANG, J. (1993). Reaching hidden populations of drug users by privileged access interviewers: methodological and practical issues. *Addiction,* 88, pp. 1617–26.

HAMMERSLEY, R. & DITTON, J. (1994). Cocaine careers in a sample of Scottish users. *Addiction Research,* 2(1), pp. 51–69.

HARRISON, L.D. (1994). Cocaine using careers in perspective. *Addiction Research,* 2(1), pp. 1–20.

HART, C.L., JATLOW, P., SEVARINO, K.A. & MCCANCE-KATZ, E.F. (2000). Comparison of intravenous cocaethylene and cocaine in humans. *Psychopharmacology,* 149(2), pp. 153–62.

HATSUKAMI, D.K. & FISCHMAN, M.W. (1996). Crack cocaine and cocaine hydrochloride: are the differences myth or reality? *Journal of the American Medical Association,* 276(19), pp. 1580–88.

JEFFCOAT, A.R., PEREZ-REYS, M., HILL, J.M., SADLER, B.M. & COOKE, C.E. (1989). Cocaine disposition in humans after intravenous injection, nasal insufflation (snorting), or smoking. *Drug Metabolism and Disposition,* 17, pp. 153–59.

LENTON, S., BOYS, A. & NORCROSS, K. (1997). Raves, drugs and experience: drug use by a sample of people who attend raves in Western Australia. *Addiction,* 92(10), pp. 1327–37.

MARSDEN, J., GOSSOP, M., STEWART, D., BEST, D., FARRELL, M., EDWARDS, C., LEHMANN, P. & STRANG, J. (1998a). The Maudsley Addiction Profile (MAP): a brief instrument for assessing treatment outcome. *Addiction,* 93, pp. 1857–67.

MARSDEN, J., GRIFFITHS, P., FARRELL, M., GOSSOP, M. & STRANG, J. (1998b). Cocaine in Britain: prevalence, problems, and treatment responses. *Journal of Drug Issues,* 28(1), pp. 225–42.

MARTIN, C.S., CLIFFORD, P.R., MAISTO, S.A., EARLEYWINE, M., KIRISCI, L. & LONGABAUGH, R. (1996). Polydrug use in an inpatient treatment sample of problem drinkers. *Alcoholism: Clinical and Experimental Research,* 20(3), pp. 413–17.

MCCANCE-KATZ, E.F., KOSTEN, T.R. & JATLOW, P. (1998). Cocurrent use of cocaine and alcohol is more potent and potentially more toxic than use of either alone: a multiple dose study. *Biological Psychiatry—New York,* 44(4), pp. 250–59.

MCCARTHY, B. & HAGAN, J. (1996). Making it: work and alternative school in the transition from homelessness. In B. Galway & J. Hudson (eds), *Youth in Transition: perspectives on research and policy.* Toronto: Thompson Educational Publishing.

MUGFORD, S. (1994). Recreational cocaine use in three Australian Cities. *Addiction Research,* 2(1), pp. 95–108.

NIDA (National Institute of Drug Abuse) (1999). *Cocaine Abuse and Addiction.* NIDA Research Report: http://www.nida.nih.gov/researchreports/cocaine/cocaine3.html.

PARKER, H., BURY, C. & EGGINTON, R. (1998). *New Heroin Outbreaks Among Young People in England and Wales.* Crime Detection and Prevention Series, Paper 92. London: Police Research Group, Home Office.

PATTON, M.Q. (1990). *Qualitative Evaluation and Research Methods,* 2nd edn. London: Sage Publications.

POWER, R. (1994). Some methodological and practical implications of employing drug users as indigenous fieldworkers. In M. Boulton (Ed.), *Challenge and Innovation: methodological advances in social research on HIV/AIDS* (pp. 97–111). London: Taylor & Francis.

RAMSAY, M., BAKER, P., GOULDEN, C., SHARP, C. & SONDHI, A. (2001). *Drug Misuse Declared in 2000: results from the British Crime Survey.* Home Office Research Study No. 224. London: Home Office.

RAMSAY, M. & PARTRIDGE, S. (1999). *Drug Misuse Declared in 1998: results from the British Crime Survey.* London: Home Office.

SHARP, C., BAKER, P., GOULDEN, C., RAMSAY, M. & SONDHI, A. (2001). *Drug Misuse Declared in 2000: Key results from the British Crime Survey.* Home Office Findings, 149. London: Home Office.

UKADCU (United Kingdom Anti-Drugs Co-ordination Unit) (1999). *Second National Plan.* London: Cabinet Office.

VEREBY, K. & GOLD, M. (1988). From Coca leaves to Crack, the effects of dose and routes of administration in abuse liability. *Psychiatric Annals,* 18, pp. 513–20.

14

Crack Dealing, Gender, and Arrest Avoidance

Bruce A. Jacobs
University of Missouri–St. Louis

Jody Miller
University of Missouri–St. Louis

Arrest avoidance has become a fruitful topic of inquiry in recent years (cf. Cromwell, Olson and Avary 1991; Dunlap, Johnson and Manwar 1994; Jacobs 1996a, b; Paternoster 1988, 1989; Sherman 1993; Stafford and Warr 1993; Waldorf and Murphy 1995; Wright and Decker 1994, 1997). This is consistent with the prominent role deterrence theory has come to play in explaining offender decision-making. Whether deterrence in general, and arrest avoidance in particular, are gendered processes is speculative and hard to know. Some research indicates that women and men experience sanction-risk management in the same way (Piquero and Paternoster 1998; Smith and Paternoster 1987). Other studies suggest that gender differences, for instance in risk tolerance or responsiveness to external threat, affect how women and men perceive the impact of being caught and punished (Finley and Grasmick 1985; Hagan, Gillis and Simpson 1985; Richards and Tittle 1981).

In trying to answer these questions, prior work has focused on potential differences in moral development (cf. Gilligan 1982), socialization and responsiveness to social control (Finley and Grasmick 1985; Hagan, Gillis and Simpson 1985), stakes in conformity, and perceptions of public visibility (Richards and Tittle 1981). Empirically, the bulk of research has centered on relatively minor offending such as marijuana use (Richards and

Tittle 1981; Smith and Paternoster 1987), drunk driving (Piquero and Paternoster 1998), theft, gambling and tax evasion (Richards and Tittle 1981). Comparatively little is known about how gender shapes arrest avoidance behaviors among active offenders involved in serious street crime. Nor is much known about the ways gender stratification shapes the situational context of arrest-risk management among female street criminals (but see Decker, Wright and Logie 1993).

Although relatively few women participate in serious street crime, recent evidence suggests that women and men involved in these activities often have similar situational motivations (Miller 1998a; Smith and Paternoster 1987:157; but see Daly 1994). Similar motives, of course, do not necessarily translate into equivalent processes of arrest avoidance. In fact, given the ample evidence that gender inequality is a salient feature of most criminal subcultures (Maher 1997; Maher and Daly 1996; Miller, 1998a, 1998b; Steffensmeier 1983; Steffensmeier and Terry 1986), it is likely that women's sanction-eluding practices are filtered through and by the gendered contexts in which they operate. With this in mind, our study seeks to provide new insights into threat management as it interfaces with the "situational foreground" of offending, and to demonstrate the ways in which arrest avoidance tactics are embedded within, and influenced by, street stratification. We draw from the experiences of active female crack market participants.

ARREST AVOIDANCE

Conceptually, arrest avoidance is grounded in Gibbs' (1975:33) notion of restrictive deterrence—a "reduction in the frequency of offenses, including strategies or tactics employed by individuals to evade detection, identification, or apprehension that have the effect of reducing the frequency of offenses." Recently, Jacobs (1996b:376–377) refined the concept to include probabilistic and particularistic forms. The former refers to a reduction in offense frequencies based on a "law of averages" mentality, the latter to criminal restraint based on tactical skills offenders use to make themselves less likely to be arrested. In the latter, offenders manage risk through a variety of tactics intended to obscure illicit activities, defy detection, and prevent apprehension. Risk management is particularly challenging when offenders face time constraints and must process information rapidly, where predators lurk, or where police surveillance is omnipresent. This is the position in which many street-level crack dealers find themselves, and it makes them an ideal population for investigating arrest avoidance tactics.

To survive economically, street-level sellers typically must move as much product to as many different customers as possible in contexts where competition often is suffocating. High customer turnover, rapid-selling retail units (some priced as low as $3), and the lack of access to private settings in which to do business (Dunlap, Johnson and Manwar 1994; Johnson, Hamid and Sanabria 1992) render discreet selling out of reach for many. Excepting the possibility of cultivating a small but loyal cadre of repeat customers—a risk-reduction strategy not always available—sellers must develop alternate methods if they are to have any chance of avoiding detection.

Several studies provide evidence of (male) crack dealers' arrest avoidance techniques. Jacobs (1993, 1996a) describes the perceptual shorthand dealers use to identify undercover officers. Worden, Bynum and Frank (1994:97) discuss tactics such as becoming "more circumspect about where and to whom [dealers] sell" and "keeping smaller amounts of drugs on hand" (Worden, Bynum and Frank 1994:110). Sviridoff and Hillsman (1994:20–21) talk about "moving selling locations indoors, devising schemes to reduce hand-to-hand exchanges, and moving out of the selling location after sales." Both Jacobs (1996b) and Johnson and Natarajan (1995) provide detailed descriptions of offenders' methods of handling drugs, buyers, and environments to minimize police surveillance and decrease apprehension risk. Each study documents, for example, how dealers choose selling locations with the intent of decreasing the likelihood that they will be watched and/or caught. Both articles also report how dealers use different techniques for handling drugs (such as hiding them on their person or in the environment, and using mediational devices to make exchanges with buyers) to minimize the probability of being caught with drugs (or at least, with a significant quantity). These and other measures take on added importance for female crack sellers because of the gendered nature of street crack markets.

GENDER STRATIFICATION WITHIN CRACK MARKETS

Crack's emergence in the mid-1980s is generally believed to have caused a widespread democratization of street drug markets. Because crack is both inexpensive and highly addictive (at least psychologically), the drug resulted in increased demand that existing distribution networks were unable to meet (Fagan 1994). Crack rapidly expanded opportunity structures for street-level drug selling—facilitating access to supplies, offering controlled selling territories, and creating entry-level dealing roles with only minimal training and start-up capital required (Johnson, Hamid and Sanabria 1992). These shifts were accompanied by "simultaneous changes in the social and economic contexts where drugs are bought and sold" (Fagan 1994:180). Specifically, deindustrialization in recent decades ushered in conditions of entrenched poverty, segregation, isolation, and social service declines in many inner-city communities (W. J. Wilson 1996). This led to expanded participation in informal economies, including the drug economy (Fagan 1994).

For the most part, however, democratized opportunities have not extended to women. Urban crack markets remain highly stratified by gender, and women's activities continue to be restricted by male-dominated street drug networks (Bourgois 1995; Dunlap, Johnson and Maher 1995; Fagan 1994; Maher 1997; Maher and Daly 1996; Ratner 1993). However, scholars disagree about the totality of such restriction. Some researchers argue that new opportunity structures indeed *have* facilitated women's entry into drug distribution networks and lessened their confinement to narrow income-producing strategies such as sex work (Fagan 1994; Sommers, Baskin and Fagan 1996; Taylor 1993; N. Wilson 1993). Baskin, Sommers and Fagan (1993:408), for example, suggest that increased economic marginality and the growth in drug markets have resulted in a lessening of social control over women, increasing the time they spend on the streets, their identification with street role models, and the desire to live the "high life" along with males (see also Bourgois 1995, chapter 6). Nancy Wilson (1993) argues that it is women's ties to domesticity that have presumably increased their participation in the drug economy. She suggests that while domestic ties have traditionally limited women's involvement in street crime, the nature of crack markets is such that a home base, which provides a place for drug preparation and discreet transactions, can be beneficial for conducting business.

In both instances, such arguments assume that *shifts* in women's drug activities are part and parcel of increased *autonomy* (Maher 1997:18; Miller 1995). Research, however, has documented the relative rarity of successful independent female dealers (Dunlap, Johnson and Manwar 1994, 1995; Fagan 1994; but see Sommers, Baskin and Fagan 1996). Maher and Daly (1996:472), for example, report that of the 200-plus women they came into contact with during three years of fieldwork in a Brooklyn drug market, they "did not discover any woman who was a [drug] business owner, and just one who worked as a manager." When women are involved in drug sales, they typically are relegated to peripheral roles such as selling irregularly, selling or renting drug paraphernalia, or copping drugs for others (see Maher 1997; Maher and Daly 1996). Even Fagan (1994:210), who argues that crack markets *have* offered expanded opportunities for women, recognizes that "women sellers hold positions within drug-selling organizations that are skewed toward lower status roles and away from management-ownership status."[1]

In particular, the institutional structure of the drug economy—including its homosocial reproduction, sex segregation and sex-typing—limits women's participation (Maher 1997; Steffensmeier 1983; Steffensmeier and Terry 1986). The violence associated with the crack economy further restricts women's involvement and justifies their exclusion (see Bourgois 1989; Maher and Daly 1996:482). Perceived as unreliable, untrustworthy and weak by male street offenders (Steffensmeier and Terry 1986), women are shunned as would-be criminal associates and, in the aggregate, find themselves with deficits in "criminal capital"—the connections, ties and pull that come only with extensive and enduring involvement in illicit street networks (see Hagan and McCarthy 1997).

Within this gender-stratified context, a small number of women who have managed to carve out a selling niche of their own (low-level as it may be) must operate. In addition to confronting many of the same risks and challenges as their male counterparts, they face unique circumstances that are indisputably gendered. Our goal here is to explore how gender shapes and mediates their dealing experience—paying specific attention to arrest-risk management. The data's larger conceptual implications are addressed, particularly as they relate to dynamic interchanges between gender and emergent street crack market conditions.

METHODS

This research is based on interviews with female crack market participants operating on the streets of St. Louis, Missouri. St. Louis is a medium-sized midwestern metropolitan area (population: 2.2 million) with a central city population of 360,000. Like other post-World War II rust-belt cities of its general size and type, St. Louis has suffered rapid deindustrialization, population loss, resource deprivation, and urban decay. Historically, St. Louis has had one of the largest illicit drug markets in the midwestern United States. In many neighborhoods, crack, heroin, marijuana, and PCP are sold openly and available throughout the day—particularly on the city's troubled north side. St. Louis arrestees have demonstrated persistently elevated rates of cocaine-, opiate-, and marijuana-positive urine specimens—rates among the highest of the 23 cities measured in the Drug Use Forecasting program (DUF 1996). Street markets here can best be characterized as "freelance" (Johnson, Hamid and Sanabria 1992); there is little evidence of hierarchical interdependence, role specificity, or functional division of labor between or among sellers (Jacobs in press).

We targeted active sellers for interviews. Although total institutions afford the chance to obtain data from drug dealers without the risk of harm associated with "street" interviews

(Agar 1973), collecting valid and reliable data may not be possible there because incarcerated offenders "do not behave naturally" (Polsky 1967:123; Sutherland and Cressey 1970:68; Wright and Decker 1994:5). Studies of incarcerated offenders also are susceptible to the charge of being based on "unsuccessful criminals, on the supposition that successful criminals are not apprehended or are at least able to avoid incarceration" (McCall 1978:27). Traditional methods—such as household surveys—likely would not identify active offenders in the first place because they "cannot produce reliable samples," they are inefficient, and because most hidden populations (such as crack sellers) are "rare" (Heckathorn 1997:174).

We used snowball sampling to locate respondents, a strategy modeled directly after that used by Wright and Decker (1997) to study armed robbers. As Wright and Decker note, the most difficult part of using this technique is making the initial contacts. Our first respondents were recruited by a specially trained fieldworker. An ex-crack dealer who had helped the first author on previous projects, this person had developed a reputation for trustworthiness among fellow criminals. Trading on this reputation, he initiated the recruitment process by approaching female offenders with whom he was familiar. Some of these contacts still were dealing crack; others remained involved only partially. After explaining the project to them—and stressing that the police were not involved—he asked them to participate in interviews and to provide information about other potential contacts who might prove useful. Twenty-five offenders were interviewed, all by the first author.[2]

In an attempt to build a more representative sample, we recruited respondents from a number of networks and points of operation. This minimized the chances of tapping into only one or two groups of criminals. Such measures are not foolproof, and offenders outside the penetrated networks remain unknown. The representativeness of a sample of active offenders can never be determined conclusively because the parameters of the population are unknown (Glassner and Carpenter 1985; see also Wright and Decker 1994). The most we can claim is that the sample appears to be representative, in general terms, of the population of female crack dealers known to the interviewees.[3]

Like Adler's (1985) cocaine traffickers, our respondents oscillated in and out of dealing, selling here and there when they needed money, had more drugs than they cared to use, wanted to help others looking to score, or were presented an opportunity too good to pass up. The quantities these offenders typically sold were small, the average sale being $20 (though individual sales could range from $50 to $200). The median number of days offenders reported selling crack per week was four (n = 24). Their self-reported median gross monthly income from crack sales was $2,500 (n = 21); their median educational attainment was the 12th grade (n = 21), and their median age was 32 (n = 25; range 18–56). Eighteen of our 25 respondents reported never having been arrested for crack dealing, one reported being arrested and released, and two reported being arrested and prosecuted (four did not respond). Consistent with our knowledge of low-level crack sellers' use patterns, most respondents used the crack they sold (Johnson, Hamid and Sanabria 1992).[4] All respondents were African American. Seventeen were unemployed at the time of interview, six were employed (n = 23). Readers should keep in mind that all these numbers reflect respondent reports and must be interpreted with care; independent validation of such figures is inherently difficult.

The interviews were semi-structured and conducted in an informal manner. They revolved around a basic set of questions that focused on the offenders' dealing techniques and arrest avoidance strategies. As with all such research, other potentially fruitful topics presented themselves during the course of our study. The first author attempted to follow up on these topics in later interviews, even though this meant that only a subsample would be able to comment (see also Wright and Decker 1997). The nature of open-ended qualitative interviewing is such that not all topics can be anticipated and or all offenders asked the same questions about issues that emerge later, often serendipitously, during the research process (Henslin 1972:52). The fact that responses became repetitious indicated sufficient topical covering, but this could have been an artifact of the sampling design. The sample's purposive design prevents us from claiming to have achieved theoretical saturation.

Interviews took place in quiet, secure places. The first author took extensive notes during interviews (street offenders often associate mini-recording devices with the police), and filled in remaining details after the interviews finished. He reproduced quotes as accurately as possible, and every reasonable effort was made to capture what respondents said and how they said it. Bracketed words indicate his own additions or substitutions to explain or amplify their statements. Some mistakes are inevitable during such a process, yet this need not be devastating. As Van Mannen (1988:56–57) notes, imperfections are an unavoidable part of fieldwork, given the complexity of the enterprise. As in all interview research, some respondents were more helpful than others—either being more articulate, informed, knowledgeable, or candid about a particular subject or focal area. We have chosen quotes that capture the essence of the particular theme or topic under discussion, and every effort has been made to represent them from a wide array of offenders.

Though skeptical at first, most interviewees relaxed and opened up soon after interviews had begun. A number of offenders seemed to enjoy speaking with someone "straight" about their criminal experiences; it may have provided some sort of outlet for them to disseminate their expertise and teach a "square" a thing or two about street life. The secrecy of criminal work "means that offenders have few opportunities to discuss their activities with anyone besides associates, a matter which many find frustrating" (Wright and Decker 1994:26). Moreover, active offenders have certain skills and knowledge that researchers lack (Berk and Adams 1970:107), and this asymmetry may empower them to open up or open up sooner than they otherwise would. The fact that respondents may see something in the research that benefits them, or an opportunity to correct faulty impressions of what it is they actually do (Polsky 1967), only facilitates openness. A small sum was paid to respondents in appreciation of their time and effort, and this seemed to help catalyze participation as well.

The internal validity of our data, finally, warrants comment. We were intruding into the lives of individuals engaged in felonies for which they could receive hard time. How could we know they were giving us the "straight story?" How could it have been in their best interest to give incisive, accurate comments about their lives, when divulging such details might ultimately undermine their success as criminals? As others have noted, "interviewees are people with a considerable potential for sabotaging the attempt to research them" (Oakley 1981:56), since "every researcher could be a cop" (Yablonsky 1966:vii). Though street criminals have a stereotypical image for lying or avoiding the truth more than others, there is little evidence to support this claim (Maher 1997:223). The validity and reliability of self-report data have been carefully assessed by a number of researchers, all of whom conclude that self-reports are among the best, if not the best, source of information about serious criminality (Ball 1967; Chaiken and Chaiken 1982; Hindelang, Hirschi and Weis 1981). Indeed, the most accurate self-report designs are those that ask questions about serious offenses, and those that involve face-to-face data collection—our technique—rather than impersonally administered surveys (Huizinga and Elliot 1986). This is not to say that offenders' reports are immune from "exaggerations, intentional distortions, lies, self-serving rationalizations, or drug-induced forgetfulness" (Fleisher 1995:80), but they appear to be less susceptible than some might think.

As for external validity, the purposive nature of our sample means that our findings must be considered exploratory. Nonetheless, they may expand our understanding of how such offenders think and act in real-life settings and circumstances. The research setting—St. Louis—also would seem to provide findings relevant to a wide array of other cities, particularly in the Midwest.

ARREST AVOIDANCE THROUGH CONTEXTUAL ASSIMILATION

Dealing is a punishable offense carrying de facto legal sanctions. With no available "safe haven," street-level sellers must minimize their risk of detection in other ways. This is particularly true for females, who must assimilate into a highly threatening and sex-segregated world. Given that public images in modern society become the primary basis for attributing motive to the actions of unknown others (Wirth 1938), female crack dealers sought to "accomplish" discretion by creating images of themselves and their behavior consistent with a non-offending identity. We refer to this process as contextual assimilation. Specifically, in their appearance and behavior, respondents attempted to blend into the environment and portray someone who would not be suspected of drug dealing. The ostensible purpose of such assimilative tactics is to prevent apprehension, but these measures provide protection from predators as well.[5] The women often drew from gender to achieve this objective. The strategy has four principal components: projected self image, stashing, selling hours, and routine activities/staged performances.

PROJECTED SELF-IMAGE

Projected self-image refers simply to conveying a sense of normalcy and ordinariness in one's demeanor and physical appearance to observers "not in the know." Female crack dealers described conveying such an image in a number of ways, for instance, by avoiding the adoption of "typical" (male) dealer behaviors and by dressing in ways they perceived as not calling attention to their actions. Offenders also took advantage of police perceptions of both addicts and women on the streets to conceal further their dealing.

By and large, these women rejected blatant methods of dealing. Such behavior was perceived to be characteristically male. This meant, according to one respondent, not "standin' on the streets, seein' a car go by, runnin' behind them, flaggin' em down, try to catch the m_____. That's the worst way to get caught up. Don't know what you runnin' up to." Indeed, (young) male street sellers, as one respondent put it, were perceived to "terrorize" would-be buyers, running around saying " 'I got the s___t,' actin' like [they] gonna beat 'em up if they don't buy from [them]." A number of respondents scoffed at such behavior because it was indiscreet. Indiscreet dealing, as Mark, Kleiman and Smith (1990:85) note, is "both more noxious and more susceptible to [police] control than discreet dealing: more noxious because it is more . . . obtrusive on the sensibilities of others, more susceptible to control because open dealing can be observed" and participating vendors provide easy targets for police investigation.

In a related sense, projected self-image meant effecting a mundane physical appearance. Fancy clothes, jewelry, accessories, and other status items—typically associated with male "ballers" and "new jacks" (cf. Hagedorn 1994)—were thought to be police magnets: "You know, diamond rings, gold, Rolls Royces . . . when you jump out in a crowd. That brings heat, gets you busted." Respondents either dressed "like a lady, you know, sandals, hair down, a dress" (so the cops would think twice about stopping her), or as another put it, "dressed down," wearing causal attire like blue jeans, long johns, or sweat pants to look like a "resident." It helped that police in the area did not believe women were dealing.[6] Women knew this and used it to their advantage. As one explained, "Poh-lice see a woman on the streets, walkin' or somethin, they think she lookin' for somethin' or is prostitutin' [and are not likely to stop]."

Some went a step further in their depiction of the mundane, portraying down-and-out users whom they believed police would not think worth the trouble of a case. Arguably, this was effective for those who called the streets home. "What the f__k you lookin' at me fo'," recounted one such seller yelling to officers about to stop and search her. "I just goin' to the store." The officers stopped and did make a search, finding one of three straight shooters (pipes). "'Where's the dope?'" the police asked. "It's on the shooter, m_____' b___h," she claimed to retort. "Push it through and you'll see it, but you better not lose the m_____ [stone]. You throw it, I get it." As a friend and fellow seller commented of this encounter, "They [police] won't really f__k with users [make a case on them or turn them into informants] unless they be weak [timid, scared]. She ain't weak so they don't f__k wi' her." Though particular details varied, all of the women presented a self-image at odds with that of the prototypical dealer as a means of avoiding detection.

Presenting a non-dealing self image was an insufficient tactic by itself. In addition, dealers had to develop a repertoire of drug-handling techniques to ensure that if police did approach them, they could continue to conceal their activities. A primary way they accomplished this was through stashing.

Stashing

For female dealers, three forms of stashing emerged: hiding drugs to sell on their person, hiding them in or around their homes, or secreting them in some undisclosed location on the streets. Which form or forms of stashing were used depended primarily on where an offender was dealing. Selling from or near one's home allowed women to stash drugs somewhere on the premises, while street-dealing required alternate methods.

Women who hid drugs in their homes described creative methods of concealment. One seller claimed to place her stash inside the hollow shaft of a curtain rod that hung right on her front door. Another reported stashing her rocks in a tin box under a secret board over which her pit bull slept. A third said she secreted her crack in a big bowl of popcorn, sitting right on the living room coffee table: "Poh-lice come in and they be lookin' for obvious places [e.g., under mattresses, floors, in ceilings]," implying they would never believe contraband to be hidden in plain sight. "You gotta think the way they think," she concluded. A fourth reported mopping her floors daily with ammonia, soaking the baggie she kept the crack in with ammonia, and burying it in the ashes of her wood stove, ashes also soaked in ammonia: "Them [police] dogs can't smell nothin' with that ammonia—it take away the scent."

Women who didn't have a home to sell from, or who chose to sell on the streets, kept rocks on their person and/or hidden in the nearby environment. One seller talked of hollowing out the earmuffs she wore during wintertime, placing the rocks inside. She also reportedly wore so-called "hustling pants," sweat pants worn over jeans with a small hole cut in the former, near an inner jean pocket, for easy access. "I keep a few rocks in the corner o' that jean pocket. They easy to hide," she claimed. In the event of a police search, it was easy for officers to miss those rocks: "That's what kept me on the streets so long." A number of women considered on-person stashing effective because public strip searches of females were prohibited in the jurisdiction. Police could not conduct them unless or until they took suspected offenders down to the station. There, a female officer had to do the search. Meanwhile, the trip provided offenders the opportunity to discreetly slide fingers of cuffed hands into their rectum, for example, to remove bagged rocks and slide them into the crevice of police car seats. One dealer claimed to crush and stuff a "whole fifty" (about a half gram) in this way; another was amused because police were riding around with crack in their cars unawares, courtesy of wily offenders like her. Vaginal stashing could circumvent the need for such measures by giving offenders the chance to claim they "needed a pad" first: "Ain't nobody gonna go down there after that," one offender mused.[7]

Hiding drugs in the environment was considered less risky because drugs could not be found in a pat down or body search. Crack could be buried underground, placed inside littered bottles, or in vacant buildings:

> I'd just go out my back door with my dog, like I was walkin' it, usually at night. 'What you diggin' for?,' I'd say to him [in case anyone was around]. Go over there, make a little hole, and put the rocks down in it. It wasn't nothin' suspicious [because it just looks like I'm checking what my dog is doing].

Another appeared more acutely aware of legal statutes as they pertained to "constructive possession" of stashes. Constructive possession is a police term referring to the ability to attribute ownership of contraband to some suspect when it lies within a certain proximity:

> I makes sure it [stash] be 250 feet away. The law say they [police] can give you a case if it be 150 feet away [constructive possession] so I be extra sure. Plus I pays a tweeker [addict] to keep close by to make sure it don't get f__ked wi'. If he [tweeker] trip [tries to steal the stash] I tear his m_____' head off.

While it is highly unlikely that this seller actually measured the distance with precision, such reports are nonetheless instructive in underscoring the process by which particular sanction threats trigger definable responses.

Bourgois (1995) and Jacobs (1996b) both describe similar stashing techniques among mostly male dealers, in crack houses and on the streets, respectively. Popular stash spots in houses include places such as inside electrical sockets, video game machines, and linoleum wall paneling (Bourgois 1995:110). The street dealers in Jacobs' sample (drawn from very similar St. Louis neighborhoods as the women explored here) used both on-person and environmental stashing. On-person stashing was mostly oral (between the upper lip and gum or under the tongue) or digital (in one's hand), although some dealers described more innovative hiding places: in their hair, inside the bands of baseball caps, between ankles or toes and socks, taped to an armpit, or inside the rectum (Jacobs 1996b:370). Street dealers retained larger quantities of drugs in nearby locations for convenient access when they needed to restock. Typically the drugs were wrapped in plastic and buried, hidden in soda cans or bottles, or in bushes.

Selling Hours

Women's decisions about when to sell further facilitate the process of contextual assimilation. Deciding what time of day to offend is one of the most important choices any offender must make. Risk of apprehension varies greatly throughout the day (Wright and Decker 1994), and some women had hard-and-fast rules about when they would and would not sell: "9 a.m. 'til 7 p.m.—those were my hours. After that, don't come knockin' 'cause the shop be closed," one commented.

Rules also could be created to coincide with the pulse of street life. One offender, for example, waited until 1:30 a.m. to stop serving:

> As long as the [liquor] sto's be open, poh-lice just think you be goin' the store, 'specially if you gots a bag or somethin.' But you be out like at 2, 3 in the mornin,' you can't be tellin' no poh-lice you be visitin.' [The stores are closed and] nobody in their right mind would do that [visiting].

Another dealer, conducting transactions off her pager and driving to meet customers, said she "stayed open" until around 3 a.m.: "Three [a.m.] OK to be out 'cause that's when the taverns all close. It just look like you be drivin' home or somethin'." Dealers who continued to transact after "excusable" hours lost the anonymity mass society otherwise provides. The longer into the night dealers stayed out, the more risk they assumed.

The decision to cease or continue (holding supply and demand constant) seemed to be determined largely by greed, with some dealers extending their hours near the first of the month when public transfer money hit the streets. Customers might spend an entire month's welfare check on crack, and the potential windfall was too much to pass up: "When things be clockin' and boomin,' I stay out 'til 3, 4 in the mornin,' sometimes all night," one explained. "Customers comin' in and they geekin' and tweekin,' and you just take your chances." At such times, a useful defense (for some) appeared to be a kind of sixth sense telling sellers whether the neighborhood was "hot [under surveillance]." "Tripping off your geeks," as one put it, or inferring police presence from customer behavior, helped to render such judgments: If police were indeed rolling through the area, buyers might act more cautiously or furtively than normal. Buyers who called the streets home, wandering at times aimlessly in search of crack, were especially good behavioral markers.

No matter the time of month, the scene tended to become more desperate later at night. Addicts typically scrounged together change and singles ($1 bills) or simply begged for credit, hoping to get a vestigial nugget. This did not bode well for any dealer, whether they had closed shop or not, because turning "fiends" away was risky. As one seller explained, "You don't kick geekin' people out. If they short [of money], do the sale anyway. They gotta be close, though [nearly have sufficient funds]. If I brush'em off, that's when they get mad [and go to the police, especially] if I'm the only one they could get it from. If you stingy, you won't have any good luck." Revenge informants are common sources for drug cases and can mean trouble for tightfisted dealers (Williams and Guess 1981).

For dealers selling out of houses late into the night, hostility from neighbors was a very real possibility. Noise and traffic might trigger late-night phone calls to police, a dire threat. Cultivating positive relations proactively was therefore critical. Cultivating refers to "courting and wooing activities . . . employed with the intent of either directly or indirectly gaining a reward" (Bigus 1972:131). Brief salutations when coming or leaving home, informal backyard conversations, and small gifts of home-cooked food could thus be quite valuable. As one illustrated, "I always be havin' barbecues so I be sendin' over plates [to the neighbors], you know, pork, ribs [and such]. On Sundays I cook turkey and dressing and send that over." Not all dealers, of course, needed to go to such lengths because neighbors often were users themselves. For neighbors who were not, reciprocity building was essential (Gouldner 1960). Reciprocity, a norm in virtually every aspect of social life, involves a "mutually contingent exchange of benefits between two or more [parties]" (Gouldner 1960:164). For female crack sellers, offers of pleasantries or home-cooked food could promote silence about behavior that may have otherwise been reported, a benefit of untold value.

Routine Activities/Staged Performances

Goffman (1963:88) notes that deviants who try to pass as normal must be alive to all "aspects of the social situation which others treat as uncalculated and unattended. What are unthinking routines for normals can become management problems for the discreditable." Respondents were keenly aware of this, and on occasion, executed the process of contextual assimilation by integrating drug transactions with other social activities. They did so in two ways: incorporating drug dealing into pre-existing routine activities, and creating staged performances to camouflage drug sales and allow them to proceed unnoticed.

As Wirth (1938:1) describes, human relations in mass society as "segmented, transitory, anonymous, and generally lacking in intimacy." Using such attributes to their advantage, some dealers drew from the on-going bustle of daily life to conduct business, insulate deals from observation, and make their illicit activity look normal. One seller, for example, claimed to deal from a local playground, waiting for customers who knew she was there to approach her: "I'd just go there and act like I was playin' on the swingset, basketball court. The playground's kinda' out the way of things [where she would talk and make the transaction at some point during the interaction]." On one occasion, this particular dealer had reportedly just copped $500 worth of crack when police arrived: "They be checkin' all the guys [on the street] they always catch but left me alone out there, thinkin' I was just one of them girls who just hung 'round the scene." The young males to whom she referred reportedly were not even aware of the extent of her dealing. "Why her little ass always at that park?" she claimed to overhear them say. "They [males] knew I was slingin' but they thought only one or two stones."

Another dealer described conducting business in a way that gave the appearance she was "conversatin" or giving directions to her buyers. Customers would call ahead of time, telling her what they wanted. Then:

> I'll just go up to the [customer's] car window on the street and just start conversatin.' I'd bend down and it look we just be talkin' 'bout directions. The radio be on loud, I wouldn't be actin' nervous or anythin' [not looking around, being paranoid, and so forth] so it'd look like just a normal conversation. Then I'd kind of bend down, lean over, drop the rocks [take the money, and be on my way].

A third exploited summer barbecues as performance settings:

> Yeah, like 4th of July, summertime, holidays, we get barbecues goin' in the backyard. [Big ones you know, so] it's real natural for a lot of different people [buyers] to come holler at ya' [make a buy]. Everybody around [neighbors, police] think it just be a big barbecue but people be purchasin' the stuff [crack] right out my backyard.

Staging performances was a related but distinctly attractive means of covertly conducting business. Performances enlisted active participation from drug customers, illustrating the notion that "those who share [discreditability] can rely upon mutual aid in passing" (Goffman 1963:97). Such performances were designed to throw off onlookers that a transaction was indeed occurring. One way to do this was to arrange to meet customers at local restaurants, markets and stores—conducting transactions inside. These so-called "organizational foci" (Feld 1981), or entities around which joint activities revolve, are "diffuse" in the sense that interactions within them are fleeting and not subject to intense supervision. Participants shop or eat and leave, generally being indifferent to the activities of unknown others. Sellers could exploit these setting characteristics, while using the foci's physical structure to insulate against possible police surveillance. Commenting on the value of dealing from the restaurant and lounge scene, one offender explained:

> I'd meet my customers at lounges at night, you know, after work. Sometimes they'd come out to the car or I would just go in, sit down and talk, have a drink and dinner. You know, just make it look normal. [The transaction would be done during this and apparently, nobody would suspect anything].

Another added, "it's easier to sling [deal] in clubs, taverns, lounges and such. People be drinkin' and socializin,' you know partyin.' You can see who be up to what and who be wantin' what." The lounge scene provided a legitimate organizational focus in which to conduct business. Socializing and drinking being its core activities, transactions synergized nicely and could be made without drawing undue attention. Filling stations also were reportedly quite useful:

> I'd have a customer meet me at the gas station and I'd be fillin' up my car. Then I'd see the customer and he'd come over and start talkin' to me. I'd say 'where that money you owe me?' It be like a pretend thing. He'd say he got it and then we'd make the exchange: I'd drop the rock in his hand as I took the money at the same time with the same hand [so it would appear to onlookers as if he were making a repayment]. Then we just stand there for a little while [still in conversation]. But you wanta make it as quick as possible. You don't want to make it a rush thing [though], just talk long enough to get the sale off [and make it look like a normal conversation].

Conventional sites may be the best venues for street-level sellers to deal precisely because they are not deviant. Taking transactions away from the street corner and vacant tenement into places like restaurants, grocery stores, and gas stations, deals can be demarginalized and given a "natural" feel. The last places drug transactions are thought to "go down" may be the most valuable ones to use. Public order crimes always stand out less when integrated into and diluted by the normal flow of social activity.[8]

Other sellers employed staging methods similar to what Jacobs (1996b) calls transactional mediation. Transactional mediation refers to the practice of using props, people, and geography to camouflage drug dealing. It generally is used only with regular customers because each party fears getting burned. Since crack users tend to be repeat customers, such exchanges are commonly understood "recipes for social action" (Schutz 1967) and have generalized subcultural currency:

> I'll go into the corner store, the buyer'll see me comin' and he'll put a 20 [dollar bill] on the ledge right before I go in. I'll take it, go in the sto' for a little while, buy somethin', then come back out, see 'em, and give 'em the rock like I'm shakin' their hand and conversatin.' You just gotta be clever and smooth.

Toting props to transactions was another useful staging method. Lauderback, Hansen and Waldorf's (1992) female gang member-drug sellers, for example, brought their infants to transactions to throw off the police: "[It's] kind of like a decoy, we have our strollers and stuff and babies, they [police] don't usually bother us" (63). One seller said she brought boxes of food, household cleaner, or grocery bags to customers' homes—making it appear as if she were running an errand. Or, she acted as if she were coming over to pick up something either owed to her, or left there by her sometime before. "You got those canned goods and boxes I left in the basement? You knew I was comin' over," she reportedly would speak loudly enough for any around to hear. After going inside and making the sale, she would exit with the aforementioned items, affirming the apparent mundane purpose of her visit.

Staging was integral to the use of public communication lines as well. Telephones are instrumental to drug dealing, and coding dialogue while using them protected transactions from possible tapping (Natarajan, Clarke and Johnson 1995). For one dealer, saying 67th Street meant "meet me at the liquor store," 74th street meant the filling station, and the "corner store" meant just outside the house. For others, locational phrasing was unnecessary because "every individual customer has their own meetin' place so you know where to go," as one put it. Quantity-coding, however, more often was required because sellers needed to know how much crack to bring: "They call and say 'meet me at five,' that means they want a fifty [and you just go]." Another spoke in greater detail:

> It doesn't matter what the sentence be as long as you put a number in it. Like a customer'll say, "you got change for a quarter?" That means they want a quarter-ounce. Or, "can I borrow a half-cup of sugar?" That mean they want a half-ounce. Or I might say, "I thought you was comin" over at 8 o'clock. That referrin' to an eight-ball.

The point was not to "talk plain" (directly) about things, but use some creativity to try and throw things off.

Pagers, commonly known as "beepers," could be even more useful by precluding the need for dialogue. Typically, customers would dial a dealer's beeper number, punch in a code identifying themselves, press the "∗" key to create a space on the beeper display, and then a number depicting the quantity they wished to purchase. Such tactics eliminate conversation and insulate communication from tapping. A pager can create problems, however, in the event its owner is arrested. As one dealer explained, "if you in jail, [your pager is still on] and poh-lice be monitorin' all them numbers." Law enforcement can use such information to their advantage, possibly making additional cases or using monitored numbers as leverage with which to "flip" callers into informants. "I had two [pagers]," the above offender noted, but the police seized them and "busted a bunch of people [buyers and sellers trying to contact me]."

DISCUSSION

Female crack dealers use various techniques to avoid detection, obscure illicit activity, and prevent apprehension. We have presented four techniques of contextual assimilation: projected self image, stashing, selling hours, and routine activities/staged performances. Our findings suggest that offenders can be quite flexible in adapting to seemingly constrictive drug market circumstances, and generate ways to use available avenues to their advantage (see also Ryan 1994). Next, we examine how gender stratification shapes arrest avoidance. In doing so, we seek to broaden our understanding of arrest-risk management, exploring how its operation is embedded within, and influenced by, sex-segregated street networks. We also address collateral effects on women's prospects for career advancement, and their vulnerability to predators.

It may be useful to think about these sellers' actions in light of Kandiyoti's (1988) notion of "patriarchal bargains"—women's strategies of action as they arise within particular sets of gendered constraints: "Different forms of patriarchy present women with distinct 'rules of the game' and call for different strategies to maximize security and optimize life options with varying potential for active or passive resistance in the face of oppression" (Kandiyoti 1988:274). The crack ecosystem is oppressive in many ways, presenting a number of risks for women (Bourgois and Dunlap 1993; Maher 1997). Participating in a gender-stratified illicit economy where violence, aggression, and coercion are ubiquitous, women receive no special protection for being female (Dunlap, Johnson and Maher 1995). In fact, they may be perceived as particularly easy targets for street predators (Miller 1995, 1998a, b).

One reason women do not attain positions of prominence in street drug markets is their purported difficulty in grappling with the masculine conduct norms that flow from gender-stratified crime networks. A "don't mess with me," "crazy" self-presentation is essential for self-protection in the dog-eat-dog world of the streets, and some commentators maintain that women, in the eyes of male offenders and their networks, lack the requisite toughness and capacity for violence to establish this persona (Maher and Daly 1996:471; see also Fleisher 1995; Miller 1998a,b). Perhaps the prudent selling practices reported in this paper obviate the need for this presentation of self. Invisibility to the police can also translate into invisibility to street antagonists, and eluding confrontation may be the best way to deal with emergent threat. Adopting these practices appears to open a window of opportunity for women in some urban locales.

Yet this window does not exist solely because of effective concealment. Street offenders generally are presumed to be male (e.g., Wright and Decker 1997), and crack sellers almost exclusively so. One simply does not expect to see females slinging rocks or slinging them in any great quantity. When inner-city women are perceived to be offending, it often is within the narrow confines of sex work or addiction. Urban male-dominated police forces, in particular, are notorious for selectively enforcing law violations and law violators (Visher 1983). More often than not, officers ignore women dealers in favor of "more threatening" male offenders.[9]

The nature of inner city life also is such that women's visibility on the streets can be construed by police as involving activities other than drug dealing. Because they are often heads of households, and tend to be embroiled in networks of familial and other relationships in their communities (Collins 1990; Stack 1974), African American women who appear to be walking down the street to the local store or visiting friends may enjoy a measure of freedom greater than that of their male counterparts. The implication is that they have a "legitimate" right to be out at these times in these places, so police need not dwell on them. Young black males, by contrast, often are over-scrutinized in such contexts (Anderson 1990; Tonry 1995). Excluding those females who are "obviously" involved in crime—the emaciated addict or blatant streetwalker—urban black women enjoy a community status that has the potential for deflecting scrutiny. White female offenders in primarily African American neighborhoods usually cannot say the same, nor can offenders who stand out in some other way (e.g., sellers who export their trade to foreign neighborhoods where they may find it more difficult to blend in [see Maher 1998; Smith and Visher 1980]). The nature of freelance, St. Louis-style crack markets undeniably assists in the blending process, providing inner-city (black) female dealers greater latitude in making decisions about where, when, and how they sell. This makes them better able to draw on gender, and on the routine activities of street life, to conceal their activity.

The techniques described in this paper are not necessarily gendered. Any street drug dealer—male or female—can use them to deal any drug, including crack. Indeed, a number of studies (e.g., Jacobs 1996b; Johnson and Natarajan 1995) paint a portrait of risk management among male street sellers similar—but not identical—to that presented here. Male discretion, particularly that of young, black, curbside crack dealers (the modal streetcorner seller and roughly equivalent to the women explored here), often is situational rather than global. Typically, they will try to reduce their immediate risk of arrest but leave their longer-term vulnerability to chance (Shover 1996). Indeed, the imperatives of "street culture"—conduct norms that guide, direct, and shape behavior on the corner—dictate that it is in male offenders' immediate and best interest to seek the opposite of discretion (Bourgois 1995; Decker and Van Winkle 1996; Fagan 1992; Wright and Decker 1997). On the streets, status is paramount; it flows from respect, respect from "rep," rep from attention, and attention from conspicuousness (Anderson 1990). Posturing and obtrusive toughness have a currency all their own. Status-item consumption and its ostentatious display do, too: the money provided by street offending, and by crack selling in particular, fuels an often intense pursuit of consumerism (Bourgois 1995). To the extent that "badness" and affluence can be embodied together in a dealing style, male street sellers become closer to membership in the mythic "aristocracy of the streets" (Wright and Decker 1997; see also Anderson in press).

They also come closer to getting caught; attention is valuable but it can be decidedly treacherous. As some of the women reported, posturing male "ballers" and "new jacks" often are the first ones to be singled out (by police or predators) as prototypical street drug dealers. Females are not held to, nor need they measure up against, the same standard. In this way, women may be freer to exercise discretion. Self-presentations can be tempered. Perhaps because they face less pressure to conform to the "flash" of street culture, females also may be more successful in channeling available discretionary income to rent and bills. This may help explain why a number of women in our sample had access to homes and vehicles from which to deal—a decided advantage for those trying to be discreet—and why young men in similar street samples largely do not (Bourgois 1995; Jacobs in press; MacCoun and Reuter 1992). Even when young black male dealers attempt to integrate dealing into conventional settings (in the way a number of the women reported here did), their perceived lack of fit in these places can sometimes make them appear as blatant as if they were rushing a customer on an open streetcorner (cf. Anderson 1990; W. J. Wilson 1996 on presentational skills and social capital among male street culture participants; see also Bourgois 1995; Maher and Dixon in press).

Admittedly, some of these propositions are speculative. We do not wish to reify or over-state gender differences in behavior. Rather, we seek to underscore the notion that "cultural pre-scriptions and mandates are filtered through prevailing gender roles," and that male–female differences in behavior probably exist at the aggregate level (Messner and Rosenfeld 1994:69). These differences may be particularly pronounced in street culture, where sex-segregated conduct norms can have an exaggerated influence on behavior (Maher and Daly 1996). Ultimately, it seems fair to say that street culture excludes and restricts female deal-ers, even as some of these offenders are able to turn these obstacles into a resource.

Discretion does have its downside, however. It may restrict female sellers' clientele. Contextual assimilation techniques take more time and effort than simple street-corner exchanges. To some degree, transactions must be organized, contexts prequalified, and be-haviors choreographed. Staging areas or routine activity-based selling venues may be ideal for concealing transactions, but they also can be inconvenient. For users, they might delay the next high; for dealers, they absorb time otherwise spent on procuring additional sales. Dealers who use these techniques must find buyers who are sufficiently patient—not an easy task given the "here and now" orientation of many crack market participants.

Given that both the police and even other (male) dealers may be unaware of a discreet dealer, potential buyers also may be fooled. It is plausible that such persons will turn in-stead to more obtrusive, more accessible streetcorner dealers to make purchases. That is almost surely true of impulsive crack addicts, but it may be equally applicable to inexperi-enced users who lack street smarts. Novices, suburbanites, or chippers (infrequent users) are precisely the kind of buyers who prefer discreet vendors for fear of robbery or arrest, but lacking criminal capital, they also will have the most difficulty finding them. Even if located, sellers may not want to deal with them; conventional wisdom holds that strangers shouldn't be sold to, since unfamiliar buyers could very well be narcs (Jacobs 1993).

Some unknown number of discreetly-minded buyers, therefore, may be turned away empty-handed. These are lost sales which could be completed almost invisibly and with lit-tle risk of incurring legal sanctions. In the aggregate, their effect could be profound, par-ticularly if large numbers of shallow-end, "wannabe" users hear that they cannot buy crack and fail even to try. The extent to which potential customers who want access to discreet sellers have been cognitively locked out of street markets, and the extent to which that, in turn, contributes to drug market stagnation, remain open empirical questions. Whether the individual career trajectories of discreet female (and perhaps male) sellers are thwarted by the same dynamics is a related matter deserving future attention.

Such considerations take on added importance in the context of crack's decline (see Jacobs in press). Nationwide, powerful anti-crack conduct norms have arisen in response to the personal and social devastation wrought by the drug. Quantitative indicators recently have documented meaningful and significant reductions in rates of crack consumption in major cities across the country, resulting from both desistance among previously active users and decreasing rates of initiation among new users (see Golub and Johnson 1997). Street crack markets in decline may trigger plummeting customer-to-dealer ratios, at least in the very near term (assuming a stable pool of dealers and excepting "boom periods" of transactional activity, such as near the first of the month, when demand temporarily spikes

[Maher 1998]). If dealers must vie for a fixed or shrinking number of sales, they may become less selective about their clientele and generally less discreet about how they do business. Such changes may be more detrimental to female sellers than to their male counterparts. Assuming increased competition and greater market volatility, even discreet women dealers likely will face a heightened risk of victimization from male sellers out to protect their declining business. This may make women's contextual assimilation more necessary, and also more burdensome. If women react, for example, by retreating more and more to private or out-of-the-way settings, it may become prohibitively difficult for them to attract customers from a declining pool of buyers. Dedicated locations also may be easier for predators to spot and target; the more secure a dealer thinks she is, the more vulnerable she actually may become. Fixed locales, finally, may be more susceptible to social control because traffic can be more easily observed coming and going.

Our findings are exploratory in nature and based on a limited sample with restricted generalizability. Inevitably, discretion is situational and open to significant variation. Stealth also is probably a tendency to behavior rather than behavior itself; individual, group, and contextual variables will condition the outcomes, as will the strong demand-side influence of evolving police tactics. Moreover, to the extent that crack dealers use the product they sell, consumption and discretion are likely to be inversely related. Dazed by intense or prolonged periods of crack smoking, threats of legal sanctions can become "remote and improbable contingencies" (Shover, 1996,102) that offenders need not fret over. Nevertheless, to the degree that discretion continues to be mediated by and channeled through street-based sex stratification, gender differences in offenders' approach to sanction-avoidance are likely to persist. In the end, discreet sellers—whether female or male—bear the difficult task of creating an invisible visibility, making their whereabouts known to customers but obscure to police and predators. How they accomplish this delicate balance is a matter of considerable interest, and promises to be a fruitful topic for future inquiry.

ACKNOWLEDGMENTS

The research on which this article is based was funded by Grant No. S-3-40475 from the University of Missouri Research Board (UMRB). Points of view or opinions expressed in this paper are those of the authors and do not necessarily represent those of the UMRB. We would like to thank Bob Bursik, Scott Decker, Lisa Maher, Rick Rosenfeld, Richard Wright, and Norman White for their helpful comments and criticisms on earlier versions of this paper.

NOTES

1. It is important to keep in mind that there are variations in crack markets across sites, including differences resulting from who participates in and controls markets, and how selling locales are structured (cf. Maher and Daly 1996:466). Moreover, whether crack markets are organized around "freelance" or "business" models affects the nature of women's (and men's) involvement (cf. Dunlap, Johnson and Maher 1995; Johnson, Hamid and Sanabria 1992). Most work discussed in this section is based on studies of more organized crack markets than those found in the current study site.

2. Six sellers (of the 25) who claimed to have recently desisted were included in the sample. Including them was intended to diversify the sample and to provide perspective from those who no

longer feared legal sanctions. Perhaps this made them feel more secure and comfortable about what they disclosed. In addition, they served as internal validity checks for active offenders who may have more to hide.

3. We used criteria from the literature to guide the referral process. Rather broad-ranging and reflective of the variable and often vague nature of participation street-level crack dealing involves, these criteria called for someone who trafficked on streets, public throughways, or from houses, one or more days a week, who had done so for at least six months, to a number of customers per day, and who grossed between $300 and $3,000 a month from all activity relevant to street crack sales (e.g., selling crack, carrying drugs for someone, steering customers, and so forth [cf. MacCoun and Reuter 1992]). Although the eligibility criteria are fairly straightforward, they are inherently difficult to apply in the real world of street dealing. It is possible that a few of the respondents (outside the six desistors) fell out of the parameters in some form or fashion. This was virtually impossible to prove, however; moreover, it seemed a waste to turn away potentially valuable respondents for the sake of adhering to a somewhat arbitrary operational definition of eligibility (see also Wright and Decker 1994:23).

4. Since crack use is accurately stigmatized on the streets, we did not wish to undermine interview rapport or threaten the research by asking respondents directly about their use. Though this may be a limitation, our fieldworker confirmed that many, if not most of the offenders, did indeed use. Since only a small percentage of the offenders reported being arrested while dealing, it appears that they were successful in not allowing their use to increase their risk of detection.

5. Our focus here is on threats from law enforcement, and we limit our empirical analysis to that topic. Moreover, we are concerned specifically with contextual assimilation as it relates to women's drug dealing, to the exclusion of other aspects of illicit income generation and drug activities. This means we take a somewhat reductionist view. For a more comprehensive analysis of women's roles in the drug economy, see Maher (1997).

6. This of course assumes police are concerned with arresting dealers rather than other street offenders. Crack-downs on prostitution or drug use would likely differentially target women rather than overlook them. As such, our assessment is both offense- and context-specific.

7. Strip searches of male crack dealers also were reportedly barred. "They can't make you do that [a public strip search]," explained one respondent from Jacobs' study (in press). "You can beat the case cause they broke the law they self. Make you pull your pants down in front of everybody. There be all kinds of witnesses. They [circuit attorneys] gonna throw out the case."

   This does not mean that the police did not conduct public strip searches. Jacobs himself reports being strip-searched during a traffic stop with an informant. Some officers have perfected a technique that avoids the need—sliding the edge of their open hand forcibly upward from outside the offenders' clothing into their crotch and rectal areas. Its noninvasiveness and perceived utility in detecting caches of rocks of varying sizes made it popular among officers who "knew" a particular suspect was dealing, but for situational and/or legal reasons, could not make the suspect disrobe on site. No woman from the present study reported this technique being used on them—perhaps in part because the 50-person unit dedicated to gun/drug enforcement had only one active female officer on it roster (female officers were the only ones authorized to do body searches of female offenders).

8. This may only be true in the short-term. To the extent that police initiatives over time displace street dealing to "conventional sites," normal citizens may become increasingly affected by the negative spillover associated with drug sales (e.g., intimidation, disputes, violence). As public order deteriorates, tighter police enforcement is likely to follow, resulting in future but-as-yet unknown forms of adaptation by sellers (cf. Maher 1998).

9. Confirmatory evidence of this comes from over an eight-month period in which the first author participated in multiple and lengthy ride-alongs with drug police in the study area. Rarely (perhaps once or twice) did he witness them stop a woman on the streets specifically for suspicion of drug dealing. Beyond the likely role of institutionalized sexism, females' relative immunity

may also be tied to the freelance nature of the crack business in the study site. Based on research in a more organized crack market, Maher and Daly (1996) report a brief period in which drug organizations used female labor for dealing precisely because the police did not target them as dealers. Soon thereafter, police caught on and began cracking down on females, making their forays into drug dealing short-lived.

REFERENCES

ADLER, PATRICIA A. 1985. Wheeling and Dealing. New York: Columbia University Press.

AGAR, MICHAEL 1973. Ripping and Running: A Formal Ethnography of Urban Heroin Addicts. New York: Seminar Press.

ANDERSON, ELIJAH 1990. Streetwise. Chicago, Illinois: University of Chicago Press.

ANDERSON, ELIJAH In Press. The Code of the Streets. Chicago: University of Chicago Press.

BALL, JOHN C. 1967. "The reliability and validity of interview data obtained from 59 narcotic drug addicts." American Journal of Sociology 72:650–654.

BASKIN, DEBORAH, IRA SOMMERS, and JEFFREY FAGAN 1993. "The political economy of violent female street crime." Fordham Urban Law Journal 20:401–417.

BERK, RICHARD A., and JOSEPH M. ADAMS 1970. "Establishing rapport with deviant groups." Social Problems 18:102–117.

BIGUS, ODIS E. 1972. "The milkman and his customer: A cultivated relationship." Urban Life and Culture 1:131–165.

BOURGOIS, PHILIPPE 1989. "In search of Horatio Alger: Culture and ideology in the crack economy." Contemporary Drug Problems 16:619–649.

BOWGOIS, PHILLIPPE 1995. In Search of Respect: Selling Crack in El Barrio. Cambridge, Massachusetts: Cambridge University Press.

BOURGOIS, PHILIPPE, and ELOISE DUNLAP 1993. "Exorcising Sex-for-Crack in Harlem: An Ethnographic Perspective from Harlem." In Crack Pipe as Pimp: An Ethnographic Investigation of Sex-for-crack Exchanges, ed. Michell S. Ratner, 97–132. New York: Lexington.

CHAIKEN, JAN M., and MARCIA R. CHAIKEN 1982. Varieties of Criminal Behavior. Santa Monica, California: Rand Corporation.

COLLINS, PATRICIA HILL 1990. Black Feminist Thought. Boston: Unwin Hyman.

CROMWELL, PAUL, JAMES OLSON, and D'AUNN W. AVARY 1991. Breaking and Entering: An Ethnographic Analysis of Burglary. Newbury Park, California: Sage.

DALY, KATHLEEN 1994. Gender, Crime, and Punishment. New Haven, Connecticut: Yale University Press.

DECKER, SCOTT H., and BARRIK VAN WINKLE 1996. Life in the Gang. Cambridge, Mass.: Cambridge University Press.

DECKER, SCOTT, RICHARD WRIGHT, and ROBERT LOGIE 1993. "Perceptual deterrence among active residential burglars: A research note." Criminology 31:135–147.

DRUG USE FORECASTING (DUF) 1996. Annual Report. Washington DC: National Institute of Justice.

DUNLAP, ELOISE, BRUCE D. JOHNSON, and LISA MAHER 1995. "Female crack sellers in New York City: Who they are and what they do." Unpublished paper.

DUNLAP, ELOISE, BRUCE JOHNSON, and ALI MANWAR 1994. "A successful female crack dealer: Case study of a deviant career." Deviant Behavior 15:1–25.

FAGAN, JEFFREY 1992. "Drug selling and licit income in distressed neighborhoods: The economic lives of street-level drug users and dealers." In Drugs, Crime, and Social Isolation, eds. Adele V. Harrell, and George E. Peterson, 99–146. Washington DC: The Urban Institute Press. Fagan, Jeffrey 1994. "Women and drugs revisited: Female participation in the cocaine economy." The Journal of Drug Issues 24:179–225.

FELD, SCOTT 1981. "The focused organization of social ties." American Journal of Sociology 86:1015–1035.

FINLEY, NANCY J., and HAROLD G. GRASMICK 1985. "Gender roles and social control." Sociological Spectrum 5:317–330.

FLEISHER, MARK S. 1995. Beggars and Thieves: Lives of Urban Street Criminals. Madison: University of Wisconsin.

GIBBS, JACK P. 1975. Crime, Punishment, and Deterrence. New York: Elsevier.

GILLIGAN, CAROL 1982. In a Different Voice: Psychological Theory and Women's Development. Cambridge, Massachusetts: Harvard University Press.

GLASSNER, BARRY, and CHERYL CARPENTER 1985. "The feasibility of an ethnographic study of adult property offenders." Unpublished report prepared for the National Institute of Justice.

GOLUB, ANDREW, and BRUCE D. JOHNSON 1997. "Crack's decline: Some surprises across U.S. cities. Research in brief." Washington DC: National Institute of Justice.

GOFFMAN, ERVING 1963. Stigma: Notes on the Management of Spoiled Identity. Englewood Cliffs, New Jersey: Prentice-Hall.

GOULDNER, ALVIN 1960. "The norm of reciprocity." American Sociological Review 25:161–178.

HAGAN, JOHN, A.R. GILLIS, and JOHN SIMPSON 1985. "The class structure of gender and delinquency: Toward a power-control theory of common delinquent behavior." American Journal of Sociology 90:1151–1178.

HAGAN, JOHN, and BILL MCCARTHY 1997. Mean Streets: Youth Crime and Homelessness. New York: Cambridge University Press.

HAGEDORN, JOHN M. 1994. "Homeboys, dope fiends, legits, and new jacks." Criminology 32:197–219.

HECKATHORN, DOUGLAS D. 1997. "Respondent-driven sampling: A new approach to the study of hidden populations." Social Problems 44:174–199.

HENSLIN, JAMES M. 1972. "Studying deviance in four settings: Research experiences with cabbies, suicides, drug users, and abortionees." In Research on Deviance, ed. Jack Douglas, 35–70. New York: Random House.

HINDELANG, MICHAEL J., TRAVIS HIRSCHI, and JOSEPH G. WEIS 1981. Measuring Delinquency. Beverly Hills, California: Sage.

HUIZINGA, DAVID, and DELBERT S. ELLIOTT 1986. "Reassessing the reliability and validity of self-report delinquency measures." Journal of Quantitative Criminology 2:293–327.

JACOBS, BRUCE A. 1993. "Undercover deception clues: A case of restrictive deterrence." Criminology 31:281–299.

JACOBS, BRUCE A. 1996a. "Crack dealers and restrictive deterrence: Identifying narcs." Criminology 34:409–431.

JACOBS, BRUCE A. 1996b. "Crack dealers' apprehension avoidance techniques: A case of restrictive deterrence." Justice Quarterly 13:359–381.

JACOBS, BRUCE A. In Press Dealing Crack: The Social World of Streetcorner Selling. Boston, Massachusetts: Northeastern University Press.

JOHNSON, BRUCE D., and MANGAI NATARAJAN 1995. "Strategies to avoid arrest: Crack sellers' response to intensified policing." American Journal of Police 14:49–69.

JOHNSON, BRUCE D., ANSLEY HAMID, and HARRY SANABRIA 1992. "Emerging models of crack distribution." In Drugs and Crime: A Reader, ed. Thomas Mieczkowski, 56–78. Boston, Massachusetts: Allyn and Bacon.

KANDIYOTI, DENIZ 1988. "Bargaining with patriarchy." Gender and Society 2:274–290.

LAUDERBACK, DAVID, JOY HANSEN, and DAN WALDORF 1992. "Sisters are doin' it for themselves: A black female gang in San Francisco." The Gang Journal 1:57–70.

MACCOUN, ROBERT, and PETER REUTER 1992. "Are the Wages of Sin $30 an Hour? Economic Aspects of Street-Level Drug Dealing." Crime and Delinquency 38:477–91.

MAHER, LISA 1997. Sexed Work: Gender, Race and Resistance in a Brooklyn Drug Market. Oxford: Clarendon Press.

MAHER, LISA 1998. Personal Communication. (July 1)

MAHER, LISA, and KATHLEEN DALY 1996. "Women in the street-level drug economy: Continuity or change?" Criminology 34:465–492.

MAHER, LISA, and DAVID DIXON. In Press. "Policing and public health: Law enforcement and harm minimization in a street-level drug market." British Journal of Criminology.

MARK, A., R. KLEIMAN, and K. D. SMITH 1990. "State and local drug enforcement: In search of a strategy." In Drugs and Crime, Volume 13, eds. Michael Tonry and James Q. Wilson, 69–108. Chicago, Illinois: University of Chicago Press.

MCCALL, GEORGE 1978. Observing the Law. New York: Free Press.

MESSNER, STEVEN, and RICHARD ROSENFELD 1994. Crime and the American Dream. Belmont, Calif.: Wadsworth.

MILLER, JODY 1995. "Gender and power on the streets: Street prostitution in the era of crack cocaine." Journal of Contemporary Ethnography 23:427–452.

MILLER, JODY 1998a. "Up it up: Gender and the accomplishment of street robbery." Criminology 36:37–66.

MILLER, JODY 1998b. "Gender and victimization risk among young women in gangs." Journal of Research in Crime and Delinquency 35:429–453.

NATARAJAN, MANGAI, RONALD V. CLARKE, and BRUCE D. JOHNSON 1995. "Telephones as Facilitators of Drug Dealing." European Journal on Crime Policy and Research 3:137–153.

OAKLEY, ANNIE 1981. "Interviewing women: A contradiction in terms." In London, Doing Feminist Research, ed. Helen Roberts, 30–61. London: Routledge and Keegan Paul.

PATERNOSTER, RAYMOND 1988. "Decisions to participate in and desist from four types of common delinquency: Deterrence and the rational choice perspective." Law and Society Review 23:7–40.

PATERNOSTER, RAYMOND 1989. "Absolute and restrictive deterrence in a panel of youths: Explaining the onset, persistence, desistance of offending, and frequency of delinquent offending." Social Problems 36:289–309.

PIQUERO, ALEX, and RAYMOND PATERNOSTER 1998. "An application of Stafford and Warr's reconceptualization of deterrence to drinking and driving." Journal of Research in Crime and Delinquency 35:3–39.

POLSKY, NED 1967. Hustlers, Beats, and Others. Chicago, Illinois: Aldine.

RATNER, MITCHELL S. 1993. Crack Pipe as Pimp: An Ethnographic Investigation of Sex-For-Crack Exchanges. New York: Lexington Books.

RICHARDS, PAMELA, and CHARLES R. TITTLE 1981. "Gender and perceived chances of arrest." Social Forces 59:1182–1199.

RYAN, KEVIN 1994. "Technicians and interpreters in moral crusaders: The case of the drug courier profile." Deviant Behavior 15:217–240.

SCHUTZ, ALFRED 1967. The Phenomenology of the Social World. Evanston, Ill.: Northwestern University Press.

SHERMAN, LAWRENCE W. 1993. "Defiance, deterrence, and irrelevance: A theory of the criminal sanction." Journal of Research in Crime and Delinquency 30:445–473.

SHOVER, NEAL 1996. Great Pretenders: Pursuits and Careers of Persistent Thieves. Boulder, Col.: Westview.

SMITH, DOUGLAS A., and RAYMOND PATERNOSTER 1987. "The gender gap in theories of deviance: Issues and evidence." Journal of Research in Crime and Delinquency 24:140–172.

SMITH, DOUGLAS A., and CHRISTY A. VISHER 1980. "Sex and involvement in deviance/crime: A quantitative review of the empirical literature." American Sociological Review 45:691–701.

SOMMERS, IRA, DEBORAH BASKIN, and JEFFREY FAGAN 1996. "The structural relationship between drug use, drug dealing, and other income support activities among women drug dealers." Journal of Drug Issues 26:995–1006.

STACK, CAROL 1974. All Our Kin: Strategies for Survival in a Black Community. New York: Harper and Row.

STAFFORD, MARK, and MARK WARR 1993. "A reconceptualization of general and specific deterrence." Journal of Research in Crime and Delinquency 30:123–135.

STEFFENSMEIER, DARRELL 1983. "Organization properties and sex-segregation in the underworld: Building a sociological theory of sex differences in crime." Social Forces 61:1010–1032.

STEFFENSMEIER, DARRELL J., and ROBERT TERRY 1986. "Institutional sexism in the underworld: A view from the inside." Sociological Inquiry 56:304–323.

SUTHERLAND, EDWIN, and DONALD CRESSEY 1970. Criminology. (8th ed.) Philadelphia: J. B. Lippincott.

SVIRIDOFF, MICHELLE, and SALLY T. HILLSMAN 1994. "Assessing the community effects of tactical narcotics teams." In Drugs and Crime, eds. Doris L. MacKenzie and Craig D. Uchida, 114–128. Thousand Oaks, Calif.: Sage.

TAYLOR, CARL S. 1993. Girls, Gangs, Women, and Drugs. East Lansing, MI: Michigan State University Press.

TONRY, MICHAEL 1995. Malign Neglect: Race, Crime and Punishment in America. New York: Oxford University Press.

VAN MANNEN, JOHN 1988. Tales of the Field: On Writing Ethnography: Chicago, Illinois: University of Chicago Press.

VISHER, CHRISTY A. 1983. "Gender, police arrest decisions, and notions of chivalry." Criminology 21:5–28.

WALDORF, DAN, and SHEILA MURPHY 1995. "Perceived risks and criminal justice pressures on middle class cocaine sellers." The Journal of Drug Issues 25:11–32.

WILLIAMS, JAY R., and LYNN L. GUESS 1981. "The informant: A narcotics enforcement dilemma." Journal of Psychoactive Drugs (July–September):235–245.

WILSON, NANCI KOSER 1993. "Stealing and dealing: The drug war and gendered criminal opportunity." In Female Criminality: The State of the Art, ed. Concetta C. Culliver, 169–194. New York: Garland Publishing.

WILSON, WILLIAM JULIUS 1996. When Work Disappears. New York: Knopf.

WIRTH, LOUIS 1938. "Urbanism as a way of life." American Journal of Sociology 14:1–24.

WORDEN, ROBERT E., TIMOTHY S. BYNUM, and JAMES FRANK 1994. "Police crackdowns on drug abuse and trafficking." In Drugs and Crime, eds. Doris L. MacKenzie and Craig D. Uchida, 95–113. Thousand Oaks, California: Sage.

WRIGHT, RICHARD T., and SCOTT H. DECKER 1994. Burglars on the Job. Boston, Massachusetts: Northeastern University Press.

WRIGHT, RICHARD T., and SCOTT H. DECKER 1997. Armed Robbers in Action. Boston, Massachusetts: Northeastern University Press.

YABLONSKY, LEWIS 1966. The Violent Gang. New York: MacMillan.

15

Street Status and the Sex-for-Crack Scene in San Francisco

Harvey W. Feldman, Frank Espada, Sharon Penn, and Sharon Byrd

❖

Cocaine has a rich and florid history. In the past, its enticing effects captured the imaginations of world-famous leaders and thinkers: Sigmund Freud, Robert Louis Stevenson, Thomas Edison, Sarah Bernhardt, Queen Victoria of England, Pope Leo XIII, and even the fictional character of Sherlock Holmes (Horowitz 1974). Prior to the invention of crack, cocaine enjoyed a reputation in the United States as an elite, if dangerous, drug because of its expense and its association with the jet set, highly paid athletes, and popular entertainers. In San Francisco, the crack cocaine scene has tended not to be associated with the intellectual elite or with prominent figures in literary or professional circles. Rather, it became a preferred drug of the underclass in inner-city neighborhoods.

The word *crack* as it relates to cocaine first appeard in the *New York Times* on November 17, 1985. Michael Aldrich (1986), an ardent bibliophile, reported since that first article that thousands of press stories appeared in the years following. The reports have emphasized the negative aspects of crack: the violence connected to trafficking, the damage to careers of athletes when they test positive for drugs, and the painful physical symptoms of newborns attributed to crack-using mothers. In short, the public media has portrayed crack as the monster drug of the late 1980s and early 1990s. More significantly, the crack fad has coincided with a legitimate HIV/AIDS epidemic and has raised serious questions about its potential for increasing the rate of HIV infection because of the reputed connection between its alleged aphrodisiacal effects and risky sexual activities. In San Francisco, where the AIDS epidemic had hit with full force, this concern elevated the importance of crack, not simply as a drug that caused physical harm but one that had the potential of disaster on a par with Armageddon.

SAN FRANCISCO RESEARCH RESPONDENTS

Respondents for the study in San Francisco were recruited by Community Health Outreach Workers (CHOWs) who, under the direction of the Youth Environment Study (YES), were assigned to provide HIV/AIDS education to out-of-treatment injection drug users, their sexual partners, prostitutes, runaway youth, and, in recent years, crack smokers. The YES CHOWs were asked to select known crack users in their respective communities and to refer them to the study. Forty respondents were selected: thirty-four females, five males, and one transsexual. Respondents came from four communities and populations: the Western Addition, a predominantly African American community; the Mission District, where Latinos were the majority population; the Tenderloin, a transition zone and sex trade area; and the Polk Gulch, one of the major gathering areas in San Francisco for homeless and runaway youth.

In selecting respondents for the study, we did not state specifically that they must have histories of trading sex for crack, only that they should acknowledge their own extensive crack use and have street reputations as crack users, which CHOWs could confirm. Later respondents were selected on the basis of their use of crack as well as their known participation in the sex trades as street prostitutes. The respondents were typically poor people from poor neighborhoods with high unemployment rates. Interviews were carried out in the natural environments of the respondents. The preferred setting was a respondent's home; when this arrangement was not possible, interviews took place in restaurants, in interviewers' cars, or on park benches, usually close to the action of the street. Forty interviews were carried out, tape-recorded, and then transcribed into typescript. The senior author read and analyzed the interviews with the aim of developing appropriate conceptual categories that captured the various aspects of both individual crack smokers and the social context of crack use. The major emphasis of data collection was on the exploratory interview with limited participant observation.

General Characteristics of the Population

Most respondents were people of color, with African Americans and Latinos predominating. Respondents recruited from the homeless/runaway youth populations were, for the most part, Caucasian. In the beginning phases of the study, we emphasized recruiting female respondents because it was believed that females rather than males would be the individuals offering sex and receiving crack and that they more than males would be vulnerable to HIV infection and other sexually transmitted diseases. Later, we attempted to balance this recruitment strategy and interviewed males who had purchased sex in exchange for crack in order to gain some understanding of the interaction between these consenting parties. In addition, one transsexual participated who was both a street prostitute and a heavy crack smoker.

Families

Respondents in this study generally came from what could be termed dysfunctional families. In almost all cases, the parents had separated, and as children, respondents were sent to live with relatives or placed in foster homes. The family life that existed was often complicated by parental drug or alcohol use and frequently accompanied by violence. When asked about her early childhood, for example, Lynn, one of the few women in our study who traded sex directly for crack, provided a vivid description of violence in her family of origin:

> Like I said, my father was an alcoholic and he used to get drunk a lot of times and gamble and come home and ask my mother for money and she would tell him she wouldn't have it. And he beat her. One time he pulled a shotgun on my sister because she tried to pull him off my mother. But that happened all the time. They were always fighting. All the time. One time she had a busted lip and I went for him and I tried to hurt him because he hurt her. And it just got bad.

In less dramatic description, Caroline, a crack smoker and heroin injector, described her family as scattered and criminal: "I'm my mother's only daughter. She has another son but she don't see him. My father has about twelve kids. He's passed away now. All my brothers and sisters use [take drugs] and are in and out of the penitentiaries except my mother's son. He's in the air force."

In all cases, respondents either grew up in or moved to neighborhoods in San Francisco where drug use was prevalent and where crack cocaine became a popular street drug. Even where families were intact, the social or neighborhood environments typically contained street scenes in which respondents participated in gang activities that included stealing, fighting, and early drug consumption. In rarer cases, respondents reported growing up in families that were highly religious, overprotective, and restrictive. In these cases, families were usually ignorant of the individual's secret sexual or drug indiscretions.

The overriding feature of respondents' view of their families was parental inability to be loving and nurturing because of the parents' own personal needs and difficulties, some of which included problematic involvement with alcohol and drugs. It was surprising to discover how many of our respondents were exposed as children to their parents' drug use in the home. In one case, a young woman reported that her mother sold "crank" (methamphetamine), and access to it led to her first drug experience. The shift in initiation to drug use from the peer group to parents among a minority of respondents was a surprising finding and clearly different from earlier studies that pictured parents as both ignorant of illicit drug use and disapproving.

In some cases, female respondents reported being either sexually molested or raped as children by male members of the family, especially by stepfathers. Almost without exception, respondents described being abandoned, turned over to grandparents or stepfathers, or placed in foster homes. Despite these early experiences of neglect and, in some cases, of sexual abuse, many of the respondents reported consisent efforts to maintain contact with their parents and sought whenever possible to present to them a conventional image of themselves.

Given their early experiences, it was not unexpected that few respondents established stable families of their own. They frequently selected unreliable partners, some of whom exploited them or provided their initiation into drug use and encouraged or approved of their selection of prostitution as an occupation. One woman described her three consecutive male partners whom she either married or with whom she lived as (1) a con man in and out of jail and a "junkie," (2) a husband who died of alcoholism, and (3) her current boyfriend, who uses crack heavily.

Many of the respondents reported having children. Only a few of them were able to care for the children in a consistent fashion. Some of the children had been removed by the courts; others were living with relatives or in foster homes. Those who were active in drug dealing or had other steady but illegitimate hustles were proud of the fact that they provided regularly for their children. Most respondents expressed a general dissatisfaction with their current lives and looked to their children as a source of motivation to make what they described as a change for the better: stopping drug use and adopting an orthodox life-style. Sadly, their children's lives appeared in many cases to be a repetition of their own family experiences. And even if our respondents did not have an immediate plan to alter their present situation, they projected a wistful desire to modify their lives and at some future, undefined time raise their children in a conventional fashion.

Education and Employment Histories

Most respondents implied that education and attendance at school was not a significant part of their growing up. While they did not report great difficulty with school, the majority of our respondents dropped out before high school graduation. The topic of school and education was not of great importance in their lives, and it appeared unconnected to either their current life situation or future plans.

Almost all of the respondents readily stated that the major portion of their incomes came from illegitimate pursuits, most commonly prostitution. We believe that this finding, however, is an artifact of our own respondent selection since the majority of them were recruited at sites known as prostitution strolls. With few exceptions, respondents were economically marginal—even those prostitutes and shoplifters who claimed to earn substantial amounts of money. One crack dealer who operated a crack house stated that much of his money supported a heroin habit and the sixteen children he had fathered by several different women. In maintaining his heroin use and valiantly striving to remain a responsible father, he was not the picture of the successful ghetto crack dealer portrayed in the media (*Time,* May 9, 1988). According to Larry, his expenses greatly outweighed his profits: "In cash I use about five hundred dollars' worth of dope between crack and heroin. Cash money from my pocket after I drop twenty dollars toward this child and ten dollars to this child and this woman get ten dollars because of this baby, I come up with a hundred dollars a day if I'm lucky." The few who held legitimate jobs did so for only short periods of time in low-paying menial labor or dead-end jobs such as fast food operations. A small minority received welfare or disability benefits. Respondents were noticeably outside the conventional economic system of the city, and income from legitimate sources was negligible.

Some of the respondents had rather sophisticated approaches to shoplifting, prostitution, or drug dealing. Carmen, a particularly energetic illegitimate businesswoman, stated pride in her ability to "boost," claiming great skill in each step of the necessary operations from the actual stealing to the way she selected customers. Usually shoplifters would steal from department stores and then search out customers or known "fences." In contrast, Carmen was pleased with her skill in stealing and was especially proud of her ability to organize purchasers and the respectful way they treat her:

> Oh, yeah, I got my clients. I got clients I call up and tell me to get in a cab and come over. I get in a cab, they pay for the cab. There's a joint [marijuana] waiting for me or a hit [crack] . . . you know. And I throw everything on the bed, and they say, "I want this and that, and that, and that, and that." And I say, "Give me two or three hundred." And they say, "Here." And they pay for my cab back, and I'm gone. I have very good clients. Because they know I'm the best.

For most respondents, however, illegitimate activities were more opportunistic. The women were generally street prostitutes who "picked up tricks" in specified "cruising" areas. Some had steady clients and could depend on them for a regular income. Occasionally prostitutes would steal from clients, but this occurred only rarely, not with regular "dates," and only when the opportunity was presented.

Overall, we would describe the economic condition of our respondents as "getting by." Even for respondents with regular illegitimate schemes, their inability to budget their money or to control their drug and alcohol consumption, in conjunction with their periodic attempts to meet family responsibilities, combined to limit their ability to accumulate savings. As a result, their general outlook reflected their economic situation: planning was on a day-to-day basis with only sketchy visions for some distant future, most of which entailed a more conventional life and escape from their present environment. Almost without exception, they attributed their failure to escape their environment and their inability to implement plans for conventional living to personal defects of character, exemplified for them by their involvement with crack and other substances.

Drug Histories

Although the study focused primarily on crack smoking, the respondents' drug histories illustrated that crack was not their only drug selection. Almost without exception, respondents reported having used a wide variety of drugs. Most of them had begun their drug-using careers very early with alcohol. One woman claimed that when she was 3 years old she drank with her alcoholic father and was similarly introduced to marijuana when she was 6 years old. Although all respondents stated that they smoked crack on a regular basis, there were often parallel patterns of heavy use of other drugs, most often alcohol or, in a minority of cases, heroin. In some instances, respondents reported alcohol or heroin as their primary preference. It was common for respondents to admit that they were physically dependent on alcohol or heroin but not physically dependent on crack, even if they experienced what they described as a periodic and uncontrolled desire for it. A substantial portion of the respondents claimed that alcohol was a pleasant companion to crack, a cooling and balancing counterpoint to the jangled effects crack often produced. Moreover, while crack was a drug they used on periodic binges, alcohol was often consumed daily. In the words of one female respondent, "I drink like a sailor."

The most distinguishing feature that appeared to account for simple or complex drug histories was *age*. Older respondents had typically experimented with dozens of different substances and tended to report using drugs as they appeared as fads during a past era. For younger respondents, their move into crack smoking did not entail wide experimentation with gateway drugs. They generally had experience with one or two introductory drugs and then moved quickly from alcohol or marijuana use directly into crack and/or speed, which were often interchangeable or progressive.[1]

Although our study singled out crack for special attention, respondents in our study considered three other drugs equally compelling, with similar or more serious consequences: alcohol, heroin, and speed. Unlike heroin, which developed identifiable physical symptoms of tolerance, respondents understood that crack did not produce physical dependence and that they should *not* experience extreme discomfort if they suddenly stopped using crack.

Learning About Crack

At the time of the study, crack had become a major drug selection for all our respondents, even for individuals for whom other drugs and narcotics competed for priority. Respondents typically reported that their introduction to crack was through a friend or a close associate. Surprisingly, respondents in San Francisco stated that they had first heard about crack not through the street grapevine but through the mass media, particularly television. In the past, Brecher (1972) noted how the media, under the guise of reporting news, served to advertise new drugs and thereby "create" an interest and curiosity about them. This media phenomenon appeared to be the way interest in crack developed in San Francisco: widespread media reporting of it on the East Coast served to generate interest among members of the San Francisco street scenes who had already made commitments to drug careers; and once crack was introduced into the street systems, experimenters gravitated to it. The respondents selected for this study became devotees.

Another feature of crack that accounted for its instant popularity was the general reputation that powdered cocaine traditionally held among street system participants. Prior to the introduction of crack, drug users in the street scenes of San Francisco considered cocaine an *elite* drug, if not *the* elite drug, not only for its high cost but for its association with successful public figures in the worlds of entertainment and athletics. With snorting, the effects were usually quite subtle, mildly pleasurable, and cleary expensive (Waldorf et al. 1977). When freebasing developed, the notion, if not the exact chemistry, of preparing cocaine for smoking became common knowledge on the street. It was unusual, however, for the average street person to possess the necessary materials, the know-how to prepare them, or the money to purchase the drug and its paraphernalia to carry out freebasing.

The introduction of preparing cocaine for smoking by cooking it with baking soda offered a number of advantages over former ways of ingesting it. First, and most important, it lowered the cost dramatically and made "rocks" or "hubbas"—the street name in San Francisco for small amounts of crack cocaine—available to even the poorest street participants. Rather than being merchandised in bulk, small rocks could be sold for five or ten dollars, thus making one or two "hits" financially accessible.

Second, cocaine's reputation as a high-status drug made it a product of special importance to a ready market of users who were eager, even enthusiastic, about experimenting with a drug that was symbolically associated with success in life. What had been embellished by myth and the popular media allowed the common man and woman in the absence of legitimate career accomplishments to enjoy vicarious association with the rich and famous.

Finally, the initial physical effects smokers experienced—a "head rush" and a sudden exhilaration—were initially so pleasurable that users, delighted with the immediate and powerful lift in spirits, found themselves with an overwhelming desire to repeat the experience.

These three features—cocaine's elite reputation, its marketing convenience and low cost, and its gratifying effects—accounted for the quickness and persistence of the crack phenomenon among the populations we studied in San Francisco.

Because of crack's relative cheapness and popularity, combined with widespread unemployment, the role of street dealer became an available and valued occupation in low-income neighborhoods (Williams 1989). Rather than the notion of cocaine's being available from only jet set distributors, almost any poor man or woman (or daring adolescent) willing to chance arrest and assault from competitors could enter the crack business and enjoy an income that was superior to whatever legitimate opportunities were available for persons with limited work experience or little formal education. With the proliferation of small-time street dealers, crack became ubiquitous on the streets of inner-city neighborhoods so that persons eager to experiment with it could buy it cheaply from street mechants they knew and trusted.

THE ATTRACTION OF CRACK: THE SETTING AND THE DRUG

Much has been written of the importance of the social context of drug use and of the necessity of understanding the influence of these contexts in shaping drug selection, drug experiences, and drug careers (Zinberg 1984). Street drug ethnographers over the past twenty-five years have noted that the adventure associated with the action of urban street scenes has been a significant motivating factor for both inducing individuals to experiment with illicit drugs and then to continue using them (Sutter 1966; Feldman 1968; Preble and Casey 1969). Participating in the street scenes of San Francisco was part of the attraction of crack use. Shanine, a young prostitute whose considerable earnings went largely to crack use (and to clothes), explained this feeling-state in the following interview:

> *Interviewer:*   The feeling I'm getting from you is that you have been giving a lot more thought than you said as far as quitting crack and getting out for awhile.
>
> *Shanine:*   I mean I want to, but it's like this place is so . . . . Sometimes I have so much fun that I don't want to leave. Because, I don't trust too many people . . . . But my associates—I'm not going to call them my friends because you have no friends out here . . . . You know, I just get out of there and get to talking and bull_____g . . . . You know, I just like to go out a lot. I don't know, I just have fun.

Shanine went on to explain that when she left the area—in this case, the Tenderloin—she was drawn back to the neighborhood, not necessarily to the use of drugs but to the excitement and pace of living there. Another respondent in response to being asked what caused her relapse to crack put her answer in the context of the neighborhood: "The environment. Being out there. It's like a trap, you can't get out of there."

Our emphasis here is to underscore the importance of the social context and the way use of crack (and other drugs) facilitated participation in these action scenes. From a street perspective in which a fast-paced life required alertness and energy, crack had a distinct beneficial function.

ROUTES INTO CRACK SMOKING

When crack appeared in the marketplace, recruits came from three sources: old-time heroin users (some in methadone programs), persons with histories of extensive drug experimentation, and young street participants who were attracted to new adventures associated with "partying."

Heroin Users

Use of cocaine in conjunction with heroin dates back to the 1880s (Feldman and Beschner 1988). Traditionally, users have reported that the interaction of the two drugs—often called "speedballs"—enhanced both drug effects. For heroin users with either steady habits or currently stabilized in methadone maintenance programs, smoking crack allowed them to regain the valued sensation of the "rush"—that sudden, intense pleasure when a narcotic is injected. Experienced heroin users compared the rush from smoking crack with its counterpart of injecting heroin. For them, the new phenomenon of crack smoking was a rediscovery of a lost but prized sensation. Pat, one of the old-time heroin users in our study, explained the practicality of crack smoking for him: "I got into this smoking of crack because I can't feel dope [heroin] over the methadone and I can't get a hit [injection] anyway; I don't have any veins." Caroline, an experienced heroin user prior to her experimentation with crack, reported how the mixture affected her and prompted her to continue mixing the two drugs:

> *Interviewer:*   What's the difference [between crack and heroin]? How does crack make you feel differently from heroin?
>
> *Caroline:*   Well, one's a downer and the other one's an upper. So it's like when you're loaded on the heroin, you're down and you're nodding. And you take a hit of crack. It's kind of like it kicks the heroin and it kicks the crack. And it gives you one big giant feeling.

For the heroin users in our study, crack became an important supplement to their regular use of heroin (or methadone). Even for individuals heavily addicted to heroin and with a clear preference for it, like Caroline, the lure of crack remained a mysterious and powerful attraction: "It's just something about it when you take that hit and feeling good; it just makes you feel like you just want more and more and more."

Drug Experimenters

Other drug users with less inclination for drug preferences usually experimented with crack as it became popular among their street acquaintances. Crack became simply another one of the many drugs they tested. In comparing crack to previous drug experiences, it most often ranked high in preference and sometimes became the fatal attraction other confirmed crack smokers reported.

Party Types

Partying was a route into crack smoking taken by young women who were usually curious conventional types from middle-class or religious families. They usually defined themselves as "good girls" who were attracted to life in the fast lane. Although they admitted to minor transgressions in their adolescent years, such as smoking marijuana or having premarital sex, they were unconnected to street action scenes, which both horrified and fascinated them. They viewed their own move into regular crack use as a descent into wicked activities that contrasted sharply with their earlier depictions of themselves. They were usually introduced to crack use by a close friend who was similarly oriented toward partying. Shay, who came from a conventional family and spent a year and a half in college, described how her initiation to crack smoking was the outgrowth of friendship and her twenty-seventh birthday:

> I was with some friends. Some friends turned me onto this s___. They bought the powder, and the rock already, a case of wine—red and white mix. Beer, champagne. We went to my house and they pulled out their pipes and all that. I never had experience with that before. He told me they wanted me to try some. So the guy put a little piece of rock in a pipe, and he told me he'd give me experience in how to hit it. Act like you're smoking weed [marijuana] but just don't suck hard. Just pull it in nice and easy. When you see the smoke coming, then let it cloud up real white and then start pulling it in. And then you hold it a little bit. You hold your nose and go [respondent sucks in air]. And a little bit more out your nose and a little bit out your mouth. Then let it all out your mouth and nose and just totally exhale until you let it all out of your system. Let all the smoke out. And I got one hell of a hit which I'll never forget. I heard bells for three or four minutes . . . . I can't explain it. It's a feeling like, "Ooooh, I want to do this again. Give me some more of that." I like the way—you can't compare it to alcohol. You can't compare it with weed. It's a kind of feeling that you feel like you're on clouds. You feel like you're in heaven.

THE LURE OF CRACK: MORE AND MORE AND MORE . . .

Almost without exception, respondents expressed a paradoxical attraction and antipathy for crack. They seemed to cling more to the promise of its first pleasures than to any enduring satisfaction it brought. A common theme underscored the intense enjoyment of the initial experience followed by a losing struggle to have that intense feeling repeated. Respondents were often unable to find appropriate imagery to describe what was obviously a different kind of sensation from other drug adventures, and users expressed both a desire for its repetition and a disappointment about failing to achieve it. As one respondent claimed, "The only time you get high is the first hit of a binge."

Perhaps the single feature about crack that was reported most consistently was the way it captivated the user and evoked an overpowering desire to repeat the experience. Despite what respondents implied was a feeling state that was indescribably delicious, they unanimously found fault with the inexplicable search of trying to regain the sensation. Each respondent tried in his or her own way to capture in words the appeal found in crack. The following excerpts are three examples of the many verbal attempts of respondents to express their powerlessness to control their desire for the effects of crack:

> It's just that it comes to a point when you take that first hit. After you do that, it's like you feel like you've got to get some more. It's telling you need some more . . . . Sometimes I can [control the urge] and sometimes I don't know. I'll get on the phone or I'll walk around or something. But it all depends on what type of mood I'm in. Sometimes I can take a hit and just say, "Well, that's cool." But then sometimes it's just like this urge that I just got to have it. [Lisa]

> The methadone is worse than heroin will ever be—to get off of it. When you go to jail, they detox you awfully quick. Some people been on the program for a long time—thirteen, twenty years. But this crack. I got into this and figured I could handle it. If it don't make me physically sick, I figured I could say no, but it's not that way . . . . I spend every dime I get on it with the exception of a pack of cigarettes . . . . But any money I make I'll spend on it. Any kind of money at all. What am I going to do when there's no money and stuff? I guess I could go without dinner. That's when I'm hungry and I wish I had bought something. I've never, even on heroin, I always made sure that I had groceries. I've always took care of that. But this stuff,

you really convince yourself that you don't care what you do. You get hungry. It has that much control over you. It's hard for me to deal with something like that. It's hard for me to deal with it because I'm not strong enough. And I'm too old to be doing this s___. I'll be 49 next week, on the sixteenth. [Pat]

It [crack] makes me feel good but then it also depresses you, too, when you smoke a lot of it. I have this feeling like, "God, why am I doing this . . . ?" And you want more. Sometimes it's no good. You don't get satisfied. Then it depresses you. And you're just running around. You're a crazed person. Always wanting more. It's mainly feeling that you just want more. And it just more or less runs your life, really, is what it does. [Caroline]

Crack Binges

All respondents reported going on crack binges that lasted anywhere from two or three days to a week or more. These experiences were both exhilarating and exhausting, where a kind of inner struggle went on to keep from yielding to the temptation of "more" and satisfying the urge for continuance. The theme that permeated respondents' descriptions of these binges was the struggle against the drug itself. Anita, one of the few respondents who traded sex directly for crack, admitted that she stepped knowingly into this aspect of dependence:

Anita: When I first smoked it, I knew it was a . . . controlling drug.
Interviewer: It would *control* you?
Anita: Yeh, controlling, where it seemed to control everybody that uses it.

Some users found that crack cocaine was a useful corollary to their other activities. Kim, a transsexual prostitute, found that crack kept her alert. After experimenting with heroin and other drugs, she made a conscious choice for crack because it aided her performance as a prostitute: "It's very rushy . . . . It keeps you up and alert. I got tired of nodding all the time on heroin and going to sleep on weed [marijuana] . . . . It helps me make more money."

The actual binge itself had many variations. The essential element was a compelling desire to continue smoking crack in a relatively uninterrupted pattern. Some respondents mixed business with the binge, especially prostitutes who, like Kim, found that it kept them alert. Shanine wrote letters and made entries into her diary.

None of the respondents looked on these crack binges in a totally favorable light. The most common complaint was that the initial pleasure, which was the only one they sought, did not last long, and the pursuit of recapturing it was elusive, time-consuming, and expensive. April's description was typical:

It kind of levels out and then goes so that you can't feel it hardly. It's like your want to keep smoking to get the rush and the five-minute high, but if you keep smoking it for a long time, like I did, it's like when you go to quit, you can just drop it because it doesn't give you the same high that it did at first.

Still, all the respondents stated that they were caught up in wanting more. This pursuit was the most frustrating part of the total drug experience because it did not deliver what it had originally promised. This dissatisfaction was increased by smokers' powerlessness to stop the pursuit, with the result that it drained them of energy, money, and eventually of the self-respect that goes with controlling one's fate. In several instances, respondents described the drug as having a command over them and of their being helpless once they were in its power. In fact, three respondents compared crack to a pimp, implying that they were in an undesirable subordinate relationship with the drug.

By the end of the crack binge, users reported a depletion of money and energy. The physical conditions they described were often a series of unpleasant bodily symptoms and an odd state of disquiet and regret. For the period of time they submitted to the temptation and remained under the drug's influence, there was, at least in the beginning, a sense of exhilaration, a "head rush" that came on suddenly and gloriously and then drifted quickly away. Although successive "hits" did not produce the same intense exhilaration, smokers remained committed to pursuing that elusive sensation they found so gratifying.

At the end of the binge, the most common complaints were related to the physical wear and tear that came from fatigue and lack of sleep. Each user reported negatively on this condition, one claiming that "it ties up your legs and muscles"; another said that it "makes me look tired, worn out." At the end of the binge, users more or less caved in and slept from exhaustion. Many crack smokers were keenly aware of the drain on their health and took special care to eat regularly and dress neatly when they were not on binges.

Controlling Binges and Quitting

While there was unanimity on the pleasures and pains of crack use, there was divergence of opinion on quitting and seeking drug treatment. Most of our respondents had at one time voluntarily attempted to stop smoking crack. During their initial period of abstinence, they reported a physical state of chronic irritability. One respondent's attempt to quit produced a condition that was decidedly unpleasant:

> *Interviewer:*   Tell me how you felt the two days that you were off.
>
> *Shanine:*   Like a b____. I was crabby at everybody. I tried to sleep. Matter of fact, I did sleep. I slept most of the time . . . . But I kept waking up . . . . I'd sleep for an hour and then wake up.
>
> *Interviewer:*   And then what?
>
> *Shanine:*   I'd want a hit. Try to eat and go back to sleep. Try and fill myself up so I'd go back to sleep.
>
> *Interviewer:*   So that went on for how long?
>
> *Shanine:*   For like a day and a half. Probably not even a day and a half . . . . I couldn't go out there and be around everybody and tolerate all that bull____. Sometimes I just have to be high, you know, to tolerate everything. To tolerate those tricks [prostitute customers]. Everything. I can't stand some of them.

Other respondents stated a desire to break out of the pattern of chronic use but expressed a personal helplessness in managing the task alone. Kim, the sexually active transsexual who found crack functional to her prostitution, typified the sense of mystification in coming to grips with the compelling nature of her desire for the crack high: "To tell the truth, I wanted to get off it, but I just couldn't get off . . . . I tried to stop on my own, but I couldn't do it." For some respondents, the lack of an immediate support system to pave the way for drug treatment provided the explanation for their limited motivation: "[There's] a long way to go," one woman said with sad resignation, "and nobody there to help me."

Drug Treatment

Only a minority of respondents had ever entered drug treatment programs or even considered it. For those who had, the problem drug that motivated them to treatment tended to be heroin rather than crack. For individuals who had voluntarily entered drug treatment programs, the experience was either unsuccessful or unsatisfying. After enjoying the freedom of street life, they found that residential programs were too regimented. For heroin users who had recently taken up crack use, methadone maintenance was an option. Once they entered treatment, however, their pattern was to supplement methadone with street drugs, which for our population was primarily crack, it was the exceptionally motivated client who cooperated with treatment regimes and reduced the use of street drugs.

The major tension between crack-smoking clients and drug treatment programs was the discrepancy between the treatment program's demands for conventional behavior and the nature of street life, whose excitement and adventures were intertwined with drug consumption. The crack smokers we selected were geared to perform in the street systems of their choice, and they viewed the options for treatment as having to give up valued activities, even those they often defined as dissatisfying or harmful. As a result, drug treatment was not a significant part of their world, and it rarely entered into their conversations.

SEX HISTORIES AND CRACK USE

Almost without exception, respondents reported having early sexual experiences. For the women, the most common age for their first experience was 13 years old, but a number of them claimed to have been sexually molested or abused when they were younger. Remembrances of these instances of sexual abuse were always described with bitterness and resentment toward the offender, who frequently was a stepfather. Others claimed to have had sexual encounters with other family members (e.g., brothers and/or cousins).

All of the respondents had been sexually active prior to their use of crack. In most cases, they were introduced to sex in some mutually determined act with an intimate for whom they claimed either affection or love. In some cases, alcohol eased the introduction, but none of the respondents believed that drugs or alcohol was the "cause" of their sexual motivation or the source of their desire. The prostitutes in our study did, however, associate their entry into street prostitution with the use of crack or, in a few cases, heroin.

Few respondents claimed to be sexually excited by crack. In fact, the opposite reaction was the more common description. Rather than crack's acting as an aphrodisiac, women often stated that it reduced their interest in sex. One woman when asked whether crack excited her sexually claimed flatly, "You don't be in the mood at all." Berta, a prostitute and sexually active woman throughout her life, explained how crack made sex repellent:

> He'd [a date] always said, "Come and smoke some." So, one day I smoked some. Ain't no such thing as having sex after that s__t. You talk about some pussy, I'll kill you. It takes away my sex drive. It just, I have no emotions whatsoever. Okay, I'm froze to death. Even when I was shooting cocaine, same thing.

For men, the sexual response to crack was more ambiguous. While they associated crack with sexual activities, they found that it tended to undermine their ability to maintain erections and to ejaculate. These sexual encounters, usually fellatio, were seldom totally satisfying for either the man or woman since the woman's aim was to complete the act as soon as possible and acquire the crack and the man's desire was to sustain the sex act indefinitely. Under these circumstances, sexual encounters often veered off into power plays rather than sessions of erotic sexuality.

Most sexual encounters were carried out in the privacy of apartments, hotel rooms, or automobiles. When these encounters took place in crack houses, they were often performed where others could observe. Women who participated were quickly identified as "toss-ups" or "crack whores." Some of the men who used crack as a lure for quick and dirty sex also recognized its theatrical value, one stating: "For a little crack, you can make them act like circus animals." The consequence for the women was assignment to such low status that local descriptions of them were in dehumanized terms, and the stigma they felt was bitter and burning.

Stories of "crack whores" and "toss-ups" abounded even though other sexual encounters that involved crack were far more frequent. These stories were used principally as anticrack propaganda to illustrate crack's evil powers. Although they were atypical situations, they were used as dramatic evidence of the destructive nature of crack smoking. Most sexual encounters involving crack, however, entailed a business component that consisted of mutual agreements between consenting partners. These encounters generally took three forms: opportunistic situations, sale of sex for money, and sexual favors for crack.

Opportunistic Situations

Opportunistic situations to exchange sex for crack presented themselves spontaneously and depended on the willingness of the individual to capitalize on their availability. A male prostitute in our study, for example, came across two gay men in one of San Francisco's gay neighborhoods. Having known the men from previous experiences, he was invited to participate in a group sex arrangement where crack was an inducement. According to his report, they said, "You come over and spend the night and party, and you can get as high as you want." The respondent, trying to clarify the distinction between this arrangement and being a "toss-up," stated, "Look at it logically . . . . I'm not a toss-up and was going to buy it anyway. And if it's there . . . . "

Sex for Crack

Although respondents referred to sex-for-crack exchanges throughout the study, they tended to be more common in discussion than in practice. Furthermore, the exchange of sex for crack for many of our San Francisco respondents did not always have overtones of degradation in which the woman was a demeaned and subordinate participant but more closely resembled a bartering situation. Anita explained how she negotiated sex for crack, not as a way of begging or losing control but as a way of eliminating an unnecessary and intrusive financial proceeding:

Anita:	I only come out at night. You know, a lot of times I don't get paid. I exchange. It's understood from the get-go.
Interviewer:	Exchange for what?

Anita:	Exchange for crack. It's like, I've got so much amount of this and I want you to do this. Although sometimes they don't tell me right off. But it's understood.
Interviewer:	If you understand it, how do you understand it?
Anita:	Oh, just because they say something like, "You want to smoke?" You know, so right there it's not for free.
Interviewer:	It's an exchange for sex.
Anita:	And sometimes they have a quarter-ounce. You know, they have to have big dope because I'm not a twenty-dollar [prostitute] . . . you know, wrong person.

When the exchange of sex for crack was made in lieu of currency and the price in crack was carefully calculated, the encounter was called "working a twist." In this circumstance, crack was a substitute for money. And the woman involved maintained control over the exchange unlike the "toss-up" when her negotiating power was absent. Rather than viewing the activity as a severe loss of status and self respect, "working a twist" was a convenient but not degrading way to satisfy the desire for the crack high. Caroline, a heroin addict primarily, explained the circumstances in which "working a twist" fit in with her prostitution:

Interviewer:	When did you first exchange sex for crack?
Caroline:	I'd say within the last three years on and off.
Interviewer:	About how many times during a thirty-day period do you do that?
Caroline:	Maybe three times . . . because it's really not that necessary. I mean I can keep track and I always have money because I do date. So I can always buy my own crack. But there is sometimes when I get down and out, and I want some crack and somebody will come along and say, "Hey, let's work this twist" or whatever. Then, yeh, I'd get crack in exchange instead of money.

Other times, exchanges of sex for crack were expedient and convenient methods to continue a binge. Rather than being sought after, they were frequently the result of partying, which was not associated with being demeaned. Lynn, whose social life frequently centered on partying, explained how she had her first "twist":

Lynn:	The first time I did it, I was high. I was really tweaking. I mean I had my high beams on. I was really mellow. I was real high. But we didn't have no more drugs. It was like three in the morning. And we still wanted to get high.
Interviewer:	Who's we?
Lynn:	Me and my two friends . . . . And we were over my friend's house. And the dope man came and he had bags of rocks. Bags of rocks. We was like trying to get credit from him, and he knew we was high. He wasn't going to give it to us. And he was like, "Well, suck my dick and I'll give you all a rock." That's how I first started.

In these situations, the exchange of sex for crack was not necessarily a humiliating experience, and several of the women remembered them in highly favorable ways. Shay recalled that her first experience in exchanging sex for crack was a mutually satisfying sexual encounter that developed when she worked the stroll as a prostitute:

> This was the first time it happened. And he asked me if I wanted to have sex. I said, "Sure." [He said,] "I got some rocks." I said, "I beg your pardon?" "I got some rocks but I'm going to pay you up front for your services before we even get into anything because I don't have no money." So, he had a hundred dollars of dope. "I'm going to give you [an inaudible amount]. You can take that with you and we can smoke what we have left." He gave me three rocks and we smoked the rest. I gave him head . . . . He gave me some head. And we really had a nice time.

Other women, particularly young ones new to the drug scene, found that more streetwise crack users and dealers readily exploited them. Michele, a young prostitute, explained how she participated in sex for crack in the beginning stages of her crack career and then rejected the practice, preferring the independence and finances of prostitution for money: "I was getting cheated on the deal. That's why I started coming out here [on the stroll]. I used to go over there a couple of times a week. And he wanted me to do his cousin and his friends. Most of it was oral sex . . . . He was a dealer."

When young women discovered that their youth had market value in the sex trade, they frequently stopped performing sexual acts for crack. Instead they entered prostitution as beginning professionals. This choice gave them control of their finances and prevented their developing reputations as toss-ups and crack whores.

Sex for Money for Crack

Most of the respondents we selected insisted that they never traded sex directly for crack, although they acknowledged entering and remaining in prostitution as a primary means for earning money, much of which was spent on crack. The intermediate step of working for money—prostituting or "boosting"—was to them an important distinction, one they saw as distinguishing them from "toss-ups." The women had little hesitation in describing their work as prostitutes and were candid about the sexual favors they provided and the cost of each activity; but most of them were adamant about preserving a self-image that was not totally driven by a passion for drugs. The issues of pride and self-esteem appeared to allow them to define their financial exchanges as business rather than an obsession for drugs or loss of inner control. By receiving money rather than drugs, they were able to avoid the kind of dependency relationship with males that they perceived as subordinate and degraded. In managing their own finances, they were able to have options for other purchases, such as buying food, clothes, toys for their children, and the like.

The most important feature in exchanging sex for money was their achievement of independence. Although they admitted that much—in some cases, most—of their income was spent on crack, they were able to maintain their individual autonomy. As young businesswomen, they controlled their money, and that aspect of financial independence preserved their self-esteem. This does not mean that during encounters with "dates" they did not smoke crack. They would share crack with customers or accept it in amounts that were equal to their standard prices. In some cases, if a crack smoker was on a binge of crack, she might drop her price to induce a customer. As Anita stated, "On hubbas, it [the price] used to go down to forty bucks for half-and-half [part vaginal sex, part fellatio]." But even on crack binges, the majority of respondents maintained the principle of a monied transaction. Several of the women voluntarily underscored the importance of money transactions and spoke of them with a sense of high moral integrity.

STANDARDS OF BEHAVIOR: FAMILY AND PERSONAL RESPONSIBILITIES

Similar to the rules that governed the exchange of sex for crack, respondents determined specific standards of behavior in other spheres of their lives that they tried to keep crack use from corrupting. They placed rather strict moral values on behavior associated with family responsibilities. Many of the women had children and tried within their means to be caring parents. Anita, for example, set limits around where her prostitution activities would take place. Since her daughter lived with her, she would not bring "dates" to the house. This decision set an ethical boundary for her—a kind of bottom line below which she would not fall. By retaining a private resolve, she was able to preserve the sanctity of the dwelling she shared with her daughter and a view of herself as a caring mother who had not been totally degraded by crack use. "No," she insisted. "That's family. That's out."

Perhaps the most important measure of maintaining respectability even during crack binges was preserving a good appearance. For the prostitutes in the study, a good appearance was necessary for business reasons since it was crucial that they project an image of sexual appeal. It was, however, the audience of friends and peers that influenced whether crack binges and sustained drug use had taken its toll on an individual. Respondents were sensitive to negative comments about the physical effects of crack binges, and women especially went to great lengths to look fresh and healthy. During those periods when crack binges drained them of energy, women would frequently withdraw from circulation until they recovered sufficiently to rid themselves of telltale signs of weariness and exhaustion. As one respondent claimed, "I stop calling people and would stay away. I don't want people to see me like that." When women in the midst of fatigue would appear dirty or disheveled on the street, it was a signal that they had surrendered a valued principle, and it marked a descent in their local status.

SOCIAL TYPES AND HIERARCHICAL ORDER

There appeared to be a hierarchy of local social types in the crack scenes of San Francisco. Its underpinnings were determined in at least two ways: by control over the direction of one's life and by the degree of participation in the monied economy. At the high end of the hierarchy were individuals who controlled their crack consumption and earned top dollar in whatever field of legitimate or illegitimate pursuits was valued in the study communities. At the bottom of the hierarchy were those who had lost control of their crack use and exhibited to a highly competitive street system personal weakness that allowed others to exploit them. If a person was sexually exploited and humiliated, their sexual services as well as their personal worth within the neighborhood system were devalued. As persons at the bottom of the prestige scale, they became subject to ridicule and scorn. In essence, they were the failures of the street system with little to offer except quick and dirty sex, performed more for the amusement of onlookers than for any sexual excitement of the encounter.

In between, there existed a complicated set of measures that each individual employed to determine whether he or she rose or fell within the local status scheme. The place where a prostitute performed her sexual favors, for example, provided one measure. Lower status was accorded prostitutes who accepted "car dates" and carried out their sexual activities in the darkness in an automobile. Higher status was conferred on those whose sexual encounters took place in hotel rooms or private apartments.

Of greatest importance in determining an individual's local status was Management of immediate family. Individuals who had the wherewithal to support themselves and their children were generally looked upon with a measure of respect. This achievement need not, however, be visible financial support. Sending children to live with relatives indicated that a level of responsibility had been accomplished; placing them in foster homes denoted inadequacy or failure as a parent.

Too often crack use and crack binges provided respondents with evidence of their inability to manage the expected roles of parent or spouse, particularly during and after episodes when crack smoking overrode all other priorities. Such failures in the performance of these valued family roles induced self-loathing and depression. Many of them expressed feelings similar to Diane's, who stated bleakly, "I hate myself sometimes . . . . It's just me in this world, all by myself . . . . I feel that way with or without crack." Her sense of chronic melancholy and loneliness was not uncommon. Like others in the study who expressed disappointment with their general condition, with crack she could periodically lift her mood, if only momentarily. For a few sweet moments, a "head rush" replaced her depression, and the potency of crack revitalized her. And the sudden surge in energy became a soothing counterbalance to a life that moved alternately between anguish and danger.

AIDS KNOWLEDGE, RISK OF HIV, AND SEROLOGY

San Francisco's model for managing the HIV/AIDS epidemic has become world famous. As the HIV epidemic moved from the gay community to injection drug users, sexual partners, and people of color, strategies for prevention and education took new shapes. In 1985, when San Francisco public officials first addressed the probable movement of the epidemic into the drug-injecting networks, the drug treatment establishment and the San Francisco Department of Public Health proposed that the only approach to preventing the spread of HIV among intravenous drug users was to recruit them into drug treatment programs, where they would presumably abstain from injecting drugs and thereby be protected from infection. Under the leadership of the YES project, a San Francisco agency that specialized in applied ethnographic research, the Mid-City Consortium to Combat AIDS pioneered an effective street-based strategy. It consisted of utilizing ethnographic findings as the basis for sending outreach workers into the natural hangouts of drug users, where they provided AIDS education and distributed condoms and one-ounce bottles of bleach to disinfect needles. During the time data for this study were being collected, the YES project deployed some thirty outreach workers and field supervisors and passed out bottles of bleach with such regularity and consistency that on the street bleach may have been better known for its capabilities of disinfecting potentially contaminated needles than it was for doing laundry. Other agencies added to the prevention effort and provided posters, pamphlets, comic books, billboards, and video-tapes addressing the connection between sharing contaminated hypodermic needles and HIV infection. In San Francisco, the term CHOW—the acronym for "community health outreach worker"—had worked its way into the street idiom and become as well entrenched as the slang for crack. AIDS workers gave away thousands of condoms every day. During the heyday of this outreach effort, there was hardly a hidden population of injection drug users in the city of San Francisco that had not been targeted for street-based intervention.

With such a concerted, if politically jumbled, AIDS prevention program, it came as no surprise to discover that the respondents selected for this study, particularly the prostitutes, were AIDS aware. As a result of intensive health outreach strategies, respondents had acquired a working knowledge of the HIV epidemic and generally put into practice those measures that would protect them against infection. One of the significant findings of our research in San Francisco is that where AIDS educators penetrate drug-using networks and establish positive, helping relationships, members of the target groups will practice risk-reduction methods. This appears to be especially applicable with street prostitutes when they have the wherewithal to negotiate transactions on an equal basis with customers. These women reported consistent use of condoms in those business transactions, and the results of their serological testing provided some evidence of their truthfulness.

As we examined the street systems in San Francisco and the drug scenes found in them—both in this study and over the past four years—it became apparent even under the best of prevention circumstances which social types were more vulnerable to HIV infection. In San Francisco, it was clear that the AIDS message had reached those drug-using networks and those individuals who had been targeted by the outreach effort. What this study specifies is that a wide variety of social types exist in low-income, urban communities, most of whom can be reached with the street-based intervention methods we have developed. Crack smokers were neither unresponsive nor uncooperative with these public health measures. In fact, the existence of injection drug users, who had adopted crack smoking and had been the primary target of the original street-based outreach, were the focal points of AIDS education within their respective communities. In their way, these injection drug users as they mingled with crack smokers became ad hoc AIDS educators within those networks that were not primary targets. As a result, crack smokers profited from the prevention effort even when they themselves had never met or talked with an outreach worker. While their use of crack may have been problematic to society for reasons of morality good taste, it did not appear that crack smoking automatically put them risk for AIDS.

There were, however, among those populations who lived on the margin outside the law social types whose self-esteem and local status were so low that infection with a deadly, incurable disease was of little, if any, concern. As we looked at the various crack-smoking social networks and their hierarchies of local social types, it was readily identifiable that among our target group, as street status diminished, activities that could lead to HIV infection increased. In San Francisco, one of these social types was the crack toss-up and those with social standing only slightly above them. These individuals, both male and female, periodically slipped into unsafe sexual practices, not simply because they were intoxicated at the moment or driven by their desire to seek another hit on a crack pipe. They were at risk because in assessing their present reality, they did not in the silence of their hearts believe that their lives were worth preserving. And while San Francisco may have produced a world-renowned AIDS model, it had not even in its best, most financially secure days found an intervention strategy to address this class of at-risk person.

During the latter part of this study, forty crack smokers (thirty-five females and five males, one of whom was a transsexual) were recruited to be tested for HIV and other sexually transmitted diseases, principally syphilis. Of the thirty-nine confirmed results—one lost due to a missing consent form—there were four individuals who tested seropositive for HIV. Of the four seropositives, three of them were injection drug users, all of them males. The other person who tested positive for HIV infection was a young African American female who had never injected drugs and had only limited drug experience other than crack.

While the numbers in the serological study were far too small to draw definitive conclusions, the fact remains, no matter how slim the data, that 30 percent of the males—who were also drug injectors—tested positive for HIV antibodies while only one female (less than 4 percent) was HIV infected. If we were to employ these data as a measure of tracking the HIV epidemic in our target communities, then we would have to conclude that in San Francisco the HIV epidemic outside the gay community remains with the injection drug users. The future direction the HIV epidemic takes regarding new infections in low-income communities, we believe, will depend largely on how well our health agencies can access or continue to access injection drug users and keep their infection rate low. Because of his role in exchanging sex for crack, the injection drug user has great potential to spread HIV to female sexual partners, particularly individuals at the lower end of the status hierarchy. Given the limited data, however, we should not assume anything more than noting the potential of this possibility. As long as the seroprevalence rate among the injection drug users remains low, as it has with an aggressive outreach program, this potential can be contained.

PREDICTING THE PATH OF THE EPIDEMIC

At this juncture, it is fair to ask, based on this study, what role, if any, crack would play in the spread of HIV/AIDS in San Francisco. The answer seems to depend on three factors: identifying as precisely as possible where the present infections are located, identifying those behaviors and activities that would predictably transmit the virus, and assessing the education and prevention methods that would interrupt what would otherwise be the natural path of the epidemic.

In San Francisco, the overwhelming percentage of HIV infections remains among gay males. If San Francisco does, in fact, have a model system of intervention, it tends to be in the treatment of HIV/AIDS and not necessarily in preventing its spread. Most services for HIV/AIDS have been directed primarily to the gay community. Just how crack smoking would extend the epidemic within the gay community has, to the best of our knowledge, not been researched, and our study would not contribute any information to that aspect of the potential spread of HIV. Several ongoing intervention programs address the issue of sexual disinhibition attributed to drug and alcohol consumption among gay men. To the degree that the annual seroconversion among gay men in San Francisco in recent years has dropped to under 1 percent, it can be assumed that crack smoking has not become a major variable in HIV transmission within the gay community.

Among out-of-treatment injection drug users, seroprevalence stabilized at approximately 15 percent during the four-year period that the CHOW program was in operation. What had not been identified until this study was the potential role crack-using, injection-drug users might play in transmitting HIV to females who may or may not be their permanent or regular sex partners. If crack smoking is an activity that has potential for spreading HIV infection in San Francisco, then injection-drug users must be considered central figures in the equation. Our study indicates that injection-drug users are not simply sexually involved with steady partners but appear to play a significant role in the exploitation of toss-ups, although this phenomenon needs further ethnographic exploration. To the degree that the infection rate among injection drug users rises, then the potential spread of HIV increases. In San Francisco, as long as the seroprevalence rate remains low, the possibility of sudden increases of HIV among crack-smoking females is not likely, although this may not be true for other sexually transmitted diseases (or in other cities).

To assess the possibility of a surge in seroconversion, it would be necessary to examine the methods for addressing prevention of HIV infection among injection drug users and their female sexual partners. As we noted, as long as an intervention structure existed that penetrated these hidden populations in San Francisco and provided consistent education and prevention to injection drug users and their partners, the seroprevalence rate remained steady, with only slight annual increases between 1 percent and 3 percent (Moss 1989). Since December 31, 1990, however, the YES/CHOW program has been shut down. To the best of our knowledge, there has been no alternative plan in San Francisco to replace it with a comparable street-based intervention strategy. Given the absence of the consistent distribution of condoms and the discontinuance of the daily distribution of bleach at the street level and the way those activities served as reminders to populations that had been originally described as hard to reach and difficult to serve, it is not unrealistic to speculate that the incidence of high-risk behavior, such as sharing contaminated needles without disinfecting them, will rise. Whether Prevention Point, the bootleg volunteer needle exchange program in San Francisco, which reaches approximately 6 percent of the estimated 16,000 injection users (Rubens 1990), can substitute for the missing outreach effort remains to be determined. What was once a highly optimistic outlook for managing the HIV epidemic among injection drug users in San Francisco has taken a frightening turn, and crack smoking, which did not appear to have a significant future in accelerating the spread of HIV, may now have an unanticipated opportunity.

NOTE

1. Brecher, in his classic report for the Consumers Union, discussed and classified methamphetamine (speed) and cocaine in the same category, most notably because of the similarity of their pharmacological effects—the elevation of mood, the decrease in hunger, indifference to pain, and the antifatigue properties. In fact, Brecher attributed the boom in cocaine smuggling during the late 1960s to the successful banning of the precursor chemicals for the manufacture of speed (Brecher 1972:302).

REFERENCES

ALDRICH, M. R. 1986. "Crack (Garbage Freebase)." In *Cocaine Handbook: An Essential Reference*. San Francisco: And/Or Press. Second Edition.

BRECHER, E. M. 1972. *Licit and Illicit Drugs*. Mount Vernon, N.Y.: Consumers Union.

FELDMAN, H. W. 1968. "Ideological Supports to Becoming and Remaining a Heroin Addict." *Journal of Health and Social Behavior* 9(2) (May–June).

FELDMAN, H. W. and BESCHNER, G. 1988. "Ten-City Report on 'Speedballing.'" Prepared for the National Institute on Drug Abuse. Unpublished.

HOROWITZ, M. 1974. Editor's Preface to *History of Coca: The Divine Plant of the Incas*. By W. G. Mortimer. San Francisco: And/Or Press.

LAMAR, J. V. 1988. "Kids Who Sell Crack." *Time,* May 9.

MOSS, A. R., P. BACCHETTI, and D. OSMOND. 1989. "Seroconversion for HIV in IVDUs in San Francisco." Abstract number T.A.O. 11, Fifth International Conference on AIDS, Montreal, Canada, June.

PREBLE, E., and CASEY, J. H., JR. 1969. "Taking Care of Business—The Heroin User's Life on the Street." *International Journal of the Addictions* 4(1).

RUBENS, N. 1990. "A Needle a Day . . . " *San Francisco Bay Guardian,* November 21.

SUTTER, A. G. 1966. "The World of the Righteous Dope Fiend." *Issues in Criminology* 2.

WALDORF, D., S. MURPHY, C. REINARMAN, and S. MALONE. 1977. *Doing Coke: an Ethnography of Cocaine Users and Sellers*. Washington, D.C.: Drug Abuse Council.

WILLIAMS, T. 1989. *The Cocaine Kids: The Inside Story of a Teenage Drug Ring*. Reading, Mass.: Addison-Wesley.

ZINBERG, N. E. 1984. *Drugs, Set and Setting: The Basis for Controlled Intoxicant Use*. New Haven, Conn.: Yale University Press.

16

The Lives and Times of Asian-Pacific American Women Drug Users

An Ethnographic Study of Their Methamphetamine Use

Karen A. Joe

INTRODUCTION

During the latter part of the 1800s, Asians represented a small proportion of the nation's immigrant population. Chinese, Japanese, Filipinos, and Asian-Indians were the primary Asian ethnic groups moving to the United States (Chen 1991). A common misconception of the times, fueled by racism, was that "the Orientals" (in particular, the Chinese) presented a threat to Americans because of their cultural differences and their alleged addiction to opium. Ethnic myths emerged with Asian men being portrayed as the "inscrutable Fu Manchu" and the "opium loving Oriental" (Sante 1991). The "Oriental woman" brought other dangers as well; she was the promiscuous and erotic creature who could turn into the evil Dragon Lady or the submissive China Doll (Tong 1994).

Since the passage of the 1965 United States immigration law reforms, Asian-Pacific Americans have become the most diverse minority population in the United States. At least 32 different Asian-Pacific American ethnic groups now reside in the United States. Asians are also the fastest growing group with an increase of 5 million during the last 20 years

Adapted from "The Lives and Times of Asian-Pacific Women Drug Users: An Enthnographic Study of Their Methamphetamine Use," by Karen A. Joe, 1996, *Journal of Drug Issues,* 20(1), p. 199. Copyright 1996 *Journal of Drug Issues*. Adapted by permission.

(Chen 1991). In 1990, the Asian population climbed to 7.3 million, and by 2020, is expected to reach 20 million (*Honolulu Advertiser* 1993). With the complexity and diversity of Asian-Pacific Americans—across ethnic origins, cultures, languages, regional dialects, socioeconomic levels and historical waves of immigration—they have been cast in a number of contradictory roles. While many of the historical depictions of the "mysterious Oriental gangster" and the "erotic Asian femme fatale" continue to persist, contemporary portrayals of Asians, paradoxically, also cast them as the diligent, hardworking and obedient "role model minority."[1] In this latter scenario, they are typically described as a population with few social problems, especially crime and illicit drug use.

As a result of such stereotypes, Asian-Pacific Americans drug-use problems are often neglected in research studies (Joe 1993; Kuramoto 1994; Austin et al. 1989). As recently noted by Zane and Sasao (1992), there is a critical need for empirical information on the substance use issues of this diverse minority group. A number of studies (Chi et al. 1989; Kitano and Chi 1985, 1986; Johnson et al. 1987) on drinking patterns among Asian-Pacific Americans have made important inroads into alcohol research, discrediting popular stereotypes about the nondrinking Asian-Pacific American and underscoring the variations in the cultural values toward alcohol consumption among different Asian ethnic groups. Drug research on Asian-Pacific users, however, has not made similar progress. The paucity of information on drug use among this "hidden population," especially Asian-Pacific American women, has created barriers to moving beyond existing stereotypes and has hampered the formulation of a theoretical foundation (Zane n.d.; Sue 1987) and the development of culturally relevant and effective treatment programs.

This paper challenges the persistent stereotype of the passive yet exotic Asian-Pacific American woman, and is concerned with uncovering the complexities of the lives of a group of women drug users and their strategies for coping with and managing their problems. I first consider existing drug-use studies on Asian-Pacific American populations and offer a path to building a theoretical foundation for understanding their use patterns and problems. Essentially, the combined use of ethnographic data and the grounded theory approach provide an important methodological and theoretical vehicle for uncovering the hidden dimensions of use among hard-to-reach populations such as Asian-Pacific Americans. I then turn to examine the ways in which the cultural claims in their lives interact with and shape their initiation into and continued use of illicit substances based on an ethnography of female methamphetamine users in Hawaii.

RESEARCH ON DRUG USE AMONG ASIAN-PACIFIC AMERICANS

The small number of studies on drug use among Asian-Pacific Americans have primarily involved survey research with household and student populations (Sue et al. 1979; Newcomb et al. 1987; Trimble et al. 1987; Skager et al. 1989). According to these studies, Asian-Pacific Americans report less drug use than nonAsian-Pacific Americans, however, a number of methodological problems make it difficult to access the prevalence and the factors associated with use among different Asian ethnic groups. As Zane and Sasao (1992) point out, these studies typically have had relatively small sample sizes, represent student-age populations, and more acculturated groups like Chinese and Japanese. Absent from most of these studies are those who are at high risk such as immigrants, refugees, and the economically marginalized. Treatment-based studies have not clarified prevalence issues as they also tend to have relatively small samples, lump different Asian ethnic groups to-gether, and reflect the experience of those who have been able to access services (Zane and Sasao 1992; Kuramoto 1994). Treatment staff indicate that language differences, lack of awareness of services and social resources, and cultural beliefs (e.g., shame, guilt) account for low utilization rates (Joe 1990).

In addition to problems of estimating prevalence rates among Asian-Pacific Ameri-can populations, very little is known about the social-cultural factors associated with their use patterns. In this regard, alcohol research and mental health studies on Asian-Pacific Americans indicate that stressful life events such as competing cultural demands and obli-gations, economic marginality, and family and kinship networks are critical factors to con-sider in understanding drug use patterns.

The family and extended kinship networks among Asian-Pacific Americans are par-ticularly important to investigate as two diametrically opposing patterns have been identi-fied as being related to health and social problems. On the one hand, the family—its ties, loyalties, cultural expectations, and beliefs—can serve as a significant source of stress as the individual tries to develop a sense of autonomy, often in an extended multigenerational household, and, in turn, contribute to deviance and health-related problems (Hunt et al. 1995; Loo 1991). On the other hand, the demands, values, and structure of Asian-Pacific American families can have a preventive effect (Zane and Sasao 1992).

Clearly, the few existing survey research studies on Asian-Pacific Americans are an important first step to ascertaining drug use patterns and problems. However the "close-ended" nature of the social survey approach limits the depth of our understanding of how the family may foster or hamper drug use. In this approach, assumptions must be made about how the family is structured and operates, and respondents' experiences are neatly fitted into preconstructed categories. As Zane and Sasao (1992) note, many substance abuse studies on Asian-Pacific Americans have not taken into account cultural and generational differences.

By contrast, a qualitative approach offers an invaluable method for uncovering and fully exploring the distinct experiences and problems associated with drug use among hidden pop-ulations like Asian-Pacific Americans. The multiple methodologies of qualitative research are intended to provide an in-depth understanding of social phenomenon guided by a commit-ment to the naturalistic, interpretive, perspective (Denzin and Lincoln 1994). As such, theory building begins by describing the world from the individual's viewpoint and examining the constraints of everyday life (Denzin and Lincoln 1994.) In this way, the analyst navigates through culture from the individual's place of reference rather than prematurely demarcate "what is relevant" from "what is not" as is required in close-ended survey questionnaires.

The ethnographic approach and its dialectical process of data gathering and analysis (Agar 1993) have been instrumental in moving beyond the stereotypical views of the "dou-ble deviance status" of women substance abusers and in "unpacking" the ways in which cultural norms of gender affect the everyday life of women and their drug use. Rosenbaum's (1981) landmark ethnography of women heroin users revealed the gendered constraints and the "narrowing of options" they experience with prolonged use. Recent ethnographies of the sex-for-crack exchange have dispelled the demonized portrayals of women crack users and uncovered the patriarchally driven subordination of women into the "secondary 'sec-ondary labor market' " of the informal drug economy (Maher and Curtis 1992:225; see also Bourgois and Dunlap 1993).

As demonstrated below, the ethnographic approach is crucial to dispelling the passive and erotic stereotypes of Asian-Pacific American women and to breaking away from preconceived notions of the Asian-Pacific American family structure. Through in-depth interviewing and field observations, it was possible to uncover the complex ways in which different Asian ethnic family systems foster or hamper initial and continued use of drugs among women.

THE ICE AND OTHER METHAMPHETAMINE STUDY

The Setting

Health and law enforcement authorities grew increasingly concerned in the mid-to-late 1980s over the emergence of ice and other forms of methamphetamine. Many believed that ice, a smokable form of methamphetamine, had already reached "epidemic" proportions in Hawaii, and would become the drug of the 1990s (*San Francisco Chronicle* 1989; *Newsweek* 1989; Miller and Tomas 1989). Hospital and emergency room reports indicated that this central nervous system stimulant had a highly addictive quality within a short period of use, and was also connected with several physical and psychological problems, including insomnia, hypertension, emaciation, irritability, and depression. Aside from the limited information available from clinical and treatment populations, little was known about the demographic, social, and cultural attributes of methamphetamine users. Clinical staff in Hawaii reported that the state's diverse ethnic population, including its Asian-Pacific American populations were using ice. Moreover, they observed growing numbers of young women and housewives using ice as a diet suppressant (Miller 1991).

The Research Design and Methods

The data are drawn from a cross-cultural community-based study of moderate-to-heavy methamphetamine users in Honolulu, San Francisco, and San Diego. These three sites were selected because each one was associated with the highest usage and problems in the United States. Also, the predominant mode of use differed in each of the sites. While San Francisco had a significant rate of intravenous use, San Diego had a high rate of nasal use. By contrast, Honolulu users primarily smoked ice. Interviews were conducted with 150 active users in each site (see Morgan et al. n.d.). This analysis is based on Honolulu interviews with 37 women of Asian-Pacific American ethnicity.

Respondents had to meet four criteria in order to be interviewed: (1) had to live in the targeted locale for at least 2 years; (2) had to be 18 years of age or older; (3) ice or another form of methamphetamine had to be their stimulant of choice; and (4) used an average of at least 0.5 grams per month during the last 12 months.

After the research staff conducted 6 months of focus groups and interviews with community agencies and officials, we were able to identify the characteristics of preliminary target user groups. We hired and trained interviewers who were culturally sensitive to the targeted user groups and who were very familiar with the local methamphetamine scene (i.e., former users, personal contacts). Given the targeted sampling frame, interviewers began to develop chain referrals based on their contacts.

The interview involved two steps whereby respondents discussed, in a taped in-depth session, their life histories, the qualitative aspects of their drug-use history, their experiences and consequences of using ice and other illicit drugs, including changes in their relationships with others. During the second half of the interview session, the respondent was asked a series of questions from a quantitative questionnaire. Questions ranged from personal and family traits to drug-use patterns, health status, and criminal history. The duration of the interviews was between 2 and 2.5 hours.

One other source of data from which this analysis draws upon stems from the ethnographic field notes taken by two of our female interviewers of mixed ethnicity and one Samoan male interviewer who had access to several *Honolulu* user groups and spent between 6 months and 1 year in the field with them.

ASIAN-PACIFIC AMERICAN WOMEN ICE USERS AND THEIR FAMILY TIES

Who are They?

As Table 16–1 shows, our female respondents represent the ethnic diversity of Hawaii. The majority of the sample, however, identified as Hawaiian (54%) and Filipina (30%).[2] The Hawaiian, the Portuguese, and to a slightly lesser extent, the Filipino women, were of mixed ethnicity; this reflects the complexity of ethnicity in the state. Nearly all of the women were born in the United States, usually Hawaii, and only two of the Filipinas immigrated to the United States during early childhood. The Samoan and a few of the Filipinas report that their parents were immigrants.

Overall, the women's median age was 27 years.[3] Over one-half of the women (57%) had never been married, but had at least one child (60%). Among those women with children, 68% of them were living with their offspring.

Overall, 40% had obtained a high-school diploma and another 30 had dropped out prior to completing the 12th grade. Because the state's major industry is tourism, the most readily accessible job opportunities are in the service sector, particularly in the hotel, restaurant, retail, and construction businesses. Overall, 38% of the women supported themselves during the last year through a job, and most of them worked in retail or clerical positions (19%). Others principally supported themselves through government assistance (30%), their family (22%), or illegal activities (11%). The majority of the women (54%) were living in poverty, with a yearly income of $10,000 or less.

Growing Up in Chaos

Several themes emerged from the qualitative interviews which underscore the strained interplay between economic marginality, and the cultural traditions and norms of Asian-Pacific American families. Many of our female respondents grew up, in various degrees, in an extended family network, known locally as the ohana system (Joe 1995). Ohana derives from Hawaiian culture, and historically referred to the family clan and its strong sense of solidarity, shared involvement, and interdependence. This kinship system has changed over the decades as Hawaii's culture has come to reflect the blending of its various Asian and Pacific Islander populations and their cultures. In contemporary Hawaii, ohana has retained the traits of cooperation and unity, but extends to persons who are not necessarily blood-related, but closely connected to the family and considered part of the social support system (Handy et al. 1972; Pukui et al. 1972).

TABLE 16–1 Personal Characteristics of Asian-Pacific Women Methamphetamine Users

	Chinese (n = 1)		Filipino (n = 11)		Hawaiian (n = 20)		Japanese (n = 1)		Portuguese (n = 2)		Samoan (n = 2)	
	n	%	n	%	n	%	n	%	n	%	n	%
Age												
18–25 yrs	0	0.0	5	45.4	9	45.0	0	0.0	0	0.0	2	100.0
26–35 yrs	1	100.0	4	36.4	8	40.0	1	100.0	1	50.0	0	0.0
36–45 yrs	0	0.0	2	18.2	3	15.0	0	0.0	1	50.0	0	0.0
Education												
11th gr or less	0	0.0	4	36.4	5	25.0	0	0.0	1	50.0	1	50.0
12th grade	0	0.0	4	36.4	10	50.0	0	0.0	0	0.0	1	50.0
College: 1–3 yrs	0	0.0	2	18.2	5	25.0	1	100.0	1	50.0	0	0.0
College: 4 +	1	100.0	1	9.0	0	0.0	0	0.0	0	0.0	0	0.0
Lived with most until 18 yrs												
Both parents	0	0.0	8	72.7	8	40.0	1	100.0	2	100.0	1	50.0
One parent only	0	0.0	1	9.0	7	35.0	0	0.0	0	0.0	0	0.0
Other relative	1	100.0	1	9.0	5	25.0	0	0.0	0	0.0	0	0.0
Other	0	0.0	1	9.0	0	0.0	0	0.0	0	0.0	1	50.0
Marital status												
Never married	0	0.0	7	63.6	12	60.0	0	0.0	1	50.0	1	50.0
Married	1	100.0	3	27.3	3	15.0	0	0.0	0	0.0	1	50.0
Separated/divorced	0	0.0	1	9.0	5	25.0	1	100.0	1	50.0	0	0.0
Number of children												
None	0	0.0	6	54.5	7	35.0	1	100.0	1	50.0	0	0.0
One	1	100.0	0	0.0	3	15.0	0	0.0	0	0.0	2	100.0
Two	0	0.0	1	9.0	3	15.0	0	0.0	1	50.0	0	0.0
Three or more	0	0.0	4	36.4	7	35.0	0	0.0	0	0.0	0	0.0
Percent living with Children	1	100.0	3	60.0	8	61.5	0	0.0	1	100.0	2	100.0
Presently living with												
spouse/partner	1	100.0	1	9.0	10	50.0	1	100.0	0	0.0	2	100.0
Children only	0	0.0	1	9.0	3	15.0	0	0.0	0	0.0	0	0.0
Family	0	0.0	4	36.4	4	20.0	0	0.0	1	50.0	0	0.0
Friends	0	0.0	3	27.3	1	5.0	0	0.0	0	0.0	0	0.0
Other	0	0.0	2	18.2	2	10.0	0	0.0	1	50.0	0	0.0
Primary source of income during last 12 months												
Professional	0	0.0	0	0.0	1	5.0	0	0.0	0	0.0	0	0.0
Clerical/retail	0	0.0	4	36.4	2	10.0	0	0.0	0	0.0	1	50.0
Skilled-manual	0	0.0	0	0.0	3	15.0	0	0.0	0	0.0	0	0.0
Unskilled	0	0.0	1	9.0	1	5.0	0	0.0	1	50.0	0	0.0
Govt. asst.	0	0.0	3	27.3	7	35.0	0	0.0	0	0.0	1	50.0
Family	1	100.0	2	18.2	5	25.0	0	0.0	0	0.0	0	0.0
Illegal Activities	0	0.0	1	9.0	1	5.0	1	100.0	1	50.0	0	0.0
Income during last 12 months												
$5,000 or less	1	100.0	2	18.2	5	25.0	1	100.0	0	0.0	1	50.0
$5,000–10,000	0	0.0	4	36.4	7	35.0	0	0.0	0	0.0	1	50.0
$10,001–15,000	0	0.0	2	18.2	1	5.0	0	0.0	0	0.0	0	0.0
$15,001–20,000	0	0.0	1	9.0	1	5.0	0	0.0	1	50.0	0	0.0
$20,001 and above	0	0.0	2	18.2	6	30.0	0	0.0	1	50.0	0	0.0

In Hawaii, today, where the cost of living is among the highest in the United States, this extended family arrangement acquires new meaning in the Western economic context. The extended family system offers financially strapped families a readily accessible and stable source of help and relief. Over 70% of all the women in this study came from working and lower working-class families where their fathers, when employed, worked principally in skilled and unskilled labor-intensive jobs. Seventy percent of their mothers worked in similar occupations. Overall, 18% of the women reported that they had lived principally with other relatives—grandparents, aunties, uncles, cousins—until adulthood. One-fourth of the Hawaiian women indicated that they had grown up primarily with relatives. Our respondents' life histories, however, suggest a more complex pattern whereby many lived between households, shifting constantly from various relatives to their parents.

The ohana system acts not only as a resource for economically strained families, but also as a source of relief for heated conflicts within the family. With only a few exceptions, women described growing up in tension-filled households. While the ohana system provides relief, it can also introduce intergenerational gaps.

> Mary is a 23 year old Chinese Hawaiian woman who is the fourth child of six. Her mother has been married three times, and her children are from different marriages. Mary never knew her father. Mary's older sister was sent to stay with their rich aunt, and as Mary angrily reflects, "the spoiled brat grew up in another lifestyle." By comparison, Mary and her younger brothers lived with their grandmother in the early childhood years. While Mary contends that she was sent to live with her grandmother to "take care of her and to help her with the house and cook", in light of her young age, it is more probable that her mother relied on her own mother to help care for two of her children while she worked and tried to look after the other children and a physically abusive husband who suffered from severe diabetes. Mary returned to her mother's home in her teen years to help her mother take care of her diabetic stepfather. She describes her childhood as "difficult" and adds, "when I was growing up, I never had anybody to talk to. Just grandma, and you know how that goes." [446]

Part of the tension in the family was due to financial worries, but also to the presence of alcohol and other drug use by one or both parents.

Several studies report a high incidence of family problems among female substance users including parental alcohol and drug abuse and domestic violence (see Inciardi et al. 1993; Ettorre 1992). As Table 16–2 shows, overall, 84% of the women indicate that at least one of their parents drank alcohol. Nearly half of the parents used marijuana, and over one-third of them used cocaine. Alcohol appeared to be the most problematic. Forty percent of the women report that their parents' had problems with alcohol. The proportion very likely is higher as many more attempted to normalize their parents' level of alcohol use and problems when describing their life histories.

> Joanne, a 44 year old homeless Hawaiian Filipina, states that her father consumed several cases of beer on the weekends, but was only a "recreational drinker" because he "never missed work due to his drinking" and, most importantly, provided for his family. She had her first drink at 22 years of age when her father became seriously ill and died, and, "for the next ten years stayed in an unconscious drunken state by noontime everyday."[551]

> Lani is an 18 year old Filipina, and lives with her parents and siblings. Her parents and her older sister immigrated to the United States, and she and her younger brother were born in Hawaii. She hints that her father drinks too much, but has been a very "good provider" for the family. She

TABLE 16–2   Parents' Use and Problems with Alcohol and Drugs By Ethnicity

	Chinese (n = 1)		Filipino (n = 11)		Hawaiian (n = 20)		Japanese (n = 1)		Portuguese (n = 2)		Samoan (n = 2)	
	n	%	n	%	n	%	n	%	n	%	n	%
% Parent(s) used												
Alcohol	1	100.0	10	90.9	17	85.0	1	100.0	1	50.0	1	50.0
Marijuana	1	100.0	4	36.4	11	55.0	1	100.0	0	0.0	1	50.0
Cocaine	1	100.0	4	36.4	7	35.0	1	100.0	0	0.0	0	0.0
Speed	1	100.0	1	9.0	6	30.0	0	0.0	0	0.0	1	50.0
Heroin	0	0.0	0	0.0	0	0.0	0	0.0	0	0.0	0	0.0
Other	1	100.0	1	9.0	3	15.0	0	0.0	0	0.0	0	0.0
% Parent(s) problems with												
Alcohol	0	0.0	4	36.4	9	45.0	0	0.0	1	50.0	1	50.0
Marijuana	0	0.0	1	9.0	3	15.0	0	0.0	0	0.0	0	0.0
Cocaine	0	0.0	2	18.2	1	5.0	0	0.0	0	0.0	0	0.0
Speed	0	0.0	0	0.0	2	10.0	0	0.0	0	0.0	0	0.0
Heroin	0	0.0	0	0.0	0	0.0	0	0.0	0	0.0	0	0.0
Other	0	0.0	0	0.0	2	10.0	0	0.0	0	0.0	0	0.0

attributes the constant fighting between her parents as well as with her to herself rather than to any problems the father might be having with alcohol. She believes that the strain at home is due to her parents' perceptions of her as being "too Americanized", "uncontrollable". When the conflict flares at home, she seeks refuge at her aunt's house, where, she says, "they understand me." [463]

Parental alcohol or drug use was typically connected with violence. More than 40% of the females describe their home life as violent. In some cases, the intensity of the violence was extreme as Susan, a 19-year-old Hawaiian woman, recalls her "unhappy" childhood.

From about five years old, Susan remembers that her father would routinely beat up her mother to the point where she would be unable to walk. Subsequently her father would come looking for her or her mother would take out her own anger and hostility by beating on Susan and her siblings. Both parents were heavily involved in drugs, and her father was a dealer. She describes having a loose family structure as her father had several children by other women.

While growing up, she was exposed to many "adult" situations including drug deals and hanging out in bars. Her father was sent to prison for hanging a man on a fence and beating him to death while drunk. At 14, an unknown teenage male raped her at a family function. She tried to isolate herself, but when her mother learned of the incident, punished her for "promiscuity" by repeatedly hitting her on the head and sending her to a group home for troublesome teenagers. [462]

In some cases, the violence was expressed through sexual assault.

Jacky is 20 years old, and of Hawaiian, Korean, and Filipino ancestry. She has one older brother who she has not seen since she was six when they were both placed in foster care. Her mother died when she was five. She and her brother lived with the step-father who was an "abusive drinker" and sexually molested them repeatedly. This went on for one year at which point, six year old Jacky stabbed her stepfather for sexually abusing them. Although she does not have a clear recollection of the stabbing incident, she does remember having her arm broken by her step-father while he was trying to sexually assault her. [537]

Another important dimension of the family centers around the cultural expectations of Asian-Pacific American women. This was clearly felt by women who were living in chaotic family situations as well as those few who described their family life as "normal." In traditional Samoan families, gender relations are organized around Polynesian traditions of male dominance, separation, and obligation (Joe and Chesney Lind 1995). While Hawaiian customs were similar to the Polynesian model of separation, this was severely altered with the death of Kamehamehakunuiakea in 1819, and subsequent arrival of the missionaries (Nunes and Whitney 1994). Although the Hawaiian system retains some male domination features, it is the women who have "learned the ways of the malihini (strangers). Women adjusted to and became clever at cultural and economic transactions with the new world" (Nunes and Whitney 1994: 60). At the same time, however, Hawaiians, who are the most marginalized group in the state, have accommodated to poverty through normalizing early motherhood, high dropout rates, and welfare dependency for girls (Joe and Chesney Lind 1995). In modern Filipino families, girls and women have been socialized according to colonial cultural and religious, usually Catholic, norms that emphasize the secondary status of women, girl's responsibility to their families, and the control of female sexual experimentation (Aquino 1994).

Cultural expectations about "being a good girl" combined with economic marginality and heavy parental alcohol consumption erupts into violence. Helen, a 38-year-old Filipino, Hawaiian, Portuguese woman, recalls her childhood years:

> I come from a family of six children and I'm the fourth. We are all scattered. One brother is in prison and one passed away. When we was growing up we lived with both my parents. They stayed married until my dad passed away. Home was very strict. My dad was an alcoholic so he couldn't hold a job. He always had a strict hand on us. Discipline kind. He was either drunk or coming down from a hangover when he hit us. My mom was the one that went to work. Beatings were all the time from my dad. Severe kind with belt buckles.

> The last time my dad hit me was when I was 17 years old. He found out that I was smoking cigarettes. I was almost 18. My youngest brother was able to drink with him, smoke cigarettes, and pot with him! But not me. The boys could do what they wanted. My mom wasn't the one to discipline us. She really had no say in it. [449]

Coping Strategies in Managing Family Chaos

The women's first response is to endure the turmoil in their families. Given the extended kinship network, some women stayed with relatives when the situation at home became unbearable. As Whitney (1986) points out, local cultural norms stress that "outsiders" not be brought into family problems, and children's respect for their elders should be shown through deference. In his clinical work with young adult Asian-Pacific American male alcoholics, those who were physically abused tended to retreat temporarily to a relative's house and were unable to negatively evaluate their parents' abusive behavior (Whitney 1986).

The majority of women, however, eventually, could no longer endure the chaos and family violence and sought refuge in one of two ways. Approximately one-half of them believed that the best strategy for dealing with the violence in their own home was by starting their own family and became pregnant in their teen years. Marty, a 34-year-old Hawaiian, Chinese woman, describes the process:

> My parents were working. Then in the fifth grade, we moved, and . . . . my father got sick, mom had to go on welfare. Things started not working out for the family. My parents was fighting, my father used to give my mother lickings every time and put us down. They were strict. We pretty much rely on each other [the siblings].
>
> I never did get along with my dad. I don't know why. I've always tried, cleaning up, never had to be told what to do, I took care of my sisters and brothers. Cleaned the house, cook, did all kinds of house chores, but my father couldn't stand me . . . . I couldn't take it anymore, so I got about to the seventh grade, that's when I met my husband. I wanted to get married but I couldn't. So I got pregnant, my first daughter, about a year after that, I quit school already. I came home, I told my mom I wanted to get married. So she gave me consent. My father, never. So I forged his name . . . I was 15 years old. Stayed with my husband and never went back home. Only went back home once in awhile to give my mom money and see how she doing. [411]

Other women took a different path and escaped the violence by running away, living periodically with friends, relatives, or on the streets, and sometimes turning to prostitution for survival.

> Linda is 28 years old and of Hawaiian Caucasian ancestry. Her parents divorced after her birth, and she has never known her mother. She and her sister were raised principally by her grandmother. Her father raped her and her sister, in addition to constantly beating them. The sexual abuse started when she was nine and continued until she ran at 12 years of age by "hopping on a bus to Waikiki" and getting lost. She had been in and out of foster homes and on the streets, but this break was permanent. She hooked up with a girl in her 20s, "I watched her, she was a prostitute. I asked her how to do that cause she had a lot of money. She taught me the ropes and I went for it. I made my money and stayed away from home. I lived out of hotel rooms." [510]

The problems these women confronted, usually from an early age—poverty, gendered expectations and obligations, parental alcohol and illicit drug use, violence, living on the streets—underscore the complexities of Asian-Pacific American families, and raise questions about their initiation into drug use, especially ice.

Initiation into Drug Use

As Table 16–3 shows, the majority of women have used alcohol, tobacco, marijuana, cocaine, and crack.[4] Over one-half of them reported regular use of tobacco, alcohol and marijuana. Many of them report experimentation with psychedelics (46%) and speed pills (54%), but few used these substances regularly. Less than 30% of them have tried PCP, quaaludes, or tranquilizers, and even fewer women have used ecstasy, opiates, heroin, and inhalants.

According to their life histories, the most common pattern in their initiation started with alcohol, tobacco, marijuana, cocaine, and then went into ice. Initial use of crack varied, with some women moving back and forth from ice to crack depending on availability. Their peer groups from school and the neighborhood, and/or family members usually introduced them to alcohol, tobacco, and marijuana during their early teen years.[5] In some

TABLE 16–3   Lifetime Use of Alcohol and Drugs of Asian-Pacific American Women Ice Users (n = 37)

	Never		At Least Once		Over 100×		Over 1000×		Over 2000×	
	n	%	n	%	n	%	n	%	n	%
Alcohol	1	2.7	6	16.2	10	27.0	7	18.9	13	35.1
Cocaine	7	18.0	12	32.4	11	29.7	4	10.8	7	18.9
Crack	11	29.7	13	35.1	3	8.1	4	10.8	2	5.4
Heroin	33	89.2	3	8.1	1	2.7	0	0.0	0	0.0
Inhalants	32	86.5	3	8.1	2	5.4	0	0.0	0	0.0
Marijuana	0	0.0	5	13.5	12	32.4	4	10.8	16	43.2
MDMA	36	97.3	1	2.7	0	0.0	0	0.0	0	0.0
Opiates	36	97.3	1	2.7	0	0.0	0	0.0	0	0.0
PCP	29	78.4	7	18.9	1	2.7	0	0.0	0	0.0
Psychedelics	20	54.0	12	32.4	4	10.8	1	2.7	0	0.0
Quaaludes	30	81.1	5	13.5	2	5.4	0	0.0	0	0.0
Speed pills	17	45.9	13	35.1	7	18.9	0	0.0	0	0.0
Tobacco	2	5.4	0	0.0	3	8.1	3	8.1	29	78.4
Tranquilizers	27	72.9	6	16.2	3	8.1	0	0.0	1	2.7

cases, the family member was a parent, usually the father, or an uncle. Evie, a 27-year-old Chinese woman, remembers the setting when she began smoking marijuana:

> When I was 11. Yeah, my first hit. My first joint. He [father] rolled a joint. Back then, they used to have those little rolling machines and my dad would have ounces of weed in his freezer. So we'd sit there eating ice cream and rolling joints and making bags. Then the boys would come over, hang out. My dad was, he was hanging out, he was involved in underground entertainment so he knew all of the entertainers, all the promoters, artists, drug dealers, he always had hip parties. (401)

Women continue to use alcohol, tobacco, and marijuana with their peers and family members. Eventually they are introduced to cocaine, but by this point, the family member is usually a sibling, cousin, or other relative. As indicated earlier, many have tried to leave home for short- and long-term relief from the family chaos. One 32-year-old Hawaiian Chinese woman recalls her route into alcohol and illicit drugs, which paralleled the accounts described by other female respondents:

> Our next door neighbor was this mother who had seven kids. My two brothers were going with their two sisters. I was 13 at the time I started drinking . . . . Pakololo [marijuana] I don't remember . . . . My girlfriend asked me if I ever tried acid before. I said no. My sister was already taking it . . . .
>
> I was 16 when I graduated. That's because I graduated a year early. When I was 17, I moved with my uncle because he was running this condominiums so I was like a maid. I was making $7 an hour! My cousin was a mason there. He was like maintenance on the grounds. That's

when I first, I didn't know to, what to feel. We went into this place where my aunt and uncle would let us kick back in. He asked me if I wanted to try it [cocaine] . . . I had alot of friends that had coke or I'd be in the house and they'd be weighing their coke and I didn't want to do it . . . He gave me a line and told me to stick the straw in the nose and he showed me. He did one first and told me to just do that. I did it and we went back into my uncle's place . . . I panicked and said I'll never do this s___ again. And I didn't not until later. Later I was doing alot, lines, mega lines. [405]

As Table 16–4 indicates, the majority of women (62%) were first introduced to ice from 1988 to 1992. While nearly all of the Filipinas started during this period (82%), 45% of the Hawaiian women tried ice earlier, between 1984 and 1987. Given the broadening of their social networks from the use of other drugs, there were several sources by which women first encountered ice. Approximately 46% of the women first tried ice with a small group of their girlfriends. Another 16% were introduced to ice by a relative, typically a cousin or sister-in-law. The combination of curiosity, and camaraderie with and trust of a relative or their girlfriends were often the reason for trying ice.

TABLE 16–4   Characteristics of Ice Use Among Asian-Pacific American Women (n = 37)

	n	%
Year started using		
1983 or prior	3	8.1
1984–1987	11	29.7
1988–1992	23	62.2
Average grams used per month		
1.00 grams or less	6	16.2
1.01–3.0 grams	9	24.3
3.01–5.0 grams	11	29.7
5.01–7.0 grams	7	18.9
8.01 grams or more	6	16.2
Unknown	4	10.8
Number of days used in average month		
Median	15 days	
Longest episode of use without sleep		
1 to 2 days	6	16.2
3 to 4 days	10	27.0
5 to 6 days	6	16.2
7 days	7	18.9
8 or more	8	21.6
Obtain ice primarily by		
Bought to sell	5	14.5
Bought to use	12	32.4
Received free	17	45.9
Other	3	8.1

As other studies have shown, male dealers and partners are also a significant group in introducing women to various illicit drugs (Morningstar and Chitwood 1987; Anglin et al. 1987; File 1976). Several of the younger women indicated that male dealers mediated their first encounter with ice. Like this 23-year-old Hawaiian Cacausian woman states, our female respondents were well aware that dealers usually had other motives than just increased sales.

> My girlfriend was using and she introduced me to a man who introduced her to ice. My first experience with it was good. The guy was attracted to me and the more he gave me, the more he thought I'd be nice to him. We were at his house. The year was about 1987. [516]

Thirty-eight percent of the Asian-Pacific American women first tried ice with their partner or spouse, and the experience often was associated with enhancing sex.

> That was my 23rd birthday. I wanted to go out and drink and come home and make love. I didn't want to stay home. He went to the store, bought drinks, came home and we had some drinks before we went out to a show. I got drunk, I was so ripped . . . . We came home and he said, "Here's the pipe, just inhale!" I had five big hits . . . . I was wide-eyed and ready. We smoked some more . . . we watched t.v. and hung for a while. Then we f_____ for hours! [laughs] [446]

With continued use, however, our respondents' relationships to their partners, families, and friends begins to change.

Continuing Use and Family Ties

After the introduction to ice, most of the women began using regularly. Overall, the median number of grams used per month was 3.5. Filipinas tended to use slightly more ice than Hawaiian women, reporting a median of 4 grams per month. The median number days of using ice in an average month was 15.[6] Their longest period of use without sleeping was a median of 6 days. Filipinas reported a slightly longer binging episode compared to the other women, with a median of 6.9 days.

Women first rationalize their regular use of ice in very gendered ways (Joe 1995). The appetite suppressant quality of the drug allows them to keep thin, and in turn, provides them with self-confidence. Also, the long-lasting speedy energy associated with ice allows them to clean up after their children and partners, and to transcend and enjoy the mundane tasks of domestic chores.

There were a number of ways in which they would obtain their supply, and this would vary depending on their existing financial situation. While approximately one-third principally bought their supplies, 46% received it free by "hanging around the dealers" or by running an array of errands for their supplier who was sometimes a relative:

> I started buying from one of my cousins. I used to always burn myself cause i was trying to learn how the hell to do this thing without wasting 'em. My cousin used to see me do that so she taught me . . . . I caught on that night! That's when I really felt good! I was up all night long till the next day . . . . I stayed with her for three months. They were big time dealers. They was selling big quantities. I help her clean up the house, a big big house. My auntie's house because I would help her clean and cook, she always used to give me free stash . . . . Right now, the only one supply me is my husband [who does not use]. Then check in one hotel . . . [411]

TABLE 16–5   Ice Related Problems Among Asian-Pacific American Women
(n = 37)

	n	%
Psychological and physical problems		
Anxiety	20	54.1
Chest pains	17	45.9
Depression	26	70.3
Hallucinations	19	51.4
Memory loss	17	45.9
Panic attacks	11	30.6
Paranoia	19	51.4
Seizures	2	5.4
Violent acts	15	40.5
Weight loss	33	89.2
Problems in interaction with others		
Co-workers	8	21.6
Family	18	48.6
Friends	23	62.2
Spouse/partner	24	64.9
Other personal and social consequences		
Drop out of school	5	13.5
Lost job	4	10.8
Financial problems	23	62.2
Serious accident	2	5.4
Hospitalized for mental health problems	9	24.3

With prolonged use, however, they become increasingly isolated from others—their children, partners, friends, and families. When this occurs, ice becomes medicinal.

Their isolation, sometimes periodic, stems from several sources. First, they are growing increasingly irritable with long episodes of limited or no sleep and food. As Table 16–5 shows, over half of them have experienced anxiety, depression, hallucinations, and paranoia. Many respondents spoke of periods of paranoia. The paranoia usually involved their being watched and followed by the police and by other users wanting to steal their stash, and consequently, they tried to limit their interaction with others. Second, nearly all of them report weight loss (89%). Some have grown emaciated and exhibit facial sores from tweaking and dehydration.[7] As such, they try to limit contact with their family and friends, hoping that they will not see their deterioration. Third, if the partner is also using ice, they are both becoming more irritable as a result of lack of sleep and food, and money problems. The partner's irritability often is expressed through domestic violence (Joe 1995).

Although many of these women have become isolated and have a strained relationship with their family, because of the ohana family system and its traditions, they rely on various relatives—immediate family members as well as extended kin—to manage their everyday life. This includes financial support, temporary shelter for themselves, but especially the shelter and care of their own children. While this extended kinship system provides them with a stable resource, it has the paradoxical consequence of enabling their use, intensifying dependency and further aggravating family tensions.

> Stephanie is a 35 year old Hawaiian Irish woman. While growing up, she recalls that her parents, both alcoholics, began physically beating her at five years of age with "extension cord wires, water hoses, punches, everything." She ran away, and after high school, married and became pregnant. Her husband died shortly after the son's birth in a work-related accident. She has been homeless for seven years, and sometimes stays with friends. Periodically she visits her mother and son, but adds that her ice use has "interfered" with her relationship with her mother. Her mother has been caring for her son since she has "no place for me and my boy." She regularly gives half of her welfare monies to her mother for her son's food and clothing. [475]

Like other women in this study, Stephanie takes refuge in ice as she finds her options narrowing. As she states, "I can't get no help finding me and my boy a place. So because I'm homeless, that's why I do the drug, I get so depressed cause I don't have no roof over my head for me and my boy." Ironically, her family, which caused her to run away, is one of her few remaining resources.

CONCLUSION

This paper underscores the importance of using a qualitative approach to studying drug use among hidden populations like Asian-Pacific Americans. An ethnographic strategy is crucial to dispelling popular stereotypes of Asian-Pacific Americans' passivity and women's "submissiveness," and in laying the groundwork for theory building and program planning.

Unlike mental health studies on Asian-Pacific Americans, this analysis suggests that stress from the family is not restricted to cultural and generational conflict. Social problems like drug use among Asian-Pacific American women are quite complex. From their early childhood, these women lived in the midst of heated, sometimes violent, conflict, which was connected to economic marginality, parental problems with alcohol, and distinctive cultural norms of femininity. Neighborhood and school peers, and male relatives initially introduced them to alcohol and marijuana. Over time, their user networks widen and their introduction into cocaine and ice is through friends, extended kin (e.g., cousins), and partners. Despite the long standing tension in their family and their more recent isolation from others from using ice, the cultural traditions embedded in the extended kinship system allow many to "return home."

ACKNOWLEDGMENTS

The research for this paper was funded by National Institute on Drug Abuse Grant #RO1-DA06853: "Ice and Other Methamphetamine Use: An Exploratory Study," administered through the Institute for Scientific Analysis, San Francisco, and directed by Patricia Morgan, Ph.D., Jerome Beck, Ph.D., Douglas McDonnell, and the author. The opinions and conclusions are those of the author. The author also wishes to acknowledge the Center for Youth Research and the Social Science Research Institute at the University of Hawaii for their support.

NOTES

1. See *Making Waves* (Asian Women United of California 1989) for an excellent discussion of historical and contemporary stereotypes of Asian-Pacific American women.
2. The ethnic composition of our sample reflects our field workers' attempts to capture our targeted sampling strategy. Given the "hidden dimensions" of methamphetamine use and drug use, more generally among Asian-Pacific Americans, it is not clear whether this is a precise reflection of the ethnic breakdown of this population.
3. The Hawiian women tended to be slightly older with a median age of 28 years.
4. There were no statistically significant differences between the Asian-Pacific American ethnic groups on lifetime use. Consequently, the data are presented for the total group.
5. In Hawaii, social groups often include peers and relatives, particularly cousins.
6. There were no statistically significant differences between women of different Asian-Pacific American ethnicities in relation to number of days used.
7. The term, "tweaking," dates from the 1970s during the "speed era." As Froner (1989:63) notes, "tweaking is often characterized by obsessive, detailed work."

REFERENCES

AGAR, M. 1993. Ethnography: An aerial view. In *Proceedings* of the National Institute on Drug Abuse: Community Epidemiology Work Group, Vol. II, December, San Francisco.

ANGLIN, M., Y.I. HSER, and W.H. McGLOTHLIN 1987. Sex differences in addict careers. 2. Becoming addicted. *American Journal of Drug and Alcohol Abuse* 13:59–71.

AQUINO, B. 1994. Filipino women and political engagement. The Office for Women's Research, Working Paper Series. Vol. 2. Honolulu: University of Hawaii.

ASIAN WOMEN UNITED of CALIFORNIA 1989. *Making waves: An anthology of writings by and about Asian American women*. Boston: Beacon Press.

AUSTIN, G. M. PENDERGAST, and H. LEE 1989. Substance abuse among Asian American youth. *Prevention Research Update* No. 5. Winter. Portland, Ore.: Western Regional Center, Drug Free Schools and Communities.

BOURGOIS, P., and E. DUNLAP 1993. Exorcising sex for crack: An ethnographic perspective from Harlem. In *Crack as pimp: An ethnographic investigation of sex for crack exchanges,* ed. M. Ratner, 97–132. New York:Lexington Books.

CHEN, S. 1991. *Entry denied: Exclusion and the Chinese community in America 1882–1943.* Philadelphia:Temple University Press.

CHI, I., J. LUBBEN, and H. KITANO 1989. Differences in drinking behavior among three Asian American groups. *Journal of Studies on Alcohol* 50:15–23.

DENZIN, N., and Y. LINCOLN 1994. Introduction: Entering the field of qualitative research. In *Handbook of qualitative research,* ed. N. Denzin and Y. Lincoln, 1–17. Thousand Oaks, Calif.:Sage.

ETTORRE, E. 1992. *Women and substance use*. New Brunswick, N.J.:Rutgers University.

FILE, K. 1976. Sex roles and street roles. *International Journal of the Addictions* 11:263–268.

FRONER, G. 1989. Digging for diamonds: A lexicon of street slang for drugs and sex. San Francisco:ALL-TEC.

HANDY, E.S. CRAIGHILL, and M. KAWENA PUKUI 1972. *The Polynesian family system*. Rutland, Vt.:Charles Tuttle.

Honolulu Advertiser 1993. Asian-Pacific Americans. Focus, B4. May 9.

HUNT, G., K. JOE, and D. WALDORF 1995. Born to kill? Culture and ethnic identity among southeast Asian gang members. Paper presented at the annual meeting of the Pacific Sociological Association, San Francisco, Calif.

INCIARDI, J., D. LOCKWOOD, and A. POTTIEGER 1993. *Women and crack cocaine*. New York:MacMillan.

JOE, K. 1990. Final evaluation report on the Asian Youth Substance Abuse Project to the Office of Substance Abuse Prevention. Asian American Residential Services:San Francisco, Calif.

JOE, K. 1993. Getting into the gang: Methodological issues in studying ethnic gangs. In *Drug abuse among minority youth: Methodological issues and recent research advances,* eds. M. De La Rosa and J. Adrados. National Institute on Drug Abuse Research Monograph #130: 234–257. Rockville, Md.: NIDA.

JOE, K. 1995. Ice is strong enough for a man but made for a woman. *Crime, Law and Social Change* 22:269–289.

JOE, K., and M. CHESNEY LIND 1995. Just every mother's angel: An analysis of gender and ethnic variations in youth gang membership. *Gender and Society* 9:408–431.

JOHNSON, R., C. NAGOSHI, F. AHERN, J. WILSON, and S. YUEN 1987. Cultural factors as explanations for ethnic group differences in alcohol use in Hawaii. *Journal of Pyschoactive Drugs* 19:67–75.

KITANO, H., and I. CHI 1985. Asian Americans and alcohol: The Chinese, Japanese, Koreans and Filipinos in Los Angeles. In *Alcohol use among United States ethnic minorities,* ed. D. Spiegler et. al., 373–382. Rockville, Md.:National Institute on Alcohol Abuse and Alcoholism.

KITANO, H., and I. CHI 1986. Asian Americans and alcohol use: Exploring cultural differences in Los Angeles. *Alcohol, Health and Research World,* Winter:42–47.

KURAMOTO, F. 1994. Drug abuse prevention research concerns in Asian and Pacific Islander populations. In *Scientific methods for prevention intervention research,* ed. A. Cazares and L. Beatty, 249–271. Research Monograph 139. Rockville, Md.: United States Department of Health.

LOO, C. 1991. *Chinatown: Most time, hard time*. New York:Praeger.

MAHER, L., and R. CURTIS 1992. Women on the edge of crime: Crack cocaine and the changing contexts of street level sex work in New York City. *Crime, Law, and Social Change* 18:221–258.

MILLER, M. 1991. Trends and patterns of methamphetamine smoking in Hawaii. In *Methamphetamine abuse: Epidemiologic issues and implications,* eds. M. Miller and N. Kozel. National Institute on Drug Abuse Research Monograph 115:72–83. Rockville, Md.:United States Department of Health.

MILLER, M., and J. TOMAS 1989. Past and current methamphetamine epidemics. *Proceedings* from the Community Epidemiology Workgroup. December National Institute on Drug Abuse Monograph. Rockville, Md.: United States Department of Health.

MORGAN, P., D. MCDONNELL, J. BECK, K. JOE, and R. GUTIERREZ n.d. Uncharted communities: Preliminary findings from a study of methamphetamine users. In *Methamphetamines: An illicit drug with high abuse potential,* eds. B. Sowder and G. Beschner. Forthcoming.

MORNINGSTAR, P., and D. CHITWOOD 1987. How women and men get cocaine: Sex role stereotypes and acquisition patterns. *Journal of Psychoactive Drugs* 19:135–142.

NEWCOMB, M., E. MADDAHIAN, R. SKAGER, and P. BENTLER 1987. Substance abuse and psychosocial risk factors among teenagers: Associations with sex, age, ethnicity and type of school. *American Journal of Alcohol and Drug Abuse* 13:413–433.

Newsweek 1989. The fire of "Ice." 37:7–9, November 27.

NUNES, K., and S. WHITNEY 1994. The destruction of the Hawaiian male. *Honolulu Magazine* July: 58–61.

PUKUI, M. L., E.W. HAERTIG, and C. LEE 1972. *Nana I Ke Kumu*. Vol. 1. Honolulu, HI.:Hui Hanai.

ROSENBAUM, M. 1981 *Women on heroin*. New Brunswick, N.J.:Rutgers.

San Francisco Chronicle 1989. New drug "Ice" called worse peril than crack. August 31.

SANTE, L. 1991. *Low life*. New York:Vintage.

SKAGER, R., S. FRITH, and E. MADDAHIAN 1989. *Biennial survey of drug and alcohol use among California students in grades 7, 9, and 11*. Winter 1987–1988. Sacramento:Office of the Attorney General, Crime Prevention Center.

SUE, D. 1987. Use and abuse of alcohol by Asian Americans. *Journal of Psychoactive Drugs* 19:57–66.

SUE, S., N. ZANE, and J. ITO 1979. Alcohol drinking patterns among Asian and Caucasian Americans. *Journal of Cross Culture Psychology* 10:41–56.

TONG, B. 1994. *Unsubmissive women: Chinese prostitutes in 19th century San Francisco.* Norman, Okla.:University of Oklahoma Press.

TRIMBLE, J., A. PADILLA, and C. BELL 1987. *Drug abuse among ethnic minorities.* Rockville, Md.: National Institute on Drug Abuse.

WHITNEY, S. 1986. Getting sober local style: Strategies for alcoholism counseling in Hawaii. *Alcoholism Treatment Quarterly* 3:87–107.

ZANE, N., and T. SASAO 1992. Research on drug abuse among Asian-Pacific Americans. In *Ethnic and multicultural drug abuse: Perspectives on current research,* eds. J.E. Trimble, C.S. Bolek, and S.J. Niemcryk, 181–209. New York:Haworth.

ZANE, N. n.d. Research on drug abuse among Asian-Pacific Americans. *Drugs and Society.* Forthcoming.

17

Negative Experiences on Ecstasy

The Role of Drug, Set and Setting[*]

Karen McElrath

School of Sociology & Social Policy, Queen's University, Belfast, Northern Ireland

Kieran McEvoy

Institute of Criminology & Criminal Justice, School of Law, Belfast, Northern Ireland

The availability of the MDMA (methylenedioxy-methamphetamine, "Ecstasy") as a street drug is relatively recent, having gained in popularity in the 1980s and 1990s in the United States, Australia, various European countries and elsewhere. As use of the drug has increased in parallel with its public notoriety, a quite polarized debate has emerged with regards to the drugs' effects. Contemporary folklore and much of the sociological literature suggest that Ecstasy creates a general feeling of well-being and contentment among users and facilitates social interaction (Henderson 1997; Saunders 1995; Beck & Rosenbaum 1994). Sociological research into Ecstasy use suggests that, generally, users are far more likely to report positive rather than negative effects of the drug (Shewan, Dalgarno & Reith 2000; van de Wijngaart et al. 1999; Beck & Rosenbaum 1994; Solowij, Hall & Lee 1992). Users in this literature typically describe their experiences with the drug as "fun," "loving," and "insightful" (Beck & Rosenbaum 1994: 59).[1] Although the drug is related structurally to amphetamine and may produce mild hallucinations, these effects generally are not characterized by the disorientation or major visual or audio distortions typically associated with other hallucinogens (Beck 1990).

This article appeared in 2002 in volume 34(2) of the Journal of Psychoactive Drugs, published by Haight Asbury Publications, San Francisco, CA, and is reprinted with permission. All rights reserved.

*The full study from which these data are drawn was funded by the Northern Ireland Statistics and Research Agency. Points of view are those of the authors.

The medical literature on Ecstasy tends towards a rather different emphasis, stressing in particular the negative effects of the drug. For instance, medical research involving reports of heavy, recreational, or first-time Ecstasy users has focused upon negative psychiatric, cognitive, and physical effects, and death after ingestion (see for example, McElhatton et al. 1999; McCann et al. 1998; Ellis et al. 1996; O'Connor 1994; Maxwell, Polkey & Henry 1993; Williams, Meagher & Galligan 1993; McGuire & Fahy 1991; Brown & Osterloh 1987). However, longitudinal and experimental studies of humans are limited, and a heated debate continues with regards to the dangers of Ecstasy (see for example, Betts & Betts 1999; Cohen 1998; Saunders 1995).

The present research uses data from a qualitative study of Ecstasy users in Northern Ireland. Similar to research conducted elsewhere, the overall study from which the present data are drawn found that the majority of users tended to report positive experiences with the drug (McElrath & McEvoy 1999). Several users, however, reported at least one negative experience with Ecstasy, and these effects are the focus of the present study. In this study the concept of "negative experiences" was limited to those effects that occur shortly after consumption or during the Ecstasy episode. The authors recognize that some users experience difficulties (e.g., depression, irritability, exhaustion, problems with concentration) in the days that follow an Ecstasy episode, and these after-effects have been documented in the literature (McElrath & McEvoy 1999; Parrott & Lasky 1998; Curran & Travill 1997; Beck 1990). The after-effects, however, are not the focus of the present study. The physical sickness (i.e., vomiting) that can occur shortly after consuming the drug has also been excluded. Many users describe this sickness as tolerable (Shewan, Dalgarno & Reith 2000) or in other non-negative terms; the vomiting period generally is brief, and users report that initial vomiting leads quickly to the more pleasurable "coming up" stage (McElrath & McEvoy 1999). Severe physical reactions and symptoms (e.g., liver damage, seizures) also are excluded. For the most part, then, the negative experiences of Ecstasy use explored in the present study refer more generally to adverse psychological effects (e.g., paranoia, severe anxiety, panic attacks, confusion) that occur during use.

FACTORS RELATING TO NEGATIVE EXPERIENCES

The authors believe that a major limitation of much of the medical literature on Ecstasy use concerns its failure to acknowledge the potential importance of social setting and, equally important, what this context means to the individual user. For example, medical research into the effects of Ecstasy tends to link psychiatric and adverse psychological symptoms to the drug only, or to drug combinations. By way of a corrective, the specific focus of this article is to explore the nature and extent to which set and setting contribute to negative experiences while using Ecstasy. It also examines the possible contribution of other factors as they relate to negative experiences with Ecstasy. These factors include: (1) dosage and frequency of use, (2) polydrug use that occurs during Ecstasy consumption, (3) the brands or types of Ecstasy tablets consumed, and (4) individual disposition. Each of these factors is discussed below.

Set and Setting

Set refers to "the attitude of the person at the time of use" (Zinberg 1984: 5) and incorporates the user's "past experiences (including previous drug experiences), mood, motivations . . . and expectations of the subject" (Jansen 1997: 117). These factors are said to influence the drug experiences for the user.

Setting includes the physical environment and social setting in which Ecstasy is consumed (Jansen 1997; Zinberg 1984). For Ecstasy users who consume in club venues, the physical environment can include the nature of the music, the role of the DJ, as well as safety features such as the availability of water and room temperature. Setting also includes "the set of other people present" (Jansen 1997). For example, the negative mood or experiences of a friend might affect an individual's experiences with the drug.

Dosage and Frequency

Both dosage (i.e., number of tablets) and frequency of use (e.g., weekly) have been linked to negative Ecstasy experiences. For example, Measham, Aldridge and Parker (2001) found that higher dosages of Ecstasy were significantly correlated with mood swings and amnesia. Solowij, Hall and Lee (1992) compared less frequent users (i.e., persons who had used Ecstasy between one and three times over their lifetime) with "multiple time users." Differences in "negative mood" outcomes, and mental and physical side effects were not statistically significant between the two groups. However, actual frequency of use and dosage were both positively correlated with the severity of side effects. Other research has found that the number of lifetime Ecstasy episodes has been linked to a greater likelihood of psychopathological disorders among drug treatment patients (Schifano et al. 1998). In contrast, Measham, Aldridge and Parker (2001) found no significant relationship between the frequency of Ecstasy use and negative psychological effects.

Topp and colleagues (1999) conducted multivariate analyses and identified factors that contributed to adverse physical and psychological effects of Ecstasy. Of relevance for the present study, these authors found that the number of adverse *physical* effects was associated with being female, age (younger), recent bingeing on Ecstasy (defined as using the drug without sleep for 48 hours) and higher dosage. Females and persons who had recently binged on stimulants reported significantly more adverse *psychological* effects. The authors of this study also noted that the variance explained was lower for the psychological effects model. This finding suggests that factors relating to set and setting might have represented important variables that were omitted from the equation.

Polydrug Use

Regarding polydrug use, Ecstasy users have been widely found to consume other drugs or alcohol during the Ecstasy episode (Measham, Aldridge & Parker 2001; McElrath & McEvoy 1999; Hammersley et al. 1999; Topp et al. 1999; van de Wijngaart et al. 1999).[2] Polydrug use makes it difficult to disentangle the effects of Ecstasy from the effects of alcohol and other drugs consumed during the same episode. Forsyth (1995) observed: "Such drug interaction may wrongly be attributed by the user only to the Ecstasy tablet." Adverse psychological effects have been linked with recent and extensive polydrug use (Topp et al. 1999). The use of alcohol during Ecstasy consumption also appears to contribute to negative experiences. For example, a study of drug treatment patients found that persons who had consumed Ecstasy with alcohol were significantly more likely than alcohol abstainers to display psychopathological disturbances (Schifano et al. 1998).

Individual Disposition

Medical literature and case reports have identified Ecstasy users who have had a history of psychiatric morbidity prior to their consumption of the drug, or a family history of such problems (Spruit 1997; McCann, Slate & Ricaurte 1996; Williams, Meagher & Galligan 1993; McGuire & Fahy 1991; Schifano 1991). These findings suggest that some users may be predisposed to psychiatric problems prior to drug consumption, and this factor might contribute to negative drug experiences. However, scholars have noted the difficulty in disentangling the causal connection between mental health problems and negative drug experiences (Measham, Aldridge & Parker 2001).

Other authors have suggested the possibility that the positive effects of Ecstasy may be of shorter duration among those persons for whom the drug is metabolized quickly (Winstock & King 1996). Spruit (1997, 18) noted that "anomalous MDMA metabolism" is one factor that might contribute to adverse effects. That is, MDMA appears to accumulate in some users rather than metabolize, an effect that can pose risk to particular users (Dé La Torre et al. 2000).

"Brands" of Ecstasy

Ecstasy sold in several countries is marketed in tablet form whereby the visible properties (e.g., embossed symbols, color, size, and shape) distinguish one brand from another (Forsyth 1995). Brands are also distinguished by name or label and these labels can change quickly, even weekly in some cultures (Calafat et al. 1998). This marketing strategy might be traced historically to the labeling of bags of heroin in New York City. Several years ago, Goldstein and colleagues (1984) studied the bag labeling of street heroin in New York City. Their list included approximately 400 different labels for bags of illicit heroin. They noted that bag labeling is helpful to both the consumer and the dealer. For example, the heroin users *believed* that the labels were helpful in locating good quality heroin. Additionally, the labels helped the dealers attract new customers: "Marked bags identify who the dealer is. It gives people an idea of which is the 'best stuff' "(Goldstein et al. 1984: 559). However, "Getting beat on a heroin purchase (i.e., being sold 'dummy' bags) or buying inferior quality heroin is an omnipresent risk" (Goldstein et al. 1984). In fact, "Both the verbal reports of heroin users and actual laboratory analyses of heroin confirm that a given label may contain widely varying qualities of heroin and, in some cases, not contain a legally controlled substance at all" (Goldstein et al. 1984).

An "active" dose of MDMA is approximately 80 mg per tablet (Sherlock et al. 1999). Earlier reports from Britain suggested that purity ranged from 50% to 100% (O'Connor 1994) and that MDMA content ranged from 50 and 150 mg (O'Connor 1994; Henry 1992) with an average of 100 mg (Newcombe 1992). Wolff and colleagues (1995) conducted tests of tablets marketed in various regions of the United Kingdom and found that the MDMA content ranged from zero to 140 mg per tablet. More recent reports suggest that the MDMA content in the region has declined to approximately 30 mg per tablet (Bassline 1998: 20). Sherlock and colleagues (1999) reported that slightly less than half of the 25 "Ecstasy" tablets analyzed contained no MDMA at all. Similarly, a thorough system of tablet testing in the Netherlands has found that about *one-half* of the tablets marketed as Ecstasy contain no MDMA at all (Spruit 1997).

Other ingredients, such as MDMA's "chemical cousins," MDA and/or MDEA, have been found in tablets sold as Ecstasy (Sherlock et al. 1999; Forsyth 1995; Wolff et al. 1995).

Ketamine also has been found in tablets sold as Ecstasy (Wolff et al. 1995). Shewan, Dalgarno and King (1996) reported that police seizures of ketamine-laced Ecstasy had increased in Britain since 1993. In the south of England, tablets sold as Ecstasy were in fact compressed magic mushrooms (Ashton 1992). Tablet testing in the United States has found that Ecstasy tablets have contained ephedrine, PCP, amphetamine, methamphetamine and a host of other ingredients (DanceSafe 2000). In their analysis of 107 Ecstasy tablets from various regions within the United States, Baggott and colleagues (2000) observed that 21% of the tablets contained dextromethorphan, a substance that has been linked to drug-induced psychosis.

Other reports have suggested that ingredients of Ecstasy tablets can vary, even for those tablets that are labeled with the same identifier or name (DanceSafe 2000; Sherlock et al. 1999). However, research that examines the ingredients of various brands of Ecstasy is less able to link the brand with a specific source. A brand that is produced from the same batch may indeed contain the same ingredients. Moreover, a symbol or name of a reputable brand of Ecstasy can be "borrowed" from other manufacturers but without providing the same ingredients. For example, the brand Mitsubishi held a "good reputation" in some regions of the United Kingdom, but subsequent batches of the brand were found to be 100% sucrose (http://www.ecstasy.org/testing/mitslabtest.html). Interestingly, this strategy also was observed by Goldstein and colleagues (1984) in their study of heroin markets in New York City two decades ago. That is, some heroin dealers reportedly used another's label when that label's reputation was good.

METHODOLOGY

The primary data for this study were collected through face-to-face, in-depth interviews with current and former Ecstasy users in Northern Ireland. The criterion used for interview eligibility was any use of Ecstasy. The authors used this very general criterion and monitored the sample closely throughout the study, knowing that the study criteria could be narrowed at a later date.[3] A total of 106 respondents were interviewed; however, eight interviews were discarded because of recording or transcribing problems, leaving a sample size of 98 respondents.

Several methods were used to recruit respondents for interviews. First, announcements of the study were placed in cities, towns and villages throughout Northern Ireland. Venues were chosen which might be described as nonthreatening and which were considered likely to be frequented by the target population, e.g., record or music shops and health centers. Second, advertisements were placed in a Northern Ireland club/music magazine. The ad was published in three monthly issues during the study period. Third, several local organizations were contacted and notified of the study. These agencies were diverse and included youth programs, universities and student unions, sexually transmitted disease clinics, gay men and women outreach programs, young offender programs, and drug counseling or treatment centers. On several occasions, study announcements were sent to agencies by mail, and then followed up with phone calls or visits by the researchers in order to discuss the study in greater detail. Fourth, the interviewers recruited some respondents through their own contacts and street sources. Fifth, the researchers relied upon snowball sampling or "chain referral" techniques (Biernacki & Waldorf 1981) whereby respondents were asked to refer friends and acquaintances. Sixth, in some instances, "recruiters" or "gatekeepers" were used and paid £10 (US $16) in cash for each subsequent referral and completed interview. This method, however, was monitored closely and an upper limit of referrals (usually six) from each recruiter was established. This strategy was particularly helpful in those outlying areas where the researchers had few contacts. Clubs were not used as recruitment venues.[4]

Interviews were conducted between October 1997 and November 1998. Four persons, two females and two males, served as interviewers (two of whom were the Project Directors).[5] A research instrument was developed, piloted on the first 12 respondents and minor revisions were made (these 12 respondents were included in the final sample).

Interviews in Belfast, the largest city in Northern Ireland, generally were conducted in university offices that offered a great deal of privacy, or in other venues convenient to the respondent (e.g., private homes). Interviews with respondents who lived outside of Belfast were conducted in private areas located within community agency sites or in private homes.

Respondents were assured of confidentiality and anonymity, and identified by number only. Study participants were provided with a £15 (US $24) music or book gift certificate for a completed interview. Interviews were conducted within a one- to two-hour time period and focused on issues related to first, last and usual use of Ecstasy, positive and negative drug experiences, drug use rituals and norms, health issues, and other items. Respondents were encouraged to go beyond the subject area of the research instrument when appropriate. Interviews were taped and subsequently transcribed. Demographic and drug use history data were collected at the conclusion of the in-depth interview.

RESULTS

Description of Respondents

Eighteen percent of the respondents were recruited through snowball sampling, 26% were recruited by one of nine gatekeepers, 29% learned about the research through one of the study's employees, and 27% read an ad that contained information about the study. Characteristics of the sample are reported for descriptive purposes only. One-half of the respondents resided in Belfast at the time of the interview, 46% lived elsewhere in Northern Ireland and 4% resided outside Northern Ireland. Males accounted for approximately two-thirds (69%) of the sample and respondents ages ranged from 17 to 45 years (mean = 25; median = 24; mode = 23). Social class was self-identified; 49% of respondents described themselves as working class, 46% were middle class and 5% of respondents reported being "between" working and middle class. Just over half of the sample (57%) were employed (either part- or full-time).

These sample characteristics are similar to studies conducted elsewhere. For example, in an Australian study of Ecstasy users males comprised 61% of the sample, the mean age was 27 years, and respondents' ages ranged from 16 to 48 years (Solowij, Hall & Lee 1992). In a study of participants in the Glasgow "dance drug scene" (Forsyth 1996:512), males comprised 62% of the sample, the mean age was 24 (range = 14 to 44 years), and 40% of respondents were unemployed.

Findings

Similar to research conducted elsewhere (van de Wijngaart et al. 1999), previously reported findings from these data suggested that positive feelings relating to mood, psychological and emotional well-being were by far the most common descriptions reported by respondents in the overall study (McElrath & McEvoy 1999). However, several users reported at least one negative experience with Ecstasy; yet in most instances, these negative effects did not deter people from consuming the drug again. Indeed, some respondents consumed additional Ecstasy tablets in the same evening and shortly after the negative effects surfaced, in hopes that those effects would subside.[6] The relationship between these negative experiences and a range of factors is discussed below.

Set and Setting

One objective of the present research was to identify the social setting, conditions and other factors that were present just prior to the consumption of Ecstasy and during the episode itself. In this regard, the following factors were explored: (1) set and setting, (2) the brands or types of Ecstasy tablets that were consumed, (3) polydrug use that occurred during the Ecstasy episode, (4) dosage, and (5) in some cases, individual disposition of the user. The overall results suggest that in a few instances, one factor (e.g., setting) appeared to contribute to negative experiences with Ecstasy, e.g., a forced overnight stay in an unfamiliar house, a club setting without water or a chill-out areas. A few respondents reported that negative feelings subsided after they had left an uncomfortable setting. For some respondents, *set* might have exacerbated the negative experiences, e.g., the realization that "I had taken something really bad." However, the more general pattern observed from these data was that negative experiences occurred most often from the interaction of *two or more* of these factors. These findings are described below.

Set and setting emerged as primary influences for negative experiences. In this sense, however, setting referred more generally to friends' or acquaintances' set, as opposed to the physical environment (e.g., being surrounded by strangers, room temperature). For example, respondents perceived that their interaction with others could contribute to negative experiences with Ecstasy: "I was just sitting quiet, and [my friends] said, 'You never [are] like this. Will you talk?' [And then] I was getting paranoid thinking there's something wrong with me" (female, age 18).

Similarly, when respondents observed friends experiencing negative effects of Ecstasy, they too began to feel uneasy. A male respondent initiated Ecstasy use with friends in a parked car: "my friend . . . he started to feel he was very closed in and started panicking. He had to get out of the car and go for a dander [walk] like and I sort of had a reaction to that because I didn't know what was going on . . . I wasn't used to it but he sort of came round afterwards and he was all right so I was sort of getting on [feeling better]" (male, age 17).

A male respondent described his reaction to a friend's experiences in a club. The friend had stated to the respondent, "I think these are bad Es cause I'm after being sick three times in the toilet". The respondent recalled that the friend's response had the potential for influencing his own experiences: "I don't want to hear it. That freaks you out, when you hear these are bad Es." (male, age 18).

Interactions with "knowledgeable" users who "define" the effects of the drug can contribute greatly to positive drug experiences for others (Becker 1967: 165), particularly among novice users. A female (age 25) recalled the second time that she had used Ecstasy and described that experience as being very positive: "It was apparently a really good E . . . the fellas we were with were saying that it was class [very good] and they'd been doing it for years."

Even during initiation into Ecstasy use, when some persons feel quite nervous about taking the drug, the presence of friends who had used the drug previously can reduce apprehensions about taking Ecstasy. A male respondent recalled that he was very anxious about using Ecstasy after hearing that a young woman in England had died after taking the drug. Despite his anxiety, he consumed the drug for the first time while in the company of friends who had taken the drug before. Those friends had discussed with him what to expect from Ecstasy, and although the effects of the drug for him were minimal, he described the experience as very positive. A 29-year-old male recalled that he had been quite "antidrug" prior to initiating Ecstasy use. He had experimented with other substances, e.g., LSD, but the effects of these other drugs were largely negative for him. At initiation, friends had told him that Ecstasy was not like hallucinogenic drugs. The respondent described his first use of Ecstasy as being very positive.

Some respondents reported that nearly all of their experiences with Ecstasy were negative. These outcomes could be attributed to the interaction between individual disposition and set. That is, some persons might be prone to negative drug experiences for biochemical reasons or may be predisposed to psychological problems that might surface with the consumption of certain drugs. A respondent's *set* then is influenced by these past negative experiences which, in turn, can influence respondents subsequent experiences with Ecstasy. In a sense, then, the past negative experiences "guide the trip." Further, Weil (1972, 52) suggested that "panic reactions, once they get going, are self-perpetuating." A 21-year old male in the present study had used Ecstasy on approximately 250 different occasions. He reported experiencing hallucinations both during and after several Ecstasy episodes (i.e., flashbacks). These hallucinations lasted approximately 10 to 15 seconds: "Usually . . . I'd be sweating, my heart would be thumping, I'd actually think, 'I'm going to have a heart attack or something here.' It was terrifying. I couldn't even explain what it was like to people. I told a couple of my friends, but it never happened to them. I was wondering why [my friends had not experienced hallucinations] and then I started getting paranoid thinking [that] there's something wrong with me. And then that's when the paranoia comes in."

Negative experiences at initiation do not necessarily deter people from using Ecstasy again. A female respondent reported experiencing acute paranoia during her first use of Ecstasy. She was depressed just prior to using Ecstasy, and had consumed a considerable quantity of alcohol during the episode. These other factors make it difficult to distinguish the role of individual disposition. Since initiation into Ecstasy use, she has periodically experienced negative effects involving paranoia, whereas consuming-friends in her company have had more positive experiences with Ecstasy. Individual disposition in the form of depression might be one factor that contributes to negative drug experiences; however, another possible explanation is that the initial and subsequent negative experiences are firmly "embedded" in her set.

Brands of Ecstasy

Although the present study did not include biochemical assays or tablet testing,[7] respondents were asked their views about the different brands of Ecstasy. Other research has shown that most Ecstasy users consume the drug without concern for its contents (Calafat et al. 1998). In the present study, several respondents believed that the potential effects of

Ecstasy could be determined by the brand or label, failing to recognize that differences could occur both within and across batches of the same label. "Say, your "Superdoves" are your best then your "Einsteins" then your "Playboys" or whatever. There's like a priority. There's a list of what are the best, what are the worst and what are the ones which are pretty good . . . you do hear about the kinds of pills to avoid" (male, age 26).

A male respondent reported that his favorite E was a "Double Amsterdam" but noted: "I haven't had a 'Double Amsterdam' in two years because they're impossible to get, because that's a pure one. [It's] equivalent to about 10 [other] Es."

Despite limited use of Ecstasy (i.e., five times over the lifetime), a male respondent (age 18) preferred "Doves" because he knew "exactly what's going to happen":

> *Interviewer:* Why are ["Doves"] better? What's in them?
>
> *Respondent:* To be honest I couldn't tell you, I've no idea what they cut them with, Jesus, they could cut them with talcum powder for all I know. But all I know is that I think there's more Ecstasy in the "Doves" than in the other ones because I would be as completely blocked [i.e., "wasted"] on half a "Dove" as I would be on a full "Loony Tune."

These reports suggest that respondents might choose a particular brand of Ecstasy because prior experiences with that brand were positive. Such a decision, however, fails to consider that tablet ingredients may differ both *within* and *across* batches of Ecstasy, despite the same label being used. If the effects of a brand of Ecstasy are always the same for a user, such an outcome might result from sheer luck. Alternatively, the *set* of the user with regards to the expectations of the label's effects might contribute to consistent outcomes for a particular brand of Ecstasy.

The perceived type of Ecstasy can interact with setting (i.e., other people's set) and shape the experience for the user: "I've done an E at a club and I talked to someone and I've got a negative response that's brought me way down. But usually that's been the case when the E wasn't particularly good . . . the better the E, the more able you are to dismiss other people's negative response" (male, age 34).

In some instances, however, it appears that the brand itself, or at least the contents of the particular batch, contributes to negative effects, irrespective of set and setting. For example, "Crowns" were widely available in the north of Ireland during January and February of 1998. Although it is not known whether these Crowns surfaced from the same batch (i.e., were made from the same ingredients by one manufacturer),[8] the vast majority of reports suggested that the Crowns available in the region during this period produced very positive effects. Persons who had used Ecstasy "hundreds" of times described Crowns as "the real McCoy" and the "best E that's been around." The reported dosage varied between one-half and two tablets, and most persons who had reported consuming Crowns during this time period had consumed some alcohol during the Ecstasy episode. One male noted that despite hearing positive reports about Crowns, "they never work for me." For him, Crowns did not produce negative effects; rather, they produced little effect at all. However, he consumed alcohol before and during the Ecstasy episode and had used Ecstasy nearly every weekend for approximately two years. The respondent's dosage rarely exceeded one-half tablet. These other factors (e.g., alcohol consumption, frequency of use, low dosage over time) might have contributed to the minimal effects.

A second brand, "Loony Tunes" also were widely available in the region during the same time period. In contrast to Crowns, several respondents who consumed Loony Tunes described the effects as being very negative. Many respondents reported physical illness after consuming these tablets, and friends who consumed the brand in the same setting also were ill. Zombie-like effects were reported by a few respondents. These findings held for respondents who did not consume any other drug or alcohol. One respondent who was *not* ill claimed that negative effects were related to dosage: "whenever we got those "Loony Tunes," anybody who took two or more was violently sick. There was me and a couple of other of my friends, we only took one and a half and we were all right . . . but anybody who took more than two was sick at the time and felt sick for the next couple of days. I'm not going to go back on those Loony Tunes. Yes, I'll avoid those like the plague."

Two persons reported no negative effects after consuming Loony Tunes. One drank heavily and the other consumed amphetamine, cannabis and some alcohol during the Ecstasy episode. Although the authors are uncertain as to the source of the batch, one respondent claimed that there were two distinct batches of Loony Tunes: ". . . the ones in [Town A] were supposed to be good, but [Town B—about 20 miles from Town A] got the bad batch. A lot of boys [were] sick on them and what not." Other brands also appeared to produce the same adverse physical or psychological effects for all or most of the users within a particular friendship or drug user network in the same setting.

These results suggest that most respondents perceive labels or brands as symbols that distinguish between "good" and "bad" tablets and help the user to identify the specific types of effects (e.g., "speedy") that one should expect from a particular brand. Only a few respondents believed otherwise: ". . . it doesn't matter what the stamp is at the end of the day. You can't really judge quality control [by the stamp/label]."

Polydrug Use

In some instances, respondents believed that combining Ecstasy with other drugs produced negative outcomes. For example, a 38-year old male avoided taking magic mushrooms with Ecstasy because that combination produced panic attacks for him. Two other males experienced paranoia or delusions when consuming Ecstasy with LSD but not when consuming LSD only. The former, however, had purchased drugs from a stranger, and that source might have affected his set. Several other respondents combined Ecstasy with one or more drugs during the same episode (as opposed to using other drugs to help with the come-down phase). However, it did not appear that drug combinations were more or less likely to produce negative experiences compared with using Ecstasy only.

During the initiation into and early stages of Ecstasy use, several respondents in the present study were cautious about consuming alcohol while using Ecstasy. However, alcohol consumption tended to increase considerably when people began to use Ecstasy more regularly, a finding that has been documented elsewhere (e.g., Hansen, Maycock & Lower 2001). The effects of combining Ecstasy and alcohol during the same episode were mixed. A respondent who was nearly always sick after consuming Ecstasy tended to ingest large amounts of alcohol, and during one negative experience, he reported to have consumed 25 pints of beer. However, during the interview he failed to make any mention at all of the possibility that alcohol might have contributed to his negative experiences. In contrast, several other respondents also had consumed large amounts of alcohol with Ecstasy, and described the effects as being quite positive.

Dosage

Several respondents limited their intake to 1/2 dosage at initiation, and a number of people recalled the first time they had consumed a whole tablet. During their most recent use of Ecstasy, most of the "experienced" users limited their dosage to two or fewer tablets (sometimes taking half dosages throughout the evening).

Higher dosages at initiation led to negative effects for some users, however, the authors' general observation was that other factors were present which might also have contributed to the negative outcome. For instance, a 23-year old female consumed two Ecstasy tablets at initiation and experienced hallucinations that she described as negative. She was "antidrug" prior to initiation and reported that a dealer had talked her into taking the drug: "I was actually lying on the bed and I didn't know where I was. I was completely and utterly gone . . . the things that I was seeing . . . like fur and all . . . like cotton wool on people's eyes and people's hands . . . just hanging on the ceiling . . . I didn't know what I was doing. I couldn't talk . . . . I was like stuttering and I couldn't [make] sense of anything."

In this instance, the high dosage at initiation might have produced the effects. However, the influence of set might also be important. She was resistant until a stranger (the dealer) had given her the tablets. Moreover, she reported that friends who had consumed the drug were *not* present during her initiation, thus the influence of setting and set were possible contributors to the outcome.

DISCUSSION

Similar to findings from other studies, most of the current and former Ecstasy users in the present study reported that the effects of the drug were largely positive. However, the majority had encountered at least one negative experience while using Ecstasy. Negative effects, however, usually did not deter people from using the drug again.

Set and setting emerged as important factors in producing negative effects of Ecstasy. The effect of setting, however, was largely due to friends or acquaintances *set,* rather than to the physical environment. Perhaps key to understanding the impact of set and setting with regard to Ecstasy use is the "communal" nature of its consumption. For the vast majority of Ecstasy users in the present study, consumption of the drug was associated with partying with friends, and part of a broader series of social and leisure rituals that included clubbing and attending after-hours parties. These behaviors are associated with achieving a *collective* good time. A sense that another user, particularly a friend or acquaintance who is part of the collective, is not having a pleasant experience may have a deleterious effect on the group as a whole.

Some evidence suggests that the drug itself might have contributed to negative experiences. For example, the majority of respondents perceived that different labels or brands of Ecstasy produce different effects. The findings suggest that this belief may be accurate in that several users who consumed a particular label within approximately the same period of time (e.g., within a period of two or three months) appeared to have experienced the same effects. Users within the same social network or wider drug culture will of course share information about various drugs, including the effects of drugs (Becker 1967). Moreover, the suggestive power of reports of drug effects has been documented in the literature (Lyerly et al. 1964). Although the extent to which this knowledge (e.g., a superior brand) might have affected users *sets* is not known, it is possible that *collective set* had more to do with user reactions than did the drug or label itself. It is difficult to determine, however, whether these effects were due to the contents of a particular brand or due to shared expectations about the effects of a particular brand.

Clearly, the data suggest that set and setting appeared to contribute to users' experiences in other ways. Overall the findings tend to support Becker's (1963, 56) earlier premise: "Enjoyment [of the drug experience] is introduced by the favorable definition of the experience that one acquires from others." One important factor in understanding the perceived effects of the drug, rests with the notion of *expectation*. As with users of alcohol (e.g., Leigh 1999), Ecstasy users have a range of pharmacological and social expectations about the effects of the drug. They expect to feel "loved up," "sociable," and "confident," and the way in which those feelings are best manifested is with users' interactions with others. The drug's capacity to deliver is realized through set and setting.

The present study found little evidence that factors such as dosage, alcohol consumption, or individual disposition, contributed consistently to negative drug experiences. That is, these factors appeared to vary considerably during users negative experiences with Ecstasy. However, it is difficult to distinguish the effects of these factors from aspects of set and setting. For example, slightly higher than usual doses of Ecstasy might produce negative outcomes for the user largely because the individual is fully aware of the unusual consumption pattern and expectations are not known.

Studies that examine the effects of Ecstasy are limited in that the actual content of tablets is often unknown. The present study is by no means an exception, as biochemical assays and tablet testing were not utilized. It is our view, however, that the process of labeling Ecstasy tablets serves at least three purposes. First, labels can be used as marketing devices by dealers. Second, labels serve as a guide to users who perceive that brand names can indicate a range of pharmacological effects. Third, for many of the users in this sample, knowledge of the range of brands, the perceived ability to distinguish between brands and to link nomenclature to differing effects, to have "favorites," were all part of a broader process of demonstrating maturity and familiarity with "the scene." Even among some of the younger users in the sample, nostalgic recollection of better quality Ecstasy tablets (which may or may not have been linked to varying quality of Ecstasy coming into the jurisdiction) and associated "partying" were important factors that signified that they were established participants on "the scene."

NOTES

1. This genre of literature usually acknowledges that while Ecstasy may engender feelings of empathy among users towards both acquaintances and strangers, such feelings for the most part are short-lived, and disappear by or during the comedown stage (see for example, McElrath & McEvoy 2001).

2. Ecstasy tablets can contain various licit and illicit substances so that there is a risk of polydrug use even without intention.

3. The vast majority of respondents who were interviewed during the first four months of the study resided in Belfast, the largest city in Northern Ireland. After this time, the authors narrowed the criteria for participation in the study in an attempt to interview respondents (1) from outside Belfast or (2) former users. Current users from Belfast continued to contact us but for the most part we stopped interviewing Belfast residents for a period of approximately two months. At other times, we modified the study criteria so as to avoid over representation of certain categories, e.g., middle class students.

4. The project directors chose deliberately to *not* use clubs as recruitment sources. Local folklore suggests that some paramilitary groups are closely tied to the ownership, operation or management of various clubs. Anecdotal evidence suggests that while some paramilitary groups have been linked to drug trafficking, other paramilitary groups remain opposed to both trafficking and personal use. We believed that recruitment from clubs might have generated suspicion and may have placed potential respondents and the researchers at risk.

5. All interviewers were trained during a two-week period before the study commenced. Training topics included the nature and importance of confidentiality (all staff members signed a "statement of confidentiality" and this document was framed and displayed in the main interview room), effective interviewing techniques, role playing, drug categories and effects, the local club scene (sites, locations, clientele, entrance fees, availability of alcohol, music), Ecstasy and the gay population, recruitment and sampling issues. Additional training occurred throughout the study period during discussions in staff meetings.

6. One respondent reported having great difficulties coping with the Ecstasy and despite having taken "the scariest pill" ever, he took the same brand of Ecstasy the very next night (the effects again were unpleasant but not to the degree as the previous episode).

7. Tablet testing would not necessarily resolve the issue for the user regarding the contents of tablets. In those countries where agencies are permitted to conduct tablet testing, generally the tablet is not returned to the consumer. In some instances, users might assume that a tablet with the same label as the tested tablet and from the same batch has the same type and proportion of contents. This assumption, however, has to our knowledge not been examined closely.

8. Similar to other brands, visible differences in appearance have been observed with Crowns. Specifically, the crown symbol has been described as both three- and four-pointed; speckled and not speckled. A four-pointed crown was said to contain 15 mg of amphetamine and also caffeine. A three-pointed crown examined approximately one year later contained approximately 30 mg of MDMA (Bassline 1998).

REFERENCES

Ashton, M. 1992. The emerging ecstasy problem. In: M. Ashton (Ed.) *The Ecstasy Papers: A Collection of ISDD's Publications on the Dance Drugs Phenomenon*. London: Institute for the Study of Drug Dependence.

Baggott, M.; Heifets, B.; Jones, R.T.; Mendelson, J.; Sferios, E. & Zehnder, J. 2000. Chemical analysis of Ecstasy pills. Research letter. *Journal of the American Medical Association* 284: 2190.

Bassline. 1998. Do you know what you're popping? *Bassline* July 20.

Beck J. 1990. The public health implications of MDMA use. In: S.J. Peroutka (Ed.) *Ecstasy: The Clinical, Pharmacological and Neurotoxicological Effects of the Drug MDMA*. Boston, Massachusetts: Kluwer.

Beck, J. & Rosenbaum, M. 1994. *Pursuit of Ecstasy: The MDMA Experience*. Albany: State University of New York.

Becker, H.S. 1967. History, culture and subjective experiences: An exploration of the social bases of drug-induced experiences. *Journal of Health and Social Behavior* 8: 163–76.

Becker, H.S. 1963. *Outsiders: Studies in the Sociology of Deviance*. New York: Free Press.

Betts, J. & Betts, P. 1999. *Leah Betts: The Legacy of Ecstasy*. London: Robson.

Biernacki, P. & Waldorf, D. 1981. Snowball sampling: Problems and techniques of chain referral sampling. *Sociological Methods and Research* 10: 141–63.

Brown, C. & Osterloh, J. 1987. Multiple severe complications from recreational ingestion of MDMA (Ecstasy). *Journal of the American Medical Association* 258: 780–81.

CALAFAT, A.; STOCCO, P.; MENDES, F.; SIMON, J.; VAN DE WIJNGAART, G.; SUREDA, MA P.; PALMER, A.; MAALSTÉ, N. & SAVATTI, P. 1998. *Characteristics and Social Representation of Ecstasy in Europe.* Palma de Mallorca, Spain: IREFREA.

COHEN, R.S. 1998. *The Love Drug: Marching to the Beat of Ecstasy.* Binghamton, New York: Haworth.

CURRAN, H.V. & TRAVILL, R.A. 1997. Mood and cognitive effects of + 3, 4-methylenedioxymethamphetamine (MDMA, ecstasy): Week-end high followed by mid-week low. *Addiction* 92: 821–31.

DANCESAFE. 2000. May–July 2000 results. Available online at www.dancesafe.org/past_lab_results/results_may-july_2000.htm

DE LA TORRE, R.; FARRE, M.; ORTUNO, J.; MAS, M.; BRENNEISEN, R.; ROSET, P.N.; SEGURA, J. & CAMI, J. 2000. Non-linear pharmacokinetics of MDMA (Ecstasy) in humans. *British Journal of Clinical Pharmacology* 49: 104–09.

ELLIS, A.J.; WENDON, J.A.; PORTMANN, B. & WILLIAMS, R. 1996. Acute liver damage and ecstasy ingestion. *Gut* 38: 454–58.

FORSYTH, A.J.M. 1996. Places and patterns of drug use in the Scottish dance scene. *Addiction* 91: 511–21.

FORSYTH, A.J.M. 1995. Ecstasy and illegal drug design: A new concept in drug use. *International Journal of Drug Policy* 6: 193–209.

GOLDSTEIN, P.J.; LIPTON, D.S.; PREBLE, E.; SOBEL, I.; MILLER, T.; ABBOTT, W.; PAIGE, W. & FRANKLIN, S. 1984. The marketing of street heroin in New York City. *Journal of Drug Issues* Summer: 553–66.

HAMMERSLEY, R.; DITTON, J.; SMITH, I. & SHORT, E. 1999. Patterns of Ecstasy use by drug users. *British Journal of Criminology* 39: 625–47.

HANSEN, D.; MAYCOCK, B. & LOWER, T. 2001. Weddings, parties, anything . . . , a qualitative analysis of ecstasy use in Perth, Western Australia. *International Journal of Drug Policy* 12: 181–99.

HENDERSON, S. 1997. *Ecstasy: Case Unsolved.* London: Pandora.

HENRY, J.A. 1992. Ecstasy and the dance of death. *British Medical Journal* 305: 5–6.

JANSEN, K.L.R. 1997. Adverse psychological effects associated with the use of Ecstasy (MDMA) and their treatment. In: N. Saunders (Ed.) *Ecstasy Reconsidered.* London: Neal's Yard.

LEIGH, B. 1999. Thinking, feeling and drinking: Alcohol expectancies and alcohol use. In: S. Peele & M. Grant (Eds.) *Alcohol and Pleasure: A Health Perspective.* Philadelphia, Pennsylvania: Bruner/Mazel.

LYERLY, S.; ROSS, S.; KRUGMAN, A. & CLYDE, D. 1964. Drugs and placebos: The effects of instructions upon performance and mood under amphetamine sulfate and chloral hydrate. *Journal of Abnormal and Social Psychology* 68: 321–27.

MAXWELL, D.L.; POLKEY, M.I. & HENRY, J.A. 1993. Hyponatraemia and catatonic stupor after taking "ecstasy." *British Medical Journal* 307: 1399.

McCANN, U.D.; SLATE, S.O. & RICAURTE, G.A. 1996. Adverse reactions with 3, 4-Methylenedioxymethamphetamine (MDMA; Ecstasy). *Drug Safety* 15: 107–15.

McCANN, U.D.; SZABO, Z.; SCHEFFEL, U.; DANNALS, R.F. & RICAURTE, G.A. 1998. Positron emission tomographic evidence of toxic effect of MDMA ("Ecstasy") on brain serotonin neurons in human beings. *Lancet* 352: 1433–37.

McELHATTON, P.R.; BATEMAN, D.N.; EVANS, C.; PUG, K.R. & THOMAS, S.H.L. 1999. Congenital anomalies after prenatal ecstasy exposure. *Lancet* 354: 1441–442.

McELRATH, K. & McEVOY, K. 2001. Fact, fiction and function: Mythmaking and the social construction of Ecstasy use. *Substance Use and Misuse* 36: 1–22.

McELRATH, K. & McEVOY, K. 1999. *Ecstasy Use in Northern Ireland.* Belfast: Northern Ireland Statistics and Research Agency.

McGUIRE, P. & FAHY, T. 1991. Chronic paranoid psychosis after misuse of MDMA ("ecstasy"). *British Medical Journal* 302: 697.

MEASHAM, F., ALDRIDGE, J. & PARKER, H. 2001. *Dancing on Drugs: Risk, Health and Hedonism in the British Club Scene.* London: Free Association.

NEWCOMBE, R. 1992. A researcher reports from the rave. In: M. Ashton (Ed.) *The Ecstasy Papers: A Collection of ISDD's Publications on the Dance Drugs Phenomenon.* London: Institute for the Study of Drug Dependence.

O'CONNOR, B. 1994. Hazards associated with the recreational drug Ecstasy. *British Journal of Hospital Medicine* 52: 507–14.

PARROTT, A.C. & LASKY, J. 1998. Ecstasy (MDMA) effects upon mood and cognition: Before, during and after a Saturday night dance. *Psychopharmacology* 139: 261–68.

SAUNDERS, N. 1995. *Ecstasy and the Dance Culture.* Exeter, U.K.: Wheatons.

SCHIFANO, F. 1991. Chronic atypical psychosis associated with MDMA ("ecstasy") abuse [letter]. *Lancet* 338: 1335.

SCHIFANO, F.; DI FURIA, L.; FORZA, G.; MINICUCI, N. & BRICOLO, R. 1998. MDMA (ecstasy) consumption in the context of polydrug abuse: A report on 150 patients. *Drug and Alcohol Dependence* 52: 85–90.

SHERLOCK, K.; WOLFF, K.; HAY, A.W.M. & CONNER, M. 1999. Analysis of illicit ecstasy tablets: Implications for clinical management in the accident and emergency department. *Journal of Accident and Emergency Medicine* 16: 194–97.

SHEWAN, D.; DALGARNO, P. & KING, L.A. 1996. Ecstasy and neuro-degeneration: . . . such as Ketamine [letter]. *British Medical Journal* 313: 424.

SHEWAN, D.; DALGARNO, P. & REITH, G. 2000. Perceived risk and risk reduction among ecstasy users: The role of drug, set, and setting. *International Journal of Drug Policy* 10: 431–53.

SOLOWIJ, N.; HALL, W. & LEE, N. 1992. Recreational MDMA use in Sydney: A profile of Ecstasy users and their experiences with the drug. *British Journal of Addiction* 87: 1161–72.

SPRUIT, I.P. 1997. *Ecstasy in the Netherlands: A Summary of the Results of Six Projects.* Rijswijk, Netherlands: I.P. Spruit.

TOPP, L.; HANDO, J.; DILLON, P.; ROCHE, A. & SOLOWIJ, N. 1999. Ecstasy use in Australia: Patterns of use and associated harm. *Drug and Alcohol Dependence* 55: 105–15.

VAN DE WIJNGAART, G.F.; BRAAM, R.V.; DE BRUIN, D.E.; FRIS, M.; MAALSTÉ, N.J.M. & VERBRAECK, H. T. 1999. Ecstasy use at large-scale dance events in the Netherlands. *Journal of Drug Issues* 29: 679–701.

WEIL, A. 1972. *The Natural Mind.* New York: Houghton Mifflin.

WILLIAMS, H.; MEAGHER, D. & GALLIGAN, P. 1993. M.D.M.A. ("Ecstasy"); A case of possible drug-induced psychosis. *Irish Journal of Medical Science* 162: 43–44.

WINSTOCK, A.R. & KING, L.A. 1996. Tablets often contain substances in addition to, or instead of, ecstasy [letter]. *British Medical Journal* 313: 423–24.

WOLFF, K.; HAY, A.W.M.; SHERLOCK, K. & CONNER, M. 1995. Contents of "ecstasy." *Lancet* 346: 1100–101.

ZINBERG, N.E. 1984. *Drug, Set, and Setting.* New Haven, Connecticut: Yale University.

QUESTIONS FOR THOUGHT AND DISCUSSION

Chapter 13: "Rich Man's Speed: A Qualitative Study of Young Cocaine Users," by Annabel Boys, Julie Dobson, John Marsden, and John Strang

1. What were the patterns of powder cocaine use and associated health risks among the youth?
2. What was the context of powder cocaine use?
3. What were some motivations for using cocaine?
4. What were the perceived risks associated with powder cocaine use?
5. What type of public health model do the authors advocate?

Chapter 14: "Crack Dealing, Gender, and Arrest Avoidance," by Bruce A. Jacobs and Jody Miller

1. Please describe the arrest-avoidance techniques employed by the participants.
2. How do the authors define contextual assimilation?
3. How does gender influence arrest-avoidance techniques?

Chapter 15: "Street Status and the Sex-for-Crack Scene in San Francisco," by Harvey W. Feldman, Frank Espada, Sharon Penn, and Sharon Byrd

1. Please describe the general characteristics of the participants.
2. What were the most salient factors found in the participants' drug histories?
3. How were the participants' sexual histories related to "crack" cocaine?
4. How knowledgeable were the participants about HIV/AIDS?

Chapter 16: "The Lives and Times of Asian-Pacific American Women Drug Users: An Ethnographic Study of Their Methamphetamine Use," by Karen A. Joe

1. How does ethnography assist in dispelling stereotypes of Asian-Pacific American women?
2. Please describe the social and behavioral characteristics of the participants.
3. Please describe the coping strategies invoked by the participants.
4. What role do social and familial networks play in the participants' drug using history?

Chapter 17: "Negative Experiences on Ecstasy: The Role of Drug, Set and Setting," by Karen McElrath and Kieran McEvoy

1. How are negative MDMA/Ecstasy experiences socially and environmentally related?
2. How does a person's social network contribute to the overall MDMA/Ecstasy experience?

WORLD WIDE WEB SITES

Cocaine Anonymous World Services
   http://www.ca.org/

Cocaine and Crack: Just the Facts
   http://www.tcada.state.tx.us/research/drugfacts

Erowid: Methamphetamine
   http://www.erowid.org/chemicals/meth/meth.shtml

Erowid: MDMA/"Ecstasy"
   http://www.erowid.org/chemicals/mdma/mdma.shtml

Emerging Issues

Managing Drug Use and Misuse

My story is nothing special; there are millions of people in the world today with the same. Only the names, the places, and perhaps a few of the events, are different. But our stories are always the same. They are stories of pain, of torment, of guilt and remorse; they are stories of despair and what we thought was hopelessness. And today we are recovering. I am not any brighter, any richer, any better looking, any stronger of will, or of any higher moral fiber than any other addict, alcoholic, or person who is chemically dependent.

Carl Adam Richmond, Twisted: Inside the Mind of a Drug Addict

INTRODUCTION

It is often to easy to demonize what we do not understand. Individuals who consume illegal substances are viewed as morally flawed and socially irresponsible. Moreover, society only wants to see drug-using behavior as a calculated expression of personal degeneration and escapist in motive. Therefore, the focus of section IV is on breaking through these societal myths by offering the reader an opportunity to not only understand the process of recovering from addiction, as experienced by the women and men themselves, but also to appreciate what the drug treatment community may or may not be able to provide these individuals as they attempt to struggle to live drug free.

In the first selection, "Mothering Through Addiction: A Survival Strategy Among Puerto Rican Addicts," Monica Hardesty and Timothy Black present a nonstereotypical portrait of Latina women residing in a drug recovery program in Hartford, Connecticut. By collecting a series of life history interviews, Hardesty and Black illuminate the significance of mothering for these self-described addicts.

The second selection, "Drug Use Among Inner-City African American Women: The Process of Managing Loss" by Professor Carol A. Roberts, offers a contemporary perspective on how life situations and events influence a woman's onset of drug use and corresponding trajectory. Implications for drug treatment and intervention are offered.

The third selection, "Improving Substance Abuse Service Delivery to Hispanic Women Through Increased Cultural Competencies: A Qualitative Study" by Professors Terry S. Trepper, Thorana S. Nelson, Eric E. McCollum, and Philip McAvoy, challenges many long-standing myths about Hispanic women and drug treatment curriculums. Through the use of intensive qualitative interviews, the researchers demonstrate how a culturally sensitive drug treatment program may very well aid such individuals in making a drug-free transition.

In the fourth selection, "Substance Use Prevention: An Iowa Mexican Im/migrant Family Perspective," sociologists Ed A. Muñoz, Catherine Lillehoj Goldberg, and Martha M. Dettman extend the cultural competency thesis relevant to drug treatment initiatives by arguing for an enhanced program that also addresses nondrug issues, such as acculturation. By employing a combination of focus group and fieldnote data, the researchers make a persuasive argument for the inclusion and benefits of a Latino-specific drug prevention program.

In the fifth selection, "After You've Ran with the Rats the Mice Are a Bore: Cessation of Heroin Use Among Men Entering Midlife," Professors Kenneth Mullen, Richard Hammersley, and Claire Marriott employ semistructured qualitative interviews as a method for capturing the diverse reasons for quitting and/or continuing heroin use among a sample of Scottish men. Implications for effectively treating men with a history of heroin abuse are discussed.

18

Mothering Through Addiction

A Survival Strategy Among Puerto Rican Addicts

Monica Hardesty and Timothy Black

Often the public, policy makers, and academics are quick to judge female addicts, to question their ability to parent, and to penalize them for their drug use by taking away their children. Before rushing to judgments and enacting social policies based on these premises, the mothering life of the addict needs to be examined more carefully. Important questions need to be addressed empirically. What is the bond between the addicted mother and her children? Does female drug addiction involve the pursuit of self-interest at the neglect of children? How do female addicts feel about their ability to parent? In this article, we examine the importance of mothering among a group of Puerto Rican addicts.

Our research exposes some common misconceptions about these women. Contrary to popular belief, we found that motherhood is vital. It is a lifeline into, through, and out of addiction. Although seemingly contradictory, motherhood remains central to Puerto Rican addicts and provides an anchor in an embattled and disruptive life. Motherhood serves as a survival strategy to escape problem histories, to sustain the women through drug addiction, and to repair the damage drug abuse has caused their children. Female Puerto Rican addicts recognize that they do not conform to everyone's notions of what it means to be a good mother. Nevertheless, they struggle to bridge the chasm between being a drug user and a mother. Although most falter in this struggle, they embrace a cultural ideal of motherhood in their steps toward recovery.

Monica Hardesty and Timothy Black, "Mothering Through Addiction: A Survival Strategy Among Puerto Rican Addicts," *Qualitative Health Research,* vol. 9(3), pp. 602–19. © 1999 Sage Publications, Inc.

RESEARCH METHOD

We adopt an interpretive framework that allows female addicts to be the experts of their experiences and understandings as mothers. We seek, rather than impose, an understanding of mothering by asking questions and allowing the women to construct the stories of their lives. Using a life history method for data collection, we gathered information about how they viewed themselves as mothers before, during, and after addiction. To get a more complete story, we conducted three consecutive interviews. The first interview was about family background, children, and drug history. The second interview included questions about health care, pregnancies, and Latino family values and expectations. The final interview discussed relationships with partners, social service agencies, and drug recovery.

Our sample included 20 Latina women from the Hartford, Connecticut area.[1] These women were addicted to either crack-cocaine or heroin. Because our interest was in recording a range of life histories, we interviewed a sample of women whose experiences varied. All of them had some contact with a treatment program for Latina addicts, but they were in varying stages of recovery and demonstrated varying commitments to their recovery.[2] Some were still very active in drug use, whereas others had been in the process of recovery for several years and were "clean." All were mothers except one who miscarried and subsequently was unable to conceive. The ages of their children varied from newborns to grown children. The ages of the women ranged from 23 to 48, with a median age of 29. Most abused drugs during their pregnancies. All of the women were Puerto Rican, except for one woman who was from the Dominican Republic. Fourteen of the women were born in Puerto Rico, although the majority had spent most of their lives on the mainland. Half of the women began using drugs as teens; the remainder began using in their early 20s.

We acquired consent for research from the interviewees at two different points in time. As clients in a recovery program, the women provided written consent to participate in all facets of a program evaluation. Owing to the time demands of the life history interviews and the sensitive nature of the topics, we sought additional consent. We informed them of the interview topics, offered them a small stipend, agreed to conduct the interviews at a place and time of their choice, guaranteed confidentiality, and ensured anonymity in any report of our findings.

Interviews were conducted in Spanish by Latina researchers who had worked on an independent evaluation study of a Latina drug treatment program and who had some prior contact with the women (Black & Hardesty, 1996). This familiarity, we believe, was important for acquiring candid information about the lives of the women. Due to the confidentiality and incriminating nature of some of the questions, the interviews took place in an atmosphere of safety—in the homes of the participants or at the Hispanic center after self-help group meetings. Each woman was interviewed for a total of 3 to 4 hours. The interviews included open-ended questions about a broad set of themes. Part of the interviews included specific questions concerning their attitudes, expectations, and difficulties as mothers before, during, and after drug abuse.

The interviews were taped, transcribed, and then translated into English. Following a grounded theory approach to data analysis, interview responses were coded into emergent descriptive categories, such as kin network, child-rearing practices, Puerto Rican definition of a good mother, and self-definition of a good mother, to name a few. Each interviewee's coded responses were compared with others in the sample in what is known as "the constant comparative method" (Glaser & Strauss, 1967). From these comparisons of descriptive codes, an underlying pattern of motherhood as a survival strategy throughout addiction became apparent. Rather than focusing our analysis on the differences between women, we analyzed what they have in common (Lindesmith, 1981). With a refined focus on mothering, we reexamined the descriptive codes and transcript data to achieve theoretical saturation of our emerging concepts. That is, we sought exceptions and noted variations until our concepts could account for all of the data we had collected. As analysis progressed, it became clear that participants constructed similar self-images as mothers, which were different from accepted views of female addicts and their capacity to parent. Their stories reveal that they do not accept the commonly held view that they are "bad mothers," as someone who neglects, abuses, or abandons her children in the pursuit of drugs. Instead, they develop strategies to preserve a sense of themselves as "good mothers."

Despite the strengths of the life history method, there is a shortcoming in our method of data collection. We did not interview our participants several times over the long course of addiction and recovery; rather, we interviewed them on three separate occasions within a period of 1 month. Our data, therefore, are reconstructions of their lives as women, partners, and mothers. It may be that they reinterpreted the past to present a more favorable image of themselves. However, we found them to be surprisingly frank about highly stigmatizing conduct: criminal activity, domestic violence, and shortcomings with children. Several of the women broke down and cried during the interviews, indicating these were deeply felt experiences. Also, before presenting any information in this article, we made sure that it was consistent with each participant's life history data. Although we cannot corroborate every story told about themselves and others, we accept the truthfulness of these stories.

MOTHERING ON LIMITED RESOURCES: THE PUERTO RICAN COMMUNITY IN HARTFORD

To understand Puerto Rican addicts as mothers, one must first understand the place of motherhood in the lives of Puerto Rican women as well as the larger Puerto Rican experience in Hartford, Connecticut. There are few small cities in the Northeast that illustrate the devastating effects of deindustrialization, racial segregation, and increasing concentrations of poverty among Puerto Ricans better than Hartford. Hartford has the highest concentration of Puerto Ricans of any city in the country, with 30% of the city's population claiming Puerto Rican ancestry. Five of the city's 18 neighborhoods have a majority Hispanic population, and all 5 of these neighborhoods are highly distressed communities. Take, for instance, Frog Hollow, the neighborhood with the largest Hispanic population. In 1990, 46% of families in Frog Hollow lived below the poverty line, per capita income was $7,500, 42% of families were female headed, only 47% of adults 25 years and older graduated from high school, 32% of residents did not speak English or else spoke it poorly, 18% of workers were unemployed (a rate that doubled in the 1980s), 55% of households had no vehicle, and 92% of housing units were renter occupied, while rent accounted for 47% of household income (City of Hartford, 1995).

Industrial decline, the changing labor force, and increased poverty have created conditions that are extremely difficult for many Puerto Rican families. Unemployment and underemployment, substance abuse, AIDS, discrimination, crime, violence, sexual abuse, school dropout, homelessness, and the lack of culturally appropriate social services overwhelm the Puerto Rican community in Hartford. The family-centered dispositions of the culture and the extended nature of families produce some respite against such conditions, but as local community researchers (Singer, Gonzalez, Vega, Centeno, & Davison, 1991) report,

> High levels of stress due to poverty, cramped living space, language barriers, unfamiliarity with the wider social and institutional environment, and limited culture-appropriate social programs have left many families feeling powerless, depressed, and facing a constant cycle of domestic crisis. Family violence and sexual/physical abuse of children, especially girls, are not uncommon. Young people often grow up having little or no hope, poor self-esteem, and few positive roles. (p. 65)

The traditional values of the Latino family have helped to form the backbone of resiliency among the impoverished Puerto Rican community. Extended family networks are life-saving resources in times of need (Schensul & Schensul, 1982). Because women perform the work of organizing these kin networks, it provides them with a special place in their community (Alicea, 1997). The Latino family system and its creative adaptations and nurturing dispositions can help to facilitate family interests and routines or, as in areas of concentrated poverty, can place undue stresses and strains on family members. Families can provide a refuge from a cruel world; the resilience of any community riddled by the historic realities of scarcity and exploitation is almost always rooted in kin networks (Stack, 1974). Conversely, sustaining a nurturing and stimulating home environment can be undermined greatly in neighborhoods in which legitimate income-generating strategies are limited, educational facilities underfunded and overburdened, public services debt impaired, and venues for realizing self-value severely restricted.

The reliance on family creates a cultural contradiction for the Puerto Rican woman. For Puerto Rican women, home is an anchor. Through kin work and caring for others, women find rewarding opportunities for self-expression, satisfaction, and recognition. However, because they carry the disproportionate burden of family responsibilities, home can become exploitative and oppressive (Alicea, 1997). If her core identity consists of family duty and motherhood, what happens to a Puerto Rican woman when poverty-beleaguered neighborhoods overwhelm her efforts to be a good mother? What happens when the chaos and disruption associated with economic and social marginality impede the cultural identity through which self-salvation depends? What happens when partners become abusive or "fail" in the breadwinner role? Home cannot always be a safe haven from race, class, and gender oppression (Alicea, 1997); hence, the ability to live up to family responsibilities is jeopardized. Culture can act as a double-edged sword: The failure to live up to deeply held cultural convictions about family life can foster destructive tendencies, and yet the resources from which one draws to reorient or reconstitute one's life may be the very same deeply held convictions. As we will see, the failure to live up to the ideal of being a good mother for Puerto Rican addicts can further deepen addiction at the same time that the identity of mother can become the cultural resource for seeking and sustaining drug recovery.

PROBLEM HISTORIES

Latina addicts in our study share the painful consequences of economic and social marginalization. Although the majority of Puerto Ricans socially reproduce cultural strategies for adapting to and resisting these conditions, carving out dignity and respect and sustaining communities against the odds, our participants represent the fringe that spins off into self-destructive patterns of behavior. The disruptions that constitute their life journeys begin long before addiction. For the women in our study, problems go back to their earliest childhood experiences, back to memories of instability and mistreatment in their families.

Like other female addicts (Tracy & Williams, 1991), they experienced early physical and sexual abuse involving parents and stepparents, brothers and stepbrothers, and family friends, and in a few instances, family members condoned or denied these incidents. Others recalled the damage done by decades of drug and alcohol abuse by family members, and some were initiated into the drug culture by family members. Others told stories of alcoholic fathers and stepfathers who routinely beat their mothers. When talking about these early childhood experiences, the women see themselves as fulfilling a prophecy of instability. As one participant succinctly explained, "I am unstable; my mother was unstable."

Patterns of abusive relationships carry over into adulthood, particularly in relationships with men. Like other female addicts (Amaro, Fried, & Cabral, 1990), partner abuse was common, even during pregnancy. Most had been abused by their partners, and about one third admitted they were in an abusive relationship at the time of the interview. One woman described abuse in every relationship with men. Abusive partners isolated them, dominated their everyday activities, and sometimes forced drugs on them when they struggled to quit.

The constant threats and episodes of domestic violence and the ever-increasing isolation of the victim not only deepened the trauma in the lives of these women but also served to further restrict their already narrowed life options. Of course, we do not know the cause and effect here, but the lifelong trauma of abuse created a situation in which the use of drugs may have fulfilled many needs: momentary pleasure, escape, endurance, or a respite from physical and emotional pain. Drug addiction, however, can further trap the victims in the viciousness of domestic violence. Because many of our study participants depended on their partners for drugs, to give up the abusive relationship with their partners meant taking on greater responsibilities for supporting their drug habits, which also meant reorganizing their mothering responsibilities, creating perhaps more problems than remaining in the violent situation.

Problem histories carry over and accelerate in full-blown addiction. To secure a regular supply of drugs to support their $300- to $500-a-day habits, many women sustained a relationship with a man who was a drug dealer or who had a steady supply of drugs. In this way, the women never had to leave their homes, a preferable situation for women caring for children. Our participants favored the cultural tradition of men working outside the home and women staying home to care for children. Despite the violence in the home, the women usually relied on the partner until he could no longer provide. This decision carries negative consequences because it increases one's dependency on addicted, abusive, and domineering men.

Sometimes partners were unable to meet the increasing demand for drugs, or they were caught and incarcerated. Then the women became more self-reliant and like other female addicts financed their drug habits by entering illegal labor markets (Inciardi, Lockwood, & Pottieger, 1993; Maher & Curtis, 1992). Some women began to deal drugs, an ever-increasing practice among female drug addicts (Fagan, 1994, 1995). Stealing, bartering, conning, prostituting, and pimping were other illegal strategies they employed. Most did not rely on a single method for securing drugs but alternated in their reliance on male partners, drug trafficking, theft, and prostitution.

With increased time in the heroin and cocaine street life, women became more and more encumbered with problems, a stage characterized as "full-blown chaos" (Haller, 1991). The career of the female street drug addict, with its roots in early childhood trauma and repeated physical and sexual abuse in adulthood, moved into a situation of full-blown chaos in which physical annihilation and a predatory street culture became their lives. In full-blown chaos, women become fatalistic; they express feelings of being "trapped in their situation, their histories, and eventually their drug habits" (Kearney, Murphy, & Rosenbaum, 1994, p. 147). They accept the elevated chaos and its painful consequences as normal; they adopt a belief in "the bizarre as the usual" (Woodhouse, 1992).

The addicts' fatalistic perceptions of their life courses have profound ramifications for their views of self. Female addicts internalize an identity as "loser," as having very little self-worth or self-value. They recognize a limited number of options for constructing new and different lives and often adopt a strategy of "settling for less" (Biernacki, 1986; Kearney et al., 1994). The narrowing of options that began in childhood and tightened in adulthood was squeezed in addiction (Rosenbaum, 1979). They accommodate this shrinking control over their lives by protecting the remaining options for selfhood and exert a kind of "motherhood control" (Kearney et al., 1994). Unlike male addicts, who organize their daily lives entirely around the drug—seeking money for drugs, copping, networking, rationing, and so on (Bourgois, Lettiere, & Quesada, 1997)—female addicts' life organization includes children.

Their histories as victims of sexual abuse and domestic violence and their exposure to generations of substance abuse did not deter these women from valuing family and themselves as mothers, even though problem histories make it difficult to fulfill this role. Like other oppressed Puerto Rican women, they continued to construct home as a place of meaning (Alicea, 1997). Motherhood became their symbolic anchor: a culturally reinforcing, self-sustaining identity that grounds them amidst the turmoil in their lives. Even at the point of full-blown chaos, even when women lost custody of their children, children remained central in their lives—in fantasies, yearnings, and plans—which, as we will see, results in a numbing surrender to self-destruction or becomes the seeds for recovery. By controlling motherhood, the addict sustained an identity not completely defined by her life with drugs. Such connections to children structure the experiences differently for women.

THE CENTRALITY OF MOTHERHOOD AND MOTHER WORK

The centrality of motherhood in our participants' lives is rooted in the Latino culture. Latino families generally adhere to traditional gender roles.[3] A woman's life revolves around the family and home.[4] Latinas typically hold themselves responsible for the majority of household and child-rearing tasks and stress the importance of mothers in the parent–child relationship (Alicea, 1997; Canino & Canino, 1980; Julian, McKenry, & McKelvey, 1994; Segura & Pierce, 1993). It is the woman's responsibility to provide the day-to-day care and to transmit the cultural values to her children (Segura & Pierce, 1993). Mothers occupy a special place within the Puerto Rican family and community. Cultural activities such as Mother's Day in Puerto Rico, a holiday only exceeded by Three Kings Day in gift giving and celebration, reinforce the normative standards surrounding the importance of motherhood for the Latina (Christensen, 1979). Our participants described their central role of child rearing: "Fathers go away, but mothers stay," and "fathers are part time; mothers are full time."

In the Puerto Rican culture, woman and mother are inseparable. Raising children is the primary role of a Puerto Rican woman, valued above her responsibilities as wife (Christensen, 1979). The ultimate measure of womanhood is being a mother. As with other low-income women, motherhood validates the Latina's womanhood (Gabriel & McAnarney, 1983; Shtarkshall, 1987). When discussing her children, one Puerto Rican addict explained the centrality of motherhood in her life: "I would do anything for them. I wouldn't allow anyone to harm them. It is as I told you, I am mother before woman." Failure as a mother is equated with failure as a woman. The death of a child brings unspeakable loss, a loss of self:

> My baby died, crib death, Sudden Infant Death Syndrome. I found her dead in her crib. It was too much for me. My addiction began then. I was frustrated. I was feeling lonely. . . . Crack was something really fantastic. It was like going out of this world, forgetting everything, and that was exactly what I was looking for, to forget everything. It is a way to shut out your feelings. Not facing them. Back then, it was what I wanted to do. I saw those people "getting fixed," looking so happy, blind and deaf to everything around them. I wanted to be like them. I wanted to forget everything that was surrounding me. I was having nightmares where I saw my child. I saw her crying. I wanted to get out of this world. I wanted a hole in the ground and get in there, to get into my own world.

So central is motherhood to their female identity, Puerto Rican women have been described as being unable to make the choice not to have children (Christensen, 1979); they opt to do it all rather than relinquish the role of mother.

When we asked our participants to describe Puerto Rican women, they too spoke about the importance of motherhood. They told us that a Puerto Rican woman is the caretaker of children. She cooks, cleans, and sacrifices for the children. Being there for her children gives her a sense of identity and a place within her community. Children come first in her thoughts and actions. Many described their children as more important than themselves. Through self-sacrifice, they derived a sense of self. Children became a way of marking the important events in their lives. Restricted by poverty, joblessness, and addiction, our participants indicated that motherhood is the only positive identity that they possess. Not unlike other low-income mothers, motherhood reveals the deeper meaning of the Latina's existence and provides a rite of passage into adulthood (Gabriel & McAnarney, 1983). Because a Puerto Rican mother is charged with the responsibility of maintaining ethnic values and social ties, motherhood grounds her within her community as well (Alicea, 1997; Segura & Pierce, 1993).

These cultural expectations for motherhood did not disappear when Puerto Rican women became addicted. Instead, the desire to mother intensified and became most important for defining oneself. While addicted, our participants could not, or would not, relinquish their mother identities. This maintenance of the mother identity entailed a considerable amount of work at defining oneself in a positive light in relation to one's increasingly illegal actions. The mother identity was constructed and reconstructed over the course of her addiction and recovery, an activity we call "mother work."

Doing It All

Maintaining a mother identity is not an easy task for the addict. In the beginning, she struggled to "do it all," to juggle the responsibilities of motherhood with her everyday drug activities. In a desire to preserve her connectedness to others, she guarded her mother identity.

Our participants preserved their identities by claiming to meet four requirements of mother-hood. First and foremost, a mother must continue to meet the physical needs of her children: food, clothing, and shelter. One addict described taking care of these physical needs during addiction: "I like the children to dress clean, to smell good, that they do not stink or be mucousy and that they eat." Second, she must continue to provide discipline to sustain the child's moral character. They claimed a need to use physical punishment to teach right from wrong: "I have to hit them a little bit so that they learn respect," and "good mothers know how to discipline her children. She doesn't wait until it is too late." Third, she must continue to meet the emotional needs of her child. One had to "be there for them when they need you," and no matter what they do, "you never turn your back on them." Finally, she must prevent the harm of unstable child-rearing practices. For those who experienced an abusive childhood, this meant "righting the wrongs" that happened to them as a child. It also meant preventing or repairing any harm that arose from their own actions as a drug addict.

A mother who can maintain a drug habit and take care of her children wins respect in the drug world (Rosenbaum, 1979). Being a good mother is an ongoing source of pride when mothering is maintained through the addiction. The maintenance of discipline and taking care of their children's needs for food, clothing, and shelter are essential elements of mother work. Although mother work involves taking care of children both physically and emotionally, it also involves identity management. Given the stigma placed on addicts, especially female ones, maintaining an "unspoiled" view of oneself as a good mother despite the addiction serves as a self-survival tool.

Many Puerto Rican addicts affirmed that they were good mothers during their addictions. They were able to stay on top of both their drug work and their mother work:

> You can be a good mother and be using at the same time because the love for your kids is always there. I take care of my kids. I worry about them. I see that they don't go hungry. I see that they don't get hurt. Wherever I go I take them along.

In doing it all and balancing these two lines of work, an addict divided herself into two separate spheres of existence: her habits as an addict and her life as a mother.

> I was a good mother to my child in spite of being, you know, an addict. . . . I never have taken addicts to my house! The one that used drugs in my house was me, and I kept it hidden. I did it in fear. I never dared disrespect my son by taking people to my house to get high, to drink or to smoke crack. I never dared! To me that is a lack of respect for my son. I always tried to have a house for him, a place for him to live where he could feel safe and sound. A safe home for him.

By creating a dual life, the addict attempted to maintain home as a safe haven and to minimize the effects of her addiction on her children.

This strategy of compartmentalizing one's life was accomplished more easily by some addicts than others. For one, the dual life was easier to maintain if she had enough money or a regular supply of drugs:

> If she has enough for her vice, she can be a good mother and use drugs. She has to have enough [money] to meet her children's needs. Because the most important thing is her children, more than the drug. That is what I used to do. First I had my children's things bought, then [I bought] the drug.

Many described a regular drug supply as an aid to their work in the home. Some women stated that the daily use of drugs allowed them to perform their mother role more easily and more effectively. Drugs eased a depression that immobilized some of them. They described a new level of enthusiasm that allowed them to get out of bed in the morning, to cook, to complete housework, and in general to "be there" for their children. For some, drug use provided them with a lift, a more positive outlook on life. With a constant supply of drugs, they could do it all. Paradoxically, this ability to do it all was accomplished most often through active drug dealing.

For their identity management to be successful, addicts had to reject others' standards of mothering and to avoid facing the label of bad mother. The growing tension between their and others' evaluations of their performances as mothers increased the difficulty of their mother work. Like other female addicts, our participants routinely discounted the judgments of others about their negative performances as mothers (Friedman & Alicea, 1995). They insisted that they were good mothers, which required them to meet minimal expectations of the Puerto Rican culture and to compare favorably with the negative mothering they saw in others. Some claimed they did not abuse their children as others did: "During my addiction I never mistreated my child. I never did any [physical] harm to my child. Had I seen that I was not able to handle the child, I would have given him to DCF [Department of Children and Families]." Others claimed they adhered to the cultural norms of motherhood as defined by Puerto Ricans:

> [Do you believe that a woman that uses drugs can be a good mother?] Yes. If you take good care of your children. You have a roof over them to sleep, have their food and all their clothing, take them to the doctor. That nothing is missing, that is being a good mother. Because in spite of me using drugs, I always was there for my girls, and they always had what they needed.

Those who were able to perform their responsibilities successfully experienced it as a source of pride. Those who performed marginally interpreted their efforts as a sign that they were not bad mothers.

However, not every addict could fend off all challenges to her status as a good mother. There was widespread recognition that some addicts maintained the dual roles of mother and drug user better than others:

> There are two types of drug addicts: the responsible one and the irresponsible one. I was doing drugs since I was 16 years old, and no one knew I was doing drugs because I took care of my children. The same thing happens with some of my friends. They have their homes in order, and they take care of their children. And if there is money left and they want to waste it [on drugs], they do it. That is the responsible addict. The irresponsible addict is the one that thinks first about getting high and the children come next.

Maintaining a mother identity became problematic, especially when one experienced difficulty in fulfilling her responsibilities as a mother. Over time, the juggling of addict and mother roles became increasingly difficult, and strains developed between the two lines of work (Rosenbaum, 1981). Because more time was spent in support of the drug habit, less time was given to the children and home. Some began to sense impending failure and experienced profound doubts about their abilities. Our participants recognized that in the long run, most addicts could not maintain both lines of work and told stories of some who fell completely into life on the streets.

Falling Through or Failing as Mothers

Having internalized the normative images of what it means to be a good mother, our participants lived between believing that they were good mothers and that they were bad mothers. Although proud of their achievements as mothers under duress, off and on they became exasperated with themselves as mothers. A time came when their attempts to compartmentalize their lives failed. They realized their mothering had suffered and was no longer "good enough."

As drug work competed more and more with mother work, the women in this study described themselves as less skillful in the performances of their mothering duties. When she had a reliable source of money or drugs, usually through her male partner, then she was able to stay home and be there for her children. However, when drug supplies became sporadic or when her addiction expenses skyrocketed to a $500-a-day habit, she spent most of her time and money on the drug. The search for drugs, or the money to finance them, became time-consuming and all engrossing.

Women often interpret thinking about others as caring (Dressel & Clark, 1990); for our participants, not thinking about children was interpreted as not caring. When drug work became all engrossing, the addict forgot her children; she removed from her mind their physical needs, neglected to feed them, and failed to see that they had a safe place to sleep. They stopped thinking of their children first:

> [How did drugs help you to deal with that situation?] I did not think. When I was using, I did not think, I just wanted to keep using. Worrying about getting it, I did not have time to think about my child.
>
> I lived for the drug. If they [her children] woke up and were hungry, I said, "Wait a minute." Now [that I'm in recovery] when they wake up, I say, "Baby are you hungry? Do you want to eat?" Drugs were first then.

As the search for drug money took addicts into the streets to hustle or prostitute, they left their children unsupervised for greater periods of time. Even when addicts were able to meet the physical needs of their children, they still expressed an overriding fear of emotional damage to their children. In some cases, the illegal street work led to arrest and jail time, which further curtailed their abilities to be with and care for their children. As addiction escalated, children were overlooked, neglected, or discarded. At this point in their lives, the women claimed to have lost balance; their mothering had fallen through:

> A bad mother is a woman who abandons her children. Someone that has put something else first, like me. I decided I preferred addiction over my own daughters. I put addiction first. Not being there when they take ill, not knowing if they eat or if they are fine.
>
> A bad mother is someone that gives her children away, such as I did. I did not mean any harm. I meant to do good when I did it because I did not have a place to stay. I was not going to let them stay in the halls where the homeless sleep to catch pneumonia on my account, or that they may die.

While struggling to stay connected to their children throughout addiction, the women realized that they often lost touch.

We found these points of falling through happened at key junctures in their lives. Puerto Rican addicts recognized their inadequacies when they completely disregarded their child care responsibilities. They acknowledged deficiencies when they gave their children to family members. They admitted failing when the DCF forcibly removed the children from the home. Admitting deficiencies and anticipating the loss of children further eroded the cherished identity of mother; nevertheless, they maintained mother work. They made numerous efforts to minimize these damaging effects, emphasizing their efforts as evidence of being a good mother and voluntarily transferring children into a family member's household.

For many women, the inability to sustain their responsibilities led to the loss of their children, temporarily or permanently. Their children usually were given away voluntarily:

> I thought that the baby was going to come out [born] with an addiction. But when the baby was born, the doctor told me that he was fine. Later on [when the baby developed pneumonia] I thought, "My God, don't let them take the children!" But before they took them, I gave them voluntarily to their grandparents.

These decisions were difficult and contradictory ones. On one hand, they recognized they were not performing up to expectations. Yet, on the other hand, they praised themselves for making such tough decisions. These decisions about children were an integral part of the identity struggle. From their point of view, it revealed good judgment: They knew when their children were not receiving proper care and were competent enough to send them to live with family, most often their own mother. This use of the kin network allowed them to salvage, albeit with difficulty, a good mother identity because unlike other addicts, they knew when to place a child with another family member.

The voluntary placement of children into another household is not as damaging to the mother identity as one might expect. Extended family networks and multiple mother figures are common among Puerto Rican families (Alicea, 1997; Mizio, 1974; Morales, 1995; Segura & Pierce, 1993). Puerto Rican women build a large network of relatives and close friends in their community to rely on in times of need (Alicea, 1997; Lazarus, 1984). Grandmothers, godmothers, aunts, and older sisters share mothering responsibilities as companion parents, an institutional practice known as *compadrazgo* (Mizio, 1974). These ties involve the cultural practice of *"hijos de crianza,"* a set of mutual obligations of economic and emotional support to the parent in which companion parents "raise the child as if it were one's own" (Mizio, 1974, p. 77).

The parenting bond between mother and daughter is particularly strong. Daughters experience themselves as an extension of their mothers and their mothers as an extension of themselves (Segura & Pierce, 1993). It is not unusual for grandmothers in Puerto Rican families to provide care for their daughters' children in their homes at some time in their lives (Lazarus, 1984). The strength and vitality of the "grandmother-mother-child triad" enable Latinas to feel connected to one another and empowered within their communities and families (Hernandez, 1988). That is, in their shared parenting bonds, they affirm themselves as "Latinas," women with a unique way of relating to one another through close interaction with other women in their kin networks.

Because Puerto Ricans construct family differently, we need to understand their decisions about children differently. An addict's decision to place her children in the custody of a female relative was not a complete relinquishing of mothering responsibilities; rather, it was another way of doing mother work. It was an enactment of shared motherhood that is so vital among Latina women (Alicea, 1997; Hondagneu-Sotelo & Avila, 1997). They placed their children in the care of a companion parent, one who is obligated to act on their behalf with all the love and attention of a biological parent. The reliance on a companion parent is entirely normal in the culture, and it, therefore, did not produce the kind of "mother guilt" as might be expected among Anglo women. Among the mothers in this study, this custody arrangement was preferred. It was temporary and allowed them to maintain some control over mothering. In their eyes, they were not completely failing as mothers; instead, their own mothers were standing in for them.

Another point of falling through occurs when children are removed forcibly from their home by child welfare agents from the DCF. Various transfers of custody had occurred among our participants. Some children of Puerto Rican addicts were placed in homes of relatives, but in some cases, children were placed in foster homes, and in a few cases, parental rights were terminated. The DCF's actions had the most damaging effect on their mother identities. Some feared serious damage to the mother-child bond: "[What is the worst thing they could have done to you?] To take my children away. Because the children are very attached to me. If taken away they would suffer. They [foster parents] might mistreat them." Numerous mothers feared their children would be mistreated in foster homes:

> It is dangerous for children because even foster homes have [sexually] violated girls. And DCF stays quiet and does not say anything. DCF helps some families, and it damages others for the rest of their lives. They do not understand that, the Whites.

Placement of children in foster homes violated the ethnic tradition of compadrazgo. The Puerto Rican extended family was undermined: "When they take the children away sometimes they don't place them with people from their own culture and the children suffer." The involuntary removal of children from the home produced great damage to the mother identity and, as a result, more mother guilt. The forced removal of their children was an undeniable sign of their failures as mothers. In addition to failing their children, they failed their communities as well. The placement of their children into the homes of strangers, people outside the extended family system or outside the ethnic community altogether, attacked the cultural foundation of community on which Puerto Rican motherhood, kin networks, and proper childcare are built.

Recovering the Mother Identity

The loss of children was devastating to these women. Many described it as the worst thing they could ever imagine happening in their lives. The loss of children often spiraled them further into addiction. A number stated that their drug use substantially increased when DCF became involved in their lives: "I was depressed because DCF told me that if my next baby was born positive to drugs they were going to take him away. That led me to use more drugs." Some feared that DCF would not ever return their children to them. For example, one mother feared that DCF would put her children up for a legal adoption:

> I am trying to remake my life in a correct way. But I am afraid that when the time comes and I fight for my children they [DCF] are going to say, "No!" That I can't take them back. I have that fear.

Despite numerous challenges to their mother identities, many put faith in their abilities to repair their relationships with their children and to have them returned to them. Rather than letting go of aspirations, hope became a new form of mother work. Although they had lost many things—stability, money, health, marriage, and a fulfilling sex life (Kearney et al., 1994)—they were determined not to lose their children. During the most traumatic times of their lives, they longed for their children, fantasized and dreamed about them. Like women in general, these thoughts of children were interpreted as signs of caring. Even when children were no longer present in the home, they continued to labor as mothers and discussed better ways of demonstrating to their children and others that they could be good mothers:

> When they took the girl away, they [DCF] helped me to reflect. If they would not have taken the baby away I would still be a good mother, but not to the maximum of how it should be. They took my daughter away to make me react and calm down, and they accomplished that.

Good mothers do not give up hope and do not cease their mother work just because their children are gone: "If someone takes my children away I fight for them, to get them back. They [bad mothers] don't do anything." Some mothers focused on the temporariness of the physical separation and on the permanence of the emotional bond between mother and child. The return of the child, though distant and vague in its timetable, shaped her mother work during these periods of separation:

> [Why did you want a child?] Because I need it in my life. [Why do you think you needed it in your life?] One always needs something in her life. It is good to have a child. [If you think you need a child, how come she is not living with you?] Because of the drugs. . . . [What do you value most?] My daughter. [If you value her that much, why don't you fight to have your child with you?] It is as I told you. I do not want to fight yet. I just began recovery and I do not want to relapse, having her and relapsing.

For female addicts, recovery means more than "getting clean"; it is about "creating a new life" (Pursely-Crotteau & Stern, 1996). For our participants, it was about recreating their lives as mothers. For them, recovery involved recovering the role of mother. Reclaiming one's children was the primary motive for recovery, regardless of whether one had given away her children voluntarily or had them taken away by a state agency. As one woman explained, "I have enough reasons to get into treatment—these are my children. I was in addiction and my children pushed me into treatment. What thing could [give me more strength] than my children?"

When confronting their past failures, women relived their drug experiences from their children's perspectives:

> I can imagine that they felt bad because they use to tell me, "Mama, please stop using drugs, we want the sweet mother that you were before." And I didn't care, didn't care, didn't care about my children. Drugs were more important. I was having no feelings.
>
> It was the worst experience when my daughter realized that I was under the influence of drugs. I locked myself up in the bathroom [to use]. She was little, but even being little, she knew something was happening. She had a negative attitude. She didn't want to talk to me. [How old was she?] Seven years old. She would tell me, "Mama, you are doing something wrong. I know it."

For the recovering addict to reclaim her motherhood, however, she must confront her guilt, repair the damage inflicted on her children, and renegotiate her mother identity. This was a monumental task fraught with anxiety and guilt:

> In the beginning it was very difficult for me to explain all this to my children, especially the oldest one. He is the one I offended the most. Now I feel better because he understands that I

have that disease. [Why did you say that you offended him?] Because many times I spoke ill to him and he answered me in the same way. He was mad at me. He probably noticed my problem and didn't say anything to me. I offended him a lot. Not long ago I asked him for his forgiveness.

While talking about her son's placement in a detention home, another mother was consumed with the grief of having been a bad mother:

I feel guilty. Sometimes I tell myself, you know, that is the result of my using drugs. It created in him emotional problems. He was greatly affected when I was sent to jail, that and the fact that he saw me using drugs. He has become a very rebellious child. He has no interest in school. It is the pain of seeing me using drugs.

Our participants did not measure their success in recovery by counting the number of meetings attended or days of sobriety. They measured their success relationally; they watched for, kept track of, and felt joy in their children's loving actions toward them. A child's kindness meant more than another day of sobriety. Reconnecting with lost children was essential to their recovery. They experienced frustrations when these loving actions did not happen as often as they desired because it meant they were not progressing as planned:

You see the damage you have caused them when you were in the addiction [and you want to repair it]. It is like when you try to straighten a bent stick little by little, then when you have the stick almost straight and the stick gets bent again. I would like to have more time with him [her son], but I cannot.

For the Puerto Rican addict, commitment to recovery involved commitment to one's children. For virtually all of the addicts, their motivations to succeed in recovery were to reconnect with their children and to recover the identity of a good mother. Yet, their successes largely depended on their children's willingness to participate in the process:

[How is the boy with you? Does he trust you?] Now he does. He has been living with my daughter for a year. The first year, that was a war, war over power. You know. "I am the boss, you are not." I think his fears of me going back to drugs were great, but not now. Since we are in therapy, he has been able to bring out all of his rage against me. There is more communication and trust between he and I.

It was important to the addicts that their children noticed the positive changes in them and encouraged their rehabilitation efforts:

They [used to] cry, "Mama, get out of that [drugs]. Look how ugly you are." When I finished the program, I came home and they said, "Oh mom, how beautiful you look." They said this to my face, and they kissed me.

[Even though] they wanted me to quit, my oldest even offered me her things [shoes and coat] for me to sell in order to have money to get fixed. She used to tell me, "Mom, sell these things, you can buy another for me later." They knew when I was *enferma de droga* (drug sick, in need of a fix). [Now] they ask me every day, "Have you gone to get your methadone treatment today?"

The desire to have their children back and to reclaim their identity as mother was essential yet often idealistic. It was a very difficult task because repeated drug use was intertwined with the guilt of being neglectful mothers in the past. Of their mothering tasks, reclaiming children was the most challenging, one that takes years to accomplish:

> Social services in Puerto Rico have two of my children. I have lost all of my parental rights, so far. [Is that for good?] At least it will be this way till my kids grow up and become aware that I am a different mother now. Then they will have to decide if they want to come to live with me. That will be the only way. In court, there is nothing I can do to get my children back. I can fight for the one that is here in Hartford. Still I call my children. I look for them. On June 16, I sent a present for one of the kids. I called him up and I asked him, "Sonny, would you like to come with mama just for vacation," and he said, "No mama, I don't want to go with you." I can't force them, see. It has been 3 years since they were taken away. So many things can happen in 3 years. I did many wrong things. I was wrong. I regret that, and I begged for his forgiveness. It hurts, you know, because I see that my child doesn't want to stay with me. It is not easy. Maybe I want to see the result of my recovery too soon. But I am going to continue my struggle. I am going to keep trying. I know that one day my son is going to realize that his mother was sick, but at least she went ahead—it would be bad if they had to say, "My mother was an addict and never changed."

Mother work in the recovery stage can set into motion a cycle of great expectations, failure to meet those expectations, and then drug relapse. The grand expectations of motherhood were repeatedly dashed in the actual practice of parenting after drug addiction; the failed mother identity resurfaced, and recovering addicts fell back into old drug habits in response to failure. Their abilities to embrace the possibilities of renewed relations, rather than succumb to past failures and to the obstacles to parenting, enhanced their success to recover motherhood. Puerto Rican addicts moved through this cycle of parental hope and despair several times before reaching a recovered status, a status that meant reclaiming one's place in the culture and reaffirming one's position in the family. The vacillation between the good mother and the bad mother identities fueled the movement between recovery and relapse.

CONCLUSION

Puerto Rican mothers in Hartford live on limited resources and with significantly reduced opportunities for achievement. Women confronted with limited opportunities very often seek the cultural ideal of motherhood to acquire self-value and personal identity. This identity provides a ray of hope, albeit dim, in the lives of women marked by oppression. Motherhood becomes a central way of staying connected and surviving in hard times.

Puerto Rican addicts cherished their role as mothers and performed a significant amount of mother work throughout their addiction and recovery. The nature of their mother work evolved over the course of the addiction. In the early stage of drug addiction, mothers juggled the responsibility of motherhood with their everenlarging drug activities. They constructed dual lives to shield and preserve the good mother identity. As their addictions progressed, the duality collapsed. They fell through and faltered as mothers. Their mother work correspondingly shifted; they confronted the bad mother in their past acts. Moving toward recovery, they walked the tightrope between the good mother and the bad mother identities—the bad mother image pushing them into relapse, and the good mother image pulling them out again. Finally, in recovery, they worked on their connections with their children to reclaim the good mother ideal.

The frustrations of parenting, especially in poverty environments in which resources for parenting are limited, may lead to feelings of failure, drug abuse, and neglect of children. We have found in the lives of Puerto Rican women a different story. Addicts, even in extreme circumstances, struggle to maintain their place as mothers. They juggle overwhelming and contradictory demands, fend off negative criticism, and find support in kin relations. Yes, we found that this crisis can accelerate self-destructive behavior and drug use, but it also can act as a wake-up call. Notwithstanding the devastation of poverty, marginalization, and other forms of oppression, women can and do mother. Despite the problem histories and abusive partners, despite the absorption into the anesthetizing world of drugs, and despite the damage caused to their children and other family members, these addicts moved into the frightening world of recovery where they confronted the consequences of their past failures. They did so because of their children. Motherhood is their lifeline; it provides continuity in a discontinuous life and sustains the Puerto Rican woman through the stages of addiction into recovery.

ACKNOWLEDGMENT

We would like to thank Maria Isabel Perez, Miriam Mercado, Ana Sanchez Adorno, Lizz Toledo, and Lani Davison for their assistance in conducting this research.

NOTES

1. We recruited our research participants through our work as evaluation researchers at a local Hispanic health center. The drug program at the center served only Latina addicts. It was staffed by Latina professionals and paraprofessionals who advocated a dual ideology of cultural empowerment and self-help. All sessions were conducted in Spanish and often involved cultural activities. The women expressed great satisfaction with these Latina-only services. They considered the center a safe haven.
2. The women in our sample had participated in some recovery services at a local Hispanic health center, although to varying degrees. Our sample does include active and former drug users. Still, a bias in our sample may exist in that Puerto Rican addicts who have not initiated recovery efforts were omitted. As a result, all Puerto Rican addicts may not fit the mothering profile we describe in this article.
3. Of course, deviations from traditional familial expectations vary across class, ethnic, and urban-rural populations. We intend to convey the significance that traditional gender roles still have, despite group variations among Latinos.
4. Even though many Puerto Rican women participate in the workforce, most are employed in low-skilled, working-class jobs (labor-intensive manufacturing industries or low-wage service sector jobs), which are less likely to shape identity compared with the rewards and status derived from more traditional familial roles and responsibilities.

REFERENCES

ALICEA, M. (1997). "A chambered nautilus": The contradictory nature of Puerto Rican women's role in the social construction of a transnational community. *Gender & Society, 11*(5), 597–626.

AMARO, J., FRIED, L., & CABRAL, H. (1990). Violence during pregnancy and substance abuse. *American Journal of Public Health, 80, 5.*

BIERNACKI, P. (1986). *Pathways from heroin addiction: Recovery without treatment*. Philadelphia: Temple University Press.

BLACK, T., & HARDESTY, M. (1996). *Cuidate mujer: Final evaluation report on a substance abuse program for Latina women*. West Hartford, CT: Center for Social Research, University of Hartford.

BOURGOIS, P., LETTIERE, M., & QUESADA, J. (1997). Social misery and the sanctions of substance abuse: Confronting HIV risk among homeless heroin addicts in San Francisco. *Social Problems, 44*(2), 155–173.

CANINO, I. A., & CANINO, G. (1980). Impact of stress on the Puerto Rican family: Treatment considerations. *American Journal of Orthopsychiatry, 50*(3), 535–541.

CHRISTENSEN, E. W. (1979). The Puerto Rican woman: A profile. In E. Acosta-Belen & E. Hidalago Christensen (Eds.), *The Puerto Rican woman* (pp. 51–63). New York: Praeger.

CITY OF HARTFORD. (1995). *State of the city, 1995*. Hartford, CT: Department of Planning and Economic Development.

DRESSEL, P. L., & CLARK, A. (1990). A critical look at family care. *Journal of Marriage and the Family, 52*, 769–782.

FAGAN, J. (1994). Women and drugs revisited: Female participation in the cocaine economy. *The Journal of Drug Issues, 24*(2), 179–225.

FAGAN, J. (1995). Women's careers in drug use and drug selling. *Current Perspectives on Aging and the Life Cycle, 4*, 155–190.

FRIEDMAN, J., & ALICEA. M. (1995). Women and heroin: The path of resistance and its consequences. *Gender & Society, 9*(4), 432–449.

GABRIEL, A., & MCANARNEY, E. R. (1983). Parenthood in two subcultures: White, middle-class couples and Black, low-income adolescents in Rochester, New York. *Adolescence, 18*(71), 595–608.

GLASER, B., & STRAUSS, A. (1967). *The discovery of grounded theory*. New York: Aldine.

HALLER, D. (1991). Recovery for two: Pregnancy and addiction. *Addiction & Recovery, 11*(4), 14–18.

HERNANDEZ, L. (1988). Canas. In L. Hernandez & T. Benitez (Eds.), *Palabras Chicanos* (pp. 47–49). Berkeley: University of California, Berkeley, Mujeres in March Press.

HONDAGNEU-SOTELO, P., & AVILA, E. (1997). "I'm here, but I'm there": The meaning of Latina transnational motherhood. *Gender & Society, 11*(5), 548–571.

INCIARDI, J.A., LOCKWOOD, D., & POTTIEGER, A.E. (1993). *Women and crack-cocaine*. New York: Macmillan.

JULIAN, T.W., MCKENRY, P.C., & MCKELVEY, M.W. (1994). Cultural variations in parenting: Perceptions of Caucasian, African American, Hispanic, and Asian American parents. *Family Relations, 43*(1), 30–37.

KEARNEY, M.H., MURPHY, S., & ROSENBAUM, M. (1994). Learning by losing: Sex and fertility on crack cocaine. *Qualitative Health Research, 4*(2), 142–162.

LAZARUS, E.S. (1984). *Pregnancy and clinical care: An ethnographic investigation of perinatal management for Puerto Rican and low income women in the United States*. Ann Arbor, MI: University Microfilms International.

LINDESMITH, A. (1981). Symbolic interactionism and causality. *Symbolic Interaction, 4*, 87–96.

MAHER, L., & CURTIS, R. (1992). Women on the edge of crime: Crack cocaine and the changing contexts of street-level sex work in New York City. *Crime, Law and Social Change, 18*, 221–258.

MIZIO, E. (1974, February). Impact of external systems on the Puerto Rican family. *Social Casework*, 76–82.

MORALES, J. (1995). Community social work with Puerto Ricans in the United States. In F.G. Rivera & J. Erlich (Eds.), *Community organizing in a diverse society* (pp. 77–94). New York: Allyn & Bacon.

PURSLEY-CROTTEAU, S., & STERN, P.N. (1996). Creating a new life: Dimensions of temperance in perinatal cocaine crack users. *Qualitative Health Research, 6*(3), 350–367.

ROSENBAUM, M. (1979). Difficulties in taking care of business: Women addicts as mothers. *American Journal of Drug and Alcohol Abuse, 6*(4), 431–446.

ROSENBAUM, M. (1981). *Women on heroin.* New Brunswick, NJ: Rutgers University Press.

SCHENSUL, S.L., & SCHENSUL, J. (1982). Helping resource use in a Puerto Rican community. *Urban Anthropology, 11*(1), 59–79.

SEGURA, D.A., & PIERCE, J.L. (1993). Chicana/o family structure and gender personality: Chodorow, familism, and psychoanalytic sociology revisted. *Signs: Journal of Women in Culture & Society, 19*(1), 62–91.

SHTARKSHALL, R.A. (1987). Motherhood as a dominant feature in the self-image of female adolescents if low socioeconomic status. *Adolescence, 22*(87), 565–570.

SINGER, M., GONZALEZ, W., VEGA, E., CENTENO, I., & DAVISON, L. (1991). Implementing a community based AIDS prevention program for ethnic minorities: The Comunidad y Responsibilidad project. In J. VanVugt (Ed.), *Community based research and AIDS prevention* (pp. 59–92). South Hadley, MA: Bergin & Garvey.

STACK, C. (1974). *All our kin: Strategies for survival in a black community.* New York: Harper & Row.

TRACY, C.E., & WILLIAMS, H.C. (1991). Social consequences of substance abuse among pregnant and parenting women. *Pediatric Annuals, 20*(10), 548–553.

WOODHOUSE, L.D. (1992). Women with jagged edges: Voices from a culture of substance abuse. *Qualitative Health Research, 2*(3), 262–282.

19

Drug Use Among Inner-City African American Women

The Process of Managing Loss

Carol A. Roberts

The dependence on illegal drugs such as heroin, cocaine, and marijuana and legal drugs such as alcohol, nicotine, and prescription tranquilizers has long been recognized as a major source of physical and psychosocial problems worldwide. The inception of crack, a smokable form of cocaine, in the 1980s introduced a new era in the world of drugs and accounted for staggering effects on morbidity and mortality across America (Bouknight, 1990). Cocaine and heroin are the most commonly injected drugs, and women using these drugs are one of the fastest growing high-risk groups for AIDS in North America (Shilling, El-Bassel, Gilbert, & Schinke, 1991). Illegal drug use has been described as a particularly devastating problem for women living in the impoverished inner cities of North America, where such drugs are easy to obtain and use has become epidemic (Inciardi, Pottieger, Forney, Chitwood, & McBride, 1991; Wachtler, 1990). Social consequences of illegal drug use include family breakdown, violence, crime, and homelessness, as well as transmission of infectious disease (Crystal, 1992).

Most research on drug use before 1980 focused on men (Abbott, 1994; Rosenbaum, 1981; Taylor, 1993). A growing concern with the extent and nature of legal and illegal drug use by women has led to increased research with this group in more recent years (Doweiko, 1990). After an extensive review of findings, Lex (1991) maintains that although some

Carol A. Roberts, "Drug Use Among Inner-City African American Women: The Process of Managing Loss," Qualitative Health Research, vol. 9(5), pp. 620–638. © 1999 Sage Publications, Inc.

attention has focused on women's drug use during the 1980s, efforts have failed to uncover etiological and contextual factors leading to the use of drugs by women. Much of this research has been quantitative, failing to specify gender in analysis, and many studies focused on women in treatment in which history and background of drug use were often obscured (Harrison, 1989).

This research employed the grounded theory method to explore the process of becoming a drug user and maintaining drug use as a part of life from the point of view of inner-city women currently using crack cocaine and women using primarily injection drugs such as heroin and/or cocaine.

BACKGROUND

A number of characteristics have been associated with the onset and maintenance of illicit drug use, but reports vary as to the consistency of events among women. Growing up in a dysfunctional family, parental use of drugs, emotional disorders, and physical and sexual abuse have been shown to be important factors in substance abuse (Blume, 1990; Boyd, 1993; Dembo et al., 1988; Wallace, 1990). In a mixed gender sample of 61 crack smokers, Wallace (1990) notes that a parental history of alcohol and domestic violence was reported by 27% of respondents; 28% reported physical abuse and 10% reported sexual abuse. Women in treatment for substance abuse frequently report rape, incest, and other violent childhood abuse prior to becoming substance abusers (Woodhouse, 1992). Sexual abuse history was noted to be high among African American women using crack cocaine. Within a sample of 105 crack-using women, Boyd (1993) reports that 65% had experienced at least one sexual abuse experience.

Several researchers have described the purpose of illicit drug use as a self-medication strategy to deal with painful feelings of anxiety and stress related to physical or psychic trauma. A model proposed by Gold (1980) indicates that feelings of powerlessness, low self-esteem, and anxiety result from inner conflict. Drug use increases feelings of power over conflict and anxiety is reduced. This model has been applied to explain the relationship between physical and sexual abuse and drug use by women. Anxiety and feelings of powerlessness result from abuse, which predisposes to loss of self-esteem, and drug taking relieves these feelings (Ladwig & Andersen, 1989).

A small qualitative study with two focus groups of inner-city women revealed that crack cocaine relieved symptoms of depression and trauma predating the onset of crack use and resulting trauma as a consequence of crack use (Fullilove, Lown, & Fullilove, 1992). Women in treatment have described medicating the pain resulting from childhood abuse experiences (Woodhouse, 1992). Similarly, the use of drugs as self-medication has been described by perinatal crack smokers as a symptom of greater underlying problems; for those people, crack eased the pain of feeling mentally hurt (Pursley-Crotteau & Stern, 1996).

These studies have contributed greatly to the understanding of women's drug use. However, many have focused specifically on women using crack cocaine or other groups of women in treatment. Prior to this past decade, inductive approaches to understanding women's drug use have been sparse in the literature. Rosenbaum (1981) was one of the first to describe a theory of narrowing options to explain life events and drug patterns among women addicted to heroin. The process of addiction and recovery has been described among chemically dependent nurses (Hutchinson, 1986, 1987). An anthropological view of women's marijuana use has been provided by Dreher (1984). The importance of qualitative research in presenting a comprehensive picture of causal and contextual factors contributing to drug use has been emphasized by Stimmel (1984). The existing literature lent support for this grounded theory study to extend theoretical knowledge about the process and meaning of drug use among inner-city women.

METHOD

The grounded theory method (Morse & Field, 1995; Strauss & Corbin, 1990) was selected to generate an explanatory theory that was grounded in the data. The resulting model identifies patterns in the data and relationships between patterns. This method is congruent with a feminist perspective, which guided the study and recognizes that women experience life differently from men. Participants were considered experts about their experiences, and they were interactive throughout the research process, reflecting on findings at all stages of the process (Anderson, 1991; Harding, 1987).

Participants

Twenty-four participants were purposively selected from two large AIDS risk-related studies being conducted at a southeastern U.S. university. One study was experimental, with approximately 300 participants known to be injection drug-using women. The second study was a nonintervention study, examining sexual behaviors of individuals using crack cocaine. Participants for both studies were recruited from the inner-city neighborhoods of a large metropolitan city. Staff members for these ongoing studies were given an overview of this study and guidelines for referral of potential participants. All women referred were older than age 18, were able to communicate well in English, and used primarily crack cocaine or injected cocaine and/or heroin at least twice a week. Eight additional women were recruited directly by the researcher through snowball sampling from two inner-city neighborhoods during the course of the study.

A total of 32 women were interviewed, and recruitment ceased when saturation of data was evident. The women were all African American. Not one was married at the time of data collection; 14 lived in a steady relationship with a man or girlfriend in a room or apartment; and 9 were homeless, living on the streets, in parks, or under bridges. The remainder lived with relatives or in an apartment alone or with dependent children. Seven of the women were childless. Of the children, 6 lived with their mothers (who had retained custody), 48 had been apprehended by social service authorities, 25 were living with relatives, 21 were living in foster homes, and 2 were adopted. Two women were pregnant at the time of data collection; one indicated that her child would be adopted.

Twenty-one participants used crack cocaine, often in combination with alcohol and/or marijuana to ease the "jitters" following crack highs. Crack users generally used drugs many times daily. Four crack users reported using drugs less than five times a week. Eleven women were intravenous drug users who primarily used heroin or a combination of heroin and cocaine, which was identified as a speedball. Two heroin users reported daily use. Participants ranged in age from 21 to 52 years. Heroin users were older than crack users, with an average age of 39 years. Crack users had an average age of 29 years.

Procedure

Data collection was conducted by the female researcher. Most data were collected through in-depth, tape recorded interviews lasting approximately 1 hour. Nine participants refused to be recorded, and in these cases, detailed field notes were kept by the interviewer. All interviews were conducted in a private interview room at the university project site for ongoing studies. The protocol for the protection of participants in this study was reviewed and approved by an ethics committee for human science research at the university.

All participants invited to participate signed an informed consent. Participants were asked to refrain from using names during interviews. Tape recordings were fogged for any identifying data following interviews. Fictitious names have been used in all reports, and ages are approximate. The safeguarding of all data and maintenance of anonymity and confidentiality could not be overemphasized in this study due to potential legal and social risks related to illegal drug use. Each participant was paid $15 per interview as compensation for time, travel, and greater assurance that individuals would appear for scheduled interviews. This fee was established for participants in the ongoing larger studies. Most women had to travel a considerable distance to the interview site, and some women incurred child care costs.

Women were interviewed two to four times. Interviews were generally unstructured. To ensure several broad domains of data, a loosely structured schedule of topics was used to help focus interviews on events surrounding drug use at the onset of data collection. The concept of theoretical sampling as outlined by Strauss and Corbin (1990) guided sampling and interviews as categories evolved. Participants were reinterviewed to provide more in-depth data concerning phenomena, to verify findings, and to ensure saturation of categories. Data collection and analysis proceeded concurrently, based on theoretical relevance.

Tape recordings were transcribed verbatim. The researcher kept a diary of her own feelings and perceptions following each interview. The issues surrounding drug use are sensitive and value laden. It was deemed important that the researcher be aware of her own values in order to minimize the risk that these values might sensitize participants and bias data collection. Although the researcher is Caucasian, she has had considerable experience in interviewing women of other ethnic backgrounds. All data and findings were confirmed with participants during subsequent interviews. During the analysis phase, findings were confirmed with another researcher experienced in qualitative research. Participants did not appear incoherent or confused during interviews, although many reported heavy drug use. Women reported the experience was fulfilling and welcomed the opportunity to discuss their lives.

DATA ANALYSIS AND FINDINGS

Data analysis began shortly after the onset of data collection using the constant comparison technique central to grounded theory. The first step in data analysis involved open coding (Strauss & Corbin, 1990). All phenomena relevant to the research question were highlighted on each transcribed interview and on the field notes. Following the completion of the first five interviews, these pieces of data were compared and contrasted, incident with incident, and given a conceptual label. The data from each subsequent interview were compared and contrasted to existing data, and similar phenomena were classified accordingly. New phenomena arising from the data were given a label. To reduce the number of units of data, all similar phenomena were grouped into broader categories and given a name. Properties or characteristics of each category and the dimensions of these characteristics were recorded in detailed memos and diagrams. Categories were labeled and described in terms of their characteristics and range of dimensions during open coding.

Axial coding followed (Strauss & Corbin, 1990). Data collection continued during this stage, directed by theoretical sampling to develop categories further, and connections were made within and between categories using the five elements of Strauss and Corbin's paradigm model. Causal conditions precede and contribute to the development of a category. Context includes the properties of a category and the conditions under which the phenomenon is managed or carried out. Intervening conditions act to constrain or facilitate actions taken to deal with the phenomenon. Actions or strategies serve to carry out the phenomenon within the context, and consequences are actual or potential outcomes of actions taken. Each category was analyzed using this model, and detailed memos and diagrams of relationships were generated.

Axial coding provided the basis for selective coding. Memos, diagrams, and relationships generated from open and axial coding were carefully reviewed and verified with the data and participants. Saturation occurred when no new categories were identified. A descriptive overview of the essence or most striking area of the study was compiled during selective coding. Experiencing loss emerged as the core category or central phenomenon that integrated all other categories, and managing loss emerged as the basic social process (Morse & Field, 1995) that women used to deal with painful feelings. Categories were refined and developed through interviews resulting in grounded theory.

Experiencing Loss: Childhood Experiences

Loss appeared early in the lives of the participants. A number of conditions gave rise to painful feelings of loss, including physical, sexual, and emotional abuse. Participants who suffered violent childhood experiences lost the opportunity to receive and give love, to develop a sense of self-worth, and to trust in themselves or others. Twenty-one participants experienced physical and/or sexual abuse during childhood; 7 women were raped by a father or relative, 1 was raped by a neighbor, and 3 were sexually exploited by parents to obtain money or drugs. Sexually abused women also recalled beatings or other physical abuse. Others were physically abused in the absence of sexual abuse. Victims reported deep feelings of emotional pain. Feelings included "feeling ashamed"; "feeling guilty"; "hating myself"; or feeling "hopeless," "depressed," and "angry." Women perceived childhood abuse as a form of punishment for being unable to please parents or guardians. Physical punishment was described as delivered for "no good reason" when parents or guardians often were under the influence of illicit drugs or alcohol. For example, Sabrina stated,

> Dad split after mom died; he'd beat me when he was drunk. I was afraid to go home. Older brother and sister don't care about me. I'm independent . . . never had a boyfriend, never loved no one 'cept my mom. Don't trust men.

Emotional rejection by parents left participants feeling unloved, insecure, and angry. Participants were labeled as "bad" or "no good" and described feeling unloved as children. Sarah and Marcy expressed this well:

> *Sarah:*   Really hated myself when I was a kid. No one loved me, couldn't do anything right. Mom, she beat me almost every day, never trusted me to do anything right.
>
> *Marcy:*   I got adopted by an older couple when I was a baby; they already had three boys. Mom couldn't cope with a girl, and dad had a sharp tongue when he was drinkin'. I was definitely not his daughter. He hated me. I wanted to die.

Women described their childhood home life as "bad," "violent," "strict," "boring," and "unhappy." Although guardians or parents were strict and often religious, family life was frequently chaotic and violent. Children were expected to live by conflicting values, as noted by Rosie:

> I lived with mom 'till I was 17; she was always goin' to church tellin' me I was bad—grandfather was a Baptist minister. He force me to have sex, couldn't tell my mom. She'd disown me, put me out of the house. Still bothers me—tried suicide once; it didn't work.

Participants reported feeling particularly victimized or rejected as children. Siblings who "followed the rules" at home were often favored by parents.

During childhood, many women suffered the devastating loss of a significant other through death and described the subsequent effect of this loss on their drug-using behaviors. Often the lost individual was viewed as supportive or central in women's lives, and their loss was particularly disturbing. Loss of nonsupportive and even abusive individuals was recalled as distressing for women as children because it usually meant a loss of home with the death of a single parent. Women were placed with relatives or in foster care. The following participant reflected on her losses:

> I really miss having a mom. She died when I was only 8. She was an alcoholic. I never knew my dad . . . lived with aunt 'till I was 12. Then I hit the streets . . . and dope.

Death of a loved one resulted in feelings of guilt. Some women felt that their "bad behavior" contributed to early deaths of significant others. Some deaths tended to occur after women began experimenting with drugs and were preceded by other types of loss. Jessie described her feelings of guilt following the death of her mother:

> I was 10 years old and I was stoned on pills the night mama died—I never been the same. I was scared and alone; they didn't find her 'till the next day. Feel so bad, just feel so bad.

In addition to parental death, women lost parents through separation, divorce, or desertion. Only 5 women were raised to adulthood by both parents.

Most participants reported leaving home at an early age because of family problems, rejection, and/or abuse. Some women reported that they became pregnant as teenagers and were forced to leave home by parents or guardians. The majority of women stated that they were experimenting with drugs before leaving home. Upon leaving home, women drifted into regular or heavy drug use while living with partners or friends. Others simply became homeless.

Managing Loss: Context of the Drug Scene

The environment and relationships within the environment played a major role in how women managed loss. Participants recalled that they were afforded easy access to a variety of drugs at an early age. Drugs were readily available in the neighborhood and often at home. Women reported that illegal drugs were literally sold "on the doorstep" and frequently were given away by pushers to ensure future sales. Drugs were cheap, and crack cocaine could be bought for as little as $5. Widespread drug use in most neighborhoods enhanced the development of networks among users, in which sharing and bartering drugs was common. Women recalled getting started on drugs in the company of boyfriends, girlfriends, with family members, or alone.

> Mom started me on crack at 15. She was always sittin' home and drinkin'. She'd send me for booze. Once I didn't come home with it . . . . She stabbed me in the leg. I'd do crack with my mom and trick for money.
>
> First drug I ever tried was Robitussen cough medicine . . . . We'd go to my girlfriend's house after school, blow off some steam, her mother worked, was easy. Sometimes we'd be lookouts for the drug boys; they'd give us marijuana . . . didn't like it, felt too sleepy, then I met this man . . . . He introduced me to heroin.
>
> Mom was a heavy drinker. When I was 5 I started sneakin' beer from her . . . . Did that 'till I was 13 or so . . . . Wanted to be like the ladies on Dynasty.' After mom died I lived with aunt. She was strict but she drank a lot. 'Gin was cold medicine and I got lots of colds.' Ran away at 16 and started shootin' coke with friends.

The streets provided an exciting life in the face of violence and loss. Women felt there was not much else to do in the community. They reported having "no one to talk to" when growing up; life was "depressing." The drug scene was a source of excitement. Women spoke about danger on the streets and their need for excitement.

> I love the excitement. Ya never know what's goin' to happin' next. I don't care. I worry about AIDS and gettin' busted. That's all. Friends are important—keep things off my mind.
>
> Life's like Wow, like on TV. My whole family was in the business. The streets are rough and it's worse for women, but I need the excitement.

Managing Loss: Intervening Conditions

A number of conditions served to intervene to facilitate or constrain actions taken by women to manage loss. Most women related a history of multiple losses throughout life. These crisis periods appeared to affect drug-taking behaviors, and the escalation of drug use precipitated further losses. Loss of relationships was ongoing in the lives of participants. As adults, women experienced failed relationships and continued physical, sexual, and emotional abuse. Jealousy and inability to trust a partner were cited as common problems leading to the failure of relationships. Increased drug use by one or both partners developed as a means of dealing with problems. Violence and abuse ensued under the influence of drugs. Loss of control over drugs usually resulted in loss of child custody. Ongoing loss was described by Julie, a 40-year-old heroin user:

> When I was 18, mom died. She was a woman among women, very religious. I ran from reality. I had no one. My older brother is gay. Never see him; never knew my father. I loved

my daughter's daddy. He left after she was born. HRS took her away when she was a baby. She grown now, and I've not seen her since she's adopted. It still hurts. What can I do?

Anger accompanied guilt and especially was noted by women reporting multiple losses. Tina stated,

Mom left me with my father when I was five . . . . He beat me when he was drinkin'. . . . When I was 10 he tied me to bed and raped me . . . . Left home when I was 14, started hustlin', went on the streets. Never want a man; don't trust women. I loved my brother but I don't wanna' see him lookin' like this. Had this boyfriend; he was a dope dealer . . . . Got shot in the head and killed . . . . Hurt for a day or two; better to be independent, stay by yourself . . . . This is my second baby. It's goin' for adoption, too.

Several women experienced the deaths of children. Others suffered multiple miscarriages. Women often lost control over drug use in the face of these events. Annie described the loss of her child and the subsequent changes in her drug use:

I used to do reefer 'till I lost my little girl. I had to forget. When she was 10 they called me to get her at school. She had a headache. Same night she took a convulsion and died. I got no hope, no control; stopped for 2 months in prison but went right back to crack.

Age and history of drug use appeared to be factors that influenced strategies women took to manage loss. Older (35 years or older), long-term users reported a desire to cut back on drug use. Several participants indicated that they reduced their use as they got older. Women spoke of feeling "tired" or "bored" and a need "to move on with life." A few older women acknowledged drugs were not helping them manage problems. Mary, a 40-year-old crack smoker, stated,

Sick and tired, I need a job. Crack don't help troubles. Brings back bad memories . . . . I pray a lot. Drugs make my problems worse.

Some older users stated a desire to quit using drugs, but they felt trapped, with no alternatives. The influence of old friends in the context of the drug scene and the lack of skills to find a job presented major obstacles. Maggie, a 41-year-old, stated,

I'm bored, I need to get off but I need something to do, need to get out, get some training. I know I'm screwed up . . . . I'm chained . . . . I'm tired.

The presence or absence of support in the lives of women was an important condition that intervened to facilitate or constrain drug-taking behaviors to manage loss in their lives. Often a lost person was the sole source of material and/or emotional support. Although there was a general lack of emotional support during childhood and adolescence, women stated that they sustained the abuse for fear of foster care or abandonment. Multiple losses influenced women's ability to accept or seek sources of emotional support. Some saw themselves as "loners" and "afraid to trust," that it is "better to be on one's own."

Women who maintained relationships with children or partners appeared less angry and rebellious. They experienced a number of losses, but structure, responsibility, and love in their lives helped them maintain a degree of control over drug use.

> Problems never really go away but ya get some escape. We use only at home, usually nights, weekends, when the kids are not around. I don't let drugs control me. I'm a smoker not a crack head. When drugs keep you broke and ya never satisfied, then ya know you got a problem. I cook, I clean, always have food in the house. We use money left over for drugs, and I get $30 from private tricks.

Women with a child to support and protect in spite of failed relationships with partners had some control over their drug use.

> My man took off—my boy's the only thing in life. Crack lifts the load off, but I never do it around my kid, usually on weekends. Most of my money I spend on my little boy—only use extra for crack.
>
>   He beat me to have sex. I was scared for the baby so I came here—started shootin' again—very controlled use. My daughter changed my priorities.

Women who suffered failed relationships with partners and had no children living with them reported that they progressed into heavy drug use following the loss. These losses often meant a loss of shelter or other material support as well as emotional support.

> Stayed off drugs for 4 years. He left and I couldn't take the stress. I'm back on. I went on the street after crack. Smoke as much as I can get.

In abusive relationships, women viewed the failure as a loss and often blamed themselves. Jenny described her desperate relationship prior to her homeless state:

> My man, he beat me. Eight times he beat me with the belt buckle. I tried to kill myself with Tylenol, didn't work. Started goin' to NA [Narcotics Anonymous]; he was jealous, he beat me again. Felt I deserved the abuse—he left—started hangin' out in the streets, started coke.

Loss of child custody and the opportunity to have a maternal relationship were devastating to women and resulted in an escalation of drug use. Women who had children placed with supportive relatives held out hope that someday they would get their lives together and regain custody. Older, long-term users often worried about older or sick guardians. Natasha, a 38-year-old with a 20-year history of poly-drug use, expressed her feelings this way:

> A strong mind is important. I need someone to talk to, make plans. Need to get life together, need to make the step. My kids are upset I'm on this stuff. I need to look out for 'em. Mom's diabetic, not able to do it much longer.

Women living on the street derived some emotional and material support from networks of friends in the drug scene. They sometimes shared food, drugs, and shelter. Having excess material goods to share provided them with a sense of power and some insurance for the return of favors when in need. For a few homeless women, friends on the street were viewed as the most important reason to stay on drugs.

> I need someone to treat me like a person. I want to keep my dignity; most programs don't care about that. Junkies give me more help but want me to stay on the s___.
>
>   I gotta' have my crowd. They're the most important. I'd miss them. Can't quit and give up my friends. No one to talk to at home.

Other homeless women were very mistrustful of others on the street and relied little on them to supply emotional or material support: "Hate men. Women are jealous. No support on the streets; they just wanna' see you die."

Health care and government agencies were viewed as unsupportive and were avoided if possible. Women who had been in residential or day care treatment programs generally found them unhelpful.

> I got into this treatment program. I felt like I was in the hot seat. They made me write down everything I do wrong. I left. I couldn't take it.
>
> I was sick in the hospital. There was too much criticism from the group. I hated that. I need a counselor, not a group.
>
> Been in six treatment programs; nothin' works. They say it's my attitude. They asked me to leave. No money, no cigarettes. Lots of restrictions and they give you a quiz on attitudes. Drug recovery is worse than jail, too many rules. They never give you a chance.

Some women received emotional support and support for their drug use from Alcoholics Anonymous (AA) or Narcotics Anonymous (NA). These agencies were viewed as "spiritual" and "nonjudgmental." Some attended without the intention of abstinence. Several women talked to clergy and read the Bible as a means of seeking spiritual support. Clarie and Martha found support through spiritual means.

> I started hangin' out on the streets; sometimes I talk to the minister at church. He tell me never to forget God. I read the 23rd Psalm every day. Go to NA. It's spiritual. I feel better about myself.
>
> I'm not a church goer but sometimes I talk to the priest. If I got someone to talk to, don't do as much.

Drug preference was another intervening condition in managing loss. Crack users usually used heavily and more frequently than heroin users. Crack highs only lasted a few minutes, and participants reported constantly trying to "recapture the high." All but one homeless woman primarily used crack. Most crack users acknowledged their strong dependency on the drug: "Can't help it, I gotta' have crack."

Women who shot heroin or speedballs reported more control over their use. The heroin high lasted longer. After an initial rush, woman reported a less intense pleasant sensation lasting several hours. Heroin users reported that they looked down on crack smokers and stayed away from the drug:

> I'm not an abuser, I'm a regular user. Heroin preserves the body. You eat well and you sleep well. Woman loses pride on crack.
>
> I'm not an addict. I'm a controlled user. Rock heads scare me to death. Heroin users can use casual, more responsible, in control.
>
> Heroin users never use crack. We look down on crack heads . . . . I tried rock once. The rush was frightening. Never mess with it again.

Managing Loss: Strategies

Getting high was the main strategy women used to deal with loss. Experimentation with drugs at an early age provided an easy escape from unhappy childhood experiences; it provided excitement and "acceptance by the crowd." Regular patterns of drug use or heavy drug use followed in response to past and ongoing loss.

Regular drug use involved establishing a stable pattern of drug use, usually using drugs three or four times a week or, in some cases, on weekends only. Regular use was characterized by a definite preference for a particular drug or group of drugs. During this phase of use, women described having "control over drugs" or being a "responsible user." Regular users described using drugs to "escape pressure" or "feel excitement." Drug use occurred in the company of a partner or friend who was a regular user and took place after chores were completed and children were in bed or out of sight.

Heavy drug use was characterized by making drug use the central focus of one's life. Participants described "living to use." Although some users maintained a stable pattern of regular use over many years, others progressed into using drugs several times a day after a short period of experimentation. Heavy use usually occurred after leaving home, living on the streets, or entering a partnership with a heavy user.

The high feeling was greatly influenced by drug preference. Heroin users described the high as "floating on air" and being "filled with energy" and that it "helps [them] blow off pressure." Crack smokers described "excitement" and feelings of "power" but described feeling "paranoid" and "jumpy" after the brief high. Others described being bored or depressed following prolonged use. Jenny, a daily crack smoker, said,

> I can't sleep when I'm based up. Sometimes I get bored and depressed. Don't like to feel paranoid. I feel sad, I cry.

Women stated that feeling high was a way to escape problems or bad memories. It helped them "think things out" and "stay in control." It made "problems go away." Without drugs, life was viewed as "too painful," with "too many bad memories." Highs provided an escape, but only temporarily. Crack users reported feeling tired, but as one participant noted, "Getting off—the risk is too painful." Anna described her dilemma:

> You forget your problems for 5 or 10 minutes, then they come back, so I keep basin'. I gotta' get that high, I live to use, I use to live. The good Lord will probably take me before I get off.

Getting high served to help women deal with their painful feelings of loss, but a number of other strategies were employed by women in order to survive within the drug scene and maintain their habit. These self-care strategies were often greatly influenced by the number of losses suffered, the amount of support present in women's lives, the degree of trust women held in seeking support, and how heavily women relied on drugs to manage painful feelings.

Gaining control involved learning a number of street survival skills, such as networking for drugs, food, and shelter; learning how to support oneself through the sex trade or shoplifting; protecting self from harm and violence; and taking drugs effectively. These behaviors were most characteristic of women who were very heavy users, had little or no family structure in their lives, lived by their own rules, and often were homeless. They suffered multiple losses in their lives and had little support, except what they chose to look for on the streets. They described themselves as "rebellious"; drugs helped them "control life." Nina, a 25-year-old daily crack smoker who lived under a bridge, stated,

> I need to do what I want to do. I need to be in control. I feel better and happy when I'm high. Drugs give me control. I've been hurt too many times. I've learned from the streets—don't trust anyone, protect yourself. Sometimes I get down and depressed. There's always a lot a people to talk to, but I know they don't care. I gotta' care for me.

Women living in relationships with men relied more on a partner to obtain drugs and food. They perceived themselves as less rebellious and independent than women who described themselves as "loners."

> Now I keep the faith. Got a boyfriend and apartment. He works and buys our dope for the weekends. Sometimes I worry I'll slip back—regained myself—don't have that rebellious attitude anymore.

Women living with dependent children and without partners frequently supplemented their income through prostitution to provide a better life for themselves and their children. They spoke about the influence of children on "taking care of self."

> My child is all I got. When I started to trick on the streets I'd get high and forget to use rubbers—sold everything—no food—lost weight. Now I'm more responsible.

Women who stated that they felt in control of their drug use engaged in more physical self-care activities than heavy users. Helene, a 38-year-old weekend crack smoker, stated,

> I love my body. Most women don't care. I got no sores and I always use a condom. I see how other women look bad. A strong mind is important.

Margie, a 22-year-old heavy crack smoker, related her desperate state:

> Many nights there's no sleep. Ya don't wanna' eat. I lost a lotta' weight. I'm scared of AIDS. Most of the time I use a rubber with my new dates, never with regulars. I lost my dignity; I don't care anymore. I pray I die from dope before the virus.

Heavy crack users looked frail and thin. Several had open sores on their faces and extremities. Many said they would have unprotected sex with men who objected to condom use as long as they received drugs or money. Often women did not take time to wash themselves between clients. Injection users appeared quite knowledgeable about cleaning needles and works but sometimes neglected to do so under the influence of the high. Injection drug users and the few crack users who reported controlled use appeared well nourished and in better health than heavy crack users.

Protection of self from danger involved a number of strategies. Strategies included a safe environment to get high, checking out dates, and carrying a weapon. Several women felt safer doing drugs in crack houses or shooting galleries where a "house man" or guard acted as lookout and offered some protection from violence or arrest. Other women felt safer alone or with friends or partners. Regular johns or clients who were serviced often were considered the safest protection against violence and AIDS. Potential new clients for sex were checked out. Generally, if they "looked respectable" or "walked and talked right," they were considered acceptable. A few women stated that they carried guns for protection against possible violence from unfamiliar clients.

Women sought help for physical ailments from health care officials only in times of emergency, such as drug overdoses, broken bones, or serious wounds. Women mistrusted health professionals. A few had obtained some medical care for sores at a local shelter. One pregnant woman received some prenatal care in advanced pregnancy from the same shelter. In most situations, women said that they entered drug recovery programs to reclaim custody of children and were often "forced" into recovery by a family member, social service worker, or while incarcerated.

Prayer was used by a number of women to feel better about themselves and for protection against harm.

> I pray a lot and hope the good Lord will help me. Mom is a minister—I can't talk to her. Read the psalms and proverbs. It say we all come through sin. I'm OK even if I use drugs. Sometimes, no sleep. I know I'm bad. Sundays I go to church, like to sing, pray, never use rock on Sunday.

Managing Loss: Consequences

The consequences of drug use as a strategy to manage loss depended on the degree that women relied on this strategy to dull painful feelings. Women drifted in and out of control over drug use to deal with loss throughout their lifetimes. Although drugs gave them a sense of control over life, their drug use was often out of control. Heavy users with little support and structure in their lives encountered ongoing loss as a result of their drug use. All of these women had lost custody of their children. Most were homeless. Most were crack cocaine smokers. They encountered ongoing violent experiences as a result of trading sex for drugs and/or at the hands of violent partners. They could not think of a future without drugs; several stated that they would probably die from drugs or AIDS. Physical, sexual, and emotional abuse as a consequence of drug use represented further loss in their lives and perpetuated further drug taking to manage resulting pain. Jackie, a 27-year-old woman, related how she ended up with a colostomy:

> One night last year I was with this joker and we went to a motel. He fell asleep after we smoked some crack and had sex. I had to go, so I took some money from his pocket. He came downstairs after me wid [sic] his pistol and shoot me in the stomach. They say I can have it put back normal. I need some money, so I'm hustling.

Some women who had lost control over drugs managed to regain control when they entered a relationship. Liz stated,

> Was homeless—doin' coke everyday for 9 years. Love is important—we don't do much—better since I'm off the street.

While in control, drugs provided a temporary escape from pain, and women were optimistic about the future. They talked about "getting a job," "regaining custody of children," "finding a man for the future," or "making a future without drugs." Older women with a long history of drug use, particularly heroin, stated that they were "in control" or had "cut back." While in control, women took better care of themselves and took fewer risks on the street when engaged in prostitution. They appeared to manage loss through drugs with less physical harm than heavy users.

Summary of Findings

Figure 19–1 summarizes the conceptual relationships revealed using grounded theory analysis. Causal conditions that gave rise to managing loss included losses resulting from childhood abuse, early deaths of parents or significant others, parental desertion, and parental

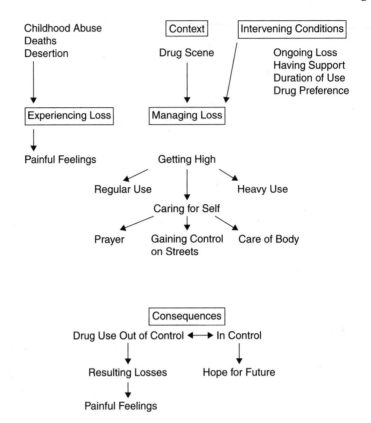

FIGURE 19–1   The Process of Managing Loss

rejection. In turn, these events gave rise to painful feelings of guilt, shame, anger, self-hate, hopelessness, and depression.

In the context of the drug scene, women experimented with a variety of drugs, which were readily available in inner-city neighborhoods. Street life provided excitement and an escape from a depressing life at home. Getting high was the major strategy used to ease painful feelings of loss. Women drifted into regular or heavy drug use within the context of the drug scene. Drug use was mediated by a number of intervening conditions. These conditions included ongoing experiences of loss, the presence or absence of support, age, duration of drug use, and women's drug preference. These conditions also influenced self-care strategies that women took to survive and live within the drug scene. Women who had suffered multiple losses placed little trust in others and developed an independent attitude. Drugs helped them to "control life," and they learned to "gain control" on the streets.

The degree of drug dependence and drug preference greatly affected how well women engaged in bodily care. Crack cocaine smokers generally used heavily, engaged in minimal bodily care, and took high risks when trading sex for drugs or money. They ate and slept poorly due to the biochemical effects of the drug and a need to recapture the brief high. Heroin users and women who smoked crack occasionally during weekends appeared in better physical health than heavy crack smokers. In general, women mistrusted health care professionals and avoided seeking help whenever possible.

Prayer was an important strategy used by many women. God was a nonjudgmental force that helped women feel better about themselves and deal with guilt feelings surrounding drug use. Women prayed for God's protection.

The consequences of using drugs to deal with painful feelings of loss depended on how much control women had over their drug use. The degree of control over drug use appeared very much affected by intervening conditions, particularly the presence or absence of support and ongoing loss in women's lives. Women described periods of slipping in and out of control over drugs. When out of control, heavy drug use precipitated further losses. Women suffered the loss of children and physical and sexual abuse as a result of trading sex for drugs, and they endured further guilt and psychic pain as a result. Drug use escalated. They expressed hopelessness and felt that they would probably die from drugs or AIDS. When drug use was in control, women felt that they could use drugs on a regular basis, and they usually had some form of love and support in their lives. There was hope for the future. When relationships and supports failed, the cycle of managing loss was reactivated.

DISCUSSION

The findings of this study confirm and extend the findings of a number of earlier studies. However, this grounded theory analysis resulted in a comprehensive model that links together many important concepts in the process of experiencing loss and subsequent drug use as a strategy that women use to manage loss. Women in this study relied heavily on drugs as a self-medication strategy to dull painful feelings resulting from trauma, especially physical and sexual abuse. These findings have been noted by a number of researchers (Boyd, 1993; Dembo et al., 1988; Wallace, 1990; Woodhouse, 1992).

Multiple trauma, including death of a loved one, loss of child custody, and physical and sexual abuse, has been documented to occur before and after the onset of crack use among women (Fullilove et al., 1992). Studying dysfunctional families of crack users, Wallace (1990) describes parental alcoholism, parental death, and childhood separation from parents as painful losses, and actual or feared loss of partners later in life reactivated childhood pain. Early childhood abuse also has been related to later partner abuse among women in methadone treatment (Gilbert, El-Bassel, Schilling, & Friedman, 1997). These losses were evidenced by women in this study, and they resulted in an increased reliance on drugs.

Participants acknowledged that experiences of loss left them with very painful feelings at an early age. Still, women had difficulty relating first drug use to a particular early experience of loss. Women described experimentation with drugs as a positive experience. Drugs provided excitement, a way to "blow off" pressures at home, a means of rebellion against strict home rules, and a way to gain acceptance from friends. These findings mirror those of Rosenbaum's (1981) earlier study of women entering the fast life of heroin in the ghetto, where drugs were common place and home life was oppressive.

The concepts of deviance and self-esteem may be important in the process of getting started on drugs. Participants in this study reported being labeled as "bad" and feeling rejected. The earlier work of Kaplan (1980) resulted in the hypothesis that early physical abuse and early sexual abuse are mutually related and are mediated by self-derogation, resulting in loss of self-esteem. According to this theory, drug use decreases feelings of self-derogation, and self-esteem may increase through membership in a deviant social group. Peer group acceptance was noted to be important for these women during experimentation and helped them feel better about themselves.

Women often reported feeling especially rejected at home during childhood and attributed their rejection to being unable to follow rules. Siblings who followed the rules received less abuse and punishment. Several women recalled that many of these "favored" siblings went on to live the "straight life" without drugs. Women could not explain why they had difficulty following rules, except that they felt angry and that they were treated unfairly as children. The issue of why some siblings growing up within the same family and environment avoided drug use, whereas others used drugs, requires further explanation.

The etiology of first drug use appears to be related to a number of complex conditions. Many participants in this study suffered physical and sexual abuse during childhood. However, the impact of emotional abuse and feelings of victimization during childhood on early drug use by women who did not sustain childhood physical and sexual abuse needs further investigation.

One of the most important findings of this study was the influence of support, structure, and love in helping women gain control over their drug use in the face of ongoing losses. These factors appeared to be highly influential in helping some women regulate their use of highly addictive crack cocaine, supporting the notion that controlled use of this drug may be possible under some circumstances (Fagan & Chin, 1989). Most of the injection drug users primarily injected heroin less than once a day. All of these women had custody of children and/or were in a relationship. However, age may be a factor in that the injection users were older than crack smokers and reported that they had managed to cut back over the years and learned to control use. The history of losses was similar among crack and injection users. Most heroin users reported heavy use of heroin or other drugs earlier in life. These findings have implications for interventions in helping women maintain support in their lives, control their drug use, and take better care of themselves.

IMPLICATIONS

The findings reveal a number of implications that might assist women who are currently using drugs and women in treatment. Health care professionals traditionally believe that interventions with drug users must have the goal of abstinence. However, there appears to be an urgent need to develop and test interventions aimed toward reducing drug-related harm among women unable or unwilling to stop using drugs, particularly heavy users who are in poor physical health. Trading sex for drugs and unsafe needle practices have implications not only for users but for society at large. Harm reduction programs, including needle exchange and education programs, are vigorously being implemented in Canada and some parts of Europe in recent years (O'Hare, 1992). Beyond these measures, inner-city women need opportunities to talk about their emotional pain, learn advocacy skills for dealing with health care and social service workers, and receive support in helping them to control or stop the use of drugs. Special support is needed in times of pregnancy, loss of child custody, family violence, crisis, and grief. The ability to maintain a home life and retain child custody greatly affected women's drug use behaviors and self-care. The large number of participants' children being raised in foster care or by relatives reflects loss of homes and the disruption of bonding between mothers and children. These children are suffering loss and are at risk to be among the next generation of drug users. Interventions to reduce the impact of loss on this generation require further study.

The loss of ability to trust professionals was an enormous concern for women and should be an important consideration in developing programs aimed toward harm reduction or abstinence. Health care and social service workers need to be sensitive to and educated about the special conditions that affect women's drug-use behaviors. Community-based efforts building on established, trusted resources such as the church may have merit for some inner-city women.

Spiritual support and prayer were important resources used by many women to help them deal with pain resulting from drug use. NA and AA were viewed as nonjudgmental programs. Spirituality may be a dimension that should be considered in other models of drug treatment. Hutchinson (1987) notes the importance of prayer among a group of chemically dependent nurses throughout their process of recovery.

Failure of drug recovery programs for women was evident in the data. Women committed to abstinence require particular attention to sex-related issues, such as codependency and abuse within partnerships. They need help in understanding how childhood violent experiences may affect future relationships. Assessment of support systems in lives of women and other intervening conditions that influence drug-using behavior appear important for helping women explore alternate ways to manage painful feelings of loss. Of particular importance to women in the inner city is the ever-present drug scene, relationships within the environment, and the lack of opportunities to move beyond this environment. Prevention and intervention strategies clearly need to address these issues.

The model describing the process of managing loss provides an inductive approach to understanding the meaning as well as the function of drug use for women using drugs within the context of an inner-city environment. Few differences were found between women who smoke crack, women who inject heroin, and women who use cocaine in terms of the meaning and function of drugs in their lives. The model may be useful in practice, especially in helping women to assess the impact of loss in their lives, but it requires testing with other populations of women using a variety of drugs within different cultural contexts.

ACKNOWLEDGMENTS

The author wishes to acknowledge the assistance of her dissertation chair Dr. P. Clunn and committee members Dr. G. Labadie, Dr. D. Ugarriza, Dr. R. Donahue (School of Nursing, University of Miami), and Dr. J. B. Page (Department of Psychiatry, University of Miami), as well as Dr. Janice Hayes. This research was completed with the assistance of a predoctoral fellowship in Transcultural Nursing, University of Miami, and a Canadian Nurses' Foundation Scholarship for Doctoral Study.

REFERENCES

ABBOTT, A. (1994). A feminist approach to substance abuse treatment and service delivery. *Social Work in Health Care, 19,* 67–83.

ANDERSON, J. (1991). Current directions in nursing research: Toward a post-structuralist and feminist epistemology. *Canadian Journal of Nursing Research, 23,* 1–3.

BLUME, S. B. (1990). Chemical dependency in women: Important issues. *American Journal of Drug and Alcohol Abuse, 16,* 297–307.

BOUKNIGHT, L. G. (1990). The public health consequences of crack cocaine. *New York State Journal of Medicine, 90,* 493–495.

BOYD, C. J. (1993). The antecedents of women's crack cocaine abuse: Family substance abuse, sexual abuse, depression and illicit drug use. *Journal of Substance Abuse Treatment, 10,* 433–438.

CRYSTAL, S. (1992). Health-care barriers and utilization patterns among intravenous drug users with HIV disease. *AIDS & Public Policy Journal, 7,* 187–197.

DEMBO, R., WILLIAMS, L., WISH, E., DERTKE, M., BERRY, E., GERTREU, A., & WASHBURN, M. (1988). The relationship between physical and sexual abuse and illicit drug use: A replication among a new sample of youths entering a juvenile detention center. *International Journal of the Addictions, 23,* 1101–1123.

DOWEIKO, H. (1990). *Concepts of chemical dependency.* Pacific Grove. CA: Brooks/Cole.

DREHER, M. (1984). Marijuana use among women: An anthropological view. In J. H. Lowenson & B. Stimmel (Eds.), *Conceptual issues in alcoholism and substance abuse* (pp. 51–63). New York: Hawthorne.

FAGAN, J., & CHIN, K. L. (1989). Initiation into crack and cocaine: A tale of two epidemics. *Contemporary Drug Problems, 16,* 579–617.

FULLILOVE, M., LOWN, A., & FULLILOVE, R. E. (1992). Crack hos and skeezers: Traumatic experiences of women crack users. *Journal of Sex Research, 29,* 275–287.

GILBERT, L., EL-BASSEL, N., SCHILLING, R., & FRIEDMAN, E. (1997). Childhood abuse as a risk for partner abuse among women in methadone maintenance. *American Journal of Drug and Alcohol Abuse, 23,* 581–595.

GOLD, S. R. (1980). The CAP control theory of drug abuse. In P. J. Letter, M. Sayers, & H. W. Pearson (Eds.), *Theories on drug abuse: Selected contemporary prospective* (pp. 8–11). Rockville, MD: National Institute on Drug Abuse.

HARDING, S. (1987). Is there a feminist method? In S. Harding (Ed.), *Feminism and methodology* (pp. 1–13). Bloomington, IN: Open University Press.

HARRISON, P. A. (1989). Women in treatment: Changing over time. *International Journal of the Addictions, 24,* 665–673.

HUTCHINSON, S. (1986). Chemically dependent nurses: The trajectory toward self-annihilation. *Nursing Research, 35,* 196–201.

HUTCHINSON, S. (1987). Toward self-integration: The recovering process of chemically dependent nurses. *Nursing Research, 36,* 339–343.

INCIARDI, J., POTTIEGER, A., FORNEY, M., CHITWOOD, D., & MCBRIDE, D. (1991). Prostitution, I.V. drug use and sex for crack exchanges among serious delinquents: Risks for HIV infection. *Criminology, 29,* 221–235.

LADWIG, G. B., & ANDERSEN, M. D. (1989). Substance abuse in women: Relationship between chemical dependency of women and past reports of physical and/or sexual abuse. *International Journal of the Addictions, 24,* 739–754.

LEX, B. (1991). Some gender differences in alcohol and polysubstance users. *Health Psychology, 10,* 121–132.

MORSE, J., & FIELD, P. (1995). *Qualitative research methods for health professionals* (2nd ed.). Thousand Oaks, CA: Sage.

O'HARE, P. A. (1992). The reduction of drug related harm. In P. A. O'Hare, R. Newcombe, A. Matthews, E. C. Bunning, & E. Drucker (Eds.), *The reduction of drug related harm* (pp. 1–14). London: Routledge.

PURSLEY-CROTTEAU, S., & STERN, P. N. (1996). Creating a new life: Dimensions of temperance in perinatal crack users. *Qualitative Health Research, 6,* 350–367.

ROSENBAUM, M. (1981). *Women on heroin.* New Brunswick, NJ: Rutgers University Press.

SHILLING, R. F., EL-BASSEL, N., GILBERT, L., & SCHINKE, S. P. (1991). Correlates of drug use, sexual behavior, and attitudes towards safer sex among African American and Hispanic women in methadone maintenance. *Journal of Drug Issues, 21,* 685–698.

STIMMEL, B. (1984). The role of ethnography in alcohol and substance abuse: The nature verses nurture controversy. *Advances in Alcohol and Substances Abuse, 11,* 19–33.

STRAUSS, A., & CORBIN, J. (1990). *Basis of qualitative research: Grounded theory procedures and techniques.* Newbury Park, CA: Sage.

TAYLOR, A. (1993). *Women drug users: An ethnography of a female injecting community.* Oxford, UK: Clarendon.

WACHTLER, S. (1990). *The state of the judiciary, 1990.* New York: Unified Court System.

WALLACE, B. (1990). Crack cocaine smokers as adult children of alcoholics: The dysfunctional family link. *Journal of Substance Abuse Treatment, 7,* 89–100.

WOODHOUSE, L. (1992). Women with jagged edges: Voices from a culture of substance abuse. *Qualitative Health Research, 2,* 262–281.

20

Improving Substance Abuse Service Delivery to Hispanic Women Through Increased Cultural Competencies

A Qualitative Study

Terry S. Trepper
Purdue University Calumet, Hammond, IN

Thorana S. Nelson
Utah State University, Logan, UT

Eric E. McCollum
Virginia Tech University at Falls Church, Falls Church, VA

Philip McAvoy
Terros, Inc., Phoenix, AZ

INTRODUCTION

Hispanic people face many issues associated with ethnic minority status in the US, including poverty, discrimination, barriers to education and employment, and drug abuse. Particularly germane to many Chicanos is the issue of illegal residence in this country, whereas

Reprinted from *Journal of Substance Abuse Treatment,* vol. 14(2), Terry S. Trepper, Thorana S. Nelson, Eric E. McCollum, and Philip McAvoy, "Improving Substance Abuse Service Delivery to Hispanic Women Through Increased Cultural Competencies: A Qualitative Study," pp. 225–234. Copyright 1997, with permission from Elsevier.

other Hispanic people face the effects of immigration, which separates them from many important resources left behind in their native countries including family, property, and culture. How issues of loss and migration are dealt with is an important facet of drug and mental health services.

Little has been reported about the unique characteristics of substance-abusing Hispanic women, in part because little has been reported about substance-abusing women in general. Most of the needs assessments, treatment models, research and follow-up projects on substance abuse focus on men—the paths that men take in their substance abuse careers, the costs to society of their substance abuse and associated behaviors (e.g., criminal acts to support drug use), and their treatment needs. Such male-oriented models do not fit women who have different "career" paths both into and out of substance abuse and different needs while in treatment. In contrast to men, women are typically more relationally oriented and their relationships, especially with male partners, exert a strong influence on their drug use (e.g., Anglin, Booth, Kao, Harlow, & Peters, 1987; Gomberg, 1993; Williams & Klerman, 1984; Wilsnack, Wilsnack, & Klassen, 1984). Substance-abusing women are more likely to be involved with substance-abusing partners than are male substance abusers. This is especially so for Hispanic women, whose self-worth is often dependent upon relationships with men. In addition, many opiate-abusing women actually begin their substance abuse careers in relationship to men (Anglin et al., 1987). One response of an Hispanic woman to her man's drug use may be to follow him into the abuse as a way of being "supportive." Although men are generally seen as undependable and not to be trusted by Hispanic women, they still serve as important sources of support and self-worth (Espin, 1985). In addition, Hispanic women tend to have children at very young ages and are discouraged from working outside the home. They are encouraged instead to focus their attention on their families and preserve their relationships with men. Even single mothers are discouraged from working and find less formal relationships with men essential to support themselves and their children.

To competently provide mental health services to all groups in society, cultural differences must be understood (McGoldrick, Pearce, & Giordano, 1985). This is especially so for ethnic minorities who are disempowered in many ways. For Hispanic women, barriers to treatment include issues relevant for all women as well as some that are unique for them. It is important, however, that issues of culture be neither exaggerated nor underplayed. Hardy (1990) discusses the "Theoretical Myth of Sameness" whereby it is too easy for therapists to assume that all families are alike. He cautions that norms which fit white, middle-class families are not appropriate when working with ethnic minorities and may be unfairly used to diagnose members of these groups as pathological or as coming from dysfunctional families when certain behaviors are the norm and are healthy for these groups. For example, many Latino families appear to Anglo therapists to be "enmeshed" with "indulgent, overprotective" mothers and "weak, absent" fathers. Although Latino families are typically involved with extended and nuclear family members to a degree that would make many New England Yankees cringe with discomfort, this does not mean that substance abuse is caused or maintained such family structures. We must look to other sociological and personal factors as explanations.

In the process of attending to cultural differences, we must not assume that all Hispanic people have similar cultural and behavioral values, based simply on ethnic background. To understand a particular individual, many factors obtain, including their legal status; socioeconomic level; education; employment history and status; migration and acculturation experience; perspectives on discrimination and racism; their relationship to their own culture and subculture; connectedness to their culture of heritage and ability to access its resources; and personal and familial values and beliefs. For example, there may be marked differences between a mother who sees herself as a "Mexican in America" and her daughter who sees herself an "American of Mexican descent" (Karrer, 1990). The issues between these two women may be very different if one has assimilated into an identity as an American whose first language is English while the other thinks of herself as Mexican and may speak English poorly, if at all.

A major criticism of mental health and substance abuse treatment for women is its lack of sensitivity to the unique needs of women. Some of these needs are instrumental— for example, dependable childcare so a woman is not forced to leave her children with former drug-using friends as she establishes her own sobriety, and safe transportation so she is not dependent on a drug-using or drug-dealing male partner to remember and be willing to take her to treatment appointments. Other needs concern how women, and their problems, are seen. In the past, women have been seen as "sicker" than men, less motivated and harder to treat, and more deviant sexually and otherwise. More recently, we are coming to understand that women's perspectives on drug use are different, that women are less likely to admit problems and use denial as a defense, require less focus on dire consequences to motivate them for treatment, and are victims of a double standard that sees a woman who uses drugs as somehow "worse" than a man who does. Women often support their drug habits and provide for the needs of their children and themselves through prostitution and informally trading sex for favors, drugs, or money. Such behavior, not observed in men, has earned them many unflattering labels.

The issues faced by all women who seek drug treatment are compounded for Hispanic women. Their culture's view of women as primarily mothers leads to less tolerance of drug use or promiscuity. In addition, the notion that taking problems outside the family is shameful makes seeking treatment harder, as does the idea that a man's machismo requires him to be protective and chivalrous toward women but does not allow women to suggest that a man is not fulfilling his role even through the act of seeking outside help. Sadly, then, substance-abusing Hispanic women are multiply jeopardized in their communities and in treatment: their lower status as women, as Hispanics, as substance abusers, and as seeking treatment places them at risk for great loss of feelings of self-worth and potential loss of support by family and other primary groups.

The literature provides us with a long list of things we must do to be sensitive to the needs of ethnic minority women in drug treatment. These things include: 1) providing competent childcare; 2) making arrangements for transportation; 3) providing bilingual treatment providers and agency staff; 4) understanding that each client has unique needs; 5) having a belief that "minority" includes strengths; 6) resources as well as needs and oppression issues; 7) having an openness to inclusion of guidance from extended family rather than encouragement to separate from an "overinvolved" or "enmeshed" system; 8) cultivating an awareness of potential patterns of coercion in the family; 9) understanding a woman's relational needs and difficulties in developing independence or interdependence with her partner; 10) understanding the typical multiple losses over several generations evident in the genograms and histories of Hispanic women; 11) understanding that acculturation and assimilation issues vary greatly within as well as between families; 12) developing an awareness of personal and treatment biases that may or may not be appropriate; 13) being careful not to individually pathologize women for what many are seeing as a social problem;

14) taking care that "cultural sensitivity" does not serve to reinforce the status quo and stereotypic sex roles (especially increased dependency); 15) being willing to see a woman's difficulties in beginning treatment, remaining in treatment, and maintaining sobriety at face value rather than as signs of denial or treatment resistance (Espin, 1987; Flores-Ortiz & Bernal, 1990; Hardy, 1990; Montalvo & Gutierrez, 1990; Saba, Karrer, & Hardy, 1990; Vega, 1992). Valuable as these directives are, they remain general in nature, and do not provide us with specific ideas about the needs of Hispanic women. Clearly, then, much is needed in the way of research on how best we can help Latina groups. Hanson (1985) has called for research that asks specifically: 1) what are the special and/or unique needs for racial and ethnic minorities that currently are not being addressed, and 2) what works best for which group? Similarly, de la Rosa, Khalsa, and Rouse (1990) call for an investigation into the role of cultural values, acculturation stress, cultural and historical differences between groups, and of various support systems (families, the church, the judicial system, and peers) in the treatment of substance abuse issues. This study represents a beginning attempt to understand the clinical needs of Hispanic women substance abusers, and how cultural factors impact our clinical research and treatment designs. Because little empirical literature exists on the subject, the present study is exploratory in nature and a qualitative design was selected because the goal was not to test hypotheses but rather to generate them (LaRossa & Wolf, 1985). This study is part of a larger project, currently being conducted in Phoenix, Arizona, which is designed to test the efficacy of couples therapy for drug abusing women.

METHODS

Sample

Data were gathered from a criterion-based sample of eight Hispanic women, six of whom were drug abusing women enrolled in our treatment program, and two of whom were local therapists. Each of the drug abusing women met our larger study's inclusion criteria: 1) they had been using illicit drugs for at least 6 months; 2) were between the ages of 18 and 35, were married and/or in a committed relationship; and 3) their partners were willing to participate in assessment and therapy. In addition, those included in the qualitative study needed to identify themselves as being Hispanic and have completed or were near completion of the therapy phase of our program. Two therapists were selected because they identified themselves as being Hispanic, worked with many Hispanic drug-abusing women, and did not know the details or hypotheses of either our larger research project or the qualitative study. The goal of having this mix of research participants was to provide us access to a broad spectrum of treatment experiences and information. In this way, data from these two sources could converge in the formulation of our findings.

Procedures

This qualitative study used intensive interviews as the basis of data collection, and a variation of the analytic induction method of data analysis (described in Goetz & LeCompte, 1984). This method was selected because the goal of the study was to elicit and thematize the views of the women research participants about how Hispanic women can best be helped in drug and alcohol treatment. In addition to analytic induction, an iterative process was used to enrich the development of the themes. With this method, the first person was interviewed using the standard interview questions, and initial themes and concepts were gleaned. Next, the second subject was interviewed, first using the standard interview questions, then going back and relating the themes developed from the first interview. The second subject was asked to comment on, add to, revise, disagree with, or elaborate those themes. Based on the second subject's responses, the initial themes and concepts were refined and subsequently presented to the third subject. This process was repeated until all eight subjects had been interviewed. All interviews were conducted by the first and fourth author, and were audiotaped and transcribed.

The actual procedures consisted of seven distinct procedural phases: 1) *A list of guiding questions* was developed by the research team, which was designed to elicit open and frank discussion about the cultural variables under investigation; 2) *Initial phone interviews* were conducted to establish rapport, explain the general purpose of the qualitative study, and to establish that the subject met the criteria for selection; 3) *Intensive interviews,* lasting from 1 to 2 hours were conducted, with the interviewer taking notes of both thematic and behavioral observations; 4) *Preliminary data analysis* was conducted as the interviewer listened to the audio tape to gather initial impressions and develop beginning themes; 5) *Intensive interviews* were done with next subject, using the question list *and* the list of initial impressions and themes as the basis; 6) Steps 4 and 5 were repeated until the last subject was interviewed; 7) *Final data analyses* were carried out to verify and refine a set of final themes across all subjects.

Guiding Questions

The following served as guiding questions for the interviews. Although these questions were not necessarily asked of each subject directly, they formed the foundation for specific questions asked in each interview. As each guiding question was addressed, the interviewer probed further and further, until the subject repeated herself and/or no new data emerged. At that point, the interviewer would go on to a different guiding question, repeating the process until all guiding questions had been dealt with.

1. What cultural group do you most identify with? Why?
2. Are you bilingual? How important is Spanish in your life?
3. What are the general *values* of your cultural group that you think are the most important?
4. What is something that we should know about Hispanic families and couple relationships that may be different from Anglo families and couple relationships? How might these differences affect whether people go for therapy or not?
5. What is the first thing you see when you walk into a treatment center or agency that lets you know whether this agency understands the needs of Hispanic clients? What tells you if they don't? How do you know if you are welcome in a treatment center or agency? If you are not?
6. Can you describe instances in treatment centers or agencies when you have felt misunderstood from a cultural point of view? Are there certain things people

said or things they did? The way the treatment center or agency is set up or operated?

7. What advice would you give a treatment center director who wanted to start a new agency that would serve Hispanic clients? What could he or she do that would help Hispanic clients feel welcome and understood?

8. When you hear other Hispanic people talk about their experiences in treatment centers, what common themes come to mind?

9. Do you think Hispanic women may have different problems getting into and staying in therapy than Anglo women? If so, what are those things?

10. Was there anything about our programs that struck you as culturally sensitive or insensitive? What could we do to make them *more* sensitive to Hispanic culture?

11. What questions did we forget to ask that we should add to the list?

RESULTS

During the course of the data analysis, 11 distinct themes emerged. Themes were included only if they were addressed by at least five of the eight women, and then agreed upon by seven of the eight when requestioned. It should be noted that there was a surprising degree of agreement throughout, with most themes being spontaneously generated by each of the women.

Important of the Family

Without doubt, the most powerful theme to emerge for the women was the importance of family. The role of the family for Hispanics, according to the women, is different than for that of Anglos, and those differences need to be understood and taken into account in clinical program development. One woman described it this way:

> "For Anglos, families are seen as a hinderance. They are what make you 'sick.' For us, families are love and support; they are what makes you 'well.'"

Several dimensions of this large and important theme were noted and are described below.

Families Are Large and Extended

All of the women came from very large families. They were insistent that the concept of an "extended" family does not apply, because, "It is just all family to us." It is important to consider the role and impact of uncles and aunts, cousins, second cousins, etc., when assessing social support and doing family assessment. (Separated quotations are from different research participants.)

> "Our families are large. Comadres and compadres [godmothers and godfathers] are as important as uncles and aunts."
>> "There is a lot of interdependence on the whole family, and that is not just those that are blood related. A lot of people play into the decisions we make. There may be uncles, aunts, all

the cousins. It's important to consider what everyone thinks. There are the comadres, the extended family. My daughter calls my sister-in-laws 'aunt.'"

"A lot of this comes from the sheer size of families, so there is more support. For us, three generations are all very important."

"Cousins are like brothers and sisters. Sometimes all are living together. You should just think that someone is always living with the family."

Your Family Will Always Be There; You Will Not Be Abandoned

A powerful subtheme emerged which suggested that, for our women subjects, the family was almost an omnipotent force. For our drug abusers, this theme was particularly important. Drug abuse is considered so unacceptable in their families that there was always the lurking fear of abandonment. However, the overriding theme for them and their families seemed to be that no matter how bad, *even if you are a drug abuser,* your family is still your family.

"We get forgiveness and redemption, especially from the mothers. Fathers more easily 'disown,' but mothers usually not. "I'm your mother no matter what you do, I'll always be there, that's what they tell you."

"You can't tell a family with a drug abuser, 'Just kick her out,' or 'If they steal your jewelry you should call the police.' You've got to be kidding! That violates one of our basic beliefs, that your family is always there for you."

This subtheme also manifested with strong values surrounding the care and nurturance of family members, from birth to death.

"Children, no matter what type of problem, are always your children. They will always have a home."

"Grandparents do not go into nursing homes. You know someone is going to be living with you."

"Parents are never a burden! We expect them to live with us when they get old."

"It is a waste to try to get us to 'separate from the family.' We will not 'divorce' our family."

Family as the First and Primary Source of Counsel

Another important subtheme was that the family is generally *the* first and major source of support and advice, much more than outside institutions and agencies, which have so often replaced the family for Anglos.

If there is a problem, we all come together. When a family member is hurt or sick, they all go to take care. When someone has a mental problem, or is depressed or confused, we go to a relative. It seems different for Anglos. You go to psychologists.

Extreme Dependency

Some of the women were concerned that the strong cohesion experienced in most Hispanic families can lead to too much dependence, especially for women. They worried that, in the case of drug-abusing women, if they perceived their family as abandoning them, they would become overly dependent on their boyfriends, even if he too were drug abusing or abusive.

"This is different sometimes for drug-women. In my family there is nothing worse than a drug addict woman. It was a shame to the family. I wanted to be close to my family, but I thought they rejected me. So I got closer to my boyfriend, even though he hit me, and didn't want me to get off of drugs. I guess I just wanted that closeness I used to have with my family. I thought he was my family, but he really wasn't."

"There is a lot of dependence on each other. I think we are made to be co-dependent."

Religion and Rituals

Although most of the women reported that they were not especially religious, they all felt that religion plays an important part in the lives of Hispanic women and their families. They believed that much of their culture and customs were tied to religion. As they expressed it, Hispanics were generally quite spiritual, and this should be understood by therapists.

"It is easy for us to talk about God. You should talk about God more in therapy."

"Actually, it's more the rituals rather than the religion. You have your baptismal, first communion, confirmation, if you're a virgin your quincinera, then marriage. All of these are very important rituals for us."

Multiculturalism and Acculturation

Each of the women insisted that "Hispanic" means different things depending upon the country of origin a family is from. However, because seven of the eight women in our sample were of Mexican-American origin, it is not surprising that most expressed values and experiences that were quite similar. Most felt that language is a primary connector; that is, Spanish is a link to other Hispanics. Out of the eight women, all but three spoke Spanish with some fluency.

They also all stated that many of these basic values were dependent upon how acculturated they and their families were to Anglo culture. However, even though some of the women were third generation and clearly acculturated, it was surprising how little their themes varied. In other words, although the *said* acculturation was a significant force in the development of their values, it appeared that the Hispanic culture was still a powerful influence.

Almost all of the participants identified themselves as "Hispanic." One called herself "Chicana" first, and stated that that was a 'political statement' rather than a cultural identity. For example, she said:

'Mexican-American' different from 'Chicana.' Many women may consider Chicana an insult. "I'm Chicana and American, but not necessarily Mexican."

Only one said that she did not want to be identified as Hispanic.

"It's always better to be white. I'm not Hispanic, I'm half white."

One of the changes that has occurred with increased acculturation is that some of the basic family structures have, by necessity, changed. There are increasing numbers of single-parent households in this community, and for some, this occurs without family support because the family is in Mexico. This can be difficult for all people, but seems to be even more so for Hispanic women, whose culture of origin typically offers so much support.

"I moved here with my husband, but he died. My family were all back in Mexico. It was really hard. I wanted to move back, but I thought it better for my kids to be here. I was really confused. Luckily, my family started to move here, first my cousins then an uncle. Finally, I got my mother here. That really helped."

Hierarchy

There is a hierarchal structure present in Hispanic families, according to all our women. The hierarchy is the mediating force behind communication, problem solving, decision making, even self-esteem, and is seen as more rigid than in Anglo families. It usually is structured by age, but other factors, such as wealth, can come into play. Each of the women insisted therapists ought to learn as much as they can about the hierarchy of a client's family when counseling her.

"Grandparents can veto parents. An adult child becomes a surrogate parent, can take on the power."

"In our family, a comadre is almost as important as a grandmother or parent."

"In my family, my mother tells me how to raise my children."

"In our family, the elder son has the power, but he was 'given' it by my grandmother. He is the one who has the heavy stresses of making sure the bills get paid, protects the rest of the family. But again, I think he is really acting for my grandmother. He would never go against my grandmother."

The Illusion of a Patriarchy

An important subtheme emerged for almost all of the women, suggesting that their families acted as if the men in the family were in charge, when in actuality the women hold the "real power." This is not an unimportant observation, given that Hispanic families wish to appear to the outside to be patriarchal, and that illusion of a patriarchy is supported by the larger culture.

"The household was hers [mother]. My father brought home the paycheck, gave it to her, she bought everything. She controlled the money. She decided on trips, when and where we'd go."

"He was physically stronger. I don't know, though, I think mom 'let' him run the family."

"On the face, men are very important, but we don't need them. Behind the doors, its the women who make the decisions. But we put that front up, give him the illusion that he's the boss. We don't buy anything big without abuela [grandmother] approving. She will have to make the payments in case something happens to him."

You should not assume men have the power just because the family acts as if he has the power.

Respect for Elders

Another important subtheme related to hierarchy that continued to emerge was respect for elders. It seemed from our women that this was not merely a cultural ideal, but supported by both rituals and generalized behaviors.

"I'm 32 years old and still won't smoke in front of my mother."

"We would never call our mother a bad name, like Anglos do. We cannot believe your TV shows where the kids bad-mouth their parents, and the audiences scream with laughter and applaud."

"Older people have wisdom. We respect them"

"You cannot raise your voice to your mother, because you cannot be angry at your mother."

"You especially show respect in front of your mother or grandmother."

"My grandfather was very wise. We always listened to him."

Separation of the Sexes

Most of the women in the study pointed out there is a strong separation of the sexes, which occurs from childhood, continues throughout adulthood, then into marriage, and the rest of family life. This has led, they believe, to a situation where the two sexes don't communicate well, as well as a pronounced double-standard with regard to sexual behavior.

"There are things that women will just not communicate to men. For example, we would talk more in detail about somebody. Men would be uncomfortable talking about it in too much detail. I think women talk about people, men talk about things."

"Men can run around on their wives, and they put up with it. My mother put up with that for years, said as long as he came home to her, and she had her kids, that was OK. I thought I would never do that, but I did the same thing. It's funny."

"I was taught that men are just different. You should obey your husband, even put up with abuse."

"Women have to stay strong and in control. Men actually are allowed to show more emotion."

Loyalty to the Family of Origin

Most of the subjects suggested that for Hispanic women there was a stronger feeling of loyalty to their families of origin than to their husbands or partners. They felt this was a particularly important thing for therapists doing couples therapy to know.

"If I have a fight with my lover, I call my family."

"You don't show affection for spouse in front of your family, you know, parents, sisters and brother. That would seem weird."

"It sort of feels like dual loyalties. Loyalty to your family is greater than to your husband, I hate to say, but I think that is true. Your husband is family, but not blood."

"Your family will always be there. Not a husband necessarily, but your family will always be there."

Privacy and the Illusion of Happiness

These two concepts emerged as part of the same theme. Hispanic families were characterized by our women as solidly entrenched systems that were almost impermeable to the outside. The result is that members of the family are reluctant to share very much about the family to people from the outside, perceive experiences that Anglo families might consider public as secrets, and always maintain the illusion of happiness, both to the outside world and even to themselves.

"Even if I know my mother is wrong I would never say 'You're wrong,' in front of other people, to her yes, but never in front of others."

"We try to keep it within the family. Like I tell my kids, if anybody's gonna help you its gonna be your family, your friends will come and go but you'll always have your family"

"We won't bring up our own family problems."

"You won't really know when you are hurting our feelings. We don't complain when we are 'racially abused.' At least not to the ones who are doing the abusing. We keep our pain to ourselves."

Concomitant with the impermeable family boundaries and protection of privacy was the notion that Hispanic families would be unlikely to open up quickly in therapy.

"It is hard for us to go to therapy and open up. Men definitely don't want to go to therapy, no matter how bad the relationship or the troubles. It's better to get divorced rather than go to therapy."

"People in my [therapy] group think I don't have feelings, because I don't open up right away. I have a lot of feelings, I just can't say them right away to strangers. If this were my family, I could tell them my feelings, though."

"If you ask a couple a question, like about their sex life, they just won't tell you."

The Illusion of Happiness

A subtheme emerged which suggested that, at least as reported by the women in our sample, Hispanic families tend to present a "happy front" for others, even if they are experiencing significant problems of which everyone is aware.

"My mother and father goes out, and they could have been arguing all day, but they'd look nice to others, to look like everything is OK."

"The problem isn't just the therapy, it's letting others know you have problems."

"You never let anyone else know you are having problems. You put up a good front. Sometimes even to ourselves."

Problems Are Addressed by Your Own Family

A theme that logically follows from the previous ones, and was addressed by all of the women in our sample, was that problems should be dealt with by the family, not by outsiders. Personal problem solving is definitely seen as an important role of the family, and if a member "needs" to get outside help, the family is viewed as inadequate and not performing its duties.

"It's bad to go to therapy. You certainly don't go for 'small' problems."

"If you and your son aren't getting along, you should talk to the family about it, not go to a stranger."

"If you have trouble with your kids, send him to an aunt or uncle. Or you just hit him if you have to."

"'Why are you going to talk to this stranger?' (a family member might ask). 'You are going to tell family secrets.' You see, image is very important."

"We don't particularly want help from outsiders. Outsiders are seen as intruders. A family should take care of itself within the family."

"You just don't let the outside world know your business, and you really don't let them know your troubles."

"None of our family went for therapy. I'm the first one, and it caused a lot of shame."

> "You must be crazy if you are in therapy. You'd never go just for small problems. The family takes care of things like that. If someone really can't handle a child, for example, he is sent to another family, but you know, still in the family."

Good of the Social Group Over the Needs of the Individuals

The women in our study suggested that Hispanics are more group conscious than individually focused. They felt this was of critical importance when doing therapy with Hispanic women, because much of current psychotherapy offers the message, "Take care of yourself first."

> "Our own needs are secondary to needs of the family as a whole."
> "Don't talk about separateness or individuality. Remind them what they are doing is for the good of the family."
> "We are for the group, not for ourselves. Hispanics are not really 'rugged individuals' as much as for the family and community."
> "I think the Catholic Church may have contributed to this. There seems to be more of a thing in the Church for not looking at yourself but for others."
> "Anglo therapists might ask, 'Can't you think for yourself, make your own decisions?' That doesn't fit for our families."

Structure of Therapy

The women, many of them having been in various forms of therapy in the past, had some strong ideas about the nature and structure of therapy for Hispanic women. The following specific subthemes emerged:

Need Family Therapy

All thought that family therapy would be an essential component of any work with Hispanic women. They also had suggestions for eliciting the support of family members.

> "You should definitely do family therapy. There is nothing 'individual' about our culture."
> "We have strong communication links. What is the use of doing group therapy when you have a built-in group? We think Americans are a little bit lonely. We can call close friends or family; we don't need to call our therapists when we have a problem. It's like a support system. But if you do therapy, shouldn't you use that support system?"
> "You cannot attend to their emotional needs, because you are not their mother. You should get the help of her mother."
> "To get other family members into family therapy, you would have to work on those already in to get them in."
> "If I am coming to therapy, and I ask my abuela [grandmother] to come, she will come, because she cannot say no to her granddaughter."
> "One way to get them in, is that everything is for the kids. They will come in 'to help the kids.'"
> "To get family in therapy, must go to a 'leader' within the family. Could be anybody. In our family it is usually the oldest of the 'uncles.'"
> "Invite the family into therapy without pressure. 'Wouldn't you like to come to help your daughter?'"

Terms of Address and Hierarchical Respect

The women in the study believed that Anglos are too informal in their relationships compared with Hispanics. They asserted that the use of formal terms of address, particularly with older people, is essential.

> "Call them Mr. or Miss. Ask what they prefer."
> "You should never address an elderly person by their first name. Anglos do that all the time, but we see that as very disrespectful. It is always 'Sir' or 'Madam.'"
> "Have kids start talking first. Ask lots of questions about the children."
> "Get kids to talk first. We love our kids."
> "If a father is there, start with father."
> "You can also start with the father. He will probably tell you the good things about the family first. That is important, so let him tell you."

Do Not Expect Immediate Openness

One mistake Anglo therapists make, according to most of the women in the study, is to expect 'quick openness' about the problem, feelings, and goals.

> "Don't expect a lot of immediate opening up at the beginning. Take your time with the family."
> "You must respect our boundaries. Don't go so quick."

Finally, *other therapy issues* emerged that may affect the success of therapy with Hispanic women.

> "Be very careful about cross-sex issues. Much better to have same sex therapist, especially for women. Their family will accept and understand it more."
> "If there is food around, offer them some. Food is very important. once you have eaten with us, you will be more accepted. We do everything around food."
> "Take into account the length of time away from the family. Family will come first, then jobs, then therapy."
> "Don't talk about politics. This has historically been very dangerous for us, and we just don't talk politics with strangers."
> "We are not as 'task oriented'—Hispanics are more people oriented."

How Agencies Can be Inviting to Hispanic Women

The women all had opinions about what would make a treatment agency more inviting for Hispanic women. From those responses, four subthemes emerged.

A Homey, Informal Appearance

All felt that the appearance and feel of the agency would be more important to Hispanics than for Anglos.

> "It shouldn't look like a hospital or clinic. Should look like a home. Image should be relaxed, homey, cozy."
> "We want the place to be friendly, open, warm."
> "At clinics, have lots of art work. Maybe of Missions."

> "Be friendly, inviting, warm."
>
> "It is really important for the place to feel comfortable. I think we are more sensitive to that than Anglos. I don't know why."
>
> "You should have lots of artwork, we are very interested in art. Like posters which represent things from Mexico."

Respect

Many of the women recounted stories of agencies where they were not treated with respect by agency staff. They said that Hispanics were particularly sensitive about that, especially because they are a minority in this country.

> "Attitude is very important. They should act like they want to serve me. Say, 'Anything we can do for you?' Then smile."
>
> "There should be attentiveness from the time you walk in the door."
>
> "If you speak Spanish to us, use the *usted* form first."
>
> "Don't ask, 'Do you speak English.' Most of us do, and it is insulting to ask. Just assume we do and if we don't we'll tell you."
>
> "Serve me. Be kind. Look at me. 'Is there anything I can do to help you?' You'd be surprised how often people don't do that."

A Culturally Diverse Staff

The women also felt seeing Hispanic members of the agency staff was a sign that the agency was open to Hispanics.

> "You do not need a Spanish speaking therapist, since most of us speak English, but it does tell us that you care enough about us if there is one there."
>
> "You should have a mixture of staff, with some Hispanics."
>
> "You should have employees from different groups. They don't all have to be Mexican."
>
> "There should be signs in Spanish."

DISCUSSION

It is clear from the many comments made by our research participants that an understanding of Hispanic culture is essential to work successfully in therapy with Hispanic women. The themes that emerged from our interviews with these women led us to see two broad arenas wherein agencies must demonstrate their ability to understand and work within the cultural views of Hispanic clients. One arena has to do with the conduct of therapy itself, and the other involves broader aspects of agency atmosphere.

Therapy

Our participants' remarks about the importance of family in the life of Hispanic women suggest the importance of including the family in therapy. However, existing models of family therapy, especially those based on Anglo values of individuality, emotional distance, and the nuclear family as the unit of treatment, may be inadequate to the task of helping Hispanic women. As our participants remind us, Hispanics live in a different familial environment than do Anglos, an environment whose values and strengths therapists must come to understand and use in the service of helping their clients. This involves a willing-ness to apply family therapy approaches flexibly and to collaborate with clients in devel-oping a strategy that will work. Our participants hint at what some of the components of such an approach might be—respect for the family hierarchy, inclusion of extended family members, validation of the efforts of clients to work for the good of their families, and an appreciation of the strengths and competencies Hispanic families have. Therapists must bear in mind, however, that there is no one "Hispanic family," rather each family is unique in its experience and level of acculturation, and this uniqueness must be understood as well. To rigidly impose on clients a model of "the Hispanic family" would be equally as insen-sitive as imposing a Eurocentric model of what families should be like. Although not said directly by our participants, it is clear from their comments that our Hispanic clients have as much to teach us about how to work with them as we have to offer them about how to solve problems. The development of a truly collaborative viewpoint on the part of thera-pists seems foundational to the success of such efforts.

Agency

Therapy does not occur in a vacuum and one cannot hope to be culturally sensitive in one's office while working in an agency that does not support such views. Our participants have a number of suggestions for how agencies might communicate their wish to understand and accommodate Hispanic clients, beginning with what they find when they walk in the front door. Perhaps must important is the presence of Hispanic staff members. Nothing else can give such direct testimony to the efforts of an agency to work competently with Hispanic clients as a willingness to hire and work with Hispanic staff. As one of our participants noted, it may not be necessary that everyone on the staff be Hispanic or speak Spanish but it is reassuring to find some brown faces among the white ones. In addition, the agency must be committed to treating Hispanic clients in a way that is consonant with their cultural expectations. Even such seemingly small things as terms of address communicate power-fully. Further, some of the traditions of Eurocentric professional practice may need to be reconsidered. Providing coffee and pastry in the waiting room may not connote inappro-priate informality to Hispanic clients but may, instead, communicate an understanding of how people connect in Hispanic cultures.

Clearly, there are limitations to the conclusions drawn from this study. Although the small sample size prevents us from generalizing our findings in a statistical sense, the close agreement among participants about the themes that emerged suggests that the findings have some usefulness. Certainly our participants make clear that cultural differences must be considered as part of the delivery of treatment services. Further, our findings can be use-ful not as the "truth" about Hispanic families but as a set of questions that need to be con-sidered and discussed to work well with specific clients. For some clients, these questions will have great relevance whereas others may find them only tangentially representative of their experience, either way, the very act of considering such issues, rather than relying on a "one size fits all" approach to therapy, communicates the therapist's and the agency's ef-forts to work ably with Hispanic clients.

This study suggests a variety of other investigations that need to be undertaken. Given that the majority of our participants were Mexican-American, it is nuclear how well their perceptions and needs reflect those of Latino people from other backgrounds. The impact of stage of acculturation on use of and needs from mental health treatment programs also bears investigation. Finally, the themes that emerged from our conversations with our participants might well form the basis for a broader survey study of a diverse Hispanic community to ascertain how universal and generalizable they are.

Although the literature provides us with a number of ideas about how to be helpful to members of ethnic minorities in treatment, these ideas remain general and not empirically derived. Through their own words and experience, the participants in our study confirm a number of these ideas and cast them in the specific form helpful to Hispanic women. Their voices bear listening to if we are to successfully provide Hispanic women with the help we wish to offer.

ACKNOWLEDGMENT

This article was supported by a grant from the National Institute on Drug Abuse titled "Couples Therapy for Drug Abusing Women," R01 DA/MH 03702-4, Robert Lewis, Ph.D., Principal Investigator.

REFERENCES

AMARO, H., & RUSSO, N. F. (1987). Hispanic women and mental health. *Psychology of Women Quarterly,* 11, 393–407.

ANGLIN, M. D., BOOTH, M.W., KAO, C., HARLOW, L.L., & PETERES, K. (1987). Similarity of behavior within addict couples: II Addiction-related variables. *International Journal of the Addictions,* 22, 583–607.

DE LA ROSA, M.R., KHALSA, J.H., & ROUSE, B.A. (1990). Hispanics and illicit drug use: A review of recent findings. *The International Journal of the Addictions,* 25, 685–691.

ESPIN, O.M. (1985). Psychotherapy with Hispanic women: Some considerations. In P. Pedersen (Ed.), *Handbook of cross-cultural counseling and psychotherapy* (pp.165–171). Westport, CT: Greenwood Press.

FLORES-ORTIZ, Y., & BERNAL, G. (1990). Contextual family therapy of addiction with Latinos. In G. W. Saba, B.M. Karrer, & K. V. Hard (Eds.), *Minorities and family therapy* (pp. 123–141). New York: Haworth.

GOETZ, J. P., & LECOMPTE, M. D. (1984). *Ethnography and qualitative design in educational research.* San Diego, CA: Academic Press.

GOMBERG, E.S.L. (1993). Woman and alcohol: Use and abuse. *The Journal of Mental and Nervous Disease,* 181, 211–219.

HANSON, B. (1985). Drug treatment effectiveness: The case of racial and ethnic minorities in America—some research questions and proposals. *International Journal of the Addictions,* 20, 99–137.

HARDY, K.V. (1990). The theoretical myth of sameness: A critical issue in family therapy training and treatment. In G. W. Saba, B. M. Karrer, & K. V. Hardy (Eds.), *Minorities and family therapy* (pp. 17–33). New York: Hearth.

KARRER, B. M. (1990). The sound of two hands clapping: Cultural interactions of the minority family and the therapist. In G. W. Saba, B. M. Karrer, & K. V. Hardy (Eds.), *Minorities and family therapy* (pp. 209–237). New York: Hearth.

LAROSSA, R., & WOLF, J.H. (1985). On qualitative family research. *Journal of Marriage and the Family,* 47, 531–541.

MCGOLDRICK, M., PEARCE, J. K., & GIORDANO. J. (Eds.) (1982). *Ethnicity and family therapy.* New York: Guilford.

MONTALVO, B., & GUTIERREZ, M.J. (1990). Nine assumptions for work with ethnic minority families. In G.W. Saba, B.M. Karrer, & K.V. Hardy (Eds.). *Minorities and family therapy* (pp. 17–33). New York: Hearth.

SABA, G. W., KARRER, B. M., & HARDY, K. V. (1990). Introduction. In G. W. Saba, B. M. Karrer, & K. V. Hardy (Eds.), *Minorities and family therapy.* (pp. 1–15). New York: Hearth.

VEGA, W. A. (1992). Hispanic families in the 1980's: A decade of research. In A. S. Skolnick & J. H. Skolnick (Eds.), *Family in transition: Rethinking marriage, sexuality, child rearing, and family organization* (7th Ed.). New York: Harper Collins.

WILLIAMS, C. N., & KLERMAN, L. V. (1984). Female alcohol abuse: Its effects on the family. In S. C. Wilsnack & L. J. Beckman (Eds.), *Alcohol problems in women: Antecedents, consequences and interventions* (pp. 280–312). New York: Guilford.

WILSNACK, R. W., WILSNACK, S. C., & KLASSEN, A. D. (1984). Women's drinking and drinking problems: Patterns from a 1981 national survey. *American Journal of Public Health, 74,* 1231–1238.

21

Substance Use Prevention

An Iowa Mexican Im/migrant Family Perspective

Ed A. Muñoz*
University of Wyoming

Catherine Lillehoj Goldberg
Martha M. Dettman
Iowa State University

INTRODUCTION

The most recent census figures show that the Latino population increased by about 58% from 1990 to 2000 (Guzmán 2001), allowing Latinos (12.5%) to surpass African Americans (12.3%) as the largest single racial and ethnic minority group in the United States (Grieco and Cassidy 2001).[1] A significant amount of foreign-born Latinos, of which the largest proportion is of Mexican descent, accounts for a considerable part of this growth (Lollock 2001). This demographic shift is evident throughout the United States and not only in regions of the country traditionally known as specific Latino regional enclaves (i.e., Mexican Southwest, Puerto Rican Northeast, and Cuban Miami). For example, in the past decade the Midwest had the largest regional proportional increase (81.0%) in its Latino population (U.S. Census Bureau 1992, 2001a). This phenomenon can be accounted for in large part by the recruitment of Mexican im/migrant laborers to work in restructured and expanding food-processing industries located in mainly rural, nonmetropolitan communities (Burke and Goudy 1999; Fink 1998;

Ed A. Muñoz, Catherine Lillehoj Goldberg, and Martha M. Dettman. Prepared expressly for this edition.

*Presently at University of Wyoming.

Stull et al. 1995). The implications of this demographic shift raise major challenges for im/migrants themselves, as well as for predominately White, rural communities of the Midwest.

Prejudice and racism directed at im/migrants from members of the dominant majority culture could result in isolation and alienation (Cuéllar and Roberts 1997), and foster the development of an oppositional identity (Rumbaut 1997). In addition, as succeeding generations of im/migrants acculturate and reject traditional cultural values of familism, respect, and loyalty in favor of American core cultural values of independence and individualism, levels of health-threatening behavior such as substance use, premarital sex, and violence tend to increase (Harris 1999; Vega and Gil 1999; Arcia 1998; Khoury et al. 1996; Barrett et al. 1991; Smith et al. 1991). In this study, substance use was the topic of focus group discussions with Mexican im/migrant families in Iowa. More specifically, investigators specializing in the delivery of substance use prevention programs recruited Mexican im/migrant parents and children to help determine if substance use prevention programs were needed among this underserved population, and if so, what would be the best method of delivery.

Mexican Latino Substance Use and Substance Use Prevention

Although the majority of scholarly literature on Mexican Latinos/as focuses on the Southwestern United States experience, there is a growing body of literature examining the experience of Mexican Americans outside of this traditional regional enclave (García and García 2002; Gamboa 2000; Valdés 2000, 1991; Maldonado and García 1995; Vargas 1993). Most of this work, however, is sociohistorical in nature and focuses on the development of Mexican American communities throughout the twentieth century and into the twenty-first century. Nevertheless, a latent theme in this work is the prevalence and control of substance use in developing Mexican communities. Investigators do acknowledge substance use within Mexican communities, but argue that its prevalence has been widely exaggerated by Anglo public officials.

This embellished perception of widespread substance use in Mexican communities has provided the justification for, among other things, the overzealous social control of Mexicans within host communities (Escobar 1999; Rosales 1999). Research documents that this phenomenon is most evident the further away Mexican communities are from long-established Southwestern, indigenous social networks. However, Mexican communities outside of the Southwest that develop strong social networks have been found to have a more favorable criminal justice experience for two interrelated factors. Strong social networks not only provide the resources in curbing law enforcement and criminal justice abuse, they also help prevent the onset and escalation of substance use in emergent Mexican communities (Rosales 1999).

To further explain, epidemiological research on Latino substance use is mixed, reflecting sociohistorical claims of exaggerated levels of Mexican substance use. Research discrepancies are indicative of theoretical and methodological inconsistencies. Ethnic subgroup identity, gender, socioeconomic, cultural, family, community, and regional characteristics all have been noted for variations in findings (Muñoz and Lopez 2000; Caetano and Schafer 1996; Chavez and Swaim 1992). Nonetheless, epidemiological research has aided etiological investigation in identifying processes that facilitate Latino substance use. Stress and familial conflict and breakup—particularly that linked with migration, acculturation, and integration—have been closely associated with increased levels of substance use. Similarly, association with deviant peer networks is very much linked with higher rates of substance use. It makes sense, then, to pay particular attention to Latino im/migrant families, and especially Latino/a im/migrant youth, who may be most vulnerable to factors that facilitate substance use (Chavez and Swaim 1992).

At issue is how to best deliver substance use prevention to Latino families and youth. To date, programs to prevent adolescent substance use have been categorized into three types. *Universal prevention* programs, designed to prevent the precursors of substance use in a general population, target *all* students in a school. *Selective prevention* programs are designed to target particular groups of the general population, such as children of substance users. *Indicated prevention* programs are for participants who are already manifesting substance use or precursors of substance use (e.g., problem behaviors) (Institute of Medicine 1994). Universal prevention programs are most feasible since school officials provide general access to all youth, thus allowing for schools to become the primary delivery point for substance prevention programs. In addition, many schools recognize that addressing potential behavioral and emotional problems early helps to improve academic achievement and success. A perceived drawback, however, can be the lack of cultural specificity of universal substance use prevention programs that could prove more beneficial for im/migrant families.

For example, the Life Skills Training (LST) program (Botvin and Dusenbury 1987) is a universal prevention program that emphasizes increasing personal and social competencies, such as assertiveness, decision making, skills efficacy, relaxation, communication, and interpersonal relations. It also includes components to increase knowledge about cigarette smoking, alcohol, and marijuana use; changing attitudes; and changing normative expectations regarding the use of these substances (Botvin et al. 1990). Although the LST program has been demonstrated to be effective with Latino/a youth (Botvin et al. 1989), researchers have raised the possibility that personal and social skills training could be more effectual if self-concept and values orientation/clarification accounting for issues of Latino/a ethnic identity are taken into account. An example here is when Latino/a ethnic identity relates to positive aspects of traditional gender role socialization, and its incompatibility with illicit substance use—machismo versus marianismo (Castro and Gutierres, 1997; Castro et al. 1991). To better accomplish this aim, culturally sensitive prevention and treatment efforts for Latinos/as should focus on the family (*familismo*), and should be characterized by personal (*personalismo*), courteous (*simpatía*), and respectful (*respeto*) mutual interactions between providers and clients (Sanchez Mayers and Kail 1993).

Even so, it has been pointed out in research primarily on Mexican American families that these broad cultural generalizations may be more specific to an abstract and exaggerated traditional Latino family. This abstraction glosses over the tremendous diversity present between and within Mexican American families with respect to specific individual and contextual factors (Cervantes 1993). Thus, selective and/or indicated substance use prevention programs may be more suitable than universal substance use prevention programs for Mexican American populations. To be sure, precise knowledge of a target population must be gained prior to program development and delivery in order to ensure maximal success in substance use prevention efforts (Sanchez Mayers and Kail 1993).

Background to the Study

Within the U.S. Census Bureau's Midwest region, the West North Central division's ten-year Latino proportional increase (123.6%) from 1990 to 2000 was almost twice that of the East North Central division (72.4%).[2] Within the West North Central division, Minnesota

(166.1%) had the largest ten-year Latino population increase from 1990 to 2000 followed by Nebraska (155.4%) and Iowa (152.7%). Nationally, these states respectively ranked ninth, tenth, and eleventh in ten-year Latino proportional increases (U.S. Census Bureau 1992, 2001a). A closer look at Iowa census data reveals that proportional increases in county Latino populations were greatest in largely rural and nonmetropolitan counties of the state. Starr County, Iowa, is a good case in point.[3] In 1990 Starr County registered a to-tal population of 38, 276 of which 98.2% identified as White. Latinos/as accounted for 0.8% of the 1990 Starr County population. During the 1990s the Starr County population increased by 2.7% to 39, 311. However, in 2000, Whites accounted for 90.4% of the Starr County population, while Latinos accounted for 9.0% of the Star County total. More telling are the net proportional and numeric changes in Starr County's White and Latino popula-tions. Overall, Whites decreased by 5.4% or 2038 persons, while Latinos increased by 1106.5% or 3,231 persons (U.S. Census Bureau 1992, 2001b).

Community leaders tie the rapid increase in the Latino population to Mexican im/mi-grant labor formally and informally recruited for work in Quickcutters Meatpacking Com-pany located in Starrtown, the county's largest city (Smith 2001).[4] In 1990, Quickcutters expanded its operations necessitating an increase in its labor force from 650 to 2,000 work-ers. Most recently, it has been estimated that 40% of Quickcutters workforce is of Latino, and primarily, Mexican origin. Although some are male sojourners, there is abundant evidence that the many newcomers are quickly sending for and or are arriving with their families. A steady increase in Starrtown building permits and a bustling Mexican commercial district pro-vides further verification of Mexican community development. Naturally, the sudden influx poses many challenges for Starrtown's Mexican im/migrants and longtime residents alike. At the root of most of the challenges are language and cultural differences. These differences, as the findings will show, play a large role in the assistance and prevention of substance use.

DATA AND METHODS

Because of its exploratory nature, focus groups were employed for the study. Focus groups consist of tape-recorded group interviews where researchers moderate a discussion among 6–12 participants on a particular topic(s) for one to two hours (Krueger 1988). This in-creasingly popular technique has been deemed a useful research methodology for studying Latino/a populations because of its cultural appropriateness (Saint Germain et al. 1993) and ability to reduce the researcher–subject gap (Madriz 1998)—that is, personal, courteous, and mutually respectful group-centered discussions. Findings presented here are from dis-cussions centering on attitudes toward and perceptions of substance use and substance use prevention programming among Starrtown Mexican im/migrant families. Research ques-tions were tailored respectively for parent and youth focus groups, and are available upon request. Investigators' fieldnotes supplemented focus group discussions and aided in pro-viding an assessment of linguistic acculturation within Mexican im/migrant families.

Potential participants for individual parent and youth focus groups were targeted from families with at least one enrolled middle school adolescent. School administrators identi-fied over thirty eligible families who were then contacted by investigators through written and verbal channels. There was minimal success through written recruitment. This outcome was anticipated due to factors such as English and/or Spanish literacy, but even more so be-cause of im/migrants' reluctance in dealing with documents from official bureaucracies, which, more often than not, are insensitive to their needs (Marín and Marín 1991). Verbal recruitment through native Spanish speakers three weeks later and one week prior to the scheduled parent focus group proved more fruitful.

During verbal recruitment study participants were informed of the project and ensured that confidentiality and anonymity were of the utmost priority. Two other factors spurred interest for focus group participation. Parents viewed the $25 cash incentive, and an additional $10 for necessary child care, as favorable. Viewed most favorable was that the focus group would be conducted in Spanish. Shortly after completion of the adult focus group, written recruitment of youth occurred indirectly through parents who provided active consent for their middle school child to participate. There was a better response to written recruitment for youth, which researchers credit to increased community knowledge of the study's aim and goal. As with the adult focus group, verbal recruitment swelled the size of the youth focus group. Youth were provided a $25 stipend for their participation. Five days before scheduled focus groups, reminders were sent to interested participants informing them of the time and place for the meeting.

All together, this process garnered seven participants for the parental focus group—two couples, a mother, a father, and a grandmother who provided primary care for her grandchildren. For parents, the length of residency in Starr County ranged from approximately one month to five years. All participants were of Mexican ethnicity with im/migration origins from Mexico and/or the southwestern United States. There was a variable degree of education among parents ranging from three to five years. Except for the grandmother, parents were approximately 35–50 years old and worked outside of the home in food processing, self-employment, and professional fields. Participating parents were married and had two to four offspring, with the majority of children born in the United States. For the youth focus group, eleven middle-school-aged Mexicans volunteered to participate—eight male and three female. The length of residency and place of origin were similar to parent focus group participants.

Focus groups were conducted at Starrtown Middle School and lasted approximately two hours. Some concern about study bias developed among investigators when several youth, who were prospective study participants for the later adolescent focus group, accompanied their parents to the adult focus group. Fortunately, parents allowed their children to attend an athletic event that was being held at the middle school at the same time of the adult focus group. In hindsight, the potentially troublesome oversight turned advantageous, as findings will show. Investigators employed a bilingual professional marketing entrepreneur to conduct and transcribe tape-recorded focus groups that provided approximately one hundred pages of data for analysis. Field observations supplemented focus group deliberations.

THE NATURE AND SCOPE OF SUBSTANCE USE AMONG IOWA MEXICAN IM/MIGRANT FAMILIES

Generally, both parents and youth did not have particularly strong negative feelings toward legal substance use—adult tobacco and alcohol use. As this mother and female teen explain, legal substance use was viewed as acceptable as long as it is kept in moderation:

> *Marcella:*   Smoking and alcohol are less harmful than drugs. And quite a few Hispanics smoke and drink at parties. Our children see this as something natural.

It's only when they see someone who's had too much to drink that they see it just as too much. But as long as they see drinking and smoking in moderation they see it as natural.

Cristina: If you're at a party or at a club, it's ok to have a beer or a wine cooler, but not a whole 24-pack.

However, generational qualifications in attitudes toward tobacco use did arise, and may be an indication of current waves of antismoking educational campaigns targeted toward youth.

Amparo (Mother):   Smoking would be easier to accept because it is easier to quit. . . . My husband and I used to smoke, but we don't anymore. . . . It is easier to stop smoking than it is to stop drinking and taking drugs.

Cristina (teen):   While you can control drinking, smoking is bad for you. It is more addictive than drinking.

Matilde (teen):   Yeah and it kills you faster cause of cancer.

On the other hand, study participants unconditionally viewed illicit substance use disapprovingly because of its highly negative stigmatization and devastating and immediate impact on family life.

Amparo (Mother):   My daughter is the one who is in middle school. She tells me she has seen the police come because they have found drugs on other students at school. She gets very nervous! I tell her, "You have nothing to worry about." She says, "Mommy they are my friends and they are going to think I also use drugs." I tell her, "That is exactly right." So she is afraid of drugs.

Santos (Father):   My godson started boxing in Mexico. A man gave him some drug and then he started buying it himself. He turned a little crazy. He went crazy from using so much. He stopped his boxing. He started getting thinner and thinner. They say he spent all day in a small room and that no one could get him out.

The data suggest that Mexican parents' and adolescents' attitudinal responses toward substance use mirror dominant American core cultural attitudes that view legal substance use in social and recreational settings as tolerable.

Often study participants' perceptions surrounding the prevalence of substance use tended to parallel attitudinal responses. That is, discussions of substance use usually focused on casual use of cigarettes and alcohol. In addition and most encouraging, the majority of participants did not perceive substance use as a major problem within their current proximal setting. Once again, however, there were some generational differences. Parents did not perceive the prevalence of substance use among Latinos/as as any different than that found in the general public.

Macario (Father):   It's not just Hispanics that like to party, all cultures have parties.

In contrast, youth felt that substance use was more prevalent for Latinos than it was for Anglos.

Investigator:	Do you think there is a lot of substance use among Latinos?
René:	Probably.
Diana:	Well mostly Latinos use more drugs than the others.
Investigator:	You think so? You think that Latinos use drugs more than other Americans.
Youth (in unison):	Yeah.

It is possible that perceptual difference in the prevalence of substance use could be due to generational differences in internalizing widely held societal stereotypes about Latino substance use (Padilla 1999) as this father's comments seem to imply:

Macario:	Our kids see movies here, and even our movies with Pedro Infante (Mexican actor 50s) . . . . They think it's nice to see him with the cigarette in his mouth with the Mariachis in the background and drunk. They think that's culture. It all depends how you see it and they always take only what is convenient to them. But I tell my daughter, take the good . . . don't just take what's convenient. It all depends on who sees it, and the monkey who climbs the tree.

Also stemming from this father's comments is the possible internalization of negative gender-appropriate roles thought to be culturally specific to Latinos, but that research consistently shows is quite characteristic of substance use. As these additional comments further illustrate, reported instances of substance use and or abuse almost without fail revolved around situations involving young males.

Amparo (Mother):	In my case, my sister's son is currently going through a situation where he has been involved with drugs. Three times he has been detained and we don't know if it is due to my sister getting a divorce. He promises that he will clean up and work but fails to do so. He was not like that. He was a normal child. He is currently in jail. My sister does not know what to do. Before my sister divorced, two years ago, he was just a child. He was in and out of jail about three times before and now he is in jail for robbery. My sister does not know what to do.
Santos (Father):	I knew this family in Utah that smoked marijuana as if it were a cigarette—children and parents. They would offer me some when I would visit them, but I never tried that.
Mercedes (Mother):	The last time we went to Mexico my son started to hang around with this boy who was 14 years old that was drinking and smoking and he started to do the same. But when we got back, my husband talked to him about it and he is no longer doing that.

Even though Latino males are more likely to use substances, females are not totally risk free as youth's talk of isolation in Starrtown implied that female abstinence may be temporary, and could change if and when more social opportunities arise.

Investigator:	What do you like about Starrtown?
Group (in unison):	Nothing!
Investigator:	What do you dislike about Starrtown?
Group (in unison):	Everything!
Ricardo:	I want to live in California. There is more of everything there— malls, parties, sports, everything.
Diana:	More Mexican stuff too, like art and stuff like that.
Cristina:	I like when I go to Mexico City. There is a lot to do!

These sentiments may be indicative of rural, small-town teenage angst, but parents voiced similar concerns. Their concerns, however, were more in the context of their children's increasing familial independence through exposure to often competing cultural and societal influences.

Macario:	Our children are being pulled by two cultures—the one at home, and the American culture, the streets, their friends. We have to understand that they don't know who to listen to. Should they listen to me, or their teacher? That's happened to me with the youngest, she will ask me how to do the homework. I will tell her do it this way. "No, the teacher says to do it this way," she says. Then do it the way you want! It's two cultures that are colliding. That's how things get away from us. It's important they understand that they are following both cultures . . . . And from what I have seen and lived, bad friendships are our enemies. And as much as we or whoever tries to get rid of bad influence . . . it is very hard . . . because when you're young and even into your 20s you think you know everything . . . and nothing can change that but yourself. I think I have won this battle as my daughters do not drink and smoke.
Marcella:	That is the way my teenager is. I am always talking to him . . . about coming home on time, studying, getting good grades. But he gets so rebellious and does not want to listen.
Santos:	When we first moved here, our boy would have friends come over to the house every day. We didn't like to have his friends over all the time. So he started going over to their house, and one day, his friends started calling him chicken because he obeyed the sign to not use the sidewalk where they had just poured cement.

As encouraging as earlier comments are about the low level of substance use among Starrtown Mexican im/migrant families, remarks indicate that processes identified in facilitating substance use for im/migrant families—acculturative stress, familial discord, and association with deviant peers—are present in this developing Mexican community.

SUBSTANCE USE PREVENTION PROGRAMMING

Naturally, parents placed a great deal of responsibility on themselves for the first line of defense against the onset of substance use.

Mercedes: I am always talking with my daughter . . . telling her why drugs are bad. "Don't do drugs," I tell her. And not too long ago my son came home from school telling me how a boy had been taken away in handcuffs because they found something. I told him, "You are not going to do that are you?" He said, "Mommy how could you think I could do that." "I don't want you doing that because it is very bad . . . you know how they took your friend, they could also take you away!" His father also talks to him by letting him know one way or another. But it's harder with my son. Sometimes he doesn't want to listen.

Oftentimes, intimate parental counseling warning children about the negative consequences of substance use occurred during leisurely situations.

Macario: Ever since the girls were little, they have watched a lot of TV and videos. Some times the programs involve drugs, like some of the soap operas. These times I use to explain how people who use drugs end up. They themselves will say "How ugly. Look how they are dying. How sad." I'll say, "Would you like to look that way one day?" "No." they will say. Of course this has limits . . . but it does help to talk to them when they are seeing it on TV.

Needless to say, parents also voiced a wish for further support and viewed school-based programs as the logical means for assistance. Their desirability for school-based programs also stemmed from their desire to avoid more extreme measures of dealing with substance abusive children.

Susana: I think that would be very good. One hour per day dedicated to substance use education, just like math. They should talk to the kids about it.

Amparo: That would be good. I don't think they talk about it a lot here in school. Maybe once a month . . . I don't know how much time they spend on it. My daughter got a certificate from the police officers from a program (DARE). Yes, I would like for her to have a class on drugs. That way they can learn about all the new drugs that are coming out, the damage that each one causes, the effects that drugs have and reactions. Yes, it would be good . . . . Before the last option I would use . . . to take them to a place where they could get help in getting off of drugs . . . to get medical help . . . if he is not going to listen to me or the school that would be the last option. Take him to a place that would help him if he wanted to stop he could do it there.

Marcella: One of my sons was saying to me that there were some kids that beat up a man and killed him and that his teacher said that she wished they had been detained for treatment. I told my boy that I would do the same if knew they were causing problems. I would rather they be in a place where they could get help, and not in prison. I would do it. It would hurt but it would hurt more to see them out causing pain to others and themselves.

Favorable attitudes towards substance use prevention programs were also present among youth, which is all the more encouraging considering that earlier discussions did not reveal a major substance use problem with either parents or youth. Moreover, Latino youth shared what they thought elements of substance use prevention programs could entail.

> *Cristina:*   You can have like after school programs to keep kids out of the streets, gangs, or whatever. Like the one program here at school is just arts and craft. You could do other things like swimming and playing soccer games, like different stuff for different days.
>
> *Miguél:*   How about fishing.
>
> *Ignacio:*   Dancing would be good.
>
> *René:*   Field trips are good too! We could go visit your school. Our ESL [English as a Second Language] teacher took us to another college to visit. We even went to a basketball game.

Latino youth's ideas are not far-fetched and can be considered as possible incentives and rewards for participation and completion of substance use prevention programs.

PROGRAM DELIVERY

Field notes from a meeting with Starrtown school district administrators early in the development of the study indicated that, at least among the children of im/migrants, linguistic assimilation was occurring at a relatively rapid pace. A school administrator present at the meeting commented that a surprising number of Mexican youth were scheduled to graduate from high school early and with honors. Yet, this "surprising" observation is consistent with research demonstrating that im/migrant (1.5 generation) and second-generation youth achieve better in school than later generations due to superior study routines acquired through learning a second language (Rumbaut 1995). This early assessment on the high rate and level of linguistic assimilation suggests that a universal school-based substance abuse prevention program could benefit Mexican immigrant youth, much like earlier research has shown (Botvin et al. 1989). However, further examination of the data suggests that a supplemental family-based component to the program could yield even better results.

The high level of English language proficiency among youth was additionally manifest through investigators' contacts with parents and youth during recruitment efforts and subsequent focus group interviews. Spanish-speaking investigators assisting with the study noted on verbal recruitment logs that youth often acted as language brokers for their parents (Buriel et al. 1998). That is, youth acted as go-betweens during initial verbal recruitment efforts, speaking in English with investigators and in Spanish with parents. Interactions during focus groups confirmed that the majority of parents were Spanish monolingual, as parents reported that they knew some to very little English. A somewhat lower than expected level of formal Spanish literacy became obvious when adult participants overwhelmingly agreed to a Spanish reading of the study's aim, which was detailed in bilingual written invitations to participate. Even more revealing were adults' animated and affirmative responses to having written consent forms read to them before they agreed to sign. And for some, signature lines were individually pointed out to participants upon their request.

Direct interactions with children attending the parent focus group further ascertained the bilingual capacity of Mexican youth and showed their English proficiency to be above average to excellent. Of particular interest here was that youth preferred to use English even when bilingual investigators communicated with them in Spanish. Investigators perceived this as a form of impression management (Bilbow 1997; St. Clair 1980) as youth may have distinguished researchers as educational authorities who are not always so encouraging to the use of Spanish within school boundaries. These early indicators of the relatively high level of English proficiency and English language preference among Mexican youth led researchers to conduct the youth focus group in English, rather than pay to have it professionally conducted in Spanish.

Upon conclusion of the youth focus group, however, there was sufficient evidence to conclude that English proficiency and preference among youth was more variable than was first thought. First of all, investigators became aware that the level of participation within the focus group appeared to be related to, among other things, whether or not a participant had a noticeable Spanish accent. Individuals who had a minimal to nonrecognizable Spanish accent participated most in the discussion, while those with a recognizable Spanish accent tended to participate less. In fact, some youth only participated when directly called on, and even then, their response was nominal. Rather than attributing this solely to a withdrawn personality, native Spanish-speaking investigators speculated that nonparticipation could also have been due to difficulty following the pace of the English discussion. Research does show that English language proficiency variability for im/migrant children is an outcome of the inconsistency among youth in place of nativity, age of immigration to the country of destination, and/or length of U.S. residency (Bialystock and Hakata 1994), factors reported earlier by youth to vary widely. This young Mexican male's comment exemplifies the unevenness and potentially rapid pace of linguistic assimilation within Mexican im/migrant families:

> *Manuel:*   I speak mostly Spanish with my parents, but with my little brother, he doesn't know any Spanish, so I have to speak to him in English.

One last instance to gauge the level of linguistic assimilation occurred through queries posed to both parents and youth on how best to conduct future work. Although parents did not perceive a special need for Latino/a program personnel for future work, they did stress overwhelmingly the need for bilingual competency among program personnel in order for their successful participation. This would be compulsory for a family-based program, while preferable for a school-based program. Bilingual competency of school-based program personnel would be preferable to provide as much continuity as possible for youth who find themselves in both predominantly English-speaking and predominantly Spanish-speaking environments. Further justification arises from the variability of English proficiency found among Mexican youth. Finally, moderate levels of Spanish language literacy among most participants and unexamined levels of English language literacy among youth recommend the need for as much verbal interaction as possible that could be incorporated into a supplementary family-based component.

CONCLUSION

There is no end in sight in the near future for the ongoing shift of the racial and ethnic composition of the United States. Continued immigration and natural population momentum from a younger Latino birth cohort will undoubtedly maintain Latinos/as as the largest racial/ethnic minority group in the United States for years to come. Because of this, continued research on this dynamic population is crucial to better understand processes of incorporation and acculturation as well as their effects on group and individual societal integration. In this study, we especially pay heed to the diversity of the Latino population when determining if substance use prevention programs are desirable, and more importantly, how they should be implemented for Mexican immigrant families in Starrtown, Iowa.

While not representative of all Latino communities, findings from the study have significant relevance for the number of predominantly White, nonmetropolitan communities throughout the United States that are experiencing a large influx and settlement of Mexican immigrant families. The perceived need and favorable attitude of parents and youth towards substance use prevention programs indicate their awareness and concern about the deleterious effects of substance abuse. Substance abuse is a hazard that both parents and youth believe can be reduced through universal school-based programs. However, the data did point to the added benefits a supplementary culturally specific family-based program can bring to Mexican immigrant families struggling with dissonant acculturation (Portes and Rumbaut 2001). Dissonant acculturation occurs when children of immigrants learn the host language and cultural values before their parents, resulting in possible role reversal and the weakening of parental authority. Hence, a culturally specific family-based program promoting consonant acculturation, or the even acquisition of English and American core cultural values, can go a long way in strengthening immigrant families.

Then again, consonant acculturation should not be misconstrued as the total abandonment of Spanish and Latino ethnic identity. As multicultural identification theory suggests, youth can successfully identify with multiple cultures without compromising their native-culture identity. Strong cultural identification serves as a source of inner strength and stability, elements associated with strong self-esteem and school adjustment. Strong ethnic identification also exerts some protective effects against substance use, but it is not uniquely protective. Protective effects are influenced by other contextual factors including parental attitudes towards substance use, peer substance use, and environmental factors (Oetting and Beauvais 1991). For all youth, value orientations that are not compatible with substance use must emphasize what have been deemed traditional Latino core cultural messages. Among some of these are value orientations and cultural messages that promote self-respect (i.e., as Latino/a); responsibility to family; and a responsibility to contribute to the community and the larger social group (Castro et al. 1994).

NOTES

1. The interchangeable terms *Latino* and *Hispanic* are both umbrella terms for those individuals who self-identify and trace their ancestry from Mexico, other Latin American countries in Central and South America, the Caribbean, and Spain. In addition, the terms *Latina* and *Latinas* are used when specifically discussing Hispanic females.
2. Michigan, Ohio, Illinois, Indiana, and Wisconsin make up the East North Central Division of the Midwest, whereas Minnesota, Iowa, Missouri, Kansas, Nebraska, North Dakota, and South Dakota make up the West North Central Division.
3. A pseudonym is employed to help protect anonymity and confidentiality.
4. Pseudonyms have been employed to help protect anonymity and confidentiality.

REFERENCES

ARCIA, E. 1998. Latino parents perception of their children health status. *Social Science and Medicine* 46:1271–74.

BARRETT, M. E., and G. W. JOE. 1991. Acculturation influences on inhalant use. *Hispanic Journal of Behavioral Sciences* 13:276–96.

BIALYSTOCK, E., and K. HAKUTA. 1994. *In other words: The science and psychology of second-language acquisition.* New York: Basic Books.

BILBOW, G. T. 1997. Cross-cultural impression management in the multicultural workplace: The special case of Hong Kong. *Journal of Pragmatics* 28(4):461–87.

BOTVIN, G. J., E. BAKER, L. DUSENBURY, S. TORTU, and E. M. BOTVIN. 1990. Preventing adolescent drug abuse through a multimodal cognitive-behavioral approach: Results of a 3-year study. *Journal of Consulting and Clinical Psychology* 58(4):437–46.

BOTVIN, G. J., and L. DUSENBURY. 1987. Life skills training: A psychoeducational approach to substance use prevention. In *Psychoeducational interventions in schools: Methods and procedures for enhancing student competence,* eds. Charles A. Maher and Joseph E. Zins. New York: Pergamon Press, pp. 46–65.

BOTVIN, G. J., L. DUSENBURY, N. BAKER, S. JAMES-ORTIZ, and J. KERNER. 1989. Skills training approach to smoking prevention among hispanic youth. *Journal of Behavioral Medicine,* 12(3):279–96.

BURIEL, R., W. PEREZ, T. L. DE MENT, D. V. CHAVEZ, and V. R. MORAN. 1998. The relationship of language brokering to academic performance, biculturalism, and self-efficacy among latino adolescents. *Hispanic Journal of Behavioral Sciences* 20(3):283–97.

BURKE, S. C., and W. J. GOUDY. 1999. Immigration and community in Iowa: How many have come and what is the impact? Paper presented at the annual meeting of the American Sociological Association, Chicago, Illinois.

CAETANO, R., and J. SCHAFER. 1996. DSM-IV alcohol dependence and drug abuse/dependence in a treatment sample of Whites, Blacks, and Mexican Americans. *Drugs and Alcohol Dependence* 43:93–101.

CASTRO, F. G., and S. GUTIERRES. 1997. Drug and alcohol use among rural Mexican Americans. In *Rural substance abuse: State of knowledge and issues,* eds. Z. Sloboda, E. Rosenquist, and J. Howard. National Institute on Drug Abuse Research Monograph 168, DHHS Pub. No. (ADM) 97-4177. Washington, DC: Supt. of Documents, U.S. Government Printing Office, pp. 498–530.

CASTRO, F. G., M. P. HARMON, K. COE, and H. M. TAFOYA-BARRAZA. 1994. Drug prevention research with Hispanic populations: Theoretical and methodological issues with a generic structural model. In *Scientific methods for prevention intervention research,* eds. A. Cazares and L.A. Beatty. National Institute on Drug Abuse Research Monograph 139, DHHS Pub. No. (ADM) 94-3631. Washington, DC: Supt. of Documents, U.S. Government Printing Office, pp. 203–32.

CASTRO, F. G., E. V. SHARP, E. H. BARRINGTON, M. WALTON, and R. RAWSON. 1991. Drug abuse identity in Mexican Americans: Theoretical and empirical considerations. *Hispanic Journal of Behavioral Science* 13(2):209–25.

CERVANTES, R. C. 1993. The hispanic family intervention Program: An empirical approach to substance abuse prevention. In *Hispanic substance Abuse,* eds. Raymond Sanchez Mayers, Barbara L. Kail, and Thomas D. Watts. Springfield, IL: Charles C. Thomas, pp. 101–14.

CHAVEZ, E. L., and R. C. SWAIM. 1992. Hispanic substance use: Problems in epidemiology. *Drugs and Society* 6(3–4):211–30.

CUÉLLAR, I., and R. ROBERTS. 1997. Relations of depression, acculturation, and socioeconomic status in a Latino sample. *Hispanic Journal of Behavioral Sciences* 19:230–38.

ESCOBAR, E. J. 1999. *Race, police, and the making of a political identity: Mexican Americans and the Los Angeles Police Department, 1900–1945.* Berkeley: University of California Press.

FINK, D. 1998. *Cutting into the meatpacking line: Workers and change in the rural Midwest.* Chapel Hill: University of North Carolina Press.

GAMBOA, E. 2000. *Mexican Labor and World War II: Braceros in the Pacific Northwest, 1942–1947.* Seattle: University of Washington Press.

GARCÍA, G., and J. GARCÍA. 2002. *The illusion of borders: The national presence of Mexicanos in the United States.* Dubuque, IA: Kendal/Hunt.

GRIECO, E. M., and R. C. CASSIDY. 2001. *Overview of race and Hispanic origin.* Census Brief 2000: C2KBR/01-1. Washington, DC: U.S. Census Bureau.

GUZMÁN, B. 2001. *The hispanic population.* Census Brief 2000: C2KBR/01-3. Washington, DC: U.S. Census Bureau.

HARRIS, K. M. 1999. The health status and risk behaviors of adolescents in immigrant families. In *Children of Immigrants: Health, Adjustment, and Public Assistance,* eds. Donald J. Hernandez, Committee on the Health and Adjustment of Immigrant Children and Families (U.S.), and Board on Children, Youth, and Families (U.S.). Washington, DC.: National Academy Press, pp. 286–347.

INSTITUTE OF MEDICINE. 1994. *Reducing risks for mental disorders: Frontiers for preventive intervention research.* Washington, DC: National Academy Press.

KHOURY, L. E., G. J. WARHEIT, R. S. ZIMMERMAN, W. A. VEGA, and A. G. GIL. 1996. Gender and ethnic differences in the prevalence of alcohol, cigarette, and illicit drug use over time in a cohort of young Hispanic adolescents in South Florida. *Women and Health* 24:2.

KRUEGER, R. A. 1988. *Focus groups: A practical guide for applied research.* Beverly Hills CA: Sage.

LOLLOCK, L. 2001. *The foreign born population in the United States: March 2000.* Current Population Reports: P20-534. Washington, DC: U.S. Census Bureau.

MADRIZ, E. 1998. Using focus groups with lower socioeconomic status Latina women. *Qualitative Inquiry* 4(1):114–28.

MALDONADO, C. S., and G. GARCÍA. 1995. *The Chicano experience in the Northwest.* Dubuque, IA: Kendall/Hunt.

MARÍN, GERARDO, and BARBARA VANOSS MARÍN. 1991. *Research with Hispanic populations.* Applied Social Research Methods Series, Volume 23. Newbury Park, CA: Sage Publications.

MUÑOZ, ED A., and DAVID A. LOPEZ. 2000. Latino/a substance abuse/dependency: Effects of assimilation? *Latino Studies Journal* 11(1):50–69.

OETTING, GENE R., and FRED BEAUVAIS. 1991. Orthogonal cultural identification theory: The cultural identification of minority adolescents. *International Journal of Addictions.* 25 (5-A-6-A):655–85.

PADILLA, LAURA M. 1999. Social and legal repercussions of Latinos' colonized mentality. *University of Miami Law Review* 53(4):769–85.

PORTES, ALEJANDRO, and RUBÉN G. RUMBAUT. 2001. *Legacies: The story of the immigrant second generation.* Berkeley: University of California Press.

ROSALES, F. ARTURO. 1999. *¡Pobre Raza! Violence, justice, and mobilization among México Lindo immigrants, 1900–1936.* Austin: University of Texas Press.

RUMBAUT, R. G. 1995. The new Californians: Comparative research findings on the educational process of immigrant children. In *California's immigrant children: theory, research, and implications for educational policy,* eds. Rubén G. Rumbaut and Wayne A. Cornelius. La Jolla: Center for U.S.-Mexican Studies, University of California, San Diego, pp. 17–70.

RUMBAUT, RUBÉN G. 1997. Assimilation and its discontents: Between rhetoric and reality. *International Migration Review* 31(4):923–60.

SAINT GERMAIN, M. A., T. L. BASSFORD, and G. MONTANO. 1993. Surveys and focus groups in health research with older Hispanic women. *Qualitative Health Research* 3(3):341–67.

SANCHEZ MAYERS, R., and B. L. KAIL. 1993. Hispanic substance abuse: An overview. In *Hispanic Substance Abuse,* eds. Raymond Sanchez Mayers, Barbara L. Kail, and Thomas D. Watts. Springfield, IL: Charles C. Thomas, pp. 5–16.

SMITH, G. 2001. Marshalltown adapting to influx of immigrants. *The Associated Press State and Local Wire*. February 16, Marshalltown, IA.

SMITH, S. S., J. W. GEORGE, and D. D. SIMPSON. 1991. Parental influences on inhalant use by children. *Hispanic Journal of Behavioral Sciences* 13:267–75.

ST. CLAIR, R. N. 1980. Language and the politics of culture: Structural parallels. *International Behavioural Scientist* 12(1):23–44.

STULL, D. D., M. J. BROADWAY, and D. C. GRIFFITH. 1995. *Anyway you cut it: Meat processing and small-town America*. Lawrence: University Press of Kansas.

U.S. CENSUS BUREAU. 1992. *Statistical abstract of the United States 1992 (112th edition)*. Washington, DC: U.S. Government Printing Office.

U.S. BUREAU OF THE CENSUS. 2001b. Iowa—County: Race and Hispanic or Latino 2000. Online Basic Facts Geographic Comparison Table: *http://factfinder.census.gov/servlet/BasicFactsTable?_lang=en&_vt_name=DEC_2000_PL_U_ GCTPL_ST2&_geo_id=04000US19*.

U.S. CENSUS BUREAU. 2001a. *Hispanic or Latino origin for the United States, Regions, divisions, states, and for Puerto Rico: 2000*. Census 2000 Summary File 1: Census 2000 PHC-T-10. Washington, DC: U.S. Census Bureau.

VALDÉS, D. N. 1991. *Al Norte: Agricultural workers in the Great Lakes Region, 1917–1970*. Austin: University of Texas Press.

VALDÉS, D. N. 2000. *Barrios Norteños: St. Paul and Midwestern Mexican communities in the twentieth century*. Austin: University of Texas Press.

VARGAS, Z. 1993. *Proletarians of the north: A history of Mexican industrial workers in Detroit and the Midwest, 1917–1933*. Berkeley: University of California Press.

VEGA, W. A., and A. G. GIL. 1999. A model for explaining drug use behavior among Hispanic adolescents. *Drugs and Society* 14:57–74.

22

After You've Ran with the Rats the Mice Are a Bore

Cessation of Heroin Use among Men Entering Midlife

Kenneth Mullen
Psychological Medicine, University of Glasgow

Richard Hammersley
Health and Human Sciences, University of Essex

Claire Marriott
Psychological Medicine, University of Glasgow

INTRODUCTION

Most of the research that has concentrated on the problem of drug use has focused on the difficulties of youth and adolescence (e.g., Barnard and McKeganey 1994; Plant and Plant 1992). Youth shifting from the use of "soft" to "hard" drugs, in particular heroin use, is a major concern. Research has thus investigated the predisposing factors that lead to serious drug use—in particular, peer group pressure and familial influences (Segal 1991; Kandel 1990). Although a lot is known about the factors that may initiate drug use and lead from soft drug use to more serious drug use, little research has been exclusively focused on the factors that either lead to cessation of drug use, or conversely, to the stabilization of use at potentially dangerous levels. With the exception of one American study (Biernacki 1986),

Kenneth Mullen, Richard Hammersley, and Claire Marriott. Prepared expressly for this edition.

this is particularly true of research into heroin use. The pathway from dependence is an important topic, as it is just as necessary to know how to stop young people from taking drugs and moving onto more serious drug use as it is to prevent them from starting. The cost of continuous drug users on the community, by way of crime, health service use, and unemployment, is also considerable.

Work on alcohol and tobacco has shown the importance of understanding lay concepts for predicting subsequent use of these substances (Denzin 1987; Mullen 1987). Such in-depth inquiry can uncover key elements in the immediate cultural conditions of a person's life that lead to moderation or cessation of alcohol and tobacco use. Research on male Glaswegians in midlife demonstrated the importance of changes in lifestyle factors in achieving moderation and cessation. Such changes could often be improvements in personal relationships, housing, or work conditions (Mullen 1993).

If we turn to research on the influence of cultural factors on illegal drug use, this again has primarily focused on youth subcultures, increasingly viewing the issue from a postmodernist perspective (Pearson 1987; Parker et al. 1988). A handful of qualitative studies, however, have looked at illegal drug use of people in an older age group (Cohen 1989; Reinarman et al. 1994; Klingemann 1991). The most important is that of Stimson and Oppenheimer (1982; Oppenheimer et al. 1979), who in 1976 followed up people who had been attending drug dependency clinics in 1969. Their study is important because it showed that 35% of clinic attendees in 1969 had stopped using opiates by 1979. They also found that those who had been addicted to heroin and who had stopped did not replace their dependency on heroin by dependency on other drugs. Most had become "social drinkers." The characteristics of those who had stopped were as follows: The general trend was for them to have made major changes for the better in their lives: their pattern of friendships had changed, most were working, and they were more likely to be in permanent accommodations. This trend raises the issue of temporal order: did their lives change and then they ceased to be users? Or did they cease to be users and then their lives changed? To answer these questions calls for an in-depth approach. Recent work on this cohort, although not of a qualitative nature, demonstrates the possibility of tracing and contacting a clinic population over long time periods (Tobutt et al. 1996; Oppenheimer et al. 1994).

Work on alcohol and tobacco use has shown the importance of family relations in moderating use (Mullen 1993). Research found that marriage minimized health-damaging behaviors, and the presence of children gave extra benefits to the psychological health of respondents. Little research of this nature has been undertaken regarding illegal drug use maintenance or cessation. But the ethnographic work that has been carried out on heroin (Biernacki 1986; Pearson 1987; Parker et al. 1988) and cocaine (Cohen 1989) shows just how relevant such issues may be. Pearson (1987) found that individuals who managed to break the cycle of heroin addiction often stressed the importance of steady relationships with girlfriends or boyfriends or contact with family. Klingemann (1991) similarly found that of 70 people who had remitted from heroin use without treatment, 29% cited changes in social interactions with significant others as the main cause. Remitters also appeared to have experienced high levels of exposure to stressful life events in the year prior to remission. Biernacki's American study (1986) showed that although respondents had great difficulties constructing an alternative social identity to that of "heroin user," this could be accomplished.

There have been a number of qualitative studies of Scottish heroin users during the 1980s (McKeganey and Barnard 1992; Taylor 1994), but these have focused on the lives and health behaviors of young, current injectors. From these studies, the generation who began using heroin in the mid-1980s seems to be somewhat different from the earlier generation studied by Stimson and Oppenheimer. They appear to be more uniformly working class or unemployed, and in some ways, less isolated from their community. The latter also may be due to the different nature of social cohesiveness in London compared to Glasgow or Edinburgh. From the mid-1980s onward, heroin injecting was less unusual than it had been previously in Scotland and probably also less unusual than it had been in London at the time that Stimson and Oppenheimer's sample began. Perhaps, then, this implies that heroin injectors from the mid-1980s would be less deviant in other ways. The importance of studying the experiences of different cohorts of drug users has been acknowledged in Oppenheimer's most recent work (Tobutt et al. 1996; Oppenheimer et al. 1994).

This might be good or bad for cessation in midlife. People who are less deviant and marginalized may find it easier to reintegrate into nonheroin-using life. Alternatively, people with these characteristics may be more likely to sustain or control heroin injecting longer, compared to those who have more problems or those who "hit bottom."

The aims of our study were to trace the "new heroin users" who had been in treatment in Glasgow during the 1980s and to compare those who had quit with those who had not. We used qualitative interviews (Strauss 1987) with men, to build on previous work about male substance use in middle age. The effect of treatment on these men's lives was considered as well.

METHOD

We were of course very much aware of all the ethical issues involved. Consent for follow-up had not been given when initial treatment had been offered. Some men might be living new lives with people who were unaware of their prior heroin use. In addition, there was a more general issue: can "informed consent" apply ten years later in new life circumstances?

Bearing these issues in mind, we developed a five-point plan to minimize these problems: (1) the men would be identified from 1980s clinic records; (2) they would be traced forward to their current general practitioners (GPs); (3) the GP would be contacted to discuss men's current lives; (4) if contact would cause problems, then no contact would be made; (5) otherwise, contact would be made.

Unfortunately, we soon encountered setbacks with our initial plan: the Social Work Department destroys most records after five years. Psychiatry records do not separate substance-dependent cases. Available records rarely recorded a current GP. These setbacks gave us a lot of insight into the difficulties of developing studies on heroin use. Even prospective studies, with consent, may lose clients whose treatment needs and contact are minimal. These problems, combined with the ethical considerations, raise serious doubts as to whether retrospective studies—that is, studies not planned from treatment onset—of people who have received drug treatment are feasible.

We therefore decided to use an alternative approach. We contacted men still known to drug treatment agencies and snowballed from these men to others. An alternative would have been to use ethnographic methods to contact users at street level. Time and limited resources precluded this.

Our method was to interview men who had quit and men who were current heroin users. Twenty-six men aged over 28 who had received drug treatment were interviewed.

The mean age of the sample was 34 years. They had been using heroin from between ten and twenty-five years. At the time of interview, they had been off heroin from six months to seven years.

Often they had tried, and for a limited time had been successful, in coming off heroin at earlier stages of their using career. They had also been in and out of services over a number of years. At the time of use, they lived in disadvantaged housing, either in the poorer council housing, or in mixed tenement (i.e., low rise flats) properties.

Semistructured interviews lasted forty-five minutes to two hours, were tape-recorded, and transcribed (see Lindesmith 1963; Dowell et al. 1995). Here, we report some of the findings related to cessation and relapse, illustrating key points with quotations from the transcripts.

FINDINGS

Cessation of Use as It Relates to Treatment

We discovered that men had received several bouts of treatment over the years, often including (a) detoxification, (b) residential rehabilitation, and (c) self-help groups. In other words, they had made repeated attempts to quit with, and without, treatment. Experience of different treatment regimes is an integral part of heroin injectors' life histories, rather than treatment providing a one-off cure.

We also discovered that men had lives that were in some periods more normal, in some respects, than the chaotic stereotype suggests:

> At the time [when starting serious heroin use] I don't think I did [get addicted], you know in my mind I didn't get addicted. I was still able to hold a job down. I've got a trade, I'm a slater and plasterer to trade. I was always able to get money. (R14)

An ex-dealer:

> I've had all the money, enough to buy a house at one time, three motors, a motorbike, all sitting outside my ma's house. I'd the wardrobe of a fitba' manager probably and stacks of jewellery. (R24)

This man had also been married throughout, although his wife had also received counseling and he had slept rough at another point in his life.

Users described how heroin use blocked other activities and normal responses to events.

> I'd like to travel and do all the things I thought when I was younger I would like to do. Years go by very quickly when you're stoned you know and you just get into a rhythm like that, you just don't notice that life's going on and things aren't changing much for you. (R4)

Interviewees reported that having a drug habit made everything else seem unimportant:

> "It's like replacing all the other problems with one great big problem." Although the drug habit presents a terrible burden for the user, in a strange way it solves (masks) other problems—Survival is on a day to day basis, where risk of overdose, or being attacked by a dealer/money lender, etc., is faced daily. Having a nice home or paying a bill, or holding together a relationship do not seem important in the face of these threats, and so, the heroin user is no longer

worried by the things that he at one time might have been. Being a heroin user, or junkie, has taken away those problems.

It was seen to control everything in their lives; they never had the time, inclination, or money to do anything else. They tried to stop when they became tired of this aspect of heroin use:

> Just getting fed up with it. It's not easy with all the hassle that's involved . . . . I'm fed up with anything that controls my life. Like I can't go on holiday without worrying about if I can get drugs there. It's no fun going on holiday if you go through some cold turkey sort of thing. (R4)

> Successful cessation tended to occur after repeated attempts and repeated treatments until it was the "right time" for them to quit. "Tried to come off of drugs through other people's pressure but every opportunity I sneaked through the door. It wis'nae my time. But when the time comes I believe you will know it."

> "Withdrawal is easy . . . but when my time came I just knew it." (R0)

They could give the reason that they had stopped for self—to reclaim control of their life, and to build up self-esteem and self-value. This was the most frequently given reason. Many of the men said that you could not stop until you really want to for yourself: "At the end of the day it must come down to me, it doesn't matter where you are" (R9).

They often stated they had just had enough; they had a maturation process, they had grown out of it. This often included the idea of hitting rock bottom, or reaching his "personal gutter." They believed they had got as low as they could go without dying.

Quitting involved major life changes, often getting a job:

> So I went back, went there and worked a couple of months and they said, 'right do you want to start painting here?' Aye and I fulfilled that part of it. (R24)

Several men also talked of moving away to England to quit, only to get back into heroin there, or after moving back to Glasgow. Men also tried to quit in order to take more responsibility for their children.

Some respondents had stopped for the sake of others—for example, because the court had asked for drug rehabilitation instead of giving a custodial sentence (respondents believed this was an ineffective way of stopping), or for wife, children, or parent. Respondents also said they had stopped to avoid prison; this included avoiding a lifestyle of crime and violence.

Birth of a child or loss of custody of a child (in a court case) was also mentioned:

> I've got two kids. That's a reason I want off as well. I've never really done anything, well I've done things for my kids but I could do a lot more, in fact I should do. I'm separated from her but I can still see the kids everyday if I want, but I'm always thinking of heroin first, so I've never took them on holiday or anything. That's the kind of thing I want to start doing before it's too late. (R3)

People also stopped because of physical problems through injecting, for example, deep vein thrombosis, frequent overdose, simply not having any veins left to inject, or not wanting to take the next step of injecting into more dangerous areas such as the neck or groin. Or being sick of having to have something; one interviewee described it as "like a monkey on my back," an old metaphor about a drug habit.

Relapse

It should be noted that many respondents had made several attempts to stop, only to relapse some time afterward. Relapse tended to occur after quitting without really accepting the problem or wanting to stop.

> You've your own personal gutter—you've got to have a desire to stop. (R0)

They stopped, but not "sincerely," or under coercion (e.g., jail). They started use as soon as possible.

> The day I was walking out of there [prison], I had it clear as a bell in my mind that there was no way that I was going to use. But the minute I walked through the gates that was what was in my head; that I've got to go and get a charge. All the things I had lost, my house, all my family knew I was in the jail, so I knew they were kind of blanking me as well, and all my self-esteem was back to [inaudible] . . . facing me right in front of me, and at any other time all I had know what to do with it was to run away from it using drugs, to run away from my own mind.

Relapse might occur when returning to old haunts and life circumstances.

> Just circumstances. I might bump into the main man who's a dealer, and he's looking great and I'm feeling terrible and I say, aw, come on gie me some. Within a few hours I feel great. (R4)

Association with other drug users and with areas where drugs are available (temptation) are constant dangers. Furthermore, other users can become jealous when an addict in the area becomes clean. They can try to tempt the person back into using, and when someone is newly clean, this offer can be very hard to resist. Several men mentioned that their "jagging pals" are not true friends, although they must have spent considerable time with them. One man, who was particularly articulate (drug worker himself) put it a bit differently—"Once you have stopped you have nothing in common with users because all they talk about is drugs and their lives revolve around obtaining and using them."

Restarting can occur on release from prison. Even men who have sworn while in prison that they will stay clean and not get a habit again, nor get involved in the criminal lifestyle, will start to use on their first free day because they feel like they "deserve a party." This soon escalates into a habit again.

Relapse could occur in response to life difficulties, including excessive alcohol use.

> Initially it [heroin] is good, it's a good feeling, and if you're worried about things that are getting you down, then it's a lot quicker than going to get drunk.

> Lost a court case for access to my wee lassie I got outside my marriage and just went right off the rails. (R24)

Emotional problems are not dealt with either—they are blocked out by the heroin and overshadowed by the need for heroin. The user becomes emotionally dead. Once clean, all the reasons that contributed to him starting in the first place are still there, but usually a lot worse—the monotony and relentlessness of life and often, money is owed to money lenders or dealers. Personal relationships will often have suffered, so the user may find himself alone to face a "clean" life, with emotions becoming overwhelming, and life's problems being insurmountable. For different people, the "emotional deadening" might involve different frequencies of heroin use, and this varies across the life span. During periods of heavy use, users might be "deadened" almost all the time. However, during lighter periods, they might use heroin a few times a week, but still as an escape from their problems, which allows them to avoid dealing with those problems.

Relapse could also occur because of the tedium of a life without heroin.

> After you've ran with the rats the mice are a bore . . . After coming into normal society things are boring, you're no always up there, so things are boring. (R25)

And again:

> When I got out of prison I was off the methadone and I refused to go back on the methadone, so I went back to heroin. I was back in the same environment, boredom as well. (R3)

Users often said that there was nothing else in life to replace the heroin habit once they stopped, so over time they tended to restart. The habit gives direction and focus to life (albeit unpleasant) so the user has something to do every day and one main purpose in life. Once clean, all the reasons for having to get up and go out are sometimes lost. It has been likened to losing a job. Also, of course, the realization that his life has nothing else to offer also contributes to the user the feeling that he may as well not bother staying clean, that he is useless, and so on, and that the easiest solution is to take drugs to forget.

A lot of this discussion alerts us to the importance of triggers for initiating relapse. These may be of an immediate or of a general nature:

- A major stressful event may trigger reusing, for example, losing access to a child, a father's death.
- Once clean, the user may try to use heroin recreationally, or may be tempted to have "just one hit," but then this use escalates and he soon develops a habit again.
- Peer pressure or encountering people wishing to sell heroin. As one respondent said: "You realize eventually you cannae do it a couple of times, you cannae dabble, a lot of people think that you can dabble, you can't dabble with heroin . . . . A lot of it is down to peer pressure as well, bad company and peer pressure, and naiveness as well."
- Using other drugs—especially alcohol—can lead to loss of self-control and reuse of heroin. It seems very difficult for an ex-user to just use once, even while drunk, without beginning regular use again.
- Eventually, if a user has stopped for someone else, then his willpower may be lost, he will not maintain his "clean" because he wants to use again, and will eventually.
- Some men simply like heroin, and do not like the experience of life without it, so they choose to use again.

Avoiding Relapse and Staying Off

Avoidance of relapse was found to require four properties. First, the effective management of negative events and emotions served as an insulator against continuing a drug-using lifestyle. For instance, the theme of the boredom of everyday life and how this needs to be guarded against was frequently mentioned:

> It's just learning to accept that such is life. (R25)

And as another respondent put it:

> Trying to accept the rest of your life abstinent is hard.

And again:

> Life is a bore, ye cannae be on a high all the time, so I'm starting to deal with that as well.

Respondents were also very clear about the necessity of filling up their time so that they wouldn't become bored. R20 avoided boredom with volunteer or community work.

Second, the individual was required to learn how to avoid high-risk situations, which could trigger a relapse episode. Our respondents were aware of these situations and guarded themselves from them. One interviewee was particularly clear about this:

> What made it a lot easier for me, it was when I got out the rehab I could have started hanging about with people on the street, old haunts, but I didnae, I stayed away from it all, and if I wisnae here [at a drug agency] or at [a voluntary agency] or [a religious agency] I used to be in the house, so it was always within a wee circle, so I had quite a network of support. (R24)

And later in the interview,

> But I think that's kept me, because I was in the safe areas, I used to get picked up at the house took to the [religious agency], then back up the road getting ran everywhere. All that kind of helped. I always say that if I hadn't had that support network, it was quite unique. (R24)

Another respondent said,

> I have also restricted my movements round here, I don't go along certain streets, I stay away from central areas. Because that's dangerous situations, you've always got that wee demon in your heed that's saying aye, you might be feeling a wee bit bored . . . at four o'clock, you might have had a bad day. . . . So you had a bad day there and you're going home to sit in the hoose yerself, so that's you. . . . So if you meet somebody at the wrong time, at the wrong point when you're feeling at a low ebb, it's still too easy. (R25)

What we witnessed allied to the avoidance of high-risk situations was the establishment of new support networks. This was expressed clearly by those attending Narcotics Anonymous, but it was also the case with others (see R14).

A third property, a personal commitment to quitting, served as a barrier against relapse for our respondents. Such a commitment was intimately tied to one's maturation. For example, once people believed they had reached a particular point in their drug-using career, then this personal commitment would seem to give added strength against relapse. Respondents often spoke about reaching a personal low point that gave them the desire to stop. For some (see R20), going into a rehabilitation unit was seen as a clear turning point, a clear benchmark. Heroin use was seen as wasted years of no achievement and an unwillingness to accept responsibility. Becoming aware of hitting rock bottom had made them make a clear decision. For some respondents, we witnessed not merely a readiness to quit but also a conscious preparation to give up heroin use.

A fourth property relates to their perceived change in personal and social identity. The concept of multiple realities is important; a person can awaken from a period of drug use to the reality of everyday life with all its periods of boredom and tedium. For these reasons, visible indicators of change are necessary; the person has to recognize that in some respects he has changed his lifestyle and changed his identity along with it. Indicators of a changed reality are needed. One respondent described being allowed to handle money as part of his volunteer work:

> Nobody ever trusted me, wouldn't even trust me to take the dog for a walk in case I sold it, and there was somebody giving me four hundred pounds. So that was a big boost . . . that comes back to the reason I geid up drugs, because people just didn't trust me, didn't like me, didn't even want to tell me what time it was. But now people who walked across the street to avoid me are handing me an envelope with four hundred pounds in it . . . people are trusting me which means you are a good person . . . . It means an awful lot to me, because I've never been trusted since I was knee high to a grasshopper. (R25)

Another interviewee stated,

> But I think what helped me through was that I was still working with people that were using, I would say maybe 90 percent of the people who came into [the religious agency] were using, either alcohol or drugs. But I was at the other side of the counter. (R24)

As we can see, several successful quitters followed a career path into drug counseling. As another respondent stated,

> I work on the Narcotics Anonymous programme, based on a 12-steps programme learning complete abstinence and I know myself that the first drink I have, that my head is going to be splitting the next day and the first thing that I am going to be looking for is a hit.

Such changes in identity often involve aspects of helping others, to somehow pay back or make amends (clearly expressed by R20).

Such changes of identity also involve respondents in the management of stigma. In their descriptions of becoming heroin users, we have numerous accounts from respondents about their relatives involved in stigmatizing activity and keeping users away from the rest of the family. Mothers did not allow respondents near their other sons and daughters. Wives kept children away from users. And indeed, throughout their heroin-using career there were still attempts at concealment:

> There's a lot of things I haven't done. You hear people speaking about injecting themselves in the groin, using it there so their partners, relatives wouldn't see it. I used the back of my hands and feet . . . I've got quite hairy arms. . . . I could hide it and it would be no problem, my brother, my friends didn't know at all. (R20)

But in general, issues of stigma are noticeable by the fact that they are not put center stage.

The new identity of ex-user does not therefore carry negative stigma, but on the contrary, carries with it positive qualities. In fact, rather than change this identity back into passing as a "straight" person, they adopt the identity of "recovering user" or "reformed user." And again, the twelve-step approach of Narcotics Anonymous was obviously important for some in transforming stigma.

CONCLUSION

We can thus see the importance of triggers or cues in the environment, which either stop people from using heroin, make people relapse, or prevent a person from relapsing. Such reaffirming (positive) cues include a reestablishment of trust with social networks, financial responsibility, and a reintegration of the individual into the larger social community.

It was also clear from the interviews that there are no naïve older heroin users. Most have been through a series of treatment regimes, and they know the jargon of different treatment philosophies. This raises a fundamental question about how discourse concerning heroin dependency evolves. Rather than thinking in terms of "lay" or "professional" discourse, it might be more productive in seeing how the two have involved and influenced each other (cf. Davies 1997).

Four particular aspects of these older respondents' depictions of their lives contrast with some of the stereotypes of addiction. First, and most generally, there is an issue of whether addiction is a state or not. Many accounts, including the discourse of Narcotics Anonymous and the disease model, view addiction as a state, even a permanent state. The lives of these men suggest that addiction is better seen as a developing process that commonly includes periods of heavy addiction, periods of treatment, periods of abstinence, and periods of substance use that deviate markedly from the model of daily use of heroin.

Second, these men had not generally severed all contacts with the "normal" world of family and friends. They felt guilt and pressure, particularly from the family, to stop. This could contribute to managing to stop. In some cases a new person, new partner, or new child helped trigger stopping. Continued pressure from existing family members could also create a vicious cycle of guilt and drug use to manage guilt, creating more guilt as discussed earlier.

Third, there is a clear possibility that heroin use delays maturity, particularly if one sees "maturity" as emerging through learning to cope with life's demands. Heroin use makes simple but extreme demands and blocks off attending to other demands. "The years pass quickly and you realize that you've wasted a lot of time, a lot of money, and you've wasted a lot of health."

And as another respondent stated,

> The first thing that goes is your personality, and it comes back and it's as if you've got a double attitude, because of all the time you've missed, because it's like being in a coma, it's as if you've been asleep, and things have happened, and things have happened, and people have been telling you, and it's awfully strange you know, and you start crying and things like that, for the slightest wee thing. But that's just the way it is, feelings coming back, you've been numb.

Fourth, there is the long-recognized issue of alcohol and other substance abuse. Some of the time during these men's lives with heroin, that habit could take a back seat to others. Alcohol was a major problem. Sometimes relapse to heroin use occurred while drunk. Other times alcohol replaced heroin as a heavy daily habit. One man reported using heroin to deal with hangovers.

Heroin use had been a dominant influence on these men's lives. During some periods, heroin had been their influence and interest. Nonetheless, it would be a mistake to view heroin as the sole influence on these men's behavior during the time of their lives with the drug.

In conclusion, our study discovered that the "new heroin" users closely resemble those studied by Stimson and Oppenheimer (1982). The long-term effects of treatment may be impossible to assess numerically. Treatment of heroin dependence may be better assessed as the management of a chronic problem rather than as a single intervention with a quantifiable outcome.

From these results we believe that long-term management should seek to build up the positive aspects of a client's life. Individuals should be taught to develop alternative ways of managing negative feelings rather than simply eliminating the negative drug-related aspects. They, and those counseling them, should also be prepared to achieve gradual improvements rather than being disappointed by anything but rapid change.

ACKNOWLEDGMENT

The authors wish to thank Dr. Iain Smith and Dr. Audrey Hillman for all the help and advice they gave throughout the duration of the project. The research was funded by a grant from the Scottish Chief Scientist Office; grant number K/OPR/15/9/F7.

REFERENCES

BARNARD, M., and N. MCKEGANEY 1994. *Drug misuse and young people: A selective review of the literature*. No. Centre for Drug Misuse Research: University of Glasgow.

BIERNACKI, P. 1986. *Pathways from addiction: Recovery without treatment*. Philadelphia: Temple University Press.

COHEN, P. D. A. 1989. *Cocaine use in Amsterdam in non-deviant subcultures*. Institute for Social Geography: University of Amsterdam.

DAVIES, J. B. 1997. *Drugspeak*. Reading: Harwood.

DENZIN, N. 1987. *The alcoholic self*. London: Sage.

DOWELL, J, G. HUBY, and C. SMITH. 1995. *Scottish Consensus Statement on Qualitative Research in Primary Health Care*. Dundee: Tayside Centre for General Practice.

KANDEL, D. 1990. Parenting styles, drug use and children's adjustment in families of young adults. *Journal of Marriage and the Family* 52:183–96.

KLINGEMANN, H. K. H. 1991. The motivation for change from problem alcohol and heroin use. *British Journal of Addiction* 86:727–44.

LINDESMITH, A. R. 1968. *Addiction and opiates*. Chicago: Aldine.

MCKEGANEY, N., and M. BARNARD. 1992. *Drugs and sexual risk: Lives in the balance*. Milton Keynes: Open University Press.

MULLEN, K. 1987. The beliefs and attitudes of a group of men in mid-life towards tobacco use. *Drug and Alcohol Dependence* 20:235–46.

MULLEN, K. 1993. *A healthy balance: Glaswegian men talking about health, Tobacco and Alcohol*. Aldershot: Avebury.

OPPENHEIMER, E., G. STIMSON, and A. THORLEY. 1979. Seven-year follow-up of heroin addicts in abstinence and continued use compared. *British Medical Journal* 2:627.

OPPENHEIMER, E., C. TOBUTT, C. TAYLOR, and T. ANDREW. 1994. Death and survival in a cohort of heroin addicts from London clinics: A 12-year follow-up study. *Addiction* 89:1299–1308.

PARKER, H., K. BAKX, and R. NEWCOMBE. 1988. *Living with heroin: The impact of a drugs 'epidemic' on an English community*. Buckingham: Open University Press.

PEARSON, G. 1987. *The new heroin users*. London:Basil Blackwell.

PLANT, M., and M. PLANT. 1992. *Risktakers: Alcohol, drugs, sex and youth*. London: Tavistock/Routledge.

REINARMAN, C., S. MURPHY, and D. WALDORF. 1994. Pharmacology is not destiny: The contingent character of cocaine abuse and addiction, *Addiction Research* 2(1):21–36.

SEGAL, B. 1991. Adolescent initiation into drug-taking behaviour: comparisons over a 5-year interval. *The International Journal of Addictions* 26:267–79.

STIMSON, G. V., and E. OPPENHEIMER. 1982. *Heroin addiction: Treatment and control in Britain*. London: Tavistock.

STRAUSS, A. L. 1987. *Qualitative analysis for social scientists*. Cambridge: Cambridge University Press.

TAYLOR, A. 1994. *Women drug users: An ethnography of a female injecting community*. Oxford: Oxford University Press.

TOBUTT, C., E. OPPENHEIMER, and R. LARANJEIRNA. 1996. Health of cohort of heroin addicts from London clinics: 22 year follow up. *British Medical Journal* 312:1458.

QUESTIONS FOR THOUGHT AND DISCUSSION

Chapter 18: "Mothering Through Addiction: A Survival Strategy Among Puerto Rican Addicts" by Monica Hardesty and Timothy Black

1. How do the participants define "motherhood"?
2. How does "motherhood" affect the participants' success in drug treatment?
3. How do the authors challenge the prevailing stereotypes concerning female substance users?

Chapter 19: "Drug Use Among Inner-City African American Women: The Process of Managing Loss" by Carol A. Roberts

1. How do life situations and events influence the onset of drug use and changes in drug-using behaviors for the participants?
2. How do the women define "loss"?
3. What is the role of violence in the lives of these women?
4. What are the long-term implications of the authors' findings?

Chapter 20: "Improving Substance Abuse Service Delivery to Hispanic Women Through Increased Cultural Competencies: A Qualitative Study" by Terry S. Trepper, Thorana S. Nelson, Eric E. McCollum, and Philip McAvoy

1. How do the authors define "cultural competency"?
2. What type of drug treatment modality do the authors advocate?

Chapter 21: "Substance Use Prevention: An Iowa Mexican Im/migrant Family Perspective" by Ed A. Muñoz, Catherine Lillehoj Goldberg, and Martha M. Dettman

1. What kind of drug treatment curriculum do the authors argue for?
2. How is ethnicity related to successful drug treatment prevention?

Chapter 22: "After You've Ran with the Rats the Mice Are a Bore: Cessation of Heroin Use Among Men Entering MidLife" by Kenneth Mullen, Richard Hammersley, and Claire Marriott

1. What factors determined successful cessation of heroin use among these men from Glasgow?
2. What were specific relapse triggers for these participants?
3. How would you incorporate the authors' findings into a treatment program for heroin dependency?

W O R L D   W I D E   W E B   S I T E S

Treatment Improvement Exchange
   http://www.treatment.org/

Substance Abuse and Mental Health Statistics
  http://www.drugabusestatistics.samhsa.gov/

Drug Treatment Forum
  http://www.atforum.com/

Drug Policy Alliance
  http://www.dpf.org/homepage.cfm/

National Center on Addiction and Substance Abuse at Columbia University
  http://www.casacolumbia.org/

National Institutes of Health
  http://www.nih.gov/

Index